Disenchanting the Caliphate

COLUMBIA STUDIES IN INTERNATIONAL AND GLOBAL HISTORY

COLUMBIA STUDIES IN INTERNATIONAL AND GLOBAL HISTORY

Cemil Aydin, Timothy Nunan, and Dominic Sachsenmaier, Series Editors

This series presents some of the finest and most innovative work coming out of the current landscapes of international and global historical scholarship. Grounded in empirical research, these titles transcend the usual area boundaries and address how history can help us understand contemporary problems, including poverty, inequality, power, political violence, and accountability beyond the nation-state. The series covers processes of flows, exchanges, and entanglements—and moments of blockage, friction, and fracture—not only between "the West" and "the Rest" but also among parts of what has variously been dubbed the "Third World" or the "Global South." Scholarship in international and global history remains indispensable for a better sense of current complex regional and global economic transformations. Such approaches are vital in understanding the making of our present world.

Anne Irfan, *Refuge and Resistance: Palestinians and the International Refugee System*

Michael Francis Laffan, *Under Empire: Muslim Lives and Loyalties Across the Indian Ocean World, 1775–1945*

Eva-Maria Muschik, *Building States: The United Nations, Development, and Decolonization, 1945–1965*

Jessica Namakkal, *Unsettling Utopia: The Making and Unmaking of French India*

Michael Christopher Low, *Imperial Mecca: Ottoman Arabia and the Indian Ocean Hajj*

Nicole CuUnjieng Aboitiz, *Asian Place, Filipino Nation: A Global Intellectual History of the Philippine Revolution, 1887–1912*

Mona L. Siegel, *Peace on Our Terms: The Global Battle for Women's Rights After the First World War*

Raja Adal, *Beauty in the Age of Empire: Japan, Egypt, and the Global History of Aesthetic Education*

Ulbe Bosma, *The Making of a Periphery: How Island Southeast Asia Became a Mass Exporter of Labor*

Perrin Selcer, *The UN and the Postwar Origins of the Global Environment: From World Community to Spaceship Earth*

Dominic Sachsenmaier, *Global Entanglements of a Man Who Never Traveled: A Seventeenth-Century Chinese Christian and His Conflicted Worlds*

Perin E. Gürel, *The Limits of Westernization: A Cultural History of America in Turkey*

Will Hanley, *Identifying with Nationality: Europeans, Ottomans, and Egyptians in Alexandria*

Simone M. Müller, *Wiring the World: The Social and Cultural Creation of Global Telegraph Networks*

Richard W. Bulliet, *The Wheel: Inventions and Reinventions*

Adam Clulow, *The Company and the Shogun: The Dutch Encounter with Tokugawa Japan*

Alison Bashford, *Global Population: History, Geopolitics, and Life on Earth*

Samuel Moyn and Andrew Sartori, eds., *Global Intellectual History*

Heonik Kwon, *The Other Cold War*

Steven Bryan, *The Gold Standard at the Turn of the Twentieth Century: Rising Powers, Global Money, and the Age of Empire*

For a complete list of books in the series, please see the Columbia University Press website.

DISENCHANTING THE CALIPHATE

The Secular Discipline of Power in Abbasid Political Thought

HAYRETTİN YÜCESOY

Columbia University Press
New York

Columbia University Press
Publishers Since 1893
New York Chichester, West Sussex
cup.columbia.edu

Library of Congress Cataloging-in-Publication Data
Names: Yücesoy, Hayrettin, author.
Title: Disenchanting the caliphate : the secular discipline
of power in Abbasid political thought / Hayrettin Yücesoy.
Description: New York : Columbia University Press, 2023. |
Series: Columbia studies in international and global history |
Includes bibliographical references and index.
Identifiers: LCCN 2022055391 | ISBN 9780231209403 (hardback) |
ISBN 9780231209410 (trade paperback) | ISBN 9780231557924 (ebook)
Subjects: LCSH: Abbasids—Politics and government. | Abbasids—History. |
Islamic Empire—History—750-1258. | Islam and politics. | Caliphate—History. |
Power (Social sciences) | Political science—Philosophy.
Classification: LCC DS238.5 .Y83 2023 | DDC 909/.09767—dc23/eng/20230315
LC record available at https://lccn.loc.gov/2022055391

Cover design: Milenda Nan Ok Lee
Cover image: The Picture Art Collection / Alamy

To my mother and in loving memory of my father

Contents

Preface ix

Acknowledgments xv

List of Early, Umayyad, and Abbasid Caliphs, 632–861 xix

Introduction: Critical Reflections on "Islamic Political Thought" 1

1. Caliphal Practice 27
2. The Language of Imamate 49
3. Political Prose Revolution 82
4. The Disruptive Language of Siyasa 106
5. Deconfessionalizing the Caliph 134
6. A Theory of Imperial Law 162
7. Territorial Consciousness 189
8. Reimagining the People of the Empire 223

Conclusion: Releasing Siyasa from the Imamate 255

Conventions and Spelling 263

Notes 267

Bibliography 331

Index 357

Preface

Disenchanting the Caliphate: The Secular Discipline of Power in Abbasid Political Thought is about opening a space of contemplation on the value of secular political languages in the histories of Muslim peoples. Taking a critical stance toward the modern scholarly and public over-religionization of the Muslim subject, it focuses on a remarkable discourse of good governance and political temporality in a foundational period in their histories. A common wisdom in Western public discourse today is that the histories and cultures of the Muslim peoples have been defined in religious terms in a way that European and North American societies have not. Seemingly innocuous statements such as "Islam is a way of life" and "Islam does not distinguish between state and religion," or questions of the same order ("Why are Muslim countries unable to modernize and democratize?" "How can one reform and modernize Islam?") have regularly underscored the idea that Muslim peoples are different. This assertion (which essentializes Islam and what "it" does) is accompanied by an astonishing supposition that the ulema, more than any other social body, have represented Muslims and held the authority to speak for the tradition. How does this mythology still sound authoritative and convincing?

Regretfully, even the post- and decolonial scholarship's deconstructive efforts aiming at provincializing Europe and its knowledge forms have been leveraged to embolden authoritarian, nativist, and chauvinistic political discourses in the global south, including Muslim societies, in the name of cultural authenticity only to circle back to the initial rhetoric of Otherness. What has also been encouraging this form of treatment and representation is the recent spectacular implosion of Islamist movements in countries where they have been able to form a governing body. This development has made speaking about Islam and

Muslims harder without invoking images of theocratic violence and oppression, incompatibility with modern life, and the lack of civic and political culture to guide Muslims in the contemporary world. In brief, this shared peculiarizing and over-religionizing language has come to define the terms of the contemporary debate about Islam and Muslims.

One way to develop a critical decolonial language is to operate with a new "problematic" and pursue a different agenda. My argument in this book is that political thought traditions prevalent in the caliphal world in the middle decades of the long eighth century diverged in two dialogic regimes of rationality: the religious governance of the ulema elaborated in what I call "imamate discourse" and the secular politics of lay bureaucrat literati expressed in the discursive tradition of siyasa. Initially emerging in the crucibles of imperial bureaucracy and separate from "scholastic" knowledge connected with mosques and ulema, siyasa discourse exposed the distinction between the ulema-centric idea of the caliphate (*khilāfa*) and royal authority (*mulk*). The dialogic engagement between the two shaped the contours of not only the Abbasid caliphate but also world-historical thought traditions from the mid-eighth century onward.

As an intervention that changed the discursive landscape, the idea of siyasa disenchanted politics.[1] The proponents of siyasa intervened from two directions. First, they foregrounded the idea of good governance as an endeavor distinct from the practice of religious piety. Second, they opened a new field of deliberation in which temporal political moralities (philosophical, ethical, realist) were expressed and elaborated. By making a non-ulema-centric sense of political reality in an epoch in which religious scholars imagined only a community of faith and its governing body, the proponents of siyasa conceptualized governance as a craft of building satisfaction through the rational and practical calculation of the contingency in consideration of the outcome. In other words, in presenting the idea of good governance in the adab-siyasa political thought tradition, I hope to point out how the discourses of the lay bureaucrat literati helped steer the caliphate away from the practices of a "confessional state" championing a particular creed in governance toward a new path.[2] While these professionals defended religious faith as sacred meaning of life and a moral foundation of orderly society, they also argued against its representation as the regulator of political practice.

Viewed from the vantage point of doing rather than describing, their discursive practice worked not as an additional "more of the same" opinion in a static space or as a conviction of certain individuals but as a disruptive argument about the art of government. Just as urban planning generates a new consciousness of the topography in the imagination of the affected inhabitants by linking various parts of the terrain in a new way, the pioneering lay bureaucrats of the Abbasid caliphate produced a discourse that interjected, in an already occupied intellectual space, a new mode of sociopolitical practice, which I call the worldly ethos of adab-siyasa. In fact, one may characterize their intervention as an attempt of deliberative empire building commonly associated with the European early modernity.

Some may object that the terms of the discussion themselves are European and thus incongruent in other contexts, and that engaging the subjects of politics and secularity in this way only enhances Eurocentrism. First, I am aware that in elaborating my argument through the juxtaposition of secular versus religious languages of politics, I cannot escape engaging our present-day hegemonic discourse about either secularism/religion or Islam/Muslims. It will be clear to the reader, however, that the proper analytical site for the discourse of "Islamic political thought" is not the histories of "Islam" and the "Muslim peoples" (any more than the label the "Dark Ages" is for the "Christian peoples") but the terms and the framing of this conversation in contemporary debate. Second, while I understand the "intent" of such an argument, I cannot help but see the orientalizing subtext of construing a notion of European exceptionalism from the back door. When this view is voiced in the global South, it risks erasing or concealing global forms of secularity by holding too tight to the notion of "European exception." By asking not to problematize the non-European global historical archive from the vantage point of democratic humanistic sensibilities, the argument stifles historically informed conversations on global participatory political values and further corners intellectuals into defending and reinventing authoritarian aspirations in the name of tradition and resistance. This argument also exposes a patronizing posture in prejudging not only what non-Europeans can and cannot say but whether they are entitled today to aspire to participatory and consensual politics. Why should this endeavor be any different from how one studies gender, slavery, labor, and power in world history? One can discuss the connections (and the distinctions) between politics and religious faith without mirroring European modernity's truth claims. And finally, I hope the reader will see that I am using the idiom secular/secularity as a metaphor, Wittgenstein's ladder so to speak, to reach beyond the immediate and highly polluted semantics of the terminology in contemporary discourse. What I am looking for is not an alternative "master narrative" but rather a space of new possibilities created by disruptions that I think better characterize the history of political reflection.

I should also add a comment here about linguistic discourses to clarify how I differ from scholars who examine political thought from the perspective of a "picture theory of meaning" whereby language functions as a tool to describe an external reality and access meaning that exists outside the actual expression.[3] I focus instead on what language "does" and what it is "used for." This entails that

I read primary-source texts not with the hermeneutic aim of understanding authorial intentions or uncovering the authors' beliefs but with the purpose of analyzing statements as *interventions*. Inasmuch as statements function in an already socially and discursively occupied field, they cannot be merely ideas and beliefs thrown into a vacuum or added to the catalog of existing ideas. Statements produce specific effects and are dialogic (contextual, connected, and interactive). They challenge and reinterpret other verbal utterances and are challenged and reinterpreted by others. Assessed from this standpoint, the statements of the thinkers I study comprise more than verbalization of their thoughts and beliefs. Taken as "discursive practices," they are, rather, interventions into the political debates of their time, to support and promote positions and resist others. In this attempt, I find useful the analytical position taken by the Cambridge school of political thought, represented by people such as John G. A. Pocock[4] and Quentin Skinner.[5]

As it will also be evident, I draw on the work of literary theorists and scholars in the humanistic disciplines who emphasize that speech acts constitute the world rather than merely describe it. John Austin's intervention on language as performance, namely, in pondering how expression does more than postulate or describe, but also performs, mobilizes relations, and enables capacities, resonates with what I am trying to accomplish in this study.[6] To mitigate the social disconnect apparent in such a position on language, however, I rely on Mikhail Bakhtin's dialogism that "verbal discourse is a social phenomenon"[7] and Michel Foucault's observation that statements are embodied in technical processes, in institutions, in patterns of general behavior, in forms of transmission and diffusion, and in pedagogical forms that at once impose and maintain them.[8] In this regard, I am convinced by Pierre Bourdieu's "social" critique of Austin that the illocutionary force of an utterance is irreducible to discourse. Rather, it is tied to the social position of the speaker, who derives his or her authority from the accumulated symbolic capital of the group, "which makes *all* the difference."[9] In invoking the connection between verbal utterances and the social web, I thus notice the way verbal expressions and specific practices of knowledge constitute their referents from a socially defined position.

To flesh out my main points, I focus on the early Abbasid period, whose intellectual vibrancy shaped politics and political thought for many centuries afterward. I have organized the book with an introduction and eight chapters, which explicate my main argument through five themes (chapters 3 to 8). The introduction discusses the conceptual and methodological bases of the study. Therein, I assess the historiography of the field to substantiate my claims about critical decolonization of political thought and lay the groundwork for my arguments about good governance.

Chapter 1 focuses on the empire-building efforts of the Umayyads and the Abbasids in order to trace the developments that underpinned the competing memories and representations of the caliphate in the mid-eighth century. The chapter considers the dialectic of two major developments which led to political reflection on the caliphate. One was related to the militarization and imperialization of the faith community that entangled faith with imperial politics and led to substantial theological divisions that tore the faith community apart. The other was the formation of the empire, with its complex structures and practices, that prompted interest in political reflection dedicated to improving administrative efficiency and political control.

Chapter 2 analyzes the early texts of the imamate in the eighth century to clarify key aspects of its language. It argues that the discourse on imamate emerged from the late seventh century onward as the political language of the ulema, who defined and guided the caliphate as "pastoral authority" and imagined social organization to be a religious affair coterminous with the religious community. The chapter then looks ahead to two early juristic texts of the late eighth century in the context of the emerging siyasa to capture the change of mood and style in the imamate's language.

Chapters 3 and 4 explore the Arabic political prose's emergence in the mid-eighth century at the intersection of developments that brought together the Umayyad administration and the new class of bureaucrats. By reviewing the biographies and writings of key figures, these two chapters capture the critical sociocultural underpinnings and the strategic aspects of their discursive practice, which set siyasa on a separate path from the imamate. Chapter 3 examines the rise of political prose in the "Sālim School of Siyasa" to illustrate how the late Umayyad bureaucrat literati tapped into the *longue-durée* imperial practices in the region to develop a new frame of deliberation echoing the hybridity of their vision of governance and the precarity of their social standing. Chapter 4 spotlights Ibn al-Muqaffaʿ's (d. ca. between 755 and 757) life and political writings, in particular the "Epistle on the Caliph's Privy," as a disruptive and pioneering archetype of siyasa text. It elaborates on Ibn al-Muqaffaʿ's writing as a remarkable example of government rationality and a new foundation of thinking incompatible with that of the ulema. It argues that by the mere form of its articulation in writing—let alone its content—the "Epistle" signified an unusual conceptual voice that exposed, for the first time in the history of the caliphate, a vision of empire that made sense of the political reality beyond its meaning as an affair of the religious community. It is the contention of this chapter that the worldly tenor of siyasa cannot be appreciated without regarding the adab tradition and its worldly and cosmopolitan character.

In chapters 5 to 8, I read Ibn al-Muqaffaʿ's "Epistle" contrapuntally to expose its larger dialogic context and as a launching pad to discuss several key themes. Chapter 5 addresses the distinction between the caliph of the imamate and the sovereign of siyasa to shed light on the key aspects of sovereignty in political discourse. It observes how siyasa was envisioned as a craft of bringing the sovereign under the law through a regime of moral cultivation, adab, which included disciplining the ruler in right conduct, inculcating the codes of propriety and ethics, and encouraging him to acquire the practical skills necessary to be an effective ruler. It also explicates how siyasa was seen as the art of practicing governance through alleviating problems by normalized and agreeable means and aspiring to foster a climate of satisfaction among the subjects to keep a sustainable social order. The chapter then probes the question of divine providence and political virtue.

Chapter 6 considers the intersection of law and political authority. It contends that the notion of "law for the empire" potentiated a new legal practice to compete against the idea of "empire for the sacred law," as advocated by the ulema. As a way to translate brute force into legitimate power, a modality to normalize control, this new understanding of law reshaped existing relations by channeling loyalty in public matters from the sacred law of the ulema to the sovereign. The chapter argues that this legal deconstructive effort was meant to rationalize the process of legislation to make neither the ulema nor even the sovereign, but the "procedure" itself, the axis of legislation.

Chapter 7 explains the reinvention of imperial topography as an administrable territorialized landscape, otherwise imagined in the idioms of faith and of the religious community. It shows how, in siyasa discourse, the empire was not simply a bequest of the believers or merely an aggregation of cities, villages, roads, and peoples inherited from the Umayyads and now happened to be ruled by the Abbasids. It was imagined, rather, as an organization with its own structures and relations and an association that is constituted rather than received.

Chapter 8 accounts for the governmentalization of people in the realm as imperial subjects, which distinguished them from the faith-subject of the imamate. It clarifies how, in siyasa discourse, the Abbasid realm was reimagined as a constituted sociopolitical order under the supreme authority of the ruler, comprising the army, elite, and common folk as major imperial estates. This classificatory intentionality did not merely shape the elites' and the common folks' role in the empire but in fact transformed the anonymity of discrete imperial functionaries and subjects into an identifiable or named collectivity (ruling class and common folk) under the sovereign's rule.

The conclusion to the book provides an overview of the main points of the study. I hope my book helps challenge the monopoly of the ulema-centric public and academic arguments about the character of political thought in the histories of the Muslim peoples.

Acknowledgments

During the arduous journey of writing this book over the course of more than half a decade, numerous individuals and institutions contributed in constructive ways. I am much indebted to Shawkat Toorawa for sharing with me the digital copies of Aḥmad b. Abī Ṭāhir Ṭayfūr's *Kitāb al-Manthūr wa al-Manẓūm*, which contains Ibn al-Muqaffaʿ's "Epistle on the Caliph's Privy" and other writings. Laura Doyle has never hesitated to offer her knowledge of world history and critical studies and many inspiring comments on various sections of the book. Hüseyin Yılmaz shared his immense knowledge of Ottoman history and political thought along the way. I cherish the many conversations we have had about Ottoman and Abbasid political thought traditions, which no doubt enriched the content of this study. Cemil Aydın offered invaluable critical suggestions from the perspective of global history on the structure of the book and the historiography of the caliphate in the nineteenth century, which helped me navigate the difficult terrain of the late nineteenth century to clarify my argument. Ahmet Karamustafa has been a friend and generous reader whose incisive and constructive feedback on the book has been precious. I am grateful to Ahmet Kaylı for offering his expert knowledge of manuscripts. I am indebted to Michael Cooperson for his comments on chapters 3 and 4 and for his strategic comments about the craft of translation. Istvan Kristo-Nagy generously suggested new readings that escaped my attention and commented on two chapters of the book. John Renard's nuanced comments made me rethink the structure of several chapters. Asma Afsaruddin's erudite intervention in various parts of the work helped nuance some of my points and reconsider others. I thank Himmet Taşkömür and Cengiz Şişman for their judicious comments on several chapters and for useful conversations on the state of scholarship in the field. I am indebted to Armando Salvatore and Necati Polat for their cogent remarks on the introduction. Wael Hallaq and Garth Fowden kindly and inspiringly commented on the draft they received. Gerald Lampe graciously made available his dissertation on Ibn al-Muqaffaʿ and the "Epistle." I hope he will not be disappointed when he finds that I frequently diverged from his translation. I am grateful to the anonymous readers who commented on the manuscript constructively. They saved me from some embarrassing mistakes and made me aware of points I had missed. I am indebted to Aram Shahin for forwarding to me several useful articles. I fondly remember the many delightful conversations with the late Sabri Orman about this book and the history of economic thought. Matthew Tillier kindly shared his article on al-ʿAnbarī with me. I am indebted to Timothy Nunan and Dominic Sachsenmaier for their sound advice on numerous points and on the final shape of the manuscript. Caelyn Cobb and her colleagues, Monique Laban, Kathryn Jorge, Milenda Lee, Peter Barrett, and Kalie Hyatt, at Columbia University Press skillfully guided me through the production process from beginning to end.

The School of Abbasid Studies has been truly a welcoming scholarly collectivity from which I learned immensely. I thank the member and nonmember colleagues for making the biannual meetings a learning feast, which continues to motivate me. I am also indebted to the international research collective of scholars who are devoted to decolonial and a longue-durée thinking under the World Studies Interdisciplinary Project (WSIP) at the University of Massachusetts Amherst. My book project has been inspired by the questions and conversations in the meetings of WSIP over several years. If I must single out a few names in the collective besides Laura Doyle, I must note Mwangi wa Gĩthĩnji, Simon Gikandi, Sheldon Pollock, Johan Mathew, and Annette Damayanti Lienau for their input about my presentations on Ibn al-Muqaffaʿ. I am thankful to the hosts and attendees of the conference "Ties That Bind: Mechanisms and Structures of Social Dependency in the Early Islamic Empire" at Leiden University, and the discussant of my paper Noëmie Lucas, for the engaging discussion. Kazuo Morimoto and the participants at the symposium "In Quest of a Proper Polity: Political Discourses in the Early Abbasid Period" at the University of Tokyo deserve a word of gratitude for their collegiality. Hatsuki Aishima and the other panelists on the roundtable on *The Wiley Blackwell of History of Islam* at the National Museum of Ethnology in Osaka, Japan, contributed their learned and collegial discussion about studying and writing about the history of Islam.

Colleagues at Washington University in St. Louis, John Bowen, Michael Frachetti, Aria Nakissa, Tim Parsons, and Jim Wertsch, offered their candid opinions on various sections of the book in the long history of its making. The colleagues in the departments of Jewish, Islamic, and Middle Eastern Studies (JIMES) and history, the Global Studies Program, the McDonnell International Scholars Academy, and the history department at my previous institution, Saint Louis University, deserve a mention for their support. Muhittin Macit and Ferruh Özpilavcı generously facilitated access to the manuscript resources in the Turkish Manuscript Directorate's collections during my research. I am indebted to the following colleagues and friends for their contributions in various ways during my research and writing: Naz Zeynep Atay, Peri Bearman, Dilek Çalgan, Jared Conrad-Bradshaw, John Curry, Kurt Dirks, Fred Donner, Nadia El Cheikh, İhsan Fazlıoğlu, Carol Jenkins, Fred Kameny, Hugh Kennedy, Fatemeh Keshavarz, Burhan Köroğlu, Gary Leiser, Joshua Mantel, John Nawas, Oya Pancaroğlu, Mehmed Özkan, A. J. Robinson, Andrew Sobel, Lynne Tatlock, Ali Tekcan, Joya Uraizee, Gerhild S. Williams, Ceyda Yücesoy, and Annalisa Zox-Weaver. A word of gratitude goes to my students for their perceptive questions and comments in my courses, particularly those who braved enrolling in "the history of Islamic political thought."

Knowing well that knowledge production cannot be separated from a state of mind and feelings, I acknowledge my friends A. Vural Ak, Mustafa Şentop, Süreyya Er, and Erol Çatalbaş for the many engaging conversations on scholarly and not so scholarly matters. In numerous occasions, Vural has even graciously facilitated my mobility in Istanbul. My brother Çetin and his wife Hatice went out of their way to make my stays in Istanbul comfortable and productive. I also thank my friends in St. Louis for the frequent warm gatherings. My gratitude to the anchors of my life, my family members Mukadder, Ahmet Suad, and John Berat, goes beyond words. They have been with me all along in this quest. It is still sweet to acknowledge Ahmet Suad for his feedback on the introduction.

Several institutions should also be acknowledged. The Center for the Humanities at Washington University in St. Louis has funded my summer research trips on several occasions. The American University of Beirut, the Orient-Institut in Beirut, the King Faisal Center for Research and Islamic Studies in Riyad, the Center for Middle Eastern Studies at the University of Chicago, Middle East Technical University, and Bahçeşehir University in Istanbul have each hosted me as a visiting scholar for a few weeks. I wrote the first draft of several chapters in the history department at Boğaziçi University during my sabbatical in 2019. TÜBİTAK of Turkey granted me a stipend for part of my residence at Boğaziçi University. My visits to the University of Jordan's lovely library brought back memories of the late 1980s when I was a Master of Arts student in the history department there. In my stays in Istanbul, I always visit my alma mater Istanbul University, where I began thinking about doing scholarship. The National Library of the Kingdom of Morocco in Rabat was a peaceful place to access resources and write in the summer of 2016. However, any views, findings, conclusions, or recommendations expressed in this publication do not reflect those of the cited individuals and institutions. I must bear the outcome myself.

List of Early, Umayyad, and Abbasid Caliphs, 632–861

Early Caliphs

Abū Bakr (11–13/632–634)
ʿUmar I b. al-Khaṭṭāb (13–23/634–644)
ʿUthmān b. ʿAffān (23–35/644–656)
ʿAlī b. Abī Ṭālib (35–40/656–661)

Umayyad Caliphs

Muʿāwiya I b. Abī Sufyān (41–60/661–680)
Yazīd I b. Muʿāwiya (60–64/680–683)
Muʿāwiya II b. Yazīd I (64/683)
Marwān I b. al-Ḥakam (64–65/684–685)
ʿAbd al-Malik b. Marwān I (65–86/685–705)
Al-Walīd I b. ʿAbd al-Malik (86–96/705–715)
Sulaymān b. ʿAbd al-Malik (96–99/715–717)
ʿUmar II b. ʿAbd al-ʿAzīz (99–101/717–720)
Yazīd II b. ʿAbd al-Malik (101–105/720–724)
Hishām b. ʿAbd al-Malik (105–125/724–743)
Al-Walīd II b. Yazīd II (125–126/743–744)
Yazīd III b. al-Walīd I (126/744)
Ibrāhīm b. al-Walīd I (126/744)
Marwān II b. Muḥammad (127–132/744–750)

Abbasid Caliphs

ʿAbdallāh b. Muḥammad al-Saffāḥ (132–136/749–754)
ʿAbdallāh b. Muḥammad al-Manṣūr (136–158/754–775)
Muḥammad b. al-Manṣūr al-Mahdī (158–169/775–785)
Mūsā b. al-Mahdī al-Hādī (169–170/785–786)
Hārūn b. al-Hādī al-Rashīd (170–193/786–809)
Muḥammad b. al-Rashīd al-Amīn (193–198/809–813)
ʿAbdallāh b. al-Rashīd al-Maʾmūn (198–218/813–833)
Muḥammad b. al-Rashīd al-Muʿtaṣim (218–227/833–842)
Hārūn b. al-Muʿtaṣim al-Wāthiq (227–232/842–847)
Jaʿfar b. al-Muʿtaṣim al-Mutawakkil (232–247/847–861)

Disenchanting the Caliphate

Introduction

Critical Reflections on "Islamic Political Thought"

Writing new histories of political thought from a critical decolonial perspective demands a theoretical and methodological commitment. One expects that many will *not* find the expression "Islamic political thought" peculiar. The phrase is regularly uttered without a second thought as a disinterested verbalization of a self-evident historical and sociopolitical reality. For this reason, the initial step must be to interrogate the framework of the discussion in terms of language and analysis. As will be clear, the act of naming something is important. It frames the object in question, creates its reality, and allows control over it by defining its boundaries. In this introduction to the book, I bring into closer focus the current approach of scholarship as a discourse whose main outcome has been a wholesale "religionization," and therefore marginalization, of major political thought traditions in world history.[1] I also explain the key terms and spell out the arguments of the study presented in this book.

Two Rationalities of Governance in "Islamicate" History

As a discursive representation of the caliphate, the imamate was a particular rationality of governance grounded in Islamic normative values. The imamate corresponded broadly to the notion of religious governance embodied in the phrase *al-imāma wa al-siyāsa*, where siyasa signified temporal politics, and imamate signified the governance of the imam (*imām*), the ruler who was meant to wield religious and secular authority combined.[2] At the imamate's core lay the requisite that the Muslim community must have a legitimate leader who would be responsible for, as al-Māwardī (d. 1058) would note later, when the term "siyasa" was no longer snubbed by the ulema, "upholding the revealed law and managing the affairs of the world,"[3] including such duties as protecting and promoting the faith, implementing laws, defending borders, leading the army, maintaining social peace, collecting and distributing revenues, and appointing administrators to undertake such responsibilities—according to the principles of the revealed (or divine) law.

Given its arguments and the foundations on which it was built, the discourse of imamate may be characterized as the ulema's political theology.[4] Some of the best descriptions and elaborations of the imamate appear in primary-source texts on creed (*ʿaqīda* or *kalām*); religious jurisprudence (*fiqh*); prophetic reports (*ḥadīth*, sayings or actions attributed to the Prophet); and sectarian disputes (*kutub al-firaq*), commonly written by the ulema, such as piety-oriented (*mutadayyin*)[5] jurists/legal scholars (*faqīh*, pl. *fuqahāʾ*), *ḥadīth* transmitters (*muḥaddithūn*), theologians (*mutakallimūn*), and other scholars from any sect or school. It is vital to note that the imamate had been the only language available to make sense of the political reality until siyasa emerged as its contestant in the mid-eighth century.

As a counterpoint to the idea of the imamate, siyasa was another discourse of constituting and representing the caliphate based on the idea of royal authority (*mulk*), in which secular political moralities were foregrounded.[6] It emerged in the crucibles of the Umayyad and early Abbasid imperial administration among a cadre of pivotal lay bureaucrat literati, who launched a discussion of politics in early literary prose writing, apart from the "scholastic" knowledge of the ulema.[7] By reacting against and relativizing the governance of the imam,[8] the proponents of siyasa created a site of a new sociopolitical imaginary. With its worldly orientation, siyasa exposed a competition between two regimes of rationality in political reflection: the political theology or religious governance of the ulema, "imamate discourse," and the secular politics of lay bureaucrat literati interested in diverse humanistic fields and mundane knowledge, "siyasa discourse." If I may repurpose Saba Mahmood's remark on the piety movement in contemporary Egypt to characterize the early Abbasid debate, as discursive practices, both siyasa and imamate performed dissimilar work in the formation of a political subject and authorized two distinct conceptions of political power, ways of life, and worldviews.[9] The dialectic of these two great traditions shaped in major ways not only the practice of the "golden age of the caliphate" but also potent currents of political thought in societies from Hotan to Cordova, extending into the age of gunpowder empires in the sixteenth century.

One sign of this great divergence is the slow warming-up of the ulema to the term "siyasa." The word hardly ever appeared in any of their texts on the imamate until the mid-ninth century. Neither ʿUbaydallāh b. Ḥasan al-ʿAnbarī (d. 785) nor Yaʿqūb b. Ibrāhīm Abū Yūsuf (d. 798), jurists of the eighth century, nor the author of the *Masāʾil al-Imāma* (*Themes of the Imamate*) in the early ninth century used the term to discuss politics.[10] Even the inventive al-Jāḥiẓ (d. 868 or 869) used it only sporadically, in vague and broad terms, despite his copious writing on the imamate. One needs to wait for the unconventional Ibn Qutayba's (d. 889) *ʿUyūn al-Akhbār* (*Selected Narratives*)[11] to see an engagement of the ulema with this terminology. Even when the word appeared intermittently in theological and jurisprudential texts alongside the term "imamate" after the mid-ninth century, its naturalization as a shared concept between the ulema and lay intellectuals took a significantly longer time.[12]

Eventually, this avant garde term appealed to the ulema as a useful concept to elaborate how they thought about politics. Like the Christian thinkers of the Renaissance in Europe reacting to the movement of humanism, or the early twentieth-century Muslim modernists' attraction to the language of science and civilization, the ulema too responded to the term "siyasa" by first refraining from using it and then recognizing its utility for their own discursive purposes. In this dialogic process, the concept acquired currency among the ulema to the degree that a religious scholar of the caliber of Ibn Taymiyya (d. 1328) coined the term *al-siyāsa al-sharʿiyya* to describe the principles of governance according to the sacred law.[13] Ibn Taymiyya's position demonstrates the ulema's pragmatic attempt to forge a new synthesis or to naturalize temporal practices of governance under the broad canopy of the shariʿa.

The ulema's strategic warming-up for a rapprochement deserves a separate study, although I elaborate on an aspect of it in the second part of chapter 2. I will focus here on siyasa as a distinct "discourse of politics." One may define "siyasa" as "a domain for the formulation and justification of idealized schemata for representing reality, analyzing it and rectifying it."[14] As Nikolas Rose and Peter Miller note, although political discourses lack the systematic and closed character of disciplined bodies of theoretical discourse, they present regularities that may be captured in the term "political rationalities." Political rationalities comprise three core aspects, which address some of the central questions in this study. First, they have a characteristically moral form and thus wield normative power because they consider the ideals or principles to which the government should be directed. They have an epistemological character in the sense that they are articulated in relation to some conception of the objects governed (e.g., people, society, nation, religious community) and embody some account of the persons over whom government is to be exercised (e.g., subjects, women). Third, political rationalities are articulated in a distinctive idiom. The language that makes up political discourse is more than rhetoric. It is intellectual machinery or an apparatus that renders reality thinkable in a certain way.[15]

One may thus read siyasa as a modality to guide and regulate human behavior to produce a reasonable (therefore, contingent) social order expected by and acceptable to its subjects. In pursuing this path, I draw on the notion of governmentality (rationality of government, the art of government), which allows me to analyze siyasa as a means of approaching the scope and practice of government, and the method of governing, to make it visible, knowable, thinkable, and practical or convenient to both the one who governs and the one who is governed.[16] I underline how siyasa's exponents discussed it as a technique of mitigation and a craft of ordering life and alleviating problems through normalized and agreeable means in order "to get things the right way," and to foster a climate of satisfaction.

As Michel Foucault wrote, governance practiced in such a way is an art involving the creative application of intuition, knowledge, and skills to management. To regulate the conduct of their subjects, rulers must know what to do. They need to know the rules of the game. For this reason, governance requires mapping out populations, classifying them as individuals, groups, and in other ways to identify, order, and control them. The mechanisms of governance are accordingly geared to achieving certain objectives: laws and taxes imposed upon subjects, and disciplinary power exercised not simply for control but to regulate people in institutions and social structures such as the military, workplaces, sites of worship, the marketplace, urban landscapes, and so forth. Rulers are also concerned with capacities and with relations between and among people as resources to be fostered. Hence, political power is exercised in several formal and informal ways, related to and outside government, extending to the family and the individual, and generating a level of concern with how to direct and manage the conduct of the governed.[17]

These points facilitate interesting possibilities in reflecting on siyasa. The mitigatory character of siyasa brings discourse closer to a position moral philosophers call "consequentialism" because governance aims beyond exercising or displaying power or bolstering the ruler's ability to defend against enemies and against the strike of (mis)fortune. Unlike the deportment in enforcing and applying the normative laws of the ulema regardless of outcome, awareness of contingency demands the acknowledgment of precarity, which is a position that invokes the sense of "secular perpetuity."[18] Facing instability demands agility and preparation to take action to solve emergent problems and manipulate affairs to maintain order. The ruler's response to contingency through siyasa's mitigative capacity gives him the means to exercise his agency. As will be discussed more fully in the following chapters, such an approach to governance, as in Ibn al-Muqaffaʿ's "Epistle," suggests a contrasting vision from that of the early imamate.[19] It is also different from that of much advice literature, which is primarily about how to bolster the ruler's ability to maintain power.[20] As an art of governing or mitigation, siyasa is rather contrary to, even the opposite of, oppression and the exercising of brute force for the sake of control. One has a sharper view of this new way of thinking about politics from the ninth century onward, when governance appeared as a major concern in the genre of the Aristotelian household management, *tadbīr al-manzil*, in which questions of order, welfare, and happiness were posed in relation to managing the self, the family, and the city.

We may probe siyasa rationality further by examining the difference between sovereignty and governance (in Ibn al-Muqaffaʿ's language, *mulk* and siyasa, respectively). According to Foucault, in precapitalist Europe "the common good" meant obedience to the law, either that of the earthly sovereign or that of God, the absolute sovereign. In each case, what characterized the end purpose of sovereignty (the common and general good), was nothing other than submission to sovereignty, which makes the end of sovereignty circular: the end of sovereignty is the exercise of sovereignty. The good is obedience to the law; hence, the good for sovereignty is that people obey it. In the political treatises of early capitalist Europe, however, government began to mean "a right manner of disposing things to lead not to the form of the common good, as the jurists' texts would have said, but to an end which is 'convenient' for each of the things that are to be governed. This implies a plurality of specific aims."[21]

As far as the distinction between imamate and siyasa is a concern for analysis, Foucault's argument about circularity better characterizes the imamate discourse. When one reflects on siyasa discourse, however, one does not have to wait for early capitalism in Europe to observe an analogous development. In siyasa, sovereignty's representation as a finality does not exclude the possible emergence of different ends or aims beyond those designed by the sovereign. In fact, any effort to isolate the sovereign by sublimating him ontologically above his subjects, and therefore requiring the transmission of his power to people through mechanisms of governance, potentiates a space of relations for multiple ends or aims, in which the difference is negotiated. This dynamic is illustrated in Ibn al-Muqaffaʿ's discussion of the elite in their role as manipulators of relations (both in the sense of constructing the sovereign and of governing the subjects) and builders of governmental institutions. It also surfaces in his discussion of obedience, where Ibn al-Muqaffaʿ avoids endorsing absolute obedience to the sovereign by referencing the revealed law, virtue, and custom. This idea is also expressed in his suggestion of writing, clarifying, making visible rules and regulations concerning, for instance, taxation. A similar sentiment appears furthermore in the procedure of legislation, in which jurists (assumed to be autonomous from the sovereign) take part in lawmaking, and in which precedents, established practices, existing customs, and rational judgment are acknowledged as regulators of the lives of subjects.

Nonetheless, the difficulty of navigating the gap between sovereignty and governance is evident in the siyasa texts. The discourse of siyasa concentrated on how to manage the unrestrained power of the sovereign so that a routine social order could be established. This point is neatly expressed in the writings of the Abbasid lay bureaucrat literati as *siyāsat al-mulk* (management of sovereignty, conventionally translated as monarchical politics). Because the sovereign cannot be forced to do what he does not want to do, siyasa presumes an inclination and a capacity in the sovereign to act with wisdom, comprehend instructions, manage power, and deploy it judiciously. In this view, although the law does not bind the sovereign, adab-siyasa cultivates him. In *The Beast and the Sovereign*, Jacques Derrida describes this concern as bringing the sovereign within the law.[22] As will come into clearer view in chapter 5 regarding *Kalīla and Dimna* and ʿAbd al-Ḥamīd al-Kātib's (d. 750) metaphor of the beast and the trainer in one of his letters, the moderating capacity of siyasa offers a way of bringing the sovereign (and the masses) within political culture and within the law so that the social order the sovereign upholds is protected from his own arbitrary power. This is not because power is corrupt but because it is destructive.

Some contemporary political theorists are reluctant to use the concept of sovereignty for the precapitalist world and in a non-European context. While this reservation is not without merit, the illustrative and imaginative value of sovereignty as a concept allows me to tie the relations of power to the production of power. Supreme political power, signified in this study with sovereignty, resembled that of shepherds over their flocks or slaveholders over their "human property." The Umayyad and Abbasid sovereign's power was produced through references to the divine right to rule, in claims to perpetual power, in assertions of the right of ownership to control the lives of the population by guiding them and compelling them to obey, and in the propagation of the ruler's independence (absolute power) from the ruled. In this model, power did not mean a transferal of authority from the community to the ruler, nor did the ruler share his power with other sovereigns (unlike the king in feudal Europe and the notion of contractual caliphate), nor did he yield to any laws besides the natural and the revealed laws over which he enjoyed only a curtailed authority. Sovereignty can thus be understood as the unifying knot of power relations. Here siyasa plays a key role as a technique of "taming" the sovereign and mitigating relations.[23]

To sum up, siyasa functions as a technology of self-cultivation (through training, education, advice, and the inculcation of ethical standards) and the control, management, and policing of the people. At a time when governance appeared as an afterthought in the timeless normative language of imamate, siyasa pointed to another way of imagining the mechanism of conveying the sovereign's power to the routine work of governance. Siyasa governance, in this analysis, is not a question of theological deliberation or religious jurisprudence but a matter of historical contingency and rational reflection aimed at producing social good. In one respect, it addresses current challenges rather than primordial questions that require timeless wisdom and universal theological principles. In another, it suggests a notion of empire in which the institutions and people constituting the empire function differently from the ulema's "religious community." Considered this way, siyasa stands for more than a self-contained *sui generis* experiment. It is a theme one can properly understand only through a world-historical consideration of politics.

Global Secularities and Early Islam

My second argument concerns the thorny question of religiosity and secularity. There are a few points to explain. First, the word "religion" (or "religious belief") is used in this study in a broad sense, as applying to monotheistic traditions separate from its modern, protestant, hollowed-out connotation, to "translate" to the contemporary ear the earlier term *dīn*.[24] *Dīn* refers to the belief in and practice of laws, commandments, ethical norms, moral values, pious ways of life, and consideration of the "here" and the "hereafter" taught to humans by the one transcendental, omnipotent, omniscient God. While the specific injunctions of *dīn* may be explicated by reason, the *dīn* itself is thought to have been constituted by divine revelation independent of reason.[25] When I intend to use the term "religion" in a stricter sense or mark a disparity in signification, I opt, in consideration of the contemporary English-speaking reader, for revealed law or divine law (*dīn*) as more comprehensive than but inclusive of the ethicolegal category of sacred law(s) (*aḥkām al-dīn*[26] or *sharʿ*, generically referred to as *sharīʿa*) following the primary-source texts used in this book.[27] Approached from this angle, both *dīn* and shariʿa signify, rather than religion in the abstract, the ulema's discursive practice, constituting and rendering reality in a certain way to create the perfect pious (worshipping, devout, dutiful, *ʿābid, zāhid, taqiyy*) subjects, who distinguish themselves from others in their thoughts, feelings, language, and way of life.

As a particular discourse or discursive practice of the ulema, both *dīn* and sharīʿa lend themselves to an intellectual and sociopolitical analysis.[28] The discourse of *dīn* and sharīʿa presents four core characteristics: (1) it is constituted in a normative body of scholarship based on a particular interpretation of the qur'anic scripture and the prophethood of Muhammad known as scholarly disciplines of the revealed law, *ʿulūm al-dīn*, or scholarly disciplines of the sacred law, *al-ʿulūm al-sharʿiyya*, which include religious jurisprudence (*fiqh*), *ḥadīth*, theology, exegesis, and so forth; (2) it is articulated in a distinct language, although varying in style from one discipline to another and from one sect to another, which remains concerned with explaining and expounding God's revelation, *al-dīn*; (3) it carries an explicit salvific message at the core of its even minor pronouncements and regulations; and (4) it aims at regulating the belief, feeling, and practice of the believer by demanding adherence to sacred laws and rituals, as constructed by the ulema.

The second point is that Ibn al-Muqaffaʿ's argument about difference between religion and reason (*al-dīn wa al-ʿaql*) in the "Epistle" must be foregrounded. According to this pioneering thinker of siyasa, each one of these two categories authorizes a distinct practice and subject. To probe this dissimilarity in the discursive construction of the sociopolitical space, it is important, therefore, to remember the notions of revealed law/the world (*dīn/dunyā*) and revelation/reason (*waḥy/ʿaql*). Ibn al-Muqaffaʿ already suggests in his *Al-Adab al-Kabīr* a distinction between the forms of engagement with religion and with the world (*dīn* and *dunyā*).[29]

Ibn al-Muqaffaʿ also notes the need for a differential treatment of religion and the body (*dīn* and *jasad*), which demands balancing the two to complete the self.[30] Viewed in the long trajectory of history, this concern for moral and mundane self-formation mobilized two distinct technologies of self-management that may be captured as caring for the body (*ṣiḥḥat al-badan/al-jasad*)[31] and knowledge/interrogation of the self (*maʿrifat/muḥāsabat al-nafs*).[32] The former signified a more worldly way of life and self-constitution, and the latter seemed more aligned with religious piety, self-discovery, and ascetic self-denial, which obscured the value of the former or downright condemned it.[33] Considering the context in which this intellectual negotiation was taking place, his intervention restructured the frame of the debate and broke open a critical gap for new intellectual and political possibilities.

Now, I must comment on the emerging notion of adab as a manner or deportment distinct from the concepts of religious dutifulness (*taqwa*) and renunciant piety (*zuhd*), which functioned as practices of moral self-formation and techniques of self-representation. Typically translated as "etiquette" or "politeness," adab, just like the word siyasa, suggested not another way of saying "manners," but the technique or art of self-discipline, self-representation, and a taste preference connected to a chain of expressions, practices, and ways of living that indicated a worldly ethos in morals, attitude, and culture.[34] Viewed in this way, adab enabled a particular sociopolitical subject, who could be distinguishable from the customary tribal noble and the fashionable pious and the pious learned.

In the discursive practices of what I call the adab-siyasa ethos,[35] akin in some ways to the Indic *arthaśāstra*, we observe a new space of reflection on issues that remained outside the interest of the evolving religious scholarly disciplines, which, on the one hand, acted as a countervailing force to the value and prestige of religious discourse and, on the other hand, developed a new knowledge structure that seemed unintelligible to the ulema. This avant garde orientation carried a sense of temporality, such as an activity, thought, and attitude with little religious justification, and was therefore unbound by religious rule. It also suggested knowledge and scholarship concerning humanistic fields, pleasures, and wealth related to this world rather than the next, and a cosmopolitan habitus.[36] What is at stake here was more than a separation of spheres of authority between the ulema and the rulers sharing identical moral values and ways of life. Rather, we see an emergent array of difference in attitudes, taste, and practices. This new sociopolitical ethos tolerated (in fact, harbored) what the ulema considered "sin," or at least the potential of sinning, and presented a contrast to, and even a critique of, crude or unprincipled piety. From this angle, what the siyasa ethics tells us is that one does not ask Ibn al-Muqaffaʿ to train the sovereign in cultivating *taqwā* nor does one seek the help of Ibn Isḥāq or Mālik b. Anas (d. 795) to master *adab al-dunyā*.[37]

As a sign of a particular sociopolitical imaginary, each of these two forms of practice represented the values of distinct sociocultural groups. One focused on urbane manners and was connected to lay intellectuals pursuing nonreligious or mundane interests in life. The other foregrounded religious devotion and was associated with the expert knowledge of the ulema. The lasting significance of this intellectual and moral path broken by these eighth-century lay scholars is that it continued to function as an entry point for later religious and lay intellectuals who reflected on governance to forge a synthesis under two dialogic epistemic domes: religious politics/religious comportment (*siyāsat al-dīn, siyāsa sharʿiyya/adab al-dīn*) and worldly politics/worldly comportment (*siyāsat al-dunyā/adab al-dunyā*).[38]

In adab-siyasa secularity, therefore, three moves are evident. Foremost, it relativizes the role of religion in political practice by introducing the notion of the sovereign who decides on matters of governance rather than of an imam bound by the community of believers and the ulema's sacred laws. It also defines religion in a manner to make it amenable to the political structure, which functions as complementary machinery rather than the determining raison d'être of social order. Last, it aims to control religion by not just subordinating it within the broader structure of the empire but also by interfering in its epistemology, which challenges the power and the autonomy of the ulema.

Reflecting on the question of secularity from this vantage point demands embracing rather than explaining away the Umayyad and Abbasid thinkers' foundational assumptions about their place in a divinely ordered universe. The question, therefore, is not about these thinkers' denial of religious truth-claims nor should it be presumed that they sought to remove religion from political enactments. It is about how the Umayyad and Abbasid lay literati envisioned "royal authority" (*mulk*) as a distinct way of governing. They defined royal authority as a form of divine grace given exclusively to the ruler to keep the earthly order and pushed back against the ulema-centric political morality for the purpose of creating a space of temporal political reflection.

A core argument of this book is that these secular practices emerged in a relational process in which the ethos of adab-siyasa diverged from the ulema's practices and simultaneously created extrareligious discursive spaces, in which lay intellectuals challenged the value of ulema's logic and authority. In the social space, the emerging secularity promoted the wielding of temporal power, the prying open of gaps in the wall erected by the ulema, and the enabling and legitimizing of a range of new practices, from epicurean activities, like playing chess, drinking wine, and building spaces for leisure and pleasure, to erudite enterprises such as demanding the recitation of the Qur'an in the vernacular and exploring intellectual fields beyond the dominant religious narratives and interests. Such practices are best appreciated not just in their own specific particularity as an end in themselves but also as signposts on a temporal direction of thinking and practice.

A Pragmatic Secularity

Writing new histories of political thought attentive to questions of religiosity and secularity calls for an antifoundational reading. It has become increasingly evident that the ideal of secularism is connected to a concrete historical condition, which includes Enlightenment modernity, Protestant sensibilities, and the scholarly discourse of social sciences and humanities in the nineteenth to twentieth centuries claiming to cleanse religious beliefs from "proper" scholarly analysis. The modern state, in turn, has reduced religiosity to a private belief and filled the gap itself to create and control its own subject.[39] Since "the return of religion" to public space in the second half of the twentieth century numerous thinkers point out how the notion of a strict separation of religion and secular life is only ideational.[40] As Talal Asad elegantly explains, the terms "religion" and "secularity" themselves belong to a semantic chain, a set of other vocabularies that bring persons and things, sensibilities, and practices together in distinctive ways in historically specific contexts. Furthermore, the religious and the secular are not confined to the realms of personal belief, intellectual judgment, or interpretation but also involve myriad practices, ways of life, and feelings that cannot be mapped onto this binary understanding.[41] In fact, rather than holding an objective descriptive value, these idioms function as signposts to given attitudes.[42] Such critical interventions demonstrate how the conditions on the sociopolitical ground are messier than the modernist theoretical neatness suggests.

However much I agree with this characterization, I am unsatisfied with its supposition. The deconstruction of the concepts of the religious and the secular as vestiges of the binary of liberal modernity has recently been taken by some scholars in Islamic studies as a free pass to overlook, or even dismiss, the debate as modern and European, and thus to paint the caliphal and sultanic traditions with the broad brush of religiosity. One issue with this stance is that since the concept "religious" is as modern as the "secular," how does rejecting one justify the embrace of the other? There is also the challenge that regardless of whether the concepts are modern, the question of secularity functions as a structuring concern, like recent awareness about the practices of gender, for rethinking the past. Denying or ignoring this problem helps only shield non-European histories from the critical treatment granted to European and North American societies. Worse yet, it empowers oppressive practices as "socially and culturally authentic" traditions in the name of religion.

In what follows, I underscore the variegated expressions of difference in the Umayyad and Abbasid writerly universe that suggest the vitality of ideas and practices that we associate with secularity (instead of secularism and secularization) in sociopolitical spaces. This is where an open-ended contestation took place, sometimes overtly and sometimes covertly, between competing political imaginaries. At the same time, I push back against the modernist ideal of secularism and its Hegelian teleology or finality (i.e., reason and science win). This is not in order to discuss the concepts of secularism and religiosity as abstract concepts imported from the modern episteme as part of a doctrine of progress and of democracy—a doctrine that typically authorized the argument of how non-Europeans failed to advance vis-à-vis "the West." On the contrary, what is interesting is the intersection of worldly and religious practices with political power, and the particular social subject each enabled in Abbasid history regardless of whether it was connected with political power.

One can take a broader view of the issue and probe precapitalist polities within the theoretical orbit of religiosity and secularity without denying the transformative nature of liberal modernity and the modern state. To begin, one notices how the precapitalist government mediated local identities just as the modern state does, and it therefore redefined and transcended particular and differentiating practices of the self that were articulated through religion. I agree that the premodern state did not have the complex state apparatuses or capacity of the modern state to penetrate the social fabric. It nonetheless shaped political subjectivity by manipulating sociopolitical structures, laws, taxation, and urban planning.[43] The transcendence of local cultural specificities appeared indirectly (unlike, for instance, the discourse of representation or the idea of citizenship in the modern states) and incrementally by favoring one cultural practice over another and, through the work of the whole system, which, over the long run, created a sort of commonality that would not exist otherwise. This sort of government manipulation was enforced by the use or the threat of government's punitive measures mostly in urban centers, where state power was more directly exercised. This dynamic appears, for instance, in Ibn al-Muqaffaʿ's argument about obedience, where he discusses the role of political power vis-à-vis a passive obedient subject and a disobedient one regardless of their particular sociocultural tradition. The subjects here are represented not by their sociocultural practice (faith, language, profession, etc.) but by their attitude toward the sovereign. Likewise, we observe a similar practice in his discussion of how to "standardize" the land tax regardless of the local identity of the farmer.

By resisting the "modern" and "premodern" binary, I am not trying to flatten temporal and geographic differences. Provincializing the modernist notion of secularity among myriad other possible global forms within the more complex canvas of world history, but without abandoning the question of a distinction between religious practices and secular ones, allows me to work with the conceptual framework of "global secularities" or "multiple secularities."[44] This vantage point enables me to shift my attention to instances in which counterbalancing responses were raised in the discourse of adab-siyasa against the ulema-centric sociopolitical imaginaries.

The term "worldliness" as a modifier or qualifier strikes me as functional shorthand, even a worthy undertaking, which helps texture the term "secular" in caliphal history. It opens the idea of secularity to different global applications without allowing the Enlightenment's secularist conception of religion to prejudge different secular practices with its yardstick. By the same token, it restricts the ulema's all-encompassing notion of transcended religiosity to dictate the terms of the discussion. We are encountering here a mode of secular practice that cannot be construed as an "incomplete" or "arrested" version that would be perfected in the Enlightenment. For this reason, one does well to practice an Aristotelian prudence in identifying the distinction between European and Abbasid secularities. The difference is in kind rather than in degree.[45]

As far as the practices we associate with secularity overlap, intersect with, and are pollinated by religiosity, and vice versa, they cannot be categorically separate, wholesale, and complete; they are fragmentary, precarious, contingent, polyphonic, and dialogic. They are in fact co-constituted. For this reason, they cannot be understood uniformly or teleologically. They are better imagined, to cite Gilles Deleuze and Félix Guattari,[46] as rhizomic, carrying the stamp of heterogeneity, multiplicity, and laterality recurrent in the relations of power and circumstances. Similar to how one might conceive of and signify gender identities in nonbinary ways, here, too, one can imagine a range or spectrum of practices and concepts developing against the dominant or hegemonic "social imaginary" of the epoch in question,[47] which represents unfinished and untheorized shifts in ways of sensing and living.[48] It should be clear from the foregoing discussion that I am interested in secularity as an epistemological and embodied-knowledge question rather than a doctrine.[49]

How we qualify secularity determines the way we examine it; thus, a further clarification of my position is in order. A good starting point is the work of Armando Salvatore and Neguin Yavari, who have characterized, similar to Leon Wieseltier's formulation of secularity,[50] distinctions in "Islamicate" histories as "soft" and "hard."[51] I see in their point a significant intervention that moves the discussion forward. However, one could argue that one observes both soft and hard forms of secularity in Islamicate histories. It surprises no one that the hegemonic religiosities in history (the Christian church, the Jewish rabbinate, the Muslim ulema) also pushed nonconforming practices to the margins, into discrete spaces as subtle practices, when they were emboldened and enabled by political power. Hence, secularity could appear sometimes as a discourse or way of living against or outside the parameters of ruling political or hegemonic religious power, which may be described as "soft." One observes such practices in the subtexts of ʿAbd al-Ḥamīd's treatise on chess, where he attacks chess players, and al-Jāḥiẓ's epistle that rails against scribes, in which he underlines their irreligiosity and impiety. Looked at from a different angle, the ulema themselves became increasingly protective of their own autonomy from the direct control of the caliphs and sultans, setting up their own separate spheres for the two authorities.

Some other practices took a "hard" form, where the rulers imposed their will on religious scholars or blocked them from determining or interfering in government practice. For instance, caliphs adapted existing pre-Islamic practices and institutions, and enacted extra-Islamic customary and ad hoc laws (fiscal, administrative, and penal). The military juntas in the Abbasid commonwealth in the ninth and tenth centuries rarely listened to the ulema in their practices. Later, the sultanic rulers of the eleventh century, such as the Selçuks and similar dynasties, openly introduced extrareligious laws in governance over and against pious objections.

To texture the discussion from my vantage point in this study, I propose to qualify the secularity of adab-siyasa as "pragmatic," with an accent on its practical and everyday aspects. In approaching the term from this direction, I want to avoid characterizing secularity as either soft or hard in a one-dimensional way. I hope instead to recognize the act it affected or mobilized and the push-and-pull character of it. The phrase "pragmatic secularity" invokes a sense of the effort made toward cultivating benefits and ensuring welfare in its temporal sense (neatly phrased as *maṣāliḥ*, *fawā'id*, or *manāfiʿ dunyāwiyya/dīniyya* in the textual sources of the eighth century onward). It also suggests the capacity to negotiate a problem according to practical logic as circumstances dictate.[52] This functional quality of secularity avoids polarizing the concepts of *dunyā* and *dīn* or adab-siyasa and shariʿa-imamate. Instead, it brings up the relational dimension of the concepts, their polyphony,[53] and the hybrid and constantly updating character of both orientations. It conveys the dialectic regulating their relations at the points of contact, which authorizes new conceptualizations and practices in the everyday spaces of governance and social practice.

It is imperative, however, to note in conclusion that given such a complex interpenetration, one cannot presume an overall "pan-Islamic" synthesis that defines "Islamicate" societies. In fact, the expectation of harmony or compatibility, no matter how well intended, under the umbrella of either religiosity or secularity—as a teleology explaining caliphal and sultanic histories—slips into an essentialist premise of a culturalist argument, which I want to avoid here. My argument is that the pragmatic and polyphonic tenor of the adab-siyasa is constitutive of the conflictual and fragmentary, rather than harmonious, dynamics undergirding governance in diverse explicit or subtle ways, depending on the context.

"Islamic Political Thought" as a Colonial Paradigm

Another guiding inquiry of this study concerns the jargon "Islamic political thought" and its cognates.[54] To put it simply, what is the function of the adjective "Islamic" in "Islamic political thought"? Despite its deceptively descriptive tone, the phrase "Islamic political thought" has been functioning over the course of a century as a discursive trope for constructing and selectively essentializing the Other, this time through its putative religious commonality. It has generated a reality whose referent is neither the histories of Muslims nor their practices but the discourse itself. If the title of the prestigious *The Princeton Encyclopedia of Islamic Political Thought* is to be taken as a benchmark, one is justified in affirming that this tradition of scholarship has produced specialists working to detail, rectify, and support the framework's fundamental assumptions.[55] One wonders what kind of secularity one could find, let alone elaborate upon, if the category of analysis is formulated in religious idioms and defined by a discourse privileging the ulema's sociopolitical ideals as the field's normative foundation and primary marker?[56]

It may not be common knowledge that the phrase "Islamic political thought" appeared during the European colonial aggression in Asia and Africa, and in the struggles against colonialism in the late nineteenth and the first half of the twentieth centuries. In this period, the European Enlightenment's triumphalist civilizational outlook, systematizing scientific discourses, and their concomitant intellectual habits and knowledge structures reshaped the language of both Orientalist scholars and Europe-oriented Muslim intellectuals. As Cemil Aydın demonstrates, colonial officers and Orientalist scholars referred to discrete peoples and empires in Afro-Eurasia as "the Muslim world" in ways that defined the Muslim peoples racially and essentialized their religious beliefs and cultures as separate from, and inferior to, that of "Western civilization."[57] Out of this colonial context, Islam emerged as a religious totality covering all aspects of life, on behalf of which one speaks and according to which one judges.

Charmed by the appeal of doing "religious science" within the "social sciences," which became a fashionable and advanced way of analyzing and knowing the natural and human worlds, Orientalists began restructuring customary knowledge practices (*ʿulūm*) under titles reflective of this remarkable epistemic shift.[58] They started writing about the colonized societies' histories and cultures in the idioms, and according to the categories, of the "homeland" and helped restructure colonized societies according to the desires of colonial empires and modern European values. Muslim activists and intellectuals too—the pan-Islamists in Afro-Eurasia—embraced and redeployed this new language and the concomitant new intellectual forms to defend themselves against the accusations of inferiority, resist colonial expansion, reform their societies to regain their lost power, and prove the Muslims' worth in the modern world. By the end of the nineteenth century, Islam was already a discourse in both Western and Muslim scholarship.

The Ottoman Caliphate and the Idea of "Muslim State"

In this political and epistemic context, the caliphate became a scholarly question in the second half of the nineteenth century. Soon after such an interest in the caliphate, the notion that Islam/Muslims must have developed a political *Weltanschauung* that cut across groups and centuries and that could be identified and studied appeared in writing as early as the turn of the twentieth century. The idea of "Islamic political thought" was thus born at the intersection of two traditions of colonial-era Orientalist and Muslim scholarship: one tradition focused on the caliphate and the other pioneered the idea of the Islamic/Muslim state.[59] The former studied the caliphate's status and future state and had a noticeable practical function, while the latter conceptualized the idea of shariʿa governance based on "reformed" Sunnite juristic sensibilities. The proponents of the latter elaborated an "Islamic" notion of politics inspired by the values of the emerging modern nation-state. Supported by the authority of the epistemic categories of the modern "social sciences" and moved by the values of the liberal political discourse, this Orientalist and Muslim "pan-Islamist" venture re-formed political knowledge by classifying and canonizing the received literary corpora on governance. Muslim and European intellectuals brought into conversation various confessional and intellectual traditions in the history of Muslim dynasties beyond the position of any single school, sect, and political regime.[60]

Considering its broad contour, Orientalist research on the caliphate followed the trajectory of colonial empires' interests in the Muslim majority regions. Orientalists paid attention to the Ottoman sultan Abdülhamid's (r. 1876–1909) world politics, pan-Islamic movements, late nineteenth- and early twentieth-century caliphate movements in Asia and Africa, and resistance to colonialism. Familiar with notions of Oriental despotism since early modernity, the talented Orientalist scholars focused on the caliphate and its history, doctrine, current state, and prospects, and movements related to it.[61] Reading historians like Edward Gibbon (d. 1794), they portrayed the "Oriental despot" as the embodiment of vices that the modern, enlightened European ruler should avoid. They did so in a language of contrasting images—"East" versus "West," "civilization" versus "barbarity."[62]

Such views spread wider than the Orientalists' work alone could achieve. Some of the most influential European thinkers had already invoked this generalized notion of difference and otherness about the East, so much so that even the most progressive voices did not feel the need to question it. Thus, Georg W.

F. Hegel (d. 1831) situated Oriental despotism in the first stage of the historical and universal movement of the spirit. Karl Marx (d. 1883) and Friedrich Engels (d. 1895) went along with the idea and explained Oriental despotism as a peculiar economic system, the Asiatic mode of production, which, according to them, prevented the rise of the middle class; led to a stagnant socioeconomic structure; and therefore allowed the hegemony of despotic power, which lacked the capacity to develop on its own without external intervention by more advanced societies.[63] In a similar fashion, Max Weber (d. 1924) bracketed Asian societies and their political structures within primitivity (or the peculiar rationality) of patrimonialism.[64]

European scholars vacillated between representing the caliphate as the most visible form of Oriental despotism, an anachronistic relic on the verge of demise, and a handy religiopolitical office for political gains by colonial governors. Already in 1868, Alfred von Kremer examined "three leading ideas in Islam": God, prophecy, and the state. The third section of the study, which comprises ten chapters, is dedicated to the development of the institution of the caliphate and to discussion of the views of religiopolitical parties (the Shiites and the Kharijites), the caliphate and the imamate, and the sultanate after the heyday of the Abbasids.[65] Even though his discussion of politics represented only a theme in a broader historico-philological study of major ideas in Islam, and therefore was closer to the style of his contemporaries, like Gustav Weil, William Muir, and Reinhart Dozy, than to later Orientalists who dedicated their studies to politics, it is notable that von Kremer allocates a section to government as one of the "leading ideas."

In the late nineteenth century, Wilfrid S. Blunt called attention to the title of the caliph as a major religiopolitical prerogative that the principal imperial powers, England, France, and the Egypt of Muhammad Ali, were eager to claim in order to mobilize colonial and state-building projects. He implied, if not suggested, transferring the caliphate to a descendant of the Prophet who would reside in Mecca and hold spiritual powers.[66] In 1903, Duncan B. MacDonald, wondering what to do with the caliphate, contemplated the possibility of presenting the "Emperor of India," that is, the British monarch, as a caliph vis-à-vis the Ottoman sultan from the point of view of constitutionalism. After a review of the history of the caliphate as a political institution from the constitutional—that is, Sunnite—position, which he calls "the theory of the Muslim State," he mentions the Shiite and Kharijite positions on the ideal caliph, and discusses, as much as a political analyst as a historian, the circumstances of the Ottoman caliphate and the global developments affecting its future. MacDonald acknowledges how presenting the English throne as the holder of the caliphate might be unconvincing; he nonetheless does not rule it out. In fact, if anything, he leaves the prospect open for such an eventuality and criticizes the English government for not being attentive to this matter. This passage is remarkable for its audacity:

> The greatest of the Sultans of Islam is undoubtedly the Emperor of India. Under his rule are far more Muslims than fall to any other. But the theory of the Muslim State never contemplated the possibility of Muslims living under the rule of an unbeliever. . . . In India, the custom seems to be to pray for "the ruler of the age" without name; then each worshipper can apply it as he chooses. But there has crept in a custom in a few mosques of praying for the Ottoman Sultan as the Khalifa; the English government busies itself little with these things until compelled, and the custom will doubtless spread. The Ottoman Sultan is certainly next greatest to the Emperor of India and would seem, as a Muslim ruling Muslims, to have an unassailable position. But in his case also difficult and ambiguous constitutional questions can be raised.[67]

Others represented the institution as an ancient relic.[68] In the same year the caliphate was abolished, Sir Thomas Arnold published his book, *The Caliphate*.[69] In this very first book dedicated to the institution of the caliphate in English, Arnold offers a useful and informative appraisal of the institution from its origins to 1924. Indebted, as he notes, to the works of Vasili Barthold, Carl Becker, Leona Caetani, Carlo Nallino, and Snouck Hurgronje, Arnold devotes brief chapters to the "Theological Sanction for the Caliphate in the Qur'an and the Traditions," "expositions" of the jurists, and philosophical and ethical writers, and describes the Shiite and Kharijite "doctrines" and other matters of concern ("the alleged spiritual powers of the caliph," "popular use of the term *khalīfa*," "the title sultan," and "the titles of the Ottoman sultan") in the appendixes.[70]

More interested in the imperial and political potential of the caliphate throughout the "Muslim world" than much else, Arnold considers the call for maintaining the caliphate as both irrational and anachronistic. Disregarding that the caliphate stood powerful as an institution and an idea globally, even as he was writing, Arnold contrasts the current views on the caliphate to that of the Holy Roman Empire. He claims that while there is "no monarch left who makes any pretension to be the successor of Charlemagne . . . there are still rival claimants for the possession of the title of Caliph" in the "Muhammadan world." He further notes that "the theory of the Caliphate is still cherished by theological students who shut their eyes to the altered circumstances of the political world, and expound the doctrine of the caliphate as though they were still living in the ninth century."[71]

Arnold describes the Turkish National Assembly's policy of abolishing the caliphate as facing the realities of life. He claims that "[a]s a political reality, or as embodying the theories that had lent importance to it in the past, the Caliphate had long been dead."[72] Yet he remains apprehensive that "[the] ideal is still cherished and is likely to survive as a hope in the hearts of Muslim peoples for many generations to come, for every Muslim regards himself as the citizen of an ideal state." To the learned as much as to the ignorant, to the devout traditionalist as much as to the modernizer acquainted with modern conditions, he observes that "this hope remains enshrined in the doctrine of the caliphate."[73]

Muslim intellectuals, too, addressed questions about the caliphate as an actual standing institution, hoping to affect its course in constructive ways. From the mid-nineteenth century onward, Ottoman officials and intellectuals began writing about constitutional monarchy, political representation, the connection between the caliphate and the Ottoman dynasty, and reforming the caliphate to meet the challenges of the time. The Pan-Islamist policies of the Ottomans carried the debate to the attention of Muslim rulers and intellectuals by advocating the spiritual leadership of the Ottoman caliph over the global Muslim community, and created conditions in which the debates about the caliphate intersected with matters of regional politics against the European empires. Many Muslim intellectuals continued to advocate for the caliphate in order to reinforce their fight against the colonizers and defend the right of Muslims for equal membership among advanced nations. The caliphate also became a rallying point to unify the global Muslim community, further calls to reform societies, and present the caliphate as a standing or ideal institution that could foster a mode of governance suitable for the time, and even as an institution the colonizers could use for their benefit.[74]

Thinking beyond the Ottoman caliphate and reforming it, Muslim intellectuals opened a new front of reflection on the forms of Muslim political organization. The outcome was a plethora of practical and pertinent publications that changed the language and vocabulary of traditional scholarship. A whole range of Ottoman intellectuals based their discussion of the caliphate and the "Muslim state" on the ideas of constitutionalism, parliamentarism, and the sovereignty of the people.[75] A few examples will suffice here. In 1898, ʿAbd al-Raḥmān al-Kawākibī used the terms *al-ḥukūma al-muqayyada* to indicate a government/caliphate checked by the laws and the constitution, and *al-ḥukūma al-dustūriyya* for a constitutional government in order to discuss caliphal rule or governance based on "Islamic" principles.[76] In Egypt, the foremost example of scholarship in this line is perhaps Rashīd Riḍā's articles in al-Manār in 1922 and 1923, which he brought together in a book titled *al-Khilāfa aw al-Imāma al-Uẓmā*. Seeing the demise of the Ottoman caliphate, Riḍā called for the independence of the Muslim world and for establishing a caliphate, which he used together and interchangeably with Islamic government, *al-ḥukūma al-Islāmiyya* or *ḥukūma Islāmiyya*, and caliphal government, *ḥukūmat al-khilāfa*, for the Muslim community.[77] Other publications in the Ottoman imperial territories and colonial and postcolonial Southwest Asia, North Africa, and India followed at an increased pace. After the demise of the caliphate, and notwithstanding the critique of it by intellectuals such as ʿAlī ʿAbd al-Rāziq, who published his renowned work, *al-Islām wa-Uṣūl al-Ḥukm* in 1925,[78] and right after the abolition of the caliphate, the term *al-ḥukūma al-Islāmiyya* gained new currency at the intersection of the independence struggles toward the mid-twentieth century and the emergence of the Islamist movements. The existing academic and political structures have assured the vitality of the nomenclature to the degree that only a few today would find problematic.[79]

The Birth of "Islamic Political Thought"

In the early decades of the twentieth century, certain Muslim intellectuals began reflecting on governance and the political revival of the "Muslim world" beyond the caliphal institution. The main question was, If not the caliphate, what? This question spurred an interest in rereading the past, reflecting on the caliphate in a deterritorialized fashion, and probing the nature of an "Islamic governance." Inspired by the universalist claims of the modern humanistic and social scientific disciplines in Europe, when the field of political thought split from its mother field to become a science itself,[80] the celebrated Indian poet and thinker Muhammad Iqbal shifted the focus of the discourse from the caliphate to "Muslim political thought." A strong defender of global Muslim revival, Iqbal was educated in Lahore, Cambridge, and Munich. He was a student of Sir Thomas Arnold in Lahore before the latter left the city in 1904 and his temporary replacement at SOAS in 1907. Iqbal's article "Political Thought in Islam" appeared in the *Sociological Review* a few months after he returned to India in 1908. As far as I can ascertain, this was the first publication in English that framed the subject using this phraseology. To enable a new intellectual space in which Muslim thinkers could elaborate forward-looking reformist ideas about governance based on the broad Islamic heritage, Iqbal discusses the Sunnite-juristic view of the caliphate (largely based on al-Māwardī's model) and summarizes the Shiite and the Kharijite positions on the imamate.[81]

Writing against the background of nearly a half-century-long Orientalist and modernist scholarship on the "Muslim world," Iqbal describes Muslims as a "nation" united by nothing other than the laws of Islam, which he presents as compatible with modern liberal values. He points out two foundations for this union: "That the Muslim Commonwealth is based on the absolute equality of all Muslims in the eye of the law" and "[t]hat according to the law of Islam there is no distinction between the Church and the State." Iqbal assumes objectively identifiable universal Islamic principles, and a politically defined religious community regardless of the various historical manifestations of Islam and the diversity of peoples.[82] His position helped the resistance against the colonial empire's policies in India through a religious justification of self-rule but affirmed the veracity of the Orientalist discourse on Muslims and Islam. The article's emphasis on political thought under such a title signaled a new conceptual direction.

A few years later, Rudolf Strothmann published *Das Staatsrecht der Zaiditen*, in which he examined the doctrine of the Zaydī imamate in Yemen. Like Iqbal's article, it discusses the Zaydī doctrine of the imamate in the framework of the history of political thought. Strothmann begins by deliberating the notion of the imamate and Muslim political thinking, expressing the idea that prophecy, the religious community, and the state in Islam form a unity ordained by God. He is convinced that instead of separation between the principles of theology and the state, Islam demands that the religious community exist in the form of a state.[83] Publications adopting the phrase "political thought" in their titles appeared more often in the 1920s-1930s, among which Gibb's are notable.[84]

In light of this line of scholarship, one needs to mention Haroon Khan Sherwani's groundbreaking publication, *Studies in the History of Early Muslim Political Thought and Administration*. Published in 1942, this work adopts Iqbal's phrase, political thought in Islam, and gives it new life in both phraseology and content. If establishing an intellectual genealogy of this field has any merit, anyone reading Erwin Rosenthal, Montgomery Watt, Ann Lambton, Anthony Black, Patricia Crone, and others would attest that Sherwani represented a turning point. Immersed in European scholarship through his Aligarh, Oxford, and Cambridge University education Sherwani surveys the political thought of several thinkers, beginning with an overall essay on the "Qur'anic State" and ending with Maḥmūd Gāwān, a high-ranking administrator in the Bahmanī sultanate of the Deccan in the fifteenth century. A collection of his previously published writings and lectures, this volume examines the political writings of Ibn Abī al-Rabīʿ, al-Fārābī, al-Māwardī, Amīr Kaʿīkāūs, Niẓām al-Mulk, al-Ghazālī, and Maḥmūd Gāwān in succession.[85]

Sherwani criticizes the lack of interest in this matter among the Orientalists and in the written histories of European political thought and describes how the neglect of Muslim thinkers created an intellectual gap that must be closed. "It would, therefore, be in the fitness of things," he remarks, "if a correct estimate is made of Islamic political thought during these centuries, an estimate which is bound to bridge the gulf which seems to exist between the Classical and the Medieval epochs, as well as to give the modern man an insight into a particular aspect of Oriental thought nearly a thousand years ago."[86] Sherwani broke ground in the sense that he did not rely on the juristic exposition of governance by the ulema. In addition to the juristic notion of the caliphate as elaborated by jurists and theologians, he included programmatically the writings of bureaucrats and philosophers as part of the "Muslim political thought."[87]

Erwin Rosenthal adopted this pioneering framework first in an article in *Islamic Culture* in 1948 ("Some Aspects of Islamic Political Thought"), and then in a monograph titled *Political Thought in Medieval Islam* in 1958.[88] In a few places in the book, Rosenthal uses variations on the same phrase, such as "political thought" in Islam and "Muslim political thought." He examines with learned detail the political views of several thinkers and helps shape the direction of the scholarship in multiple ways. He divides the history of political thought into three big branches, with some overlapping figures such as Ibn Khaldūn: the theory of the caliphate by the jurists; the writings of moralists and belles lettres and princes; and political philosophy of Muslim philosophers, which makes up the largest section of the book. Like Sherwani, Rosenthal directs his attention to individual authors and their texts rather than to the caliphate, but he differs from Sherwani by foregrounding and elaborating on the political thought tradition in philosophical writing.[89]

Published in 1968, Montgomery Watt's monograph, *Islamic Political Thought* assured the currency of this expression as a framing idea. Watt repositioned Rosenthal's philosophers-oriented approach on the juristic theory of the imamate by focusing his narrative on the ideas of the jurists and theologians rather than the philosophers. He traces political thought from the seventh until the thirteenth century as it evolved in the actual practice of the caliphate and the activities of Muslim sects rather than through the lens and texts of individual scholars, as Rosenthal does. Watt thus begins with "the Islamic state under Muhammad" and proceeds through various stages of the caliphate, the organization of the empire under the Umayyads and the Abbasids, focusing on later periods. He then examines issues related to the religiopolitical sect of the Kharijites, the formation of what he calls the religious institution, referring to the Sunnite ulema, and their political positions. Watt also provides a portrait of the Umayyad and Abbasid scribes and explains the clash between the ulema and the bureaucrats over power and prominence. He underlines the central significance of the faith community as a political body. Attentive to the political ideas in his survey, Watt discusses the breakdown of the Abbasid caliphate and the rise of the warlords, and gives a brief list of the political theorists before the Mongol conquests and an overview of the caliphate after 1258. In the last two chapters, Watt discusses the Shiite position on the imamate and contemporary politics, as part of his discussion on "Islam and occidental political ideas."[90]

Watt's work and the uncritical scholarship that followed, such as by Lambton, Bernard Lewis, Crone, and others, popularized the idea of Islamic political thought until it became a conceptual paradigm according to which particular knowledge has been produced.[91] Beyond approaching their questions mostly from a Eurocentric, liberalist, commonsensical perspective, without reflecting on their own epistemic and political assumptions, these twentieth-century scholars privileged the ulema-centric religious discourse from an "Islamic studies" perspective with a patent bias toward early centuries of Islam to discredit change as deviation from the norm or as decline rather than tackling key questions about relations, political economy, political power, and governance. Considering the global political and intellectual scene, one notices that this narrative continues to be communicated by state leaders, political and religious pundits, Islamist and lay intellectuals, academics, and the full set of other global institutions with complex vested interests.[92] Read contrapuntally, this stance cannot be explained as a mere intellectual discourse. It at once reflects and authorizes the structures of the contemporary power relations in the domestic and international fields.

A Way Forward

Fortunately, several important studies, which I critically engage, have exposed the conventional historiography.[93] Just to name a few here, Aziz Al-Azmeh treats the caliphate and later forms of rule as another iteration of the idea of kingship ubiquitous in the *longue-durée* "Near Eastern" tradition. Arguing that the older traditions of kingship in the region were transposed onto Islamic form and given Islamic textual sanction, this much learned and inspiring study is too unyielding in its assumption of continuity and similarity to notice change and the political significance of the intellectual current of secularity and governmentality that shaped the political role of faith in the empire.[94]

Wael Hallaq's erudite work is a broad comparative and interpretive survey of the legal, political, and moral histories of "premodern" Islam and the West. It makes two essential points: the modern state is incompatible with Islamic moral values and thus cannot be adopted by Muslims, and modern experiments with establishing an Islamic state have been unsuccessful in advancing an acceptable form of a genuine shariʿa state. My issue with this otherwise persuasive argument is whether it allows any role for siyasa. Explicating the incompatibility between the moral foundations of the modern state and shariʿa governance, he underlines the ulema-centric moral and epistemological tradition, overlooking the significance of temporal notions of politics associated with siyasa. I hope *Disenchanting the Caliphate* sheds another light on the question.[95]

Additional vital studies on the post-Mongol caliphate probe the question of caliphal governance as an ongoing process of revival, refinement, adjustment, and redefinition in political thinking rather than as a decline in the pursuit of justifying brute power. Accentuating the historicized moral and ideological underpinnings of political thought and demonstrating the intertextuality of cultural currents and of religious discourses, they only marginally pay attention to secular writings that revolved around statecraft, the genre of mirror for princes, and notions of imperial sovereignty. Ovamir Anjum, Mona Hassan, and Hüseyin Yılmaz examine eruditely the effects of the Mongol imperial experience on the Mamluk, Mughal, Ottoman, and Safavid imperial cosmopolitanism. What is less articulated (and less argued) in their writings is the extent to which a secular Abbasid imperial tradition might have contributed to the Mongol period and to early modern political discourses.[96]

The political thought of the Abbasid period remains understudied. Among those that address some questions I deal with in this study is Muhammad Qasim Zaman's learned study of the relationship between the ulema and the Abbasid caliphs in the eighth and ninth centuries. It argues that the caliphs collaborated and cooperated with rather than competed against or conflicted with the "proto-Sunni" ulema over religious and political authority. Sohaira Siddiqui examines the eleventh-century jurist and theologian al-Juwaynī's theological, legal, and political writings to argue that al-Juwaynī approached the caliphate/imamate as a question of refinement and adjustment rather than as a concession and apology under difficult circumstances. Zaman and Siddiqui are duly concerned with the question of legitimacy and political accommodation within the imamate's framework, but they neglect siyasa. Indeed, they seem to operate on the assumption of a ubiquitous religiosity that shapes political thinking and practice.[97]

In fact, aside from a small number of interventions critical of the Eurocentric assumptions inherent in the more conventional work, the discourse of "Islamic political thought" continues to dictate the terms of the discussion. Only few studies concerning the Abbasid caliphate actively seek to challenge the over-religionization of political thought across the Nile-to-Oxus imperial axis in the pre-Mongol period.[98] I must mention the meticulous work of Louise Marlow on Pseudo-Māwardī's *Counsel for Kings*. Marlow's exemplary contextualization of the work demonstrates the work's dialogic and intertextual character. Although Marlow does not directly address the secularizing tone of Pseudo-Māwardī's text as a work of mirror for princes, her overall analysis demonstrates that the

Counsel for Kings is a remarkable example of siyasa discourse in the early tenth century. As Marlow notes, the author is as an engaged observer. He practices multiple literary genres, religious and otherwise, and combines a wide range of perspectives, disciplines, and cultural materials to offer effective and pertinent political counsel in the first half of the tenth century Samanid Iran. Marlow encapsulates the resilience of the siyasa discourse across centuries in the ability of its proponents to combine perennial wisdom and contingent knowledge in their writings.[99]

I should also mention Yavari's insightful survey of the genre of mirror for princes literature from early Islam to the early modern era, in particular the Selçukid period (eleventh through thirteenth centuries) and the work of vizier Niẓām al-Mulk (d. 1092). In it, Yavari argues how the advice literature promoted secular values, such as reason and prudence, as a safeguard against political misfortune and loss of power. However, she does not elaborate how secularity is related to political power beyond underlining the value of prudence and reason, especially concerning the period before the Selçukid Empire, nor does she consider, as a matter of political reflection, the dynamics regulating the relations between the sovereign's power and the practicalities of governance, or what I have described as the governmentalization of sovereignty.[100] In the same encouraging line, Linda Darling's panoramic survey of the idea of the "circle of justice" across the ages, however brief on the Abbasid period, is dedicated to illuminating the persistence of the idea of social justice from ancient to contemporary times. Remarkable for its attention to nonreligious political themes and sources, this study, like the other self-described studies of "Islamic political thought," do not seek to challenge the framing and terms of the analysis in scholarship.[101]

Such promising efforts have shown that the list of anomalies in the conventional paradigm has grown too large to ignore. Half a century ago, when Marshall Hodgson challenged the same frame of analysis by setting up "the venture of Islam" in a world-historical trajectory, he coined the term "Islamicate" as a new conceptual space for studying Muslim peoples' history related to but distinct from Islam as a faith. I still find the term "Islamicate" to be a generative intellectual space to think through the thorny questions of religion and secularity. However, to relieve Hodgson's term itself from overdetermining the character of research by implying, if not demanding, the reference to "Islam" no matter what subject one studies and pinning down the histories of diverse global societies to the singularity of religion, I opt to use the concept as a step to climb beyond it. I thus shift the focus of my attention to a contrapuntal reading of the primary source texts to sound out the variegated expressions of temporality in the dynamics of sociopolitical life, which emerged at the intersection of empire building, bureaucratic formation, and prose writing. I can only hope that the effort inspires a new agenda of research in the histories of Muslim dynasties from the eighth century onward and encourages a new analytical language that can challenge the framing of the liberal epoch and move in the direction of Hodgson's and Edward W. Said's decolonial global democratic humanism.[102] The following chapters of the book commence with an outline of the caliphal practice as the structuring framework of political reflection.

1

Caliphal Practice

To analyze the discourse of siyasa, I begin by delineating the world of the literate elite whose texts I study in this book. I observe two major developments until the mid-eighth century at the intersection of self-aware political reflection. One had to do with the co-formation of faith and empire. Muhammad's community broke into multiple rival groups during the sociopolitical transformation in the seventh century, which brought the faith to the forefront of disputes and closed the door on the notion of a unified community, thus potentiating a plurality of imaginaries on faith and governance.[1] Given their positions in the empire, each of the rival groups not only shaped public piety and social practices in diverse ways but also constructed various religious epistemologies that patterned the forms of knowledge and modes of thinking about faith and politics.

The other may be captured in the caliphate's rise as an empire with its structures and practices. Only one century after Muhammad's death, caliphs ruled over a sprawling empire, from the Oxus to Gibraltar, with a complex system of political economy and sociocultural practices in the most ancient imperial geography of the world. In their efforts to manage military undertakings, control conquered territories, and administer people, the caliphs embarked on spontaneous and then self-aware empire-building programs. By the close of the seventh century, the caliphs were already leading the "new world" alongside other ecumenical rulers, which meant that, no matter how the caliphs were perceived from the "inside," they were seen as emperors or kings from the "outside." In the following, I sketch the imprints of these developments on political reflection.

The Political Trajectory of a New Social Imaginary

Proclaiming his faith within the tradition of "Abrahamic" monotheism, the Prophet Muhammad built a community of believers bound to him by a common notion of discipleship.[2] Muhammad communicated a new social and spiritual imaginary that refocused the feelings, reasoning, and practice of his followers, which we know as Islamic piety. As a development out of step with the sociopolitical context of the Hijaz, and in view of the Prophet's social praxis, as exemplified in the "Charter of Medina,"[3] and of his military and missionary activities in the peninsula, this new outlook must have inspired a new level of communal awareness among his followers.[4] Likewise, the qur'anic language about settled life vis-à-vis pastoral nomadic life[5] suggested that piety, as a communal practice, could be perfected only in a sedentary, even urban, social environment.[6] One must keep in mind, however, that community building is a process that does not always lead to "state formation."[7]

It is plausible too that qur'anic references to organized societies and to kingship only in practical terms, without affirming them or giving any directions, might have even disincentivized political aspirations. Indeed, the qur'anic scripture is noteworthy for its neglect of mentioning a political framework. The qur'anic language of God's sovereignty or suzerainty over the universe does not seem to bear on polity formation, at least not for the early Muslims.[8] The political opacity of the qur'anic text—and the apparent inattention of the Prophet to name a "successor" or delineate a procedure for governance—precludes a political road map, unless one reads the prophetic era against the background of the caliphate. Only in the later Umayyad period, for instance, does one notice a connection between the qur'anic word "caliph" and the historical caliphate emerging.[9]

For many, it was a surprise that, immediately after the death of the Prophet in 632, his close companions in Medina gathered under the leadership of the Prophet's senior disciple and father-in-law, Abū Bakr (d. 634). With Abū Bakr's election to lead, the community faced a unique challenge: a new form of authority—one based on contract, which presupposed consent and obedience. Because the caliph Abū Bakr, as a mere member of the community, could not claim the same sort of privilege or generate a similar bond of comradery as Muhammad, his authority needed to be justified and exercised. To avoid risking alienating the fragile community of believers, he could neither act like a tribal leader nor assert himself as king in a "stateless" society. No matter how well argued and accentuated, this new form of authority was a *revisionist* intervention in the sense that it differed from that of the customary pastoral nomadic notion of authority and that of Muhammad. Because it needed to be justified, it could not be but political.

Therefore, the community's transition from the voluntary association of the Prophet's congregation to caliphal governance happened in neither a smooth nor a linear manner. Multiple groups rejected as obscene Abū Bakr's and his successors' claims to authority and demand for obedience in tumultuous events later called the "apostasy wars." They perceived such advances as an aberration of Muhammad's conduct and a violation of kinship customs.[10] Strife ensued, the community split, and civil wars broke out.[11] One could describe the crisis as a yearning for love, for paradise lost, for the simplicity and bareness of communal living, which generated various notions and practices of piety (*taqwā*) and distinct representations of the past in the seventh and eighth centuries.[12]

Although no one could predict its trajectory, a new polity was coalescing on the fringes of the Sasanian, Roman, and Ethiopian imperial worlds. What made the negotiations that resulted in the election of Abū Bakr as the commander of the faithful and its aftermath consequential was the success and elevation of military campaigns to the center stage of communal activity as jihad in the path of God. Abū Bakr's determination to move against kinship groups in the apostasy wars and carry out campaigns against the Byzantines enabled the caliph to demand more compliance and loyalty from the community.[13] Once the caliphs defined jihad as a collective and programmatic military activity that they pursued, it provided them with justification to use force, as well as the means to organize the community according to military requirements, which rationalized the demand for obedience more than ever before.[14]

Military conquests shaped a transformation that proved to be contentious and multidirectional. Through the efforts of conquering and controlling new territories, the caliphs learned how to improvise sociopolitical practices, which included restructuring the community according to military priorities. By blueprint adoption or inspiration, the caliphs introduced financial, military, and bureaucratic arrangements to sustain the military momentum; surveyed farmlands and populations to levy taxes on conquered peoples; apportioned tracts of land to existing and emerging nobility to keep them in the fold; governed regions; managed migrations from the Arabian Peninsula to new territories; and settled the army and their dependents in new garrison towns at the outskirts of existing cities to energize their push into new frontiers.[15]

Considering that the cadre at the helm comprised close companions of Muhammad and their immediate descendants who did not shy away from upholding their faith as a matter of habitual practice and as the moral anchor of their activities, the faith and its practice co-formed with the polity itself. One must acknowledge that Muhammad's death marked one of the most critical turns in the community's history—the birth of interpretive authority. Because the Prophet was no longer alive to set norms and settle disagreements, the decision-making authority needed to be anchored (or not) in some other entity. This challenge led to the emergence, soon after his death, of the "scripture" and the "prophetic practice" among the Muslim community—not as formalized foundations but as signposts, reference points, and memory anchors to guide authoritative practice and hermeneutics.

One explanation for the sustained dissent, therefore, was the remarkable role of the moral authority of the Qur'an and of the memory of Muhammad. The survival of the Qur'an as an "open text," resisting the full control of the rulers and of the "interpretive cast," created a space for any member of the community to weigh in on new meaning. This interpretive potential "democratized" the scripture and made it possible for the believers to articulate diverse and contradictory opinions in ways that the rulers could not control. Given the circumstances, however, this capaciousness also meant that any mundane dissent gained a religious character and religious terminology dominated political expression. Even though references to the customary notions of justice, fairness, good governance, and tradition still implied dissent, or discontent, in "lay" language, Islamic piety became the tenor of political debate.

Compelled by the rapid changes, the leading companions of Muhammad sought compliance and conformity with the faith to ground the community and institute order. They established a scale of seniority as the basis of entitlement to privileges, prioritizing early followers of Muhammad. For instance, when the caliph ʿUmar I b. al-Khaṭṭāb and his immediate successors introduced the system of seniority and contribution to military campaigns as criteria in the distribution of military pensions, or when they instituted the year 622, when the Prophet migrated from Mecca to Medina, as the starting point of a new calendar, or when they encouraged piety and pious knowledge as desired skills in taking up public duties, they enabled capacities that created a new social order based on loyalty to, and display of, faith. The realignment of social relations according to one's standing in faith rather than (or at least prior to) customary ties of kinship, lineage, and nobility (although these distinctions reasserted themselves later, as the new system generated its own nobility) transformed the pastoral nomadic and sedentary kinship groups of the Arabian Peninsula and the conquered territories into an agrarian society, organized according to new priorities and moral values. These changes brought the scripture and the practice of Muhammad into sharp sociopolitical focus.[16]

The caliphs demanded obedience in actual political matters and in "doctrinal" opinions as their prerogative. They hoped to unite the community around their authority, quell opposition, and control the empire. But they achieved little success in pacifying dissent.[17] The "structuring community" split into factions that nurtured dissimilar positions on the faith and the caliphate. The first (656–661) and second (680–692) civil wars laid bare the competition over privileges and political leadership and propelled a debate on the meaning of faith and pious practice.[18] Pondering the big picture, one can identify several major foundational groups from 656 to 692, beyond the Umayyads, who ruled the empire:[19] the Kharijites;[20] the Shiites;[21] the "middle-of-the-roaders"; the outsiders (perplexed, remained in-between, did not want to be involved, did not feel strong enough to support one group or another, or preferred to wait);[22] and the kinship groups, whose opportunism made them instrumental and dangerous.[23]

As the opposition to the Umayyads perceived more disparity between the values of the "founding fathers" and the actual practice of the caliphs, the debate about the ethics of governance and ideal leadership of the community gained momentum. The discussion involved questions about managing the political economy, such as the control of revenue and expenditure,[24] and compliance with the demands of faith and the faithful. Much of the opposition voiced its discontent in "republican" terms (election, consultation, and consent). A few anecdotal examples illustrate the type of pushback the Umayyads encountered. Prominent figures, who clustered in the Hijaz region (Mecca and Medina), insisted on "returning to consultation." The fourth caliph's son, al-Ḥusayn b. ʿAlī (d. 680), and al-Zubayr's son, ʿAbdallāh b. al-Zubayr (d. 692), who opposed moving the caliphal seat to Damascus and envisioned a better role for Medina, accused the first and the second Umayyad caliphs, Muʿāwiya (r. 661–680) and his son Yazīd (r. 680–683), of neglecting the companions of the Prophet by not giving them a fair share in administration, of not practicing the faith well, and of not ruling according to fairness and justice. The second caliph, ʿUmar's son, ʿAbdallāh, allegedly reprimanded Muʿāwiya for designating his son as heir apparent and thus converting the caliphate to "the rule of Heraclius and Khusrau," in which the sons would inherit from the father. He made the tongue-in-cheek remark that if the caliphate had been that way, then he would have been caliph after his father.[25] The first caliph Abū Bakr's son, ʿAbd al-Raḥmān, allegedly scolded Muʿāwiya b. Abī Sufyān for naming his son Yazīd as heir apparent and for mimicking the Romans: "Don't make us act like the Romans do—whenever a Heraclius dies, a new Heraclius takes his place."[26]

Even though political and administrative restructuring after the second civil war seems to have worked against the opposition, several prominent leaders among its ranks continued to raise the call for restoring justice by returning to election and consultation. Some even justified armed rebellion against the Umayyads in defense of such values. Serious uprisings by disgruntled generals, leaders of kinship groups, and prominent nobility—such as Muṭarraf

(Iraq, 696); Ibn Ashʿath, whose supporters included several prominent jurists (ending in Iraq, 701); and the ʿAlid ʿAbdallāh b. Muʿāwiya (d. ca. 746–747) in Kufa—and the Kharijite revolts in Iraq, the Jazira in northern Mesopotamia, Armenia, and Adharbayjan—kept the Umayyads on high alert.

The more the Umayyads practiced family succession, by appointing sons, brothers, and relatives, and the more they allowed family members to function as a ruling family, the more their opponents accused them of imitating Byzantine and Sasanian monarchies and converting caliphal rule into kingship, thus violating the earlier egalitarian and consensual practice. Apart from a certain faction of the Shiites, the opponents of the Umayyads, even the quietists, idealized consultation and election as the singular mark of moral politics, good governance, and political justice.[27] It is no exaggeration to say that the demand for consultative and elective governance and the associated theological debates concerning election during the Umayyad period laid the ground for a "republican" discourse against monarchical ambitions and oppressive policies that survived the ages.

However, the Abbasid revolt stands as one of the most spectacular political events of early caliphal history.[28] The revolt promoted the idea of gathering around the leadership of "the one agreed on among the family of the Prophet," which referred to none other than a Hāshimid figure. For more than half a century, the Hāshimids, which included the houses of the fourth caliph ʿAlī b. Abī Ṭālib and the Prophet's uncle ʿAbbās, had been looking for a chance to rule, at least in Hāshimid memory.[29] From the time of al-Mukhtār b. Abī ʿUbayd (d. 687) in the late seventh century, who claimed to have operated on behalf of Muhammad b. al-Ḥanafiyya (d. 700?), the younger son of the fourth caliph ʿAlī,[30] both houses encouraged messianic expectations to guide their activities. They also forged strong links with the Kaysāniyya sect, which made up the bulk of the radical wing of the Shiites during the Umayyad period.[31] Although the movement disintegrated after the middle of the eighth century, it left an indelible mark on Abbasid self-perception.[32] With overt messianic claims and tacit allusions to the cosmic significance of the Prophet's family, the revolt spread in Iraq and its peripheries and in the eastern provinces of the empire and among the Shiite groups there.

From the perspective of the Umayyads, the empire's most problematic regions included Iraq and Khurasan, which they tried to keep under firm control—with little success. One can suggest several issues that made this region a challenge for the Umayyads and provided significant support for the Abbasids. During the initial conquest of the region, the caliphal governors intervened little in the existing socioeconomic structure to ensure the flow of revenue and maintenance of stability. Shaken by internal controversies and civil wars among the "ruling people," the Umayyad administration resorted to harsh policies to control the region, but they failed to ensure long-term stability. Instead, they provoked resentment and discontent among some of the landed nobility and common folk, who began to sympathize with sectarian groups in the region.[33] As a result, the Kharijite and, especially, Shiite opposition to the Umayyads grew in Iraq and Khurasan. The caliphs implemented a policy of segregation to control the conquerors and the natives separately. With the steady migration of the peninsular people to this region, this policy created a settler-ruling community that depended primarily on warfare, military pensions, administrative positions, and links with the center but had little investment in the province. The native agrarian nobility found ways to collaborate with the administration to protect their interests to the detriment of peasants and commoners, who became vulnerable to the interference of rulers and the oppression of landowners. As the social groups adjusted their relations to these circumstances, new socioeconomic divisions and challenges emerged. For instance, even among the ruling people, the gap between the kinship nobility and their common kin widened. Faction politics (*ʿaṣabiyya*) replaced the earlier kinship politics in the army and administration. With accelerated conversion to Islam, the differential treatment of non-Arab Muslims led to continual discontent and rebellions against the Umayyads. The intermixing of people following socioeconomic developments in the public sphere made the region a center of hybrid imperial subjects and non-Arab Muslims, which made it extra difficult for the Umayyads to sustain their policy of segregation and to defend the differential treatment of Muslims.[34] Above all, the Umayyads failed to channel the developments and thus calm the region and maintain their authority, while the opposition gained strength. In the middle of the eighth century, Abbasid propagandists rallied people behind their slogans to restore justice, and rose against the Umayyads.

In 749, clothed in black garments and raising black banners to proclaim the rise of the Muslim messianic protagonist, the Mahdi (*al-mahdī*), the revolutionary militia, marched across Khurasan from Marw to Rayy and Nihawand and arrived at the city of Kufa. There, on November 28, 749, the Abbasids proclaimed the caliphate in the name of Abū al-ʿAbbās Muhammad b. ʿAbdallāh, with the regnal name al-Saffāḥ (r. 749–754), in the main mosque of the town. The new caliph made the small Iraqi town of al-Hāshimiyya, on the east side of the Euphrates near the city of Kufa, his capital, but settled in al-Anbar. A decade later, the capital of the dynasty moved to a new imperial compound founded by the second Abbasid caliph, al-Manṣūr (754–775), in 762 on the west bank of the Tigris. He named it the City of Peace, Madīnat al-Salām.[35] In the end, the Hāshimid summons produced an Abbasid messianic imam, which marred Abbasid-ʿAlid relations from that point onward.[36] When, finally, al-Manṣūr claimed the imamate and excluded the ʿAlids, not long after the revolt, he destroyed any remaining bridge between the two families.[37]

Since the initial stages of the revolt, the Abbasids had called for a consensus candidate from within the Prophet's family as caliph, but now they established the rule of their own family. They had been eager to enlist the support of the nobility and factions in Iraq and Khurasan and to give them voice against the Umayyads, but now they faced the cold reality of satisfying and controlling them. In addition to their kin, they enlisted the support of a diverse range of groups with varying demands and goals: non-Arab Muslims, who long asked for equality and a share in privileges; Khurasani veterans, known as the *abnāʾ*, the sons of the revolt, and their allies; kinship factions, whose last foray brought the Umayyads down but who now appeared out of place because of the configuration of the revolt and socioeconomic and religious developments; active sects; and the growing community of the ulema, who demanded a greater role in shaping society. Revolutionary sectarian, esoteric, and messianic enthusiasts, once underground and persecuted, now emerged to hold influential positions in the army and administration. Because the revolt's inclusiveness generated innovative ideas on how to run the empire, the Abbasids needed to configure relations, establish practices, and build structures to co-opt these groups and address their problems.[38]

If one takes Ibn al-Muqaffaʿ's "Epistle" as a guide to understand early Abbasid practice, one gets the impression that, facing grim challenges, the Abbasids had contemplated little beyond promising to distribute spoils and revenues fairly among those who saw themselves entitled to disbursement, not stationing soldiers for long in the frontiers but allowing them to visit their homes for set periods, recognizing the rights of Muhammad's family, alleviating the burden on non-Arab Muslims, and acting piously. In such circumstances, the Abbasid family's challenge was to ride the lion, as Ibn al-Muqaffaʿ warned al-Manṣūr, without becoming its victim.

Modalities of Governance

By the time of al-Manṣūr, the caliphate had already become a heavyweight empire with an imposing presence, sharing structures and practices known in the imperial history of Afro-Eurasia (primarily the Sasanians and the Byzantines), including the region's established faith systems (Christianity, Judaism, Zoroastrianism, and Islam), aptly described by Marshall Hodgson as Greco-Roman and Irano-Semitic.[39] The caliphate differed in the sense of its particular history, but it was similar in the broad contour of its practices and institutions (conquests, administration of territories, taxation, imperial organization, architecture, and enunciation of political power).

Islam's ecumenical potential strengthened the caliphs' imperial transregionalism and helped them anchor their political self-image to a religious morality that distinguished them from other empires. The Achaemenids and their successors in Persia practiced Zoroastrianism; Romans, polytheism and then Christianity; Axumites, Christianity; Maurya and Gupta empires, Buddhism; and Chinese Han and their successors, Confucianism and Buddhism. In a similar way, the Umayyad and early Abbasid caliphs identified with Islam and participated in its formation and development in so many ways, not only for acceptability and to secure their rules to a moral anchor but also to rely on the faith for their actual imperial needs and demands, which created an economy of religious knowledge that came to define the faith's doctrines, practices, and values. As Garth Fowden has pointed out, the Umayyads were even more efficient than preceding empires in harmonizing their imperial ambitions with Islam's universalist potential.[40]

However, the Umayyad empire presents a more complex case. In assessing two monuments, the Dome of the Rock in Jerusalem (or the Umayyad Mosque in Damascus) and the Qusayr ʿAmra palace in Jordan, one observes that each monument points to a distinct dynamic of universality in the eighth century. While the first monument represents a religiopolitical universality within the *longue-durée* "Abrahamic monotheism," the second, in contrast, suggests a different world-historical imperial universalism, not moored to the rationality of monotheism. If one wishes to link the political signification of each monument to a particular discursive practice and moral position at the time, one would classify the Dome of the Rock with the imamate and the ulema, and the Qusayr ʿAmra palace with siyasa and the activities of lay bureaucrats in the Umayyad imperial chancellery.

It is only fitting that the first major architectural monument of the Abbasids was the round imperial city of Baghdad, conceived as the axis mundi and the world itself, housed within the walls of the city.[41] Despite the fact that the Abbasids shifted the axis of their interests from the Mediterranean world of the Byzantines toward the Indian Ocean and the Achaemenid-Sasanian imperial tradition, they continued to pursue universalist policies. We know, at least, that many later Abbasid historians continued to depict the caliphs as both the inheritors of ancient empires and protectors of the last iteration of God's revelation.[42]

Under the broad canopy of the empire, the caliphs ruled territories that varied in their physical, climatic, demographic, and cultural compositions by any standard of the "old world." Ideological motivations aside, the caliphs needed to govern the territories to generate surplus, to control natural and human resources, and to project strength among their subjects and abroad. Control and management compelled the establishment of administrative and military institutions to facilitate relations and form effective links between the center and its provinces, the allocation of resources from India and beyond to the Iberian Peninsula, and the execution of large-scale infrastructure (roads, irrigation canals, hostels) and prestige projects (mosques, palaces, shrines). Given the complexity of the administration in the mid-eighth century, the caliphs seemed to have appreciated that imperial lands were not a fenced hunting ground in which to pursue prey at will but a patrimony, a dominion to be protected. In the caliphal titles they preferred for themselves, one observes that the caliphs outlined their privileges but at the same time placed parameters around their authority vis-à-vis their subjects.

Four Forms of Caliphal Authority

Like other emperors in world history, the caliphs from 632 to 1258, when they were unseated by the Mongols, preferred to underscore their military commandership in their main title, "the commander of the faithful." It was the only title unalienable from the ruler in any circumstance and the one reserved for him exclusively as the mark of sovereignty. Other appellations described various aspects of the caliph's authority or the way he exercised it. Similar in many respects to the question of the attributes of God, or God's secondary attributes in theology, here, too, "ancillary" titles specified, modified, and supplemented the sovereign title in certain ways but did not replace it. Thus, the eighth-century Umayyad caliphs bolstered and qualified the authority they conveyed in the title "the commander of the faithful" by adopting three additional major "attributes." They referred to themselves as God's caliphs, messianic redeemers, and imams. After the revolt, the Abbasids also emphasized, alongside the sovereign title, the spiritual dimensions of their authority by using a wide range of messianic appellations as well as the title "imam," along with the designation "God's caliph," although the latter appeared less frequently. Referring to the ruling person by the sovereign title always indicated an acknowledgment of and submission to his supreme authority. It is noteworthy that the appellation "caliph" or "Mahdi" did not carry a similar level of strictness and exclusivity.[43]

In much of the eighth century, the caliphal titles and functions were delineated in the elementary language of early theology. Even though much of the administrative vocabulary came from ancient Arabian traditions and current military and administrative practices in a vast empire as they evolved, theology emerged as the dominant semantic field in which political idioms communicated meaning. The moral force of Islam undergirding the political and military success of the caliphate produced a discursive status quo in which the authority of the commander of the faithful was expressed in the imamate's language. Within this discursive framework, an educated individual (scholar, administrator, or other) in the mid-eighth century would be familiar with four forms of political authority—caliphal contractualism, God's caliphate, messianic leadership, and the Shiite imamate—but would find siyasa's intervention remarkable and provocative. It may be useful to describe them succinctly here, as I use them in the chapters to follow.

In brief, the term *khalīfa* in Arabic signified "successor," "deputy," "inheritor," "substitute," and eventually "vicegerent." It also suggested a sense of descending, to be a descendant of, to produce descendants, and the act of procreation and multiplying in succession over generations. As also appears in the Qur'an, the word thus connoted continuity, with differences in details but with similarity in kind, as in the act of human reproduction, generation after generation.[44] Even though the precise date of the earliest use of the title *khalīfa* to denote political leadership remains uncertain,[45] its initial circulation, as al-Qadi argues, began during the early Umayyad period, perhaps as early as the reign of Muʿāwiya, but not in connection to the qur'anic use of it in its various inflections.[46] In the political sense, the signifier might have referred to the ruler in his official capacity, as the body or entity representing the community of the faithful or standing in for God's political authority, which passed from person to person regardless of the demise of individual caliphs. Understood thus, the term connoted transferring power across generations, akin to the idea of the "king's two bodies," in which the biological body of the ruler appeared transient but the authority he represented and carried perpetual. As will be clear, the idea of "two bodies" is unmistakable in the notion of the imam.[47]

What has been called caliphal contractualism enshrined the idea of "contract" between the ruler and the ruled through the process of consultation, election, and consent (*shūra*, *ikhtiyār*, *bayʿa*) as the theoretical underpinnings of legitimate authority. The contractualists often described the Byzantine or Persian models of monarchy (described as Caesarism, *qayṣariyya*, and Khusrauism, *kisrāwiyya*, respectively) as conflicting with the consensual and contractual constitution of the caliphate. They accused the Umayyad caliphs of the intention to reduce the "community of the believers" to imperial subjects. Many of the proponents of this view identified themselves with sectarian groups (the Kharijites, the Muʿtazilites, the Murji'ites) that opposed the Umayyads.[48] Eminent figures of the nobility (such as Ibn Zubayr, Ḥārith b. Surayj, Ibn Ashʿath, and others) who rebelled against the Umayyads advocated contractualism. Many members of the emerging ulema also called for implementing the sacred law and following the practice of the "founding fathers," including the first four caliphs (variably identified).[49] The common points about the caliph included the idea that he derived his authority from the community of believers' "contract." Being a member of the faithful, the caliph was subject to the same laws as his subjects and answerable to the community for his actions. Until the downfall of the Umayyads, the idea of contractualism seems to have been a dominant opinion among the ulema.[50] An early and prominent transmitter of historical and *ḥadīth* reports, al-Zuhrī (d. 741 or 742), compiled and transmitted reports to that effect, most of which found their way into Ibn Isḥāq's *Biography of the Prophet* and other sources.[51]

In the mid-eighth century, we notice similar views being defended by the early jurists and *ḥadīth* transmitters. According to the Shiite scholar al-Nawbakhtī of the ninth century (d. after 912), the folk in this category[52] included eminent scholars such as Ibn Abī Laylā (d. 765), Sufyān al-Thawrī (d. 778), Mālik b. Anas (d. 795), and al-Shāfiʿī, who maintained that the Prophet died without appointing a successor and left the matter for the community to decide. They argued that the community bequeathed the caliphs the responsibility of keeping people together, arbitrating their conflicts, handling the administration (which al-Nawbakhtī calls kingship, *mulk*, to condemn it) and the affairs of their subjects (*raʿiyya*), making peace treaties, delegating authority to lesser administrators, organizing the army, defending the realm, punishing the obstinate, educating the ignorant, and protecting the victim.[53] Al-Nawbakhtī's claim that many of the early jurists and *ḥadīth* transmitters thought that the caliph (Nawbakhtī uses the term "imam," following the conventions of his time) had to be appointed by the exercise of rational judgment, *ijtihād al-ra'y*, or by what was congruent with reason, *yakhtārū bi-ʿuqūlihim*, suggests that such views evolved side by side with *ḥadīth*-based assertions among some of the pre-Sunnites that the Prophet appointed Abū Bakr to be the caliph.[54] Henceforth, the idea of a contract as a constitutive element of political order became a major theme in the political discourse of the following centuries.

In response, and to bypass the checks on the caliphs, which were presumed in caliphal contractualism, the later Umayyad caliphs referred to themselves as God's deputies (*khalīfat allāh*). They claimed to rule over their subjects as their spiritual guides, invested with interpretive and salvific authority. Poets of the late Umayyad period used "God's caliph" for their patrons in panegyric and elegiac poetry, and at least one coin minted for the Umayyad caliph ʿAbd al-Malik (r. 685–705) in 694 bears this title. Common in Umayyad political debates, the phrase "God's deputy" underlined the notion that God's will and support were fundamental to the caliph's authority to ensure—in expected and unexpected ways—the well-being of God's flock as His deputy on earth.[55] Consistent with predestinarian beliefs, the notion of God's deputyship as a demonstration of God's will freed the caliph from the obligation of answering to the community but constrained him within the sacred law. While the idea of communal check on the caliph faded, religious imperatives still determined and guided his political action. Although the path to office required procedures that might be considered at least nominally consensual, victory in a military confrontation to determine succession proved God's will and support. The Abbasids also continued to use this title and resisted abandoning it completely in favor of the more common appellation "imam." Whereas the ulema of the Umayyad period did not use the appellations "caliph" or "God's caliph" in a political sense for the Umayyad caliphs, al-ʿAnbarī and Abū Yūsuf used it for the Abbasid caliphs Muhammad al-Mahdī (r. 775–785) and Hārūn al-Rashīd (r. 786–809) with little reservation.

Messianic leadership constituted another major form of political authority constructed around the figure of the Mahdi, the divinely guided redeemer who would appear to restore righteousness to the corrupt world when the preordained time arrived. While connected to the ideas of the imam and God's caliph, and therefore positioned against caliphal contractualism, messianic leadership either sought the restoration of a pristine past or anticipated—or even ushered in—the age of messianic bliss. Based on a fundamental rejection of the status quo, this idea, whether it is associated with apocalyptic end-of-time scenarios or not, exerted a disruptive effect. That is, the Mahdi's authority, combining both spiritual and mundane powers, diverged from that of God's caliph and the imam in that customary and normative sacred laws did not restrict it, although it might confirm, comply with, and implement them. Rather, the Mahdi's appearance would upend the conventional sociopolitical order. On the historical scene, the idea of messianic leadership was claimed by the Umayyads but also unleashed a diverse range of movements by both marginal and quite established figures, who revolted against the Umayyads in the late seventh and first half of the eighth centuries.[56] One may cite here the Abbasid revolt itself as a notable example. Ibn al-Muqaffaʿ witnessed only the start of the Abbasid experimentation with messianism as rulers, which he addressed in his "Epistle."

In the same circumstances, the appellation of "imam" became widespread during the Abbasid revolt as the principal attribute of the sovereign title and a deliberate alternative to the term "caliph," but closer in its connotation to the notion of God's caliph and the idea of the Mahdi. While it had not been used by the Umayyads in any noticeable way as a political attribute of the caliph, it became common coinage among the Shiites as the main signifier of the legitimate or ideal and even sacred ruler. In this Shiite sense, the current imam was named by the preceding imam explicitly, but in private, upon specific instruction from God. By the mid-eighth century, the concept became a standard reference for Abbasid leaders and caliphs. It also spread as a common signifier of the supreme authority of the ideal caliph among a wide range of non-Shiite groups. In fact, the term replaced "caliph" as the central concept of the discourse on caliphal authority, whether the discussion involved the actual ruling caliph or the ideal one. This shift in expression is patent in Sālim b. Dhakwān's (lived in the first half of the eighth century) and Ibn al-Muqaffaʿ's texts, as we will see in the following chapters.[57]

Whereas the word "caliph" signified the ruling person (one would not be called caliph unless one ruled, claimed to rule, or had ruled), "imam" connoted the legitimate leader, whether he held an office or not. The term suggested the privilege of being designated by God for political leadership and for guiding believers to salvation through spiritual knowledge akin to that associated with Muhammad (inspiration, direct revelation of utterances) or more radical esoteric powers (incarnation, transmigration of souls, magic). Hence, the imam held comprehensive authority over previous rulings and even over the scripture. His authority among his followers entailed a relationship of master-disciple, in which the imam ruled over and guided his subjects in their mundane and spiritual lives.

As a question of practice, however, caliphal authority remained contingent on how much the caliphs could leverage it. In hindsight, the early caliphate persisted, for a few decades, as an elective, consultative, and consensual polity. The caliphal appointment observed a process (nomination-election-consent) to assert legitimate authority. One had to advance messianic claims or secure military victory to bypass the whole procedure, but even then, the procedure of consent (*bayʿa*) would take place. The practice of election and consultation seems to have emerged from the context of urban life in Mecca and Medina, the pastoral nomadic ways of life in western Arabia, the moral egalitarianism of the new faith and Muhammad's communal practice, and the balance of power among the companions of Muhammad.

Practicalities limited the number of people who took part in the election process. Only a small group of individuals (males and, depending on their prominence, sometimes females) in the cities where the caliph resided took part. Electing the new caliph and transferring power required the explicit approval and verification of an ad hoc and informal assembly that became known as "the assembly of dismissal and contract" (*ahl al-ḥall wa al-ʿaqd*). To be sure, the qualifications, identities, and duties of the members of this assembly were not listed and fixed, but the council included prominent individuals from among the high administrative and military officials and other nobility and stakeholders. Contrary to the pedantic treatment of this council in modern scholarship, it strikes me as an underappreciated genuine "republican" political institution, which certain historical contingencies impeded but never eliminated. Together with the oath of contract (*bayʿa*), it survived as the hallmark of contractual and elective authority and a model of better politics against which practices were judged.[58]

Summing up in abstract terms the succession to rule until the Abbasid revolt, one notices various "republican" and "dynastic" forms—ranging from a free election among the Quraysh tribe to succession within the family, and even primogeniture.[59] Family succession developed as the preferred way of transferring the power during the Umayyad period, despite being contentious. Designation took various forms as well (*ʿahd*, designation, therefore *walī al-ʿahd*, heir apparent), with no preference for primogeniture. It also became a customary practice as early as the seventh century to designate one or more heirs (an adult, or in certain circumstances, a minor) to secure succession in the family line. A written testament often accompanied the designation.[60] By the time of the Abbasids, designation within the family seemed an ordinary practice.

Even though the early caliphal "republican" experiment, as contextualized in world history, stood little chance of success under the duress of monarchical imperial aspirations, the fact that numerous groups articulated, defended, and deliberated it is significant. As Al-Azmeh remarks in his erudite discussion of monotheistic kingship, royal authority had been and continued to be, for many centuries after the caliphate, the most ubiquitous and durable form of rule in Afro-Eurasia. One appreciates that, in the bigger picture, the early caliphal, Roman, and Greek republicanisms represent a short-lived anomaly in world history until early modern times.[61]

Construed in hindsight, the earliest caliphs enjoyed an authority that bridged theological and juridical spheres. Several later Umayyad caliphs claimed theological and juridical authority, as the Damascene Abū Zurʿa (d. 895) suggests. He reports that the Umayyad caliph al-Walīd I (r. 705–715) attempted to force the judges to follow Khālid b. Maʿdan's (d. ca. 722) verdict on a particular case.[62] ʿUmar II (r. 717–720) also seems to have tried to combine legal rulings into one universal code but abandoned this project, according to Abū Zurʿa, for fear of eradicating the companions' rulings, which had been taken by the judges as precedents.[63]

Since the early eighth century, the caliphs seem to have controlled the judicial administration, but the jurists determined the content of the law, provided their judgments did not interfere with political decisions and did not threaten the survival of the ruling caliph and his family. By the time the Abbasids became caliphs, the legal rulings of the jurists had become a major body of legal opinions and precedents that shaped the legal practice of caliphal rule.[64] In effect, the ulema's sacred law operated as the functional arm of caliph's authority—but also as a check on it.

Under the best of circumstances, the caliphs functioned as the supreme rulers of their domain and, with rare exceptions, remained in office for life. They were visible to their subjects through several institutional and sociocultural modalities (their residences, ceremonies, processions, patronage, pardons, gifts, administration of justice, taxes). Several symbols (later referred to as *shārāt al-khilāfa*) were reserved exclusively for them and represented their authority. As early as the seventh century, the sermon (*khuṭba*) during the Friday prayer in the main mosque in town, in which the preacher mentioned the name of the ruling caliph, indicated sovereignty. The caliph often led the Friday prayer in the capital and joined the hajj ritual in person at least once during his reign. At other times, he delegated such tasks to administrators for proper execution on his behalf. Mention of the ruling caliph's name in provincial mosques, the minting of coins bearing his name, and the playing of the trumpet at the gate of his residence during prayer times were also considered to be the recognition of his authority.[65]

Structure and Meaning

Like other empires, the caliphate pursued the idea of conquering new lands and ruling over the habitable world. By the time the Abbasids took over in 750 CE, the caliphate had expanded into territories from the Iberian Peninsula to the Indus Valley. While the Abbasids gained no additional territories, they still followed a routinized policy of conquest by organizing seasonal raids (called summer and winter raids) into Central Asia and Byzantine lands in Anatolia.[66] Territorial expansion occurred through two main methods: military conquest and various arrangements of incorporation, as the situation on the ground required. Besides finding new material and human resources, the energy to conquer and expand even more resulted from an ideology of conquest, whose content, emphasis, and persuasiveness varied from time to time.[67]

Imperial territories were politically constituted and flexible. As Umayyad power manifested itself in normalized ways from the beginning of the eighth century, the centers of gravity in Syria and Egypt differed from the outlying provinces. Based on the relative importance of the provinces, there emerged in practice a distinction between core and periphery. Although the "imperial core" did not define an exclusive "homeland" for the ruling family or the ruling people in any sense of permanence, Ibn al-Muqaffaʿ noticed soon after the Abbasid revolt a particular Syrian loyalty to the Umayyads and solidarity in the region, which suggests that a distinction between core and periphery had taken root.

In the core zone, the caliph held the center and the tightly controlled provinces, often governed by close kin or protégés of the caliphs who dwelt in provincial capital cities (*amṣār*). As far as one can tell, besides the imperial core, Syria, the regions of the Umayyad caliphate encompassed three or four provinces (*wilāyāt*): Ifriqiya and the West; the Jazira and the North; and Iraq and the East. Khurasan was acknowledged sometimes as an independent province, if not counted in the province of Iraq and the East. Each province contained smaller administrative districts, from towns down to villages or farms (*qarya*, *rustaq*, *tassūʿ*), which were supposed to have their own administrators, full-time or part-time, charged with revenue collection and keeping order.[68] The periphery also included more remote provinces administered by other parties, who might enjoy a certain autonomy from Syria. This practice accounts for the willingness of the caliphs to negotiate their authority, and share it with lesser potentates when necessary or expedient.[69]

By blueprint appropriation or inspiration, the caliphs recycled many of the existing structures and practices that they encountered in Afro-Eurasia to govern their empires better. From the Umayyad ʿAbd al-Malik b. Marwān's administrative and military reforms onward, the caliphal imperial structure grew in complexity. The caliph built the central and provincial administrations, and launched a large Arabization program and currency reform by minting imperial coinage. Subsequent caliphs also developed their military, which expanded from modest army units based on the human resources of kinship groups to a more professionally trained and organized force of mixed Arab and non-Arab soldiers under the early Abbasids. A layered system of administration with imperial and provincial scribes, governors, judges, and tax collectors had been functioning by al-Manṣūr's time.

Much of the administrative work took place in offices (*dawāwīn*, sg. *dīwān*), the function of which evolved from maintaining registers of soldiers to actual offices holding such registers, and to administrative offices (chancelleries) under the early Abbasids. The field of responsibility of the *dīwāns* varied, and included, until the second half of the eighth century, military administration (*dīwān al-jund*), fiscal expenditure (*dīwān al-nafaqāt*), land tax administration (*dīwān al-kharāj*), postal services and intelligence (*dīwān al-barīd*), the office of the caliphal seal (*dīwān al-khātim*), official correspondence (*dīwān al-rasā'il*), the office of official dress (*dīwān al-ṭirāz*), and others.[70]

The provinces were governed by officials (known as *ʿamīl*, *wālī*, or *amīr*), who were often appointed by the caliph and oversaw military, administrative, and fiscal affairs. In each case, the governor worked with a staff assigned to him, which included a body of guards (*shurṭa*) to keep order, and a judge (*qāḍī*) to settle legal cases. Lower-level administrators in the provinces were selected from the local nobility and supervised by a governor, regularly sent from the center (and often a member of the ruling family itself) from among those with known service to the caliph.[71] Local subordinates satisfied two functions. They helped the upper administration maintain the implementation of laws, collect taxes, keep order, adjudicate disagreements, pacify insurrections, disseminate cultural norms, and represent the caliph. They also voiced local concerns and demands to the upper administration but did not always follow an established chain of authority.[72]

A malleable frontier zone (*thughūr*, *ʿawāṣim*, *ribāṭ*) separated the Umayyad territories from the outside world. Any territory beyond the frontier remained a potential target of military conquest. The new territorial acquisitions were subordinated either fully by establishing direct control or in part by affording some autonomy to the controlled region (vassalage) through certain arrangements. In the later Umayyad period, dividing the world into morally distinct spheres, such as the house of Islam and house of war (*dār al-Islām* and *dār al-ḥarb*), and still later, also the domain of peace treaty (*dār al-hudna* or *dār al-ṣulḥ*), appeared in discourse, although everyday reality accommodated overlapping and hybrid zones.[73] The Umayyad and early Abbasid art and narratives testify to the imagination that the world beyond the caliphate contained "civilized" and "barbaric" societies, each of which required different rules of engagement.

In terms of its peoples and cultures, the caliphate was a heterogeneous polity. A cross-section of the Umayyad subject population beyond the ruling family included the military, civil servants, the scholarly class, merchants, artisans, farmers, the urban poor, pastoral nomads, war captives, and slaves. Confessional differences, and dissimilarities in language, culture, ethnicity, age, and gender added further complexity to this mosaic. Like the rulers of other empires, the Umayyads, and after them, the Abbasids, acknowledged, created, and maintained differences among their subject populations. Conversion, association with the elite, and the possession of critical skills enabled social mobility, however modest, which prevented the empire's elite and ruling class from sealing themselves off from the rest of society. The story of the non-Arab Muslims who played a critical role in the Abbasid revolt is a good example of the venues for social mobility.[74]

Sociocultural difference was thus unavoidable. Ideological and moral incentives encouraged the ruling elite and the dominant groups to acknowledge diversity as a reality of life. There was also inevitability. Unlike nation-states, which use advanced mechanisms to integrate their territories, older empires were ineffective in controlling and monitoring their territories because they lacked the ability and capacity to do so over distance. The empire's inability to control and monitor far-flung territories made adapting to difference more practical and even desirable.[75] The caliphs created and exploited differences among their subjects and, by this means, forged various relationships with them. They allowed communities—confessional or otherwise—to maintain their own social and cultural traditions, however truncated, and recognized multiple legal conventions.[76]

Loyalty and submission rather than cultural similarity seem to have guided the Umayyad caliphs in their relations with their subjects.[77] The tension between difference and tendencies toward homogenization led to hybridity in various walks of life, from ethnicity to language, to art, to confessional dogma, because the exigencies of ruling over extensive lands demanded regular and sometimes intensive and abrupt, voluntary or forced interchange among peoples. One outcome of such governing practices was the migration (voluntary and forced) of people, along with their skills, ideas, and goods. The migration of Arabic kinsfolk with, and after, the army to Khurasan, the Anatolian frontier, and North Africa, for example, required amassing huge resources and bringing thousands of people from different regions to help in construction and provide services. Another result was tangible change in the lives of ordinary people in urban centers—in their diet, beliefs, cultural conditions, and aspirations.[78]

The caliphate established political, legal, and economic institutions to manage people, control territories, and enable connections within and beyond borders. The caliph appointed administrators, judges, and military personnel; secured and defended his realm; collected taxes; maintained order; ensured the welfare of his subjects; enacted rules and regulations; waged wars against enemies; protected the faith; and intervened as the ultimate arbiter in disagreements and conflicts. In case of any actual or perceived violent threat to their rule (rebellion, dynastic claims), the caliphs seem to have felt free to improvise military punitive measures as much as their power and means allowed. Yet caliphal authority expanded and contracted depending on the extent of resistance to it by the provincial and central nobility, sectarian communities, military factions, administrators, and the ulema.[79]

Because the imperial administration depended on human and material resources beyond the capacity of any single region or polity, rulers accepted—in fact, created—a multiplicity of legal frameworks and ad hoc arrangements to deal with their provinces and tributaries and thus ensure the uninterrupted flow of resources they needed. These included honoring a diverse set of traditions and conventions in various regions; absorbing military, administrative, and fiscal laws (some reaching back to ancient Mesopotamian societies); and upholding various religious practices and codes. The mores and legal rulings of the jurists (which were later called the shariʿa) formed one such system, which advanced to center stage from the mid-eighth century onward.

Bifurcating Intellectual Capital

To govern, the caliphs needed professional skills, and they encouraged intellectual activities that could help. They recruited individuals to serve at various levels of the administration, advise on affairs, and carry out bureaucratic tasks. As the Umayyad administration expanded and grew more complex, the demand for civil administrators increased, providing new opportunities in the central and provincial administrations for those with professional skills. The rise of the scribal or secretarial class is rooted in such empire-building activities.[80] This class of administrators came into view in late Umayyad times but rose to prominence in the aftermath of the Abbasid revolt.

It is worth noting at the outset that in the seventh and eighth centuries, the imperial functionaries in the Umayyad and early Abbasid bureaucracy were both non-Muslims (*dhimmī*) and non-Arab Muslims (*mawālī*, clients) because the ruling population was reluctant to accept administrative positions. The peninsular Arabic-speaking nobility looked down on farming, shunned administrative work, and shirked at trade. Instead, they preferred positions in the military, governorship, and judiciary to protect their status and prestige. This situation lasted more than a century, even after ʿAbd al-Malik's reforms in the late seventh century, leaving the "clients" and the non-Muslim experts almost the only group functioning in the bureaucracy.

If one takes the Umayyad scribes as an illustrative example, one observes high-charged professionals, many of whom hailed from families with imperial service under the previous imperial administrations, with impeccable professional skills and impressive Islamic acculturation. Patronized by the caliphs, governors, and other high-ranking officials, these bureaucrats shaped military and civil administration under the Umayyads, when such skills and services were needed in the empire-building efforts. Competent in the tedious details of statecraft and administration, equipped with knowledge and linguistic skills, and adept at producing students and apprentices to perpetuate their professions, the scribes played a larger role than was expected. While many performed low-level duties, some became high-level imperial administrators and others leading experts in various branches of knowledge outside religious scholarship, as we will see later.

Concurrently, the emergence of the ulema as an empire-wide learned elite represents one of the most consequential developments of the seventh century. Although their learning and scholarship developed outside the control of the caliphs, often as a form of resistance, soon the ulema became essential to the rulers, as both friend and foe. With their activities, the ulema informed the daily life of imperial subjects and functioned as a mechanism to normalize imperial power. Among them, the "middle-of-the-roaders" were poignant. They were scholars of religious jurisprudence, *ḥadīth*, exegesis, grammar and language, and other related branches of knowledge who did not identify with emerging sects in the eighth century that opposed the Umayyads but pursued a "middle road," which would be called Sunnism in the late ninth and tenth centuries.

Claiming to represent the founding fathers, the Prophet, and the community of believers, and by their sheer knowledge in religious matters and piety, the ulema harnessed noticeable authority among imperial subjects, the elite, and the rulers themselves. Hailing from Arab and non-Arab backgrounds, they became desirable specialists by the rulers—as collaborators and maintainers of the caliphate; as intermediaries between the rulers and their subjects through both formal judicial and administrative transactions; and as scholars, pious people, sages, teachers, and wise men.[81] The Umayyads forged relations with the ulema, many of whom also often served as instructors, judges, and even administrators.

They have been called proto-Sunni or *jamāʿī* scholars,[82] but one does well with pre-Sunnite.[83] Because none of the labels help us understand their political position, however, I classify them as part of the emerging religious and political "establishment" that supported, allied, or cooperated and collaborated with the ruling caliphs. Although these pre-Sunnite ulema held competing loyalties and represented a spectrum of views in the early eighth century, they still maintained a discursive cohesion by centering their attention on the notions of "community" (*jamāʿa*) and "tradition" (*sunna*) and dedicating their efforts to studying religious themes.

The comfort of being supported by the rulers did not settle their contention with the caliphs over authority. Their scholarship and interaction with the masses in various social spaces gave them eminence as interpreters of the scripture and defenders of the faith, which put them in a precarious position vis-à-vis the caliphs. As long as the jurists monopolized religious scholarship (*fiqh*, *tafsīr*, *ḥadīth*) and made up the learned expert elite, the caliphs had no choice but to negotiate with them. Although this arrangement did not impress the emerging bureaucrats in the central administration, it benefited the ulema to cooperate and collaborate with the caliphs.[84]

While many did so in various religious, judicial, and administrative tasks—or as propagandists of the caliphs—many others maintained a calculated distance from the Umayyad caliphs, in response to practical demands. Such ulema devoted much of their activity to matters that seemed irrelevant to governing. In fact, if one wishes to characterize the mood of the ulema in the mid-eighth century, "resentment of politics" would be a suitable expression. The late Umayyad decades witnessed a growing chasm between a substantial segment of the ulema and the caliphs. This rift eroded the moral ground of the ruling family and left them alone against their opposition. When the Abbasid revolt occurred, many of the ulema placed their bets with the Abbasids and continued to cooperate and collaborate with them in the following decades. While it is an oversimplification to portray the ulema as the mouthpiece of the Abbasid caliphs, they produced a particular practice and network of relations within the orbit of Abbasid politics.[85] Their intervention in political discourse will be more evident in the following chapters.

To sum up, I have described not how the caliphate grew out of the Prophet's conduct nor how it unfolded from its roots in religious principles, and therefore was condemned to remain a theocracy, but how the ruling and literate elite in Umayyad Syria and Abbasid Iraq created as much as navigated the sociopolitical world in which they lived. Spelling out the intellectual and political questions that compelled the mid-eighth-century thinkers to produce different representations of the nondirectional lived reality of the past helps explain how they made sense of their contemporary realities, intervened in them, and imagined multiple trajectories for the caliphate. The next chapter studies the idea of the imamate as one such form of representation to highlight major aspects of its politics.

2

The Language of Imamate

To elucidate the early language of imamate, I will scrutinize several mid-eighth-century texts. I begin with the Umayyad political theology, as communicated in the short letters of the caliphs al-Walīd II b. Yazīd (r. 743–744) and Yazīd III b. al-Walīd (r. 744), which I read against the background of the debate on the ideals of election and succession. I then discuss the religiopolitical concerns of the ulema, which I characterize as "prepolitical" or "elementary," beginning with the *Kitāb al-Irjā'* (*The Book of Postponement*) attributed to al-Ḥasan b. Muhammad b. al-Ḥanafiyya (d. 718?), the "Epistle" of the Kharijite Sālim b. Dhakwān (lived in the late seventh or first half of the eighth century), and Muhammad b. Isḥāq's (d. 767) the *Biography of the Prophet*.

One important aspect of the ulema's discursive orientation is that they underlined the collective body of the community (*umma*) as the basis of any political structure claiming to belong to it. They correlated governance directly with religious principles and pious morality, and held firm to the idea, as an article of faith, that the imamate (either the actual or the ideal) embodied the only legitimate authority to enforce religious obligations, organize communal life according to and as a fulfillment of the revealed law, and pursue military activities to defend the community and expand the territories. In voicing contractualist arguments (the notions of election, consultation, and the accountability of the ruler) and maintaining the view that the rule of the caliphs differed from that of kingship, many members of the ulema criticized the Umayyads.[1] At the same time, they kept a distance from the day-to-day operation of the empire. Whether they were interested in universal principles dealing with faith and its community, carried a sense of resentment toward politics, or defended theological principles that appeared too normative to relate to the contingencies of the moment, they offered only little actionable knowledge and mutable regulations in response to acute challenges.

I then read early juristic writing in the second half of the eighth century to capture the outcome of the engagement between the ulema and the caliphs through two self-aware tracts: ʿUbaydallāh b. Ḥasan al-ʿAnbarī's letter to the caliph al-Mahdī and Abū Yūsuf's *Book of Taxation*, which he wrote for Hārūn al-Rashīd. One of the effects of this development is seen in the middle-of-the-road ulema's mode of calculated distance from the Umayyads. Their position vis-à-vis the rulers morphed into a willingness, even fervor, for alliance with the Abbasid caliphs, as reflected in their writings. Another crucial development occurred in their texts. The new "style" of writing represents a stage in the political language of the ulema that may be described as "imamate discourse in practice." Ostensibly developing under the discursive pressure of siyasa, the ulema's change of mood and style ended up helping to define the caliphate in jurisprudential-theological terms and also shaping religious jurisprudence in the caliphate's image in public and political matters.

Formations of the Ulema-Centric Political Theology

It may be fair to state that the Umayyads always governed while battling the ghost of election and consultation. In addition to the opponents of the caliphs, claimants also included some members of the Umayyad family and even certain caliphs who sympathized with constitutional sentiments. Among those rulers, one might cite Yazīd III, who raised the banner of the ideals of consultation, election, and consent in his move against his cousin al-Walid II as the bases of righteous and legitimate authority. However, the Umayyad rulers regularly claimed either that they inherited the caliphate from the third caliph ʿUthman, were entitled to it in the arbitration agreement between ʿAlī and Muʿāwiya, acquired it from the Prophet himself, or God graced them with the caliphate.[2] Besides emphasizing their mundane, practical abilities and qualifications, they asserted that God guided and blessed their decisions and made them a refuge for people during calamities. The political rhetoric of the caliphs and the panegyric poetry addressed to them since the beginning of the eighth century suggest that the caliphs defined their rule as divinely sanctioned and that they highlighted the theological and salvific quality of their authority. As one of the most celebrated Umayyad poets al-Farazdaq proclaimed about his patrons, "the earth is God's, who granted it to his deputy (*khalīfa*); the friend of God will never be defeated," they enlisted their ability to hold on to power as proof of their right to rule.[3] ʿAbd al-Malik b. Marwān underlined his authority as God's deputy (*khalīfat allāh*) by minting coins featuring this designation.[4] As long as their power continued with God's will, the Umayyad caliphs and their supporters argued, they were entitled to complete loyalty and submission. Murji'ite and Kharijite opponents of the Umayyads also shared much ground with them in seeing governance as an affair of the community of believers, although each developed their arguments from different points of departure.

Ruling by Divine Decree According to God's Law

In both al-Walīd II's and Yazīd III's letters, the caliph's title "the commander of the faithful" is qualified consistently with the appellation "God's caliph" to underline once and again the reception of divine approval. What is noteworthy is that, while both caliphs portrayed rule in their letters as a divine responsibility and privilege, they defined their authority as demarcated by divine commands and coterminous with the religious community. In this capacity, the caliphs not only governed their "disciples" in their mundane lives but also guided them to salvation by executing God's will on earth. In his letter to his governors requesting allegiance to his sons al-Ḥakam and ʿUthmān, as the newly appointed heirs apparent, the Umayyad caliph al-Walīd II defends his authority as an inheritance from the prophets and the deputyship of God in the world. On this basis, he demands obedience and loyalty as his God-given right. The caliph warns that God punishes those who abandon obedience to the caliph, for God has commanded that he be followed and upheld. It is through obedience to the caliph that the earth is made firm and the heavens stand erected.[5]

To explicate its political underpinnings, I will bring the letter into closer focus. In an intensely elevated theological tone, akin to an esoteric justification of political authority, the caliph al-Walīd II anchors his request for compliance in his being God's caliph. The prophet Muhammad inherited and succeeded previous prophets, the caliph argues, in carrying and transmitting God's message. God established the community of the faithful through his messenger, who restored his servants to faith and salvation after they had gone astray. God explained his law, he continues, through the Prophet and sealed his revelation by gathering the messages of previous prophets in Muhammad's summons. The caliph reminds his audience how the Prophet's conduct, his activities, and his way of building the community offer an example for others to follow and emulate. The Prophet, al-Walīd II explains, preached God's summons to his people, acted according to the will of God, and taught his community the knowledge of divine will. God correspondingly graced those from among his people who accepted the faith and adhered to his messenger's call with being part of an honored community of faith (*umma*).

In this scenario, al-Walīd II highlights the special significance of God's caliphs as His deputies on earth and the duty of the community to follow the revealed law. He reminds his listeners that God assigned His caliphs as deputies to follow in the path of His Prophet. They are responsible for implementing God's decree (*ḥukm*) and executing His legal sanctions (*ḥudūd*) and observing the requirements of His regulations (*farā'iḍ*) and His rights (*ḥuqūq*). They have the right and responsibility to defend Islam, uphold the foundations of the faith, protect the believers from the forbidden, deliver justice (*ʿadl*) among His servants, and restore order in His lands.

Al-Walīd II explains the need to obey the caliphs. The heavens and the earth, he argues, are supported by the power of obedience. The caliphs of God, he reminds the governors, followed one another in guarding the inheritance that the prophets left and over which God made the caliphs deputies. None from the believers, he warns, can dispute their right without God cutting them down, and they cannot secede from their community without God destroying them, nor can they hold their caliph in contempt or question the decree of God (*qaḍā Allāh*) concerning the caliphs, without God subjugating them to the caliphs. Through the caliphs, God has preserved His servants on earth and made obedience to them the path to understanding and happiness, and decreed disobedience the cause of their destruction.

Thus, promises al-Walīd II, those who correctly obey God's caliphs are the friends of God who will attain rectitude and be singled out for good fortune, both in this world and the next, unlike those who forsake it and forfeit both this world and the world to come. He then explains the elevated status and responsibility of the caliphs in executing divine will and holding true to their covenant with God. He maintains that God has prepared His caliphs for the perfect practice of honorable deeds. From the time God deputized a caliph as the commander of the faithful, the caliph has not had a greater preoccupation or concern than this covenant because of his knowledge of its preeminent role in improving the affairs of the Muslims.

At the end of the letter, al-Walīd II explains the appointment of his heirs apparent and highlights his expectation of obedience and compliance with his orders. As the commander of the faithful, he argues, he has deemed appointing two heirs best so that his subjects may be in the same position as those before them. This, he argues, is in harmony with universal order and spiritual perfection, which brings a respite of ample hope and inner tranquility, a flourishing state of concord, and a knowledge of the situation that God has established as protection.

Al-Walīd II then names his heirs, his sons al-Ḥakam and ʿUthmān, and asks his governors to pledge allegiance to them. Both of his sons, he asserts, are persons whom God has created for this purpose and fashioned them for it. They are graced with the best virtues in respect of plenitude of insight, soundness of adhering to the revealed law, superabundance of manliness, and knowledge of what is right. He concludes with the necessity and virtue of pledging allegiance to his sons so that prosperity, common good, and the state of security and protection endure without interruption.[6]

The letter is a bold commentary on political power and a defense of mundane action through radical theological arguments, placing the governance of people at the heart of salvation history and constructing a political cosmology more remarkable than the actual incident (designation of heirs apparent) that prompted it. In a noteworthy way, the caliph erases the possibility of other arguments, thus leaving no space between order and chaos. From the pulpit of authority, the caliph pushes against anti-Umayyad political cosmologies and against opposing groups, including the Kharijites and the Shiites—if not by name, then by argument. The letter is a reminder of the Umayyads' efforts to anchor their authority in a pre-encoded universal order for which they do not seem to have an alternative.

None of the heirs apparent mentioned in the letter stood a chance of becoming caliph. The fact that al-Walīd II deploys so much theological ammunition to convince and compel his governors to comply with his order reveals the tumultuous circumstances of the time and the precariousness of the caliph's authority, even within the Umayyad family itself. That is why the caliph eschews two of the most obvious political issues of the time, consultation and election, which had a direct bearing on wording the letter and the designation of the heirs apparent. While the letter operates at the level of salvation and compliance with theological imperatives, it shows no interest in discussing governance in the sense of distributing power, organizing empire, and structuring relations to administer the land.

This incongruity became a rallying point for his contender and cousin, Yazīd III. Yazīd III's letter to the people of Iraq announcing the death of his cousin al-Walīd II and the beginning of his reign exhibits similar references to God's decree, God's deputyship, and the obligation to pursue a pious life and fulfill God's purpose on earth under a divinely sanctioned caliph, who guides the community of the faithful to salvation. In trying to justify the killing of al-Walīd II by the members of the delegation, whom Yazīd III had sent to convince al-Walīd II to relinquish his title, he bases his claim on his responsibility to restore God's governance by upholding the principles of consultation and election in the transition of power. Yazīd III accuses the late caliph al-Walīd II of ignoring consultation and the consent of Muslims, despite his efforts to urge him to do so.[7]

Yazīd III begins with the statement that God chose Islam as the true revealed law, and approved and purified it. God stipulated in it, he informs his audience, certain obligations, which God enjoined or prohibited, to test the obedience and disobedience of His servants. God perfected in the faith every good deed and then took charge of the faith to preserve its purity. God guarded those who observed His legal sanctions (*ḥudūd*), protecting them and making them cognizant of the merits of Islam. Yazīd III then reminds his audience that the caliphs of God followed one after the other as guardians of His law, judging according to God's decree, following the "book" in doing so until the caliph Hishām died (743).

Then, the caliph continues, the authority passed to al-Walīd II, whom Yazīd III accuses of being the enemy of God. Yazīd disparages him as a violator of what God had made sacred on a scale that had never been seen by either Muslim or non-Muslim. Yazīd argues that when the misfortune of al-Walīd's rule intensified, blood was spilled on his account, and assets were taken wrongfully, he had to act against al-Walīd. He declares that he went to al-Walīd to convince him to mend his ways and ask God and the Muslims for forgiveness by disavowing his behavior and the acts of disobedience to God that he had dared to commit.

After seeing the intensity of the disapproval of him to the point of rage and realizing that the caliph would not change his ways, Yazīd claims, he spurred some men to action against al-Walīd. He defends his response that the delegation he had sent called on al-Walīd II to set up a council of consultation, *shūra*, in which "the Muslims might consider for themselves whom to invest with authority from among those they agreed on," but the caliph, whom he disparages as "the enemy of God," did not agree to that.[8] Negotiations, he recounts, thus failed, and the caliph was killed. Yazīd III was then declared the new caliph.

Yazīd III wrote the letter to announce the transition of power and inform the people of Iraq that they were now in a superior position: their rulers were the best men among the people and equity and justice were spread out for them. Yazīd III then calls the people of Iraq to listen to and obey his authority and whomever he may deputize to succeed him from among those agreeable to the community. He reassures them that they should expect the same righteous action from him: "I shall act among you in accordance with the command of God and the practice, *sunna*, of His Prophet, and I shall follow the way of the best of those who have gone before you."[9] In arguing against the previous caliph, Yazīd III also articulates some of the fundamental and shared theological arguments of his time concerning the idea of righteous rule defined by divine commands and the notion of governance built on the pivotal role of the community of the believers.

An Early Islamic "Conservativism"

The early Murji'ite position suited the Umayyads. One might be surprised to read that the debate over free will and predestination had anything to do with politics. However, the eighth-century Umayyad caliphs spoke about this matter in their sermons and testaments to their heirs apparent. Their scribes penned letters to administrators and opposition figures defending their patrons. As the Umayyads defended their authority through claims of God's will, fate, and providence,[10] they produced an opposition that also marshalled arguments of free will to hold them accountable for their actions.[11]

ʿAbd al-Ḥamīd's letter to the caliph Hishām seeking guidance on how to deal with a group of Qadarite (those who supported free will) soldiers among the military is a good example of such writings. The letter does not address the question of training or disciplining the soldiers but rather of correcting their doctrinal beliefs so that they conform to those of the caliph. If we consider ʿAbd al-Ḥamīd's letter as a proxy for the caliph, both appear not only alarmed by the circulation of theological doctrines not sanctioned by the caliph but also presume the imposition of theological uniformity on soldiers to be a desired goal.

ʿAbd al-Ḥamīd attacks the Qadarites in the army as a group of misguided soldiers and stubborn transgressors. He accuses them of infringing upon God's right to decide how He dispenses His will and thus arrogating to themselves the privilege of partnering with God in managing the affairs of the world. In what they utter, he claims, they oppose the most fundamental tenets of the faith and sound more like a "group of Christians" who have no regard for God's will or any concern about the peril of trespassing or lessening God's sovereign power (*sulṭān Allāh*) and His capacity to act (*qudrā*). The scribe continues to inform the caliph that he prevented such individuals from spreading their "false beliefs" among other soldiers by threatening them with severe punishment. ʿAbd al-Ḥamīd asks the caliph to advise him on how to proceed because the caliph has the right to reprimand and punish them for their deviance. ʿAbd al-Ḥamīd defines one's position on free will as not only a principle of the faith and a sign of belonging in the community but also an acknowledgment of the authority and legitimacy of the caliph.[12]

In the same religiopolitical milieu, we encounter the question of the faith status of the grave sinner (what is the faith status of a person who commits a grave sin?) as a political argument concerning the Umayyad caliphs and their authority: If the Umayyads were grave sinners (the reasons included killing without a just cause, oppression of subjects, laxity on major religious obligations), would they still be part of the community of the believers and therefore authorized to lead and entitled to obedience? The question led to a thorny theological debate about the meaning of faith, the relationship between faith and practice, and the status of the believer.

Conventionally, the problem of the grave sinner in heresiography included a neat discussion involving three parties. The Kharijites, seeing faith and practice as one (there is no faith without practice), considered the Umayyads to be unbelievers and therefore condemned their authority as illegitimate.[13] Pro-Umayyad theologians, including those known as the early Murji'ites, seeing faith and practice as separate entities (one might be a grave sinner but still a believer and thus a member of the community), considered the Umayyads believers, part of the community despite their sins, and hence entitled to obedience as caliphs.[14] Another group (they were later called the Muʿtazilites) took a middle position and placed the grave sinner in a "station between the two stations," that is, between faith and infidelity, neither believer nor disbeliever, and thus did not condone or condemn the Umayyads.[15]

Written perhaps by a prominent member of the ʿAlid nobility in Medina, the *Kitāb al-Irjā'* explains succinctly the Murji'ite position in this debate. It records a moment of the imamate discourse in its "prepolitical" state. Not more than a pamphlet, this brief text dates to a time around the Abbasid revolt in 750,[16] which makes it perfectly contemporary with Ibn al-Muqaffaʿ, who addresses the theme of obedience as a question of sovereignty rather than of faith status, as we will see in chapters 6 and 8. Structurally, the letter reflects the oratorical conventions of its time and the theological language of the late Umayyad and early Abbasid decades. It reads like a sermon or declaration of faith, arguing the speaker's position on the faith status of the earliest caliphs (the letter calls them *imāms*), which was a common way of discussing one's position on controversial doctrinal issues and on political questions concerning the caliphs.

The *Kitāb al-Irjā'* is not a political pamphlet but one that touches on political questions and defends a position (such as legitimate authority) from the standpoint of their theological value. For instance, "How does postponing or refraining from judgment on the faith status of the caliphs after ʿUmar I determine one's faith?" is the kind of question the letter tries to answer. Although varying positions on this question remain in the background unarticulated, they oblige the author to spell out his own position because they are assumed.

In a brief manner, the letter addresses several issues in the following order:[17] it begins with a discourse on the foundations of the faith, the significance of recognizing and following the scripture and divine revelation, Muhammad's prophecy and undertakings, and the formation of the community during his time. It sketches as a question of faith the controversies of the first civil war (which it calls civil discord, *fitna*) leading to the murder of the third caliph ʿUthman and its aftermath, the division of the community in the civil war and its bearing on one's faith, and the faith status of the sinner as related to the positions of those who participated in the civil war. The statement on the declaration of faith explains the Murji'ite perspective on faith as "postponing judgment" to God on the individuals who had taken part in the controversies after the reigns of the first two caliphs, Abū Bakr and ʿUmar. It also offers a defense of the Murji'ite position against its critics, launches a polemical refutation against the Saba'iyya sects,[18] and concludes with a statement of faith according to the Murji'ite creed as constructed in the letter.

The letter is also a declaration about, or position statement on, the legitimacy of past and current caliphs, who no doubt faced actual challenges from their opposition. By postponing judgment on the caliphs' controversial actions, the pamphlet affirms the faith status of the caliphs as believers and declares them part of the community, which makes them entitled to obedience. Evaluating the question from a conformist position, the letter is concerned with the faith status of the caliphs after ʿUthmān as a starting point of dispute, which suggests that the voice in the text is settling for a low threshold of piety to accept the legitimacy of the caliphs.

Bearing in mind the high bar that had been set for the first two exemplary caliphs by the Umayyad opposition (including this pamphlet), its compromise about the grave sinner would sound morally corrupt to the interlocutors of the Murji'ites because the letter gave the impression that the Murji'ites were unconcerned with even major religious obligations. While the pamphlet assumes the caliph's faith as a precondition of his legitimacy, it lacks specificity, has no bearing on the current governance, and presents no political knowledge beyond vague religious norms and piety of the caliph assumed as a framework for organizing society. Like its dialogic discourses, whether from the Umayyads or their opponents, the text shows no awareness of the challenges of governing faced by the rulers in actual time.

Theology of Resistance

Sālim b. Dhakwān's "Epistle" (*risāla*) is an early theological (*kalām*) text of an ʿIbādite Kharijite from the periphery, which engages in polemics against the Murji'ites and against hostile Kharijite groups, such as the Azraqites, the Najdites, and some quietists.[19] The "Epistle" resembles in structure the *Kitāb al-Irjā'* because both begin with an extended preliminary exhortation on piety and faithfulness followed by a reminder of Muhammad's mission; then discuss the dissension in the community, launch polemics against opponents, and defend their positions; and end with a declaration of faith and recapitulation of their positions.[20]

A much longer piece than the *Kitāb al-Irjā'*, the "Epistle" displays an elementary form of dialectic argumentation interspersed within the text. It retains the style of oral rhetoric. In hindsight, one may situate it, given its more sustained argumentation and specialized language, closer to prose than *Kitāb al-Irjā'*.[21] The "Epistle" consists of four parts, as Patricia Crone and Fritz Zimmermann point out. After starting with the preliminary appeal for piety, Sālim explains, in the second part, the origins of the faith, namely, God's grace in showing the right way to humans, the mission of Muhammad and the formation of the community of the faithful, and the completion of the mission by showing the criteria by which to distinguish those who believe from those who do not. He goes on to discuss dissension concerning the caliphs among the believers after Muhammad through recognizably Kharijite arguments and themes. His primary aims are to explain his position on the conduct of the caliphs through the first civil war, to show the reasons for his position, and to justify the emergence of the sect.[22]

In the third part, Sālim engages polemically with opponents. He first argues against the Kharijite maximalism (i.e., the Azraqites, the Najdites, and their splinter groups). Next, he refutes the Murji'ites and another group, which he names *al-Fatana*. He lays out objections against the various Kharijite positions and explains their errors or radicalism of accusing other Muslims with disbelief. He refutes the Murji'ites for being hesitant to take a position when they must, thus violating the principle of being clear on issues of faith. Second, he challenges them on the basis of their association with "kings," which he uses pejoratively for caliphs, and for refusing to count their "kings" as infidels, even though, he argues, they agree that their "kings" are sinners. He finds the Murji'ites contradicting both the Qur'an and their own arguments.

The curious group, the Fatana, which must signify the devoted Umayyad supporters, also goes astray, according to him, on two counts. First, they claim that, whereas imams may declare war on any offending member of the community, the members of the community are prevented from fighting against offending imams.[23] Second, they profess not to know whether God will reward or punish "kings" in the hereafter. He complains that they are thus worse than the Murji'ites; while the Murji'ites classify kings as believers, they do at least disown them as sinners in this world and consign sinners to Hell in the next.

In part four, Sālim summarizes where he stands and what he asks of others.[24] He begins by listing the salient points covered in part three; recapitulating points already made; and even adding new ones against the Kharijite maximalists, the Murji'ites, and the Fatana. He concludes his "lecture" by asking the erring parties to mend their ways and embrace the correct belief:[25]

> We disapprove of any Muslim undertaking to serve with the kings of their people (*qawm*) as long as the latter continue in the error of their ways. For if a Muslim individual campaigns with them and thereby calls upon their "enemies" to obey them, he will be calling upon them to obey people he professes to be infidels. But he must not call upon others to obey the kings, for if they respond and obey them, he will have to disown them; and if they separate from him and do not obey them, he will have to deem it lawful to fight them. He who fights along with kings is in one of two positions: either he will be siding with them in full approval of their cause, or else he will be helping them and strengthening their sovereign power (*sulṭān*) despite reservations.[26]

Sālim references qur'anic verses extensively (more than 150 times), either verbatim or by paraphrasing or allusion.[27] He uses the word *sunna* to connote the established practice of the Prophet and his immediate caliphal successors, and seems to assume it to be a legitimate source of legislation besides the Qur'an. He thus mentions precedents (*sunan*) that ʿUmar I set as legally binding on Muslims because "the Muslims" had been consulted about his appointment and he himself continued to consult them on how best to follow the Qur'an and the *sunna* of his predecessors, the Prophet and Abū Bakr. In Sālim b. Dhakwān's view, none of the rulers after ʿAlī, to whom he refers as kings (*mulūk*), met these conditions.[28]

Remarkable in its clarity, the "Epistle" is a good example of the idea of the imamate from the perspective of someone opposing the Umayyads as oppressive kings. If the *Kitāb al-Irjā'* represented, by Sālim b. Dhakwān's standards, a declaration of a "reluctant loyalist" selling his faith to kings, Sālim might have been accused of being a naïve critique who lacked the knowledge of political practice. Despite the difference in argument and position, however, the text shares a similar discursive plane with the Murji'ite *Kitāb al-Irjā'* and the Umayyad rulers' addresses. Like the *Kitāb al-Irjā'*, the "Epistle" does not develop a political goal or offer a practical agenda. It underlines religious obligations, purity of faith, the faith status of the caliph, and the faith value of his actions but offers not much beyond them. Apart from the dichotomy it draws between the ruling imam and king (*imām* and *malik*) and the references to the Qur'an and the community in electing the leader, the "Epistle" remains oblivious or at least inattentive to governance on the ground. It offers no critique of practice nor a path to a better one, other than demanding "correct" faith and adherence to piety embodied in action, both of which make good points for rallying support against the established order but do not offer specific steps to guide actual practice.

One does not have to labor much to characterize the "Epistle," like the other texts in this chapter, as a prepolitical discourse in theology, to which politics remains accidental. It also reveals that, whether one uses doctrinal, jurisprudential, *ḥadīth*, messianic, or historiographical idioms, "theology" remains the only language available to anyone who wished to make sense of political practice. Its distinct language not only describes political reality in a theological way but also shapes the discourse about it by inviting and compelling others to engage the question on the author's own terms.

Pre-Sunnite Caliphal Contractualism

Ibn Isḥāq's historiographical representation of the death of the Prophet offers insight into some foundational aspects of the pre-Sunnite ulema's vision of the caliphate in the mid-eighth century. Ibn Isḥāq (d. 767) was a contemporary of the later Umayyad and first Abbasid caliphs. The grandson of an Arabic-speaking Christian war captive from the village of ʿAyn al-Tamr in Iraq who became a client of the Āl al-Muṭṭalib in Medina after converting to Islam,[29] he pursued a scholarly career. Ibn Isḥāq operated in the circle of *ḥadīth* transmitters in Medina and might have harbored ʿAlid sympathies, which he recast as Abbasid loyalty after the revolt. As customary among many of his peers, he had been collecting reports about the life and deeds of Muhammad and had traveled for that purpose before he made his way to Iraq a few years after the Abbasids announced their caliphate in 750. He sought patronage at the court of al-Manṣūr (r. 754–775) in Hira and later followed the caliph to Baghdad, where he died. He presented a version of his *Biography of the Prophet* at the request of the caliph to his son Muhammad, then a small child, who would later become the caliph al-Mahdī.

Ibn Isḥāq conceived the work as a universal history in three parts, beginning with the creation, continuing with the biography of the Prophet, and ending with his activities and the early debates among his companions over leadership. Although the text survives only in later recensions,[30] its outline makes clear how reports are organized to draw a historical contour for the community (*ḥadīth*-reporting alone could not accomplish this task) and order the past by the contemporary state of its author's knowledge and priorities. My point is that Ibn Isḥāq does not simply report the past but "transforms" it by bringing it up in a historiographical modality grounded in the eighth century.[31] Even his historiographical terminology narrating Muhammad's activities under such labels as *sīra*, *maghāzī*, and so forth, is unmistakably organizational in the sense that it guides the attention of its readers toward a certain direction and establishes the terms of the discussion.

Representing and constructing a shared perspective among the mainstream ulema,[32] Ibn Isḥāq offers a foundation story, a narrative that demonstrates the communal and faith-related underpinnings of the caliphate. He appears interested in figuring out the connection between the Prophet and the caliphs, making sense of the division of the community on the question of leadership, and posing the question of leadership as a matter of contractual delegation of power from the community to the caliph. Like both his contemporaneous colleague Sālim b. Dhakwān and the author of *Kitāb al-Irjā'*, Ibn Isḥāq operates on the assumption that the Prophet communicated God's laws, built a community of faith, showed it the correct way of living, and left the question of leadership of the community open to its discretion so that the community would unite under one of its members.

In doing so, Ibn Isḥāq reconstructs what must have been an extraordinary turn from "prophetic authority" to "political authority" as only a rite of passage whose outcome the community already knew. Ibn Isḥāq uses his discretion to deduce politics from the life story of the Prophet. He offers a historiographical representation of the past in the hindsight of caliphal history, the empire-building activities, and the political practices of his time. He recalls the events surrounding the Prophet's death from the vantage point and demands of an established order with which he aligns, even though some of his reports, once read separate from the organizing telos of the overall narrative, suggest a state of disorientation in which actors seem to be struggling to make sense of their mundane reality.[33]

Representing the past through the prism of the ulema's gradualist and middle-of-the road prudence, and yet grounded, like his sectarian interlocutors, in the foundational idea that the caliphate (but not the particular caliph) was implicit in the Prophet's mission and had to do with faith, he avoids any suggestion that the transformation of community to polity depended on circumstances and the discretion of the community. In this "political" light, his readers would imagine the biography of the Prophet in the framework of the leadership dispute, anticipate the caliphate, highlight the authority of Abū Bakr and ʿUmar, prioritize the Muhājirūn over the Anṣār as the main stakeholders, shelve the Anṣār's position,[34] sympathize with an argument against the Kharijites and the ʿAlid Shiites, pass over the Shiite imamate claims—which in their own ways kept altogether different memories of the event—normalize the Qurayshite monopoly on the caliphate, and marginalize the view that saw no connection between the caliphate and the mission of Muhammad.[35] Ibn Isḥāq could not have supported a position resembling that of the Kharijite Najadāt or the later Ṣūfī-Muʿtazilite anarchism.

The act of recounting the life of Muhammad, therefore, did more than transmit reports in a text composed of anecdotes of events. It reorganized the fragments of the Prophet's life, which it attempted to represent in a coherent and teleologic story line to yield a particular meaning. We see such historiographical discretion in the accounts of the initial caliphal disputes. Ibn Isḥāq describes in some detail how Abū Bakr was elected by acclamation because of his seniority and life experience, close companionship with Muhammad, and standing in the community, in addition to his piety and praiseworthy character. Ibn Isḥāq also notes how Abū Bakr accepted the oath of allegiance (*bayʿa*, performed in the gesture of a handshake) in the Saqīfa portico, where deliberations over who should lead the community after the death of Muhammad took place. The broad congregation of the Muslims subsequently confirmed the pledge in the mosque of Medina.[36] Ibn Isḥāq's contemporary ulema framed the act of acclamation following this precedent as two stages: the restricted or private pledge of allegiance, *al-bayʿa al-khāṣṣa*, and the public pledge of allegiance, *al-bayʿa al-ʿāmma*.[37] The teachers and senior colleagues of Ibn Isḥāq had already emphasized the deliberation at the Saqīfa as a paradigmatic indicator of elective, consultative, and consensual government as opposed to kinship-chieftainship, kingship, and tyranny.[38]

Within this framework, Ibn Isḥāq cites a sermon by Abū Bakr, which he claims the caliph delivered to the congregation at the mosque of Medina soon after his election, explaining how he would lead:

> I have been given authority over you, but I am not the best of you. If I do well, help me, and if I do ill, then put me right. Truth consists in loyalty and falsehood in treachery. The weak among you shall be strong in my eyes until I secure his right if God wills; and the strong among you shall be weak in my eyes until I wrest the right from him. If a people refrain from fighting in the way of God, God will smite them with disgrace. Wickedness is never widespread in a people, but God brings calamity upon them all. Obey me as long as I obey God and His messenger, and if I disobey them, you owe me no obedience. Arise to prayer. God have mercy on you.[39]

This exemplary model of good governance and high moral discourse on politics is a "republican how to govern" checklist common among the late Umayyad ulema. Its language, the concerns it raises, the relations it discusses and supposes, and the potential it enables strike the reader as a "structuring" intervention that shaped the early ulema's contractualism. It envisions the caliph as a leader put in charge through the process of election and presupposes consent between the elected caliph and the members of the community. Both the caliph and the community are depicted as agreeing to abide by what is assumed to be the shared values of the community, which the report implies are piety, justice, equality, emulation of prophetic practice, fighting in the path of God, accountability, and safeguarding the welfare of the community. It suggests that the community's consent to the leader's privilege of wielding power on its behalf generates the corollary obligation of obedience as long as the terms of delegation of authority or contract are satisfied. The significance of this vision is its acknowledgment of political authority as contingent, contractual, and authoritative within the stated terms.

For the same reason, the report rationalizes the birth of political authority after the death of the Prophet. Notably, in depicting Abū Bakr and ʿUmar in this and other reports demanding obedience as a precondition of leadership, Ibn Isḥāq marks the transition from the "communal" to the "political" in the sense that the new authority, unlike the Prophet's, had to be continually supported, justified, and defended in order to remain enforced and authoritative. One can only appreciate the aptness and the relevance of the following remark attributed to ʿUmar I on the occasion of the funeral arrangements of the Prophet in one account of the ninth-century *ḥadīth* transmitter al-Dārimī (d. 869): "There is no Islam without community, no community without leadership, no leadership without obedience."[40] Ibn Isḥāq also underscores the notion of obedience in several reports involving Abū Bakr and ʿUmar I because it marked the most critical distinction between pastoral nomadic and kinship "statelessness" and the new social imaginary that Islam communicated, as al-Shāfiʿī (d. 819) also observed several decades after Ibn Iṣḥāq: political leadership (*imāra*) embodied a new form of authority, which would work through delegation and obedience, unlike the authority based in kinship.[41]

On display in Ibn Isḥāq's account of the death of the Prophet is therefore a core question of the ulema concerning the limits and the religious justification of political power. Ibn Isḥāq's text suggests an attempt to bridge the gap between prophetic authority based on faith and caliphal (political) authority based on contract and consent. Although his text eschews any useful knowledge about actual matters of governance, it still presents a "republican" sense of politics—one that is more communal, more reverent to various forms of piety, and much more limited and egalitarian than both the emerging discourse on kingship and later jurisprudential piety. As I stated above, Ibn Isḥāq also unveils a shift that separates the Umayyad period's ulema, who stayed an arm's length away from the caliphs, from their Abbasid counterparts, who cozied up to the caliphs, as we will see in the next section.

Imamate after Siyasa: The Governmentalization of Religion

Here I turn to the late eighth century to demonstrate how the ulema began elaborating the imamate as a concern of governance. I see this development as an outcome of the transformative impact of siyasa on the ulema. My contention is that Ibn al-Muqaffaᶜ's and his colleagues' disruptive intervention burst the bubble of the imamate as the dominant language of politics. Siyasa created an intellectual environment in which it was no longer possible to think about governance without also evoking siyasa. The attitude of the proponents of the imamate after the mid-eighth century encouraged dialogic engagement with the caliphate, in which the ulema adopted or emulated the political knowledge of siyasa. They initially did so without ever citing the term for several decades. From this radical shift of posture, one surmises that the ulema, realizing the disconnect between their ideals and actual matters of rule, marshalled their intellectual capacity to coordinate between abstract theological principles and the practicalities of governance, such as specifying what justice entailed in the treatment of people, deciding legal cases, taxation, regulating markets, and others.

Before I discuss al-ᶜAnbarī and Abū Yūsuf, I should spotlight here a remarkable political perspective. This is necessary not only to demonstrate the multidirectional trajectory of the imamate's discourse but also to warn against an undue overgeneralization. As we have seen, the label "imamate discourse" refers to diverse views on the origins of the caliphate and the proper form of governance (messianism, the imamate of the Kharijites, Shiites, pre-Sunnites). I also use it to signify certain anarchist positions to argue that the debate about the imamate generated enough moral and intellectual tension to prevent it from becoming a sealed-off discourse. The case I am raising here is the political arguments of the "Sufis of the Muᶜtazila."[42] Still holding on to the idea of organizing sociopolitical life according to the requirements of the revealed law, a cadre of "disillusioned" pious learned and sectarian scholars raised their voices against the idea of organized polity and empire and interrogated the idea of the imamate starting from its very foundations. They rejected the rapprochement between the caliphs and the ulema as unjustified accommodation of an oppressive rule through religious arguments.

Instead, the Sufis of the Muᶜtazila articulated an anarchist position that did away with the imamate altogether. Reacting against the imperial status quo, they condemned the caliphate as another form of ordinary kingship (*mulk*), which they saw as deeply alien to scripture and prophetic practice. In opposing religious (and rational) arguments for the imamate and rejecting the authenticity of the *ḥadīths* attributed to the Prophet about it, they challenged the foundations of the imamate. They maintained that establishing a ruling imam from among the Muslims stemmed from neither a rational necessity nor an essential creed of the revealed law. Barring that, the ruling imam, they explained, should at least not enjoy any broad temporal or salvific authority and not be elected for life.[43]

Contextualized in Baghdad's intellectual milieu, their views reflect the values of an urban, scholarly, and engaged circle of people whose level of dissatisfaction with the existing order made them interrogate its underpinnings.[44] One may dismiss their dissenting voice as marginal, but I see it as another "island of meaning"[45] in the orbit of imamate discourse, which created its own historiographical representation of the past, similar to what other sects and groups did.[46] By narrativizing the Prophet's actions or life events as not leading to "imperial" political authority, they produced a vision at odds with various versions of the ulema-centric ideals of the imamate, which invariably organized the Prophet's life around the question of the caliphate/imamate from the start, like the ones treated below.

A Juristic Archetype of the Imamate

My first working example is ʿUbaydallāh b. al-Ḥasan al-ʿAnbarī (b. ca. 718–724, d. 785), who served as the judge of Basra during the reign of al-Mahdī. After years of service in the judiciary, he wrote a letter of advice to the caliph to effect improvements in the fields of revenue collection, management of farmlands, and the administration of justice consistent with jurisprudential religious precepts.[47] According to Wakīʿ, who transmitted the text in his *Akhbār al-Quḍāt*, al-ʿAnbarī wrote the letter to al-Mahdī in 775, at the beginning of his reign.[48]

Al-ʿAnbarī (in reference to the al-ʿAnbar clan of Tamīm, the founding tribe of Basra) was born into a prominent Arab family of Basra in the late second or early third decade of the eighth century. His father, al-Ḥasan b. al-Ḥusayn, was a reputable scholar and *ḥadīth* transmitter. His grandfather, al-Ḥusayn b. Malik, served as governor (*ʿamīl*) of Maysān for ʿUmar I. Al-ʿAnbarī is known for his expert knowledge of law, poetry, lexicography, and Arab genealogies, and for practicing law according to the Basran school of religious jurisprudence, thus favoring *ra'y* or rational judgment.

In 773, the caliph al-Manṣūr named him the judge of Basra and, like his predecessor, the governor in charge of prayer in the city. His responsibilities included delivering the Friday sermon on behalf of the caliph at the main mosque. He combined these two positions until 775, when al-Mahdī, soon after becoming caliph, withdrew the governorship to entrust it to ʿAbd al-Malik b. Ayyūb al-Numayrī, but confirmed him in his post as judge, which he occupied until 783 or 784. In his fifties when he wrote the letter, al-ʿAnbarī might have hoped to attract the attention of the newly appointed caliph to either advance his career or to display the expected charitable loyalty to his profession.

Al-ʿAnbarī was dismissed perhaps because of a disagreement with the caliph on some administrative decisions, two of which at least related to taxation and land allocation.[49] Al-ʿAnbarī's legal arguments with the caliph during his judgeship strained their relationship. On several occasions, he contested the caliph's orders regarding how to administer public lands and taxes. Al-ʿAnbarī seems to have sided with the local people and actively resisted al-Mahdī's request to increase the land tax levied on the farmlands of Basra. He also opposed al-Mahdī's personal intervention into two or more litigations regarding disputed rural properties. Thus, we have here a professional who served as a judge in the Abbasid administration and who forged a personal acquaintance with the caliph himself without surrendering his juridical and administrative authority.[50] The following generations remembered his exemplary conduct and his contribution to judicial autonomy.

Al-ʿAnbarī wrote his letter without solicitation from the caliph himself to address what he saw as the pressing political questions of his time. In a straightforward and impressive manner, he advises the caliph on how to improve the administration in the four major areas of the frontiers, judiciary, tribute levied on non-Muslims, and legal alms levied on Muslims.[51] In his frequent use of qur'anic verses and *ḥadīth* reports, and his inclusion of pious phrases, exhortations, warnings, and explicit references to end-of-time portents and the hereafter, al-ʿAnbarī foregrounds legalistic piety as the defining aspect of his overall political outlook.[52] Notable for his grasp of the administrative structure of the caliphate and the institutions comprising it, the author impresses the reader with his cultivated manner of guiding the administration toward his own juristic political sensibilities.

With its practice-oriented content, his letter marks a transition from the abstract doctrinal pronouncements examined earlier in this chapter to the practical advice of the later ulema. The letter demonstrates the jurists' gradual realization of the political value of their knowledge in actual matters of governance, beyond its value as a keen political observation of a prominent and independent-minded judge, who is convinced that the administration would run more efficiently if it were guided correctly. Al-ʿAnbarī thus produces an archetypal text of religious-jurisprudential perspective on the imamate. In fact, he spells out a legal method, a remarkable new development, not yet widely shared among the jurists.

As we will see in the next two chapters, the letter is intertextually related to ʿAbd al-Ḥamīd's and Ibn al-Muqaffaʿ's political prose, in particular the "Epistle on the Caliph's Privy" by Ibn al-Muqaffaʿ (common themes include the army, judiciary, revenue, taxation), even though it advocates competing sociopolitical values and is anchored in a distinctly dissimilar epistemic framework. Whether by inspiration or even blueprint, the text evidences a transposition of style (political, practical, specific), known to be practiced by bureaucrats, into jurisprudential writing. It thus pioneers a prose form of political "advice" hitherto unfamiliar among jurists. Seen in this way, the letter represents one of the earliest jurisprudential texts confronting the challenge of political practice in fields outside legal matters, making it dramatically different from the earlier texts I have examined.[53]

The text follows a pattern of presentation comparable to peripatetic letters, sometimes rhetorical, interspersed with qur'anic verses, lines of poetry, *ḥadīths*, and personal or biographical anecdotes. It opens with a theme found in other imamate texts explaining the foundations of the community (God, the prophets, the scripture, pious ancestors, and their practice) and moves to discuss current issues of administration and to remind the caliph of the rewards and punishments in the earthly life and in the hereafter. The letter is also remarkable for its allusions and references to end-of-time expectations, urging the caliph to do good before it is too late. As the survey and evaluation below illustrate, the letter offers a compelling narrative of the meaning of caliphal rule, and expands noticeably the vocabulary and the scope of discourse on the imamate.

In his assessment, al-ʿAnbarī reveals how he conceives the Abbasid governing structure. One estate of the administration is the army, which he discusses in the context of managing conquests and protecting the frontiers efficiently. Another estate is the judiciary. The administration must have an efficient and fair legal system, led by the caliph but maintained by the jurists, following the jurisprudential methodology explained in the letter. He anchors the legal system in the religious jurisprudence of the jurists, which differs from the legal model offered by Ibn al-Muqaffaʿ, as we will see in chapter 6. The third estate has to do with the revenue gained from the land tax on non-Muslim farmers and its distribution. Here, too, he organizes the practice according to jurisprudential principles, and seeks conformity with them. Al-ʿAnbarī's acknowledgment of the presence of "protected people" as one of the constituent elements of the realm warrants mention here because Ibn al-Muqaffaʿ's "Epistle" does not name them as such. Alms or obligatory ritual charity (*ṣadaqa*), as another form of taxation levied on Muslim subjects, constitutes the fourth estate. As a religious obligation, it needs to be collected and distributed according to specific religious principles and traditions. It is worth mentioning that

Ibn al-Muqaffaʿ's text does not even acknowledge this sector as a matter of discussion.

Al-ʿAnbarī begins his letter by praising the caliph after his inauguration, whom he honors as a recipient of God's grace and support. He depicts the caliph as the model ruler of a righteous community, fulfilling God's will on earth as it approaches the end of time. Following a convention of his time, he prays for the caliph's comfort and health and for receiving support from righteous individuals. He lauds the caliph for his knowledge of God's book, of the practice (*sunna*) of His Prophet, and of the conduct of the past caliphs. Explaining the reason for composing the letter, he expresses his feeling of responsibility toward God and the caliph to give advice to the latter, thus to improve the administration of affairs.[54]

Al-ʿAnbarī stresses the importance of safeguarding the realm for the believers and the faith, which he describes as a blessing bestowed by God to complement and perfect the believers' faith and submission. God, he asserts, wants to unite the community of the faithful and increase their love for each other, and He wishes (al-ʿAnbarī adds in paraphrased verses) to make supreme their revealed law, which He has chosen for them. Furthermore, He wishes to complete His blessing over them by making them deputies (*yastakhlifu*) on earth, as He has done for the communities before them. God wants to replace their fear with tranquility so that they believe in Him alone and not associate partners with Him.[55] Al-ʿAnbarī thus bonds the administrative functions of the caliphate to the caliph, whom he presents as the chief guardian of God's laws among the faithful, the deputy of God, the father of his subjects, and the divinely supported leader who guides his community to righteous living and welfare.

As in the previously introduced letters discussing the imamate, al-ʿAnbarī outlines "the foundations" in patently jurisprudential-pious language and with paraphrases from qur'anic verses. With His grace and bounty, he informs the caliph, God dispatched the Messenger as He had in the past, followed by the righteous caliphs (*al-khulafā' al-rāshidūn*) and the leading and trustworthy jurists (*al-a'imma al-fuqahā' al-ṣiddīqīn*). God wanted the believers to worship Him alone and be His sincere servants. God tried the first generation and those who followed its members, who acted according to the light of the scripture (*al-kitāb*). They are, al-ʿAnbarī continues, the rightly guided and rightly guiding ones, the God-fearing imams, the loftiest nobility (*al-hudāt al-muhtadūn, al-a'imma al-ʿā'idūn*, and *al-ashrāf al-akramūn*), the ulema, the caliphs, the innocent, and the pious. They are the ones who deserve to be followed. Through their pious deeds and actions, the realm becomes straight, God's path is followed, God's commands are implemented, and entitlements are distributed justly until such time as the regions (*bilād*) become stable, people obtain their deserved status, frontiers are fortified, and enemies are defeated. He assures the caliph that God has made the faithful the inheritors of countries, territories, and wealth through the undertakings of the prophets and the caliphs.[56]

After an elaborate preamble that makes the case for the caliph as the supreme leader, chief legislator, and righteous believer who follows the pious tradition, al-ʿAnbarī turns his attention to matters of governance by highlighting in broad pious terms the value of governing with justice, being watchful of one's subjects, and the due obedience to the ruler to secure order. He greets the reign of the caliph as a time of renewed energy among his subjects and expresses his hopes for prosperity and rectitude under the authority of the caliph. He compliments the caliph for upholding justice, leading his subjects to righteousness, and implementing God's orders by following the path of the previous imams, whose qualities he notes in the preamble. Al-ʿAnbarī wishes that, in this way, believers may attain a lofty station in the hereafter, and the caliph's subjects (*raʿiyya*) may experience love, compassion, tranquility, and welfare. He encourages the caliph to observe justice and implement what is right among the people. In addition, he compares the position of the caliph as God's deputy to that of a compassionate father concerned for his children's well-being, watchful of their weaknesses and errors, merciful toward them when a reasonable explanation is given for their misbehavior, careful to protect their dignity, and willing to take responsibility for their affairs.

God has bestowed upon the caliph, he resumes, the power of grace and support, which obliges his subjects to listen to and obey him and be at peace with his rule (*samʿ wa ṭāʿa wa sukūn*), which will help them keep their conduct straight and filial relations virtuous. With God's grace, he notes, the caliph may rule over communities (*jamāʿāt*) and the land (*bayḍa*). Al-ʿAnbarī completes his praise of the caliph and of his reign with a proverb, which suggests his awareness of the unique value of governing, encouraging al-Mahdī to continue acting according to justice: "The commander of the faithful knows what has been said in the past, namely, that one day of a just imam's rule is better than sixty years of worship—in this kind of contest rulers should compete."[57]

The judge then moves to advising on administration and explaining justice that he is asking the caliph to implement. He lays out his recommendations in four categories: the frontiers (*thughūr*), the law (*aḥkām*), tax revenue (*fay'*), and the *ṣadaqa* tax.[58] With regard to the frontiers and the military, as both ʿAbd al-Ḥamīd and Ibn al-Muqaffaʿ had dealt with in the "Testament to the Crown Prince" and the "Epistle on the Caliph's Privy," respectively, he informs the caliph that stable rule depends on the help of courageous men, educated by experience, who should be compensated, together with their soldiers, with satisfactory pensions (*ʿaṭā'*) and in-kind pay (*arzāq*) as long as they are called to duty.

They should not be left alone to rely on whatever they have gained from the spoils (*ghanā'im*) they seize during campaigns. Rather, they should be given extra pensions and favors whenever they successfully conquer territories. The caliph should deploy brave, vigorous, and strong men to combat the enemy so that they perform their duties in the best way. Their virtuous deeds should be noticed and rewarded in their lifetimes and perpetuated among their descendants in accordance with their entitlements. Others will notice the benevolence shown to such veterans, he reminds the caliph, and will be encouraged to compete for success.

Perpetuating conquest benefits in progeny dates to the practice of ʿUmar I. The question became a point of contention during the Umayyad period, leading to controversies, rebellions, and momentous military confrontations between the provincial administration and the center due to its implications for wealth allocation, ownership, and control of the land.[59] For this reason, al-ʿAnbarī's position was critical. Even though al-ʿAnbarī presents the matter gently to his patron, he effectively proposes a change in the methods of taxation and of financial control. As he concludes this brief section on the frontiers, al-ʿAnbarī cautions the caliph (on the authority of a jurist from the generation of the Successors, the generation succeeding the Companions of the Prophet) that the Prophet had forewarned that not being watchful of borders would threaten the community. The caliph should therefore always be vigilant about the frontiers because they were ramparts (*ḥuṣūn*) protecting the faithful (*ʿibād*) and securing peace (*sakan*) in the realm. Keeping order on the frontiers posed, he states, a challenge and a test, and God had entrusted the caliph with this responsibility. One will be rewarded for fulfilling this responsibility in the measure that one bore the burden of it.[60]

Compared to the candid posture in his suggestions on the military, al-ʿAnbarī seems guarded about giving advice on the law and judges, perhaps because he sees a conflict of interest there. He explains that his current duties as a judge should neither discourage nor prevent him from offering his counsel to the caliph as far as his knowledge permits because his appointment as judge is only temporary. It will change soon either because of "separation in life"[61] or because of death, which is why, he stresses, his strongest appeals are intended for others rather than himself. First, he advises, judgments must be rendered according to what is in the "Book of God." If one does not find the answer there, then one must render judgments according to the "Sunna of the Prophet of God." After that, one must judge according to the "consensus of the leading jurists" (*al-a'imma al-fuqahā'*), if one does not find a relevant ruling in the Sunna. Finally, one determines according to the "independent ruling of the judge" (*ijtihād al-ḥākim*) because he is given authority by the ruling imam to fulfil this duty, in consultation with the people of knowledge (*ahl al-ʿilm*).

As for employing the judges (*ḥukkām*), he recommends that the least one can expect from them is heightened piety (*al-waraʿ*) and intelligence (*al-ʿaql*) to avoid blame. If the appointees are also endowed with understanding (*fahm*) and knowledge of the "Book and the Sunna," they satisfy the basic requirements of their duty. And if the judge's qualifications exceed what is necessary—such as having resolve and discernment, insight into human behavior, and perceptiveness about how to examine confused cases in which people complain about each other—the judge approaches perfection. Al-ʿAnbarī encourages the caliph to take such individuals into service when found. The caliph needs to establish those persons firmly in their positions, assign them a high rank, support them, encourage them, and empower them to execute their judgments. The judge and his auxiliaries (*aʿwān*) and his scribes (*kuttāb*) should be allotted ample salaries (*arzāq*). Al-ʿAnbarī concludes his proposal by remarking that the judiciary (*al-ḥukm*) stands at the forefront of public duties (*al-aʿmāl*) and that the caliph fulfills the role of a leader (imam) by governing and supporting them.[62]

Concerning tax revenue from the conquered lands (*al-fay'*), he advises that it must be collected according to custom (*bi-sunnatihi*) from those who are subject to it, with lenient adjustments matching the means of the population so that they have enough to meet their needs and those of their lands, their auxiliaries and their families, and the poor among them. Likewise, al-ʿAnbarī recommends, one way of managing taxation is to report taxes annually. This practice would help the regions (*bilād*) flourish, the milk flow in abundance, and the revenue of the land tax (*al-kharāj*) increase, which would be fairer to the subjects (*al-raʿiyya*). Thus, he reasons, easing the burden of the tax-paying subjects by reducing the amount of tax on them would generate a yield several times higher when their lands become prosperous, and their remaining shares would be more abundant than would be the case by ruining them and devastating their regions.

It is only right, al-ʿAnbarī advises, to respect the conditions granted to the beneficiaries of a peace treaty—that is, the non-Muslim subjects of the caliph. He warns that he witnessed near his home two different practices of the same tax policy with different outcomes. The first one related to an area of farmland he visited within his district, where the assigned tax and sharecropping (*muzāraʿa*) guidelines that had been granted to its population were respected. There, the proceeds of the land tax (*kharāj*) exceeded the revenue collected from the surrounding villages (*kuwar*). The second one, he says, is where a similar practice was not respected. There, the outcome was contrary to justice and injurious to the peasants. Despite the caliph al-Manṣūr's written edict to Sawwār b. ʿAbdallāh, the judge of Basra, ordering him to respect the conditions granted to farmers who had already paid their taxes in advance (*al-muzāriʿīn al-mutaqabbilīn*) as stipulated, al-ʿAnbarī warns the caliph that he saw one of these farmers complaining that he was forced to pay a tax amount several times more than the agreed-upon sum.[63] Al-ʿAnbarī advises the caliph to prevent such erratic practices, which are detrimental to revenue and contrary to the fair treatment of farmers.

Moving on to discuss expenditures and the collection and disbursement of tribute revenue (*fay'*), al-ʿAnbarī refers to the Qur'an to explain why the caliph should disburse in perpetuity part of the revenue collected from the conquered lands among certain groups of people. Once collected, the tribute must be distributed equitably according to the customs in force (*ʿalā sunanihi*) and according to qur'anic commands laid out in five verses in the suras Ḥashr (four verses)[64] and the Loot (one verse),[65] which he selectively quotes. According to his interpretation of the quoted verses, he recommends that the caliph dispense a portion of the revenue gained from tribute to the descendants of the Emigrants (*Muhājirūn*), the Helpers (*Anṣār*), and to other entitled Muslims after them, as their share in perpetuity. In support of his recommendation, he cites the practice of ʿUmar I and urges the caliph to follow the tradition on this matter. He encourages the caliph by noting that the ruling imam of the subjects (*imām al-ʿāmma*) should be diligent concerning the distribution of revenue, with proper adjustments to privilege some in relation to others for their virtues, their seniority in Islam, or their exploits in the pioneering conquests of earlier times. For the rest of the people, he advises, the caliph should act equitably. Al-ʿAnbarī also warns the caliph that respecting the practice of the Prophet and of ʿUmar I requires that the caliph reserve only one-fifth of spoils for himself.[66]

As advice on the religiously obligatory *ṣadaqa* tax (alms, *ṣadaqāt*) and its collection from those who are subject to it, al-ʿAnbarī recommends, following Abū Bakr and ʿUmar I's practice: to consider it as a tax regulated by the administration rather than a charity left to individual discretion. He alerts his patron that an individual must neither pay more than his obligatory part (*farīḍa*) nor be allowed to pay a lower sum or overrate its value. He then reminds the caliph that the Prophet had warned about observing the limits set forth concerning the alms, saying, "Whoever goes beyond the bounds in almsgiving is like one who refuses to pay it." The caliph must therefore charge alms on grain, fruits, and other goods, according to customs (*sunan*) that "Muslims know and practice."

Citing the relevant verse in the Qur'an, he reminds the caliph that legal alms must be distributed among the beneficiaries whom God has specified in His scripture in a manner that the ruling imam sees fit, depending on exigent needs in each of the specified categories. The caliph should not include as beneficiaries any people not listed in the stipulations nor exclude any of the specified people from receiving alms. The caliph should not deprive the inhabitants of a locality of the benefits of their portion of the legal alms unless they can afford the deficit or subsist without it for a year, until the next cycle of alms distribution. If their welfare is assured for a year, they can be excluded from the alms for a year to benefit the poor closest to their locality. The caliph should also collect from non-Muslim (*ahl al-dhimma*) merchants under his authority double what Muslim merchants pay, per ʿUmar I's practice. It is the practice, too, al-ʿAnbarī reminds the caliph, that foreign merchants (*tujjār al-ḥarb*) pay when they arrive in Muslim lands the equivalent of what foreigners (*ahl al-ḥarb*) take from Muslim merchants when they visit their lands.[67]

These four areas constitute, al-ʿAnbarī notes, the functions entrusted to the caliph concerning his subjects. He reminds the caliph that there is no room for independent reasoning (*ra'y*) on issues specified in the "Book of God" and the "Prophet's practice" for anyone. The rules regarding these issues must be followed and respected. As for other matters that the ruling imams and the people encounter but for which neither the scripture nor the Prophet's practice sets forth any rule, the caliph is the sole authority. Al-ʿAnbarī acknowledges the authority of the caliph, stating that no one can bypass the one in charge of the affairs of Muslims (*walī amr al-muslimīn*) and the ruling imam of their collective body (*imām jamāʿatihim*), nor can anyone decide without him. Indeed, his subordinates must take matters to him for the final decision and must submit to his verdict.

Two additional recommendations that complement the previous four remind the caliph of consequences, practical and spiritual. The first is to consult righteous and trustworthy people (*ahl al-dhikr wa al-amāna*)[68] on the work of the civil servants (*ʿummāl*). The second is to give everyone what they deserve by rewarding those who do excellent work and censoring those who do misdeeds or revoke their privileges and replacing them with other qualified individuals. It is also useful, he notes by telling a proverb, for a governor (*wālī*), to lead effectively, not to overestimate what is being done well, even if the work is significant. On the other hand, the caliph should not underestimate excellence or neglect it because those who do good are happy with the blessing that will be prescribed for them, whether small or large. Virtuous deeds accumulate and cancel bad ones. One should not neglect to be scornful of any mischief, even if it seems small, because no evil is innocuous.[69] He warns the caliph that the work of today should not be postponed until tomorrow. Under certain circumstances, obligations accumulate, and some work must inevitably be neglected for the benefit of others.

Al-ʿAnbarī concludes with additional exhortations: one must also hasten to do outstanding work among the people and in the privacy of one's soul, referring to the prophetic *ḥadīth* urging believers to hurry at the sight of the portents, which he assumes that the caliph has already heard. Next, al-ʿAnbarī launches into a discourse on the portents of the end of time, which the caliph should know to avoid hastening the Hour: the rising of the sun at sunset, the antichrist (*al-dajjāl*), the beast of the earth (*dabbat al-arḍ*), the annihilation of humans, and the neglect of the affairs of the common people (*amr al-ʿāmma*). One can never be certain, he warns the caliph, when these signs will appear—tomorrow morning or even tonight. To support his assertion, he cites reports attributed to the Prophet about the imminence of the Hour, which are well attested in later compilations of *ḥadīth*, such as "I have been sent as close to the Hour as these two fingers, and the Prophet would join his forefinger with middle finger."[70]

To encourage the caliph to act, he elaborates further. How is it, he asks, that so many years and ages have elapsed since these statements?[71] He then recommends that the caliph gather before his lofty presence (*bi-haḍratihi*) a group of individuals selected from the inhabitants of the cities (*al-amṣār*) who are trustworthy and who know the prophetic practice, and who have experience, reason, and piety. The caliph should ask for their advice on governing the people, setting regulations that affect them, and delivering his judgment in cases of injustice (*maẓālim*) that are brought before him. Al-ʿAnbarī encourages the caliph to seek help and advice even though, he notes, in His generosity, God gave him superior knowledge in the scripture and the laws (*sunnatihi*). He reminds the caliph that the affairs of the community, which God has entrusted to him, concern both the peoples of the east and the west and that some duties demand so much time from the caliph that he cannot devote himself satisfactorily to others. Such circumstances dictate that the "people of trust and knowledge" would be of great assistance to him.[72] To support his recommendation, he cites two qur'anic verses in which God advises the Prophet to consult the community of believers even though he was privileged to receive revelations and was more virtuous and more knowledgeable than any of his disciples. After citing these verses,[73] he mentions the virtues of the Companions of the Prophet because they formed the most meritorious community. According to this verse, they are also distinguished by the virtue of consulting each other in managing their affairs.[74]

Already, al-ʿAnbarī notes, the people of the caliph's realm have been pleased to know that he makes public appearances to address their needs. They furthermore pray to God to increase the caliph's ability to administer their affairs swiftly, strengthen his patience to do so, and bolster his power to administer their affairs in this way. Al-ʿAnbarī explains to the caliph that it is a manifestation of justice when a ruler looks after the affairs of his people (*al-walī ʿalā amr al-raʿiyya*) with devotion.[75] He conveys his hope that the caliph's knowledge of justice, his piety, strength, and discernment will lead him to do what is best for his soul and make the best decisions. He reminds the caliph of the consequences for those who close their doors in the face of the needy and the poor. Thus, the caliph should remember to approach them with compassion. Al-ʿAnbarī concludes his letter with a prayer that God may grant the caliph mercy and grace; make his reign just; inspire him to treat his subjects with benevolence, clemency, and mercy; and privilege him with his subjects' attention and obedience.[76]

Al-ʿAnbarī writes with an awareness of the priority of the revealed law (*al-dīn*), whose framework he outlines briefly but clearly, to governance. He asks the caliph to follow the methodological procedure outlined in his letter and to encourage the jurists under his authority to do the same: the caliph should legislate first by looking for answers in the scripture, then in the prophetic practice, followed by the consensus of the leading jurists, and by using his rational judgment. In his capacity as the deputy of God (*khalīfat allāh*), al-ʿAnbarī seems to assume, the caliph has the fundamental duty of judiciously interpreting and implementing the revealed law and protecting it, which is also the raison d'être of his authority. It is patent in his text as it is in Abū Yūsuf's that the caliph is given a more capacious religious authority than the jurists of the ninth century onward allowed. Later jurists refrained from addressing the caliph as God's caliph precisely because it suggested an authority that seemed too comprehensive.[77] By the time of al-Māwardī in the tenth and eleventh centuries, the juristic caliph had already been defined as subordinate to the community and a mere defender of the juristic law.

In this delicate balancing act, al-ʿAnbarī acknowledges more so than the later jurists the caliph's prerogative to make legal decisions. However, al-ʿAnbarī was also aware that he wielded no institutional power (practical or administrative tools) to compel the caliph to follow the legal principles and methodology outlined in the letter. In a measured advisory tone, he could only encourage the caliph to consult with jurists and the trustworthy "people of knowledge" and to consider the moral, pious, and legal guidance. For this reason, the letter is better read as an acknowledgment of administrative and legal "subordination" (as distinct from cooperation or competition) of a legal scholar to the caliph as long as the caliphal administration upheld the moral underpinnings of the sacred law and the religious principles of the jurists.

A main question in this regard has to do with the authority over the law and the function of the ruler in the realm. In acknowledging the caliph as the deputy of God and the imam of his community, al-ʿAnbarī already undermines juristic authority. In the same manner, by *not* emphasizing the independent authority of the jurist over the law vis-à-vis the imam, he unduly enhances the caliph's authority. While al-ʿAnbarī proposes improvements on caliphal administration according to juristic reasoning and expertise, he does not spell out any balancing procedures beyond exhortative warnings if the caliph "transgresses." When al-ʿAnbarī advises, he does so only within the political and administrative structure already in place, not as an alternative to it—and not against it. Consequently, a "shariʿa-compliant" caliph, as far as al-ʿAnbarī is concerned, was not a foregone conclusion.[78]

To assess the positionality of the letter, one also needs to consider the posture of other groups and factions at the time (the Kharijites and the Shiites) from the Abbasid administration. Compared to their standpoints, al-ʿAnbarī falls squarely within the ruling class as a participant in the Abbasid rule, an insider who assesses the practice for administrative efficiency, and an enabler of Abbasid politics. Rather than reveal a conflict between al-ʿAnbarī (and, by extension, the jurists) and the Abbasids, his letter speaks with a tone ready to make the jurists the legal and religious establishment of the empire.

Al-ʿAnbarī writes from the high moral ground of an assumed universal order. Far from the dissenting voice of sects and the passionate tone of *Kitāb al-Irjā'* or Sālim b. Dhakwān's "Epistle," calling from the margins, eager to argue to convince or accuse the opponent, his letter establishes (or represents) by its very language the order of things, the norm that should be followed, and from which one would only deviate or break away. It offers the caliph a legal framework that normalizes the revealed law for the caliphate, not by arguing against it but simply by stating and explaining it for the uninformed. The letter strikes the reader as a bold demonstration of the confidence the jurists gained after they had established strong bonds with the Abbasids in the second half of the eighth century. In this regard, Abū Yūsuf's text, the *Kitāb al-Kharāj* (*The Book of Land Tax*), marks a milestone, as I examine below.

Imperial Turn in Juristic Discourse

If al-ʿAnbarī advised al-Mahdī to make the sacred law of the jurists the law of the caliphate by informing him of it, al-Rashīd himself would be compelled to ask Abū Yūsuf to tell him how he should do it.[79] Yaʿqūb b. Ibrāhīm Abū Yūsuf is known as the chief judge (*qāḍī al-quḍāt*) of the Abbasid caliph Hārūn al-Rashīd and the foremost student of Abū Ḥanīfa, the eponym of the Ḥanafī school of law. He was born in Kufa about 730, hailing from a family of Arab ancestry in Medina, hence his patronyms al-Anṣārī and al-Kūfī. His great-grandfather was reputed to have been a young person in Medina during Muhammad's time. He studied prophetic traditions (*ḥadīth*) and religious jurisprudence (*fiqh*) in Medina and Kufa under heavyweight scholars such as Mālik b. Anas, Abū Ḥanīfa, Layth b. Saʿd, and others. He seems to have lived in Kufa until either the caliph al-Hādī or al-Mahdī appointed him judge in Baghdad, where he lived afterward. Al-Rashīd conferred upon him the new title of chief judge. While the authority and function of this office evolved gradually, the caliph not only consulted Abū Yūsuf on the administration of justice, financial policy, and related questions but also on the appointment of other judges across the regions, to make the judicial administration more centralized. Abū Yūsuf laid the foundations of an institution of juridical administration that functioned routinely and flourished after his death.[80]

Taking Ibn al-Nadīm's *al-Fihrist* at face value, Abū Yūsuf must have composed numerous works, but only one seems to have survived: *Kitāb al-Kharāj* (*Book of Land Tax*).[81] Compared to his mentor Abū Ḥanīfa, he relied more on *ḥadīths* in legal opinions and judgments and took a more reserved position about relying on independent reasoning or rational judgment (*ra'y*). It is possible, as some of his contemporaries suggested, that Abū Yūsuf's career as a judge led him to change his opinion on numerous legal questions.[82] Thanks to the development of prose writing, the spread of written works, and the flourishing of the paper manufacturing industry in Baghdad, the jurists produced a substantial amount of scholarship, aiding the Abbasids beyond the adjudication of legal cases. It is fair to suggest that his position and his scholarly work brought his fellow jurists into a remarkable partnership with the caliphs as part of the ruling class.

As far as his political loyalties are concerned, he might not have been a partisan of the Abbasids but rather a good public servant who allied with the existing caliphal system and was invested in its success.[83] Similar to the intellectually gifted scribes of his time, Abū Yūsuf put his work at the service of the imperial bureaucracy, even though his moral compass sometimes pointed in a different direction. This does not mean that Abū Yūsuf was daring in his engagement with the Abbasids about their religious and political memory and self-image. At least, his text's tone and the examples he cites do not indicate it. In an attempt to construct a linear caliphal trajectory from Abū Bakr to his patron, he must have ignored their Hāshimid Shiite background and sectarian Kaysānite affiliation. An indication of his "pan-caliphal" political position surfaces in his citation of the first four caliphs and the Umayyad ʿUmar II as ideal caliphs whose conduct is taken as setting a precedent. It is also apparent in his argument about the collective probity of the Companions of the Prophet as legitimate and trustworthy sources of legal judgment and religious values.

The practical dimension of siyasa must have inspired both Abū Yūsuf and al-ʿAnbarī to envision a practice that meshed religious principles with the political body of the empire, which I have called a governmentalization of religion. As Abū Yūsuf notes in his introduction, the *Kitāb al-Kharāj* was meant as a guide to the caliph, who asked him to explain and expound on how he should act in matters at his discretion to avert oppression from his flock (*raʿiyya*) and to benefit their well-being.[84] The text is, in fact, an extended response to questions posed by the caliph Hārūn al-Rashīd on land tax, landholding, poll tax, customs duties, legal alms, religious communities, imperial subjects, rebels, criminal justice, legal and ethical principles, and associated topics related to various aspects of administration. Overall, the work deals with structuring and regulating taxation and clarifying the legal status of farmers living off the land. Although Abū Yūsuf is concerned with financial questions, he offers opinions on a range of administrative matters, including warfare and the status of non-Muslim subjects, to present a set of legally sanctioned rules, principles, and values to guide al-Rashīd's policies and administrative practices. An overview of the introduction of the *Kitāb al-Kharāj* will show its dialogic connection to the discourse of imamate and its positional difference from siyasa after the mid-eighth century.

Like al-ʿAnbarī's much shorter letter, *Kitāb al-Kharāj* begins with an initial exhortation encouraging the caliph to comply with God's commands, habituate pious acts, and observe justice in administering his realm according to religious principles and the practice of the early pious generations and thus store virtuous deeds for a felicitous eternal life in the hereafter. According to Abū Yūsuf, the caliph can expect success and the loyalty of his subjects only after he follows this righteous path. Beyond making specific recommendations on actual policy matters, Abū Yūsuf measures administrative success not by the outcome of a policy but by the devotion of the administrators to religious principles and the community's righteous practices, which he sets forth as the source of earthly and eternal fulfillment (*ṣalāḥ*).

In an oratorial address on good rule and good governance from a jurist's perspective, Abū Yūsuf cautions the caliph that God has appointed him to look after the affairs of his community as shepherd and trustee, and gave him a supreme position, which can lead to great reward if it is rightly occupied and to severe punishment if it is not. He describes the position of the ruler vis-à-vis God as that of a shepherd to an owner, and the one between the ruler and his subjects as that of a shepherd to his flock. The happiest of shepherds on the Day of Resurrection before God, he reminds the caliph, will be the shepherd whose subjects were happy under his authority. A building not based on awe of God cannot last, he warns his patron, for God will smite its foundations and destroy it on top of him who built it or helped to build it. The caliph should not squander the command that God has given him over this community and not put off today's activity until tomorrow, otherwise he will be lost.

The caliph is charged with dispensing justice in matters entrusted and assigned to him by God. He must therefore actively seek to rule well, avoid bias toward any party, suppress his anger, and aim for righteousness and fear of God. The caliph should prefer the hereafter to the pleasures of this world; treat subjects fairly and equally in enforcing the ordinances of God; strive for unambiguously defined aims; and follow a well-trodden path, well-established practices, and recognized legal sources so that he would be compensated for his efforts on the Day of Judgment.

Abū Yūsuf cites qur'anic verses to warn the caliph of the reckoning after death and to encourage him to act devoutly in his interactions. He informs him that obedience to and fear of God are important for the caliph because his actions are fraught with great responsibilities. God, he alerts the caliph, "has appointed the rulers to be His vicegerents on earth, and granted them the light of wisdom that illuminates the confused affairs of their subjects and makes clear to them the rights and duties about which they are in doubt."[85] He reminds the caliph that the wisdom of the rulers manifests itself in carrying out punishments and in restoring established and proved rights to their owners by absolute and clear orders. For this purpose, the revival of precedents and traditions (*sunan*) laid down by the pious and the devout is important. He cautions the caliph that "the iniquity of a shepherd spells ruin for his flock," and his reliance on anyone other than righteous and reliable officials spells disaster for the community. Abū Yūsuf closes the initial portion of his introduction with an additional appeal, and reminder, that he hopes this work that he has written will benefit the caliph and result in abundant tax revenue.[86]

The *ḥadīths* cited by Abū Yūsuf at the end of the introduction cover a wide range of topics, focusing on the governance of the pious according to the norms and worldview of the pre-Sunnite ulema, including their views on the Companions of the Prophet. In the following brief catalog, I recapitulate the content of the quoted *ḥadīths*: piety of the ruler; divine reward and punishment in the hereafter; the community of the faithful as the bedrock of righteous rule; obeying the revealed law; the right of the people to voice their thoughts and the obligation of the ruler to listen; correct belief; justice and fairness; observing correct conduct and control of emotion; dutifulness and diligence; observing merit; treating Muslim and non-Muslim subjects prudently; duty of jihad; the collective duty of the community to act on certain occasions; the merit and authority of the first two caliphs; and anecdotes about Abū Bakr, ʿUmar I, and ʿUmar II, their justice and piety, and their words of wisdom.

Contemplating its content in comparison to al-ʿAnbarī's letter, the work stands out less for its innovative outlook in terms of its conceptualization of the problem, view of the empire, and intellectual rigor, and more for its laborious craftmanship in "normal science," to use Thomas Kuhn's useful term, that attempts to solve the puzzles of a familiar terrain.[87] Its reader is struck by its legal language, including explicit systematic legal reasoning and references to sources to support arguments, and by its devoted loyalty to religious principles and values from the perspective of the emerging Ḥanafī legal methodology. The text is also remarkable for its profuse use of *ḥadīths* from, and on the authority of, the first four caliphs. The reports are complemented by chains of transmission.[88] Compared to the Qur'an-heavy texts of earlier times, including that of al-ʿAnbarī, the *Kitāb al-Kharāj* quotes qur'anic verses less frequently, in contrast to abundant citations of communal and caliphal precedents and the rulings and legal opinions of the jurists. Stripped to its core elements, the work reads like al-ʿAnbarī's letter but deals with issues in a more comprehensive way, providing more substantial discussions on many matters of administration than the brief text of al-ʿAnbarī.

From the long view of the pre-Sunnite position, Abū Yūsuf represents the convenience of forgetting the earlier contractualist principles of the ulema. The landmark aspects of early republicanism (election, consent, consultation, responsibility toward the faithful), for example, are absent from his discourse. To fill this gap, he instead prioritizes compliance with the religious precepts and the moral guidelines of the sacred law. With such proper signposts in place, Abū Yūsuf tries to keep in check, or, more correctly, manage and nurture the caliph in accordance with the religious principles of the emerging juristic sensibilities. From the pulpit of a legal scholar and administrator of justice, Abū Yūsuf creates a world in which the caliph functions only as an extension of the community of the faithful and executor of the sacred law that he and his colleagues the ulema elaborate. He portrays the caliph as ontologically equal to other members of the community and a law-abiding figure rather than as a sovereign lawgiver, despite his heightened rhetoric on the caliph's individual sublimity. As a whole, however, Abū Yūsuf does not object to the empire's structure nor does he raise any concern about the independence of the jurists as long as the caliph maintains the status quo.

In wrapping up this chapter, I must note that writing in the dialogic context of siyasa, both Abū Yūsuf and alʿAnbarī, who survived Ibn al-Muqaffaʿ by several decades, were not immune to the discursive developments happening at the center of political power. As much by their own experience and genius as by inspiration, they figured out how to governmentalize religion and transcend the earlier elementary language of the ulema. This leap helped them elaborate a practical vision that united the political body of the empire with the religious community and the sacred law. As we will see in the following chapters, re-envisioning the imamate as a question of actual governance and administration marked a development that Ibn al-Muqaffaʿ had predicted and had written against the very backdrop that enabled it.

No matter how many positions the ulema took on the caliphate, they presumed politics to be a concern of faith. As we have seen, they defined the caliphate in theological and jurisprudential terms as an institution bound by religious norms and obligations and tasked to guide the believers in faith and practice. Until they faced the challenge of the early siyasa texts written by lay bureaucrat literati, the ulema operated in a discursive space that they dominated, which made the discussion of politics merely an intra-imamate debate. In the mid-eighth century, the lay bureaucrats introduced a new language of politics that was utterly unfamiliar to and against the suppositions of religious scholars. Because what these professionals had to say did not follow the established routine, it destabilized political discourse, as I will demonstrate in the next chapter.

3

Political Prose Revolution

In this chapter, I discuss how the discourse of siyasa appeared at the intersection of the formation of caliphal bureaucracy, the sociocultural awareness of lay bureaucrats, and the development of prose writing in the eighth century. I contend that the discourse of siyasa emerged not gradually because of an accumulation of knowledge but as a rupture, with the potential to destabilize the ideal of the imamate and change the scene of political reflection.

This shift in thinking was associated foremost with a cadre of lay bureaucrat literati in the Umayyad chancellery. Many of these professionals were part of the conquered non-Arab peoples during the caliphal expansion in the seventh century who were given a social status through a "contract" of clientage (*walāʾ*)[1] in which certain peninsular Arabic-Muslim tribes were considered their guardians. Often glorified as "political realists," many of these bureaucrats worked in the central administration's high-level offices near the rulers. Because many of them were "clients," however, they also faced the challenge of being simultaneously the elite and the Other.

Through two representative figures, ʿAbd al-Ḥamīd al-Kātib in this chapter and Ibn al-Muqaffaʿ in the next, I highlight how their practice opened the sociopolitical arena to patrician professionals like themselves and labored to reorient the empire in a direction that accommodated their sociocultural backgrounds. It is worth noting that the appearance of such bureaucrat literati coincided with the fading of political Byzantinism and the rise of Persophilia, and a shift of the empire's axis from the Mediterranean to the Indian Ocean.[2]

A Landscape of Temporal Political Reflection

The texts on siyasa appeared in a milieu in which not prose writing but epic poetry, sermons, lectures, orations, short letters, qur'anic recitations, epics, brief treaties and edicts, documents, religious scriptures, *ḥadīth* reports, and legal opinions were available, no matter what one's occupation or level of education.[3] The early Umayyad caliphs used Arabic only intermittently because its script and prose techniques had not yet developed enough to meet the challenges of prose and specialized writing. Even in Damascus, the early Umayyads employed both Persian-speaking and Greek-speaking functionaries because administrative work required individuals with skills, such as reading, writing, arithmetic, administrative knowledge, intellectual acumen, and cultural literacy. These professionals were chosen from among imperial functionaries under the previous provincial administrations in the conquered lands to help build a bureaucratic practice. The caliphs continued to use the established administrative languages, Greek and Persian being two major ones, for correspondence, record keeping, and other administrative tasks. This meant that Persian continued in Iran and Iraq, Greek in Syria and Egypt, Syriac in northern Mesopotamia, and Coptic in Egypt. Similar circumstances had encouraged the early caliphs to endorse and expand the use of existing Byzantine and Sasanian mints, with minimal or no modification, in commercial exchange, distribution of payments, and taxation.

As administrative awareness increased, the demand on the part of the Umayyad caliphs for such skilled individuals incentivized competition for governmental positions and encouraged the emergence of a class of petty and high-level administrators of Grecophone and Persianate pedigree. Skilled in the art of civil and military administration, the "client" functionaries (advisers, scribes, tax collectors, administrators, boon companions) also helped to integrate local practical administrative knowledge into the caliphal system. The ongoing public and institutional changes expanded the social and political visibility of such trained professionals, fostered a professional cosmopolitanism in the ranks of Umayyad administration, and encouraged education and scholarship, which kept in check the role of kinship nobility and the incipient ulema in governmental work.[4]

It is not an exaggeration to state that the empire-building efforts of ʿAbd al-Malik and his successors revolutionized this process. The most far-reaching reforms included Arabizing administrative records in the capital and provinces of the empire, and minting coins to replace Byzantine and the still-circulating

Sasanian mints.[5] To appreciate the novelty and the revolutionary effect of this development, one must remember that, until the first half of the eighth century, Arabic was only a vernacular of the ruling people, with no developed prose writing. As the reforms were implemented, they shaped the fate of Arabic as cultural capital for social and professional mobility.

Several intersecting dynamics spurred a sustained interest in the Arabic language and made it the imperial lingua franca that we find in the ninth century. The first was related to the empire-building efforts. Administrative organization generated a demand for written Arabic and encouraged new competition for positions in the imperial administration among the scribes, between those with proficient command of written Arabic and those without. Once the imperial bureaucracy began to demand written Arabic as a skill, other languages lost their edge in the caliphal administration. Administrative functionaries were required to be proficient in Arabic and familiar with the cultural practices of the ruling people, no matter if they were native or non-native Arabic speakers. Arabic and non-Arabic-speaking literate subjects (the landed aristocracy and imperial servants of the preconquest native regions) were thus compelled to study the language and teach it to their protégés.[6] From the early eighth century onward, it became unavoidable for many non-Arab Muslims and non-Muslims (Christians, Jews, Mazdeans, and others) to learn the Arabic language and actively use it beyond imperial service, which helped Arabic become the language of imperial correspondence, administrative work, court records, and scholarship.[7]

The second dynamic that made Arabic a cultural and scholarly currency was the scholarship of the ulema. From the beginning, the Arabic language functioned as the language of religious scripture and ritual, of poetry, and of daily life among its native speakers. Liturgical requirements, interest in learning for so many reasons, scholarship in religious and other subjects, and debates and disputation among the learned elite on a wide range of practical and theoretical questions stimulated wider use of the language. Religious scholarship expanded in the early eighth century, which both encouraged and necessitated coining innovative words and idioms and defining grammatical structures to describe relations and create new meanings. Although the ulema grew slowly extraneous to much of the administration, except in the judiciary and related fields, their authority continued to increase in social life through their intellectual production, which helped spread the written use of the Arabic language.[8]

A third dynamic was the support of scholarship by the caliphs in mundane topics as a factor that incentivized the learned elite to devote attention to language. Writing and translating texts in practical mundane knowledge expanded the horizon of prose writing in the Arabic language. Because its grammar had not been formalized, and prose remained rudimentary, short, and defined by the esteem for poetry, oratory, and sacred book recitation, sustained interest in and support for this kind of scholarship and cultural curiosity stimulated work on grammar, the script (punctuation, separation of words), and simple prose, which made writing much more accessible to larger groups of people.

A fourth dynamic was the rise of political prose in tandem with bureaucratic changes and sociopolitical developments in the Umayyad eighth century. Since the institution of the chancery or Bureau of Correspondence (*Dīwān al-Rasā'il*, 690s onward),[9] whose tasks included producing chancery documents, a cadre of scribes experimented with innovative ideas and practices in the scribal craft, which went far beyond formalizing procedural and secretarial tasks in administration. Notably, politics appeared initially as the leading theme of early prose writing in the circle of Sālim b. ʿAbd al-Raḥmān Abū al-ʿAlā' (d. ca. 720) in the Umayyad imperial chancellery. It became more visible in the work of ʿAbd al-Ḥamīd al-Kātib and of Ibn al-Muqaffaʿ, who were recognized as the pioneers of Arabic epistolary style and prose literature. They were also creative figures of the translation of a substantial body of Hellenistic political wisdom and work of advice literature from Persian into Arabic.[10]

The Lay Bureaucrat Elite's Sociocultural Position

Because the *mawlā* status defined major aspects of many scribes' social standing, it is imperative to consider its implications. The concept *mawlā* (pl. *mawālī*) exercised a shaping force on the dynamics of relations in the empire since its appearance as an outcome of the conquests in the mid-seventh century. In the eastern provinces of the empire, for instance, the differential policy toward the Arab and non-Arab Muslim population gradually led to discontent in the farmlands and urban centers. Among a vast non-Muslim and non-Arab Muslim population, the Arabic-speaking Muslim ruling elite and nobility constituted only a small minority with many privileges. As the faith community expanded by conversion among the conquered peoples and changed from being a prerogative of the people of the Arabian Peninsula, the differential treatment of each class of Muslims resulted in discontent among the native Muslims. For example, the converts were forced to pay both the poll tax and the land tax levied on the non-Muslim native people from the reign of ʿAbd al-Malik onward. It took the Umayyads decades to recognize the crisis that this practice created, until ʿUmar II b. ʿAbd al-ʿAzīz abolished the differential tax policies in 718–720. However, no consistent policy existed. We know from the last Umayyad governor in Khurasan, Naṣr b. Sayyār (d. 748), that in the intervening period, Umar II's policies were ignored. Faced with this situation, the *mawālī* communities in various regions of the province demanded fair treatment commensurate with their faith status, and they staged uprisings. Their discontent encouraged many to join insurrections against the provincial administration from the 720s onward. Naṣr tried to resolve the conflict by reintroducing the reforms of ʿUmar II, but he failed. The *mawālī* communities joined the Abbasids in their revolt against the Umayyads and defeated them.[11] In the aftermath of the Abbasid revolution, the practice of clientage fell behind public developments because of its inherent instability and began fading away, although the associated cultural discourse lasted much longer.

At some level, the *mawālī's* experience must have been tragic and not too dissimilar to that in which many colonized or diasporic writers in the nineteenth century onward found themselves, as Albert Memmi notes concerning European colonialism.[12] Even the elite *mawālī* were rarely addressed by honorifics (the father of X or mother of X), as was customary for the conquerors. They were also banned from marrying Arab women (and in military service, commoner *mawālī* served as foot soldiers, receiving a meager pension, while the Arabs rode horses). To cite only one case to illustrate the circumstance, Saʿīd b. Jubayr (d. 714) was a non-Arab Muslim *mawlā* who became known for his scholarship. When the caliph appointed him judge in Kufa, he caused an uproar among some inhabitants of that city for not being qualified because "he was not an Arab."[13]

What is vital to observe here is that, by constructing a new category of people, the conquerors made a portion of the population in the empire the object of the sociopolitical power in a particular way. And by designing themselves as "guardians," they recalibrated their own identities and practices vis-à-vis the "clients" in various fields of activity: policies, forms of treatment, institutions, and discourses. When one ponders who fit the category of the "guardians," one hesitates, however, to use the word "Arab" or "Muslim-Arab" in the generic and modern sense. In terms of their background, the "guardians" were particularly powerful, Islamized, conquering, peninsular, and kinship (pastoral nomadic and sedentary) groups who were now reidentified as a privileged collectivity vis-à-vis the *mawālī*. The "guardianship" did not extend, for instance, to Christian Arabs or Jewish Arabs or other Arabs who were remote, disconnected, or "went native" in their new homes in the conquered territories, pursuing farming or crafts, or who remained urban poor.

For this reason, the system of clientage cannot be easily dismissed as a demonstration of religious or ethnic zeal or simple-minded "tribal" impulse or glorification of the Muslim-Arab ways of living over others. In fact, it reveals a sociocultural hegemony and a cultural discourse by the powerful that normalized the preferential treatment of people for the distribution of material and social privileges among the "guardians." In a remarkable way, the various forms of social distinction acquired a new dimension that was based not on tribe or faith but on ethnicity and linguistic difference—a distinction between Arabic-speaking native peninsular Muslims and non-Arabic-speaking Muslims in the conquered territories marking status and socioeconomic and political privileges.

What kind of position might this situation leave ʿAbd al-Ḥamīd, Ibn al-Muqaffaʿ, and *mawālī* elite like them in? A crucial point here, which informs my analysis in the following pages, is that, caught up in the middle of the debate about "subalternity," which I use in the Gramscian sense,[14] this elite could not imagine writing in the Arabic language as an apolitical pursuit.[15] Given their social origins, these figures were unmistakably "subaltern." They led their lives in a sociopolitical universe that afforded them privilege but forced them to negotiate between the two identities they nurtured: one by birth as inferior imperial subjects and one by work and talent as members of the ruling class. As non-Arab Muslims (ʿAbd al-Ḥamīd was a third-generation Muslim and Ibn al-Muqaffaʿ converted later in his life), they remained socially inferior to native Arabic-speaking subjects. An *ʿarab-mawlā* distinction was evident in social relations, marriage, dress, conduct, and access to resources. For instance, as driven as both appear, humility and loyalty were virtues they must have internalized emotionally and embodied in their daily comportment, especially among those considered superior to them. It would have been incongruous, for instance, had they married free Arab women.[16]

By the virtue of their professions and cultural capital, however, they escaped common urban or peasant subjectivity and achieved a higher social and legal standing than the other non-Arab Muslim and non-Muslim subjects of the empire. In part, the "boom" of urban life since the early eighth century and changes in cultural demography driven by conversion, migration, and more regular interaction eased social constraints. Certainly, imperial cosmopolitanism enabled them to transcend the structural limitations of their social status. Other, more private and local factors related to them, such as leading their lives in family circles, among close friends, colleagues, and admirers, who saw talent, character, and complex personalities in them rather than one-dimensional stereotypes of inferior status, helped them foster a sense of belonging. From this angle, their life stories do not stand out as a unique case in the history of non-Arab Muslims and non-Muslims during the Umayyad and early Abbasid caliphates.

Discriminatory practices, like the question of slavery, were part of a larger sociocultural universe that normalized and even idealized them as ontological and natural facts, which the *mawālī* bureaucrats themselves also shared. One must still remember that social exclusion and differential treatment must have tangible, day-to-day implications in the lives of these professionals. Being at once essential and dispensable, they existed in a limbo. They thus lived in a constant flux and state of anxiety, as professionals who must traverse existing sociocultural values in their day-to-day activities while leveraging their knowledge and positions to improve their status.

One may ponder Frantz Fanon's analysis as a way of understanding their situation. In *The Wretched of the Earth*, Fanon makes an acute observation about the colonized intellectuals' cultural and psychological response to their conditions. First, he notes, colonized intellectuals prove they have assimilated the colonizer's culture. Their works correspond point by point with those of their metropolitan counterparts. The inspiration is metropolitan, and their works can be easily linked to a well-defined trend in metropolitan literature. This is the phase of full assimilation. Thus, colonized intellectuals ensnared by the colonizer mimic the colonizer's taste and culture, lose themselves, and consequently become lost to their people. In the second stage, the colonized writers have their convictions shaken and decide to cast their mind back to their original culture. But because the colonized writers are not integrated with their own people—because they maintain an outsider's relationship to them—they are content with remembrance.[17] They revere the past, Fanon points out, but the culture that has been retrieved from the past to be displayed in its splendor is not their own culture; rather, the culture that is proclaimed is a racialized culture.[18] In this way, following the unconditional affirmation of a colonized culture comes the unconditional affirmation of racialized culture. It is only with liberation struggles and independence that the creation of a national culture becomes possible.[19]

I do not intend to shadow Fanon's argument to explain the conditions of the *mawālī* elite in the eighth century; I only intend to use it as an entry point, a launchpad, for approaching the question. In particular, I wish to steer the discussion away from the seemingly apolitical language of cultural history and cast a new political light on the language of lay bureaucrats like ʿAbd al-Ḥamīd and Ibn al-Muqaffaʿ. Fanon's third point does not apply to the *mawālī's* situation. The contingencies required an adjustment of positions, and the *mawālī* elite—as civil servants and defenders of their patrons—adapted gradualism, practicality, and pragmatism to remain relevant and consequential. As a result, one can better understand the conditions of some *mawālī* through the lenses of accommodation, resistance, and hybridity rather than rejection aimed at liberation.

I contend that the attitude of many of the *mawālī* professionals over several generations may be characterized as a series of shifts. They were subjugated first. Then they slowly assimilated into the dominant cultural values in empire-building activities, becoming part of the empire as tax collectors, scribes, petty and high-level administrators, advisers, and scholars. Because political and sociocultural developments provided opportunities for them, they first acknowledged the given reality, then mastered the new language and adopted the new culture. They began from the point of assimilation and integration into the conquerors' dominant life narratives and cultural values. For reasons of profession, cultural interest, and social competition, they cast their gaze back to retrieve and represent a past that they claimed as their own, which resulted in inventing a cultural past over the dominant one. Eventually, working within and for the empire and functioning within an imagined native past and current reality, they constructed a hybrid social practice that shaped the Abbasid imperial cosmopolitanism in the ninth century in important ways.[20] In this light, if ʿAbd al-Ḥamīd stood closer to integrating into his masters' world by cultural assimilation; Ibn al-Muqaffaʿ might have seen accentuating the value of his heritage as a better way to seek coexistence.

Recalling the disruptions that they and their families must have gone through, these *mawālī* elite moved beyond crude nativism. This fact alone speaks volumes about their cultural habits and political position. The outcome of this struggle molded a subjectivity with hybrid taste, which allowed this elite to be at peace with the diverse social and cultural expressions of Islam, the Arabic language, and the caliphate but to be critical of the hegemonic sociocultural practices and not shy away from disclosing, disseminating, and advocating their own social and cultural preferences. They could manipulate the conditions of their peculiar status to make a space where they not only advanced their careers at the Umayyad and Abbasid courts but also resisted the sociocultural hegemony that marginalized them.

One cannot but agree with Albert Memmi that writing in the "conqueror's tongue" might have been the only sensible option if they wanted to be heard.[21] By helping the ruler administer more efficiently, they enhanced their collective standing as a cadre of useful professionals. They also created discursive spaces for cultural negotiation—as suggested in the growing interest in ancient cultural and imperial practices among both Umayyad and early Abbasid elite.[22] Using Arabic (whether by upbringing or choice) gave them the opportunity to engage critically with a wide range of humanistic subjects in their environments. Enjoying the distinct advantage of being familiar with how the administration functioned, these bureaucrat literati devoted attention to substantial and novel questions about the ruler, rulership, and the ruling elite, and studied how to manipulate the sociopolitical circumstance to benefit the rule.

In their political writings, these lay bureaucrats addressed governance; the efficient administration of affairs, including the practical matters of routine work; and political advice in a milieu in which little else was available to assist the rulers to govern. Driven as much by imperial ambitions of the Umayyads and the early Abbasids as by the anxiety about self-image and sense of belonging among the literary elite like themselves, they facilitated access to the nonreligious written corpora of Southwest Asia. They produced a body of knowledge with a mundane and practical character that was neither sanctioned by the ulema nor geared toward elaborating a religious argument. As professionals who took a new direction separate from religious practice and knowledge pursued by the ulema, who often frowned upon leisure and pleasure and derided politics as immoral, they connected the ruling, social, and literary elite to the larger world through secular interests.

Therefore, this cadre of scribes not only helped advance the prose language but, more significantly, unleashed new political uses of language, producing more nuanced visions of society and governance. Their deployment of the language (using prose, discussing statecraft, exploring literary themes) gave their discourse "a surplus of meaning" that animated in it an illocutionary force. More consequently, however, their particular social position embedded their statements within a certain symbolic capital, which gave their language an authority that made its impact during and after their lifetimes. Hence, the more "intellectual prestige" the lay scholars acquired, the wider their discourse spread.[23]

Invariably, they also wrote about religious themes and affirmed pious morality in their writings. Even when doing that, however, they directed their readers' attention to banal and curious subjects of governance and administration, beyond their meaning in religious discourse. In a sense, these mandarins "invented" politics in social relations and reasoned from their own background in politics. Thus, they competed not just for administrative positions as a career goal but also for preeminence in shaping the content of political conduct. Because the discourse of siyasa emerged in such a context, I will discuss in the rest of the chapter how the Sālim school of siyasa played a pivotal role in the epistemic rupture in political knowledge.

The Sālim School of Siyasa

The most cited early figure in the secretarial craft, Sālim b. ʿAbd al-Raḥmān Abū al-ʿAlāʾ, was a client of the Umayyads. This pioneer chancellor of Persian ancestry joined the Umayyad administration during ʿAbd al-Malik's reign and seems to have advanced in rank until he led the chancery (*Dīwān al-Rasāʾil*) of the caliph Hishām.[24] Sālim is credited with introducing, among other secretarial procedures and standards attributed to his office, courtly protocols, such as addressing the caliph in the third person singular as the commander of the faithful (e.g., the commander of the faithful requests such-and-such) in imperial correspondence.[25] In a political milieu in which face-to-face interaction with the ruler was expected, his introduction of such a figure of speech in chancery letters fulfilled perhaps as much a practical as a political function by creating a procedural distance that further separated the ruler from his subjects and magnified his power through regulating access to him, in a similar way as the chamberlain, *hājib*, restricted personal contact with the ruler. Sālim seems to have risen to such prominence under Hishām that he seemed to function as the "gatekeeper" of the caliph. The celebrated historian of the tenth century, al-Ṭabarī, sarcastically remarks about his power: "Sālim used to act in such a way that it is as if he had appointed Hishām to the caliphate."[26]

According to the tenth-century bibliophile and bibliographer al-Nadīm, Sālim translated "letters" between Aristotle and Alexander the Great, or commissioned their translation, while refining them editorially. Familiar with Sasanian writerly culture, Sālim might well have known Greek to undertake the translation himself. The "letters" in question may be *Kitāb fī al-Siyāsa al-ʿĀmmiyya Mufaṣṣalan* (*The Detailed Book on the Governance of the Commonfolk*), or, in short, *The Book of Politics* (*Kitāb al-Siyāsa*). This work dates to the end of the caliph Hishām's reign and was written in the circle of Sālim, if not by Sālim himself.[27] Combining original composition and much translation from Greek or Persian (or a combination of both) of various Greek and Persian material in a sixth-century Hellenistic milieu, *The Book of Politics* stands as an early example of Arabic epistolary prose and as one of the earliest works on siyasa politics. As J. D. Latham notes, however, later interpolations and references to events during the Umayyad period only in vague terms makes it imprudent to use the text as an Umayyad-era work before a credible critical edition of the work is produced.[28]

This detail about his political writing suggests that Sālim engaged in political reflection and took part in sociopolitical life intellectually. His office seems to have functioned as a "school" of the scribal craft and of political thought that produced accomplished bureaucrat literati such as ʿAbd al-Ḥamīd and Ibn al-Muqaffaʿ, who shared a common professional and sociocultural background and continued his initiatives.[29] Above all, one can almost pinpoint the emergence of siyasa as a concept and tradition to Sālim's office. Branching out from his "school," the discursive tradition of siyasa evolved in two major directions: One branch "modernized" a Hellenistic-Greek tradition, as illustrated in the intellectual efforts (including *The Book of Politics* and similar work) leading up to the work of al-Fārābī later, and the other branch generated a fresh Perso-Hellenistic tradition, which we see in the work of Ibn al-Muqaffaʿ and his successors.

Unfortunately, the biographical details of the leading scribes in Sālim's office are too little known. Even the basic facts of their professional careers in the accounts of historians are a one-dimensional and cartoonish mosaic of fragmented episodes of, no doubt, eventful life stories. Among the better known, one must cite ʿAbd al-Ḥamīd b. Yaḥyā b. Saʿd (or Saʿīd), given the honorific Abū Ghālib. He was a third-generation client (*mawlā*), who was born sometime in the 680s, the grandson of a person from the ʿAnbar region in Iraq (or from Raqqa in Syria). His grandfather might have been taken captive at the Battle of al-Qādisiyya (ca. 636) and after his conversion became a client of the Banū ʿĀmir (or perhaps the Banū Umayya, as al-Balādhurī claims).[30] ʿAbd al-Ḥamīd's career, of course, indicates his hard work and talent but also tallies well with broad socioeconomic developments under the Umayyads and the concurrent gradual improvement of the conditions of the clients in Syria and the Hijaz region. For the same reason, his situation illuminates the forms of subordination that the clients endured during the Umayyad period.

His early life, like that of many of his contemporaries, is lost to us. He might have been a resident of Kufa for a few years in his youth. He learned Arabic in addition to his ancestral tongue (most likely Persian) and received an education that enabled him to begin his professional career as a peripatetic teacher of children. Iḥsān ʿAbbās rightly problematizes the form of "teaching" ʿAbd al-Ḥamīd practiced in his early career by distinguishing between instruction (*taʿlīm*) and discipline (*ta'dīb*).[31] Despite the little information we have about this aspect of his early professional life and whether he worked as an instructor or mentor, or instructor-mentor, his writing defines education as both the acquisition of knowledge and ethical formation.[32]

His personal credentials and traveling teaching career must have assisted him in connecting with established individuals, including Sālim, the chief scribe of the caliph Hishām. Sālim would become his eventual in-law (ʿAbd al-Ḥamīd married either Sālim's daughter or sister). Sālim seems to be the person who helped ʿAbd al-Ḥamīd secure a position as scribe at the Umayyad court in Damascus as early as the later years of ʿAbd al-Malik's reign.[33] ʿAbd al-Ḥamīd resided in Rusāfa, which the caliph chose as his capital instead of Damascus, until he was assigned as scribe to Marwān b. Muhammad, who had been appointed governor of Armenia and Adharbayjan in 732.

He remained with Marwān, and in 744 accompanied him to Harran, where his patron relocated to seek the caliphate for himself during the intrafamily struggle after Hishām's death. After the short and restless caliphate of Yazīd III, Marwān was declared caliph in 744, and he made Harran his residence. ʿAbd al-Ḥamīd continued to serve him there as the head of the central Umayyad chancery until the demise of both in 750. His letters for Hishām and for Marwān

II indicate an unflinching loyalty to the Umayyads. He was captured and executed either in Būṣīr, Egypt, with his master Marwān II, or in Raqqa, where his family might have resided. He was there in the company of his younger colleague and mentee Ibn al-Muqaffaʿ, who escaped death.[34]

Thanks to his students and his children, grandchildren, and great-grandchildren, several of whom served as advisers and scribes to the Abbasids and the Ṭūlūnids,[35] some of ʿAbd al-Ḥamīd's letters have been preserved, although they represent only a small part of his literary output. Only about fifty folios exist out of an estimated total of over one thousand that he produced during his career, from the time of the caliphate of Hishām until his death. This surviving corpus includes various chancery documents, letters, and private correspondence with his family on various occasions.[36]

As historical records of varying length written on behalf of caliphs, his letters reveal the political emergence of prose writing. They discuss governance; administrative issues; major caliphal activities; political and military challenges of the Umayyads and their victories; the suppression of rebels; potential dissent or actual rebellions; subversive activities; the Abbasid revolt; the question of obedience and disobedience to the ruler; civil discord; and reflections on the vagaries of life, moral education, techniques of self-discipline, and political advice.[37]

ʿAbd al-Ḥamīd differed from the previous generation of scribes. He was aware of the value of his work and keen on articulating in his writing the importance of it. In his letters, he appears as a courtier, adviser; chancery tutor; expert in the art of war; hunter; orator; author of personal and familial correspondence; and moralist, preacher, jurist, and propagandist in the service of the Umayyads. His secretarial responsibilities must have given ʿAbd al-Ḥamīd a thorough grasp of administrative procedures, which form the foundation of his discourse on scribes.[38] Although he may not have known Greek, he must have benefited from the translations and practical knowledge and skills of his contemporaries. As Iḥsān ʿAbbās notes, one may list four such individuals: his patron, the caliph Marwān II, in rhetorical eloquence; his mentor, Sālim, for Greek translations and secretarial work; Ibn al-Muqaffaʿ for Persian translations and cultural acumen; and Ṣāliḥ b. ʿAbd al-Raḥmān, who undertook the translations of the registers of the central administration into Arabic, for the details of the bookkeeping craft.[39]

Abū Hilāl al-ʿAskarī's remark that "ʿAbd al-Ḥamīd extracted and transcribed patterns of secretarial composition from the Persian tongue and transposed them into the Arabic tongue"[40] may be read as veiled sarcasm about his writing being gauche or at least inelegant. This remark attests to the transitional nature of his prose, which exposed the Arabic language to the demands of administrative and political subjects. In their often lengthy and elaborate introductions and conclusions, complex sentences complicated by equally prolonged clauses, logical flow, descriptive narration, and aversion to rhyme, his letters present an innovative form of writing, marking a tension between chancery style, which became a model for and part of the curriculum of Abbasid scribes, and epistolary rhetoric.[41] Also displaying the transitional character of his milieu between oral/aural rhetoric and prose, ʿAbd al-Ḥamīd sought in his writing both literary pleasure and functional capacity. Recognizing the tension between oratory, poetry, and prose writing, Ibn ʿAbd Rabbih (d. 940) praises him as "the first to tear open the sleeves of rhetoric, to smooth out its ways, and to set poetry free from its bonds."[42] Ibn al-Muqaffaʿ picked up this thread not necessarily from but likely with ʿAbd al-Ḥamīd, as we will see in the next chapter.

The Intertextuality of Imamate and Siyasa in Early Political Prose

ʿAbd al-Ḥamīd's early writing astounds the reader in being almost devoid of any trace of his own cultural past.[43] Much of his work is at home with, and in fact appreciative of, the Arabic cultural practices of the time, gesturing toward assimilation as a gateway into the dominant imperial culture. His later work reflects an embrace of his cultural past. The difference in content and tone of his writing suggests that he became more conscious of his "subalternity" later in life and sought some kind of reconciliation with it, and even perhaps developed a language of "us" and "them."[44] It is plausible to speak of the "early" assimilationist ʿAbd al-Ḥamīd and the "later" one, the shaken intellectual, making him a remarkable point of transition, upon which I will elaborate below.

ʿAbd al-Ḥamīd's writing spanning two decades cannot be reconciled under one conceptual umbrella. Permeated by Umayyad-Islamic values and fragments of political wisdom from the Sasanian past, his work carries the imprint of a transitional figure heading away from an assimilationist position toward one of greater cultural sensitivity to his social and cultural background. Over the course of his career, ʿAbd al-Ḥamīd develops two voices in his writing. A chronological overview of his letters suggests a break between the "early" ʿAbd al-Ḥamīd, who elaborated a theology of caliphal authority from the perspective of the jurists and theologians of his time, and the "later" ʿAbd al-Ḥamīd, who highlighted arguments in line with a rationality of siyasa. Even if one objects to the argument that the chronological order of his letters is not clear, the shift in their tone is unambiguous.

Looking at ʿAbd al-Ḥamīd's early writing, one notices how it closely follows the concerns of the imamate discourse of its time. As shown by Wadad al-Qadi in her exhaustive study of ʿAbd al-Ḥamīd's extant letters, ʿAbd al-Ḥamīd's writing explains, argues for, and defends the Umayyads in an unmistakable language of religious salvation.[45] Written on various occasions and for different parties, the letters underline the theological bases of the Umayyad authority and lack any reference to the pre-Islamic past not connected to monotheistic prophethood.[46] The texts advance political opinions in rhetorically elaborate prose with salvific provocation and pious imagery, replete with extensive references to scripture and prophetic history, and demanding the recognition of, and conformity and obedience to, Umayyad authority on this basis.[47]

Al-Qadi has already evinced a premeditated ideological argument in ʿAbd al-Ḥamīd's letters that "is almost entirely clad in a religious garb," in which political leadership enhanced with salvific authority is carefully crafted and logically defended. The caliph, for instance, appears as part of "the Qur'anic vision of human history." Indeed, his rule has the status of prophethood and thus an established exceptional relationship to God. The caliph is cast as the authority in God's final dispensation, against whom any form of dissent is firmly censured.[48] Similar to other imamate texts we have seen so far, ʿAbd al-Ḥamīd depicts caliphal authority as part of an elaborate political cosmology: God has sent messengers, of whom Muhammad was the last, to guide human beings. The Prophet established a community of the faithful, put forth laws and regulations, and showed the community the manners of pious practice and moral conduct to improve his community's devotion to God's will and ordinances. ʿAbd al-Ḥamīd presents the Prophet as the conduit of God's revelation, a community builder, and political leader who was succeeded by the caliphs, who took charge of his community as his inheritors, and who was also sanctioned and inspired by God.[49]

In the letters, the caliph is presented therefore not only as the ruler but also as the leader of the religious community. ʿAbd al-Ḥamīd situates the caliphs next to the prophets in guiding, organizing, and protecting the community of the faithful. They derive their authority not only from the Prophet but also from God Himself, as His deputies, God's caliphs.[50] The caliph is distinguished by his exemplary piety, his devotion to prophetic practice, his preoccupation with God's cause, his defense of the revealed law, and his concern with the welfare of the community in this world and its salvation in the hereafter.[51] The caliph's theological status and mission render his piety and spiritual rank necessary components of political discourse because they explain and justify the constant demand for obedience and underline the premise that the caliph played a part in witnessing God's historical plan for human beings.

For theological and cosmological reasons, the caliph is entitled to unflinching obedience, which, ʿAbd al-Ḥamīd explains, is the essential universal order, the backbone and bond of the revealed law, without which chaos and dissension would spread. Disobedience, therefore, cannot be anything other than satanic and destructive activity. The theological consequences of resisting the caliph are amply demonstrated in his letters in which he accuses advocates of free will of challenging God's will, of being erroneous, marginal, and destructive to social order.[52] He presents obedience as the price human beings have—or are enjoined—to pay if they hope to live in peace and attain salvation because "God has made obedience the basic order (*niẓām*) of the revealed law . . . its backbone (*qiwām*), and its bond (*ʿiṣma*)."[53] He thus situates governance at the heart of salvation history, in which arena the caliphs are charged with ordering earthly life by maintaining the faith community and their subjects so that social order dovetails seamlessly with the universal cosmic order.[54]

In contrast to such a doctrinal position in governance from the angle of religious piety, the "later" ʿAbd al-Ḥamīd devotes his attention to the matters of governance and improving practice. The pious phraseology notwithstanding, his tone and position begin to shift, displaying a transition from the theological mode of the imamate to the practicality of siyasa. His language is more banal, imperial idioms more explicit and forthright, the value of the *longue-durée* administrative practice more foregrounded, and the tenor of political counsel more discernible. One need not look any further than his two celebrated letters, "Testament to the Crown Prince" and "Letter to the Scribes," to capture the transition in his political writing.

"Testament to the Crown Prince" is his longest extant work.[55] It strikes the reader as a pioneering effort in the genres of political advice (*naṣīḥa*) and testamentary counsel (*ʿahd* or *waṣiyya*), which may have made its appearance even before his death, through the work of none other than his friend and mentee, Ibn al-Muqaffaʿ.[56] Already known in the region since before the advent of Christianity, the genre of mirror for princes just emerged in the caliphal context and would soon become a major literary undertaking from the late eighth century onward.[57] Seen in this light, "Testament to the Crown Prince" seems to anticipate, in form and content and in a noteworthy way, Ibn al-Muqaffaʿ's "Epistle," and thus helps us outline a literary and intellectual background for the "Epistle" extending beyond ʿAbd al-Ḥamīd and Ibn al-Muqaffaʿ.

Written in 747, "Testament to the Crown Prince" is a counsel to the heir apparent of Marwān II, ʿAbdallāh (or ʿUbaydallāh), on how to be a virtuous and effective prince and victorious military commander.[58] The immediate political context of the work is the Kharijite rebellion in upper Mesopotamia in 745, under the leadership of Ḍaḥḥāk b. Qays, during a turbulent period of Umayyad history. Occupied with his own problems in Hims, the caliph Marwān II dispatched his son and heir apparent, ʿAbdallāh, who had been in Harran, to confront the Kharijites.[59]

In its assessment of a political contingency as a subject that can be studied and reflected upon to take proper action, ʿAbd al-Ḥamīd's "Testament to the Crown Prince" presents a new and practical discourse concerning governance. It guides the reader to reflect on governance as contingency and to consider the mundane and practical matters of administration, rather than on the universal theological norms of the ulema. Expressed in a new literary style, this form of writing became a model for the later, common "advice" genre in the region, which combined two distinct but related traditions of writing at its foundation: the humanistic writing of adab and the literary forms of the epistle and the testament (*risāla* and *waṣiyya*).[60]

"Testament to the Crown Prince" contains detailed moral, political, and military advice to the heir apparent, addressing issues such as maintaining his piety and moral virtues in private and public, relations with his family and government officials, and military issues (including tactics, strategy, weaponry, and administering personnel). It explains the skills and qualities of an effective ruler in two apparent but unmarked major sections of unequal length (the first one is about one-third of the whole). The first part discusses the moral cultivation of the ruler and the common principles of moral politics. It begins by stating the problem and naming the caliph and his heir apparent. Then it enumerates the virtues of the prince and the way to cultivate the desired virtues in the ruler. Moving on to explain the proper conduct, it instructs how to cultivate the skills and disposition necessary to habituate it. The same part also advises on the prince's entourage, his skills, character, conduct, and responsibilities. The latter part presents candid and detailed practical and technical advice on military organization, administration, finances, and war tactics.[61] Although the text is situated in a political universe defined in the imamate's language, the detailed information on administration and commandership constitutes the bulk of the text and includes information from time-tested practices in imperial and caliphal past; it diverts its reader's attention from decontextualized piety toward matters of governance, the mundane tasks of managing affairs, and ways of mitigating existing challenges.

ʿAbd al-Ḥamīd opens "Testament to the Crown Prince" with a rebuke of the rebel Ḍaḥḥāk b. Qays, who also serves in the text as an antithesis of a righteous ruler, and the Kharijites. He disparages the rebel as a "desert Bedouin," who acts in the chaos of ignorance. He condemns the destructive consequences of his rebellion and accuses him of violating divine will, laws, and regulations, and of sowing discord and destruction on earth. In contrast, ʿAbd al-Ḥamīd emphasizes divine support for the heir apparent, who is chosen and supported by God as his deputy to the exclusion of others in his family.[62] The letter praises the prince by highlighting his customary virtues, and assures those who would listen that wisdom and good judgment would require that he be chosen for his position even if his appointment had not been willed by God.

He then discusses the essential virtues of a successful ruler and the ways to develop and cultivate them, some of which include self-discipline and morals, and other skills, techniques, and learned manners of proper conduct. He harmonizes the virtues of pious morality and those of an effective administrator to describe a good ruler. The crown prince must observe major religious obligations, resist whimsical desires, avoid blatantly sinful behavior, and exhibit genuine piety.[63] He should always strive to obtain wisdom through devoutness and obedience to God, accustom himself to pray each morning to show his gratitude to God, and recite a portion of the Qur'an during the day. The crown prince will gain from this exercise not only knowledge of the holy text but also moral strength and virtue. ʿAbd al-Ḥamīd warns the crown prince to be wary of fanciful human passions because they are the good ruler's enemy, and he encourages him to seek refuge in God to fight resolutely against them, however difficult and constant that may be. He flags the vanity of pride as the fountainhead of passion that will surely destroy the standing of any ruler, and he urges the crown prince to guard against it by adhering to fairness, attending to duties, and restraining passion.[64]

However, the bulk of the advice directs the attention of the reader to the mundane matters of governance as the basis of what is assumed to be monarchical rule. Expressed in a prolific and detailed catalog of proper conduct to be an effective ruler, his advice concerns two major topics, which are notable for their worldly and practical character: the moral and professional excellence of the ruler's entourage (*biṭāna*) and the scope of their work. The crown prince should choose the members of his chamber from among persons of discernment and self-contentedness, who must be good at keeping secrets, maintaining a somber appearance, avoiding behavior that is belittling or disparaging, and avoiding interference in the affairs of others. They should also exhibit self-restraint and moderation in what they do. The crown prince must avoid career opportunists who shamelessly approach him for advancement and favors. He should also consider the affairs of each member of his entourage individually to know them better and understand their positions.[65]

He warns that any matter of concern should be brought first to the attention of the relevant scribe rather than to the crown prince to obviate any undue encounter with the petitioner. The crown prince should also consult his scribe before issuing a decision on any matter brought to his attention.[66] He should make it a habit to consult several of his confidants about a matter but avoid relying on any one of them in making his decision. As for the personnel in the crown prince's chamber, he explains how to address his inferiors, respond to a question, and ask his staff about matters of concern. The prince should encourage his confidants and the elite of his chamber (*khāṣṣa*) to advocate for him and spread good news among the masses to increase hope and goodwill among his subjects. Furthermore, the prince should take an interest in the common people's affairs, help those in need, and guide those who have gone astray or remain ignorant about proper conduct. The crown prince can only gain a good reputation among his subjects and earn reward in the hereafter based on his own virtuous conduct.[67]

ʿAbd al-Ḥamīd also advises the crown prince on how to receive delegations and visitors and how to conduct himself in meetings to generate the intended effect on his visitors. He underlines the proper way of self-representation, such as exhibiting the traits of personal virtue and observing proper etiquette. He encourages the crown prince to avoid self-promotion, boasting, and overemphasizing his personal power. The crown prince should also keep his anger in check but be firm in his decisions and maintain control. He should entertain himself without excess, make eye contact with his visitors rather than fix his gaze on one or a few of the attendees in a meeting, and avoid swearing and cursing. He should pay attention to his posture; control his jests, mimics, and physical reflexes; and manage calls of nature discreetly so that he satisfies his needs without diminishing his dignity and honor.[68]

The latter part of his treatise reads like a manifesto in military administration and the art of war, with a remarkably detailed discussion. This section begins without an obvious formal break or transition in the text. The tone and the subject matter of "Testament to the Crown Prince" suggest that the scribe was addressing a dynamic situation that was currently unfolding.[69] His counsel includes practical and specific recommendations to the crown prince about the army, war, the enemy, administration, finances, weaponry, commandership, and other major matters concerning wartime and other times. The following is a list of the subjects that ʿAbd al-Ḥamīd addresses in this part of the treatise: preparing to meet the enemy after making a sound decision, commanding the army with ethical standards and demanding the same from the soldiers, marching to meet the enemy with determination and a strong belief in God's favor, the virtue of securing victory without major loss of life, trying to resolve hostility with the enemy by first approaching them with offers of amnesty and exhibiting benevolence before engaging in combat, protecting non-Arab Muslims (*mawālī*) and non-Muslim subjects (*dhimmī*) after victory, spying on and monitoring enemies, establishing an efficient and reliable intelligence system, taking precautions against the enemy's spies, administering and policing the army, maintaining military guards, administration of justice in the army, reviewing vanguards and their weapons, selecting and commanding the guards, observing the importance of guards, the significance of the army commanders, commanding the army, commanders of the horsemen, planning to meet the enemy and the manner of gearing up and marching toward the enemy, commander of the foot soldiers and his responsibility, the troops to be stationed behind foot soldiers, the order to march toward the enemy and the best way to engage it, digging ditches and building fortification against the enemy, combatting and defending against the enemy, determining to chase the enemy after battle to eliminate it, mounted soldiers and their gear and training, dividing and organizing mounted soldiers into units (of one hundred), the role of the superintendent of military offices and treasure, war tactics to weaken the enemy, and the proper attitude and morals of the model soldier preparing to meet the enemy.[70]

To state that "Testament to the Crown Prince" is the first of its kind in caliphal history is not saying much, but a few observations are in order: compared to ʿAbd al-Ḥamīd's other letters, it represents a discourse in transition from the pious and abstract doctrinal language of imamate to the practicality, worldliness, and pertinence of siyasa. It does not spell out a new notion of rulership (*mulk*), which appears more clearly in Ibn al-Muqaffaʿ's writing, but it implies and anticipates it. First, although theologically sanctioned and divinely appointed, the ruler appears as an individual who needs discipline, practical knowledge, and advice to rule effectively. It is noteworthy that religious piety; doctrinal "orthodoxy"; and establishing justice, in the sense of executing religious obligations, appear in the text, but such information does not strike the reader as relevant to ensuring success and guaranteeing effective rule. Instead, they are overshadowed by the practical information based on expert administrative knowledge and skills.

Second, contrary to what one might expect in other contemporaneous theological texts on politics, the ruler and his subjects no longer share an ontological plane. The sovereign belongs to and operates at a level beyond and above his subjects. In two instances, one notices a subtle tension between the contractualism of the ulema and the divine bestowal of sovereignty that the text is developing. One instance is where ʿAbd al-Ḥamīd uses the words "common folk" and "elite" (*ʿāmma* and *khāṣṣa*) systematically to distinguish imperial subjects from the ruler and to consciously make common folk an object of governance.[71] Considered intertextually, this ambiguously expressed difference between the ruler and the ruled comes out more clearly in his "Letter to the Scribes," where he makes an ontological distinction between the ruler and his subjects.[72] The second instance appears at the beginning of "Testament to the Crown Prince," where ʿAbd al-Ḥamīd praises the qualities of the prince and comforts his readers that wisdom and good judgment would have required that he be chosen for his position even if this had not been willed by God.[73] Sounding not radically different from the Umayyad practice of claiming God's deputyship, this emphasis on divine support nevertheless acquires new meaning when the crown prince is placed on a different pedestal than his subjects. In no other Umayyad text does one observe such a distinction between the ruler and the ruled. On the contrary, the imamate texts we have examined so far assume equality among the believers and presume no ontological distinction between the members of the community, which is the proper seat of power, and the caliph. In view of its polyphonic character (the voices of *imāma* and siyasa), "Testament to the Crown Prince" is a remarkable textual site in which the author realizes the inadequacy—if not the deficiency—of customary remedy so visible in contemporaneous discourses of the imamate to governance but has yet to produce a counterpoint.

His "Letter to the Scribes" seems to be a step in that direction in the specific case of civil servants. In this most renowned treatise of his, also written later in his life under Marwān II,[74] ʿAbd al-Ḥamīd focuses on the work and the role of the scribes in imperial administration. While he shifts away from the imamate and concerns himself with the actual matters of governance, he does not yet present the formal or preconceived destination we identify as siyasa or *tadbīr*, although he is one of the pioneers of epistolary writing to use these idioms in such a political way. Considering the details he offers in "Letter to the Scribes," one is convinced that he must have used information, with the aid of his colleagues, from Sasanian administrative literature to compose it.[75]

As an inventive piece, "Letter to the Scribes" highlights four essential qualities that should be cultivated and nourished in a model scribe: proper training and education in the details of the craft, acquisition of proper morals and ethical behavior commensurate with status and class, good manners in performing the work, and display of solidarity with peers.[76] A model scribe, according to ʿAbd al-Ḥamīd, needs instruction, including rigorous training, to attain the professional and ethical qualifications for his craft. He should have expert skills in what he does, which includes gathering sufficient information in fields of knowledge so that he can quickly grasp the essence of any matter before it is fully explained to him in detail. A good scribe must take initiative in seeking and acquiring knowledge and in nurturing the good manners associated with it.[77] He should have a respectable understanding of the faith, beginning with a knowledge of the Qur'an and major religious obligations (*farā'iḍ*). He must have a perfect grasp of the Arabic language in both spoken and written forms. The scribe must also develop impeccable writing skills and make an unswerving effort to train his hand for an elegant script and related skills. He must not neglect a knowledge of arithmetic, which he regards as a foundational discipline for those who are charged with administering taxes. In addition, the scribe must understand poetry, which he should learn and memorize, and be versed in Arabic and Persian history.[78]

To survive "office politics" and succeed, an exemplary scribe must also embody the best practices of ethical behavior and moral conduct. He should avoid the cardinal and minor vices that can ruin a career in office (such as arrogance, overambition, slander and backbiting, extravagance) and avoid immersing himself in luxury and excess in the material aspects of daily life, which would inevitably bring him failure and disgrace. An ideal scribe exhibits the virtues of professional dignity (such as adaptability, propriety, etiquette of occasion, impartiality, attentiveness, discretion, devotion to duty) and recognizes personal limitations and vulnerability.[79] He should also nurture unswerving loyalty to colleagues of equal rank and to superiors, and show kindness and consideration to his inferiors, retired or active, young or old, thus promoting cooperation and encouraging professional solidarity.[80]

The text requires acknowledgment of the new vocabulary it uses. Throughout the letter, ʿAbd al-Ḥamīd praises and dignifies scribes as the sustainers of kingship (*mulk*) and maintainers of the affairs (*umūr*) of kings. It is through the scribes' good governance and wise political decisions (*tadbīr* and siyasa),[81] he argues, that God improves the king's sovereign power (*sulṭān*), taxes are collected, and regions (*bilād*) prosper. Their knowledge and work are so critical to maintaining power and control that no king or governor can do without them. They are "the ears through which the kings and governors hear, the eyes through which they see, the tongues through which they speak, and the hands through which they strike."[82]

A voice of this sort must have sounded strange to its audience (one thinks of the *ḥadīth* folk, jurists, theologians) in the late Umayyad political context, not just for how it explains governance but for its language. One way to read "Letter to the Scribes" is to consider it, like Al-Qadi does, as an effort to construct an identity for the scribes in Umayyad administration so that they are distinguished by their profession.[83] The letter does indeed explain the qualities and skills that scribes need to distinguish themselves from other groups working in the imperial administration. While I agree with this assessment, I fear it may not fully appreciate the innovative spirit of ʿAbd al-Ḥamīd's contribution. What "Letter to the Scribes" also does is that it envisions and animates a community of professionals, which would shoulder the transfer of the sovereign's power to governmental practice. It draws a blueprint for secretarial practice, which builds on the idea that mastering professional knowledge and observing the sociocultural etiquette are necessary skills for a model scribe, without excluding a notion of religious piety as a matter of self-formation and public self-representation. Besides outlining the responsibilities that scribes must shoulder to represent and wield the sovereign's power, "Letter to the Scribes" urges scribes to acquire qualifying skills and manners not just to satisfy the routine and established requirements of administration but also to set up the mechanisms responsible for both generating and driving governance. With such innovative ideas, the letter marks a singularly important intervention in the late Umayyad milieu: it tries to cultivate a roundly educated imperial servant tasked to rationalize the administration.

ʿAbd al-Ḥamīd's intervention is critical at another level as well: the performative aspect of his language. It defines rather than describes the political reality. Naming scribes as a collectivity and their work as a "craft" brings the class of scribes into being. It transforms discrete individuals working for the caliph in managing his various tasks and duties, cooperatively or individually, into practitioners of a profession with whom they identify as a "class."[84] One is trained and educated in secretarial work as craft. One sets certain standards and regulations for it and for its practitioners. One develops a method of assessment for it, according to which one measures practice as good or bad. The letter therefore makes their activity a vocation and a career that can be studied, improved, and perfected, regardless of any external moral or theological code, just like possessing the skills necessary to work as a carpenter, a goldsmith, and so forth. By doing so, he creates, consciously or not, a new imaginary of politics.[85]

ʿAbd al-Ḥamīd builds his argument about the vital role of scribes upon a brief but substantial discussion of social order and the ontological separation of the sovereign from his subjects. He divides humanity into two broad categories: the folk broadly, which includes the scribes, the most privileged of whom are only a select few; and prophets, messengers, and kings, who are above any human collectivity. In fact, the latter are not a class but individuals selected by the grace of God and elevated above other humans. "God, most high and sublime," he tells his colleagues, "has made human beings after prophets and messengers, may God have mercy on all of them, and after honored kings, crowds of subjects (*sūqa*, pl. *suwaq*),[86] and assigned to them various crafts from which He produced their common livelihood."[87] God made the crowds of subjects into different classes or crafts (*ṣunūf al-ṣinaʿāt*) so that they might earn their sustenance. Among these classes, the author addresses the scribes: "God has made you, the assembly of scribes, into the noblest class as the people of cultivated manners (adab), of manliness, of modesty, of discernment, and of authority."[88] Thus, the status of the class of scribes as the elite among the masses can never be close enough to challenge that of the sovereign because they do not share the same ontological plane; they do still occupy a place of honor above the common folk, which allows them to mediate between the ruler and his subjects and assist in governance.

This discourse is another way of arguing subtly that the human being is a *zoon politikon*, which authorizes a distinct sociopolitical imaginary. To be sure,

ʿAbd al-Ḥamīd does not discuss this *longue-durée* Aristotelian idea—he assumes it and operates accordingly.[89] He presumes that humans have the natural capacity and cultural ability to attain dignified lives, but only through political life. He also suggests that social order stems therefore from human beings' natural aptitude for cooperation with others, from their respective stations in the social hierarchy through the division of labor, and from the mediation of the division of labor by the sovereign. Being necessary and virtuous, because it settles the conflicts arising from humans' divergent interests and improves their conditions, sovereignty is the backbone of the social order.

It is here that he sees scribes play a critical role.[90] "Through you," he encourages his colleagues, "kingship (*mulk*) becomes well-ordered and the affairs of kings are coordinated, and through your management and governance (*tadbīr wa-siyāsa*) God improves their power, gathers their strength, and causes their lands to prosper." By reason only of their craft and skills, he reassures them, "the sovereign needs them to execute the greatest tasks of his dominion and those of the governors in any large or small matter of governorship. No one among them can dispense with the scribes."[91]

Spotlighting the function of secretaries in this way enables ʿAbd al-Ḥamīd to elaborate on the art of administration and the learned techniques of control. At the same time, problematizing the secretaries' work becomes a means to shift the attention from theological normativity, which does not respond to practical concerns in the daily practice of governance, to the question of contingency, of professional skills, and of prudence in political conduct. Bearing in mind this instance and other occasions in "Letter to the Scribes," one observes that ʿAbd al-Ḥamīd prudently shifts the axis of political discourse from the generic faith community (*umma*) and faceless crowds distinguished only with few generic qualities (as was evident in the imamate texts of his time) to people in a variety of social positions and categories (common folk, elite, group, people, flock, creatures, God's servants; *ʿāmma, khāṣṣa, ahl, nās, raʿiyya, khalq, ʿibād*), which renders them political rather than religious.

It would be an overstatement to say that he is secure in his intellectual position. He nevertheless gestures toward the idea of governance as an art of ruling over people for ensuring mutual benefit and agreeable outcome (siyasa and *tadbīr*). He uses novel and established idioms (siyasa, *mulk, malik, tadbīr*) with a nuance, which invoke a new imaginary of politics, connecting the caliphate discursively to the established political vernaculars of the region. The qur'anic words *mulk* and *malik*, for instance, appear unburdened by the negative baggage evident in the ulema's debates on kingship and caliphate. He does not use the word "king" pejoratively and does not put the faith status of the ruler, which he accepts as is, at the center of his attention. It is worth noting here that the word *mulk* soon became the standard signifier of monarchical authority, without the stigma attached to it, among the ulema.

Finally, "Letter to the Scribes" is also remarkable for what it leaves out. ʿAbd al-Ḥamīd does not touch upon election, consultation, consent, and the rest that percolated in Umayyad political controversies. Compared to Sālim b. Dhakwān's implacable language of a sectarian opponent or Ibn Isḥāq's pre-Sunnite normativity and measured contractualism, as we saw in the previous chapter, ʿAbd al-Ḥamīd's "transitional" writing discusses matters from the perspective of a bureaucrat wanting to improve practice. Not surprisingly, Sālim b. Dhakwān and ʿAbd al-Ḥamīd drift apart concerning the ruler: Sālim opposes the Umayyads and is not interested in improving practice, but he strives to clarify his stance, argue against opponents, and explain why the Umayyads and their supporters were damned. ʿAbd al-Ḥamīd, siding unapologetically with the Umayyads, is unconcerned with sectarian argumentation or with explicating or debating the Umayyad rulers' faith status, which he takes for granted. Rather, he seems more attentive to how to nurture the ruler morally *as ruler* and advise the caliph who is already in place to rationalize governance by improving its practice—a perspective that became one of the key features of the royal advice genre later in the Abbasid caliphate thanks to the work of his mentee and colleague, Ibn al-Muqaffaʿ.

As we have seen, the lay bureaucrats' siyasa facilitated an unusual conceptual possibility by the mere form of its articulation in writing, let alone its content. What was coalescing in the Sālim school of siyasa was, for the first time in the caliphate's history, a vision of empire that made sense of the political reality beyond its meaning as an affair of the religious community. This new language also promised to sideline the "republican experiment" of the early caliphate in favor of a monarchical rule akin to other world-historical empires spanning the area from Rome to Pataliputra. In investigating the work of Ibn al-Muqaffaʿ in the following chapter, I will show in more detail the disruptive impact of adab-siyasa on the prevailing moral and political views.

4

The Disruptive Language of Siyasa

In this chapter, I discuss the pioneering perspective of Ibn al-Muqaffaʿ to highlight the disruptive intervention of siyasa. In the first section, I examine his life story and political writing as a frame of reference of a new imaginary of politics. I introduce the "Epistle on the Caliph's Privy" as a remarkable representative of government rationality related to the political prudence of monarchy. It is useful to remember that the discourses of the imamate at the time imagined social organization to be coterminous with the religious community and the normative universal principles of the revealed law, regardless of outcome. Siyasa, on the other hand, arose from a dissenting epistemological and moral sensibility that recognized historical contingency as the basis of political practice.

Ibn al-Muqaffaʿ was concerned with the knowledge of practices required for good governance, with tested techniques of administration, and with historical knowledge thought to be useful to guide the ruler in his practice. His intervention could not be restricted purely to knowing more about governance or offering supplementary routine information for practice. He also attempted to create politics; find politics in relations; and governmentalize structures and practices that had, so far, been thought to be innocent of it. Therefore, being a bold political manifesto underscoring the structuring value of siyasa in Abbaṣid political thought tradition, the "Epistle" represents a discourse of deliberative state building usually associated with the modern state.

In the framework of the "Epistle," I also discuss how siyasa necessarily intersected with secular values of urbane conduct, civility, cosmopolitanism, and the art of good living, expressed in terms like *dunyā*, adab, and *ẓarf*. Probing secularity as an expression of a particular social practice and affective state or attitude more than intellectual reflection suggests a profound distinction between the manners of religious piety and worldly desires, where one was pegged to the religious morality of the ulema and the other associated with the urbane manners of lay intellectuals.

A Lay Bureaucrat-Littérateur's Résumé

An anecdote connects ʿAbd al-Ḥamīd and Ibn al-Muqaffaʿ in a tragic way, reflecting the siyasa discourse's emergence from its fragmentary beginnings to its more self-conscious iterations. In the frightening months after the Battle of the Zab in January 750—if we trust al-Jahshiyārī—the Umayyad scribe ʿAbd al-Ḥamīd sought shelter with his younger colleague and friend Ibn al-Muqaffaʿ in a safe house near Raqqa. They were fleeing the Abbasids, who, after defeating and killing the Umayyad caliph Marwān II, were intent on capturing and punishing those who had cast their lots with him. One day, the two were going about their business inside the house when they were spotted and apprehended by an Abbasid squad. The soldiers asked which one of them was ʿAbd al-Ḥamīd so that they could arrest him. Both responded, "I am." Fearing that the soldiers might rush upon Ibn al-Muqaffaʿ and execute him, ʿAbd al-Ḥamīd intervened to assure them of his identity: "Have some mercy. I have birthmarks. Have some of you watch us and dispatch others to ask those who sent you about these birthmarks to verify my identity." They agreed. He was then identified and taken away for execution, and Ibn al-Muqaffaʿ was set free.[1]

Born Rōzbeh (meaning "the blessed one" or "the fortunate one" in Persian), Ibn al-Muqaffaʿ was a mentee, colleague, and friend of ʿAbd al-Ḥamīd. The Abbasid revolt destroyed his improving career prospects under the Umayyads, so Ibn al-Muqaffaʿ charted a new path for himself as a scribe and reorganized his career goals. Soon after the collapse of the Umayyads, Ibn al-Muqaffaʿ entered the service of the Abbasid family in Iraq and enjoyed a successful but short career with them until he suffered an even more tragic end than his mentor a few years later for entirely different reasons.[2]

Ibn al-Muqaffaʿ was born in southern Iran in Gōr (al-Ghūr), present-day Firozabad, the old capital of the Sasanids, around 720 CE to a Persian family of midlevel nobility and administrators under the Sasanians.[3] His father, Dādūya (Dādōē or Dādhuwayh), had worked for the Umayyads in Khurasan, possibly as a tax collector for the governor of Iraq al-Ḥajjāj b. Yūsuf or Khālid al-Qaṣrī.[4]

Ibn al-Muqaffaʿ grew up in Basra—arguably the most vibrant and cosmopolitan city of the caliphate at the time—as a client of Āl al-Ahtam.[5]

A native speaker of Persian, Ibn al-Muqaffaʿ benefited from his client-family's eloquence in Arabic and the town's robust cultural, intellectual, and professional life. He must have received a rigorous instruction in Arabic.[6] His professional knowledge of middle Persian is remarkable. He may have mastered five "languages" or dialects of Persia, three of which were no longer living languages. These were written in seven different scripts, several of which were still in use.[7] Whether his proficiency in languages and scripts is exaggerated or not, he must have acquired advanced education either in his family as part of a tradition or through some form of Persian educational structure that still survived in Persia.

In his early years, he would visit Basra often. He became a resident of it after the Abbasid revolution. In Basra, early and later in his life, he socialized with a group of intellectuals best known for their literary talents and "unorthodox" views (from the standpoint of later standard jurisprudential Sunnism), such as Bashshār b. Burd.[8] He appears to have converted to Islam after the routing of the Umayyads (he is cited as a Manichean or Zoroastrian) with the encouragement of his patron, the Abbasid ʿĪsā b. ʿAlī, the uncle of the caliphs al-ʿAbbās and al-Manṣūr, and changed his name from Rōzbeh (teknonym, Abū Amr) to ʿAbdallāh (Abū Muhammad). However, when one reads his "Epistle," one notices no sign of a recent conversion or a shallow understanding of Islamic religious themes; on the contrary, its relevant passages read like an erudite critical reflection penned by someone steeped in religious knowledge.

He pursued his father's profession and served the Umayyads and then the Abbasids in various advisory and secretarial capacities in multiple locations in Iraq and Iran. In the eventful years of the 740s, he served as scribe in Shāpūr, Fars, for Masīḥ b. al-Ḥawārī, soon after the appointment of ʿAbdallāh b. ʿUmar b. ʿAbd al-ʿAzīz as governor of Iraq (743–744). Later, in Kirman, he worked for Yazīd b. ʿUmar b. Abī Hubayra, the last Umayyad governor there, and after Yazīd's death, for Yazīd's brother Dāwūd. He also briefly served Marwān II with ʿAbd al-Ḥamīd. He witnessed the end of the Umayyad dynasty and the execution of his patrons and his friend and mentor, ʿAbd al-Ḥamīd, by the Abbasids.[9]

After the fall of the Umayyads, he successfully associated himself with the paternal uncles of the first two Abbasid caliphs, which may show his nonpolitical loyalty to his profession to work for any ruler,[10] ambition-driven quest for power, or personal reputation leading to his recruitment. Through his work and his skills, Ibn al-Muqaffaʿ joined the circle of prominent members of the Abbasid family. He served ʿĪsā b. ʿAlī and his brothers Ismāʿīl b. ʿAlī, the governor of al-Ahwaz and Mosul, and Sulaymān b. ʿAlī, the governor of Basra. He lived in Basra, which from 751 to 757 was governed by Sulaymān b. ʿAlī.[11]

He interfered in the Abbasid intrafamily feud between the caliph al-Manṣūr and his uncle ʿAbdallāh b. ʿAlī, who had rebelled against al-Manṣūr. When ʿAbdallāh b. ʿAlī lost his bid, he was allowed to stay in the custody of his brother Sulaymān b. ʿAlī, for whom Ibn al-Muqaffaʿ worked. Fearing dire consequences, Sulaymān asked him to draft a letter of pardon (*amān*), on behalf of his brother ʿAbdallāh, for the caliph to sign, which Ibn al-Muqaffaʿ did. Al-Manṣūr might in fact have signed the letter, but his next move suggests he was not happy with the pardon and even less happy with the wording of the letter. Given the vulgar language of the "pardon letter," the caliph, we are told, became offended. When he inquired about the scribe, he was told that it was "a scribe called ʿAbdallāh b. al-Muqaffaʿ in the service of your uncles."

Once the caliph felt himself in a stronger position, he ended his arrangement with his uncle's family. He replaced Sulaymān b. ʿAlī as governor of Basra with Sufyān b. Muʿāwiya al-Muhallabī (February 757), which spelled misfortune for Ibn al-Muqaffaʿ. Sufyān b. Muʿāwiya, as the narrative goes, might have held some grudge against Ibn al-Muqaffaʿ from a few years back for siding with the governor of Shāpūr, Masīḥ b. al-Ḥawārī, against him. Other reports claim that Sufyān had been the subject of Ibn al-Muqaffaʿ's derision and ridicule on more than one occasion. According to the narrative, he therefore had compelling reasons to see Ibn al-Muqaffaʿ suffer. When the caliph sought to punish Ibn al-Muqaffaʿ, as Ibn Khallikān and al-Jahshiyārī suggest, he instructed the vengeful Sufyān b. Muʿāwiya to do the job, which he might have undertaken in a most ghastly manner.[12] Another account suggests that Ibn al-Muqaffaʿ committed suicide after he was captured and taken to al-Manṣūr for punishment.[13] The date of his death is given variably as 755 and 757. He might have been in his mid-thirties, but possibly much older, in his fifties.[14] One of his sons, Muhammad, appears in the service of al-Manṣūr as a scribe a few years later.

In a sarcastic remark, Ibn Khallikān relates that Khalīl b. Aḥmad, the linguist and author of *Kitāb al-ʿAyn*, used to say about Ibn al-Muqaffaʿ, after having met him, that his knowledge surpassed his rational discernment (*ʿilmuhu akthar min aqlihi*).[15] Unanimously, sources report him as a person of eloquence and manners, and a gifted observer who thoroughly knew this administrative-scholarly tradition as a professional scribe and person of scholarly erudition. They point out his profound knowledge of the details of the administrative profession, his excellent command of Arabic prose, and his gift of translation, all of which helped advance his reputation.[16]

His contemporaries and later generations of literate professionals disagreed on whether to praise or condemn him for his political views, cultural loyalties, and former faith. His writing suggests that he cared about his Persian roots and the cultural practices associated with his background.[17] He might have subconsciously harbored raw visceral feelings toward the ruling people's native culture, perhaps witnessing a renaissance as nostalgia for desert life and for the authenticity and simplicity of Bedouin ways. His work and position earned him a reputation for being a Shuʿūbī, that is, a person who refuses to acknowledge the superiority of the Arabs and thus seeks division and strife rather than unity.[18]

In the office politics of the Umayyad and early Abbasid bureaucratic circles, his rivals accused him (both during his life and after his death) of not only *zandaqa* (Manicheanism, also heresy) but also of being a pseudo-Muslim, crypto-Manichean, and ʿAlid-supporter. He was even accused of writing a refutation of the Qur'an.[19] That he might have written a work as a refutation of the Qur'an remains possible. Such work would be self-sabotage, however, for such a driven and careerist person who worked for the Umayyads and the Abbasids since his youth. To this, his professional career does not attest. Indeed, it would also go against the principles and values he espouses in his writing. Might he have written a refutation during the Abbasid revolt for someone belonging to a fringe sect in Khurasan, including someone around Abū Muslim, in the hope of new patronage? It is probable and would tally well with his professional opportunism, but we have no information to confirm it.[20]

Given his recent conversion and his life after his espousal of Islam, if we do not assume that conversion signifies a moment of decision when puzzle pieces fall in place and suddenly changes everything, we may even reason that he always remained in between and in transition. In any case, his alleged heresy had little to do with his downfall because Manichaeism stayed under the radar as a major public concern until the reign of al-Mahdī onward.[21] His death may relate to a cause he discusses in his writing: a wise adviser should avoid at all costs to interfere in political controversies and bid on the wrong horse. One might consider his eagerness to defend ʿAbdallāh b. ʿAlī against al-Manṣūr to the extent of writing, if he indeed wrote it, the scathing letter of safe conduct on his behalf in an abhorrent language such an opportunistic interference in family matters.[22]

He might have been stigmatized by not being able to serve in the court of the first two Abbasid caliphs to the degree that he accepted writing the letter of safe conduct against the caliph. Clearly, he lived the last part of his life as a disgruntled careerist who tried hard but unsuccessfully to work as adviser to the caliph, Umayyad or Abbasid. This disappointment may explain his presumptuousness in still writing the "Epistle" to al-Manṣūr about "how to run the empire," even though he was not asked to do so. One still wonders how Ibn al-Muqaffaʿ, who had turned against his patrons, the Umayyads, only half a decade earlier, and even sided with an Abbasid contender against the current caliph barely a few years before he wrote the "Epistle," could still expect to be convincing to the caliph.

In narrative representations of his personality, Ibn al-Muqaffaᶜ comes across as a driven person with extraordinary talent and ambition, an adventurous climber who could be condescending and supercilious at times, which might have contributed to the tragic end of his life.[23] Accusations aside, he seems to have been eager to move upward from his position as a scribe, without concealing his background. He worked for the empire and strived to be at its center. Whether through his translations or Arabic prose compositions, he seems to have aimed in his intellectual production at creating a new meaning out of existing practice that resonated with the cultural orientation of *mawālī* imperial elite like him.

One of his substantial contributions was maintaining an active engagement with Persianate cultural and scholarly traditions through writing and translating. One must acknowledge the subversive and destabilizing character of his writing: he questions the established wisdom and authority not only in political practice but also in long-term habits and thinking. In his quest to assemble an idealized, often sentimentalized, Persianate political culture as a model for the caliphate in his work, he both asserted its relevance to the current political reality and used it to resist the emerging cultural hegemony. He functioned as a translator, literally and figuratively, to transpose elements from both worlds to generate a hybrid political discourse and praxis fitting the new empire, which he idealized for the caliphate.

Far from seeking to replace the caliphate with the putative Persian empire, he wrote to create a ruling class with the capacity of rising above the pressures of the cultural hegemony, encourage a political practice that appreciated the *longue-durée* imperial history in the region, and alleviate a sociopolitical imbalance among the ruling class.[24] It is pertinent to note here that the accusation that Ibn al-Muqaffaᶜ operated as a Shuᶜūbite demagogue centered precisely on this kind of pushback against a cultural hegemony and political privilege that had been building since the imperial expansion in the mid-seventh century onward.[25]

Siyasa Texts as Political Disenchantment

Ibn al-Muqaffaᶜ's known works address political questions. In his compositions and translations, Ibn al-Muqaffaᶜ opened a window onto the world of empires and imperial governance, and directed the attention of his peers to new frontiers of political knowledge. One needs to approach his work as the tip of an iceberg. Considering the audience of his work and the curiosity it created among those who traded with it in diverse ways and those who carried it forward in thought and action, his writing exposes a major intellectual trend one must assess in terms of the ripple effect it created.

While this statement makes a point about the inspiring and impactful language of Ibn al-Muqaffaᶜ, it does not say much about its originality. To claim that his writing agreed with the political writing of his time would be an underestimation of the disruption it caused. One cannot truly appreciate the significance of his work by simply elaborating on it as a routine contribution to the discussion in a depoliticized and stable sociopolitical space. Rather, his work is best understood as a form of discursive practice that disrupted the status quo and shaped a new reality. By centering his prose on politics and writing about it in a variety of ways (as fable, advice, a collection of wisdom, translations of various works), Ibn al-Muqaffaᶜ shaped the way others thought and wrote about politics.

When his work is evaluated in context, one is struck by the narrative purposefulness of his writing and the originality of its content. At the root of his writing is, of course, a fundamental assumption about the value and power of writing—about its potential to create and change reality, to translate thought and desire into action. It shows his evident trust not only in the world-changing quality of writing but also in governance as a commendable and positive force for the common good. This marked a significant step in a milieu in which political practice was frequently associated with corruption and immorality and a cause of dissension.

The breadth of Ibn al-Muqaffaᶜ's work and scholarly interests justifies examining him as both a scribe and as an intellectual in his own right.[26] A perusal of the remaining part of his written work shows that he was a talented prose writer, even if one discounts many of the epistles and books falsely attributed to him. Primary sources cite his keenness to use the capabilities and techniques of languages in which prose writing had long been established (such as medieval Persian) to create new forms of expression in the Arabic language.[27] They praise his dedication to prose writing as having the same vigor as ᶜAbd al-Ḥamīd but guiding it in a new direction. Although his critics appraise his writing as stiff, dry, and archaic, one must acknowledge that it represents a benchmark of a new style of writing.[28]

Ibn al-Muqaffaᶜ's writing both perfected and surpassed ᶜAbd al-Ḥamīd's. If ᶜAbd al-Ḥamīd represented a figure in transition who was not ready to question the theological arguments of the imamate and did not challenge the cultural hegemony (couched as "Arabic" following the encounter with the Other in more regular and mundane ways, the development of urban life, and the corollary expansion of intellectual interests), Ibn al-Muqaffaʿ made clear that siyasa was distinctive from and challenging to that of imamate. His work on politics, as an archetype separate from the elementary forms of the imamate, was rooted in this condition of hybridity. He explored broad imperial themes beyond Umayyad theological and Arabic cultural interests that would, after his death, become a major genre of political writing and of inquiry, embracing transcultural humanistic disciplines in its folds. Even a cursory review of his work would prove an intellectual genealogy extending to Persian, Indian, Greek, and Arabic-Islamic sources. He actively sought ancient, time-tested imperial cultural practices for emulation, which was not evident in ʿAbd al-Ḥamīd's writing.[29]

Despite the clumsiness of his prose, he would impress his critics over the ages as the preeminent Arabic prose writer and an all-time celebrity of Arabic literature. In fact, many centuries later, another giant, Ibn Khaldūn (d. 1406) of North Africa, discussing his own work on politics, acknowledged Ibn al-Muqaffaʿ for his contributions to the subject. Feeling the need to explain where he differs from Ibn al-Muqaffaʿ, Ibn Khaldūn praises the earlier scholar for tackling many of the problems he treated in his work, including political matters. He asserts, however, that Ibn al-Muqaffaʿ did not substantiate his ideas satisfactorily with arguments but stated matters in passing in the flowing prose and eloquent verbiage of a rhetorician. Ibn Khaldūn credits himself that he, on the contrary, did a full study of the subject.[30]

It is exactly this sentiment revealed by Ibn Khaldūn that I wish to hold up to scrutiny here. Siyasa, as exemplified in the work of Ibn al-Muqaffaʿ, emerged precariously, bearing the imprint of its dialogic context in which the imamate, however incipient and vague its concerns and question about governance, was the language of political reflection among the learned and ruling elite. Ibn al-Muqaffaʿ deployed his work as a disruptive intervention that laid a new foundation of thinking and offered a new language of politics one could no longer ignore, regardless of what position one took.

Ibn al-Muqaffaʿ is most famous for composing the celebrated animal fables *Kalīla and Dimna*, which stands at the foundation of the literary genre of fables and bestiaries in the Arabic language.[31] This work is the translation of a middle Persian composition based on Sanskrit sources by one Borzoe (Barzawayh) of the sixth century, who was alleged to be a court physician of the Sasanian Anūshirvan Khusrau. Unfortunately, we do not have the early version of the text. What we have are much later reworkings of his putative translation in a wide range of languages, which cannot be considered Ibn al-Muqaffaʿ's actual work.[32] Despite *Kalīla and Dimna*'s concern with themes mostly related to the imperial court, its fundamental entertaining value made it a major source of inspiration for later writers and gave it a much wider audience, not only in Arabic but also in numerous other languages, for centuries. By telling stories through animals, it delivers time-tested moral lessons, practical advice, and political wisdom from the past for those interested in propriety in their relationships, primarily with rulers and those who associate with them in a variety of settings.

Ibn al-Muqaffaʿ wrote a preface for this work and translated the rest with substantial editing to suit his circumstances.[33] The sage Bidpai (Baydaba), responding to the request of the Indian king Dabshalim, narrates the stories included in the book. In the first story, events develop around the lion Binkala and the deceitful jackal Dimna. The other fables (involving a crow, a rat, a gazelle, and a tortoise; owl and crow; monkey and tortoise; rat and cat; king and bird; lion and jackal; king, vizier, queen, and the wise; lioness and horseman; monk and his guest; traveler and goldsmith; prince and his companions) tell stories of sovereignty, governance, true friendship, watchfulness against the enemy, the rotation of fortune and misfortune, the dangers of ignorance and lack of expertise, avoidance of making enemies, caution in trusting vengeful persons, restoration of relations with subordinates, avoidance of harming others because of the possibility of receiving the same in return, the risk of making choices, bestowal of favor on the unworthy, fate and the inevitable consequences of divine judgment, and other themes of timeless wisdom. Its fables are about human nature and relations and about cultivating and educating those who are endowed with sovereign power.

In his putative introduction, Ibn al-Muqaffaʿ summarizes the possible readership of the work, from those who wanted to read fables to those looking for a deeper meaning: "This book is a work of parables and stories composed by the people of India, who sought to incorporate into it the most eloquent speech they could find in the style they preferred. In order to make their intentions comprehensible, scholars of every nation and tongue have employed a variety of devices and means when presenting their arguments."[34] To explain the content and the meanings of the text, he informs his readers that "because such a book combined entertainment with wisdom, the wise would study it for its wisdom, and the simple for its value as entertainment; young pupils and others would be delighted to read it and it would be easy for them to memorize."[35]

Referring to the work's allegoric language, Ibn al-Muqaffaʿ prepares the potential audience for the depth of its meaning: "When the young person reached maturity and grew in knowledge, he would ponder what he has memorized—as it had been recorded and inscribed in his heart without his knowing its true nature—and would come to realize that he had acquired a great treasure. . . . The reader thus needs to know the method used to compose the book, otherwise he will not comprehend its intention or realize what can be gained from it."[36] Ibn al-Muqaffaʿ then discloses, as if he were expecting an audience unfamiliar with the genre, the meaning beyond the apparent literal wording of the text. "The first requirement for anyone studying this book is to begin with a deliberate reading: the object should not be to get to the end of the book, but to uncover its meaning and to understand and reflect on what is being read. No one will benefit from the book if his sole concern is to reach its end without thoroughly understanding what he is reading."[37]

In a universe in which human and animal worlds were connected as creations of God, fables served more than a metaphoric and metonymic purpose; that is, they were more than a vehicle to carry and convey human values or represent them. The author therefore cautions the reader: "You must realize that the book has an inner meaning still to be learned and that you will not benefit from the outward sense until you become acquainted with the inner meaning—just as unshelled nuts bring no benefit until you crack them and extract their kernels."[38] In their own way, the fables bring together and mark a border between the "human" and the "animal," in sociopolitical and cultural rather than biological fields. As I will assess later in chapter 5, fables pose questions about social order, political power, sovereignty, and being subject to contingencies.

Abbasid and post-Abbasid bibliographers and biographers attribute a few translations of an eminently political nature to Ibn al-Muqaffaʿ. *Khuday-nāma*, *ʿA'in-nāma*, *Kitāb al-Tāj*, *Sakisaran*, and *Letter of Tansar* are among the major ones attributed to him, some spuriously. Unfortunately, none of them survives in the original and those for which we have fragments from diverse sources cannot be relied on to reconstruct Ibn al-Muqaffaʿ's translation and adaptation. Nevertheless, the themes explored in these works and their broad content and language reveal the cultural and sociopolitical direction toward which Ibn al-Muqaffaʿ headed.

Khuday-nāma was a chronicle of Persian kings, hence, its well-known name *Siyar Mulūk al-ʿAjam* or *Siyar Mulūk al-Furs*. Partly legendary, partly historical, *Khuday-nāma* tells the story of imperial rule, with its kings, royal family, warriors, and social classes working to maintain social balance under royal authority, which such literature highlights as the prerequisite of political success. Its narrative entertains as it informs. Its advice on governance and military affairs is interspersed with stories, aphorisms, and practical wisdom, which resembles and revives the *andarz* genre of Sasanian literature.[39] Like its middle Persian original, Ibn al-Muqaffaʿ's Arabic version has not come down to us with the exception that Ibn Qutayba's *ʿUyūn al-Akhbār* may have preserved fragments from it. Al-Ṭabarī in his *Tārīkh* also may have obtained some of his information about pre-Islamic Persia from it.[40]

Our information on the content of *ʿA'in-nāma* (*The Book of Proper Conduct*) is even more negligible. The original *ʿA'in-nāma* appears to have been a Sasanian work (or a collection of several works) devoted to courtly conduct. Ibn Qutayba's

ʿUyūn al-Akhbār contains numerous passages that the author claims he quoted from *ʿA'in-nāma*. The work deals with court manners and customs, military tactics, archery, divination and physiognomy, and polo. It portrays a world in which strictly regulated social classes fulfil their duties under the authority of an omnipotent king.[41] Another work, *Kitāb al-Tāj*, deals with the imperial biography of Khusrau II Parwiz and seems to be written as royal advice (mirror for princes, *adab al-mulūk*).[42] Ibn al-Nadīm claims that it was a biography of Khusrau I Anūshirvan.[43]

Ibn al-Muqaffaʿ also translated a work called *Sakisaran*, which, according to the historian al-Masʿūdī, commemorated the glorious deeds of heroic rulers from the Persian past such as Rustam and lsfandiyār. The work became a source of inspiration for a later generation of Persian poets who produced epic poetry or accounts of pre-Islamic Iranian history. The most renowned among them is Firdawsī (d. 1020) who, in his celebrated *Shāhnāma* (*Book of Kings*), narrates the history of preIslamic Iran in verse. It might have preserved some content from the lost middle Persian work translated by Ibn al-Muqaffaʿ.[44]

The *Letter of Tansar* is also a political tract from middle Persian literature in the sixth century. Ibn al-Muqaffaʿ's translation did not survive. What we have is its thirteenth-century Persian translation by Muhammad b. al-Ḥasan b. Isfandiyār (Ibn Isfandiyār) included in his *History of Tabāristān*.[45] Tansar, who is the presumed author of the letter, was a Zoroastrian priest and adviser to the first Sasanian king, Ardashīr I (r. 224–240). The author is known for his work to establish a canon of scripture and religious orthodoxy to promote conformity under imperial rule. The letter serves as a warning to King Gushnasp, urging him to submit to the rulership of Ardashīr, "the king of kings."

In the first section of the *Letter of Tansar*, Tansar praises Ardashīr's stable rule, which Tansar claims was maintained by keeping the social groups in their ranks through the wise use of power and administrative skills. The next section includes lessons on humility, intelligence, forbearance, and other qualities using stories and quotations from ancient sages. Among the major themes to promote order in the world is one about the interdependence of religion and kingship, which the text describes as twins. Another concern is maintaining the equilibrium of social order by keeping the four social groups in their own ranks. First is the clergy, including priests, judges, ascetics, temple-guardians, and teachers. The second includes the military, comprising cavalry and foot soldiers. The third contains the scribes, including writers of official communications, accountants, writers of chronicles, poets, and physicians. And the fourth has the artisans, including land tillers, cattle herders, merchants, and traders. An additional topic is about how the "king of kings" is the sole authority entitled to amend tradition to establish a better one. Without depending too much on inferences from a thirteenth-century rendition of it, one may conjure that the *Letter of Tansar* underlines four pillars of a stable rule: a powerful king; equilibrium among social classes; a reasonable arrangement of cooperation (because they are assumed separate) between religion and kingship; and mechanisms of control to maintain this order in perpetuity, which is the craft of politics. These themes appear in one way or another in Ibn al-Muqaffaᶜ's other work and are unmistakably assumed in the "Epistle on the Caliph's Privy."[46]

Some other translations attributed to Ibn al-Muqaffaᶜ are spurious, others probably so, including *Bilawhar and Yudasaf*,[47] portions of Aristotle's *Organon* (from a middle Persian translation),[48] and other Aristotelian and Greek philosophical work.[49] Among the compositions attributed to him, only two survive: *Kitāb al-Adab al-Kabīr* and *Risāla fī al-Ṣaḥāba*. A brief text of political aphorisms known as *Yatīma* may also belong to him.[50]

Al-Adab al-Kabīr (also known as *al-Durra al-Yatīma*), which, according to Iḥsān ᶜAbbās, could be the second part of the original larger book,[51] is a short piece of political and practical wisdom composed for rulers or governors, such as his own patrons, aspirants to office, and ranking office bureaucrats. *Al-Adab al-Kabīr*'s prose is interspersed with poetic, aphoristic, and oratorical expressions, providing evidence of a remarkable transitional text in initial stages of prose writing ready to unleash the potential of the language beyond poetical expression and strictly administrative manuals to various humanistic interests. It also displays more compositional self-confidence in expressing the author's point of view, who appears no longer reluctant to articulate the value of Sasanian imperial moral virtues, practices, and political protocols useful in the late Umayyad courtly milieu.[52]

The work is about adab, in this context "political virtue," which entails more than self-representation. Adab is also a regime of conduct to guide moral formation and the cultivation of virtues of civility for good judgment and effective interaction with peers, subordinates, and superiors.[53] Along with the other work of Ibn al-Muqaffaᶜ, it breaks new ground for a genre of political writing that we may classify as "political virtue" or "royal conduct" (*adab al-siyāsa, adab al-mulūk*) or "advice to kings" (*naṣīḥat al-mulūk*), which includes but is not limited to etiquette. It advises monarchs on how to display courtly manners, foster moral traits fitting their status, nurture a royal conduct for an effective rule, and embody political virtue as a lifelong habit or a way of life.[54]

Bearing in mind its current form, *Al-Adab al-Kabīr* is organized roughly around ten themes of varying lengths that sketch the principles of virtue for monarchs and their associates, which, if we trust al-ᶜĀmirī, might have been inspired by the Avesta.[55] The first is a synopsis of why ancient (Sasanian) courtly culture and knowledge were indispensable for those in positions of power. In the second, one reads about the virtue of recognizing the basic principles of moral formation, conduct, and relations. The third involves instruction in the required virtues for effective rulership and effective conduct. Next comes a discourse on the privy of the sovereign, the politics of serving in that capacity, and how to avoid its pitfalls and take advantage of its benefits. In addition, it describes the required knowledge and grooming that the courtly associate needs in order to receive acceptance and favor at court and to avoid the monarch's anger and disdain. Furthermore, it discusses how to navigate relations with colleagues and competitors, and how to work on refining certain skills and manners. The fifth focuses on friendship (or collegiality), which he associates with the ability to forge permanent bonds; sustain them by fidelity, loyalty, and devotion; and protect them against corrosive forces. He subsequently discusses succinctly the techniques of cultivating patience in the sixth, the merits of knowledge in the seventh, and the virtue of generosity in the eighth. In the ninth theme, he offers a longer discussion on adversaries and on acquiring attitudes and strategies to address envy and rancor, and on nurturing the good qualities of modesty and good morals with respect to power and money, and then in tenth theme he delves into the topic of controlling sensual desire for women, and other pieces of advice.[56]

Al-Adab al-Kabīr's relatable pieces of wisdom contrast with the acuteness and urgent relevance of the "Epistle on the Caliph's Privy".[57] The "Epistle" is a rare and brief piece of writing on actual political practice. Far from being a restrained piece of advice, which takes the conventional order for granted, it advises on how to meet the challenges that the Abbasid ruler faced. It is concerned with the here and now: pressing challenges, empire building, the details of governance, political culture, and ways to naturalize the sovereign's power—a blueprint for establishing effective monarchical government. Besides its keen observation of the current political and administrative circumstances, it gives its reader an audacious and cogent perspective on how to stabilize the revolutionary volatility according to new principles. Therefore, the significance of the "Epistle" demands a dedicated discussion.

Governmentalization of Sovereignty

The "Epistle on the Caliph's Privy" is about good governance.[58] It is a brief account of around five thousand words that reads like a manifesto, a policy report, a political proposal, and a list of what to do and how to do it. The internal evidence, language, and references to historical figures in the text indicate it was written after the Abbasid revolt, at the beginning of the second Abbasid caliph al-Manṣūr's reign, sometime between 754 and 757. It does not name the addressee, but the caliph al-Manṣūr was the intended recipient.[59] The "Epistle" is not always specific or clear in terms of the *dramatis personae* to which it refers or alludes; but it includes a few incidents and names that help better contextualize its content. Whether for reasons of political correctness or professional courtesy, there is little specific ad hominem attacks in it. It also avoids naming sects and groups and their controversies (the Shiites, Kharijites, Muʿtazilites, etc.), although it deals with their discourses throughout the work. Ibn al-Muqaffaʿ wrote it as the Abbasid family was trying to learn about ruling after al-Manṣūr won the major battles against his rivals. He might have been seeking a new patron or hoping to get closer to the caliph instead of remaining a provincial adviser in the service of a family that seemed to have lost its fortune (Banū ʿAlī) after submitting to al-Manṣūr. The "Epistle" thus might have been a way for Ibn al-Muqaffaʿ to exhibit his skills and usefulness to be hired at the court of the caliph.

As far as we know, Ibn al-Muqaffaʿ wrote this letter on his own volition without solicitation from the caliph, which makes sense because he remained noncommittal during the Abbasid revolt, and he was a career opportunist who bet on the wrong horse after the death of al-Saffāḥ, so much so that he wrote an unsparing letter of safe conduct to the caliph on behalf of his rival, the anti-caliph ʿAbdallāh b. ʿAlī, who failed in his bid against al-Manṣūr. Whether the "Epistle" reached the caliph we do not know, but we need no endorsement from the caliph to appreciate the creativity and impact of its discerning analysis. Ibn al-Muqaffaʿ died soon after writing it, having received no promotion but anger instead.[60]

An impressive number of nineteenth- and twentieth-century scholars have already discussed it and its author from various erudite but commonsense liberal perspectives that never question their own fundamental assumptions about the Umayyad and Abbasid worlds. Current studies present the "Epistle" as a remarkable spark in a continuum and a "realist" assessment of Abbasid caliphal practice, but they problematize neither its language nor the discursive context defined by the ulema. Impressed by the "practical" tone of the "Epistle," modern scholars have articulated several arguments that shed light on how the "Epistle" presented the Sasanian political culture as a model for the caliphs; addressed the failures of the caliphate; attempted to resolve the crisis of legitimacy after the Abbasid revolt; diagnosed the shaky ground on which the new caliphate rose; or offered, as Said A. Arjomand argued, a "comprehensive program of revolutionary reconstruction which foreshadow[ed] both the integrative and centralizing long-term consequences of the Abbasid revolution."[61]

I do not dismiss these points, but I think Ibn al-Muqaffaʿ's more remarkable contribution lies in his disruptive voice that interrogates some of the fundamental assumptions of his milieu concerning political authority and governance. As we have seen, the caliph's faith status and piety were a paramount concern of the ulema. In their political imagination, the central questions of politics were related to the compliance of the caliph's conduct with the religious requirements they formulated: the faith-value of obeying or disobeying the caliph, the faith status of the first four caliphs, and the role of the community of the faithful as the guardian of the faith. They framed their calls to fairness and justice as implementing God's laws among the believers. The political discourse of the "Epistle," on the other hand, accentuated the empire and its political constitution and the sovereign and his power. The "Epistle" aims at building a sociopolitical order under the authority of the "absolute possessor" of the world by divine sanction. By the mode of its expression, it denaturalizes the imamate discourse and pushes back against the increasing pressure of the ulema, who sought to structure the Abbasid administration according to jurisprudential values and principles.

As a way of orientation and to prepare the reader to comprehend its impact in an already semantically occupied field against which it worked, an outline of its contents is in order. The "Epistle" discusses the following themes, in order of their appearance in the text:[62]

(1) Praise of the caliph, grounding sovereignty. The virtue of humility and justice in governing people.
(2) The role of the learned, value of rational judgment, merit of counseling, merits of the sovereign concerning his attention to inquiry and advice.
(3) The army and the caliph. Discipline, control and organization of the army, manual of conduct. Caliph's authority, the question of obedience to the caliph and to God, revealed law, interpretation, and judgment. Religion and reason and how and when each should be followed. Obedience to and privileges of the caliph in matters of command and administration. Tax administration and administration of the military. Promotion and assignment of duties in the army. Training and education of the army in ethical skills. Pension of soldiers and method of compensation. Surveillance of and intelligence in the army.
(4) Iraq and Khurasan. Merits of the people of Iraq and Khurasan, challenges facing the caliph concerning the elite in Iraq. Law, diverse and conflicting opinions. How to regulate and control legislation, supervision by the caliph. Causes of the diversity of judgments, reasoning by analogy.
(5) Controlling Syria. What to do with Syria. Critique of current practice. Pacifying discontent and rebellion in Syria.
(6) Caliph's privy, the *ṣaḥāba*. Dealing with courtly elite, noble associates, and advisers. Merits and attributes of useful associates.

(7) The Abbasid family.
(8) Administration of the land tax. Good practices of fiscal administration.
(9) Honoring the Arabian Peninsula.
(10) Discourse on nobility and common people. Need for and function of nobility. Improving the state of the common people through nobility.
(11) Praise.

As a record revealing an imperial scribe's participation in the process of empire building, it is a disruptive and inventive text. Except for its archaic language, it hardly resembles any writing of its own period. One needs to labor hard to find a work like it in the eighth century. As a genre, it is neither a writing in religious jurisprudence, *ḥadīth*, *kalām*, poetry, storytelling, advice on virtue and bravery, nor is it about ancient Arabic political nostalgia. It is also not a text of moral exhortation or of a mirror for princes, like his *Al-Adab al-Kabīr*. In its intertextual and dialogic space, it impresses its reader as a foundational text of political analysis, which stands distinct from the prepolitical reflection of the sectarian thinkers and of the middle-of-the-road ulema who became major figures in the early Abbasid period. It may have been inspired by ʿAbd al-Ḥamīd's earlier work in its style (prose, subject matter, language) and genre (policy manual, report). Two of his letters might have served as a model for the "Epistle": "Letter to the Scribes" and "Testament to the Crown Prince." While no work of ʿAbd al-Ḥamīd or of anybody else among his contemporaries and earlier pairs with the "Epistle" in terms of the themes it discusses, the "Letter to the Scribes" and the "Testament to the Crown Prince" invoke the functionality, practicality, realism, and style of the "Epistle." It may not be far off to claim that what ʿAbd al-Ḥamīd wrote concerning scribes and the crown prince, Ibn al-Muqaffaʿ did on an imperial scale in a much more direct way.

As a new reading of the political practices and discourses of its time, the "Epistle" represents a turn in political thinking. When compared to the other contemporaneous texts on governance, it strikes the reader as an exceptionally insightful piece of writing showing that the question of how to rule went beyond the functional knowledge of administrative duties to theorizing about what Pierre Bourdieu has described as "the structuring structure." Its unusually direct discourse on politics proceeds not in the abstract and timeless language of a moral self-construct of the ruler and his courtly elite—the kind we see, for instance, in his *Al-Adab al-Kabīr* or *Kalīla and Dimna*, and numerous similar works later—but in the specific themes of imperial authority (the sovereign, territory, law, military, and courtly elite). This point dovetails with another observation concerning the "Epistle's" conceptualization of governance: the absence of any reference to the Sasanian notion of the circle of justice.[63] Ibn Muqaffaʿ was familiar with the idea, although this text does not explicitly suggest it.[64] On this occasion, Ibn al-Muqaffaʿ seems to be foregrounding a political model closer to a pyramid. Here, the sovereign, as an ontologically distinct being, functions at the apex of the social pyramid and is supported by the military and civil elite, who assist him in governing the subjects.

When one ponders why Ibn al-Muqaffaʿ might have neglected the mention of the circle of justice, two possibilities present themselves. Given that he did not aim to offer timeless advice but rather practical information about pressing issues, which the model of the circle of justice did not offer, he might have seen it as irrelevant to the revolutionary order after the Abbasid revolt. More pertinently, the rise of the ulema with claims of autonomy as a major sociopolitical force might have compelled Ibn al-Muqaffaʿ to rethink the whole model. Given Ibn al-Muqaffaʿ's emphasis on the elite as the empire-wide enablers of the caliph, one wonders where in the circle of justice he would fit the ulema, whom he saw as unruly, without disturbing the model's theoretical integrity? This question might have given Ibn al-Muqaffaʿ enough reason to put the idea on the back burner on this occasion.

The "Epistle" demonstrates Ibn al-Muqaffaʿ's political optimism. It reflects the scribe's recognition of the empire as a framework of life, its peoples and cultures beyond and above the ruler's ephemeral priorities and rationality. The resolute dedication of its author to address the most fundamental questions of the Abbasid dynasty points to, on the one hand, how this discourse overshadowed the evolution of the caliphate and the potentialities it unleashed.[65] This was an outlet to steer the caliphate in a direction that conformed to established imperial practices in the region. In the aftermath of the Abbasid revolt, when the Umayyad structures, relations, and social order had broken down and multiple directions presented themselves to the ruling family, it remaps in writing (the day after the revolution, so to speak) the inherited topography as a political landscape. It conceives and thus actually constructs the empire in discourse before it materializes on the ground. I do not suggest that ideas about how to administer effectively had not been raised before. What I mean is that the notion of good governance as a separate question from the universals of theology and from the religious notion of justice was being elaborated on its own merit and with the intention of empire building.

What the "Epistle" did therefore was more than just bringing the Abbasids face to face with their predicament or offering them practical information to stabilize their rule. It directed the attention of its readers, whether governors, judges, advisers, or caliph, to conjure up in their imagination a larger political structure above and beyond their own positions in it, and as an entity larger than the collective body of the Muslim community. The "Epistle" brought the practice of governance to the consciousness of its readers and showed them the framework of their lives from an unexpected new angle.[66] It enabled them to reimagine the ulema-centric "house of Islam" as a realm, a polity, a political landscape under the sovereign, that purported to function according to a particular governing rationality. In fact, (the putative) Ibn al-Muqaffaʿ in the *Letter of Tansar* describes the transference of sovereign power to the mundane task of governance (or the proper form of the deployment of the ruler's power) as the rational law of world rulership, "*qānūn-i ʿaql-i jahāndārī*."[67]

The genre of mirror for princes presents a vision that assumes good counsel as the only means to check the overwhelming power of the sovereign. As I have noted at the beginning of this study, what is noteworthy about the "Epistle" is that it distinguishes between the sovereign and government (*mulk/malik* and siyasa) and underlines the value of establishing procedures that add layers between the ruler and his subjects in dispensing power. Still subtle and vague, this distinction potentiates a political space in which different end purposes, "little" life worlds, and little "finalities" that are not determined or controlled by the sovereign, emerge. These guiding structures and principles grounded in the anxiety about getting things right to produce mutual benefit (such as a tax code that is suitable to the farmer, laws to promote predictable and safe living conditions) potentiate additional tasks for the government beyond guaranteeing obedience to the laws of the sovereign for the sake of obedience, as the following chapters will show. Hence, looked at from another vantage point, the "Epistle" governmentalizes the people of the empire by making them the objects of governance. What we are encountering in Ibn al-Muqaffaʿ's political writing is no less than a penetrating intervention in the prevailing sociopolitical ways of his milieu.

The realism of Ibn al-Muqaffaʿ's political analysis and his conceptual orientation strikes any reader familiar with the textual world of the eighth century as a thought-patterning intervention that carved out an imperial social order from the mundane flow of events otherwise made meaningful only in religious discourse. He introduced a political vision that relativized the language of the jurists. Whereas Ibn al-Muqaffaʿ underlined an imperial social order inclusive of, but broader than, religious obligations, the ulema's texts highlighted faith, the community of the faithful, and religious guidance and law as a framework of righteous governance. Ibn al-Muqaffaʿ did not abolish religion from politics, but he distinguished between the jurists' imamate and the lay bureaucrats' siyasa. What therefore makes his "Epistle" more than just the good advice of a scribe is his imagination of government as part of a temporal sociocultural ethos expressed by lay bureaucrats in the new siyasa prose. As an intellectual effort, one leg of his cultural and conceptual compass rested in the caliphate's history and in the late Umayyad–early Abbasid realities. The other leg extended to the imperial traditions of Afro-Eurasia, to the Achaemenid-Sasanian complex in particular. In the following section, I will illustrate the worldly political ethos of the "Epistle" as part of a broader adab-siyasa orientation connected with the Umayyad and Abbasid lay bureaucrats.

The Secular Ethos of Adab-Siyasa

Islam launched a new "social imaginary" and a narrative of life for its followers. One observes that sociopolitical practice under the early caliphs and the Umayyads upheld the values of the conventional wisdom and Islamic piety. The spread and deepening of Islam through proselytizing activities, social incentives, and power structures demanding pious practices allowed for subsuming the values of conventional wisdom under the umbrella of piety, which fostered a value system based on Islamic morality in sociopolitical life. As the empire continued to adhere to Islamic piety and as the moral values of Islam expanded among the ruling elite, nonconforming or dissenting practices were appropriated or modified to be embraced, or they were abandoned as aberrations connected to paganism or impiety. While secular practices continued to exist as long as they did not clash with political priorities and dominant religious practices, the language to discuss life practices became enmeshed with religious morality in tandem with the development of writing and religious scholarship.

However, the transformation of the community into an empire forced the faithful to generate boundaries of resistance against the infringing religiopolitical authority. One facet of the new dialectic was that the consistent credal and salvation claims of the caliphs as guides of the believers and the religious policing of public life incentivized escape from government power and the "orthodoxy" it demanded. Incongruence obtained a "heretical" character: the dissenting voices were branded as heretical and impious, and the dissenters positioned themselves against the orthodoxy, that is, religious views supported by the political power. The emergence, right from the beginning, of multiple Islamic pieties that competed for sociopolitical power exposed each other to critique from within and without, as one observes in the disputes of heresy and nonconformity. The outcome of such developments in the eighth century included both confessional isolation and the growth of secular practices, which resisted the ulema-centric pious morality and way of living.

Another aspect was the secularizing orientation of the caliphs, which included harboring mundane imperial practices and fostering artistic-architectural expressions. As I have noted in chapter 1, the Dome of the Rock and the Qusayr ʿAmra palace in Jordan, for instance, communicate different orientations and sensibilities, reflecting competing forms of devotion and pleasure. Taken as spaces of activity apart from their architectural and artistic value, these structures suggested distinct ways of being and doing, and diverse models of propriety. Neither a temple nor a secular monument, the Dome of the Rock appears to be a commemorative edifice to rehabilitate Jesus as a monotheist prophet through the veneration of both Moses and Muhammad. By the time the Dome of the Rock was built, this spot might have already been revered by the Muslims as the location from which Muhammad ascended to the heavens.[68] As Oleg Grabar argues, its inscriptions and mosaics suggest that the building proclaimed the new faith and empire in the city of the older two traditions of the revealed law, Judaism and Christianity. On the one hand, it recognized and sanctified anew the Jewish sanctuary and incorporated the "restored" memories of Abraham and Jesus, among others, to highlight the new dispensation of monotheism with Muhammad. On the other hand, it set up the crowns of Byzantine and Persian kings as an offering around the center of the monument.[69] It expressed therefore a religiopolitical sentiment that included an announcement of, and invitation to, the new faith and a declaration of the supremacy of the empire protecting and embodying it.[70] One may not be far off to read the monument as a text representing the cycle of paradise, the Judgment Day, and the Resurrection, and thus the imminent fulfilment of God's promise in Jewish, Christian, and Muslim prophecies.[71]

The Qusayr ʿAmra palace complex, on the other hand, is a secular monument dedicated to the use of the Umayyad caliph as a desert post and leisurely dwelling, suggesting interest in mundane pleasures and esthetics. Reflecting on the fresco on the wall of the main hall inside the palace, one gets a new sense of piety and imperial universality not well aligned with the somber message of the Dome of the Rock. The fresco features six rulers, a family of monarchs: Caesar (Qayṣar), Khusrau (Kisra), Roderic (the Visigoth king), the Negus of Ethiopia, and two whose labels are lost, possibly the emperor of China and the Khaqan of the Khazars. They stand next to each other in one room, appropriately dressed and in full control of their gestures, waiting to greet or greeting, as it were, the one absent from the scene, the Umayyad caliph, as if he were receiving their homage. The patron, most likely Yazīd III, was thus making a claim to world rule, as the king of kings among the renowned kings of the time.[72]

Social attitudes and cultural expressions were also part of the dialectic between the religious and the mundane. In this context, citing ʿAbd al-Ḥamīd's attack on the game of chess may prove useful. Analogous to the objections against coffee drinkers in sixteenth-century Cairo or Istanbul,[73] chess in Damascus seems to have become a matter of moral and social concern related to public order for ʿAbd al-Ḥamīd. Otherwise, an *adīb* himself (and in the "secularizing" faction, if one asks al-Jāḥiẓ), ʿAbd al-Ḥamīd takes the hard line here. He portrays the game as an impious, devilish distraction from beneficial work, a senseless waste of time, and a detriment to devoting one's time to prayer in the congregation. According to him, chess is a terrible pastime that keeps those who play day and night away from proper remembrance of God. It erodes their morality and prevents them from pursuing pious acts. Agitated by the spread of this habit, he also condemns it for provoking too much enthusiasm, foul language, and unruly companionship in saloons and gathering places (*al-andiya wa al-majālis*). This textual instance not only reveals the social morality of the "early" ʿAbd al-Ḥamīd but also illustrates the intersectionality of distinct ways of living and the precarity of secularity amid pressuring and infringing practices.

Viewed from the other side, the governmental mechanisms of control, such as the police (*shurṭa*)[74] and the market inspector (*ṣāḥib al-sūq*, later *muḥtasib*)[75] to monitor conduct in social and public spaces, made visible the nonconforming practices, including those associated with secularity. Not satisfied with the measures taken, ʿAbd al-Ḥamīd rushes to criticize the complicity of the ulema and the people of wisdom and of seniority for not resolutely condemning the playing of chess, and asks the authorities in urban centers on behalf of his caliph to ban this practice and pursue those who still continue to indulge in it by taking their names off of the pay register and subjecting them to other punishments.[76] Thus, it is evident that when the hard and soft techniques of control faltered in the usual everyday cycle of life, around the workplace, the temple, and the house, new spaces of activity, such as saloons, markets, bathhouses, and taverns, emerged where new sociocultural moralities shaped distinct ways of living.

Yet another dimension concerns the lay bureaucrats' social ethos of worldly civility, adab. As a concept, a method of training and education, etiquette of behavior, sociopolitical outlook, and a particular taste, adab was central to the political writing of the lay bureaucrats in the circle of Sālim.[77] They helped expand the semantic range of the term from teaching, training, and inculcating proper social manners and civility in the individual to a mundane attitude in life practices and worldly literary production. In the beginning of the eighth century and perhaps earlier, the term "adab" connoted proper training and education; praiseworthy social manners; and, as William E. Lane notes, the rules of discipline to be observed in the exercise of a function, such as that of a judge or governor, and in the exercise of an art, such as that of the disputant, the orator, the poet, or the scribe.[78] In the mid-eighth century onward, it signified gentlemanly, urbane, cultivated, and cosmopolitan social skills and taste and the practice of such skills, as inspired by the mundane concerns of the elite rather than the jurisprudential and theological norms of the ulema. In this sense, adab may have been used together or competed with another term, *ẓarf*, to denote worldly social etiquette or refinement (*ẓarīf*, pl. *ẓurafāʾ*, a person who is refined, even dandy). *Ẓarf* seems to have been in use since late Umayyad times onward to connote a gentlemanly and cosmopolitan manner and mode of conduct as distinct from the forms of pre-Islamic *muruwwa* (manliness, manly virtue) and Islamic piety (*taqwā*, *zuhd*, and *waraʿ*).[79]

To give an example, ʿAbd al-Ḥamīd was a teacher or trainer (*mu'addib*). As fitting in his circumstances, he uses in his writing the word in administrative and political context to mean work discipline or ethics, proper conduct, manners, and propriety. When one reads it in reference to the training and work of scribes and the description of the leadership qualities and the desired manners of the crown prince, one notices a nuance that separates it from what the word for good morals (*khulq*, *akhlāq*) elicits, but one gets no sense of it being recognizably distinct.[80] In Ibn al-Muqaffaʿ's use, the term acquires a political meaning in a discernibly separate sense from good morals and piety (*taqwā*, *waraʿ*). One can hardly read *Al-Adab al-Kabīr*, for instance, without attending to its political relevance. The title *Al-Adab al-Kabīr* here may even signify not the literal "greater adab," meaning the hefty principles of the etiquette of conduct, but "political adab," that is, the adab specific to the ruler and rulership as opposed to that of the common individual.

This topic brings up an interesting point about political virtue. On the one hand, Ibn al-Muqaffaʿ uses the word "adab" in this work to refer to learning, social skills, moral manners, etiquette of conduct, secular interests, and manly virtues. In short, the word connotes a disposition that elicits respect, recognition, and dignity through strictly controlled embodied language (speech, facial expression, clothing, grooming, motion), and a cosmopolitan intellectual refinement. On the other hand, as advice on political virtue, *Al-Adab al-Kabīr* deals with the conduct of the ruler and those serving him. It portrays a sovereign who differs from the one described in the discourse on the imamate by the ulema, which glorifies a ruler who is supposed to be a God-fearing person following the ulema's religious morality. Ibn al-Muqaffaʿ's ruler is concerned with wielding power well after having nurtured a disposition to do so, but the foremost concern of the ulema's imam is to satisfy the requisites of his piety.

The development of writing and scholarship also created spaces of secular expression in literature, sciences, and other mundane subjects as separate from pious practice and legal-theological scholarship. Secular knowledge that combined humanistic and other bodies of learning was neatly expressed in the word *maʿārif*. This term signified pursuing mundane knowledge (arithmetic, medicine, astrology, and ancient knowledge), associated with the translation activities sponsored by the later Umayyad rulers and the Abbasid al-Manṣūr, as separate from the knowledge of the revealed law (*fiqh*, *ḥadīth*, *tafsīr*, and others) from the early-eighth century onward.[81] We also see the term "adab" being used to denote literature in the sense of both the knowledge of and scholarship about any field of learning (grammar, poetry, oratory, artistic prose, administration, rulership, advice, historical knowledge, social relations) not connected to religious disciplines (such as qur'anic studies, exegesis, the study of Prophetic *ḥadīth*, and religious jurisprudence) and the "sciences" (such as astrology, medicine, and others). As a humanistic undertaking, adab in the sense of pursuing literary interests seems to have emerged in the mid-eighth century and spread widely from the beginning of the ninth century onward.[82]

Not unexpectedly, the ulema attempted to restrict the meaning of knowledge (*ʿilm*) to religious disciplines (*al-ʿulūm al-sharʿiyya*) as opposed to mundane or secular knowledge (*maʿārif*) but were challenged by those who pushed back against them.[83] Ibn al-Muqaffaʿ seems to resist the idea of restricting the term *ʿilm* to religious knowledge.[84] In his *Al-Adab al-Kabīr*, he advises his reader to love *ʿilm* and pursue its requirements. When Ibn al-Muqaffaʿ reminds his reader that *ʿilm* is of two kinds, one satisfying utilitarian benefits (*manāfiʿ*) and the other leading to the refinement of the intellect (*tadhkiyat al-ʿaql*), he suggests a notion of knowledge broader than the religious one.[85] Approaching knowledge this way created a dynamic in which the language of mundane learning and governance (*maʿārif*/adab-siyasa) began to split from religious learning and governance (*ʿilm / imāma*), which bothered piety-oriented ulema partly because this new orientation created spaces over which the ulema did not have any authority. For this reason, the debate about the moral and religious value of *ʿilm* outlasted the eighth century, as is nicely articulated from the perspective of a religious sensibility by al-Ghazālī in the eleventh century, who divided *ʿilm* into two moral categories: praiseworthy (*maḥmūd*) knowledge and blameworthy (*madhmūm*) knowledge.[86]

Similarly, adab evokes the notions of worldliness (*dunyawī*), relating to the world and to human rationality (*ʿaql*). Worldliness represented a distinct sensibility from what was thought to institute and be connected to revealed law (*dīn*, *tadayyun*)[87] and sacred law (*sharʿ*), including thoughts, feelings, and practices resulting from and suggesting being religious.[88] The term *dunyā*/*dunyawī* ("the world"/"worldly") in such uses almost always recalls a sense of temporality, near as opposed to far, this present world as opposed to the hereafter (*waqtī*),[89] the natural world as is with no religious value attached to it, and pleasures and wealth related to this world. It also refers to a separation from religion/religiosity (*dīn*/*dīnī*), that is, activity, thought, and attitude with no religious basis or justification and not bound by religious rule, and knowledge or scholarship outside or other than religious fields of knowledge.[90]

The dialectic of religion/world created a productive tension. In a noteworthy moment of calculated nostalgia, Ibn al-Muqaffaʿ remarks in the opening of his *Al-Adab al-Kabīr* that "the religious person (*ṣāḥib al-dīn*) among these ancients was more eloquent about his religion both in knowledge and practice than the religious person of today, as was the worldly person (*ṣāḥib al-dunyā*) similarly better in eloquence and grace."[91] Regardless of what he is referring to, what is remarkable in this statement is the assumption that religious and mundane affairs involve discernibly different rules of engagement. Each demands a way of living not always compatible with the other. Describing the Indians, al-Masʿūdī in the tenth century also uses the word *tadayyun*, for instance, to make this kind of distinction when discussing their wine-drinking habits: "The Indians refrain from drinking wine. They despise its consumption not because of religious sensibility (*lā ʿalā ṭarīq al-tadayyun*), but because they wish to stay clear from bringing on their intellect what would cloud it and take it away."[92]

The tension between the two orientations might have emanated from the idea of the Fall. In the foundational assumption about human beings, the Fall affected a separation that cost the loss of perfect harmony and condemned humans to carrying the burden of balancing both worlds. Remarkably, unlike many of the ulema who downplayed the significance of the distinction and downright condemned the world/worldliness by prioritizing religious piety, the lay bureaucrats spotlighted manners of living and comportments that sought to balance the demands of both worlds by acknowledging the separation. In *Al-Adab al-Kabīr*, Ibn al-Muqaffaʿ has this to say about caring for one's soul and body:

> The basic principle in religion is to believe the faith the right way, avoid grave sins, and fulfill firm religious obligations. Persevere in this as if you were a person who could not afford to be without it even for the duration of the blink of an eye and one who knows that if he is deprived of the thing, he is destroyed. If you can enhance this to the level of acquiring knowledge about religion and worship, then this is better. The basic principle of caring for the body is not to burden it with any food, drink, or sexual activity except what is light. If you can know all the things that benefit and harm the body, and how to benefit from all that, then this is better.[93]

What Ibn al-Muqaffaʿ is hinting at is that caring for one's soul and body requires distinct strategies, knowledge resources, and manners, and that life is about balancing these two sides to cultivate self and guide practice. Just to illustrate how this distinction was always the subject of updating interpretations from various positions, I should quote a later thinker, al-Māwardī, who nicely expresses what I am trying to capture in the eighth century. He would acknowledge this distinction as a reasonable and useful parting of views and manners of acting in his book, if we trust its attribution to him, *Adab al-Dunyā wa al-Dīn*, which may be rendered as *Worldly and Religious Ethics*: "There are two kinds of adab: the adab-shariʿa and the adab-siyasa. The adab of shariʿa satisfies religious obligations and the adab of siyasa makes the earth prosper. Both are connected to justice, which assures the well-being of the rule and the prosperity of the regions. For whoever abandons performing religious obligations harms himself and whoever devastates the earth injures others."[94] Although al-Māwardī, like Ibn al-Muqaffaʿ, seeks to combine the two foci under one umbrella from his own discursive angle, he recognizes the distinction and therefore the range of positions in between. Inspired by al-Māwardī, Ibn al-Ḥaddād in the early thirteenth century in Mosul also restates this core matter in saying that "there are two kinds of politics: governance of religion (*siyāsat al-dīn*) and governance of the world (*siyāsat al-dunyā*). The former leads to the fulfillment of religious obligations and the latter leads to making the earth prosper. Both are connected to justice, which assures the well-being of the sovereign power (*sulṭān*) and the prosperity of the lands (*ʿimārat al-buldān*). For whoever neglects religious obligations harms himself and whoever devastates the earth injures others."[95]

To bring back politics and social positionality of lay bureaucrats to the discussion of worldliness, a stop at the treatise "On Censure of the Ethics of Scribes" by the early ninth-century literary giant and Muʿtazilite apologist al-Jāḥiẓ is useful. Hiding behind his ad hominem attacks on the "scribes," al-Jāḥiẓ was warning against "popular" discursive and embodied practices that were giving birth to worldly, albeit precarious, destabilizing ways of living since the early eighth century. His discussion is exceptional for its clarity concerning the link between worldliness and heresy, nonconformity, religious laxity, cosmopolitan culture, and political ambitions.[96] In a facetious, entertaining, and at times distinctly comedic tone, al-Jāḥiẓ launches a frontal attack on the "scribes" of his time, their morals, and their ways of life as being incongruous with Islamic morality and established norms. Identifying them as a collectivity reaching back to the Umayyad period, al-Jāḥiẓ begins his treatise by condemning the "ignobility of their characters and morals" with directed attacks on some of the most renowned Umayyad and Abbasid scribes, including Sālim, ʿAbd al-Ḥamīd, and Ibn al-Muqaffaʿ.

Among the traits al-Jāḥiẓ mentions to disparage them, irreligiosity, heresy, and moral laxity reign supreme. They are hypocrites, a sinful and impious group who do not conform to the norms of the established religiosity but keep longing for Sasanian values. Even, he fumes, a novice scribe's first display of talent is "an attack on the organization of the Qur'an and a judgment that the sacred book contradicts itself." Clarifying that the novice scribe is only an illustration of the group, al-Jāḥiẓ adds sarcastically that this novice "also shows his cleverness by declaring the reports transmitted from the Prophet false and by disparaging those who have passed on these traditions." The novice's dislike of and irreverence to pious ancestors are so farfetched that "if someone praises to him the Companions of the Prophet he grimaces at their mention and turns away from their merits." He attacks the scribes for not even having the intention of being pious. He claims that "no scribe has ever been seen to make the Qur'an his evening companion, its study his banner, gaining knowledge of the revealed law his emblem, or memorizing reports of the Prophet's words and deeds as his prop."

For al-Jāḥiẓ, the problem concerning them is never a simple negligence or shortcoming; it is a deliberate aversion to a pious life. This attitude, he asserts, was a common trait among them. He continues to list the allegations about their habits: if one of them is observed to mention some matters of piety, the person first would do it awkwardly and with no grace. If anyone among them "chooses to strive to gain knowledge of the Prophet's words and deeds and to occupy himself with references to the books of the scholars of religious jurisprudence, his peers find him tedious, and his friends think him sick." And if a scribe conducts himself that way in earnest, al-Jāḥiẓ resumes, peer pressure to persuade him to do otherwise mounts and thus compels him not to abandon his customary habits or attempt to do something not of his nature or out of character for him.[97]

This giant literary figure continues to denigrate scribes for their eccentricity, snobbishness, and antagonism toward the ulema. He accuses them of looking down on anyone daring to challenge their knowledge, skills, and manners. He claims they belittle even the most luminous of the ulema: "If Shurayḥ[98] is cited, the scribe takes exception to him. If al-Ḥasan[99] is portrayed to him, he finds him tedious. If al-Shaʿbī[100] is described to him, he considers him dull. If Ibn Jubayr[101] is brought up, he calls him ignorant. If al-Nakhāʿī[102] is presented, he belittles him." Instead of seeking the knowledge of the revealed law and expertise in such disciplines, al-Jāḥiẓ claims, even the novice scribe among them prefers to wade in muddy waters, speculating on abrogated or otherwise ambiguous verses in the Qur'an, rather than following the known and conclusive ones, and rejecting reports on the grounds of lack of eyewitness testimony.

Condemning their knowledge, the sources of their knowledge, and their intellectual interests, al-Jāḥiẓ further denounces them for being enchanted by what he characterizes as books of passing value, recent "popular" books, and books on Greek logic.[103] Despite their limited knowledge and slight accomplishments, al-Jāḥiẓ complains, they are full of themselves, excessively ambitious, and greedy. He continues, stating that it does not take much for even a novice scribe among them to believe that he is a great and irreplaceable expert in various branches of knowledge. As soon as a novice can memorize some eloquent catchwords and scholarly anecdotes, quote some maxims of Bozorg Mehr[104] and the *Testament of Ardashīr*, read the epistles of ʿAbd al-Ḥamīd and the siyasa of Ibn al-Muqaffaʿ, make the *Book of Ma[r]dak* the source of his wisdom, and stick to the book of *Kalīla and Dimna* for insights, he thinks he has it all. The novice sees himself qualified to advise the caliph and entitled to a position of responsibility in the administration.[105]

Al-Jāḥiẓ is also apprehensive about and even envious of the cultural capital they mustered. He chastises and disparages the common folk, *al-ʿāmma*, for being enamored of them. Common folk take scribes as models, he laments, admire their literary talents not because they know the scribes or are associated with them but because they are foolish to the degree that they are fascinated by them.[106] Thus concerned about the popularity and consequences of the scribes' work, al-Jāḥiẓ is unsparing about their "true" motivations. Not appreciating, not even acknowledging the work of the great religious scholars and the people of piety, the scribes, he warns, display an unabashed Persophilia and advocate a brazen religious laxity. They are so blatant in their ways that they do not even hide their longing for the times of the Sasanian rule. They prefer to discuss the political strategy of Ardashīr Papakan, the policy of Anūshirvan and the so-called good order of the lands under the Sasanians, al-Jāḥiẓ marvels, instead of informing themselves of the opinions of great religious scholars and pious luminaries.[107]

His characterization of the "ethics of scribes" speaks volumes about the contested claims on agreeable ways of living, of feeling, and of knowing. His treatise helps us understand better the avant garde sociocultural and intellectual position of the "scribes" and the multifarious ways in which secular manners appeared in the early Abbasid world. It displays how varying moral positions generated different knowledge structures, social practices, and cultural moods. It also shows the level and character of the competition among the Abbasid elite over wielding power in governance and informing social practices. Evaluated in the context of our discussion about the lay humanists so far, al-Jāḥiẓ's treatise demonstrates, in fact, the power of their discourses and social practices, which bothered al-Jāḥiẓ. Despite al-Jāḥiẓ's objections, the proponents of the adab-siyasa outlook did indeed harness enough authority to redefine the terms of the debate over sociopolitical life. Only a few decades later, for instance, another giant figure of the ulema, Ibn Qutayba, was bold enough to write his hefty *Etiquette for the Scribe* (*Adab al-Kātib*), as if writing against al-Jāḥiẓ, which attempted to incorporate authoritatively the secretarial profession and its adab-siyasa-oriented outlook into an ulema-centric worldview.

As should be clear by now, both this chapter and the previous one sought to recover, through the biographies and works of ʿAbd al-Ḥamīd and Ibn al-Muqaffaʿ, the questions that this generation of non-ulema intellectuals confronted in their writings. In tracing their biographies, I attempted to illustrate the ingenuity of their critique of the prevailing moral and political assumptions in their lifetimes and elucidate the content of their intellectual production.[108] As we have seen, the lay bureaucrats constructed a discourse that was at peace with the *longue-durée* political and sociocultural traditions of their worlds without dismissing the sociocultural manifestations of Islam (although many criticized the cultural hegemony ethnicized as "Arabic"). Whether translating from Persian or writing in Arabic, they communicated a cosmopolitan world-historical awareness that allowed them to produce a hybrid discourse and cultural orientation away from their own potentially reactionary nativism and the confessional militancy of the ulema. To shed additional light on the groundbreaking nature of their intervention in political thought, the following chapter will discuss the notions of sovereignty and virtue.

5

Deconfessionalizing the Caliph

This chapter elaborates on how Ibn al-Muqaffaᶜ reimagined the caliph, in a patently contradistinctive way to the notion of the caliph in the imamate discourse, as an "independent" sovereign with the political agency that enabled him to face the challenges of his contingency. Carl Schmitt's question (who is the sovereign or who decides?) about sovereignty seems to be appropriate to begin the inquiry.[1] If the ruler cannot decide on the exception, he claims, then sovereignty is meaningless. Ibn al-Muqaffaᶜ would readily agree with the statement. Although his sovereign is the one who decides on the exception, is he above the law? Are there any limits to his will? Could one speak about the sovereign's "obligation"?

An evaluation of sovereignty is followed by a discussion of political virtue. The main question is: How is political virtue conceivable if sovereignty is a gift of God? By reading Ibn al-Muqaffaᶜ's text from the perspective of political virtue, that is the ability of the sovereign to rule not only by self-cultivation to obtain stately skills but also, more fittingly, by practicing good governance beyond the bare task of maintaining his power, I argue that Ibn al-Muqaffaᶜ operated with an understanding of the problem as a dialectic between contingency and agency, which produced a different ruler than the caliph in the imamate discourse.

Sovereign as Beast

In view of the four forms of caliphal authority noted in chapter 1, Ibn al-Muqaffaᶜ's project of creating a "monarch" from the caliph comes into better focus when we pay attention to the notion of sovereignty that is foregrounded in his writing. From the start, both Ibn al-Muqaffaᶜ and his mentor ᶜAbd al-Ḥamīd were discussing a different kind of ruler than the one explained in the imamate texts, although the titles referring to him (the commander of the faithful, imam, or caliph) were the same. In ᶜAbd al-Ḥamīd's and Ibn al-Muqaffaᶜ's use, the word for monarchical sovereignty or kingship, *mulk*, carries a central and constructive meaning. It no longer connotes unrighteous tyranny but a form of divine grace or favor, often signified in the word *niᶜma*, as I will discuss in more detail later in this chapter.

The word "sovereignty," *mulk*, itself precedes Ibn al-Muqaffaᶜ. It had been used in pre-Islamic Arabia, had appeared in the Qur'an, and had been widely circulated among the learned and political elite in the controversies of the Umayyad period. The root *m-l-k* signifies "to possess" and "to dominate." Several verses in the Qur'an mention kingship and king (*mulk*, *malik*) to signify the Egyptian pharaohs and for the stories of Moses and Joseph, which suggest the knowledge of empire forms in the Fertile Crescent.[2] In reference to the ancient Hebrews, a verse describes how the Israelites ask Moses for a king to lead them in warfare,[3] and reminds its audience that David was given a kingdom[4] and the Israelites were made kings over other nations.[5] Except for one verse, "When kings enter a country, they despoil it, and make the noblest of its people its meanest; thus do they behave,"[6] the Qur'an seems to take no particular stance for or against kingship. The qur'anic reference to God's kingship and kingdom, *mulk* and *malakūt*, and governance or decree, *ḥukm*, did not seem to strike its earliest readers as political and legal,[7] but the words king (*malik*) and kingship (*mulk*) came up in Umayyad debates almost always as an accusatory mantra to denounce certain Umayyad practices as anticaliphal, which the pious ruler should avoid if he was sincere in his belief.[8] In the discourse of siyasa, *mulk* becomes a necessary structuring condition of human collective life and gift of divine origin, given only to the ruler to maintain social order.

In his political writing, Ibn al-Muqaffaᶜ uses the concept of sovereign power, sometimes directly and sometimes between the lines, but always as the axis of his political vision. To indicate the sovereign's power, he uses *sulṭān*; for the estate he is controlling, he uses *dawla* ("fortune," "estate") and *wilāya* ("rulership," "reign"), *walī*, *walī al-amr* (pl. *wulāt al-amr*) ("ruler," "caretaker"). When he refers to administrative and military officials who derive their authority from the sovereign, he uses *amīr* ("commander"), *wālī* ("ruler," "governor"), *ra'īs* ("chief," "leader"), and *qā'id* ("military commander"). Ibn al-Muqaffaᶜ does not address the caliph as king (*malik*), although he uses *mulk* ("kingship," "sovereignty," "dominion"), to refer to his patrimonial monarchical authority.

Ibn al-Muqaffaᶜ describes the caliph as "God's trustee" in the world and assumes that sovereignty (*mulk*) is of divine origin, a kind of divine gift, grace, favor, or blessing.[9] In the preamble to the "Epistle," he explains that God preserved the caliph by destroying his enemies, quenching his thirst for vengeance, strengthening his position on earth, and granting (*atāhu*)[10] him its possession (*mulkahā*)[11] and access to its treasures.[12] In his "Letter to the Scribes," ʿAbd al-Ḥamīd also discusses divine favor, *niʿma*, as a gift given only to prophets, messengers, and privileged kings.[13] This privilege of being graced by the divine effulgence[14] elevates the ruler to an ontological category above social ranks and classes, which allows God's absolute power to pass to him (*sulṭān*) so that he governs the people of the earth.[15]

The word *sulṭān* itself had been used in the Qur'an in a theological sense to refer to "absolute evidence to prove something" and to absolute authority. From the Umayyad period onward, its semantic range might have included its Aramaic cognate *sholtan*, denoting "power and authority" in a political sense. Later, this noun was used as an appellation for noncaliphal rulers from the late tenth century onward—the Selçukid rulers used it as their official title in the mid-eleventh century, and it denoted political power based on military strength.[16] But already Ibn al-Muqaffaʿ uses it regarding the absolute authority of the ruler and as the threshold measure of having true sovereign power.[17]

The ruler is given power precisely to control people and establish order on earth so that human life reflects the wisdom of God, which is to do good and become fulfilled, *ṣalāḥ*.[18] Ibn al-Muqaffaʿ begins his "Epistle" by warning against social dissension and oppression in order to make a point about establishing order in the world through the rule of the sovereign.[19] This allusion to producing "public" benefit through the connection between politics and virtue suggests an Aristotelian understanding of politics, which Ibn al-Muqaffaʿ might have become familiar with during his upbringing or through his scholarly and professional contacts in the circle of Sālim, who is credited, as I have noted, with the translation of pseudo-Aristotelian political writings.[20] Attaining virtue or being and doing well, as the purpose of politics, became a major area of focus among later Abbasid philosophers such as al-Fārābī, who discussed various political systems in terms of their potential to lead the city dweller to a virtuous life, or what is sometimes rendered as happiness, *saʿāda*.[21]

Theoretically, the power attained by divine right cannot be circumscribed nor is its holder subject to rules and regulations meant for his subjects.[22] Ibn al-Muqaffaʿ's monarch is touched by the grace of God, like the prophets, which puts him in a separate category from the rest of his subjects. Nonetheless, the following passage illustrates the crucial question that the contradiction between absolute power versus liability poses for ʿAbd al-Ḥamīd and Ibn al-Muqaffaʿ. It is also an insightful portrayal of the distinction between the sovereign of the siyasa and the caliph of the imamate. To explain the scribe's relation with the sovereign, ʿAbd al-Ḥamīd uses the metaphor of the work of the animal trainer. The scribe, ʿAbd al-Ḥamīd asserts, resembles the animal trainer (*sā'is*) who uses the best techniques and strategies (*ḥadhq, ḥīla, adab*) available to him in performing his craft.

> You know that a person who oversees an animal (*bahīma*), if he is skillful in dealing with it, he seeks to know her character. If it is inclined to gallop, he takes precautions with its hind legs. If it is ungovernable, he does not goad it when he is riding it. If it is inclined to kick, he takes precautions with its forelegs. If he fears that it will bite, he takes precautions with its head. If it is restive, he gently subdues its desire to go where it wants to go. If it persists, he pulls it slightly to the side, then loosens its halter. In this description of the trainer of the beast and in the gentleness of his training (siyasa), there is a proof and manner (adab) for him who governs (*sāsa*) the people, interacts with, serves, and associates with them.[23]

ʿAbd al-Ḥamīd's metaphor captures the most crucial aspect of sovereignty in the siyasa discourse: the unique value of sovereign power and its enigma. First appearing in writing in any substantial way in the circle of Sālim and in ʿAbd al-Ḥamīd's letters in particular, the word "siyasa" signifies the work of the sovereign in dealing with his subjects and the work of the scribe responsible for instructing and advising the sovereign through learned techniques of discipline and education. ʿAbd al-Ḥamīd advises the scribe to convince the sovereign to avail himself of counsel, instruction, and education so that he learns the skills to control his impulse and exercise his power with discretion to produce agreeable results. He assumes that one can train the ruler to maintain, enhance, and represent his power through wise action and effective rule.[24] However, he also assumes, a priori, that the ruler can likewise undermine and dishonor the gift of sovereignty by misconduct, mismanagement, and injustice.[25]

Like *tadbīr*, siyasa indicates in the previous passage not top-down command or forceful suppression but reaching the goal of improving conditions (*iṣlāḥ*) by strategizing, by managing with stratagems, mutuality, and consent. However, there is a deeper reason than "educating an uncouth person in proper manners" to explain why the metaphor in the passage mixes animal with human, wild horse with trainer. ʿAbd al-Ḥamīd seems to respond to the question of the untamable quality of power associated with sovereignty. If one cannot force or oblige the sovereign to act in a certain way or dismiss him, how can one stabilize his power and habituate in him a stable temperament that would allow him to govern predictably? How, in short, can one train the wild horse not to kick arbitrarily?

Looking at sovereignty from this angle recalls the question of political meaning in fables. In *The Beast and the Sovereign*, Jacques Derrida provides an illuminating analysis of the similarity and difference between the figures of the beast and the sovereign vis-à-vis the law. Derrida argues that both the beast and the sovereign share the same status because they remain outside the law. Whereas the beast is beneath the law and cannot be a proper subject of the law, the sovereign is above the law or alongside the law and, although responsible for implementing the law, cannot be held accountable to it.[26] In such a context, ʿAbd al-Ḥamīd's siyasa offers a way of convincing or training the sovereign to remain within the law so that he does not act against the very social order he is supposed to uphold.

How to manage the brute power of the sovereign is a central question in Ibn al-Muqaffaʿ's writing too. In his celebrated book of fables, *Kalīla and Dimna*, he provides his readers with one of the most illuminating examples of the new notion of sovereignty. One story is about an animal kingdom ruled by the lion Binkala. A smart, ambitious, but deceitful jackal named Dimna, not content with his own circumstances and wanting more prestige and influence, cozies up to the king to impress him with his wit and intelligence, against the advice of his brother Kalīla. In trying to eliminate his competitor, a bull, who has been the king's faithful companion, Dimna spreads malicious rumors about him. Convinced by what he has heard, the king becomes suspicious and irritated, and kills the bull. Soon after he kills him, however, he realizes that his friend was in fact innocent. The king expresses sorrow, but the offense has been done. Being a fair king, the lion punishes Dimna for his crime of seeking "his own advantage by way of the injury of another." The story ends with the wisdom of "justice served."

Justice is indeed served, but only if one does not problematize the lion's status. Analyzed from the perspective of the sovereign's power and the law, the story sums up the question of the ultimate independence of the sovereign from justice. The lion, having the power, kills the bull because of Dimna's allegations against him, not because of any certainty. Binkala does this wrongfully, as the narrator knows, then realizes his mistake and punishes the jackal for his crime of staging the whole chain of events and in revenge for the innocent bull. Binkala has now committed two acts of murder. Yet he receives not even a reprimand for his malfeasance. The tale lets the lion escape with a sense of regret induced by his own conscience for committing a crime, for having done something wrong, and for having acted out of imprudence. But he faces no legal consequence simply because the lion is the lawgiver who executes the law but is never subject to it. He is the restrainer who is never restrained.[27]

Knowing well that the sovereign's "condemnation" to the solitude of omnipotence can induce erratic impulses and lead him to act beyond convention, Ibn al-Muqaffaᶜ wishes to protect the ruler from undue critique. In his political advisory *Al-Adab al-Kabīr*, he assesses the ruler's status from the perspective of his subjects. In counseling those who intend to accompany the sovereign, he advises that they should not measure matters between themselves and him by what they "know of his moral-standards for moral-standards are annulled with sovereignty."[28] The point here, of course, is not the immorality of the sovereign in commonsense language but that conventional moral standards do not apply to the sovereign because he is above or outside them.

There is another thought-provoking anecdote in *Al-Adab al-Kabīr* in which Ibn al-Muqaffaᶜ reminds the putative ruler that he should not get angry, because he already has power. He should not lie, because no one can force him to do what he does not want. He should not be parsimonious, because he is one of the least people to fear poverty. He should not be hateful, because his power is greater than the pretenses of all people. Nor should he swear oaths, because he does not need to swear oaths.[29] As the anecdote suggests, the craft of siyasa, in the sense of inculcating the desired qualities of leadership in the ruler and advising him on proper action, to encourage him to deploy his power constructively, becomes the only means to restrain the sovereign and bring him within the parameters of social order.

To explicate ᶜAbd al-Ḥamīd's remark on the "trainer" further, let's briefly dwell on the question of representation. If the sovereign is independent but his power must be transformed into a tolerably regular pattern of action for proper governing, the ruler would need a fitting form of representation to project his power beyond the exhibition of crude force. To phrase it as a question, how should one represent the sovereign so that his power or its exercise is effective and agreeable? Ibn al-Muqaffaᶜ seems to ponder the issue, which is a remarkable display of the positional difference between the ulema and Ibn al-Muqaffaᶜ. In his *Al-Adab al-Kabīr*, he alerts his reader to this question:

> As far as earthly life goes, a ruler only needs to make two kinds of decisions: the kind that strengthens (*yuqawwī*) his sovereign power (*sulṭān*) and the kind that embellishes (*yuzayyin*) its image in people's eyes (*nās*). Of the two, the decision made in order to increase his strength (*quwwa*) merits the most consideration. The decision to embellish the image of his power is easier and works best for cultivating many supporters. Although strength comes from embellishment, and embellishment originates in strength, the matter of governance goes back to its basis and its fundamental principles.[30]

This remark is worthy of closer attention for several reasons. It strikes me as recognizably marginal to the political discourse of the time, even to ʿAbd al-Ḥamīd's writing, which, as we have seen, distinguishes itself from the imamate but shies away from "representation." It describes and enables a new practice of rulership that considers politics as a function of relations between the ruler and the ruled and even seems to advocate a "soft" consequentialism. It also seems to distinguish between political power and its representation, where the possibility of "manufacturing" various representations of power becomes integral to politics. Establishing this novel dialectic between political power and its image produces its own technologies of representation in which embellishing one's image—or, stated differently, dressing up the naked power of the sovereign to strengthen and sustain it—is made part of political morality. This is in contradistinction to any notion of an arbitrary exercise of power or the notion of theologically normalized universal truth as an end, regardless of the consequence.

In the imamate's language, with its various versions noted earlier, one assumes compatibility of inner self and outward conduct, between political constitution and practice. This correspondence, or the compatibility, is the crux of moral sincerity because it actualizes and reflects one's character and inner self. This is also true of faith, of course, the minimum threshold of which is sincerity. We should recall that, in the Umayyad period, major political debates about committing a grave sin and the status of the sinner, the definition of hypocrisy, and the nature of faith (whether faith is verbal articulation, inner belief, or both; whether faith increases or decreases) involved precisely the problem of faith and practice and their compatibility, and whether the rightly guided or the Umayyad caliphs had the moral integrity and sincerity to claim legitimate political authority. The caliph of the imamate discourse is expected to embody this kind of sincerity and to function within and according to scriptural guidelines, satisfying his contractual obligation. He would be in varying degrees subject to the scrutiny of his community or of the ulema as the guardians of the faith and the community.

Unlike the circumscribed and derivative power of the "jurisprudential" caliph, who cannot be other than always dressed in a certain garb because of his "contractual" commitment (*bayʿa*), the power of Ibn al-Muqaffaʿ's sovereign lies in establishing norms and instituting laws but does not depend on them. Outside the subject population over which he rules and ontologically isolated from them, he is the unconstrained "beast" who constrains everybody else. Ibn al-Muqaffaʿ's passage thus subverts the notion of compatibility of self and its representation. It decouples the self from its image and allows representation to increase political effectiveness.

Understood in this way, Ibn al-Muqaffaʿ's ruler no longer makes sense within the ulema's vision of the imamate, which, by definition, cannot be other than making the caliph dependent on the community of believers and sacred law. Ibn al-Muqaffaʿ, on the contrary, unshackles the caliph from the "juristic" bonds of the ulema by giving him independence. What is crucial here is that, by intervening from this angle, Ibn al-Muqaffaʿ opens up an intellectual space to discuss the sovereign as a subject of adab and siyasa rather than of theology of the imamate and religious jurisprudence, which aim at cultivating the virtue of pious dutifulness and abstention (*taqwā* and *waraʿ*) as the primary quality of the righteous ruler. The outcome is, of course, an altered political practice.

What Does Siyasa's Caliph Do?

In his *Al-Adab al-Kabīr*, Ibn al-Muqaffaʿ speaks about three kinds of authority as modalities of rule: the authority of revealed law, the authority of strength, and the authority of whimsical temptation. "The authority of revealed law," he says, rests on the fact that "when a revealed law is established for the subject people, it gives them what is important for them and imposes on them what they must do. This makes them content and makes the resentful among them settle down and submit like content people." "The authority of strength" assures "the execution of orders, even if it is met, as sometimes happens, with antagonism and resentment. The antagonism of the weak will never hurt the power of a strong man." Finally, "the authority of whimsical temptation is merely an hour of amusement, and then eternal destruction."[31] In each model, a different political reality is created. In his "Epistle," Ibn al-Muqaffaʿ seems to suggest the first, the sovereignty of revealed law, combined with the second, the authority of strength. He, however, warns the caliph against the third authority. What is remarkable here is both his recognition of religious faith as a social institution that the ruler must consider and his utter utilitarian mobilization of it as an element of social control.

To achieve the intended goal of governing, the sovereign's power must be disciplined, and his singularity must be "translated" into practice. In other words, the sublimity and independence of sovereignty must be bridged into the inter-relational canvas of social order. This is the inflection point of the transcendence of the sovereign and the multiple details of managing relations in the empire, where unrestrained power must be molded into a productive and sustainable form of authority. In this kind of setting, the imperial institutions govern relations and the elite plays the role of the "tongue of the common folk" in the sense of informing the ruler of their conditions and interacting with the subjects to guide them so that they attain in their own way virtuous lives (*ṣalāḥ*).[32]

How does one characterize the political rationality of siyasa and *tadbīr*? Both words cover a range of meanings.[33] They may be described as a particular way of governmentalizing sovereignty (*siyāsat al-mulk*). According to lexicographers, the root verb *dabbara* (from the root *d-b-r, dubur*, "the hindmost," "the end") and the verbal noun *tadbīr* connote cleaning up after something or someone; to do, to manage, direct, administer, govern, take care of something or someone; to act prudently with consideration of the issues or results of affairs and exercising, forecasting, or forethinking by anticipating the outcome; to consider or forecast the matter or results of the affair or event; to look into something, consider it, examine it, or study it repeatedly to understand it. It evokes a sense of devising, planning, or strategizing a thing against another because doing so requires consideration of the issues or results of the affair. One says someone manages, conducts, orders, or regulates the affairs of the provinces or country in this sense.[34] It may have been derived from Aramaic, as in Syriac *dabbar*, "to run, govern, administer something." In the qur'anic text, too, as a corresponding contemporaneous dialogic text, it refers to the power and will to govern (direct, regulate, arrange, manage) the affairs (*yudabbiru al-amr*)[35] and the deliberate and careful reflection, mediating and thinking upon something (*yatadabbar*).[36]

In the eighth-century texts, we see the term *tadbīr* used in the above sense. Ibn al-Muqaffaᶜ uses it in the sense of governance of the empire and in close association with siyasa. The ruling imam, he argues, must be obeyed "in the use of rational judgment (*ra'y*), governance (*tadbīr*), and rule (*amr*), whose bridle God has placed in the hands of the imams."[37] In another place Ibn al-Muqaffaᶜ repeats the same principle that God "relegated other matters of ruling and governance (*al-amr wa al-tadbīr*) to rational judgment, and God gave the right of rational judgment to holders of authority.[38] On another occasion, he uses the word about God in the sense of managing or executing the affair by forecasting or forethinking. In praying for the success of the caliph, he underscores divine omnipotence: "there is no power and no strength save in God. He is the Master of creation, the Holder of power who decides the affairs of people and manages (*yudabbir*) their destiny with great power and preexisting knowledge."[39] Ibn al-Muqaffaᶜ uses the word when he remarks about handling the status of different legal judgments in the past, that "some people manipulate or manage (*yudabbir*) them one way and other people manipulate them another way."[40] *Tadbīr* therefore is about relation, negotiation, process, manipulation of things, and management of affairs rather than having crude power with the autonomy to deploy it whimsically as the privilege of sovereignty.[41]

The verb *sāsā* (from the root *s-w-s*, "to tend," "to manage") and the verbal noun siyasa are used in the sense of managing or tending the animals and training them. Their semiotic chain may extend to biblical Hebrew *sūs* ("horse"). Among Bedouin groups in the Arabian Peninsula, it was used to mean the tending and training of animals; hence the word *sā'is* ("groom," "conductor," "manager," or "trainer"). "Siyasa" connotes ruling or governing the subjects; presiding over their affairs as a commander or governor to command and forbid them, and governing the individual who governs others, and governing self. ʿAbd al-Ḥamīd al-Kātib uses the word "siyasa" in one of his letters to describe it as governing the affairs of the empire and managing the ruler himself. It is thus used in both an active and passive sense, such as ruling and being ruled, commanding and being commanded, disciplining someone and being disciplined. It is also synonymous with *tadbīr*, to signify managing a thing in such a manner as to position it in the right way or bring it to a proper state. In general terms, it is rendered management, statecraft, rule, government, governance, and politics. It seems to have been connected to the ancient idea of the ruler as the shepherd and director of his human flock, and even perhaps also with the idea of the "man on horseback" as a symbol of authority.[42] In the "Epistle," Ibn al-Muqaffaʿ states: "Concerning the subject of this courtly assembly, the *wazīr*s and scribes in charge under the caliphate of the Commander of the Faithful did an exceedingly appalling job, corrupting dignity, decorum, and politics (siyasa), attracting malicious people, and driving away the good ones."[43] In this sense, the word refers to governance, which functions on the basis of mutuality and negotiation, and is linked to reason, discretionary opinion, and civil conduct. From the ninth century onward, the term "siyasa" became a pivotal concept of political discourse outside the strict discussion of the imamate.[44]

I should pause here on the question of managing "affairs" (*amr/umūr*) to make the point about the "Epistle's" worldly tenor on governance from another angle. *Amr* and its plural *umūr* ("affair," "thing," "business," "situation," "command," "rule") is the single most frequently used idiom in the "Epistle." The semiotic chain of the word is long, but it need not consume the discussion here. When Ibn al-Muqaffaʿ uses the word, apart from the instances when he uses it straightforwardly to mean "commanding" (*amara, amīr al-*), it signifies a condition, state or status, affair, thing, dispensing or disposing affairs, governing the affairs, and managing affairs (*waliy al-amr*). Analogous to Michel Foucault's argument about the "government of things," Ibn al-Muqaffaʿ uses the word *amr/umūr* to insert an additional layer into governance, in the sense of getting involved in governance and paying attention to details in governing and in regulating relations, like the artful manipulation of affairs and dispensation of tasks that the words "siyasa" and *tadbīr* connote. Thus, siyasa as an art or a craft goes beyond "taming" the primal impulse of the power holder or the stubbornly focused attention on maintaining power.[45] The sovereign would not only rule but also govern the affairs of humans with other humans and with material things; their transactions and interactions; and the state of their conditions, including their spirituality.

These points concerning power and its representation bring the discussion to the meaning of caliphal titles. Contemporary scholars have already discussed various connotations of the caliphal titles, which illuminate critical aspects of his rule. In the following, however, I will pursue this theme through the theoretical insight of Louis Althusser on ideology by prioritizing practice and doing rather than believing and being.[46] I will shift the axis of my inquiry from what these titles *are* to what they *do* in context to extrapolate some leads on the difference between siyasa's caliph and the imamate's caliph and get a better sense of Ibn al-Muqaffaᶜ's intervention. What does the commander of the faithful do? Given the brevity of the "Epistle," Ibn al-Muqaffaᶜ never attempts to define any of the caliphal appellations but seems to use them in specific ways to construct the sovereign he envisions. Counting the number of times each word related to the sovereign appears in the "Epistle" may be useful. The appellation *amīr al-mu'minīn* appears fifty-seven times, more by far than any other title used in the text. In contrast, the title "imam" and its augmented and nuanced form in the plural (*a'immat al-hudā*) appear twenty times, fifteen of which occur in the specific context of whether the imam should always be obeyed. One appears regarding the "imams of guidance" immediately after Muhammad, another concerns the future imams following the example of the current one, and three other references are related to the need of the common folk (*ᶜāmma*) and the elite (*khāṣṣa*) for a leader. Ibn al-Muqaffaᶜ never uses the titles "the Mahdi" and "God's caliph" for his patron, but he uses "imam." The appellation "God's caliph" (*khalīfat allāh*) appears only once in unspecific plural form (*khalā'if allāh*). The title "caliph" (*khalīfa*, pl. *khulafā'* or *khalā'if*) appears only five times in relation to the companionship related to, and the companions of, the caliph (*ṣuḥbat al-khalīfa, ṣaḥābat al-khalīfa*) and the caliph's "reign" or "office," with no additional qualification and in distinction to another caliph's reign, as in "the *wazīrs* and scribes in charge before the caliphate of the Commander of the Faithful" and "the companionship of the caliph became a laughing matter."[47] Ibn al-Muqaffaᶜ uses the title in a generic sense to refer to the reigning caliph's administrative position but addresses his patron as "the commander of the faithful," as in the following remark: "Despite this, one could find his way and grab what he liked until he was permitted an audience with the caliph, taking precedence before many of the descendants of the Emigrants and the Helpers (Muhājirūn and the

Anṣār) and before the close relatives of the commander of the faithful and the people from the distinguished houses of the nomadic Arabs."[48]

As far as the text is concerned, the appellation "caliph" satisfies a function, but it falls quite short of the glory the Umayyads wished to evoke with it. It seems as if the word conveys, in everyday language, the official position of the sovereign and meets the required threshold of respect in addressing the caliph, but it would not, by itself, dignify the person holding the office in the same way that the titles *al-mahdī*, *khalīfat allāh*, and "imam" would. In the following remark, for instance, Ibn al-Muqaffaᶜ uses *khalīfa* in a minimalist sense, in what appears to be a sweeping criticism of the first two Abbasid caliphs: "So, in authorizing entrance to, and sharing, his company . . . the caliph places a great store on people concerning their noble lineage and prestige and their exploits in war."[49] In contrast, Ibn al-Muqaffaᶜ addresses the caliph consistently with the military title, "the commander of the faithful" (*amīr al-mu'minīn*), to signify his sovereign authority.

In world history, because empires depended on conquest and military strength, their rulers emphasized their military commandership and were addressed by such titles.[50] This was also true for the caliphs, who were expected to lead the efforts to conquer new lands and guard their territories against attacks from outside and insurrections from inside their realm. Indeed, the caliph was addressed as "the commander of the faithful" as soon as military commandership became his principal task. This practice dates to the reign of the second caliph ᶜUmar I (634–644), even during the caliphate of Abū Bakr beginning in 632. It was used for ᶜUthmān (r. 644–656), but documents date it in Muᶜāwiya's reign (r. 660–680). Whether or not the caliphs conquered new territories,[51] military prowess continued to define the caliph as his most prominent quality. By the time the Abbasids came to power, the title had already become indisputably the most obvious sovereign title.[52] The military might of the sovereign was supported by the political economy of the empire and by the discourse of jihad, which organized people and resources to feed military operations.

As a matter of historical practice, the commander of the faithful was expected not only to be of faith but also to lead in it and act on its behalf. The function of the signifier "the believers" in the title changed over the course of time.[53] Initially, it helped to distinguish the conquerors from the pagan Arabs and reflect their religious charge as well. It also marked the difference between the conquerors and the natives of the conquered lands. Moreover, naming the leader this way signified the form of association and organization that the initial Muslim community hoped to establish. Although kinship privilege (such as the appearance of the Qurayshite lineage as a fundamental requirement for leadership almost immediately after the death of the Prophet) asserted itself, the use of the title "the commander of the faithful" suggests a dialectic between the more customary naming conventions based on kinship and the avant garde practice of referring to the caliph primarily by his faith affiliation. The continual use of the title reveals that a sociopolitical imaginary based on religious deeds rather than kinship took hold early, as seen in ʿUmar I's policy of classifying those who were entitled to a pension from the spoils of war according to their seniority in Islam.

When the non-Arab subjects of the empire began converting to Islam, the title became even more representative of the faith community by the sheer fact of prioritizing the faith rather than the kinship or ethnic background of the ruling people. The commander was not of the "Arabs" or "Quraysh," but of the "believers." As the caliphs themselves realized by coming into closer contact with the lands they conquered, their faith affiliation connected them to a rich heritage of monotheistic faiths and empires in the region and enabled them to make greater claims about their roles in world history. Caliphal diplomatic correspondence during the Umayyad period reveals that the caliphs identified themselves as the commanders of the faithful in their foreign correspondence, but they were addressed as kings (of the Saracens) by their fellow emperors.[54]

To grasp the dialogic context of Ibn al-Muqaffaʿ's position and recognize how disruptive his use of titles might have been in his milieu, one needs to remember the circumstances of the Abbasid revolt and the revolutionary army that Abū al-ʿAbbās and al-Manṣūr led.[55] Ibn al-Muqaffaʿ wrote the "Epistle on the Caliph's Privy" when revolutionary and sectarian enthusiasm was still high. Many Abbasid loyalists, including many in the military, were convinced of the salvific powers of the sovereign, as Ibn al-Muqaffaʿ points out.[56] Ibn al-Muqaffaʿ pushes back, in fact overtly, against this revolutionary enthusiasm and the practice of revering the commander of the faithful as a salvific master. His proposal flew in the face of the Abbasid-Shiite self-image and exposed Abbasid messianism as an erroneous cognition when, for many in the military who were supporters of the Abbasid Summons, messianic leadership and esoteric comradery within the Abbasid family were the only reality.

However, Ibn al-Muqaffaʿ's effort to divest the sovereign of esoteric powers originating in a specific divine commission in the manner of a Kaysānite or Shiite imam was not a simple neglect of piety or a reckless irreligiosity. On the contrary, Ibn al-Muqaffaʿ advanced instead a notion of sovereignty with the assumption of a "deconfessionalized" religious morality that endowed the ruler with absolute authority as expressed in two core terms, *sulṭān* and *mulk*, and dissociated him from the ulema's constraints. Making the sovereign parallel to prophets who are handpicked to communicate God's message to people, Ibn al-Muqaffaʿ redefines sovereignty, *mulk*, as a particular form of divine grace or favor (*niʿma*) conferred upon certain individuals to the exclusion of others, who inhabit a plane shared by ordinary people but belonged to a different ontological category. This "absolute" divine bestowal of sovereignty renders the act of ruling over people a sacred calling, far from being a communal affair created to address the needs of the community, which Ibn al-Muqaffaʿ never brings up in any of his discussions.

In his discourse on the army, for instance, the wedge between the two notions of power comes to light. Even in the most critical circumstances, in which Ibn al-Muqaffaʿ cites claims circulating among the soldiers about the miraculous powers of the caliph ("if the Commander of the Faithful were to order the mountains to move, they would move, and if he ordered that the worshippers turn their backs to the *qibla* in prayer, it would be done"), he unequivocally dismisses these claims as baseless and censures them as a cause for disorder and a detriment to the authority of the caliph.[57] While Ibn al-Muqaffaʿ acknowledges the messianic and esoteric enthusiasm among the military commanders and the supporters of the Summons, which had carried the revolt forward, he not only dismisses the practical value of such enthusiasm in political reality but also condemns it.

Building on ʿAbd al-Ḥamīd's elementary "practical" advice on the army for his patron Marwān II but going beyond ʿAbd al-Ḥamīd by theorizing on the subject of creating a "professional" army, Ibn al-Muqaffaʿ suggests issuing a written manual comprising rules and regulations to outline the obligations and authority of army personnel according to rank and function. Conceiving a military outside sectarian concerns and kinship loyalties, he asks the caliph to organize military administration according to this manual to consolidate it formally and regularize how the sovereign interacts with the commanding leaders and soldiers. Ibn al-Muqaffaʿ envisions the caliph as the ultimate commander-in-chief who directs the military's administration through the chain of command and oversees the military's perfection by prioritizing military skill and talent rather than the informality of revolutionary zeal and sectarian discipleship.[58]

Framing caliphal authority outside its esoteric and sectarian semiotics is evident in Ibn al-Muqaffaʿ's use of the appellation "imam," which comes into a better view in his discussion of obedience, as I will examine in more detail in chapter 6.[59] Two points are important to note here: one relates to the caliph's authority and the other to his being a model for and inspiration to the nobility. Ibn al-Muqaffaʿ depicts the caliph as the final authority in decision making and the supreme administrator of his domain who is above the social ranks. The caliph, whether in person or by delegation, appoints his administrators as he wishes, organizes and approves policies, makes and executes laws, sets rules, establishes procedures to maintain social order, acts as the protector of his subjects against infringement and violation, assures the effective operation of the administrative machinery of the empire, and monitors its work. The caliph controls and manages the finances and ensures the collection and distribution of revenues according to his discretion.[60]

In his capacity as imam, the ruler is also the legislator in chief. Ibn al-Muqaffaᶜ's commander of the faithful controls the law by creating, implementing, and enforcing it. Without preempting my discussion of this matter in more detail in chapter 6, I should state how the sovereign functions as a lawgiver. Ibn al-Muqaffaᶜ discusses the exemplarity of the "imams of right guidance" in reference to the caliphs who came before the Umayyads and generically at the time of "the rightly guided imams after the Prophet" to anchor the practice of good governance to long-standing Islamic tradition.[61] He envisions a commander of the faithful who enjoys broad legal powers, one of the most significant of which is legislation. Ibn al-Muqaffaᶜ subsumes lawmaking activity under the caliph's authority and gives him the right to oversee the production of laws and supervise the administration of justice to maintain order. He is unequivocal about demanding unencumbered authority for the caliph in matters involving military operations, collecting and distributing revenue, appointing and dismissing administrators, issuing verdicts made through rational judgment, and carrying out legal sanctions and sentences.[62]

However, Ibn al-Muqaffaᶜ also concedes a point in the field of ritual. While he affirms "that the imam should not be obeyed when he disobeys God, concerns the firm divine obligations and legal sanctions (*ᶜaẓā'im al-farā'iḍ wa al-ḥudūd*) over which God has given no one any authority (*sulṭān*)," he underscores the ruler's sweeping powers that obedience can only be to the imam "in using rational judgment, governance, and rule (*ra'y, tadbīr, amr*), whose bridle God has left in the hands of the imams."[63] He restricts the discretionary power of the sovereign over known rituals and major obligations as outlined in the Qur'an and established in sound practice. By doing so, he decouples on practical grounds political authority from its salvific and esoteric attributes, which results in a check on the sovereign's power and on the power of the sacred law of religion.

While Ibn al-Muqaffaᶜ glorifies and separates the revealed law from the interference of the ruler, he restricts its political role noticeably. He subordinates the religious to the political without authorizing the sovereign to enjoy complete control of it.[64] With this guiding framework, Ibn al-Muqaffaᶜ's commander of the faithful holds the tools to control the law but functions without the privilege of the Shiite imam, God's caliph, and even the Abbasid messianic ruler.[65] One must acknowledge the originality and remarkably destabilizing impact of this approach on its environment. It calls for a restructuring of "religion" (revealed law) in a way that gives the caliph comprehensive authority over one part of it but protects the other part from his interference and allows sacred law (*sharʿ*) to function as a component of a larger sociopolitical structure less burdened by the protocols of the jurists.

To fulfill such tasks, in Ibn al-Muqaffaʿ's vision, the caliph needs functionaries (military and civil servants, advisers, nobles, family members), who have the capacity to transform the sublimated sovereign power to the governance of "little things," *umūr*, that is, institutions, social relations, families, markets, individuals, and others.[66] Visualized as a pyramid, his realm consists of three broad estates: the crown at the top, then below him the aristocracy (or nobility) in the Aristotelian sense, followed by the common folk, with the latter two collectively making up the flock (*raʿiyya*), imperial subjects.[67] The commander of the faithful functions as a leading exemplar, imam to be emulated by the nobility (*khāṣṣa*) whom the masses (*ʿāmma*) follow in pursuing the good and the praiseworthy. He is the axis and anchor of his realm who represents the norm, which the nobility upholds to inhabit the proper manners, prosper, and function among the masses so that they lead dignified and virtuous lives. The sovereign, with the grace of God, according to Ibn al-Muqaffaʿ, gives the elite their credibility and strength to satisfy their duties among the masses, protects them against those who would discredit them, unifies their opinions, and shows them their distinguished place among the masses who look up to the elite to live by the rules of propriety.[68] The commander of the faithful is therefore not merely a ruler. He is the exemplar of virtues, the ultimate model for the elite, and the manifestation of divine grace and power among his subjects, to which I must turn now.

The Dialectic of Sovereignty and Providence

How does one account for "political virtue" or "political agency" where accountability is not a proper criterion and sovereignty is merely a divine beneficence (*niʿma*)? The objectification of sovereignty in governance also poses a question of virtue. This is not just because representation (that is, portraying the ruler one way but not the other) seems to cancel virtue but also because the sovereign power is absolute and therefore not subject to the moral standards of regular humans. I have already noted that, for Ibn al-Muqaffaʿ, sovereignty (*mulk*) is a divine grace. I noted ʿAbd al-Ḥamīd also sees this grace as a special favor bestowed only upon prophets, messengers, and privileged kings.[69] The textual context of the term in the "Epistle" suggests that *niʿma* is a gift more likely given as a favor to someone who perseveres. Like the Hermetic idea in antiquity that consequential visions are divine gifts to deserving individuals, grace or providence also seeks to dignify those who have the potential to rule. However, one cannot gain it by merely seeking it. A divine beneficence, *niʿma* owes its recipient nothing. God can take it away from an individual for no reason. In the preamble and throughout the "Epistle," Ibn al-Muqaffaʿ directs the attention of the caliph again and again to the idea that all power belongs to God, who is the lord of creation, the ruler (*waliy al-amr*) who judges what happens in peoples' lives, and governs their affairs with great power and preexisting knowledge.[70]

Despite this candid acknowledgment of the arbitrariness of divine grace, Ibn al-Muqaffaʿ emphasizes the dialectic between *niʿma* and action. He reminds the caliph of his own diligent efforts to overcome his challenges and underlines how God favored the caliph against his enemies so that he can establish his sovereignty (*mulk*) in the world unhindered.[71] It is God, notes Ibn al-Muqaffaʿ, who maintains the caliph "on the right path and strengthens his authority by granting him protection and a long reign."[72] The *niʿma* is the reassurance to the caliph that God relieved him of the harm of his enemies to allow him to devote his attention to doing good work.

In emphasizing the current felicitous state of al-Manṣūr, Ibn al-Muqaffaʿ referred to various serious challenges the caliph faced until he secured his position. The collapse of the Umayyad system unleashed new rivalries. Abū al-ʿAbbās and Abū Jaʿfar needed to establish a new status quo. The Qaysī tribes refused to accept the new regime and openly rebelled. Some of the Khurasanis, those military soldiers and militia from Khurasan who had made up the Abbasid army, became wary of the growing power of the dynasty and of having to share their power with other groups.[73] Each of the three powerful stakeholders, Abū Jaʿfar, ʿAbdallāh b. ʿAlī, and Abū Muslim, began maneuvering to secure his interests and outmaneuver his rivals. None seemed convinced that the revolt had ended. When al-Manṣūr succeeded as caliph, Abū Muslim was still the independent ruler of Khurasan, commanding the Khurasanis, and he established deep roots there in the name of the Abbasid Summons. The caliph's uncle, ʿAbdallāh b. ʿAlī, the veteran commander of the battle that Marwān lost at the Zab River, was also a powerful governor general of Syria, with support from the Khurasanis and the Qaysī faction. When al-Manṣūr's political maneuvering and attempt to pit these two rivals against each other did not produce the expected outcome, the rivalry became an open military confrontation between the caliph and his two challengers. A new status quo emerged only after the military defeat of ʿAbdallāh b. ʿAlī and Abū Muslim. The former renounced his claims after being defeated by al-Manṣūr and lived in virtual captivity. Abū Muslim was killed in an ambush by order of the caliph, who then went on to reconcile his leading supporters.

Knowing these challenges, Ibn al-Muqaffaʿ makes his point about the connection between divine grace, the capacity to face challenges, and the magnanimity of returning the favor through judicious conduct. On the few occasions where Ibn al-Muqaffaʿ paraphrases qur'anic verses, at the beginning of the text in the same section where he discusses how God favored the caliph against his enemies, he mentions the story of Joseph's perseverance. He makes his point about both sovereignty and grace and suggests how facing challenges might be part of the attribute of those whom God chooses for leadership. Just like Joseph, the caliph must rise to the occasion. "When God's grace (*niʿmat allāh*) was conferred upon him and God gave him sovereign authority (*mulk*) and taught him something from the interpretation of visions, ordered his affairs, and brought him joy by reuniting him with his parents and his brothers," Ibn al-Muqaffaʿ encourages the caliph that Joseph "praised God, Most Exalted Glorified, for His grace, and then thought no more of his plight, and knew[74] that death and the afterlife were preferable."[75] In this anecdote, God bestows His grace on someone who has struggled to overcome his plight and who reciprocates with appropriate diligence and action to honor the divine favor.

To avoid speaking about *niʿma* only in the semiotic context of its religious background as God's beneficence or grace, I should point out that the term also connotes the sense of comfort, softness, happiness, and delight, like a pleasant wind.[76] It refers to chance associated with stars and time, and the fortuitous cloud at the peak of a mountain that shadows the ground from the heat of the sun, the lavishness and evanescence of owning cattle, and the alertness of ostriches (*naʿāma*) to their surroundings and the manner of their fleeing when scared.[77] The *niʿma* signifies therefore divine favor, luck, munificence, comfort, and the sense of precarity. Pondered in this larger context of feeling and meaning, the term belongs to a semiotic chain that grounds its signification in two lineages, which are molded together in Ibn al-Muqaffaʿ's discourse.

One lineage branches off from the Islamic and monotheistic notion of divine grace, which was part of political vocabulary since the early caliphate, as elaborated by the ulema. The other one extends wider, like its cognate word, *dawla*, to a terminology associated with the older notions of grace, luck, beauty, fortune, and gift from above, as found in Southwest Asia and the Mediterranean, including the Persian *khvarana/khwarra* and *farr*;[78] the Indo-European *khar*, *kharis* (*kharisma*); and the Greco-Roman *Fortuna* in the semiotic chain.[79] In the Persian notion of divine glory or splendor, for instance, favor is expressed in *khvarana/khwarra* or *khvarra* and divine light or divine effulgence in *farr-i īzadī*. Mary Boyce elucidates the semiotic range of the concept in pagan Iran, where the deity Ashi appears to represent the good fortune that anyone might experience through luck (and due sacrifices), with the term *khvarana/khwarra*, which signifies divine grace that descends on those favored by the gods, endowing them with exceptional power and prosperity.[80] Kings and heroes obtain fame and splendor through *khvarana/khwarra* until it leaves them, changing their state from fame and glory to that of loss and misery.[81]

Although Ibn al-Muqaffaʿ does not deal with this topic as a theoretical problem, his discourse on sovereignty rests on the assumption of *niʿma* and its cognates as a new polyphonic register of political fortune connected discernibly to these two separate genealogies. The word appeals to Islamic religious morality as divine grace or providence without appearing confined to the forms of grace constructed by the jurists and other sectarian ulema. In his use, the concept recalls instead the older notions of fortune and glory in the sense of divine grace unrestricted by or unrelated to the limitations of religious legal norms or religious piety. Such a notion of divine favor puts Ibn al-Muqaffaʿ at odds with the ulema's approach to rulership, in which the ruler's authority is rendered "weak." In the texts of the imamate that we have examined, rulership simply represents a vehicle to implement God's laws and ensure the prescribed righteous living. Al-ʿAnbarī, for instance, speaks of organizing people according to a system of righteous living explained in religious texts and practices, and portrays true happiness as the actualization of the rules and regulations in the scripture, where political authority remains extraneous to the dynamics of religiously righteous living. The late Umayyad caliphs also emphasized their divine right to rule. They described themselves, or were touted thus by loyal poets, scribes, scholars, and other kinds of devotees, as God's caliphs, the trustees of God, the mine of kingship, and the locus of governance and leadership (*khalīfat allāh, amīn allāh, maʿdan al-mulk, maqarr al-siyāsa wa al-riʾāsa*) and claimed messianic prerogatives as Mahdis. The power assumed in these appellations entitled them to conquer the world, restore faith, and establish universal justice before the end of time.[82] Viewed from the perspective of the imamate discourse, however, even their claims to divine favor constrained their political authority by pegging it to religious obligations.[83]

Thus, the shared use of the term *niʿma* is not about producing a binary or dichotomy between the religious and secular senses of the term but about suggesting a new political orientation, a counterpoint to the religious framing of the term. Whereas in the former, the caliph's authority or the presence of the divine grace is judged and validated by the degree to which the caliph's actions are compatible with and in compliance to scriptural, doctrinal, and jurisprudential imperatives, in the latter, divine favor itself, by its sheer bestowal and presence as power, authorizes agency and acts as a structuring principle, according to which a stately morality is built.

As is apparent in Ibn al-Muqaffaʿ's proposal on the law, the sovereign is supposed to observe religious obligations, but he is not bound to the jurisprudential religiosity's prescriptions or to observing common pious morality. The siyasa's *niʿma* demands that the sovereign honor religious priorities and pious morality, but political success is not solely about or satisfied by them. The *niʿma* is concerned with political practice or action that allows only a restricted role to religious morality in governance.[84] As such, it results in a reduction of the role of the ulema's prescribed religiosity in public matters and requires the sovereign to act beyond the constraints of sacred law in meeting his challenges.[85]

Ibn al-Muqaffaʿ communicates a similar sense of grace or favor in his use of *dawla*. The word *dawla* ("state," "turn of fortune," "turnaround," "to alternate"/"alternation," "victory," "reign," "rule") was associated with the fortune of the Abbasids after they defeated the Umayyads. It described the state of being victorious and assuming rulership after the success of their Summons (*daʿwa*), which emphasized the deliberate struggle toward acquiring political leadership. *Dawla* thus comes after *daʿwa*. Ibn al-Muqaffaʿ uses *dawla*, in the sense of "reign" or "rule" and even "the rule of the Abbasid family" by fortune, in the following statement as an indefinite noun: "Then this 'fortuitous state' (*dawla*) was established" or "then there was this 'fortuitous state.' "[86] In his discussion of unidentified recent rulers or governors, he uses the word in the sense of a downturn in affairs, alternation, degeneration of affairs akin to corruption: "the case of assistants by whom the rulers are afflicted[87] and who, although they do not help the rulers do good, cannot be removed by the ruler because of their influential position and because of the fear of a possible reversal (*dawl*) and corruption (*fasād*) if he troubles them or reduces[88] what they have in their hands."[89] *Dawla* carries, then, an element of luck or chance similar to the word *dāʾira* (turn, circle, contour, calamity), which conveys the sense of alternating turns not fully calculable or predictable, like the wheel of fortune. He uses the word in this sense in the following statement to express a wish of good fortune in an active military confrontation: "the turnabout will be in favor of the commander of the faithful (*al-dāʾira li-amīr al-muʾminīn*)."[90]

Ibn al-Muqaffaʿ tries to make sense of "history" as a continuum with a trajectory, which may be manipulated by taking initiative. "Turnabout" and the shift of "fortuitous state" may occur following a pattern in the mundane flow of time. In his *Yatīma*, Ibn al-Muqaffaʿ (if he wrote it) makes an interesting observation about time, rulership, and virtue. Beginning with the rhetorical question of "what is time?" he gives a thoroughly political answer. "Time is certainly the people. And the people are only two categories of men: the ruler and the ruled. And the times are four kinds, depending on the conditions of the people." He then states each one of them: "The best time is the one that combines a virtuous ruler with virtuous subjects. . . . Then comes the time in which the ruler himself is virtuous but his subjects are corrupt. . . . The third time is when his subjects are virtuous, but the ruler is corrupt. . . . And the worst time is the one that combines the ruler and his subjects in corruption."[91] In this passage, assuming that the desired "time" is the first one and epochs differ from each other, he seems to suppose a transition from one "time" to another not necessarily in any order but because of the ruler's and his subjects' action. This idea of epochs, analogous to the theme of the turn of fortune and misfortune, which is also a matter of concern in his other work *Kalīla and Dimna*,[92] presupposes an agency beyond the absolute arbitrariness of providence and fortune.[93] Likewise, when Ibn al-Muqaffaʿ reminds the caliph in the "Epistle" how God delivered him victorious against his enemies just like Joseph, he praises him for rising to the occasion by showing his gratitude in the form of moral conduct and by being prudent in his governance.

For this reason, *niʿma* is not utterly inexplicable. While there is still a point in arguing that divine grace as God's will renders political virtue (and communal justification of power or legitimacy) mute, my argument is that "divine favor" in Ibn al-Muqaffaʿ's use allows a form of human agency and the will to fight against threats. Even if *niʿma* or *dawla* explains, without itself needing an explanation, why a particular person but not another is granted favor, it also demands that the ruler act. A diligent ruler is one who organizes mundane life and governs (*tadbīr* and siyasa) prudently by leading his subjects to a good life, similar to how prophets organize and improve peoples' spiritual lives, to reciprocate with the privilege of receiving divine grace.[94] The siyasa's *niʿma* demands, therefore, qualities similar to those praised in the notions of *khvarana/khwarra* and fortune, especially the aptitude of agency to manipulate circumstances.

Rational Judgment as Political Virtue

Viewed in this way, as Louis Althusser and Quentin Skinner elaborate about fortune and virtue in their studies of Machiavelli,[95] Ibn al-Muqaffaʿ's stance lends itself to an analysis from the angle of the dialectic between *niʿma/dawla* and *tadbīr*/siyasa as expressions of agency and virtue. Problematized as history or contingency, *niʿma* is a substitute or metaphor for the challenge the sovereign must always confront. The unpredictable nature of the challenge forces the sovereign to act by always evaluating his circumstances, mitigating problems, proactively warding off dangers—in short, governing prudently lest the *niʿma* withdraw from him. Virtue in this scenario is nothing other than the political agency of the sovereign in facing the contingencies of history.[96]

Ibn al-Muqaffaᶜ uses multiple signifiers, clustered together in the preamble of the "Epistle" and in other places in the text, to indicate the stately conduct and manners of the caliph. They include making a firm determination (*ḥazm*); to determine upon something (*hamm*); resolve, determination, deciding upon something (*ᶜazm*); rational judgment (*ra'y*); industriousness, agility (*nashāṭ*); to fix, improve, and make better or more complete (*ṣulḥ, iṣlāḥ, istiṣlāḥ*);[97] striving to obtain something (*ṭamaᶜ*); merit, superiority (*faḍl*); to labor, to make, to act (*ᶜamal*).[98] One among them, *ra'y*, commonly defined as "discretionary opinion," "rational judgment," or "independent opinion," presupposes all of the aforementioned qualities of agency and seems to be more pertinent as a distinct political virtue. The word is used in the text in a range of broad commonsense and politically perceptive ways, including "vision," "perspective," "sound opinion," "sagacity," "perspicacity," and "considered judgment."

The virtue of exercising *ra'y*—that is, to take proper action based on rational judgment—is the site of political astuteness. *Ra'y* in this sense is not just an erudite opinion but also a performative locution, a speech-act through which the ruler executes his will. Ibn al-Muqaffaᶜ uses the term primarily in the sense of the political discretion of the ruler for what is good for leadership. Rational judgment is a sagacious way of dealing with subjects.[99] It is also a virtue whose holders the ruler should seek and encourage.[100] In the preamble of the "Epistle," Ibn al-Muqaffaᶜ praises the caliph for possessing the commendable trait of encouraging the person of sound opinion (*dhū al-ra'y*) to offer useful information[101] or point of view to advise him on a course of action in a positive direction. He also uses it in the sense of knowledge or knowledge produced through diligent work (*iᶜmāl al-ra'y*) to fulfill a task at hand and a spiritual insight or inspiration to arrive at a perspicacious judgment.[102] It is a quality that encourages the caliph to listen to skillful, learned individuals with specialized knowledge of statecraft, scribes, and the established nobility to make decisions and govern with confidence,[103] as the passage below illustrates:

> God has done for the Commander of the Faithful the nicest favor by removing those who would associate themselves with his authority, but with a manner and opinion (*ra'y*) different from his until God put him at ease, and He secured him from their misdeeds thanks to proof of their guilt and reasons which they had accumulated against themselves and thanks to the strength God has bestowed upon the Commander of the Faithful to act with sound judgment (*ra'y*) and regard to divine satisfaction. God humbled his subjects to the Commander of the Faithful by combining in him leniency and mercifulness. If he shows leniency to anyone . . .[104] it neither comes from weakness

> nor from an expectation of flattery. And if he is harsh with anyone . . . such an attitude comes from neither a tendency toward violence nor an unreasoned transgression.[105]

The term "rational judgment" therefore signifies much more than a casual sense of giving advice or articulating an opinion. As a privilege of the sovereign, *ra'y* signifies practical knowledge that the ruler uses to govern effectively; political discretion and insight leading to good governance beyond maintaining crude power; and successful leadership, which is the virtue itself. It is a virtue related to the political rationality of decision making and in fact to the underlying logic of governance and politics, *tadbīr* and siyasa, which informs the modus operandi of the ruler and his associates. As governance must follow the requirements of sound opinion, proper governance cannot be an arbitrary or tyrannical domination in which predictable, reasonable, and bearable action is not expected. Because rational judgment is also a measured response to contingency, it stands distinct from the doctrinal pronouncements of the jurists (and sectarian enthusiasts), which may not be pertinent to the circumstance.

In keeping with this logic, one infers that, while sovereignty may be conferred on an individual because of courage, routine succession conventions, or military victory,[106] the chance of preserving and maintaining it depends on the ruler's ability to act. Ibn al-Muqaffaʿ reminds the caliph that God has secured him from the misdeeds of those associates of his who conspired against him and that, thanks to the caliph's sound judgment and determination to act, God has humbled his subjects to him.[107] One surmises therefore that the least the sovereign can do is to embody a stately disposition commensurate with the grace of sovereignty, which sums up the virtue. In praising the caliph, Ibn al-Muqaffaʿ notes that God has cleansed the caliph of disagreeable characteristics and has given him leadership qualities (insight, good intentions, prowess, and determination), and moral values to anchor them (regard for divine satisfaction, leniency, and mercifulness), so much so that even the ignorant among the people, let alone the knowledgeable, observe these qualities in his conduct.[108] In summary, if divine grace can be managed and honored at all, it is done through the ruler's judicious actions rather than through religious piety alone.

To further explicate the distinction between religious piety and prudent action that I have argued, I should pose the following question: How can the sovereign deal with, mitigate, or manage the *niʿma*, so that he causes it to not withdraw from him? It is a crucial aspect of Ibn al-Muqaffaʿ's *niʿma* that, unlike the pietistic and mystical notion of grace, it operates dialectically with effective rule. In the preamble of the "Epistle," Ibn al-Muqaffaʿ's prayers for the caliph suggest a complex interpenetration of agency, divine will, grace, and the slippery political space in which the sovereign must operate. As I have noted, it is God, Ibn al-Muqaffaᶜ says, who made the caliph virtuous and conferred upon him the favor (*niᶜma*) of shining with a praiseworthy disposition. He reiterates that the sovereign must be alert to the challenges he faces by weighing his actions and enlisting the assistance of his advisers.[109] Although the ruler may not be able to control the *niᶜma*'s course completely, he can still act according to its requirements to enable a "negotiation" between his conduct and providence to prolong his rule.[110]

Constituted thus, *niᶜma* requires the exercise of authority with prudence and without the unreasonable use of brute force. The proper response to the gift of divine grace requires a particular stately temperament, a calculated response to contingency. The sovereign must always be on alert and nimble. In a poetical and suggestive statement, Ibn al-Muqaffaᶜ reminds the caliph of the risk involved in not being energetic: "Thus, along with ambition comes effort and along with despair comes relinquishment of hope.[111] Seldom does hope decrease without the ease of life departing as well. The demand of a despairing man is feebleness while that of a man of ambition is firm decision."[112] Therefore, the ruler should seek political virtue in firmness of decision and right action rather than relying on providence. It does not escape the reader that, although Ibn al-Muqaffaᶜ presumes no tension between a proper stately posture and leniency or mercifulness, he is aware of the risk of appearing either weak or brutish. An effective ruler does not rely on naked violence in matters of governance but governs firmly without being brutish and shows mercy without appearing weak. "If he shows leniency to anyone," Ibn al-Muqaffaᶜ commends the caliph, "it neither comes from weakness nor from an expectation of flattery." If he is harsh with anyone, "such an attitude comes from neither a tendency toward violence nor an unreasoned transgression."[113] A prudent sovereign therefore needs to balance firmness and determination with tenderness and magnanimity in action similar to Joseph's behavior during and after his plight[114] but not lose sight of his dependence on strength, as Ibn al-Muqaffaᶜ reminds the caliph concerning the defeat of his enemies.[115]

Although the favor may not obey one's desires even if one shows the proper gratitude, it may still be dialectically related to the sovereign's political astuteness and personal merit, including good character traits and intelligence. Regarding the qur'anic passage discussing Joseph's predicament and his exemplary gratitude for God's favor, Ibn al-Muqaffaᶜ advises and cautions his sovereign that providence is honored best with the practice of virtue.[116] What makes a sovereign effective should therefore be sought in acting in political terms by reasoning and soliciting opinions, examining matters, making choices based on inquiry, and being firm in decisions. This is pleasing to God and is a reason for divine favor.[117] In his praise of the caliph, Ibn al-Muqaffaʿ makes the point about coordinating good morals with effective action as the preferred virtue the sovereign should seek. "How honorable it is,"[118] he affirms, "for these items to be means for every great accomplishment of good deed which is judged meritorious in this world and the hereafter, today and tomorrow, for the elite and the masses."[119]

No matter how hard the ruler tries, divine grace can still be taken away. Unlike *Fortuna*, which carries whimsical impulse, the force of luck here is endowed with the power of immediate or postponed reckoning. The *niʿma* can wait patiently to strike. Ibn al-Muqaffaʿ implies this aspect of the *niʿma* repeatedly, with or without using the word. *Niʿma* could be withdrawn for reasons of sudden death, sickness, or military defeat as well as the vices of incompetence, ingratitude, negligence, maladministration, oppression, and tyranny. Instead of speculating about the *niʿma*'s withdrawal, he foregrounds the causes that may hasten political failure such as maladministration rather than pious shortcomings. Ibn al-Muqaffaʿ makes his points by commending the caliph for his good actions, reminding him of the work to be done, and condemning the Umayyad rulers for their transgressions. Unlike the caliph, "the evil Umayyad rulers," he declares, "used to combine with their ignorance, vanity and self-indulgence." Regardless of how many correct and authoritative opinions or pieces of information they received, they chose to pursue baseless arguments.[120] He warns the caliph that when the Umayyads and the enemies of the caliph had chosen the path of arrogance and self-indulgence, they prompted their defeat and ruin.

If virtue is necessary for effective rule and for meeting the demands of *niʿma*, proper handling of administration is part of it. To succeed, the ruler needs to nurture the essential qualities of leadership: determination and ambition. Ibn al-Muqaffaʿ praises the caliph as a good and effective ruler who has an inquisitive mind, listens to others, conducts himself with decorum despite enjoying the rank of royal dignity, gives more thought and consideration to his subjects than to his own family, and explains his actions to those who are subjected to them.[121] The caliph, Ibn al-Muqaffaʿ commends (and instructs) his patron, shows due diligence in supervising his subordinates but, at the same time, does not spare effort to coordinate and collaborate with them in dispensing their duties so that he can avoid missteps leading to failure or, worse, descending into tyranny. The caliph, Ibn al-Muqaffaʿ notes, works industriously for the prosperity of his community (*umma*). He appears more concerned with the welfare of his subjects and with what improves[122] their condition in his dominion (*sulṭān*) than some of his governors.[123]

It follows that the sovereign must have the power to act. There is an inherent link between sovereignty, virtue, and obedience. Ibn al-Muqaffaʿ dwells on the question of obedience at some length to shore up an absolutism that, except for the practice of religious rituals and carefully delineated religious legal sanctions, concentrates authority in the sovereign. But, again, if obedience is all there is to be concerned about, what is the difference between a tyrant and good sovereign? Here Ibn al-Muqaffaʿ produces political virtue not from the obedience of subjects compelled by brute force but from the consensual obedience of people satisfied by good governance. Ibn al-Muqaffaʿ engages this question against the background of some of the most enduring debates in the eighth century among the proponents of various sectarian theological groups, who, as we have seen, wanted to effect change in the post-revolt circumstances.

I have already argued how the problem of obedience to the ruler came to the forefront of discussion concerning sociopolitical organization and communal self-image after the death of Muhammad. In the eighth century, the questions of coercion, of the right to exercise power, of the duty to obey the holders of authority, and of who controls the revealed law became hallmarks of theological and political debates as the faith and the empire grew. First, as I have discussed in chapter 2, the Umayyads and their allies adhered to and even promoted predestinarian ideas to demand unfettered obedience to the will of God. The idea of personal responsibility and free will became a common conviction among many of those who opposed the Umayyad caliphs. By Ibn al-Muqaffaʿ's time, many religiopolitical sects, including the Kharijites and the Qadarites, and many jurists had been advocating free will and rejecting the idea of wholesale obedience. They raised the slogan of "no obedience to anyone in disobedience to God" to check caliphal authority and underscored the ability of the faithful to engage the revealed law as their inalienable right. Second, the Shiite arguments, especially the one by the Kaysānites and other maximalist groups regarding the authority of the imam being spiritual, esoteric, and legislative, extending beyond just governing a realm, continued to stir heated debates among the concerned. Ibn al-Muqaffaʿ launched his discourse on obedience from the perspective of the sovereign's authority against the background of the various positions on free will and obedience in the eighth century.[124]

Ibn al-Muqaffaʿ addressed the question of when one must or must not obey the caliph (referred to as the imam in the "Epistle") in such a discursive and political context. He first introduced this topic in his discussion of the army, and then brought it up later concerning legislative authority of the caliph.[125] Unexpected as it may sound, Ibn al-Muqaffaʿ downplayed the esoteric and sectarian overtones of the title (such as the notion of infallibility [*ʿiṣma*] in the Kaysānite idea of the imamate) to underscore instead a notion of moral and legislative authority better understood in the context of divine grace (*niʿma*, *dawla*). Ibn al-Muqaffaʿ presents a ruling imam who governs his realm absolutely and functions as the legislator in chief and moral guide but is not entirely like the Kaysānite imam who enjoyed spiritual authority, which overlapped with the prophetic one and was therefore not the subject of obedience and disobedience.

His argument against unconditional obedience to the caliph in his discussion of obedience and the law, as I will examine in chapter 7, is instructive because it makes the idea of legitimate political dissent possible by pointing to the value of consent. Obviously, Ibn al-Muqaffaᶜ's political vocabulary does not have the words to describe dissent as one would today, but he notices that disagreement does not always have to emanate from a flaw in character or from heretical intent, although both may be plausible reasons. It might also result from taking different moral positions on affairs about which the sovereign may be at fault or his policies inefficient. About the discontent of the Syrians who were defeated in the civil war, for instance, Ibn al-Muqaffaᶜ explains to his patron that the outbursts that are feared from the Syrians could be prevented if the people of Syria were treated justly. To elevate the discussion to a reasonable discursive level rather than confine it to outburst of an unruly people who deserve punishment, he even theorizes that "sovereignty (*mulk*) does not leave a people without also leaving behind resentment, which causes them to become agitated, but this agitation ultimately causes their suppression and removal."[126] What I am suggesting is that, considered as a question essential to politics rather than as a contingency, the negotiation of dissent becomes, in Ibn al-Muqaffaᶜ's approach, part of political virtue and a sign of good governance.

In analyzing Ibn al-Muqaffaᶜ's text, I have illustrated how in Ibn al-Muqaffaᶜ's use, the word *niᶜma* is connected to the semiotic chain of both siyasa and imamate. The crucial aspect of the new political morality is that it differs from the charge of the imamate, which privileges the sovereign to function as representative of the divine and thus remains morally immune to the consequences of contingency as long as theological obligations are satisfied. In imamate discourse, the sovereign's success or failure is not a result of his practice as ruler but of the proper execution of sacred law and the practice of individual piety *regardless* of outcome. In siyasa discourse, however, the ruler can hope to enlist the company of the *niᶜma* or *dawla* only by facing the contingency in a stately manner through procuring the political astuteness required for governing and maintaining an effective administration.

I have also elucidated how the notion of sovereignty in siyasa granted the ruler ultimate independence. Someone accustomed to the argument in the imamate discourse would be startled by hearing a statement on the independence of the sovereign. Notwithstanding the idea that the ruler of the imamate discourse derived his authority from God through various modalities, as noted, the way he dispenses it is restricted by the scripture and the community. Sālim b.

Dhakwān would never agree with Schmitt nor would al-ʿAnbarī or Abū Yūsuf if one pressed them to the limit. This is because they would not know what to do with the scripture, the community, and the associated "republican" practices of contractual governance if they affirmed Ibn al-Muqaffaʿ's logic.

To conclude, Ibn al-Muqaffaʿ's intellectual experiment with political virtue tapped into two traditions. One tradition extended to the early caliphal practice in the seventh century and expressed religious piety associated with the semiotic range of *taqwā*, which is evident in the texts of the ulema we have discussed. The other one was connected to the avant garde adab-siyasa ethos associated with a broader, deconfessionalized ethos of proper conduct that took contingency and responding to it through rational judgment into account. The idea of sovereignty in siyasa facilitated a space to acquire virtue through political astuteness in facing the contingency rather than religious piety. In the following chapter, I will discuss one of the critical questions in the "Epistle on the Caliph's Privy" on good governance and political virtue—the law as an inalienable function and prerogative of the sovereign.

6

A Theory of Imperial Law

Controlling legislation and law occupies a substantial portion of the "Epistle on the Caliph's Privy." Ibn al-Muqaffaʿ's discourse on law is directed at creating a social order intended to function according to the rules and regulations of a monarchy. As with other institutions and regulations in the empire, the law for Ibn al-Muqaffaʿ was also a mechanism to translate brute force into legitimate power, a modality to normalize control and reshape existing power relations by channeling loyalty in public matters to political power and toward the ruler. If the sovereign's power could be governmentalized in law, it would gain the authority to demand compliance from his subjects so that they obeyed orders in a normalized and routine fashion. At the same time, it would restrain the jurists (and other ulema) who, by compelling the faithful to submit to their guidelines, might divert the loyalty of the governed from the ruler and encourage resistance to his power. In other words, Ibn al-Muqaffaʿ intervened with a game-changing epistemological position in his legal proposal to more than control the revealed law (*dīn*) or curb the autonomy of the jurists vis-à-vis that of the caliph, but instead to create a law that was imperial rather than religious, thus reducing the religious law of the ulema to just a legal body, among others, and the ulema themselves to functionaries in their capacity as legal/religious experts.

One may express this tension as a conflict between "religion" and "politics." While Ibn al-Muqaffaʿ acknowledges the revealed law as a source of public morality and a social given, he understands the necessity of defining it as a contingency and a technique of control to aid effective governance and social equilibrium. As Jürgen Habermas reasons on the question of state power and religious legitimacy in world history, Ibn al-Muqaffaʿ sought, on the one hand, to establish a convincing connection between political power and the law, which derives from religious beliefs and practices, to ensure the obedience of imperial subjects. On the other hand, he warned that the sovereign might become too reliant on a legitimizing power external to his control if the revealed law remained independent of his interference. The sovereign could make the revealed law stable by organizing and sanctioning it, but he could not avoid the fact that his power rested on an unstable foundation.[1] Ibn al-Muqaffaʿ does grapple with the revealed law's double use and proposes a legal framework to fortify the sovereign's power by subsuming part of the revealed law under imperial law, which falls under his authority. Ibn al-Muqaffaʿ thus pushes for "law for the empire," which authorizes a new political practice and an alternative path of legislation, as we will see below.

The Critique of Religious-Legal Thought

As far back as ancient times, empires built legal structures and institutions to control and manage people and enable regulated contacts within and beyond their borders. They worked with a multiplicity of existent legal structures and conventions for the most efficient control. The caliphate too, from its inception in the mid-seventh century, accommodated multiple legal traditions and ad hoc arrangements to regulate its relationship with its subjects, namely, administrators, the military, the people in the provinces and tributaries. In addition to issuing laws of their own, the early caliphs honored a diverse set of customs in various regions, including military, administrative, and fiscal regulations and traditions, and upheld the existing communal and religious practices as legal norms to facilitate relations. The "Islamization" of the legal practice began with the jurists in the eighth century and made up only a portion of the legal landscape, even though Islamic legal thought established a discursive hegemony as conversion to Islam accelerated, the complexity of the imperial sociopolitical system required more regulation, and the learned pious devoted their attention to explicating ritual and legal matters in and for a sprawling empire.

The emergence of a religious jurisprudence brings several developments to mind. With the centralization efforts of the Umayyads in the eighth century, one sees a more systematic procedure of appointing judges to major cities in the empire, which led to the formation of a formal process of legal proceedings. This required hiring support staff and keeping records. A distinction between judge and mufti (legal counselor or a person with nonbinding authority to issue legal opinions on actual or theoretical cases) and the legal scholars (*fuqahā'*) emerged. Major centers of activity (Medina, Kufa, Basra, Sanaʿa, Damascus) became hubs of legal knowledge, where aspirants received an education and debated with peers and mentors. This soon led to the appearance of legal authorities who gained a reputation much beyond their local fame.[2]

Legal consciousness brought the qur'anic text into a new intellectual focus as a source of legal knowledge, encouraged reflection on the legal use of "precedent" (*sīra*) and "established practice" (*sunna*), and stimulated theories on the use of rational judgment (*ra'y*) in drafting legal opinions. The growing complexity of legal thinking and the breathtaking diversity of legal issues led to a gradual specialization in addressing various human activities and communal matters. As the scope of law expanded, theoretical reflection on legal matters acquired an independent character, out of the control of the ruler, and divergent methodologies or paths of legal reasoning appeared. A consequence of this development was the proliferation of differing legal opinions and rulings on ritual, transactions, and actual minor and major legal cases. It provided a working system that the caliphs and the ulema seem to have rationalized as an ongoing practice, or a practice in progress, to help solve legal issues as they arose. This practice continued until the Abbasids inherited and fostered it.[3]

By the time Ibn al-Muqaffaʿ wrote his "Epistle," jurists in Iraq, Syria, and the Hijaz (Mecca and Medina) had already produced a substantial body of religious-legal thought based on their individual interpretations and methodologies, in contact with, but independent of, political supervision. Because their practice was not regulated by any scholarly authority, conflicting rulings were expected, and existed in abundance. Juridical work guided the everyday life of people as legal opinions were solicited freely and became enforceable discrete rulings and laws in courts. The law guided moral conduct and regulated the practice of rituals, transactions, social relations, and even governance. The caliphs solicited opinions from jurists in their administrative undertakings, in the adjudication of legal cases, and other needs. The postrevolt circumstances created a new opportunity for a rapprochement between the jurists and the Abbasids, who were moving toward collaboration and cooperation without overt attempts to undermine the independent work of the jurists. Ibn al-Muqaffaʿ intervened at that juncture.

Since the early twentieth century, scholars have assessed Ibn al-Muqaffaʿ's proposal for its effect on Islamic law and the caliph's authority. Scholars seem to agree that Ibn al-Muqaffaʿ's proposition was fresh and pertinent, if shortsighted, in addressing the administrative and political challenges of the new dynasty. In explaining the meaning of Ibn al-Muqaffaʿ's proposal, two arguments have emerged. One sees in Ibn al-Muqaffaʿ's view an ability to control sacred law by subsuming legislation under the caliph's authority, and thus unify the law in the empire. The other argument points out that, following a Sasanian tradition, Ibn al-Muqaffaʿ attempted to make the caliph the supreme leader of the religious community by giving him the authority to legislate in matters related to the revealed law. Scholars concur that, as jurists succeeded in controlling sacred law and establishing hegemony over legal epistemology, Ibn al-Muqaffaʿ's proposal failed to receive the attention it deserved and thus remained a theoretical reflection disconnected from the realities on the ground.[4]

In each argument, the question of religion and politics/ulema and caliphs has been raised, but the modern notion of "Muslim society," in which "Islamic law" has been relentlessly characterized as the structuring principle of sociopolitical practice, has muted its implications.[5] As far as I can see, the debate has remained a confined discussion on diverse ways of deploying Islamic law and recalibrating the caliph's religious authority. While I share the view that Ibn al-Muqaffaʿ's discourse on law was political, in the sense that his argument would bolster the caliph's power over religious law, I contend that his concern was primarily about the sociopolitical or public facet of law *in general*, not merely about religious law in particular. For this analysis, I will differentiate between divine (or revealed) law (*dīn*), sacred law (*sharʿ*, *aḥkām al-dīn*), and religious jurisprudence of the ulema (*fiqh*).

Ibn al-Muqaffaʿ engages the theme of law in his discussion of obedience to the ruling imam and of the relation between "religion and reason" in the specific paragraphs dealing with the army. He appraised the legal situation as disordered, contrary to the common good and justice, and detrimental to the authority of the caliph. He offered his views on mitigating what he described as legal chaos and eliminating the divergent judgments of the jurists by subsuming legislation under the caliph's authority. Looking for ways to curb the autonomy of the jurists and purge conflicting legal judgments, he suggested that the caliph establish a procedure for legislation by which to create an empire-wide legal code under his direction and control, which would be binding for the judges and which the caliph would implement throughout the empire. In legislating, the caliph would refer to the scripture, the authenticated tradition (including prophetic practice), legal precedent, and his rational judgment to issue his rulings and thus establish a practice the future caliphs would follow. In particular, rational judgment (*ra'y*, as a facet of intellect that is separate from the revealed law) is evident in his treatment of legal questions but is also found throughout the text as an underlying principle of thinking, social practice, and governance.

What dovetails with making the law imperial is the language and the vocabulary he uses that would tip the scale in favor of the caliph. Instead of using religious idioms, such as "permitted" or "prohibited" (*ḥalāl* or *ḥarām*), Ibn al-Muqaffaʿ

insists on using imperial ones, such as "sovereign statute" or "imperial edict," issuing orders, verdicts, commands/rules, rational judgment, written documents, executive action (*amr, qaḍā, ḥukm, ra'y, kitāb, imḍā'*) to explain the caliph's practice. Considered from a political perspective, this move not only decentered the existing legal practice privileging religious jurisprudence but also pushed back against the state of legal plurality from the perspective of the sovereign's authority.

Viewed in the circumstances of its timing and the groups it targeted, Ibn al-Muqaffaᶜ's legal argument is noteworthy for the critique it raises against the existing legal conventions, the discursive space it opens for public legal discourse, and the political morality that lays bare the difference between royal authority and the idea of the imamate. One can also read it as a frontal attack on the status of some influential sociocultural groups that had already been in place or were coming to prominence with the Abbasid revolt. Their inner fracture and conflictual relations notwithstanding, these groups included the community of the jurists themselves and the nascent *ḥadīth* transmitters, who had spread far and wide enough to compel the caliphs to seek their support as political allies, as well as the messianic-esoteric revolutionary groups whom Ibn al-Muqaffaᶜ so eagerly wanted to be reined in but who were not ready to surrender to an established order that marginalized them.

As I will examine below, Ibn al-Muqaffaᶜ envisions a system of law that combines under the supreme authority of the caliph three codes with different regulatory frameworks. The first code is the temporal or "positive law," which is based on the rational discretion of the caliph. This legal code is meant to order political and public life in the empire. It is dynamic and expansive. The second code is the sacred immutable law, which comprises the firm and restricted major religious rulings and the obligations of ritual worship based on the sacred book and the authenticated tradition. The role of the sovereign here is only to supervise its execution and implementation. It is narrow in scope and codified, and therefore fixed. The third code is discretionary sacred law, which comprises the rulings on what is considered ambiguous in the revealed law. It is also left to the regulation and rational discretion of the caliph. Like the first code of law, it is dynamic and mutable.

Political and Legal Premises

Ibn al-Muqaffaᶜ's first foray into the question of law involves whether the ruler should be obeyed when he contradicts God's command, which he immediately links to a "Cartesian" distinction that he draws between "religion and reason." Unlike the jurists who reasoned on law from the vantage point of theological universals regardless of the historical context, Ibn al-Muqaffaᶜ envisions a pioneering legal model based on religious and rational foundations. It is critical to remember here that Ibn al-Muqaffaᶜ engaged legal questions from the perspective of a particular field of knowledge. He was neither a religious scholar nor part of the community of religious knowledge. As a scribe with a humanistic background, he was interested in effective legal practice in the empire. To understand the legal proposal of Ibn al-Muqaffaᶜ better and to explicate his argument, I will assess the moral and epistemological foundations on which it was built by spotlighting two themes in the "Epistle": obedience to the imam and the dialectic between "religion and reason" as a space to imagine the political function of rational judgment.

Obedience to the Imam

To follow up on my earlier succinct discussion on obedience in the context of political virtue, the absence of an organized or institutionalized clergy to represent the revealed law bothered Ibn al-Muqaffaᶜ. This seems to have raised an important political and administrative question for him: How should one organize the revealed law so that it enhances the presumed social order efficiently? To be sure, Ibn al-Muqaffaᶜ does not phrase his contention this way but his critique of the legal situation demonstrates that he acted on this question. He notices the political challenge in the conflict between the sacred law and the sovereign, and seeks to resolve it in a manner that eschews the expediency of proposing complete obedience to the caliph or submitting to the broad autonomy of the revealed law. He takes the complicated route of a nuanced analysis that involves a discussion of universals and epistemology. He poses the question as a matter of negotiation, which, if one thinks for a moment about the possible practical steps, suggests a dialogue and collaboration among the parties involved, including the ulema, the sovereign, and the relevant administrative functionaries who will work out the details. This is as close as one gets to an acknowledgment of the distinction between revealed law and political power and of the need to mitigate the contest between the two.[6]

Ibn al-Muqaffaᶜ begins the elaboration of his position by setting up a scenario in which one group argues that there must be "no obedience to a creature in disobedience to the Creator."[7] According to this view, the ruling imam who orders disobedience to God should not be obeyed, whereas anyone other than the ruling imam who commands obedience to God should be obeyed.

The other group argues to the contrary that the ruling imam must be obeyed in all circumstances. It maintains that, whether or not the ruling imam obeys or disobeys God, his subjects are not in the business of judging and therefore interfering in the authority of their ruling imam. Evaluated not in the abstract but in the circumstances of the post-revolution caliphate, Ibn al-Muqaffaᶜ's observation targeted specific groups among the ulema, sects, and the supporters of the Abbasid Summons. In the following passage, he makes several points with major theoretical significance.

> We have heard a group of people say, "No obedience to a creature of God in disobedience to the Creator." They constructed this expression of theirs in a twisted manner and said, "If the imam orders us to disobey God, then he deserves to be disobeyed, and if anyone other than[8] the imam orders us to obey God, then he deserves to be obeyed. Thus, if the imam is disobeyed when he is disobedient to God, and if someone else is obeyed when he is obedient to God, then the imam and the other person are equal in the right of obedience."[9] This is a well-known saying, which the devil has found as an excuse for renouncing obedience to the imam[10] and achieving what he aspires to, so that[11] people will be all alike and no imam would take charge of their affairs, and they would have no weight against their enemies. We have heard others say, "On the contrary, we obey the imams in all our affairs, and we do not investigate their obedience to God or disobedience to Him. None of us is responsible for scrutinizing them. They are the holders of authority (*wulāt al-amr*) and people of knowledge (*ahl al-ᶜilm*). We are the followers (*atbāᶜ*) and have the duty of obedience and submission." This expression is no less harmful than the previous one in weakening the sovereign authority (*sulṭān*) of the imam and disparaging obedience[12] to him, since it leads to heinous[13] and abominable consequences, which consist of permitting disobeying God openly and unequivocally.[14]

Here, Ibn al-Muqaffaᶜ engages head on with one of the most enduring problems of political authority in facing religious power: To what extent is the sovereign entitled to obedience? The main question not only puts him into a direct dialogue with the theological arguments about the subject in the eighth-century imamate's discourse but also allows him to shift the direction of the conversation toward another horizon in which "religion" is decentered and relativized vis-à-vis reason and politics.

Both views, Ibn al-Muqaffaᶜ argues, are wrong. In both cases, the ability of the sovereign to act virtuously is impeded. The first one elevates regular individuals to the level of the ruling imam and grants them equal rights to obedience, which threatens the foundations of political authority and the social order. The second position is harmful too because it permits disobedience to God openly and belittles the very practice of obedience and the authority of the ruling imam. Ibn al-Muqaffaᶜ pushes back against the two positions that he neatly describes, but what he is truly resisting is the underlying assumption in both arguments that the meaning of God's word is accessible to the faithful through their own interpretations. In his assessment, even the sovereign does not have an unfettered right of access. While the sovereign has the authority to interpret God's word, he can never pretend to control or monopolize its meaning.

Interested in the social and political aspects of religious practice and the social space where the sovereign's power and authority are at stake, Ibn al-Muqaffaᶜ pursues an opening to aid the sovereign in regulating or managing the divine word rather than competing against it. In the first argument ("No obedience to a creature of God in disobedience to the Creator"), he sees infringement on the sovereign's authority by the faithful, who are assumed in the statement to have the power of interpretation of the divine word and therefore the authority to question the sovereign. If we understand for a moment the phrase "obedience to God" in the passage above as meaning God's word, which seems to be what Ibn al-Muqaffaᶜ is trying to get across here,[15] the first argument triangulates the revealed law between the faithful and the sovereign, where the obligation requiring obedience (1) is autonomously authoritative on its own by virtue of being part of the revealed law and (2) is accessible, as far as its meaning is concerned, to any reasoning believer, including the sovereign and his subjects. This privilege of access to meaning renders the revealed law knowable by the faithful, who determine the meaning of God's message based on their own interpretation. From a political standpoint, Ibn al-Muqaffaᶜ finds such a notion of ubiquitous or shared privilege, that is, the power to access the meaning of the revealed law with no higher or institutionalized authority, detrimental to the sovereign's authority because it almost renders him irrelevant or, worse yet, incapacitated.

Concerning the second position ("we obey the imams in all of our affairs"), Ibn al-Muqaffaᶜ also notices a dimension that undermines the sovereign's authority and erodes social order. While the triangulation of the revealed law between the sovereign and the faithful remains the same, the sovereign gains, through the unreasoned submission to his will, too much discretion in exercising his power, which insinuates witting neglect of the revealed law and engenders apathy because the imperial subjects' aspiration here is not constructive or aimed at maintaining good order—rather, it is only concerned with obeying power passively in a pessimistic way. Ibn al-Muqaffaᶜ notices that, while unconditional obedience relieves the sovereign from constraints, it does so only at the cost of rendering the revealed law mute, making the faithful complicit in willful neglect, and inhibiting political virtue. Such a deliberate disregard of obligations diminishes the political and moral authority of the sovereign to the point of disregard and communicates ill will, which leads to the corruption of social order.

If both positions on the question of obedience to the ruling imam ("no obedience is due to a creature of God in disobedience to the Creator Himself" and "we obey the imams in all of our affairs and we do not investigate their obedience to God or disobedience to Him") are equally objectionable because they undermine the authority of the sovereign and the revealed law or at least do not produce political benefit, what should the caliph do? Ibn al-Muqaffaʿ suggests a strikingly imaginative solution in which the power of the sovereign and the revealed law, applied correctly, become effective and supreme, each in its own realm. In a move little appreciated by scholars, he proposes an argument that offers a new reading of the practice of the revealed law and of political power. Ibn al-Muqaffaʿ brings the discussion to the role of the revealed law in sociopolitical life.

> People of merit and proper direction said, those who said that "no obedience is due to a creature of God in disobedience to the Creator Himself" are correct, but they are not correct in annulling (*taʿṭīl*) obedience to the imams and in ridiculing[16] obedience. Those who acknowledge obedience to the imams in that which they ascertained were also correct, but they were not correct in granting obedience in what they were uncertain about[17] in all affairs. As for our affirmation that[18] the imam should not be obeyed when he disobeys God, that is in the firm divine obligations and legal sanctions (*aẓā'im al-farā'iḍ wa al-ḥudūd*) over which God has not given anyone sovereign authority (*sulṭān*). If the imam prohibits ritual prayer, fasting, and the pilgrimage, or forbids the legal sanctions (*ḥudūd*) and permits what God has forbidden, he has no authority (*amr*) to do that. On the other hand, our affirmation that obedience can only be to the imam is in that which any other person should not be obeyed. It is in the use of rational judgment, governance, and rule (*ra'y, tadbīr, amr*), whose bridle God has placed in the hands of the imams. No one else has either a say or right of obedience in such matters as raiding and returning from military operations; collecting and distributing revenue; appointment and dismissal of functionaries; judgment made through use of rational judgment when there is no trace of precedent (*athar*); carrying out legal sanctions and rulings (*al-ḥudūd wa al-aḥkām*) according to the scripture and the tradition (*al-kitāb wa al-sunna*); waging war with the enemy and disengaging from it;[19] and carrying out transactions on behalf of Muslims.[20] All of these matters and similar ones are a part of the necessary obedience to God, Most High and

Sublime. No one among the people has a right over them except the imam. Anyone who disobeys the imam in this regard or deserts him brings destruction upon himself.[21]

In this extraordinarily rich paragraph, Ibn al-Muqaffaᶜ makes two broad moves concerning obedience to the sovereign. First, he divides the revealed law epistemologically into two categories. He postulates that certain parts of the revealed law are beyond the authority of the sovereign. These parts consist of the major ritual obligations, prohibitions, and penal laws, assumed to be unambiguous and fixed, and thus closed to reasoning. No one has the authority to alter, supplement, or forbid God's legal sanctions or to permit what God has forbidden. The sovereign, like any other faithful Muslim, must submit to these requirements. By fixing these injunctions and rituals, he also makes them visible and protects them against the interference of the ruler and jurists. In contrast, the other part, as he explicitly acknowledges, comprises the contingent pronouncements. These include any provisions other than what is specified in the first part of the divine law and are subject to reasoning and interpretation, which he addresses both in this passage and in other passages.[22] His critical intervention here is that the caliph is endowed with the sole authority or perhaps, more accurately, the higher authority of reasoning (to interpret, specify, promulgate, and validate) in the second category of divine law. One consequence of this argument is that the laws thus enacted or confirmed, although they can still be reconstituted in sacred law in a variety of ways, may no longer be disregarded at will, at least legally, on religious grounds. As imperial edicts and sanctioned pronouncements across imperial lands, they would be enforceable by authorities, unlike the existing juridical judgments, which were, according to Ibn al-Muqaffaᶜ, inconsistent from legislation to implementation.

Second, Ibn al-Muqaffaᶜ distinguishes the political from the religious by setting boundaries to the latter in matters of governance. Deconstructing Ibn al-Muqaffaᶜ's legal discourse this way allows me to expose a new field of reasoning beyond the jurists' epistemological framework.[23] Ibn al-Muqaffaᶜ enables a "secular space" beyond the parameters of the revealed law, where conventional or practical rationality rather than religious injunctions informs legislation and judgment in public matters, which he places under the legal discretion of the sovereign. Ibn al-Muqaffaᶜ is quite open about reserving the right of rational judgment, governance, and commandership, and the entitlement to obedience in political matters, for the ruling imam alone, which he discusses in some detail. The ruling imam, he reasons, must be obeyed in all matters other than the major religious obligations and rulings, to which he himself is subject as a believer. He must be obeyed in military tasks and in governance (such as collecting and distributing revenue, appointing and dismissing functionaries) and in enacting and executing legal judgments, such as making legal decisions through the use of rational judgment when there is no reported precedent, carrying out legal sanctions and rulings according to the "book and the tradition," deciding when to engage and disengage the enemy in warfare, and conducting affairs on behalf of Muslims.[24]

To comprehend Ibn al-Muqaffaᶜ's vision of the field of legislation as a political question, we need to keep in mind a legislative procedure that includes two fields of reflection as the foundation of the law: (1) the rational legal field falls outside the revealed law and is subsumed under the authority of the ruler, who would legislate according to his discretion, and (2) the sphere of the revealed law, which Ibn al-Muqaffaᶜ divides into two epistemologically distinct subcategories: (a) the religious ordinances that are unambiguous and specific are fixed and not open to discretion or rational deliberation (e.g., one does not eat pork, or one performs the ritual prayer), and (b) those pronouncements of the revealed law, because the instruction is ambiguous, that need clarification and rational reflection. Pondering both, we know that Ibn al-Muqaffaᶜ restricts the authority of exercising discretion in the first category to the ruler alone. In the second category, he creatively invents a space for political agency in religious-legal structure to make the caliph more than a mere administrative arm of the jurists in the following way. Item 2a is sealed off from rational reflection (one would assume that the application or implementation of obligations still requires certain functional reasoning to explain and specify how). The obligations, legal and otherwise, in this category should be upheld because they are stated and specified in "the scripture and the tradition" (*al-kitāb wa al-sunna*) where the *sunna* acquires as a strong authority as the *kitāb*.[25] In item 2b, a judgment must be based on authenticated prophetic practice (*sunna*) and legitimate precedent (*sīra*) or promulgated through a judicious legal analogy (*qiyās*) before the final approval of the caliph.[26] The final decision to render a religious-legal opinion as the law rests with the sovereign alone, who is the final decision maker. The jurists remain free to voice their opinions during the process of legislation until the "law" has been enacted.[27]

In this "historicist" perspective, Ibn al-Muqaffaᶜ's remarks on *athar* ("attested precedent" or "a trace of authoritative practice") and *sunna* (defined as "established practice") further restrict the jurists and underline the boundaries of the revealed law. He articulates this point as part of his discussion of "religion and reason" when he notes that the ruler deserves obedience only when he carries out the rules of the divine judgments and the traditions.[28] By anchoring a particular religious practice or decision to authoritative tradition or attested precedent and custom, Ibn al-Muqaffaᶜ curtails what he sees as the proliferation of various contradictory practices spinning out of control. Thus, his point is also an argument against the emerging trend among the ulema (jurists and *ḥadīth* transmitters) of establishing religious (legal or ritual) decisions based on a single report (*ḥadīth*) attributed in a variety of ways to the Prophet and his companions, which they considered "written *sunna*."

One consequence of shoring up the law epistemologically in this way to shape its public role as complementary to political authority was the new role the ulema would play in the new structure. On the one hand, his proposal authorizes a sacrosanct "core" in the revealed law and seals it off from the sovereign to prevent his interference in it. By the same logic, the core is also off-limits to the ulema apart from their serving as maintainers of the faith, which Ibn al-Muqaffaᶜ seems to have taken for granted. On the other hand, by singling out the sovereign as the sole authority to reason on other public or political matters, regardless of whether they are considered by the ulema to be part of religious discourse, he reduces the power of these scholars to that of legal administrative functionaries with circumscribed legislative privilege and autonomy. As I will address shortly, however, limiting the authority of the ulema does not prevent them from taking part in the process of legislation but instead fine-tunes their role. Considered as an intellectual possibility, Ibn al-Muqaffaᶜ's point is an attempt to direct the duty of obedience in public matters to the ruler rather than to the ulema and reduce the friction over authority between the two in favor of the caliph. This difference comes to better light in his discussion of the sovereign's authority within the framework of "religion and reason" and the use of rational judgment.

The Dialectic Between Religion and Reason

Ibn al-Muqaffaᶜ was not a philosopher but a political thinker who perceived theoretical and epistemological questions from a practical perspective. His arguments about the value of religious guidance vis-à-vis the sovereign's authority emerge from a "theory" of knowledge about the duality of "religion and reason," which he addresses during his discussion of obedience. His short passage on the subject, albeit minimalist, stands out as a pioneering and bold foray into the complex world of the revealed law and epistemology. Not that "religion and reason" had not been a matter of deliberation in Arabic before Ibn al-Muqaffaᶜ. To the contrary, both words appear on numerous occasions in the Qur'an among other semantically connected words to signify a way of practice or law ordained by God (*dīn*) and the innate human capacity to understand and reason (*ᶜaql*). Echoing the larger dialogic context of Byzantine and Sasanian theological and philosophical traditions, the pioneering theologians and jurists became interested in reason and reasoning (among the Qadarites and the Muʿtazilites) as a discipline in the service of theological argument in the eighth century, partly also to respond to the ambiguity of the qur'anic text. At least among the ulema, revelation as the foundation of knowledge had emerged as a major idea, although instrumental rationality still guided both theological and jurisprudential thinking as a matter of common sense.

Ibn al-Muqaffaʿ raises the discussion to a political level by naming the question of "religion and reason," which had escaped the previous theologians and jurists of his milieu. In a penetrating analysis of the distinction between the two, he defines revealed law as the knowledge stipulating rituals and obligations that are beyond human capacity, interference, and control. Religion, as he sees it, meets human needs and aspirations as grace from God in matters in which the intellect fails, becomes insufficient, or is incapable of comprehending. Thus the revealed law must, by definition, provide guidance in a limited way. Reason, on the other hand, refers to the innate, God-given human capacity to think and act constructively, without or separate from religious guidance. Unlike the foundational assumption of the ulema about religion as the comprehensive universal truth, Ibn al-Muqaffaʿ relativizes it vis-à-vis reason. The critical point is that Ibn al-Muqaffaʿ constructs this "Cartesian" duality of "religion and reason" by describing and defining it along two sources of authority, prophetic and political. This is how he encapsulates the problem:

> These two matters (*amrān*) can only be distinguished from one another by a great proof from God, Most High and Sublime. God has made the sustenance (*qiwām*) of people and the proper condition of their lives now and in the hereafter in two natural gifts (*khalla*): religion and intellect (*dīn wa ʿaql*). Their intellect could not, even if the favor of God, Most High and Sublime, has been great upon them in having intelligence, gain knowledge of the right religious guidance (*hudā*), nor could it deliver people to the satisfaction of God without the favor which He perfected for them as a grace in the form of revealed law (*dīn*), which He ordained (*sharaʿa*) for them and by which He made receptive the hearts of those whom He meant to guide. Moreover, if the revealed law, which has come from God, had left no word out from the rulings (*aḥkām*), rational judgment (*ra'y*), command (*amr*) and all that can occur and happen to people between the day when God sent His messenger, God bless him and grant him salvation, and the day when they meet him in the hereafter and had been the subject of a firm divine decree (*ʿazīma*), they would have been charged to do what they were not capable of doing. They would have become too confined by the revealed law to which they adhere, and He would have

> imparted to them more than what their ears could hear, and their hearts could understand. Their minds and hearts, which God had bestowed upon them, would have wandered in confusion. Their intelligence would have been futile. They would not have needed it at all and would have used[29] it only in matters already regulated by revelation. But God has granted them revealed law which their rational judgment (*ra'y*) would not absorb[30] as was stated by the devout worshippers of God, "We would not have found the right path if God had not guided (*hudā*) us."[31] Then He relegated other matters of rule and governance (*al-amr wa al-tadbīr*) to rational judgment (*ra'y*), and He gave the right of rational judgment to holders of authority (*wulāt al-amr*). There is no stake for the people in this matter except to make suggestions when consulted, to respond when invited, and to advise sincerely in private.[32] A ruler does not deserve this obedience unless he carries out the major divine decrees and the traditions (*al-ʿazā'im wa al-sunan*), which[33] carries a similar meaning.[34]

One must acknowledge that this passage destabilizes rather than complements the existing knowledge about "religion and reason" in not only politics but also epistemology. It is not a disinterested description of these two "faculties" of knowledge and authority for the sake of clarity and information. Ibn al-Muqaffaʿ wants to create a duality and make a case for reason against what he sees as infringement on it by the revealed law as defined by the ulema. One would have little reason to hesitate at this point to read the "people" in the passage ("there is no stake for the people in this matter") as also signifying the ulema. He explains succinctly the independent authority and function of each "innate faculty" residing in human beings without suggesting a necessary conflict between them.[35] Instead, he emphasizes their utility for humankind, which is none other than ensuring good living and eternal salvation. As natural characteristics inalienable to the human being, both are ontological equals. They ensure welfare and order in people's lives by satisfying diverse needs. They are the moral and social components of their lives that make them complete. These remarks may thus be interpreted as an attempt to sketch, without using the specialized vocabulary of theologians or philosophers, in lay language an epistemological distinction between "physics" and "metaphysics" so to speak to place politics in the former category. Indeed, Ibn al-Muqaffaʿ brings up this subject in the discussion of obedience to explain his argument concerning the authority of the caliph against the claims of loyalists and opponents.

After distinguishing "religion and reason" as the two ontological foundations of human life and as gifts from God to ensure the happiness of human beings, Ibn al-Muqaffaʿ continues by describing the critical role of the revealed law in human welfare and salvation. He does so in a remarkable rhetorical way that enables a moral and intellectual space for reason. He underlines the utility and significance of the revealed law and acknowledges the limitation of reason in achieving perfect felicity or salvation only to arrive at the conclusion of confirming and expanding the role of reason in human life. He describes the revealed law foremost as a kind of knowledge that appeals to hearts rather than minds in guiding the believer to salvation (*hudā*) and clarifying one's obligations toward God. In this view, the revealed law appears constricted to matters of salvation and divine obligation, to which reason cannot respond. He then pivots to qualify what he just articulated to make space for the human intellect. Ibn al-Muqaffaʿ launches a brief but condemning rebuke of what he describes as the absurd dead end of overdoing religion. While the revealed law, he argues, is the only path meant to guide humankind to salvation and a pious life, which reason alone cannot do, it is not meant to prescribe the details and activities of life. Once the revealed law intervenes in every detail of life, it loses its value and becomes a hindrance rather than a guide. In view of this explanation, one appreciates the logic behind Ibn al-Muqaffaʿ's jarringly contemptuous rejection of what he sees as overreach by the ulema to make the revealed law a cause of suffering rather than salvation.

Deconstructing the role of the revealed law in this way paves the way to his argument about reason. As a form of knowledge and an ontological category like the revealed law, reason is at the foundation of most human activities, politics being the primary one in which Ibn al-Muqaffaʿ is interested. While reason remains secondary in matters related to salvation, it is the primary faculty that guides human beings in matters on this earth and enables the capacity to judge because contingencies ("all that can occur and happen") require managing life and maintaining social order. After establishing the authority of reason in guiding social life, Ibn al-Muqaffaʿ does not hesitate to restrict the privilege of political discretion (*ra'y*) to the rulers. Given his overall view of social organization, it is not surprising to see him excluding the "people" from exercising political discretion, even as they carry the responsibility of making suggestions when consulted and responding when invited. This is a point that circles back to his argument about the question of obedience to the ruler. To explicate his argument further, however, I need to discuss briefly his assessment on the application of "rational judgment" in legal practice as the prerogative of the ruler.

Ibn al-Muqaffaʿ uses *ra'y* as an inalienable right of the caliph and a commendable virtue in fulfilling his tasks. His distinctive political reading of the term *ra'y* is evident in his encouragement of his patron to appreciate and solicit opinions from those who can offer good ones, which he unmistakably codes as distinct from religious knowledge, so that the ruler can use them to act prudently. In his discussion of the elite, Ibn al-Muqaffaʿ also emphasizes the importance of useful and sound knowledge (*ra'y*) to warn the caliph to be wary of the opinions of those who gained sudden and recent fame, erratic enthusiasts, and opportunists who would offer any opinion to please the caliph. In legal reasoning, Ibn al-Muqaffaʿ codes the term *ra'y* with the opinion expressed in cases where revelation remains silent, a discretionary opinion on how to interpret an undetermined religious judgment, a subjective and independent point of view, an opinion that can thus be falsified, and even an arbitrary judgment that should be dismissed.[36] In this sense, the word is used in contradistinction to the improvised opinion, arrogance, ignorance, and imitation.[37] For instance, one might produce unscrupulous opinion or perfect an already sound opinion. There might be multiple compatible or incompatible rational judgments, but when opinions support each other, they would cause even more assurance and a better outcome. Unless an opinion is judged abhorrent, it would reflect positively on the intelligence and character of the person articulating it. Offering a good opinion might be a desirable quality, but it is better when supported by action.

What I want to say about the word's polyphonic legal character is better explained in its dialogic context. Even among the jurists, the idea of rational judgment in the mid-eighth century still functioned as a major principle of legal work. As Wael B. Hallaq convincingly notes, in Iraq at least, where rational judgment was considered among jurists a legitimate way of knowing and judging, before *ḥadīth*-provoked suspicion arose against it for being irreverent to prophetic practice, the word had already been used to distinguish secular intellection from revealed knowledge (*naql*, *naṣṣ*) or established practice (*sunna*). In legal discourse, it specified a rational judgment or the passing of judgment on a case by independent reasoning, that is, what seemed commonsensical given the circumstance, or by reasoning and judging when scripture and established practice remained silent. In the initial decades of the eighth century, the notion of rational judgment became a major principle of legal reflection during an age when prophetic practice (*sunna*), as reconstituted textually in *ḥadīth* reports, had not yet been regarded as an exclusive source of law. The prophetic *sunna* represented only one source among other established practices (*sunan*). *Sunna* sometimes signified an established practice without referring to any specific content, similar to how other established practices were used. Yet many of the references to the prophetic *sunna* had a specific content, at least as far as the law was concerned, which became more authoritative and superior to other established practices.[38]

At the time, the jurists still considered prophetic *sunna* separate from *ḥadīth* and did not yet embrace the idea of *ḥadīth* being its verbal expression. In fact, they flagged some reports as contradicting established *sunna* or *sunan*, in part because of the fabrications of prophetic materials. Although some jurists and *ḥadīth* transmitters sought to support some of their legal views by referencing prophetic and companion reports, they had not yet formulated a principle allowing exclusive reliance on prophetic *ḥadīth* or on the reports of companions and successors. Still, the authority and piety associated with the idea of *sunna* aided the spread of *ḥadīth* among nonspecialists and provided an incentive for false attributions to the Prophet in inventive ways by scholars; preachers; storytellers; and, of course, rulers, among others. The late Umayyad caliphs and the Abbasids from the reign of al-Manṣūr onward became interested in patronizing transmitters of any *ḥadīth*, authentic or spurious, that would support and help them rule. Ibn al-Muqaffaʿ cites this confusion as one reason for conflicting legal judgments because this practice encouraged the collection and writing of *ḥadīth* and contributed to forgery and misattribution.[39]

When the gradual emergence of *ḥadīth* cast a shadow of suspicion on rational judgment in legal reasoning among jurists and others after the middle of the eighth century, the signification of *ra'y* shifted from rational judgment to "arbitrary reasoning" or "fallible human view," as opposed to sound judgment by transmitted report. *Ḥadīth* transmitters promoted prophetic reports as an authoritative method in religious learning and legal work to replace rational judgment. Once *ḥadīth* became evidence and a basis for legal opinion, its counterpart, rational judgment, *ra'y*, came under attack, and was associated with the rejection of *ḥadīth*. Those who practiced *ra'y*—or the folk of rational judgment, *ahl al-ra'y*—were frowned upon for their aversion to *ḥadīth*. The phrase "the folk of rational judgment" became a commonplace signifier of scholars in Iraq. It later became a hallmark of the Iraqi school of religious jurisprudence, championed most famously by Abū Ḥanīfa and his pupils. From the early emergence of the adherents of *ḥadīth* in the first decade of the eighth century or soon thereafter, the folk of rational judgment were represented as being antagonistic to *ḥadīth* and, not unexpectedly were suspected of being impious or at least lax.[40]

This development occurred during the lifetime of Ibn al-Muqaffaʿ. Although he was writing when the balance had not yet tilted toward the *ḥadīth* folk (*ahl al-ḥadīth*), his angst about this problem comes out in his critique of legal scholars. Wanting to clear the path for the caliph to issue legal judgments and resituate the work of the jurists according to the priorities of imperial social order, Ibn al-Muqaffaʿ reins in the revealed law to authorize temporal rational reflection as a self-conscious activity distinct from theology to govern thinking and practice. In politics and law (the authoritarian tone of his proposal notwithstanding), he thus prioritizes reason as the regulating logic of statecraft and draws new boundaries for religious rationality in legal matters.

Imperial Law and the Idea of Codification

Consistent with his overall imperial vision, Ibn al-Muqaffaʿ assesses the emerging legal status quo as not just a source of confusion and injustice but also as an infringement on the authority of the caliph. Concerned with the efficient control and management of the law, he describes the legal scene as confusing and chaotic and rebukes judges in various regions and cities for producing different and contradictory rulings on similar cases with impunity. He accuses them of laxity in implementing verdicts with no regard to consistency or showing no remorse for malfeasance, even though their judgments would lead to capital punishment, defile women's honor, or cause loss of property. Ibn al-Muqaffaʿ is unsparing:

> Among the things that the Commander of the Faithful takes into consideration regarding[41] these two metropolises and other cities and districts (*nawāḥī*) is the disparity between the contradictory rulings, which has become so momentous as to affect human blood (capital punishment), the genitalia of women (sexual access), and possessions. Thus, where ruling on blood and the genitalia of women is regarded as lawful in Hira, it is regarded as unlawful in Kufa. A similar disparity exists in Kufa itself. Thus, what is regarded as lawful in one district is regarded as unlawful in another. However, despite its variety this disparity of rulings continues to be in effect concerning the blood of Muslims and their women. Judges whose orders and judgments are valid continue to judge by it. Yet there is no group among the Iraqis or Hijazis who have examined this matter and have not clamored with self-flattery about what they have done and have not looked down on all the rest. This situation has forced them into doing things that have startled[42] the discerning people who hear about them.[43]

Reading this passage, one is struck by the acuteness of his characterization of the legal scene. It both captures the core dynamics of religious jurisprudence as a field of reflection and practice and solicits a reformist response to change to the status quo. Pointing out methodological rather than epistemological questions and building on his broader discussion of the subject in the "Epistle," Ibn al-Muqaffaʿ criticizes what he portrays as arbitrary rulings and inconsistent reasoning. He rebukes such an "everything goes" kind of carelessness as leading to legal chaos, to the detriment of justice, the caliph's authority, and social order. His statement is in fact so convincing that one can miss the fact that Ibn al-Muqaffaʿ was the marginal who resisted the ongoing practice. Remember that jurisprudential work was an activity of independent jurists operating voluntarily and autonomously in informally connected small epistemic communities that gathered around a distinguished thinker. It is clear from Ibn al-Muqaffaʿ's critique that such collectivities had already been formed at both regional (the Hijaz and Iraq) and city levels (Basra, Kufa, and Hira). The field of religious jurisprudence remained amazingly competitive and diverse until the systematization of methodologies and the popularity of certain legal schools curbed legal plurality in the ninth century.

After describing the ongoing situation as harmful, Ibn al-Muqaffaʿ lays out its causes to substantiate his proposal on how to reform the process of legislation and improve the implementation of the law without diminishing the sovereign's authority. He first tackles the methodology of the jurists and raises pivotal points about their practice.

> As for the one among them who claims that he must follow the established practice (*sunna*), he makes what is not *sunna*, a *sunna*, to the point where this leads him to shed blood without authoritative evidence and proof for the matter that he claims is a *sunna*. If questioned about that, he cannot say that some blood was shed at the time of the Prophet—God bless him and grant him and his family[44] salvation—or the rightly guided imams after him. If he is asked, "Whose blood was shed according to this practice (*sunna*) that you claim?" he responds, "That was done by ʿAbd al-Malik b. Marwān or one of those Umayyad governors (*umarāʾ*)." In the matter of fact, he embraces rational judgment and becomes extremely infatuated by his attachment to his own opinion to express, on a serious matter concerning the Muslims, a point of view that is not shared by any other Muslim. Moreover, he is not alarmed by having done so alone, and by having administered the sentence while admitting that it is an opinion of his, which is not based on either a written document (*kitāb*) or an established practice (*sunna*).[45]

The question for Ibn al-Muqaffaʿ in this passage is the abuse of the authenticated precedent (including but not limited to the Prophet's practice) and of rational judgment, which lead the jurists to insist boastfully on upholding marginal opinions not shared by any other jurist, conflating what is actually an unauthoritative precedent (the practice of the Umayyad governors and caliphs) with an authoritative, established practice (*sunna*), and issuing arbitrary judgments with no documented support. These inconsistent ways and the lack of rigor, he reasons, cause them to present wrongfully what is not an authenticated practice as genuine, which consequentially causes harm to people.[46]

What I also want to underline is the mention of writing/written document in this context as a credible source of law. Mirroring his position on documenting in writing any matter of significance related to governance, Ibn al-Muqaffaᶜ here too makes his case that legal judgments can be based on an applicable and credible written document, presumably such as the one he suggests the caliph leaves behind for subsequent rulers to consider in their legal work, as I will cite in the following passage. He proposes a process whereby the caliph can consolidate legal practice under his legislative authority and intervene administratively before he makes his final decision. The following passage explains his proposal and the groundbreaking epistemological and methodological intervention he is making:

> If the Commander of the Faithful could see fit to order that these divergent judicial rulings (*aqḍiya*) and practices (*siyar*)[47] be submitted to him recorded in a written document (*kitāb*) along with what each group (*qawm*) claims to use as an established practice (*sunna*) or analogy (*qiyās*); if the Commander of the Faithful would examine these documents and render on each case his opinion, which is inspired by God (*yalhamuhu*); if he would adhere tenaciously to this opinion and prohibit litigation (*qaḍā*) contrary to it; and write it in a comprehensive codex (*kitāb*), we could hope that God would make these judgments, which mix[48] the accurate with the erroneous, into one correct code, and we could hope that the unification of judicial practices would be evidence for unification of the rule (*amr*) consistent with the opinion (*ra'y*) of the Commander of the Faithful and corroborative of his language. Then another imam would proceed to do the same and so on until the end of time, God willing.[49]

This is a thought-provoking suggestion that does not fit the conventions of his time. One notices first that the corrective action, according to Ibn al-Muqaffaᶜ, begins with writing and collecting the divergent rulings and practices along with the supporting evidence on which they are based to be submitted to the caliph for review rather than legislating anew through a body of scholars appointed for this task. He is therefore not rejecting the jurists but trying to incorporate them into a legal system controlled by the administration. The practical outcome of his argument is to keep the jurists engaged in the legal work and encourage them to reflect on the law and offer opinions on theoretical and actual cases, knowing that there is a process in which opinions would be vetted.

The proposed method allows the jurists to reflect independently on legal cases but also creates a procedure for a higher review of "proposed" legal opinions (and the supporting evidence) that scrutinizes and approves or declines them by way of a competitive vetting process. Those that are approved would be adopted as law, placed in a codex for permanency, and handed down from generation to generation to be implemented, amended, and supplemented by successive rulers. This means that no single opinion would be enacted as law without the approval of the caliph, and no court would arbitrate based on judgments that have not yet been endorsed.

Although the jurists' playing field is noticeably restricted, the new system would keep the channels of collaboration between the caliph and the jurists open without infringing on their juristic autonomy—they would be part of the legislative process without being allowed free rein in the judiciary. Because not all religious guidance is politically pertinent, Ibn al-Muqaffaᶜ does not address or push back against the authority of the ulema on matters not related to or not conflicting with the sovereign's authority, which allows them to operate in a legal and religious field with a capacity to shape and elaborate religious principles and practice as long as they do not interfere with imperial authority. One presumes that religious scholars would continue to have discretion to advise on or determine the nature of rituals, address questions related to practice, and reflect on other fine matters of the revealed law and the scripture that had no major bearing on political discretion.

A consequence of this legislative arrangement is that the legal opinions of the jurists would be trimmed down as part of a larger legal structure and subjected to a procedure of amendment and approval to be enforceable as laws. Understandably, changing legislative activity in this way would radically alter the dynamics of legal reflection and the priorities of the jurists. Its impact on them would be far beyond bringing them into a closer collaboration with rulers. It would also render them subordinate to the higher authority of the caliph and of the group he would assemble to administer the task. This would be another way to encourage or compel the jurists to write for the governing authority (because legislation, legal practice, and the implementation of the law would be under the direction of the political authority) rather than for colleagues or whomever would be the subject of those laws. It is not an overstatement to say that the proposal would make the legislative activity an entirely administrative undertaking (like taxation or other bureaucratic duties) as long as the jurists remained willing to ponder questions and offer their views.

This last point brings me to another aspect of the proposed change. What Ibn al-Muqaffaᶜ suggested could be successful only if scholars submitted to its requirements and the ruler maintained this arrangement and the firm control of his empire. If the caliph's control weakened while the social power of the jurists continued to increase, there would be little to prevent the emergence of two parallel tracks of law: the sovereign's law and the jurists' law, the latter operating outside or under the radar of governmental control, whereby the opinions and rulings of the jurists would be applied but not officially sanctioned. One observes a similar workaround later, albeit in a different form, between *ʿurf* and shariʿa, *yasa* and shariʿa, and *qānūn* and shariʿa.

Ibn al-Muqaffaʿ's argument is remarkable for another reason. It evokes the discussion of the king's two bodies, the biological and the legal. I wish to highlight two points that indicate the continuity of the legal body of the ruler. One relates to the capacity of the sovereign to issue laws and the other to his capacity to transfer the laws to future generations. The caliph issues the law following a certain procedure, and he is inspired by God in making his final decision, which separates the act of declaring laws from the ruler's other functions dictated by his biological body. It is worth noting that I do not read the "inspiration" cited in the passage in the confessionalized sense that assumes an immediate or specific divine directive to pick one opinion or the other. In the way Ibn al-Muqaffaʿ uses it here and in other passages in the "Epistle," the verb signifies divine support in the form of grace, like *niʿma*,[50] associated fittingly with the notion of the dignity or the aura of the office. It refers to the decision-making capacity that the sovereign attains when in office. As part of divine sanction, therefore, inspiration privileges the ruler with additional insight to make sound decisions. The second point pertains to the sovereign's privilege of handing down the laws to future generations, which suggests a notion of the transfer of sovereignty across generations. While the biological body of the caliph dies like any other human being, the legal body of the caliph survives his death. Royal dynasties often explain this idea using the metaphor of the genealogical tree.

In view of the ongoing discussion, I want to make a few additional remarks about Ibn al-Muqaffaʿ's legal interrogation. Considering his argument about the distinction between "religion and reason" and the use of rational judgment, I contend that Ibn al-Muqaffaʿ wanted to keep the jurists involved in legislation, which compelled him to discuss methodological and epistemological questions. Had his strategy been limited to concentrating the power of legislation in the hands of the sovereign alone, there would have been no need to discuss methodology and epistemology because the sovereign would decide the law regardless of what the jurists recommended. Instead, he took the more arduous route of arguing about what was and was not an established practice, *sunna*, the validity of legal precedents, and the proper manner of pursuing legal analogy for the common good. After suggesting how to consolidate legislative activity, Ibn al-Muqaffaʿ launches a discussion on why legal judgments might differ and how to manage legal questions to ensure a desirable outcome. He makes a full stop on legal analogy.

> As for different judgments, they are something handed down (*ma'thūr*) from past generations, but there has been no unanimous agreement on this, so some people manage (*yudabbir*) it one way and other people manage it another way. Thus, one examines a judgment to find out which of the two parties is worthier of approval and which of the two choices is closer to being just. These different judgments can also come from a rational judgment (*ra'y*) achieved through the application of legal analogy (*qiyās*), which has diverged from other views and spread, containing an error in the principle of analogical comparison. It thus is introduced into a case of analogy based on a dissimilar example. These different judgments can also come from adhering too heavily to legal analogy (*qiyās*).[51] Consequently, whoever wants to adhere to *qiyās* and never depart from it in matters of the revealed law and judgment (*ḥukm*) falls into quandaries, treads in dubious paths, and shuts his eyes in order not to see the abomination, which he knows and sees very well. He refuses to abandon it [*qiyās*], repugnant as he is to abandon practicing legal analogy. Indeed, legal analogy is a guide by which one can infer what is good. Thus, if what it leads to is good and virtuous, it is adopted, but if the result is something bad and objectionable, it should be abandoned, because *qiyās* is not an end in itself.[52] The seeker desires not the *qiyās* itself, but what is good and virtuous, and what delivers justice to people who deserve it. If something were already straightforward for the people, and was directed from where it should be, that is the truth of the circumstance, and the devices of analogy would thus be disregarded.[53] Therefore, if one wants to lead according to veracity, he will not be bound by it [*qiyās*]. Such is the case if a man said, "Do you order me to always be truthful and never tell a lie?" His answer would be "Yes." Then, if he were asked to say repeatedly, "Must I be truthful with regard to such and such?"[54] until he would say "Do I tell the truth[55] in the case where a man dashing off in pursuit of a fugitive asks me to indicate where the latter was located so that he could harm him or kill him?" In this case his adherence to *qiyās* would be invalid. The correct view (*ra'y*) for him would be to abandon that *qiyās* and resort to what has been agreed upon unanimously, the good and the virtuous.[56]

Ibn al-Muqaffaᶜ registers two principal causes of legal disagreement and explains how to mitigate them. One has to do with disagreeing on the meaning of a judgment or practice reported from past generations. His "legal historicism" enables him to include existing practices without infringing on the sovereign's authority. In such cases, he suggests, the sovereign is to examine (*naẓar*) the differing views on what has been reported and decide—to choose one of the views—according to his discretion. He seems to consider "what has been reported" (*ma'thūr*) from the past generations (*salaf*), who, one may assume, were well-regarded people/rulers, to be of binding authority or approaching that level of credibility. The sovereign needs only to choose the view that he thinks best fits the circumstance and leave out the rest. This point refers back to his discussion of conveying laws to the future generations in the sense that he expects the caliph to respect existing laws.

The second cause is erroneous logic or flawed method in arriving at an opinion through a faulty application of legal analogy (*qiyās*), which is far riskier and more harmful than the former. Ibn al-Muqaffaʿ's intervention tells us much about the emergence of *qiyās* as a legal methodological principle but does not exclude other forms of *qiyās* as part of rational judgment. Legal analogy (without being named as such) was initially practiced as early as the beginning of the eighth century among Iraqi jurists as a method under the broad umbrella of rational judgment, following a long tradition of legal thinking in the region reaching back to Sasanian times. By Ibn al-Muqaffaʿ's time, the use of *qiyās* was common in the region and already named *qiyās*, even though its technical and methodological principles had not yet been established or commonly agreed on among the jurists. That al-Shāfiʿī repeatedly calls the jurists of Iraq the "folk of *qiyās*" indicates that they used this procedure more extensively than others during his lifetime. By the end of the eighth century, the term *qiyās* became widespread among the ulema and signified a specific form of legal analogy.[57] The fact that Ibn al-Muqaffaʿ elaborates on this subject in such a brief text demonstrates his frustration with what must have been a practice in vogue among the jurists in Iraq in the mid-eighth century.

Ibn al-Muqaffaʿ's argument suggests that legal analogy was a recognized but not yet formalized and methodically defined practice among the Iraqi jurists, who seem to have been using it in a variety of ways. After acknowledging the place of analogy as a methodological device (*dalīl*) in legal reasoning, Ibn al-Muqaffaʿ recommends that it should be used sparingly to arrive only at what is commendable. He complains that legal analogy is applied in a manner that is contrary to the principles of reasoning, pointing out that a jurist's adherence to analogy excessively would have him make judgments contrary to the common good. It would also confine one's life to unreasonably detailed religious rulings that few would follow. Analogy, he asserts, is not an end in itself but a method by which to infer the good. One should abandon it whenever the expected outcome is harmful and objectionable, as one should not do analogical reasoning to produce harm.

Theoretical and Practical Implications

Codifying and objectifying the law in this way recalls an imperial legal tradition in the region that aimed at making the law a modality to ensure the compliance of the subjects and to act as a check on the power of the ruler. On the one hand, Ibn al-Muqaffaʿ insists on outlining or specifying regulations in manuals so that the rules governing relations are known by both the administrators and the subjects of the regulations. This is true for his advice on the army, taxation, and the law. On the other hand, by revealing the law and outlining responsibilities and rights, Ibn al-Muqaffaʿ exposes the government to a check by those who are subject to the law. The law may allow the sovereign an increased power and control; it also empowers his subjects by making the law visible to them and by enabling them to refer to it in settling disputes and disagreements among themselves and against the government. This trade-off is, as one may expect, a response to an old problem that the rulers had faced, which compelled or encouraged them since Hammurabi to spell out the laws and thus agree to circumscribe their own power in return for stability.

Certain aspects of Ibn al-Muqaffaʿ's argument also strike me as a reaction against an "axial age" problem that made the critique of political authority from the perspective of religion possible. As Habermas put it, the reference to a divinity beyond the world released the mind from the narratively ordered flood of occurrences under the sway of mythic powers and enabled the individual quest for salvation. "Once this transformation has taken place, the political ruler could no longer be perceived as the manifestation of the divine but only as its human representative." The ruler, like any other person, became subject to the nomos, which remained theoretically independent of his will. "Because the axial worldviews make both legitimation and the critique of political authority possible at the same time, 'the political' in the ancient empires was marked by an ambivalent tension between religious and political powers. Though the religiously backed belief in legitimacy can well be manipulated, it is never totally at the disposition of the ruler."[58] Observing a similar foundational challenge, Ibn al-Muqaffaʿ offers a way to normalize the legal tension by setting boundaries to the legal authority of the caliph and of the jurists. On the one hand, he attempts to prevent the jurists from infringing on the caliph's authority by issuing discrete and conflicting rulings without any check. On the other hand, he does not stipulate that the caliph hold a uniliteral authority over the law. Ultimately, Ibn al-Muqaffaʿ proposes a nuanced and workable compromise that encourages cooperation between the ulema and the caliph rather than a top-down monopoly of the ruler over the law. While he expects that jurists will still produce various competing legal opinions as developments required, one generation after the next, he envisions a legislative check on their work in order to weigh suggestions against one another, vet those that do not fit, and submit the remaining few for final approval by the ruler to be enacted as law. The proposed system would encourage the jurists to compete against one another not in the market of the believers but in the corridors of the administration to propose "bills" that they would deem most likely to succeed. Such a practice would create a regime of legal knowledge noticeably different from the one the jurists and their collaborators among the *ḥadīth* folk were practicing at the time.

With Ibn al-Muqaffaʿ's intervention, the law acquired the character of the "law of the land." Unlike the jurists' universal laws, which derived from the divine and aimed to establish rules for righteous living that were theoretically applicable anywhere, Ibn al-Muqaffaʿ's proposed law code was designed to respond to imperial contingencies. Like his overall position in the "Epistle" on administrative, military, and financial matters in the empire, the law too would regulate the lives of imperial subjects for the purpose of maintaining the ruler's power as well as the stability of the social order. In this scenario, the ruler as the legislator in chief would be concerned with the law not as the function of a profession or an act of mere piety but as a sociopolitical utility to generate a manageable rhythm of life among subjects. Hence, Ibn al-Muqaffaʿ's argument about the law makes human life an object of power. The law's three bodies (imperial, divine, and the combination of both), as I have argued, were meant to be not merely a body of rules interested in punishment, prohibition, and condemnation. While the laws would include an element of that, they would also be expected to function as a mechanism to normalize the conditions of life so that the social order would be bearable to the people constituting it.

On this subject, one would not object to the argument that the caliphs were already combining imperial-secular rulings and religious laws like those Ibn al-Muqaffaʿ was suggesting. It is plain, however, that the jurists were trying to recalibrate caliphal practice according to their own principles. They had already made substantial progress in gaining power in the field of law. Ibn al-Muqaffaʿ's intervention at this juncture was therefore critical. If nothing else, it denaturalized the caliphal practice and the ulema's jurisprudence by naming a new legal vision and elaborating it intellectually as a choice. If indeed the caliph al-Manṣūr intended to make the legal opinions of the prominent jurist Mālik b. Anas (d. 795) the primary law code of the Abbasid administration, he might or might not have done so by listening to Ibn al-Muqaffaʿ's advice. What is more notable is the fact that he did see the need to do that, which confirms Ibn al-Muqaffaʿ's foresight. Mālik b. Anas also responded with an argument that confirmed Ibn al-Muqaffaᶜ's critique of the jurists. If we assume Mālik b. Anas responded to the caliph, he rejected the caliph's desire on the ground that the opinions of other scholars were also legitimate and that there was nothing in the tradition to favor one opinion over another except for individual preference. This was a view that upheld the status quo.[59] Ultimately, the caliphs clashed with the ulema on exactly the points that Ibn al-Muqaffaᶜ had predicted.

Unfortunately, there is no recorded response to Ibn al-Muqaffaᶜ's "Epistle." One would expect, however, that his proposal would not tally well with the expectations of two groups. First, the revolutionary enthusiasts and the caliph himself might have considered Ibn al-Muqaffaᶜ's legal proposal too dismissive of Abbasid messianism. In the circumstances, when the caliph and his supporters led (or took part in) the most esoteric, maximalist, sectarian, and messianic movement of the eighth century, the scribe's portrayal of the caliph might have come across as too profane to be a salvific master. Second, the ulema would see his views as subversive. In this regard, Ibn al-Muqaffaᶜ's challenge was larger than sorting out the relations between the jurists and the caliph politically. As we have seen, it involved resolving the potential clash between the revealed law and the rational law, which his own proposal created. The ulema were steadily moving in the direction of the Islamization of the entire legal discourse when he pointed out the need for sorting out the functions of "religion" and "reason" as a question of statecraft. Although he offered a way to do so by defining religion and reason as divine gifts, equally capable of leading people to happiness as long as they are kept in their defined domains and are monitored by the ruler,[60] the very creation of a rational legal space separate from the ulema's jurisprudential discourse would generate a pushback from the ulema.

Finally, as must have been apparent to readers so far, Ibn al-Muqaffaᶜ's language is strikingly different from that of the jurists and revolutionary enthusiasts. Compared to the ulema's juristic language, with its attendant idioms and jargon, his language is that of statecraft. Although some contemporary scholars indict him as being an amateur in the legal discipline, partly because he does not explain the subject in the language of the jurists, what is evident in his text is that his lay language gave him the critical distance from the jurisprudence (*fiqh*) of the ulema to consider it not a natural, self-contained activity but one among other existing legal traditions in the region and part of imperial laws.[61] In the following chapter, I will explain how the legal "historicist" and "territorialized" notion of the law aligns with his imagination of the caliphate as an imperial landscape.

7

Territorial Consciousness

Imagining a Political Landscape

The main point of this chapter is that Ibn al-Muqaffaᶜ's envisioned empire represented not just an aggregation of cities, villages, roads, and peoples inherited from the Umayyads and now ruled by the Abbasids. It was an organization with its own structures and institutions, and an association that was constituted rather than received, cultural rather than natural, which suggests a political awareness more than a naked realism concerning how to normalize political power. It is true that the empire had been in the making for a century if one takes the early caliphal military conquests as a benchmark, or at least half a century since ᶜAbd al-Malik's administrative reforms. But his deliberate reflection in writing on the meaning of the imperial topography to rebuild it as a "political landscape" was a pioneering intervention.

Moving away from the enthusiasm of the revolt and the universalism of the ulema, Ibn al-Muqaffaᶜ defined the empire spatially within a certain territory as a geopolitical entity even if that meant severing certain limbs from the realm, as with North Africa and the Iberian Peninsula, which he does not include in his political calculus. This political awareness coincided with the caliphal shift of the axis from the Mediterranean to the Indian Ocean, which incidentally anticipated the "grand split" between Baghdad and Cordoba.

In this chapter, I clarify how Ibn al-Muqaffaᶜ's imaginative framework of a territorialized empire differed from the idea of religious community expressed only in the idioms of faith. I will first examine the discursive construction of Iraq-Khurasan and its military as the axis of the empire and how the Arabian Peninsula was reimagined as the ancestral sacred home of the Abbasid dynasty.

I will then deal with Syria's reconstitution as a subjugated province. I conclude the chapter with an assessment of why North Africa and al-Andalus may have been left out of the imperial territories.

The Orient of the Umayyads

One is justified in claiming that the Abbasid revolt did more than substitute one dynasty for another at the helm of the empire; it also dismantled the sociopolitical order, including its geopolitical structure. After the Abbasid victory, the axis of the empire shifted to the peripheries in the east and the west, and the imperial core in Syria imploded. In the east, Iraq and Khurasan became the center of the new empire while in the west, the North Africa–Iberian Peninsula complex became the hub of another independent empire. Until they accepted the new reality, the Abbasids acted on the assumption that they ruled over a landmass stretching from the Iberian Peninsula and Morocco in the west to the eastern frontiers of Iran in the east. For the first two Abbasid caliphs, the question of how to control the territories, what to do with the Umayyad institutions and structures, and how to implement their own ideals were open-ended questions. The uncertainty was a symptom partly of competing groups that pushed in different directions and partly of the bewilderment that ensued when the established order collapsed, leaving in its wake a vacuum of power that from the beginning pitted the participants in the revolt against each other.

As we have seen in chapter 1, implementing efficient policies required more substantial efforts than expressing discontent, which makes Ibn al-Muqaffaᶜ's intervention additionally valuable. He shifted the attention of the caliph toward the challenges of governing and proposed steps to build the postrevolt empire in a specific way. Pondering this circumstance at a time when multiple possibilities still presented themselves, Ibn al-Muqaffaᶜ suggested a road map to define the Iraq-Khurasan region as the core of the empire rather than relocating to Syria, which was the imperial core of the Umayyads. The critical point here is that his suggestion was not a simple affirmation of an actual condition. It was an imaginative proposal that involved the calculation of multiple steps. He first recognized that the dynasty needed a core support to survive and that Iraq and Khurasan should be chosen for that purpose. He observed that those two regions were distinct from each other not just geographically but also socially and culturally. Seeing the potential of amicable interactions between them, he suggested forging bonds among them as the best course of action to protect and marshal support for the caliph. He also predicted the challenges to come and warned the caliph about the dangers inherit in this project of "social engineering."

Ibn al-Muqaffaʿ makes a case for the Iraq-Khurasan region by highlighting the military as the core power and foundation of rule. While his advice on the military did not emerge as an "out of the blue" idea with no precedent, it was nevertheless reformist and bold. The closest example one may cite as precedent is ʿAbd al-Ḥamīd's "Testament to the Crown Prince," in which he laid out his recommendations for how to manage the army that the heir to the throne commanded. As an author and a colleague of ʿAbd al-Ḥamīd, Ibn al-Muqaffaʿ would have been familiar with the text and might have even been inspired by it. However, because there is no reason to think that ʿAbd al-Ḥamīd's writing had been widespread or well known beyond a small circle of administrators and scholars close to the court, Ibn al-Muqaffaʿ's recommendations would still strike the caliph and the revolutionary enthusiasts after the revolt as noteworthy.

The Empire's Military Foundation

In the opening paragraphs of his "Epistle," immediately after the preamble, Ibn al-Muqaffaʿ launches a discussion on how to reform the military. Considering its terse tone, the discussion strikes the reader as an audacious proposition that might be euphemistically described as a Leninist program (seizing and naturalizing power) proposed against a Trotskyist project (permanent revolution) dominating the postrevolutionary Abbasid milieu. In the months after the revolt, the Syrian army was dismantled by the Abbasids and replaced with the Khurasanis, who were being stationed in various centers and frontiers of the empire. The initial (or the revolutionary) Abbasid military replacing it comprised a body of soldiers in large numbers hailing from diverse Persian, Arab, or Perso-Arab roots (the Khurāsāniyya or Ahl Khurāsān), including various kinds of peasant and urban militia.[1] It also included tribal militia and Umayyad regiments who had switched their allegiance to the Abbasids.

The caliph al-Manṣūr seems to have acted robustly to mitigate his military challenges. He overcame his two major rivals, his uncle ʿAbdallāh b. ʿAlī and the celebrated commander Abū Muslim. In the meantime, al-Manṣūr reorganized the military to curb clan factionalism. While favoring the Yamanī faction, which had supported the Abbasids in the revolt, the caliph also tried to forge ties with the Qaysī faction, which had defended the Umayyads and reluctantly sided with ʿAbdallāh b. ʿAlī in his bid for the caliphate. Moreover, the caliph incorporated many of ʿAbdallāh b. ʿAlī's leading supporters in the administration and recognized the power and contribution of the Khurasani "sons of the revolt," *abnā'*, by choosing them to govern the province of Khurasan and administer its tax revenues. In hindsight, al-Manṣūr would appear building an elite military force composed of Arabs and *mawālī*, which he supervised through Khurasani military commanders, hoping to eliminate the danger of strife among kinship collectivities in his administration.

In the postrevolt circumstances, however, it would have been ostentatious to call the troops an organized army, even though the "trademark" of the Umayyad military, namely, its "tribal" makeup, had been dissipating, and kinship ties and loyalties were weakened. In one respect, the soldiers had no tribe to worry about; they displayed a strong loyalty to the new Summons; a manifest sectarian enthusiasm; and a reverence for the "family of the prophet" and the caliph himself. But, if we trust Ibn al-Muqaffaʿ, they also engaged in a stiff competition for lucrative positions and wealth and lacked military training. Additionally, despite their success in the Abbasid revolt, the soldiers received their pensions only in a disorganized and inconsistent manner, which threatened their morale. This was one of Ibn al-Muqaffaʿ's complaints about the military administration.[2]

Without knowing whether the caliph shared a similar perspective or would accept his advice as an agreeable course of action, Ibn al-Muqaffaʿ characterizes the current state of the revolutionary army as suffering from four major flaws: chaos detrimental to soldierly conduct caused by fanatical and overzealous leaders, confusion and bewilderment among soldiers, disorderliness and lack of military training, and conflicting opinions about the limits of caliphal authority. To train and reorganize the soldiers so that they respond efficiently to what Ibn al-Muqaffaʿ sees as a substantial political and administrative necessity, he suggests specific steps to take. After acknowledging the merits of the Khurasani army and the devotion of soldiers, he unambiguously recommends that the caliph look beyond the esoteric and messianic bond of discipleship that the revolutionary morality espoused if the caliph wished to achieve the soldierly ethics and training required of an effective military. He also recommends restricting military duties to military tasks by reassigning the responsibility of tax collection, which had been done by the military, to administrative offices. This reform would allow soldiers to be well trained in their craft with no distraction, and it would protect the farmers from their potential abuse. In effect, he suggests the creation of two separate institutions, one for the administration of the military and the other for the administration of land tax. Pondering his suggestions, one is justified to presume that while his advice was prompted by an evolving situation, it was also a calculated response aimed at a long-term impact: guiding the army to function according to the training they receive so that the caliph felt comfortable to entrust the dynasty's fate in the hands of a normalized military.

Lest the modern reader of the "Epistle" be persuaded by Ibn al-Muqaffaᶜ's reformist tone concerning the army and not ask why, in fact, his argument had any merit, a note on the army's standing is in order. Looked at from the perspective of the caliph, Ibn al-Muqaffaᶜ might have been "inventing" a problem by setting up a dichotomy between what one may call the "revolutionary army" and the "institutional military" that others did not see. After all, this was the same army that defeated the Umayyads, brought the Abbasid family to power, and even handed a decisive victory to al-Manṣūr against Abū Muslim and against his uncle, thus defending the family against the ᶜAlid claimants. One would also venture to say that the Abbasid caliph might have found the advice on the military unreasonably confining, even perhaps belittling, in light of the caliph's authority as the ruling imam and the messianic guide of his realm. Why should the caliph be dissatisfied with such an army and why should anyone listen to Ibn al-Muqaffaᶜ? Asking this question allows me to shift the analytical axis of my assessment from "reality" to language and to evaluate Ibn al-Muqaffaᶜ's position as one among other ways of representing the empire and the state of the army.

Considering that Ibn al-Muqaffaᶜ wrote at the beginning of a new era, after the revolt in which the Abbasids had yet to establish policies and practices, his intervention meant more than a portrayal of the scene or critique of the current circumstance. It also represented an attempt at providing a road map for building a powerful military force by reforming it and by reorienting its operation to fit an imperial order. This is not a problem he discusses theoretically. Pondering the suggestions he makes about the military in the dialogic context in which he writes, however, I would argue that he flips the revolutionary pyramid upside down, from its current orientation of creating an "empire for jihad" to organizing "jihad for empire." Ibn al-Muqaffaᶜ seems to redefine the goal of military operations from being a theological pursuit to being an imperial endeavor without attempting to deny its theological underpinnings or significance. Remaining consistent with his overall vision in the "Epistle," he rationalizes and politicizes military operations according to imperial priorities, which includes jihad as a source of strength but no longer the driving purpose of conquests, at least not to the extent that it is observed later in al-ᶜAnbarī's and Abū Yūsuf's texts.

Religious Devotion Versus Soldierly Virtue

Ibn al-Muqaffaᶜ assesses a revolutionary and zealously sectarian army of jihad. He notices the fervor and enthusiasm, the good qualities of loyalty, zeal, and humility in the Khurasani soldiers. He praises the sincerity, chastity, and purity of their intentions, and commends their honorable position among the people for their virtues and soldierly distinction. Whether the revolutionary soldiers had in fact embodied these qualities is irrelevant as far as the author's discursive strategy is concerned; the point he is making is that an ideal soldier needs such martial skills and moral qualities, which allows him to discuss how to attain them. Ibn al-Muqaffaʿ describes to the caliph in almost flattering terms that the likes of the Khurasani army have "never been witnessed in Islam" and that he has himself witnessed no one among other people even approaching their superiority. The Khurasanis, he notes, stand out because of traits that make them an exceptional group. They are insightful in matters of obedience, vigilant about protecting people's chastity and lives, far removed from corrupting actions, reputable among people, and a protective shield for the ruler.[3]

However, Ibn al-Muqaffaʿ is interested in discussing not the excellence of these soldiers but where they fall short, and the orientation of the military. What concerns him, and what undermines what he has just stated about the excellence of the soldiers, is that while the soldiers possess zeal and enthusiasm, they lack soldierly preparation to meet the sovereign's need. Ibn al-Muqaffaʿ portrays them as a group of arbitrarily collected individuals who, lacking a common purpose other than their seeming unbridled devotion to the leading family, the Abbasids, are oblivious to their charge and are not equipped with the training they need. In their current state[4] they roam in confusion[5] because of "fanatical and overzealous leaders and bewildered followers who are full of doubt."

After articulating this sweeping critique, Ibn al-Muqaffaʿ offers his diagnosis: if the sovereign wants them to function as well-trained soldiers, they must undergo a comprehensive program of training and discipline to improve their "military skills, opinions, and language."[6] In their current state, they are so disorganized, he warns the caliph, that "he who attacks enemies without assuring that his men agree with him in judgment, word or deed is like the rider of a lion who frighten those who see him, but is in fact more frightened than anyone else."[7]

A substantial portion of Ibn al-Muqaffaʿ's discourse on authority in the "Epistle" concerns how to mitigate and curb such revolutionary messianic enthusiasm so that their centrifugal posture does not derail the new order or prevent efforts to reach a new equilibrium. Alarmed by the heightened esoteric and messianic enthusiasm among the soldiers, Ibn al-Muqaffaʿ recommends a challenging course of action to correct their ways: the caliph should make their beliefs "straight" so that they match the military training they should receive and the soldierly conduct they must display. On this point, he goes right to the heart of the revolutionary fervor to characterize the state of the military: "Many of the opinionated talkers (*mutakallimīn*)[8] among commanders (*quwwād*) of the

Commander of the Faithful today say in their speeches, when giving orders and making claims,[9] that if the Commander of the Faithful were to order the mountains to move, they would move, and if he ordered that worshippers turn their backs to the *qibla*,[10] that would be done."[11] Sounding astonished in a religious and political sense, Ibn al-Muqaffaᶜ continues to caution the caliph that "this is talk that is seldom accepted[12] by an adversary and is rarely heard by anybody without creating suspicion and doubt."

Ibn al-Muqaffaᶜ had a point. Without mentioning names, he criticizes attitudes in such damning language that brings to mind the discursive and emotional axis of the Abbasid propaganda, the Kaysāniyya, and its sub-branches such as the Rāwandiyya, which advocated the veneration of the Abbasid family, including al-Manṣūr himself, as messianic figures. As Ibn al-Muqaffaᶜ was keenly aware, the revolutionary messianic language of the Abbasid uprising had brought to positions of power all sorts of messianic propagandists in Khurasan and Transoxiana who set out to make their imprint on empire building. The chief Abbasid propagandist and the commander of the Summons in Khurasan, Abū Muslim himself, had forged connections with the Khurasani Kaysāniyya. After his death, he even became one of the messianic figures of such sects that claimed to follow his teachings.[13] The sect Abū Muslimiyya, for instance, formed a subgroup that maintained that the imamate had passed from the first Abbasid caliph al-Saffāḥ to Abū Muslim, whom the group considered its leader. After the execution of Abū Muslim by the caliph al-Manṣūr in 755, some of his supporters maintained that a person who only resembled him had been killed and that Abū Muslim had gone into occultation.[14] One may also note the insurrection of Sunbād, a wealthy Zoroastrian from Nishapur who was an ardent supporter of Abū Muslim. Two months after Abū Muslim's execution, he revolted, claiming that Abū Muslim had not been killed and would return to rule.[15] Another revolt in Transoxiana in the name of Abū Muslim was led by al-Muqannaᶜ, the Veiled One, in Marw in 777. Al-Muqannaᶜ claimed to be divine and the incarnation of Adam, who had been reincarnated in Moses, Jesus, Muhammad, and Abū Muslim. His movement began in his native Marw and spread to Samarqand and Bukhara before ending in a spectacular suicide in a fire with the members of his family and the most loyal of his followers.[16]

Other movements and insurrections allied with Abbasid figures contributed to this milieu of heightened esoteric and messianic tide. Rizām b. Ṣābiq, one of the Rāwandīs in Khurasan, upheld the succession of al-Manṣūr to the imamate and developed a substantial following known as the Rizāmiyya. Although they refused to repudiate Abū Muslim, they affirmed that the imamate would remain in the Abbasid family until the Resurrection, when a descendant of al-ᶜAbbās would be the Mahdi.[17] A group among them even claimed the divinity of the caliph (circumambulating his palace as the sacred precinct of their "lord"), but once he repudiated them, they attempted to kill him.[18] The caliph seems to have distanced himself from the radicalism of the Rizāmiyya, but he did not renounce any claims concerning his messianic role. He is reported to have recounted in his chamber a dream in which the Prophet entrusted him with a banner until he fought against the Antichrist (al-Dajjāl).[19]

Although Ibn al-Muqaffaᶜ knew that the revolt was led by a family considered to be endowed with a messianic charge and that the adoration of the "Prophet's family" among the militia-turned-military and other supporters was pervasive and widespread, he still dared to challenge the revolutionary fervor. By marginalizing the claims as extreme without naming their source, he allowed himself to caricature and therefore demolish them as being unfounded, unconvincing, and damaging. In such a cacophony (*akhlāṭ*), as he describes the scene he is assessing, he proceeds to advise on how to restructure the military. Ibn al-Muqaffaᶜ invites the caliph to listen to those whom he called "high-minded people from among the Muslims" (*ahl al-qaṣd min al-muslimīn*). He reminds the caliph that "what they say is good for strengthening the command (*aqwā li-al-amr*), reinforcing sovereign authority (*aᶜazz li-al-sulṭān*), suppressing adversaries, satisfying supporters, and ensuring evidence of right conduct before God, Most High and Sublime."[20] Although he reveals neither those "high-minded" people nor what comprised high-mindedness, he seems to mean individuals whom he considered "sane" believers, who kept an arm's-length distance from such maximalist esoteric and militant messianic practices. Ibn al-Muqaffaᶜ's dismissal of the esoteric veneration of the caliph, coded so prominently in Abbasid revolutionary discourse, in this way was more than just unsettling. It was a "counter-revolutionary" position.

Ibn al-Muqaffaᶜ eschews the claims of the sectarian enthusiasts. He places the military under the direct control of the caliph as the commander in chief rather than a messianic master of his devotees. In this context, Ibn al-Muqaffaᶜ launches a discussion on when the ruling imam should or should not be obeyed and attempts to define the limits of the sovereign's authority. While he privileges the caliph with a firm authority over his army, he avoids any notion of messianic discipleship or the bond of esoteric fraternity that blurs the line between the supreme commander and the soldier. Ibn al-Muqaffaᶜ advises on how to start this process: "One of the things to examine about the situation of the army is that some of the ordinary soldiers among them are better than some of their officers. If they were recognized and supported, they would become a useful element and force, and this would be beneficial both for the officers above them and the troops below them."[21] One may read this statement as an innocent and good commonsense suggestion for reordering the military. Read against the background of the revolutionary fervor of the initial Abbasid decade, however, it may also be understood as recommending that the revolution devour its own children. Its cynical undertone aside, this statement pushes the agenda of replacing the "revolution heroes" with officers from the rank-and-file soldiers who, Ibn al-Muqaffaʿ argues, would do a much better job in "normal" times than that of a haphazard assemblage of militia inherited from the revolt. Said another way, his recommended course of action makes it possible to transform the military from being a collection of "street-educated" militia to an organized army with "school-educated" rank-and-file soldiers who would follow a predetermined career path based on their skills and merit.

Acknowledging and supporting the Abbasid family's tradition of trusting the Khurasani military rather than the defeated Syrian soldiers (*ahl al-Shām*), whose loyalty, according to Ibn al-Muqaffaʿ, cannot be guaranteed, Ibn al-Muqaffaʿ suggests that the sovereign writes "a customarily considerate (*maʿrūf*), eloquent, and brief manual (*amān*), containing all that they must either put into practice or eschew, a manual that is both utterly persuasive and devoid of excess." It is, he continues, "to be kept by their officers (*ru'asā'*) so that they conform to it when leading common soldiers, and some of them oblige their subordinates among the soldiers[22] at large to commit themselves to abide by it." He assures the caliph that such an initiative "would improve and correct their judgment and would serve as an authoritative guide for others and a legitimate excuse of one's behavior before God."[23]

Perhaps expecting the element of surprise in his recommendation, Ibn al-Muqaffaʿ explains why a manual such as the one he describes is needed and desirable, although the explanation itself might have struck its audience as more audacious than the actual advice. His recommendation of writing a manual to administer the military is noteworthy for several reasons. The immediate consequence, which might have been a cause of anxiety for the caliph, is that it would risk alienating many of his supporters in the postrevolt circumstances because it would require substantial changes in the military. Another audacious aspect of his recommendation was that the manual itself, as a contract and assurance of protection (*amān*) would become binding not just upon the soldiers but also upon the ruler himself, as evidence or proof in case of a disagreement. Although the caliph might alter or abolish it as a set of rules that would apply to him and to soldiers, it would still have the authority to regulate the career of soldiers and set a binding standard for their relations with the sovereign for the duration of its validity.

Military power and soldierly virtue cannot be attained without proper conduct and the right belief. Ibn al-Muqaffaʿ proposes succinctly a series of measures to train and discipline the troops as a dependable imperial army to best serve the sovereign. Operating on the assumption that different constitutions of a good soldier would lead to distinct armies, he insists on "professionalizing" the military through vigorous training in martial skills and "the right belief." To raise a good soldier and an army with a well-organized structure and a firm chain of command, he suggests establishing procedures and regulations known to soldiers and the caliph to cover the soldiers' training, education, discipline, career paths, ranks, pay, assessment, and promotion. Because creating a wholesome soldier cannot be limited to martial instruction, discipline should include ethical education to inculcate soldierly virtue as the end purpose of military training. The soldiers should build martial character congruent with the caliph's demands and cultivate a feeling of strong loyalty toward the sovereign.

Ibn al-Muqaffaʿ advises how to ensure the soldiers' proper manners (*adabihim*) so that they learn the scripture (*al-kitāb*, the Qur'an); cultivate the knowledge of tradition (*al-tafaqquh fi-l-sunna*); uphold the virtues of fidelity and integrity; and display in conduct frugality, modesty, and dislike of excess in pleasures. Citing here the caliph as an example to follow, Ibn al-Muqaffaʿ advises that the caliph needs to ensure that the soldiers distinguish themselves from "heretics" and avoid the opinions and the appearance of pleasure-seeking people by leading an austere life. "What is known about the Commander of the Faithful in his actions and in what he expresses in words," he acknowledges, "is his hatred of excess lavishness and extravagance and people who devote themselves to such matters." The caliph, he adds, is known for his love of frugality, modesty, and people who attain such qualities. He reminds the caliph to nurture such qualities among soldiers so that "they know that the beneficence of the Commander of the Faithful is forbidden to those who would hoard wealth out of greed[24] or waste it extravagantly on perfume, clothing, and excessive desire for women and concern only with climbing ranks." They should know that the caliph prefers to be charitable to those who intend to be beneficent and selfless.[25]

Ibn al-Muqaffaʿ was a realist. An empire was based on the support of military might, but that power can also turn against its benefactor. He knew that, despite the measures taken to maintain a powerful and loyal military, the ties between the soldiers and the sovereign, no matter how strong, could fail. He thus recommends that the caliph be alert about unwanted developments in the military. The caliph would monitor the military with utmost care, control its movements, and preempt any resentment or commotion that might undermine stability. He warns that "it is a facet of comprehensive and successful work, with God's permission, that nothing remains secret to the Commander of the Faithful about their affairs, their circumstances, and the innermost facts about them in Khurasan, in Askar Mukram, and on the frontiers."[26]

Recognizing the critical value of intelligence, Ibn al-Muqaffaʿ encourages the caliph not to spare any expense in monitoring the military and warns him to hear the advice of only trustworthy people concerning this matter. The caliph must not dislike spending funds on this nor avoid asking for help—again, from only the most trustworthy advisers. Overlooking a precaution would be worse than not asking for help at all. Confiding about the army in untrustworthy advisers would only result in ignorance and deceit.[27] His advice on the army intelligence is, of course, an apt observation, but it is moreover an action-enabling thought that potentiates establishing a bureau of army intelligence staffed by the most trusted advisers to gather information about the soldiers and their activities. Taking such steps would further remove the military from its current "revolutionary" state and place it under stricter administrative control, with checks and balances that would keep it in its proper place.

Civil Administration and the Military

One of the critical discussions of the army involves its finances. Here I will problematize the subject in the context of creating a proper soldier. Ibn al-Muqaffaʿ critiques the existing practice of using the military in the collection of taxes levied on farming, whether it is sharecropping by the central or provincial administration, as not just ineffective but harmful to the army and to the farmers. He suggests that the caliph, in the interest of his army, should not put any military officers in charge of the land tax, "for administration of the land tax surely corrupts the fighters." He reminds the caliph that haggling to collect taxes is not commensurate with the dignity of the military and warns that "the administration of the land tax requires humility, wickedness, and pedantry, while the position of the fighter is one of dignity and generosity."[28]

Ibn al-Muqaffaʿ's fear is that, if creating wealth becomes a priority for soldiers, it would erode military prowess and values. The soldiers would become entangled in a web of relations that had little to do with their professional responsibilities and would negatively affect the performance of their primary duty. They would have less time to devote to training, be less dependable in fulfilling military obligations, and be less skilled in their craft. He also disapproves of this form of contact between farmers and soldiers as being beneath soldierly ethics and status. The soldiers must be given a degree of isolation from the population and be freed from the burden of collecting taxes so that they can maintain their high military morale. For him, collecting taxes is nothing but an exchange of military values and dignified soldierly life for the mundane and vulgar activity of dealing with money and interacting with farmers.

His other concern about using the military to collect the land tax is the possibility of intimidating farmers, abusing taxpayers, and alienating subjects from the sovereign. Alluding to the current practice, Ibn al-Muqaffaʿ alerts the caliph that farmers in their turn have been trying to avoid soldiers because of the fear of being brutalized. He cautions the caliph that "if the soldiers become attracted by dirhams and dinars, they will bully the farmers, and if they succumb to treason, all of their affairs[29] will become corrupted, including their[30] advice and their loyalty." He fears that if military power is exercised or the threat of military violence is expressed as an option in tax collection, it will corrupt the whole cycle of production, affect tax revenue, and disturb the social balance, about which he is so dearly worried in his proposal.

An army officer who is less concerned with his professional duties than with the politics of land administration and tax revenue would become a political threat as well. Overseeing taxation would create a rift between soldiers and the ruler. If they are questioned about the decrease in the revenue of the land tax, Ibn al-Muqaffaʿ warns, their pride causes them to be resentful,[31] a situation the caliph should avoid. Once a soldier becomes an actor in financial affairs and in the politics of tax administration, he can no longer be trusted. The conflict of interest might lead him to treason and force the sovereign to review constantly his conduct, be alert to subversion in his activities, and take steps to outmaneuver him. If the soldiers were freed from this burden, however, they would be immune to the possible corrupting influence of dealing with money and could devote their time and energy to their own training, which would help them maintain an undivided loyalty to their sovereign.

Yet the caliph must pay the soldiers generously. Aware of the connection between soldiers' pensions and tax collection, Ibn al-Muqaffaʿ proposes to reform how soldiers should be paid with minimal impact on the budget and without causing discontent. The Umayyad practice had been to record the names of soldiers in the army register (*dīwān*) by their kinship affiliation and pay them annually in cash (*ʿaṭāʾ*) and kind (*rizq*),[32] with bonus gifts on holidays and other occasions. By the time al-Manṣūr became caliph, the system had broken down, and no new convention was in place. The established practice was that any revenue from the land tax went to the governmental treasury, from which the salaries were paid.[33] As a major expense, Ibn al-Muqaffaʿ argues, military pensions need careful planning and supervision. Pensions should be given at regular intervals every few months so that the soldiers know what to expect routinely. Regular payment would also stall any protest among them because of delay.

His recommendation on this subject connects a major branch of the imperial economy to the military. Let me quote this section in full:

> Regarding their pensions (*rizq*, pl. *arzāq*), it would be useful if the Commander of the Faithful would set a time when they know they will receive it, every three or four months, or over a certain period judged by him to be appropriate. It is necessary for all the soldiers to understand the reason for setting up a register (*dīwān*) and collecting their names, so that they know when they will receive their pay, in order to avoid any delay and complaints. Just one word of protest uttered in this regard by one soldier may become a grave matter. It is thus necessary to firmly shut such a door.[34] Also, the Commander of the Faithful knows the amount of the pensions they receive and the abundance of money that goes out to them.[35] He knows that if this land tax is in abundance, it is because of rising prices. There inevitably will be a recession and breakdown. Everything exists in abundance and lavish supply today. The revenue from the land tax in Iraq is high only because prices are high. Indeed, the army today needs increased pensions because of rising prices. It would be good fortune, God willing, that harm does not come to the land and that the treasury suffers no reduction by the Merciful One, lest that reflect back on the soldiers through their pensions (*arzāq*), even though they would not incur loss because they would be able to buy at a more modest price what they used to buy at a higher price in the past. So I say: If the Commander of the Faithful were to reserve a fraction of the pensions,[36] turn some of these funds into food and some into fodder for the animals to be paid in kind, then, when the price of food and fodder is determined, and their value deducted from the pensions, there would, therefore, not be an immediate decrease in their pay (*arzāq*), which they would detest. This will be a way to keep them combat ready against the enemy[37] and to relieve the treasury from being concerned about whatever they might receive later, for even if prices become high, they will still get their portion, benefiting from the surplus (*faḍl*).[38]

Because agricultural production formed the primary sector of economic activity in the empire, his belief that the army should be paid from the revenue of the land tax follows a customary practice, but Ibn al-Muqaffaʿ lays out several specific and critical steps needed to organize the finances of the military. The foremost task is establishing a procedure based on actual financial conditions. He encourages creating a register containing the names, ranks, and salaries of soldiers; clarifying the form of payment; diversifying pensions as cash and kind and adjusting them according to "inflation," and establishing a schedule for the distribution of pensions. He observes critical financial questions (production, market volatility, prices, inflation, land tax, salaries) related to the "economy" to balance expenditure and avoid setbacks so that the soldiers are kept satisfied and the treasury is unburdened.

His suggestion to divide pensions into cash and kind payments is part of the same strategy of ensuring the supply of food and fodder to soldiers, preventing drastic and immediate reduction in salaries, and enabling them to resume their military operations undistracted by financial concerns. The soldiers would not lose any benefits because they would receive in-kind payments and because the prices of their food and fodder would also increase and decrease following the fluctuations of the market. This administrative policy would also protect the treasury from the pressure of constant demands to process delayed payments during times of recession.

Remarkably, his assessment of supply and price fluctuation might be the first instance in which we encounter a discussion of inflation in caliphal history.[39] Ibn al-Muqaffaʿ reasons that soaring prices are driven by demand when the market is full of commodities. This helps tax collection because farmers can generate abundant wealth and pay their taxes. This is the ideal situation, if sustained, because it enables the sovereign to fill the treasury and pay the military without difficulty. He notices, however, that there could be a cycle of recession driven by the volatility of the market, which he explains as an act of God. Because pensions are taken out of the treasury, any volatility in revenue because of a recession would have grave implications for the ability of the treasury to pay the military. Identifying the question of salaries as fiscal, Ibn al-Muqaffaʿ, thus, offers a strategy to avoid recurring crises in the future. He aims to minimize the impact of an economic downturn on the military without also straining the budget. In adjusting pensions as a matter of policy, according to and by predicting market movements, he theorizes a way to avoid fiscal crises by monitoring inflationary pressure on revenue and expenditure.

Considering the foregoing discussion, one observes that Ibn al-Muqaffaʿ repeatedly reminds the caliph in several ways that the military cannot be a collection of individual soldiers brought together by chance, nor a community functioning according to an ethos of esoteric discipleship, in which the soldiers and the commanders play the role of brethren and masters. Rather, he presents the army as an organization composed of trained soldiers in a controlled military setting whose rules and regulations are written, whose expectations are set, and whose area of responsibility is delineated to serve the desired purpose. Considered along with his other recommendations, the fact that Ibn al-Muqaffaʿ wanted the caliph to ensure that the army functions as a "professional" military under the direct control of the caliph matches Ibn al-Muqaffaʿ's broader interests in the "Epistle." To put it in Aristotelian language, Ibn al-Muqaffaʿ suggested that a soldier could attain soldierly virtue only by discharging his duty.

The "Core People"

Ibn al-Muqaffaʿ emphasizes the people of Iraq and Khurasan in several passages in the "Epistle," but he pursues the theme of making the region the empire's center immediately after discussing the military. By the time of the Abbasid revolt in the 740s, the Umayyad Empire stretched from the Iberian Peninsula to the Indus Valley, with Syria and Damascus as its center. Like other agrarian empires, the Umayyads arranged imperial territories according to their political priorities and projected power outward from the empire's center. Although what one refers to as "the core" was never exclusively defined as a "homeland" with a specific durability, one notices the articulation of difference in discourse, in the political economy, and in the architectural investment between the Eastern Mediterranean (Greater Syria and Egypt) and the rest of the provinces.[40] The Umayyad family relied on Syrian and Egyptian elites, soldiers, and kinship groups for their administrative and military operations. While the core areas were controlled by Umayyad family members and other trusted officials, the outlying provinces were subject to various flexible arrangements of imperial oversight through autonomous vassals and even independent tributaries.

The Hijaz and Yemen were neglected provinces with no major infrastructure (roads, monuments, urban planning) because the wave of migration from these regions to major cities and frontiers had been draining their populations. The holy cities of Mecca and Medina maintained their prestige, of course, which encouraged the Marwānid Umayyads to appoint family members to govern them, but the region received little attention beyond that. In the north, the provinces of Armenia, Harran, and Adharbayjan were governed from the Jazira by members of the Umayyad family, who kept their provinces under tight control. The western provinces of North Africa and the Iberian Peninsula were a recognized part of the empire, but the actual control of them from the center was not always effective.

Combined with Iraq, Khurasan comprised territories extending to the east of the Oxus River. From the perspective of the Umayyads, it was one of the most problematic regions; they tried to keep it under firm control, with little success in the eighth century. One can note several issues that made this region a challenge for the Umayyads while offering significant support for the Abbasids. Since its conquest in the early seventh century, Iraq was an important province of the caliphate. It was the site of two thriving news towns, Kufa and Basra, which were established as garrison towns during the caliphate of ʿUmar I; a significant source of revenue; a hub of the new religious and social formations; and a center of controversies among the ruling elite, pastoral nomadic groups, and sectarian groups. During the tumultuous events of the first civil war from 640 to 660, the region became the center of Kharijite activities and ʿAlid loyalties. ʿAlī even moved his capital from Medina to Kufa to secure his position against his opponents. After his assassination in 656, the town became the cradle of Shiite sectarianism. When the Umayyads got hold of the caliphate after the assassination of ʿAlī, Syria became the center of the empire and Iraq lost prestige as a province, but both Shiite and Kharijite activities continued there against the Umayyads.

During the initial conquest under the caliphs ʿUmar I and Uthmān, the new overlords intervened as little as possible in the existing socioeconomic structure of the province. They made rudimentary administrative, urban, and then legal arrangements to minimize contacts between the natives and the Arab colonies, which were established there in garrison towns and settlements housing the soldiers and their families. If they paid the tribute, the natives and their local nobility were left undisturbed. Such policies separated the Arab and native populations of the region from each other as a means of management and control. While the policy of segregation helped the natives adjust to their new circumstances, it also allowed their overlords to interfere in their lives in a variety of ways.[41]

In the beginning, the Umayyads co-opted the native landowners and administrators, who desired to cooperate with them by acting as their agents in the region in return for certain privileges. Beginning with the governorship of Ziyad b. Abīhi of Iraq and the east in 665, however, the new administration took aggressive and punitive steps to subdue and control the region. Khurasan and further to the east were too far to be governed from Syria. For this reason, the Umayyads sometimes gave the region autonomy under strongmen and at other times placed it under direct Syrian control in the hope of better administering it, but neither arrangement seemed to ensure stability in Iraq and Khurasan.[42] On the contrary, military and administrative interference of the Umayyads and their harsh policies provoked resentment and discontent among some of the landed and ruling nobility, and early sectarian formations revolted against the Umayyads. In return, the Umayyads resorted to protracted, often violent pacification policies, but local social and political problems persisted.[43]

It would be an understatement to say that the military settlements in the broader region contributed to existing tensions. In Khurasan, for instance, Marw became the military base of the conquerors, where soldiers and their families, hailing from Basra, settled starting from the eighth century. Until the arrival of the Azd tribe, the Arab population in Khurasan comprised four main kinship groups: Tamīm and Qays (known as the northern tribes of Muḍar) and Bakr b. Wā'il and ʿAbd al-Qays (known as the Rabīʿa tribes of Yemen), which had long competed for hegemony over Khurasan even before the Second Civil War in 684–685.[44]

The efforts to control the region led to the emergence of a settler-ruling community that was attached to the caliphate. This group of administrators served in the military and administration and therefore depended on imperial pensions and the spoils of war for their livelihood. Many of them had little appreciation of the common people, farming, and crafts.[45] Having adjusted and adapted to the region, some prominent families among the Arab settlers, soldiers, imperial agents, administrators, and other officials seized on larger opportunities beyond their pensions and primary function and gained landed estates by whatever means.[46] Others took up trade in luxury goods, some even gaining enough influence and wealth to build their own militia. Many soldiers gave up their professions and became farmers or peasants; others, however, fell in the cracks of this "gold rush" and ended up among the vagabonds and the urban poor. A similar transformation took place among the local native subjects. The native agrarian nobility quickly discovered how to cooperate with the new ruling class and protect their own interests, while the commoners and the peasants lagged behind.[47]

Finding an expedient policy of quid pro quo, the governors distributed military and civil service positions among their kin and allies to secure loyalty. Clan factions competed (by both political maneuvering and violence) to receive such favors, which led to complex ad hoc alliances and rivalries among factions and among subgroups within each faction.[48] For instance, the Syro-Jaziran troops, local Arabs, and non-Arab Muslims (*mawālī*) competed for access to such power and patronage from a governor. The stakes got higher, and the conflicts among kinship factions and constituent tribes grew more frequent and violent. Even non-Arab converts to Islam in the province, who were allied to various tribes through clientage, *walā'*, were drawn into such rivalries on the side of their patron tribes.[49]

As the caliphate engaged with the region, migration continued, urban life developed with the intensification and regularity of transregional trade, and new socioeconomic divisions and conflicts emerged among the settlers and the natives. The kinship nobility of the colonists became detached from common kin because of the military and administrative positions they occupied and through investment in land and trade. The old forms of kinship politics turned into faction politics (*ʿaṣabiyya*) in the army and administration. At the same time, however, segregating the soldiers and the ruling people from the native populations lasted only for so long. The policy faltered in the initial decades of the eighth century. Towns and cities became places of more complex sociocultural and economic relations (linguistic, ethnic, racial, confessional), which paved the way for hybrid urban classes in the region.[50] The intense socioeconomic interactions, including conversion, marriage, taking on administrative and other positions, and interest in scholarship, produced hybrid imperial subjects and a growing presence of non-Arab Muslims in the province. Persian disappeared as a high language, and Arabic established itself, and the "Khurasani tongue" (Arabo-Persian) developed among the subject population as a shared vernacular. The Khurasani vernacular replaced Arabic in everyday interactions among the second and later generations of migrants in the early decades of the eighth century.[51] Its spread may be an indicator of the sociocultural transformation that took place and of the multivalent power dynamics in the province under the Umayyads.

To understand the political calculus of Ibn al-Muqaffaʿ, a remarkable corroborative anecdote may be useful here. A founding father of the Abbasid claims, Muhammad b. ʿAlī is said to have told his followers to concentrate their missionary activities on Khurasan, where they would find enthusiastic supporters unlike those in any other region. His assessment included that Kufa remained loyal to ʿAlī and his offspring. Basra and its countryside housed only ardent Umayyad-supporting ʿUthmānis. The hopeless Kharijites, Bedouin, a bunch of "rustic folks" (*aʿlāj*), and degenerate Muslims adopting Christian moral values populated the Jazira of upper Mesopotamia. Syria stayed loyal to its Umayyad lords and opposed the Abbasid Summons; Mecca and Medina still lovingly remembered Abū Bakr and ʿUmar. Only in Khurasan, Muhammad b. ʿAlī estimated, would a missionary see many supporters and hopeful enthusiasts of the Abbasid Summons.[52]

A patent Abbasid apology, the alleged reasoning of Muhammad b. ʿAlī is not anachronistic. If such an observation could be made, the fourth decade of the eighth century would be a fitting time for it. Political considerations after defeating the Umayyads encouraged the new ruling family to rely on supporters in Iraq and Khurasan. Given the uncertainty during and after the revolt, however, even the capital of the new ruling family shifted from one town to another (within only a dozen years from Humayma, Hira, Kufa, Hashimiyya, to Baghdad—all in proximity) to better manage and mitigate the risks that the new leadership faced. When Ibn al-Muqaffaʿ began his new career in the fifth decade of the century, Khurasan had already emerged as the de facto power reservoir of the Abbasid family, although the political structuring of the empire remained a work in progress.

As a person from the region, Ibn al-Muqaffaʿ knew these developments. He recognized the potential significance of the professional and intellectual capital of the Iraqi region for the empire. In particular, the metropoles there boasted sprawling urban life, socioeconomic and cultural eminence, attested seniority in the Shiite struggles in the past, and a strategic location between Khurasan and Egypt. His overall point in this matter is to mold the populations in Iraq and Khurasan into a core people to protect and support the caliph. To make a case, Ibn al-Muqaffaʿ discusses succinctly the merits of "the people of the two metropolises,"[53] Kufa and Hira in Iraq as potentially the most devoted and resourceful subjects of the sovereign. "After the Khurasanis," he asserts, "they are the people most suited to become his supporters and followers,[54] for they have intermingled with the people of Khurasan. They are from them, and they are their leaders."[55] As I will examine in the next chapter, Ibn al-Muqaffaʿ assures the caliph in another section of the text that if he desired to rely entirely on an elite among the people of Iraq, he could do so because they are unmatched "among all other people of the Qibla."[56] In a perfectly complementary way, he describes the people of Khurasan as the loyal core subjects of the new dynasty and encourages the caliph to combine them with the inhabitants of the two metropolises. The inhabitants of the two major Iraqi cities, according to his assessment, match their Khurasani counterparts in being eminent in loyalty and competence and worthy of privileges as supporters of the Abbasids.

Not being overly optimistic, Ibn al-Muqaffaʿ expects challenges in Iraq and warns the caliph about breeches of loyalty. The caliph "must assure himself of the sincerity of their loyalty"[57] and seek the help of the Khurasanis "in what he wishes to know about their affairs."[58] "In that, however," he continues "there is some burden,[59] in addition to the intermixing of people with people, Arabs with non-Arabs (*al-ʿarab bi-al-ʿajam*), and the people of Khurasan with those in the two metropolises."[60] Given the circumstances in Iraq and Khurasan after the revolt, Ibn al-Muqaffaʿ's apprehension about the divided loyalties and the competing claims on privileges was well founded. The caliph's task of creating a core people and relying on their loyalty might require efforts and facing serious challenges much beyond taking administrative precautions. While Ibn al-Muqaffaʿ recognizes the inevitability of these developments, he approaches them at the same time with a toned-down apprehension as a question of control and management. If one ponders his advice in the text about other matters, one suspects that he must have also wondered whether the policies of the Abbasids impeded the ability of this region's people to serve as the center of the empire he imagined.

Ibn al-Muqaffaʿ's most remarkable observation in this context concerns the consequences of intermixing people and the challenge of social hybridity. As I have noted in chapter 1 and here, the Iraq-Khurasan region enjoyed a complex sociocultural topography that only grew more intricate toward the mid-eighth century. Ibn al-Muqaffaʿ's comments reflect his recognition of diversity, of the hybridity and cosmopolitanism of imperial life, and of the sociocultural fault lines of the core region that were emerging after the revolt. The intermixing of people and biological hybridity carried implications for the relations of the "Arabs with non-Arabs," the status of the *mawālī*, and the distinction between the elite and the common folk. His very notice of the cultural "border crossing" suggests that he expected new developments and wanted to channel their course. On the one hand, he sees no way out of this social blending in this region, which the new ruling family needed for support and which had been happening anyway. On the other hand, for someone like Ibn al-Muqaffaʿ, social hybridity posed an unsettling problem beyond the question of controlling the emerging new social group. Would the imperial subject produced by the recent intermixing of people, and because of his "social engineering," complement or hinder the monarchical notion of social equilibrium?[61] The question of how to situate the Iraq-Khurasan region in the empire gave Ibn al-Muqaffaʿ a reason to ponder strategies for shaping the empire according to new priorities and even reassess the major pillars of his own political vision.

A Sacred Homeland

In analyzing Ibn al-Muqaffaʿ's territorial awareness, one wonders about the Hijaz and its two holy cities. His statements on the region in various places in the text suggest a leveraging of imperial might to reconstitute or reaffirm it as the "sacred core" of the empire. Ibn al-Muqaffaʿ's recommendation regarding the region as part of an imperial geography does not seem to be provoked by any urgent administrative or military problem nor by a notable revenue-producing capacity or commercial potential that needed to be addressed as a matter of reform. His interest in the region seems to be entirely related to the region's cultural and spiritual significance. Unlike the urgency evident in his other recommendations (concerning Iraq-Khurasan, Syria, the elite, army, taxation), Ibn al-Muqaffaʿ aims here to dignify the region and connect the Abbasids to their "sacred" roots. This gesture toward the sacred geography would differentiate the Abbasids from the Umayyads discursively and symbolically, too. As the Umayyads appeared oriented toward Palestine, the Abbasids would be oriented toward the Hijaz.

The Arabian Peninsula housed the two sacred Muslim cities and was the home of the ruling family's ancestors and the venerated figures of Islam. In addition, the faithful performed the major communal Muslim ritual, the Hajj, in the sacred towns of Mecca and Medina. It had also been the center of the early caliphate and a province of the Umayyad Empire, often governed by a member of the Umayyad family. Following their takeover, the Abbasids, like the Umayyads, were frugal concerning their investments in the Hijaz. They built no major roads until the reign of the caliph al-Mahdī and sponsored no major projects beyond some urban improvements in Mecca and Medina and maintaining the pilgrimage from Iraq at regular intervals. They seem to have followed the practice of the previous administration, which had excluded the Hijaz and Yemen from the "super-provinces" (eastern Arabia fell under Basra's control). This may have been done for practical reasons because the region had no active military fronts or waves of migrants. The memory of Ibn Zubayr's caliphate there in the second half of the seventh century and the building of the Dome of the Rock in Jerusalem indicate a dampened emotional attachment on the part of the Umayyads to the region. However, the region never remained a stagnant backwater. Its religious, cultural, and scholarly significance continued to grow despite urban and other physical negligence of imperial patronage. Scholars; all sorts of pious travelers and wanderers; and political marginals, including ʿAlids, found it a welcoming refuge for their activities in the mid-eighth century onward.[62]

Ibn al-Muqaffaʿ brings to the attention of the caliph a particular image of the province as a place to be venerated and one to be generous and dignified toward. He recommends a few straightforward steps. As a sign of goodwill, leniency, and sympathy, the caliph would forgive the revenue collected from the province and appoint distinguished family members and other highly regarded dignitaries to govern it. Assuming that the caliph recognizes the poignant and spiritual significance of the region, he explains his view in a concise statement encouraging an affective attention to the region: "One of the things of which the Commander of the Faithful is reminded is the Arabian Peninsula from the Hijaz to Yemen, Yamāma, and related places. It would be a suitable policy for the Commander of the Faithful, if he would consent to forego its funds, which he takes from almsgiving and other sources and choose the finest people from his own household and others to govern this province."[63] He counsels the caliph to display compassion for the province to make the Abbasid family benefit from the grace of the sacred lands. "For that would be the most perfect indication of fair conduct and the honorable statement (*al-kalima al-ḥasana*), which God has bestowed generously upon the Commander of the Faithful, including the opinion which is, by the permission of God, the guarantee and proper order of all affairs in the metropolises, military districts, frontier zones, and administrative divisions."[64] Besides his advice in this passage, Ibn al-Muqaffaʿ brings up the subject of the sacred cities in his discussion of Syria as well when he encourages the caliph to earmark some of the surplus revenue of Egypt as charity for Mecca and Medina.[65]

When viewed from a political perspective, Ibn al-Muqaffaʿ's comments may be read as a discourse about resanctifying this most important pilgrimage destination as the sacred core of the empire and the ancestral home of the Abbasid family. That the region had already been a place of spiritual veneration might have inspired Ibn al-Muqaffaʿ to endorse it anew. By flagging the region as a sacred landscape, he envisions a mechanism to normalize loyalty through the feeling of belonging and consent. He operates on two levels. On the one hand, he provides emotional encouragement to his patron for a task that he sees as integral to the practice of piety and of good governance. The sovereign's act of charity and benevolence would, he seems to calculate, promote the feeling that he is protecting the sacred lands and inspire narratives about the caliph's ancestors. On the other hand, Ibn al-Muqaffaʿ seizes upon the existence of the sacred landscape to solicit the goodwill of the inhabitants of not only the Hijaz toward the sovereign but also of other "metropolises, military districts, frontier zones, and administrative divisions."

It may be appropriate to problematize here the question of family sacrality that I have mentioned but did not treat. Ibn al-Muqaffaʿ's statements about the Abbasid (indeed, the Hāshimid) family suggest that he envisions it as a ruling family that operates both as a connection to and buffer between the caliph and his subjects socially and ontologically. While this issue may seem self-evident and even banal, it was anything but trivial during the political debates when Ibn al-Muqaffaʿ was writing. Any argument about the family status, while it dovetailed well with the Abbasids' self-claims of being "the blessed tree" and "the chosen family,"[66] bumped up against the question of election and succession among the ulema from a wide range of groups. It also evoked the heated controversies among the Hāshimites concerning the status of the house of ʿAbbās. Bearing in mind the jurists' attention to the piety of the caliph as a believer, their aversion to the notion of dynastic rule as in kingship, and their (and other groups') emphasis on election and consultation, Ibn al-Muqaffaʿ's attention to the question of family as a matter of governance and in positive terms meant that he was swimming against a substantial tide.[67]

Ibn al-Muqaffaʿ envisages the Abbasid family as a dynasty. He mentions the role of the family and, on more than one occasion, notes that the caliph's family is not only an asset to help administer the empire and provide support for the sovereign, as Ibn Khaldūn later would reason too, but also a beacon of light for the nobility and the common folk to look up to and emulate. "Moreover," he asserts, introducing his advice about the subject, "there is no part of speech by which one seeks to prove that the family of the Commander of the Faithful is superior to the people of other families, and other qualities which the people need to mention, that is not already found in his house." Ibn al-Muqaffaʿ sees evidence of that in their "eloquent and praiseworthy conversation, which is more eloquent than anything extravagant sycophants might say."[68] This expressed a vision of a dynasty, a ruling family separate from the rest, pitting monarchical rule against the contractualism of the ulema and the esoterism of the Kaysānite and other sectarians, and even against the ideas in the ongoing rift between the ʿAlids and the Abbasids.

Ibn al-Muqaffaʿ knew about the feuds among family members and between different houses (ʿAlids versus Abbasids, the family of ʿAbbās versus that of ʿAbdallāh b. ʿAlī) that had torn the family apart in the civil war and its aftermath. As we know, Ibn al-Muqaffaʿ even took an active part in some of these conflicts. He also knew that in the few years following the revolt, members of the Abbasid family were appointed commanders of armies and governors of the provinces of Iraq, Syria, Egypt, and the Arabian Peninsula. Al-Manṣūr's early political and administrative arrangements may be noted here as a backdrop to Ibn al-Muqaffaʿ's political insight. Already under al-Saffāḥ, the first Abbasid caliph, appointments reflected the reliance of the caliph on his family members. Abū Jaʿfar took charge of the governorship of the Jazira, Arminiya, and Adharbayjan; Dāwūd b. ʿAlī of Hijaz, Yemen, and Yamama; ʿAbdallāh b. ʿAlī of Syria; Sulaymān b. ʿAlī of Basra and its environs, Bahrayn and Uman; Ismāʿīl b. ʿAlī of the province of Ahwaz. Abū Muslim became the governor of Khurasan, and Abū Awn ʿAbd al-Mālik b. Yazīd became the governor of Egypt and North Africa.[69]

When Abū Jaʿfar became the caliph, he consolidated the major appointments, eliminated his rivals, and rehabilitated others such as his uncle ʿAbdallāh b. ʿAlī and the revolutionary hero and governor of Khurasan Abū Muslim. Despite the conflict with his uncle, he kept his cousins in governorships and high-level positions. He appointed ʿĪsā b. Mūsā as governor of Kufa, Ṣāliḥ b. ʿAlī of Qinnisrīn and the ʿAwāṣim, ʿAbbās b. Muhammad of the Jazira, and Jaʿfar b. Sulaymān of Medina. He also seems to have reconciled with some Umayyad nobility by appointing them to governorships. Maʿan b. Zā'ida al-Shaybānī received the governorship of Yemen, Khāzim b. Khuzayman of Arminiya, and Yazīd b. Ḥātim al-Muhallabī of Ifriqiya.[70]

However, the gap between the Abbasids and the ʿAlids grew larger as the Abbasids became more confident of their power. The Abbasids had come to power as members of the House of the Prophet (*Ahl al-Bayt*), but then they competed with the ʿAlids, who advanced their own claims within and without the Kaysāniyya movement. Both al-Saffāḥ and al-Manṣūr had attempted to win over the ʿAlid branch of the family.[71] Soon afterward, however, a new Abbasid discourse on the imamate, emerging under the second caliph al-Manṣūr, severed this link, which then excluded the ʿAlids. The Abbasids began to claim that they had inherited the imamate from the uncle of the Prophet Muhammad al-ʿAbbās rather than from an ʿAlid or Fāṭimid imam.

This last move dismantled the whole notion of Hāshimid succession and created a whole new political reality for the Abbasids and the ʿAlids alike.[72] Although the Abbasids brought prominent ʿAlids as honored guests to their courts and compensated them with large pensions, which was a noticeable improvement on their status under the Umayyads, they definitely left them out as possible candidates for the caliphate.[73] Some members of the ʿAlid family and their supporters saw the Abbasids as usurpers and refused to give up their claims. Defending their rights to the imamate, they resisted the Abbasids and went into hiding when necessary to continue their activities.[74] Other ʿAlids, such as the Ḥasanid Muḥammad b. ʿAbdallāh, known as the Pure Soul, rose in arms.[75] The Abbasids made sure that the ʿAlids remained restrained on the battlefields and in the discourse.[76]

Self-serving and therefore unconvincing aspects of his recommendation aside,[77] Ibn al-Muqaffaʿ makes a critical point regarding the significance of family ties and building bridges by transcending immediate conflicts to rally the family around the caliph, including, it seems, the ʿAlids. His message to the caliph on this matter is clear: The Commander of the Faithful should mend fences among various branches of his larger family.[78] Ibn al-Muqaffaʿ advises conciliation and reminds the caliph that "the young men of his own family, the sons of his father and the descendants of ʿAlī b. Abī Ṭālib and al-ʿAbbās b. ʿAbd al-Muṭṭalib," would help to shoulder certain responsibilities "for among them are men who, if they were offered important tasks and governmental responsibilities, could meet their challenges and become ready to take charge in other assignments."[79] This suggestion captures a critical moment in ʿAlid-Abbasid competition and points to the potential of reconciliation, which, while it never materialized, might have remained an aspiration among some Abbasid rulers until al-Ma'mūn acted on it. The caliph did in fact appoint the ʿAlid ʿAlī al-Riḍā as his heir apparent; whether an attempt at reconciliation or political cooptation, it failed miserably in the end.[80]

What binds the family together, however, is neither the bond of discipleship and revolutionary enthusiasm nor the personal merit of the caliph being a courteous family member—Ibn al-Muqaffaʿ knew the family rifts too well to reason along that line. It is the ontological status of the family that requires its members to rise to the occasion. It is a privilege that distinguishes the ruling family from the rest and makes them more meritorious than the rest.[81] Assessed in the broader world-historical perspective, this dynastic notion of family corresponds with the idea of family sacrality, which ties power to family rather than an ethnic group, similar to that of the Han and the Sasanians but unlike that of the Roman and Mauryan Empires, in which a particular ethnicity was singled out as the bedrock of political power.[82] One may conclude from the ongoing discussion that Ibn al-Muqaffaʿ was moving in the direction of building the new empire on the collective power of its core elements (the caliph, military, the core region and its people, sacred homeland, and family), which must work together properly to be effective. There is no doubt, however, that Ibn al-Muqaffaʿ's construction of the imperial center engendered its periphery, as I will discuss next.

The Western Limbs of the Empire

The periphery is a constituted political entity more than a by-product of naming the center. If the revolutionary military might and the skills of the elite in Iraq-Khurasan made this region an appealing imperial core, what should happen to Syria, the core province of the Umayyad Empire, and other territories? The Umayyad caliphate ruled over a firmly controlled central region, one that included Egypt, the Jazira, the Hijaz, and Iraq. Syria comprised four military districts (sing. *jund*, pl. *ajnād*), identified as Damascus, Palestine (with its capital at Ramla), Hims, and the Jordan (with its capital at Tiberias) populated by Yamanī tribes. The jund of Qinnasrīn populated by Qaysī tribes was created at a later date and detached from Hims.[83] From the standpoint of the Abbasids, although this province invoked a memory of subjugation and oppression, it still boasted the most distinguished and skilled professional and military personnel of the Umayyad Empire and served as a model for what Ibn al-Muqaffaʿ tried to suggest for Iraq.

Governing the Old Core as Imperial Periphery

Ibn al-Muqaffaʿ dwelled on the question of Syria as a subjugated province, even as one under a "state of emergency," that had to be controlled tightly with a plan for its gradual stabilization. His tone on this matter suggests that controlling the region for him was not about either receiving love or exacting vengeance. It was about stabilizing this province to make it governable by removing structural obstacles and mending emotional fences. He attributes the problems in Syria to two broad issues: the oppressive and incompetent practices of the new administration and the resentment of the Syrians over their misfortune. In the succinct discussion of this matter, he charts a path for the new administration in the province to resolve major obstacles that hinder the normalization of the province, which may be summed up in four points: (1) easing the administration's oppressive tactics and discovering how to control the province without exercising brute force; (2) forging more amicable relations with the Syrians; (3) creating a loyal elite from the local nobility, who are willing to cooperate and collaborate with the new administration, to encourage the masses to do the same; and (4) stabilizing the province's finances, reforming the system of distribution of monetary entitlements in government registers, and restructuring the pension apportioned to soldiers. Appreciating the emotional dimension of being subjugated, Ibn al-Muqaffaʿ shows a pathway to controlling the province and easing the ill feeling by eliminating the chief causes of discontent and restoring a routine rhythm of life, which would encourage a level of consent and a sense of loyalty among the Syrians.

With such a purposeful approach, Ibn al-Muqaffaʿ brings the region to life as a province in a drastically new way. Compared to the revolutionary tactics of the new administration, which in his eyes border on persecution, Ibn al-Muqaffaʿ's "executive summary" normalizes Syria as a critical province of the empire. He begins with a laundry list of Syrian offenses to justify its subjugation, therefore affirming its peripheral status, but quickly moves to censure the early Abbasid administration for failing to ameliorate Syrian resentment. He cautions the caliph that the people of Syria are "the most difficult people to endure and the most feared for their hostility and misdeeds," but reminds him he "should neither reproach them for their hostility nor expect affection from them."[84] Recognizing the dramatic chasm between the province's past and present state and knowing well the inferior status and function given to it at present, he advises working toward a gradual pacification and subordination of the province but never expecting total submission.

Noting that the current administration has descended to retaliating against the Syrians as the Umayyads had previously done to the people of Iraq, Ibn al-Muqaffaʿ advises the caliph to avoid such counterproductive tactics. Without pointing fingers at any specific person or administrative office, he reports in clear terms that the treatment of the Syrians has been brutal and undignified. The path of "retaliation has been taken.[85] They were dispossessed just as they had dispossessed other people. Their *fay'* revenue has been assigned to others just as they had been granted the *fay'* revenue of others."[86] He continues down the list of harmful policies as if advocating indirectly for the Syrians. They "were removed from the pulpits, the councils, and the public functions just as they had removed others whose proven merit and prowess they could not ignore. They were deprived of assembling with officials just as they had prevented others from obtaining with them a meal which their princes had put out for the common folk."[87] Suggesting that successful management should not be punitive or extractive but remedial, he strongly advises against brutal and impulsive responses not just because they are morally wrong but also because they are ineffective as a matter of administration.

Ibn al-Muqaffaʿ proposes to begin by cultivating a new elite among the Syrians. He suggests that the caliph "selects from among the Syrians a distinguished group who he hopes will do good or whose loyalty and sincerity he already knows." He continues to assure the caliph that "it would not take long before those people would separate from their companions in opinion and desire and indulge that which they were tasked to do."[88] While explaining how to establish good rapport with the rich and the powerful in Syria and various groups who are subject to such policies in the region, he advises that the caliph "treat the rich and powerful with leniency concerning their responsibilities (*khiffat al-muʾūna*) and demand a quick response from them to show their obedience (*al-khiffa fī al-ṭāʿa*), and not give preference to any of them over any other, except for a known talent (*khiṣṣa maʿlūma*)."[89]

Once the elite is convinced to settle on Abbasid loyalty and warm up to cooperation, Ibn al-Muqaffaʿ reasons, other regional nobility would seek collaboration, hoping to receive a similar favor from the caliph, which will help the caliph stabilize the province and establish his rule in Syria. Calculating that these "select" group of people would habituate and nurture a new culture of living and develop different opinions and desires from the rest of the Syrians, he expects that the people of Syria would lose their ability to bond against the Abbasids. To support his opinion and demonstrate his shrewd political reasoning, he informs the caliph that the situation in Syria is not unique and that he has seen it elsewhere among people in similar circumstances, such as among the people of Iraq, "whom the people of Syria had sought to coopt."[90]

A striking theme in the discussion of Syria is maintaining control of the province through structuring its finances to make sure that the region enjoys enough comfort. After reminding the caliph of the oppressive tactics that have been used against the Syrians, Ibn al-Muqaffaʿ asks him to change course: "So if the Commander of the Faithful desires to abandon this and similar ways of acting, if he does not adopt what he has censured, and if he does not imitate what he has detested," Ibn al-Muqaffaʿ places the caliph in a position to heed the following advice, "justice dictates that he reserves for the Syrians their *fay'* revenue and that he allocates the surplus of revenue from the land tax in the administrative districts (*kuwar*) of Syria to expenditures; and makes the surplus of the land tax of Egypt into the entitlements for the people of Medina and Mecca."[91]

A corollary recommendation concerns the control and administration of Syrian troops as part of the Abbasid military. Ibn al-Muqaffaʿ advises the new ruler to establish a military register in which to keep the names of soldiers and track them to normalize military service and to set up a pay system that the administration can afford and that soldiers would not oppose. While the caliph may still use his discretion to update the register, it would document the measure for, and record of, pensions and privileges of those whose names were recorded in it. As an ongoing task of administration, Ibn al-Muqaffaʿ recommends the caliph to "establish a register of their soldiers as their special register (*dīwān*), or he may add or delete as appropriate"[92] and "order that the army of each of the military districts of Syria be given provisions, which will be divided by drawing lots." The caliph would "balance the unequal amounts of provisions thus received so that none of the Muslims will be neglected."[93]

Ibn al-Muqaffaʿ's observations expose a complicated history and demonstrate how "realistic" and perceptive his proposal is. When the Abbasids defeated the Umayyad caliph Marwān II, his army disintegrated. Some of his troops continued to fight against the Abbasids in different regions whenever they saw an opportunity, while others switched sides in the hope of patronage from the new masters. Many Umayyad family members staged insurrections in numerous locations in Syria, but in the end, they were pacified during the reign of al-Saffāḥ. Others fled or sought accommodation with the Abbasids. As a hub of military resources, however, Syria kept its prominence long after the reign of al-Saffāḥ. During his bid against his nephew al-Manṣūr over succession, the governor of Syria, ʿAbdallāh b. ʿAlī, convinced the Syrian army in the Jazira to join his Khurasani troops and march against al-Manṣūr. It was a risky decision by the Syrians, and it did not work out well for them. ʿAbdallāh's defeat exposed the Syrians to al-Manṣūr's wrath. The Syrians had to dispatch a delegation to him asking for pardon, which he seems to have given them. Afterward, al-Manṣūr seems to have allowed the incorporation of Syrian contingents into his military within limits,[94] which aligned well with what Ibn al-Muqaffaʿ suggested for the province. However, that Ibn al-Muqaffaʿ dedicated much attention to normalizing Syria indicates that the situation on the ground was much messier than the accommodating posture of al-Manṣūr suggests.

Ibn al-Muqaffaʿ also speaks about the Syrian people's feelings. What is at stake for the Syrian people, he seems to reason, is the burden of imperial glory that they must carry. He is thinking through the question of what to do with the state of ruin when divine grace leaves a dynasty. Likely based on his knowledge of the past, he arrives—as if anticipating Ibn Khaldūn in the fourteenth century—at a general principle concerning the loss of sovereignty and the conditions of the ruling peoples after they are defeated. Ibn al-Muqaffaʿ contends that "royal authority (*mulk*) would not leave a people without also leaving behind resentment, which causes them to become agitated, but this agitation ultimately results in their suppression."[95]

This theoretically grounded and emotionally intelligent, realistic posture of Ibn al-Muqaffaᶜ manifests in his warning to the caliph that discontent and dissatisfaction may linger and that the Syrians may react against Abbasid rule. The Syrians, he observes, had become a community united by their own values, feelings, and ways to express them under the Umayyads. He reminds the caliph that their shared glory under, and because of, the Umayyads; having a common past within a particular geography; and developing common interests, grievances, ambitions, and aspirations have given them enough unity to cause disruption. They would continue to remember their glory under the Umayyads and detest those who destroyed it. As long as the longing for past privileges and glory overpower the Syrians, they will continue to pose a risk, which requires the new administration to watch them closely.[96]

A good sovereign is one who can mitigate this risk to create a favorable effect. "As for their outbursts, which are feared by those who are apprehensive about the Syrians," Ibn al-Muqaffaᶜ swears "that if they are treated justly, which has not been done so far, they are certainly not likely to revolt and commit impetuous acts." To urge the caliph to act, he explains that he is "almost certain, thank God, that they are not entangled in that penchant for disorder with anyone except themselves, and that the turnabout (*dā'ira*) in the rule at the end of the day will be for the Commander of the Faithful, God willing."[97]

In effect, Ibn al-Muqaffaᶜ defines the status of and normalizes Syria as part of the imperial periphery by bringing up the province as a political question and by suggesting a rule of conduct for its administration. His problem-solving approach to the province, the siyasa itself in his overall discourse, highlights the fact that Syria had been the center of an empire, a home to privileged groups and classes, and a distinguished military that had acquired a sense of glory and superiority. He reasons that putting an end to the arbitrary revolutionary desires of taking revenge and instituting a reasonable routine of administration would move the province toward equilibrium vis-à-vis the new dynasty. While he does not minimize the threat of insurgencies and other outbursts, he focuses on setting policies to forge new relations that ensure a desirable outcome.

To shed more light on Ibn al-Muqaffaᶜ's discourse on how to configure the various elements of the imperial topography against the background of far-reaching changes, it may be useful to cite here a portrayal of the empire by another upper Mesopotamian contemporaneous native voice.[98] The Syrian-Anatolian frontier had been a region of socioeconomic, cultural, and political coexistence and conflict for centuries between the Byzantines and

Sasanians. It continued to be an active frontier zone under the Umayyads and the Abbasids. I examine it here from the perspective of a late eighth-century Syriac text, *The Chronicle of Zuqnin* or *The Chronicle of Pseudo-Dionysius of Tel-Mahre*,[99] which includes substantial information on the transition of power from the Umayyads to the Abbasids, to clarify my argument concerning Ibn al-Muqaffaʿ's discourse on the provincialization of Syria. This work is a universal chronicle in four parts, beginning with the creation of the world and ending in 775/776, when the work must have been composed. Despite its attributions to Dionysius of Tel-Mahre and Joshua the Stylite of Zuqnin, the author is not known. Part IV of *The Chronicle of Zuqnin* deals with the reign of Justinian and continues to the year 775. The section dealing with the period between 767 and 775/776 in upper Mesopotamia contains detailed eyewitness accounts of the author on the early Abbasids, mostly the caliph al-Manṣūr, and their policies in the region and on various matters relating to the Syrian Orthodox Church in the Jazira.[100]

In the section under consideration, written only a few decades after the Abbasid revolt, there is a telling account of the region's early encounter with the Abbasids, who are accused of upending the routine of life in the region. The narrative is informed by the author's memories of the Abbasid takeover of Syria. It seems unmistakable that the narrator knew about the rancor among various houses of the ruling family, the controversies and clashes among Arab and Muslim factions and groups, dynastic change, the old and new aristocracy, and the implications of this for this region. The narrator has a dim view of the Abbasids, who are identified as "Persians" and "coming from the East"—no doubt in reference to the Persian-speaking Khurasani supporters of the Abbasids—to subdue the "Arabs"[101] and rule the land after them. According to the narrator, the Persians, described as "wearing full-black garments," are numerous, merciless, skillful, cunning, and powerful, and were foretold by prophecies to become the new lords of the lands.[102]

Rich in interesting details about the power struggle in the province during and after the revolt and the provincial resistance against the Abbasid penetration of the region, *The Chronicle of Zuqnin* discusses insurrections by Umayyad loyalists and the Kharijites, administrative changes, the demographic shifts that occurred because of population displacement, and Abbasid policies in the province.[103] It reveals that dismantling the Umayyad structure took some time and that control of the province by the Abbasids required establishing regular administrative procedures and negotiation, and abrupt punitive rather than remedial practices when expedience compelled the rulers to seek quick solutions. It also shows how the new administration's intervention altered the lives of the people in the region by restructuring relations.

The initial presence of the Abbasids in the region involved violence to quell disturbances, establish a status quo, and direct vengeance against the Umayyads and their supporters.[104] The new rulers attempted to reorganize the administration, but the actual practice shows much overlap and flexibility, which is one of the criticisms of Ibn al-Muqaffaᶜ. Imperial agents in the region included governors, tax collectors, branding agents, poll tax (*jizya*) collectors, and other administrative officials who were sent from the center. Lesser officials were appointed from within the province itself and from smaller districts to make sure that those appointees knew the local language.[105] Even village chiefs played a role, sometimes on their own and sometimes in alliance with administrative and military agents.[106] The provincial administration also worked with local informants at large to gather information about villages and towns or about the wealth of a particular locality in order to assign or collect the taxes.[107]

From the narrator's perspective, financial interests, punitive practices, dismantling of the Umayyad status quo, and empire building instead of religious confession drove Abbasid policies in the region.[108] At the time that the new Abbasid administration took charge of the region, taxation had already overburdened Muslim and non-Muslim farmers, so much so that in certain districts, many were forced to abandon their farms to escape excessive taxation.[109] We know from an anecdote illustrating another example of unfair practices that revenue concerns continued to be the driving motive for harsh policies in the region.[110] Insurrections and complaints demanding a reduction in taxes and abiding by fair practices sometimes worked, but they were often suppressed or ignored, and the taxpayers were forced to sell their products cheaply to pay their taxes.[111]

The narrator agonizes about the oppressive administrative and taxation practices, which cause the Muslim and Christian inhabitants of the region in the countryside and towns to resent the Abbasid administration.[112] Oppressive practices were not specific to non-Muslims because tax collectors, the author of *The Chronicle of Zuqnin* tells us, went into the shops of "Syrians" and "Arabs" (Suryoye and Tayyoye) and demanded payments that were to be sent to Baghdad regardless of their background.[113] The administration sometimes confiscated private property (shops, houses, fishing boats) that had not been recorded in previous censuses and added it to the *ṣawāfī*, crown property.[114] The administrators of *ṣawāfī* property operated independently from other tax collectors, and surveyed lands and taxed peasants separately.

The mutual desire to create a new status quo brought different confessional communities together and forced local patricians and the central administration to negotiate. Local dignitaries negotiated with Abbasid officials to stop harassment and thus keep farmers from abandoning their lands.[115] The Abbasid administration maneuvered to cultivate the local elite to get them to collaborate in dismantling the Umayyad governmental structure and build a new one.[116] From the perspective of the writer of the work, one notices that not religious confession but revenue, controlling and subduing the region, and reorganizing the administrative structure to fit the demands of the new rulers regulated the relations between the Syrian-Anatolian periphery and the imperial center.

To sum up this discussion, Ibn al-Muqaffaᶜ and the author of *The Chronicle of Zuqnin* might have overstated the case regarding Syria, but their points seem to have been well taken. Al-Manṣūr accorded urban Syrians an honorable but circumscribed place in the new regime, and the descendants of the Umayyad family survived as courtiers and comfortable members of Abbasid society. The countryside, however, had an altogether dissimilar experience, where opposition to the Abbasids continued. Resentment was also prolonged among some of the Syrian patricians for a considerable time and even inspired the insurrection of Abū al-ᶜAmayṭir al-Sufyānī over half a century later in the Fourth civil war.[117] In the end, Syria did not keep resisting perpetually. The Abbasids readjusted relations through various political arrangements and socioeconomic changes: the empire's political, economic, and cultural weight shifted to the east. Baghdad was built and the web of relations between Iraq and Khurasan became strong and complex, leaving Syria a subjugated peripheral region in which the opposition abandoned its dreams of resurgence and focused instead on making a few parochial demands.[118]

Discursive Erasure of al-Andalus

Undergirding Ibn al-Muqaffaᶜ's astute approach to the status of Syria is a conception of an imperial landscape in which regions are politically constituted. The imaginative nature of Ibn al-Muqaffaᶜ's imperial landscape comes into clearer view when we consider the fact that, while Egypt is linked to Syria and considered part of the administration, the territories west of it are ignored.[119] If one reads the "Epistle" without knowing that North Africa and the Iberian Peninsula (the Maghrib) were part of the Umayyad caliphate and thus a matter of immediate consideration for the Abbasids after their revolt, one would assume that such territories had no connection with the caliphate. A similar statement cannot be made about the Arabian Peninsula, which Ibn al-Muqaffaᶜ includes in the Abbasid realm without a second thought.

Ibn al-Muqaffaᶜ's lack of interest in the Maghrib contrasts with the Abbasid policies. Incorporating the provinces west of Egypt posed a major question for the new ruling family, but what and how to address this issue remained uncertain. "Experimentation" would be an apt word to describe how they dealt with the Maghrib. In 754, al-Manṣūr dispatched Yazīd b. Ḥātim al-Muhallabī, an Umayyad-era patrician, with a substantial army to suppress the Kharijites and the Berber revolts in North Africa and to take control of the region. Yazīd continued his actions against the insurrections until 772, when he entered Qairawan and restored order there. Al-Manṣūr also seems to have tried to take control of the Iberian Peninsula by supporting local insurrections there against the Umayyads, using leaders loyal to the Abbasids. He encouraged al-ʿAlāʾ b. Mughīth al-Judhāmī, a prominent patrician from the nobility of Beja in southern Spain (or Ifrīqiya, Tunisia), to revolt. He supplied him with soldiers from Ifrīqiya and appointed him the governor of Iberia or al-Andalus in the year 763. Al-ʿAlāʾ crossed the straits to Gibraltar and approached Beja with the help of a local Egyptian army division (*jund*). The insurrection seems to have grown larger with the support of additional local disgruntled aristocrats. Informed of the developments, the Umayyad emir ʿAbd al-Raḥmān I (r. 756–788) withdrew from his capital, Cordoba, to the fortress of Carmona, which al-ʿAlāʾ besieged for two months. How the insurrection played out is a good illustration of the fragility of the Umayyad rule in the Iberian Peninsula. It shows the expanding Abbasid prestige in the west of Egypt to the extent that the Abbasid support enabled al-ʿAlāʾ to cobble together such a large coalition against the Spanish Umayyads. Although ʿAbd al-Raḥmān I crushed the insurrection and al-ʿAlāʾ was killed, these events speak to the early Abbasid efforts to incorporate this region into the empire. In fact, the caliph al-Mahdī, still interested in the region as late as 777, appointed ʿAbd al-Raḥmān b. Ḥabīb al-Ṣiqlabī from Ifrīqiya as governor to maintain the fiction of de jure suzerainty over the region.[120]

Ibn al-Muqaffaʿ could not have been oblivious to the Abbasid push to control the region. Yet his willful inattention to the western province suggests that he considered the empire, in this case, against the Abbasid programmatic efforts on the ground, as a territorial entity from the perspective of controllability. By simply not discussing the Maghrib, Ibn al-Muqaffaʿ shed a light on the caliphate as a political constitution, a territorialized entity that could be mapped out, reflected upon, and therefore managed rationally. How else should one explain his neglect of saying even a word about North Africa and the Iberian Peninsula? His silence is also significant on another level. It exposes a fascinating difference in political or territorial conceptualization between imamate and siyasa. Without a doubt, the caliphs ruled over territories and people, commanded armies, appointed governors, and conquered and controlled lands. But the value of the vast territories they controlled and of what they were doing in them had been articulated only in the universal and nonterritorial language of the ulema, who concentrated their attention on the community of the believers and the sacred law rather than the empire and its territories. It is noteworthy that as late as the time of al-ʿAnbarī and Abū Yūsuf, we see no jurist attempting to discuss the empire as a territory or define its major aspects for the purpose of a better administration. Even for al-ʿAnbarī and Abū Yūsuf, the caliphate as a territorial domain appears as an afterthought, an ephemeral entity appended to sacred law and the community of believers. The caliphate is represented as the believers' rightfully inherited land, the abode of Islam (*dār al-Islām*), and the ever-flexible realm housing the collective body of Muslims (*bayḍat al-Islām*) rather than a territory, a landscape one can reason about.[121] The contrast between Ibn al-Muqaffaʿ and the jurists is stark, which is not necessarily the result of an awareness or the lack of it. As I noted above, it is a choice that reveals the conceptual and positional difference between the proponents of imamate and of siyasa.

In wrapping up this chapter, it may be useful to note how Ibn al-Muqaffaʿ's vision of empire anticipated and might have even informed al-Dīnawarī's geopolitical awareness in the mid-ninth century. The dialogic correspondence between their visions is remarkable. Ibn al-Muqaffaʿ's perceptive calculus concerning the Nile-to-Oxus region, anticipating the shift of the empire's political axis from Syria to Iraq and from the Mediterranean to the Indian Ocean, is reiterated in the opening paragraphs of al-Dīnawarī's *al-Akhbār al-Ṭiwāl*, in which an even more profound geopolitical shift to the east is observed.[122] Drawing on a much larger and diverse body of material in the second half of the ninth century and going beyond Ibn al-Muqaffaʿ's intellectual horizon, al-Dīnawarī and other scholars interested in historiographical and geographical knowledge represented the Euphrates-to-Oxus region (a more easternly modification on Ibn al-Muqaffaʿ's Nile-to-Oxus region) as the heart of the Abbasid Empire, the axis-mundi, and the best of the seven climes (*aqālīm*) of the world.[123]

A significant part of this new territorial vision of the empire is the reimagination of its inhabitants. In the final chapter, I will discuss how Ibn al-Muqaffaʿ reinvents the empire's populations as imperial subjects (masses and the elite) and move on to elaborate on the ways in which imperial subjectivity and lawfulness were linked to taxation and territory.

8
Reimagining the People of the Empire

It is my contention in this chapter that Ibn al-Muqaffaᶜ foregrounds and consistently refers to a vocabulary that suggests a notion of "imperial subjectivity" as the common denominator of the inhabitants of the caliphate. While the idioms "the flock," "the elite," "the masses" (*raᶜiyya, al-khāṣṣa, al-ᶜāmma*) had been in circulation long before Ibn al-Muqaffaᶜ, they were not yet theorized or highlighted for deliberate reflection in a political sense. He does so against the background of the moral and ontological egalitarianism of the imamate's discourse, which conceived of peoples as communities of faith and focused on constructing a pious subject who embodied the values of the sacred law in life practices.

This most comprehensive and generic term for imperial subjects, the flock (*raᶜiyya*), taps into the long-standing shepherd-flock metaphor, which assumes a bond, a structured form of relationship, a mutual dependency, yet a categorical distinction between the sovereign and his subjects. The distinction I am referring to here is more than political in the sense that the shepherd manages the flock while the latter follows the former to ensure safety and order, but it is also ontological because it pertains to the shepherd as human and the flock as animal. By combining the human with the animal, the metaphor elicits a different sense of order than the one we encounter in the animal kingdom in many fables, where animals stand for humans.

Ibn al-Muqaffaᶜ assumes a social order based on the cooperation and collaboration, however differential, of two distinct classes of people. First is the ruling class, the imperial aristocracy, which consists of the military, administrative elite, and nobility at large, the select or the elite. He reserves the task or privilege of governing for the first group, who serve in the military, the offices of civil administration, the caliphal chamber, and the less structured network of patrician collaborators around the empire. The second class is the taxpaying subjects or the common folk (*al-ʿāmma*), whether in urban centers or agricultural regions.[1] Ibn al-Muqaffaʿ represents the common folk as the object of political power and even a primordial entity that is essential to social order. While Ibn al-Muqaffaʿ consistently portrays the common folk as constituting a lower social rank, he nevertheless suggests a distinction marked by political subjectivity rather than faith affiliation between "imperial subject" and "nonentity," as Giorgio Agamben discusses with respect to "bios" and "zoe."

I note in this chapter how Ibn al-Muqaffaʿ generates new social distinctions and relations beyond faith affiliation and practices that allow the ruler to "herd" subjects toward a calculated end through political reasoning and the manipulation of circumstances. Also significant is that Ibn al-Muqaffaʿ does not just describe the elite and the common folk as established entities. Like the work of ʿAbd al-Ḥamīd on secretaries, he in fact constructs from discrete peoples and groups the ruling class and the ruled, each with specific functions, duties, and privileges. He therefore transforms their anonymity into an identifiable collectivity as imperial elite and common folk under the sovereign's rule. Examined against the background of the imamate discourse, this political intervention had significant implications for the idea of the community of the faithful and the practice of faith.

The Shepherd and the Flock

In Ibn al-Muqaffaʿ's text, the systematic use of the terms "flock," "elite," and "masses" to refer to imperial subjects represents a shift in political thinking. He uses *raʿiyya* to refer to imperial subjects over whom the caliph exercises authority regardless of their social or cultural rank, thus including the elite and the common folk alike. In his sociopolitical imaginary, the people inhabit a life as imperial subjects under the protection of the sovereign. This privilege distinguishes them by default from the people who dwell outside the empire (whom the jurists designated as *ḥarbīs* or *ahl al-ḥarb*) and whose status makes them vulnerable to justified military conquest or enslavement, payment of tribute or confiscation of property.

While Ibn al-Muqaffaʿ spares no space to discuss social diversity as a question unless he deals with the people of Khurasan and Iraq as core supporters of the new dynasty, the vocabulary he uses suggests a political vision that orders the imperial domain according to the distinction between the sovereign and his subjects beyond their confessional difference. In view of his consistent use of the term "the flock" to refer to imperial subjects, his cross-confessional recommendations concerning tax policies, which contrast with his silence about non-Muslims and his sporadic and matter-of-fact mention of "Muslims," suggest a new vision of imperial subjectivity beyond confessional affiliation. I consider this possibility an extraordinary intervention, emerging not from Ibn al-Muqaffaᶜ's "libertarian" spirit but from his desire to order social classes according to the rationality of monarchical prudence.

Ibn al-Muqaffaᶜ refers to imperial subjects in several ways. They are people (*nās*) or folk (*ahl*) of something (qualified with an attribute). When Ibn al-Muqaffaᶜ uses *al-nās*, he consistently refers to their commonality (whether he discusses small or large bodies of people) as humans compared to other creatures, assuming here, of course, certain dispositions, traits, needs, and failings as constitutive of humanness. With *ahl*, he regularly qualifies the sort of folk he wants to signify, such as people of merit, people of knowledge, people of religious jurisprudence.

Ibn al-Muqaffaᶜ also uses the word *umma* (three times in one discussion) to signify the collective body of people in the empire, without rejecting or stressing its theological meaning as the community of Muslims apart from other confessional communities.[2] For instance, it appears in the following ways: "God improves the community (*yaṣluḥ al-umma*) today or in its remaining time (*ghābir dahrihā*),"[3]God facilitates "the betterment of the community (*iṣlāḥ al-umma*) through the Commander of the Faithful," and "the Commander of the Faithful is more diligent with the situation of the community (*umma*)."[4] From the way he uses the words *umma* and *raᶜiyya*, one suspects that he implies distinct meanings. *Umma* seems broader than the totality of people in the realm, the *raᶜiyya*. Whereas *raᶜiyya* refers to the actual, contemporaneous subjects of the caliph, *umma* signifies the abstract body of people with a particular bond that brings them together during and after his reign.

Considered in the light of his broader position on sovereignty and religion, the *umma* of Ibn al-Muqaffaᶜ also differs from the one espoused by the ulema. Although the ulema had represented the caliphal realm as the domain of the community of the faithful under the caliph, Ibn al-Muqaffaᶜ seems to have selectively accentuated the word's temporal dimension. In his use, the word implies, albeit subtly, all the people under caliphal authority rather than the community of Muslims. Using the word *umma* in this more mundane and "cultural" sense anticipated the views of the historians and philosophers of the ninth century onward who used the term *umma/umam* to signify the people of a particular cultural zone (Persians, Greeks, Indians)—the assumed common trait of a people in a large region, similar to the word "civilization" today, such as "Indian civilization" or "Greek civilization," which was very much different from the sense the ulema highlighted.[5]

Ibn al-Muqaffaʿ does not make much of the words "Muslim" and "Muslims" either. When he does, he gives no impression that either (singular or plural) is a synonym of the realm's population. The word "Muslim" occurs only once in the "Epistle" as part of the verse he quotes about Joseph, while its plural form, *Muslimūn*, appears multiple times to signify the caliph's Muslim subjects in a routine manner. Ibn al-Muqaffaʿ highlights the religious affiliation of the parties involved in the discussion of the army, the law, the Syrian Umayyad loyalists, and the caliph's privy as "the elite from among the Muslims . . . and their 'common folk.' "[6] The references seem to acknowledge the supremacy of the Muslims as the ruling people but at the same time relativize them as part of a larger body of people under the caliph.

However, Ibn al-Muqaffaʿ is not forthcoming about the role of Muslims vis-à-vis members of other faiths in the empire. He must have known that he lived in a diverse social, cultural, and confessional environment, although he makes no explicit reference to other faiths. Not to make an argument from absence, but given what we have discussed so far about Ibn al-Muqaffaʿ, this glaring omission of the religious diversity of the people cannot be a matter of simple neglect or ignorance. By the mid-eighth century, the religious affiliation of the ruling people and the status of non-Muslims in the empire had already been a discussion in debates about the poll tax, differential land tax, and social restrictions on the non-Muslim and non-Arab populations. Caliphal policies accentuating the difference between the Muslim Arabic speakers and the others had been in effect for multiple generations. Ibn al-Muqaffaʿ may have seen the non-Muslim subjects as inconsequential in governance and therefore dropped their mention as a category. However, one could also argue that, by disregarding mention of their religious specificity, he wished to transcend confessional differences to forge a common imperial subjectivity (*raʿiyya*) inclusive of all, as I have noted, which tallies well with how he discusses farmers and taxation.

When the Abbasid revolt brought the status of Persianate and Khurasani non-Arab Muslims and non-Muslim subjects of the empire to the forefront, Ibn al-Muqaffaʿ must have critically reflected on the demography of the empire, in particular that of the Iraq-Khurasan region, as the "Epistle" demonstrates, where non-Arabs and non-Muslims had just become a remarkable political force. With his other empire-wide suggestions and his consistent references to the people in the empire through their political status and function (they are the flock of the caliph) and social class (they are elite and common folk) before any other marker, including religious affiliation, his silence on faith identities and communities was not accidental. For a shrewd political observer like Ibn al-Muqaffaʿ, it must have been apparent that the moment was demanding and enabling a broader category of imperial subjectivity not merely for the control of social groups in the empire but also to recognize them as subjects of the empire beside the Arab-Muslims. I hope it is clear that I am not discussing here any sort of equality but rather an upgrade of the non-Arabs from being "nonentities" dispensed with at will to "imperial subjects" with certain obligations and "rights." This point is better understood if we consider how Ibn al-Muqaffaʿ designs social order within the triangle of the ruler–the elite–the masses rather than the duality of Muslims and non-Muslims. Exactly for this reason, explicating the elite occupies a substantial space in the text, which I tackle next.

Constituting the Elite

Ibn al-Muqaffaʿ dwells at length on the people of influence to generate from them a new class of aristocracy and ruling elite. By casting his gaze on their function, he transforms their anonymity into an identifiable collectivity, which he calls "the select" or "the elite," and outlines their status in the empire. Like the construction of the notion of "working class" to describe the laboring people in the nineteenth century by defining the parameters of their practice in a larger social context, Ibn al-Muqaffaʿ facilitated a new appreciation of the empire by bringing the elite to the consciousness of his reader. By naming the elite, stating their existence, describing and defining their function, setting them up against others, and praising and criticizing their manners, he gives life to them as a category and prepares those who reflect on the empire to think about the sociopolitical reality in a new way.[7] A genealogical exploration of this term leads us to his *Al-Adab al-Kabīr*[8] and to his *Nāmah-i Tansar*, where he discusses nobility at length.[9] One should also remember the name of his mentor and friend ʿAbd al-Ḥamīd, whose "Letter to the Scribes" and "Testament to the Crown Prince" speak to the themes of court companions, the caliphal retinue, and imperial nobility. There is no doubt that Ibn al-Muqaffaʿ grounded his discussion of the subject in ʿAbd al-Ḥamīd's pioneering work and extended it in a new direction.

Although the elite belong ontologically to the subject class (*raʿāya*) together with the common folk, they are distinguished from them socially through an acquired or inherited nobility or merit. In the "Epistle," the elite appear as the learned experts, distinguished individuals with recognized skills, and people of social status or privilege who hailed from diverse backgrounds (Muslims, non-Muslims, Arabs, and non-Arabs) and from the center and the periphery. They relate to the caliph as either imperial servants or collaborators and carry a wide range of formal and informal responsibilities under varying degrees of subordination to the caliph. Collectively, they formed the pool of aristocrats from which the caliph would draw his companions and advisers.

Ibn al-Muqaffaᶜ describes them variously as people of discernment (*ahl al-naẓar*); people of knowledge (*ahl al-ᶜilm, aṣḥāb al-ᶜilm*); people of good conduct and sound judgment (*ahl al-faḍl wa al-qaṣd*); people of sound opinion (*aṣḥāb al-ra'y*); people of certain accomplishment or bravery (*sābiqa, balā', murū'a*); and people of inherited and earned nobility (*sharaf, wajh, nasab, ḥasab*), wealth (*tharā'*), merit (*faḍl*), status, and influence (*manzila, khaṭar*). One might also include other groups mentioned in the text, such as poets, storytellers, merchants, teachers, learned cosmopolitan people who fall in the broad emerging category of literati (*udabā'*, sing. *adīb*), and the ruling family members, who functioned in various branches of the civil and military administration. Looking at the background of the elite from his style of address, they are divided into two categories: those with "inherited nobility" and those with "acquired nobility," for instance, those belonging to a prominent family or exhibiting eminence in learning and scholarship. It strikes me as noteworthy that Ibn al-Muqaffaᶜ distinguishes between the elite at large (*khāṣṣa*) and the caliph's privy or his chamber (*ṣaḥāba*) as an exclusive subset accompanying the caliph.

Ibn al-Muqaffaᶜ's discussion on shoring up a competent imperial cadre is as much about encouraging the caliph to pay proper attention to selecting his collaborators and retinue as it is about forming the ruler himself morally so that he acts in a stately way. As mentors, tutors, advisers, and confidants, the elite guide and manage the ruler to unlock his capacity to govern, which ᶜAbd al-Ḥamīd calls politics (siyasa), that is, the politics of coaching the sovereign. The elite help the sovereign cultivate the right disposition (adab) of rulership so that he exercises his power in an effective and commendable way. I have already discussed how Ibn al-Muqaffaᶜ's political cosmology entails the exaltation of the sovereign as the recipient of grace or fortune, which makes sovereignty a gift that is granted, not always earned.[10] Although this gift endows the ruler with political power that cannot be fully tamed (the "beast" of ᶜAbd al-Ḥamīd and the Lion of Kalīla and Dimna) and because the ruler does not take orders and is not constrained, the elite come to play the role of the "trainer," who nurtures the stately virtues of the ruler so that he acts to meet the demands of the divine gift. Given their critical role, the elite thus work as a shield against the misfortune of neglect and willful conduct.

Ibn al-Muqaffaᶜ is therefore aware that the elite on the one hand play the role of "the trainer" who nurtures the ruler by reminding him of his role, refining his conduct, facilitating and negotiating his decisions, and ensuring the maintenance of his stately self. On the other hand, they authorize and normalize the sovereign's power by setting up governmental institutions, managing relations from the top down and bottom up, speaking on behalf of his subjects in his court (*alsinat raʿiyyatihi*) to inform him of their condition, and acting on the ruler's behalf.[11] They also function as models for others to improve their conditions,[12] and they represent him among his subjects to instill in them a sense of consent and of compliance. Because the proper execution of the sovereign's power hinges on them, they also reflect the sovereign's virtue of discernment in recognizing only the worthy individuals (skilled professionals, people with special knowledge, status, wealth, experience, bravery) as advisers.[13] By praising the desired qualities of the elite and rebuking others, Ibn al-Muqaffaʿ in fact inspires the caliph himself to act virtuously. Those who are familiar with the Aristotelian virtue of ethics might recognize here that Ibn al-Muqaffaʿ's emphasis on expert knowledge in governance tallies well with the idea that rulership would be more effective if the ruler heeds learned guidance. At least epistemologically, Ibn Muqaffaʿ's relentless focus on practice brings him into a dialogic communication with an Aristotelian ethical position.[14]

Beginning with the preamble of his "Epistle," Ibn al-Muqaffaʿ brings up the subject of consultation with experts, the value of rational judgment, and the merit of listening to good advice. After praying for the prosperity of the caliph, he commends the caliph for listening to the opinions of his privy and for his sincerity in cooperating with those who can reason.[15] He hails the commander of the faithful for his ability and willingness to combine "with his knowledge, the merit of inquiry and readiness to listen to others, whereas the evil rulers [the Umayyads] had combined with their ignorance, vanity, and self-indulgence." He continues to compliment the caliph for the virtue of supporting his opinion with evidence and demanding his subjects to do the same.[16] Ibn al-Muqaffaʿ attacks the Umayyad caliphs precisely for failing to rise to that level of virtue: they "used to be content with meekness and satisfied with baseless arguments and with no excuse for their inaccessibility if anyone had the courage to offer them an opinion or a piece of information."[17]

Keenly interested in stability, Ibn al-Muqaffaʿ finds it imperative that the caliph cooperates and collaborates with the elite in his realm to maintain order. He envisions two critical functions for the collaborators and advisers of the sovereign. Thanks to the encouragement of the caliph, Ibn al-Muqaffaʿ maintains, "the person of sound opinion (*dhū al-ra'y*) comes forward to hand the caliph information[18] about matters of which the informant doubts anyone else has apprised the caliph, and to remind him of what has been already brought to his attention."[19] The person in that capacity is therefore either "the possessor of sound opinion (*ṣāḥib al-ra'y*) who is not more than an informant,"[20] who delivers to the sovereign fresh information, or a "reminder, who reminds him of a matter about which the sovereign has already been informed."[21] Ibn al-Muqaffaᶜ accordingly reminds the caliph to seek the cooperation with, or rather consider the opinions of, experts as a practice of good governance because it is the proper way of "encouraging the righteous (*dhawī al-albāb*) to produce and implement an opinion (*iᶜmāl al-ra'y*) more diligently regarding the means by which God improves the community (*umma*) today or in its remaining time (*ghābir dahrihā*)."[22] He ends his statement with optimism—that seeing the determination of the caliph, "the righteous have begun to aspire" to witnessing prosperity, which is a wish that hopefully "will be realized at the hands of the Commander of the Faithful."[23]

As in his advice on controlling Syria by cultivating an elite among its people to mediate between the caliph and the Syrian people and to inspire loyalty to the new rulers, Ibn al-Muqaffaᶜ intervenes to show how to transform the revolutionary disruption into a calibrated social order through a selected governing elite. With their expertise and professional skills, this elite normalize political power in regulated military apparatuses and the routine of civil bureaucracy. As the elite perform their duties and live their lives, they also serve as a resource of proper guidance and models to be emulated by the common folk regarding the correct demeanor (adab).[24] In this sense, the work of the elite necessarily involves mediation and negotiation to create a bearable life for imperial subjects by safeguarding social order and minimizing fear for all.

Explaining the reason for fostering an elite among the subjects and the benefit of supervising them, Ibn al-Muqaffaᶜ informs the caliph that "the significance of this is great in two areas, one of which is the return of troublemakers to good behavior and the return of dissidents to union." Beyond the benefit of negotiation and mediation to calm dissent among the subjects, however, the elite satisfy an even greater need: the control of what is communicated to ensure unity and consistency of the message. "The other area is that no one should act with regard to any of the affairs of the masses unless a supervising eye is observing him, and no one should whisper to the masses unless a sympathetic ear is listening in his direction."[25] Keeping the channels of communication open and safeguarding the integrity of the message being disseminated among the common folk, Ibn al-Muqaffaᶜ reasons, would block any attempt at subversion. "If these are done," he promises, "the troublemakers cannot lie in wait for opportunities and seize them, and if they are not seized, the results, with the permission of God, are innocuous."[26]

In addition to occupying posts in the military and civil administration, the elite make imperial power visible through a set of empire-wide or culture-specific modalities, which also create life worlds for much of the population. Although Ibn al-Muqaffaʿ does not detail their activities, from the themes he addresses, one understands that they function as the translators of the sovereign's brute power into a functioning governing mechanism. While they veil the caliph himself from the public eye, except on certain ceremonial occasions,[27] they render his power immediately evident to his subjects. They enunciate his power and magnanimity in theatrical displays (processions, ceremonies, royal entries, coronations, funerals, public hearings), literary and artistic work (art, literature, scholarship), monumental building and urban planning (roads, bridges, mosques, palaces, public spaces), control and policing, taxation, charitable work (pardons, patronage, donations, payments in money or in kind), and theology, constructed and maintained by a range of specialists among the literate elite (ritual preceptors, the ulema).[28]

A scribe himself to an Abbasid family member in Iraq, Ibn al-Muqaffaʿ understood that, given their position, the elite constituted one of the most crucial hubs of administrative knowledge. "The people of sound opinion" among the elite provided the caliph with timely and useful information on actual matters of governance, which enabled him to make the best decisions and avoid the danger of arbitrary rule. At the very end of the text, Ibn al-Muqaffaʿ praises the caliph for strengthening the collaboration with his advisers to attain success. He reminds the caliph that, "having seen that these matters are organized by working together, and having known the undertakings of the Commander of the Faithful, according to the exemplarity of which God has united the elite of the Muslims in their desire to provide good assistance, support, and be concerned with the good of the masses," he was assured of success and a good outcome "for the common folk."[29]

It should come as no surprise that Ibn al-Muqaffaʿ asks the caliph to meet the expectations of his associates and free their minds from worry by helping them financially so that they occupy their minds only with building and maintaining order. Analogous to his recommendation on the finances of the military, here too Ibn al-Muqaffaʿ seeks effectiveness and satisfaction. Recalling the practices and wisdom from the region's long imperial history, he explains to the caliph that "every human group has its own special class of people who receive allowances when they have been formed for that purpose. They are the object of favors, they are aided in carrying out their opinions, and their livelihood is supported, so that they are free to dedicate themselves to their tasks without worry."[30] In this manner, while the sovereign relies on the skills and knowledge of his elite to ensure the satisfaction of his subjects, the elite in turn obtain their authority and political culture from the sovereign to perform their duties correctly and inspire the common folk, who look up to them for leadership and protection.

A Critique of the Status Quo

Seeing the developing circumstances as dangerous, however, Ibn al-Muqaffaᶜ points out the need for reckoning. Ibn al-Muqaffaᶜ is not pleased with the expertise and ability of certain advisers and administrators. Indeed, he accuses many of them of being ambitious but inept, greedy, and ignorant men who labor only to maximize their own benefits and are downright harmful if not removed from their posts. In light of revolutionary excitement, at a time when seniority and deeds in the revolt were now paying off, and when new sociocultural collectivities were rising to prominence around the ruling family barely half a decade after the Abbasids took over, he impatiently warns the caliph about the disparity in skills and experience between the revolutionary enthusiasts and the "rank and file" imperial servants. As on other occasions, Ibn al-Muqaffaᶜ warns the caliph that recent developments and actions of the people in charge—the elite, and the cadre in the caliph's chamber—demonstrate that corruption has been working against orderly governance. He explains that the conditions of the Iraqi elite under the Umayyads, and more recently under Abbasid rule leading up to al-Manṣūr's reign, which he portrays in grim terms, have been lamentably deteriorating.

Ibn al-Muqaffaᶜ reminds the caliph that mismanagement and oppressive policies in the past have already ruined the reputation and defamed the inhabitants of Iraq. The Umayyads used to oppress their nobility as the elite of a subjugated province through no fault of their own. He notes in certain terms that "this class of people [the elite] from Iraq has suffered from the fact that in the past the Umayyad governors of Iraq were the worst governors of all. They had subordinates who were just as bad, from the people of their provinces." Administered by governors from other provinces, the Iraqi elite suffered grave consequences and "all the people of Iraq have been held accountable for whatever burden these vile people [the governors] have brought. And the Iraqi people's Syrian enemies grabbed onto that as an excuse and held it against[31] them."[32]

As a political realist, Ibn al-Muqaffaᶜ was disappointed with the direction of the sociopolitical change he witnessed after the revolt. "We and our forefathers," he exclaims, "have met only people who were noticing in the administration weaknesses[33] that defeat sound judgment and shackle mouths."[34] Using less than polite language, he faults the current state of affairs as being outrageous: sound opinion and expert knowledge are absent from administration, opinions of incompetent individuals are upheld, practices based on weak and false opinions remain unquestioned, or decisions are made expediently to rescue the day without thinking about the consequences. A case in point about corrupt or otherwise inept administrators is "a governor who was not concerned with improvement or restoration (*iṣlāḥ*), or who, if he were concerned,[35] one could not rely upon him for sound judgment, or who possessed sound judgment but lacked energy with firmness or determination,[36] or who sought to seize the benefits for himself to the detriment of the people,[37] or who did not take enough initiative to find the resources to be collected or divided."[38]

Ibn al-Muqaffaʿ observes that where governors make strenuous efforts, their inept "assistants, by whom the governors are afflicted[39] and who are not the best of helpers to do good," fail them. "The governor has no way to get rid of them because of their position of power and because of the fear of a possible shift in affairs of the state, and fear of trouble if he provokes them or lessens their privileges."[40] Thus, corrupt supporters and dishonest assistants, who are connected in one way or another with senior administrators, remain influential because of the governor's ineptitude in not taking proper action against them and because of his fear of dismissal from his position. This situation further deteriorates because corrupt "iniquitous subjects" (*raʿiyya muttazira*),[41] who have nothing to do with fairness concerning themselves," pursue self-interests in vulgar ways. "For, if they are treated with severity, they are enraged, and if they are treated with leniency, they trespass all bounds."[42]

The grim tone in this passage is direct, coarse, and offensive.[43] Although the biting criticism is sandwiched between passages of praise and glorification, the language is nevertheless strident. If one puts aside the possibility that Ibn al-Muqaffaʿ is not overstating the case for his own career goals, why is he portraying the situation as one of utter incompetence? As Ibn al-Muqaffaʿ knew intimately through his association with many governors and administrators, the revolt had generated its own children: the Hāshimid family, the Shiite groups, the ulema, various nomadic nobilities, Quraysh dignitaries, Khurasani revolutionary figures and their social extensions, messianic and esoteric enthusiasts, and others. They were part of the new imperial class who acquired various positions and gained fame and prominence. My contention is that Ibn al-Muqaffaʿ attacked those individuals and groups that achieved certain recognition and positions of power because of their participation in the revolt, but, according to him, had no skills, culture, nobility, or understanding to make them eligible for critical positions. He recommended that the caliph not be blindsided by the urgency of the moment but develop a strategy according to which he chooses his companions, advisers, and administrators to shape the direction of his administration.

In his pursuit of reforming the administration, Ibn al-Muqaffaʿ provides a more shocking assessment: the new administration, even under the Abbasids, was not interested in anyone other than careerist climbers who were suspected of having connections with the ruling family. Given this situation, he explains, people of skill and knowledge in the province have become unwelcome by those in positions of power and have been pushed away. Reading his comments on the army in the previous chapter, one already anticipates a critique of the current situation accompanied by a to-do list concerning the Iraqi elite. Ibn al-Muqaffaʿ does so, indeed, in a manner that is even more direct than his advice on the military. His language is blunt, and it even sounds as if he were too agitated to suppress his anger, in particular when he discusses how the new administration in Iraq has been seeking and collaborating with administrators displaying gross incompetence and unbridled greed: "Then this fortuitous state was established, and your subordinates among the ministers and the agents (*wuzarāʾ wa-l-ʿummāl*) were only attached to the close or the closest individuals among those who cozied up to them, or those they had found holding some authority."[44] Given this level of favoritism, "many Iraqi individuals fell into disgrace wherever they were among the companions of a caliph—in an administrative post, a position of trustworthiness, or a place in battle."[45]

Being neglected and pushed away, those with talent sought vocations in other venues that took them away from many career paths suitable to their talent and skill set. "It was the opinion of those people of merit that they should go only where they were requested, which delayed them from becoming known and from being put to good use."[46] Not knowing or not recognizing the surrounding talent, the people in power (*aṣḥāb al-sulṭān*) would pick other, less qualified individuals for jobs and further alienate those with talent and skill who, because of their self-respect, did not ask for positions.

Ibn al-Muqaffaʿ's personal agenda aside, he did place his finger on a sore spot. Mediocre people with less talent along with downright careerists who were adept at manipulating the administrators in vulgar ways continued to fill the positions and attract other people like themselves. Ibn al-Muqaffaʿ notes this incompetence in plain terms: "If the holder of power is one of those people who govern people before he knows them, then keep inquiring about them from those who know them well, and seek to conduct a thorough investigation about them;[47] then the affairs will spin out of control and the men will fall from their proper pedestals, because people seeking positions will impress him (the governor or ruler) only by faking the best they can muster in terms of calculating when to remain silent or speak."[48]

Ibn al-Muqaffaʿ knew that the elite were not a homogeneous class, but his career had also taught him that the ad hoc administration of affairs that had been the norm so far after the revolt resulted in notoriously contradictory practices. He knew, as he himself got involved personally in some of them, that competition for favors, positions, influence, and a larger share of power became a routine reality. Influential administrators maintained a circle of patronage among peers and lower-level administrators in their respective branches of administration, reaching provincial subordinates to satisfy their ambitions and maintain or advance their positions. Incompetence and greed only hindered the efforts of administrative structuring and undermined the caliph's authority.

It is no coincidence that Ibn al-Muqaffaᶜ touches upon the universal problem of dealing with nepotism, favoritism, patronage of mediocrity, quid pro quo, and corruption in administration. He is alarmed here by what he sees as the organizational chaos that the revolution has caused. It has rendered the talented professionals of Iraq, who once worked under the Umayyad administration (individuals like him), irrelevant when new positions were being filled. No matter if the situation was as bad as he portrays, he seems to argue that replacing the career administrators, who have proven their knowledge and experience, with "revolutionaries" and their larger circle of affiliates with no attestable relevant talent and skill would only hurt the government and put the sovereign in the unenviable position of working with less than qualified people, which would cause violence to the values of the system the sovereign should rather be upholding.

Ibn al-Muqaffaᶜ alleges that the revolution and the subsequent energies spent to establish a new administration have further eroded the situation in Iraq. Appropriate channels of recruiting administrative and other staff have been eliminated or bypassed because of a lack of knowledge or because of nepotism. Only the less than desirable people were kept. "Moreover," he exclaims, "these mediocre folks are the most skilled at fraud, are the sweetest talkers, and are the most adept at persuading ministers, or being cunningly convincing to others, to be able to obtain praise in their absence."[49] Even if one resists the temptation to hire such opportunists, gossip, defamation, and conspiracies will spread. "If it happens that the governor chooses to trust for a task only a man who is not willing to commit such acts, he will invite all that same defamation from the opportunists against him. They [mediocre folk] would desire to harm him and be emboldened against him. They would visit him too often and hustle for whatever favor he has." Under such circumstances, no one would want to enter the snake pit: "If the people of merit see that, they would refrain from him and move away from him, for they would dislike being seen in a place not fitting their status or being put in a situation to compete with those who are not their peers at all."[50]

That this startling criticism is communicated so frankly in such a letter is another audacious salvo against the current administration. Indeed, it not only exposed its author to the charge of being a disgruntled careerist and greedy provincial scribe but also incriminated him as a "counterrevolutionary." However, his assessment sounds eminently convincing. The revolutionary measures removed the old elite from their positions and dismantled the existing institutions and practices. It cleared the field of administration at the discretion and under the influence of the revolutionary cadre from different levels of society: people with records of revolutionary bravery but nothing much else, well-intentioned individuals who were unfamiliar with the terrain to which they were assigned, administrators lacking competent subordinates, and brazen fortune seekers riding the bandwagon. Administrators were being chosen without a proper vetting process in the chaos of the distribution of spoils or as a reward to those who had taken part or claimed to have taken part in the revolt. This happened in a period when the caliph needed technical knowledge rather than revolutionary or religious enthusiasm to shape practices and institutions.

Overall, Ibn al-Muqaffaᶜ complains about what he sees as a loss of meritocracy. The idea of merit and recruiting individuals according to ethical standards and practical requirements from among those with applicable skills and knowledge, although a principle of good governance anywhere and in the interest of social justice, is a significant point. The damning part of his proposal from the point of view of the new administration is that he accused the revolutionary family of incompetence. Ibn al-Muqaffaᶜ cautions that as the new regime was taking shape, merit and skills were ignored by a family that claimed to uphold them. Fearing that this practice would not deliver, he advises the caliph to concentrate on building up his political core programmatically according to merit, professional skill, and customary practices of good governance.

One sees in his text that Ibn al-Muqaffaᶜ's discussion of merit is a way to coach the caliph to look for imperial servants with intellectual and moral capital so that they steer the administrative practice toward a reasonable routine in both selecting appointees based on skills and fulfilling tasks efficiently. Like his advice concerning the army, Ibn al-Muqaffaᶜ advises the caliph to flag and remove unworthy administrators from offices and from his entourage. The caliph should respect precedence, promote individuals with special talents and who have distinguished service records, and seek professionals known for their virtue and nobility.[51] Careful consideration of merit would strengthen the caliph's rule because these associates would occupy positions of status and influence that would enable them to execute the sovereign's orders, govern territories, manage taxes, administer the army, promulgate laws, serve as judges, educate and control people, inform the sovereign about the common people, and "represent" them at his court.

King's Privy and Their Ills

In keeping with this logic, Ibn al-Muqaffaʿ constructs an even more exclusive group of experts and professionals whom he calls the privy (or, as conventionally rendered, companions) of the caliph and whom he associates with the caliph's chamber. That this category of the caliph's advisers or functionaries included the ulema is obvious, but the collectivity also consists of "experts" with wider interests and skills who Ibn al-Muqaffaʿ hopes will function differently than the ulema and revolutionary enthusiasts. We do not know whether Ibn al-Muqaffaʿ or a later copyist titled the letter the "Epistle on the Caliph's Privy," but it is apt in either case because this topic appears in it at some length. The term he uses, *al-ṣaḥāba*, companions, is in the sense of counsels, advisers, courtiers, and functionaries of the caliph serving in various capacities in his chamber but neither in the sense of casual company around the caliph nor the Companions of the Prophet, which had probably been used before but was not a common term with this caliphal meaning.[52] Therefore, and in the light of the biblical phrase "the friend of the king" in ancient Hebrew and of the Greek *philos* (friend), the secularizing and politicizing function of the term in his language must be noted here, although the concept eventually lost the battle for meaning to *al-ṣaḥāba* in the sense of "the Companions of the Prophet."[53]

As part of his larger project of promoting the Iraq-Khurasan region as an alternative to the old Umayyad-Syrian core, Ibn al-Muqaffaʿ recommends—in fact, insists on—finding, employing, and dignifying the Iraqi learned and professional elite programmatically. He describes the privy as the most direct group of experts to organize political will from the sovereign down to his subjects, building it upward to the sovereign, and working it out spatially across the realm in relations. They are the closest cadre to the caliph, which helps the sovereign govern but at the same time instructs him in the techniques of moral education and the art of governance. In the initial paragraphs devoted to companions of the caliph, he reminds his patron of what this select group of the elite is supposed to do at his court: "Among the matters most requiring the ruler's scrutiny and selection is that of his privy, who are the pride of his court,[54] the ornament of his council, the tongues of his subjects (*alsinat raʿiyyatihi*),[55] the supporters of his opinion, the objects of his generosity, and the elite among the masses (*al-khāṣṣa min ʿāmmatihi*)."[56] Ibn al-Muqaffaʿ encourages the caliph to associate with distinguished individuals who were selected through a rigorous vetting process and to rely on them when he needs counsel before making important decisions and not turn a blind eye to the theater of incompetence.

Still, after the revolution, Ibn al-Muqaffaᶜ claims, the result has been just to the contrary. What was happening to the advisers was the elimination of the good and the disappearance of the rightful individual from the chamber of the caliph. In a conversational tone, he remarks that "this entourage has accomplished some wonderful deeds, which were intermixed with wrongdoing." The examples and anecdotes from his personal past lend this letter an autobiographical tone when he discusses his concerns and makes suggestions about how the sovereign should shape his chamber and select his subordinates. Resonant with his critique of the broader elite, his points about the deterioration of the administration after the revolt are nothing less than describing a "dog-eat-dog" world. He warns the caliph about how the ease of access to him became a way to gain power, which he cites as a bad practice that must end.

Assuming a voice of remarkable clarity, he conveys to the sovereign, with some self-promotion and a nostalgia for the Umayyad culture of governance, how companionship with the caliph ceased to be a position of admiration, dignity, respect, and high-level decision making because of the continuing instability.

> Concerning the subject of this companionship, the *wazīrs*[57] and scribes in charge under the caliphate of the Commander of the Faithful did an exceedingly appalling job, corrupting dignity, refinement, and politics (*al-ḥasab wa al-adab wa al-siyāsa*), attracting malicious people, and driving away the good ones. Thus, the position of caliphal companionship[58] became a laughing matter, sought after only by scoundrels and renounced by those who would have been satisfied with a lesser position. It happened that when we went to meet Abū al-ᶜAbbās, may God have mercy upon him, I was originally in the company of the upstanding leading residents of Basra. However, some of them refused to come to him. Some hid and did not appear before the caliph at all, and others fled after having been present, preferring to commit disobedience over accepting a bad position, and excusing themselves merely by arguing that the functions of scribe and the honor of being invited for service and of being present before the caliph had been spoiled. They say, "People more noble than our fathers used to seek lesser positions from dignitaries of lower rank than the commanders of our rulers today, but it was an honor and a dignity, because people who would benefit were examined and investigated. Today, however, we hear the names of so-and-so and so-and-so announced[59] without attention to seniority or any recent feats of valor."[60]

As I have already mentioned, his commentary is not a disinterested assessment of the situation. It is the reaction of a rank-and-file professional to a lost order. As implied by his language, he defends career bureaucrats who followed the proper steps of promotion and the established nobility and dignitaries who achieved their status under the routine circumstances of Umayyad rule. It is also a rebuke of the new revolutionary elite who appear to be from a cross section of the subject population but are of no account. They are lucky nouveaux riches whose only merit might be attributed to their deeds in the revolutionary period or to gaining access to the revolutionary network in one way or the other, including wheeling and dealing.

Ibn al-Muqaffaᶜ launches an even more biting critique of the new assembly of caliphal associates by citing anonymous others who allege that they "have never seen anything more amazing than these companions, such as a person who has neither acquired a refined manner nor has recognized personal merit. Moreover, opinion of him is loathsome because he is infamous among the people of his province for his licentious behavior, he has spent most of his life as a craftsman working with his hands, and he cannot demonstrate any prowess or wealth."[61] Yet, Ibn al-Muqaffaᶜ wonders, why are such individuals kept in the caliph's company and how did they become well connected?

Here too, one is tempted to characterize Ibn al-Muqaffaᶜ's position as counterrevolutionary. Looking at the text beyond Ibn al-Muqaffaᶜ, one cannot but see his argument as a description of a broader conflict between the establishment and counterestablishment in which the latter is now strengthening its own position against the discontent of the former and of those who are left out of power. From the standpoint of Ibn al-Muqaffaᶜ, what was happening might have looked like a malady, a political decline, and dangerous chaos that must be remedied for the benefit of the social and political order. He seems anxious about resolving matters that he considers outrageous, things that are not in their proper places. "O Commander of the Faithful, may God honor you," he appeals to the good sense of the caliph, "who, then, would want to be part of what is in here [caliphal administration] unless the whole justice is administered with the fear of God, Most High and Sublime, and unless matters are put in their proper place?"[62]

He is careful enough to distance himself from the new companions and their sociocultural background. He discusses several reasons why the emerging elite are unfit for the position they hold and the status they enjoy. He is pitiless: they are misfits; they lack proper education, cultivation, noble background, earned or inherited honor, and military experience. As if to allow a moment of emotional relief to convey metaphorically in poetry what his prose fails to express, he even cites two lines of poetry, following the convention of his time: "The first one said, 'People cannot cure anarchy when they have no leader. And there are no leaders if the ignorant rule.'[63] He also said, 'They made Naṣr bin Sayyār[64] their chief; he who governs the tribe reveals its aspirations (*yubayyinu*

ʿan aḥlāmihā).' "[65] In a disparaging manner, he accuses the current caliphal privy of ignorance and points out with chilling audacity that their ignorance not only solves no problem and serves no good but also reflects on the quality of those who promote them to their positions. Because such individuals do not belong to the class they pretend to be embodying now, they would harm the nobility, work against the success of the caliph, and recklessly upend the social order.

Beyond voicing what seemed to Ibn al-Muqaffaʿ a gross mismanagement, he points out structural problems responsible for generating conditions in which access to the caliph and control of privileges shifted so dramatically from the conventional nobility to newcomers. The opportunist, as I have quoted previously, "could still somehow find his way and arrive where he liked and was given an audience with the caliph before many of the sons of the Muhājirūn and the Anṣār (the Emigrants and the Helpers) and before the close relatives of the Commander of the Faithful and the people from notable Bedouin Arab families." He contrasts the inept but greedy fortune seekers with these established families. The latter included the descendants of the leading members of the nobility; the Meccan emigrants during the lifetime of the Prophet (Muhājirūn) and their hosts in Medina (Anṣār); the family of the caliph; well-regarded Bedouin Arab families; and the broader house of the Hāshimites and the other families of the Quraysh, which was by far the most prominent and influential tribe of the seventh and the eighth centuries by virtue of being the tribe of Muhammad, the early caliphs, the Umayyads, the Abbasids, the ʿAlids, and many other prominent groups and families.[66]

After reminding the caliph about the pitiful state of the prominent families, he sketches how an opportunist office seeker navigates his way to a position with generous pay: "He is compensated double the pay received by many of the Hāshimites and other leaders of the Quraysh and he is given allowances in approximately the same amount." Thanks to their guile, such opportunists cozy up to their superiors and manipulate them to achieve what they want. The opportunist "was not appointed because of noble descent, because of insight in the revealed law (*fiqh fī dīn*), because of bravery in famous, ongoing, well-known past battles against the enemy, because of recent wealth, because of aptitudes that made him indispensable, because of special abilities, or because he was a horseman, orator, or eminent scholar." The opportunist lacked qualifying skills and dispositions, "except that he had served a scribe or chamberlain (*kātib aw ḥājib*) whom he had informed cunningly that the revealed law (*dīn*) could only stand thanks to him, to the point that he caused the scribe or the chamberlain to write whatever he wanted and enter wherever he wanted."[67]

Ibn al-Muqaffaʿ emphasizes the corrupting influence of revolutionary mismanagement on the social status, prestige, and integrity of the nobility to convince the caliph to take action against the current conditions: "The wrongdoing which has sullied this state of affairs is great, and it has affected particularly the Quraysh and touched many people in general; it has made those people of merit and dignity endure great suffering and serious losses."[68] He cautions the caliph that issuing favors and privileges arbitrarily would corrupt the whole body of the nobility because it would nullify and debase merit and the time-tested conventions of royal conduct: "So, in arbitrarily empowering certain people to enter and share his company, in giving them pay and allowances, and in granting privileges in this regard to some over others, the caliph places a great penalty on people concerning their noble lineage, prestige, and exploits achieved in war."[69]

In a remarkable statement, Ibn al-Muqaffaʿ even differentiates between the caliph's personal favors and his public discretion to clarify the critical value of making "official" appointments. He reminds the caliph that "this is not a question of something like granting special favors or acts of courtesy, which the Master confers upon whomever he wishes, but is an important public (*ʿāmm*) display of justice by virtue of which one rules in favor of the descendants of the people of seniority who have records of meritorious deeds, contemporaries who are renowned for great achievements, people having won great fame in war, and people of wealth."[70] He warns the caliph that he should put an end to arbitrary practices that have produced only injustice and harm, and he should correct the wrong that has been done by administrative means, but without the use of force: "The types of injustice most in need of speedy correction or elimination are those that cause harm by disgracing and dishonoring sovereign authority (*al-sulṭān*), and the elimination of which requires little effort, does not provoke unrest and anger among the common people, and does not necessitate the use of force or cause harm."[71]

Ibn al-Muqaffaʿ's analysis takes us into the field of social and cultural conflict far beyond the old, but still potent, argument about Arabs versus Persians in the early Abbasid period. If anything, his discourse on the elite and the caliphal companions reveals his sympathy with the established caliphal sociopolitical order. He describes a textbook case of such conflict between the established nobility (upper-level administrators; urban, refined, learned companions; career army and chancellery bureaucrats; multiple generations of landowners; prominent families) and the new comers among the common folk (heroes of the revolution and their company, artisans, merchants, sectarian activists, and opportunists trying to capitalize on the new circumstances). For someone like Ibn al-Muqaffaʿ, who is convinced that mixing social classes and allowing the common people a share in governance would be wrong, the egalitarian wave of the revolt would appear alarming. As I have noted in chapter 6, he does not hide his dislike of the notion of communal egalitarianism. In the context of the obedience to the imam, for instance, he accuses those whom he portrays as wishing to diminish the authority of the caliph as wanting nothing other than making "people all alike," which, according to his estimation, is a blatant affront to the power of the sovereign.[72]

Yet his goal was not to restore the old status quo. Ibn al-Muqaffaʿ knew by personal experience that going back was impossible. He tried, instead, to build a hybrid structure of governance, to facilitate a merger and a slow transition from the current revolutionary "disorder" to the more familiar terrain of sociopolitical equilibrium. He suggested the creation of a new order in which classes were stabilized in their respective places by effective royal leadership and a choreographed body of caliph's privy. As he has attempted to do in his recommendations regarding other administrative and military matters, he aims here too to describe the qualifications for those who would be considered for the privy assembly and to outline the limits of their responsibility. The following passage sums up the broad professional principles and ethics of constituting the administrative personnel in the caliphal chamber:

> The privy of the Commander of the Faithful—may God honor him—have distinction and preeminence. This companionship is a distinguished honor for its holders and memorable glory for their descendants, and an accomplishment that deserves to be preserved and defended. It should be given only to a person who is distinguished by a special quality; or a man whom the Commander of the Faithful supposes to possess distinction resulting from familial affinity or extraordinary service rendered; or a man whose nobility, judgment, and action make him worthy of the company of the Commander of the Faithful, conversing with him, and advising him; a brave man known for and ready to display courage and who combines with it personal merit and modesty, and who can be promoted from the army to the entourage of the caliph; or a man with insightful pious knowledge (*faqīh*) who is devoted to doing good and who can be placed among the people so that they can benefit from his virtues and insightful knowledge (*fiqh*); or an honorable man who does not corrupt himself or others. As for whoever attempts to use intermediaries who can be granted companionship, he must be declined or placated with reasonable beneficence and righteousness, which do not lead to alienation and upset the order of things. Thus, the devoted companions must maintain their places and proper functions. A scribe should not have any power to either increase or decrease salaries, and a chamberlain should not have the authority to either give permission for audiences or delay them.[73]

These recommendations are a step forward to restore routine and "rationalize" administration. Ibn al-Muqaffaʿ advises the caliph to honor the old nobility; promote career administrators and military commanders; and recruit only talented persons and people possessing special abilities, such as those who rendered commendable service, and reputed scholars. He encourages him to promote those who have excelled, demote undeserving persons, and keep in place those who have proven themselves in their work. To enable an agreeable operation of governance, he advises the caliph to define the duties of the scribe and the chamberlain in a way that ensures proper control over decisions and to specify the function, responsibility, and authority of subordinates.[74] It seems as if he is targeting to remove some individuals and groups associated with the revolt and its aftermath in an effort to influence the new administration to build a formal imperial council, which would include a few select advisers who would help the sovereign govern the empire better.

The "Qualified Life" of the Masses

By deliberating on the sovereign and the elite, Ibn al-Muqaffaʿ also discusses the common folk, *al-ʿāmma*. It comes as no surprise that Ibn al-Muqaffaʿ takes the *longue-durée* view of imperial social distinction in the region for granted. He speaks about the people from the perspective of social hierarchy and presents a view that contrasts with the theoretical ontological "egalitarianism" of the ulema, above all with their discourse on the community, considered a collectivity of equal members. Notwithstanding the fact that the ulema too would adopt the discourse of *raʿiyya*, as I have noted in my discussion of the texts of al-ʿAnbarī and Abū Yūsuf, Ibn al-Muqaffaʿ's political conceptualization of the people as an "estate" (in addition to the sovereign and the elite) reflects a new notion of governance and speaks of a new political reality, one to which the ulema had to adapt. Politics proper, siyasa, in this context appears as the technique of management and control to ensure an agreeable life by which the sovereign secures the obedience and satisfaction of the masses.

Ibn al-Muqaffaʿ describes the entourage (*al-ṣaḥāba*) as "the tongues of his subjects" and "the elite from among the masses"[75] and refers to the common people as a faceless mass, the objects of political power comprised of city and country dwellers from walks of life pursuing various confessions. The common folk pay taxes and provide human power, which makes organized life possible. They are part of the social order humans have known universally, without whom the collective life would be impossible and the order would lack coherence. They are the flock placed by God for and under the protection of the sovereign, and they need proper herding to satisfy their duties and lead a good life.

However, his stance on the masses does not bring him any closer to the ulema's theoretical egalitarianism. For Ibn al-Muqaffaᶜ, the masses are dangerous and potentially devastating on account of their sheer quantity and lowly existence. While he does not elaborate on this point in the "Epistle," from the way he describes the common folk as ignorant, selfish, impulsive, and prone to be herded, he sees them as a destructive force, in the literal sense of the word. Left alone, the masses do not know how to live a dignified life and "have evil and corrupt ways."[76] They are an unpredictable flock, as he warns the caliph, which rage if treated firmly and respect no limit if shepherded with kindness.[77] Speaking of the pessimism of Ibn al-Muqaffaᶜ on this point, I should clarify that his cynicism concerns not human nature as discussed by ancient philosophers and the theologians of his time, as is often assumed, but human collectivity as a political entity and the power common folk might wield if they act together. He seems interested not in the individual "sheep" as an ontological question but rather in the flock (*raᶜiyya*) as a collective body.

To elaborate this point and better illustrate the direction of my analysis, I would like to invoke Agamben's discussion on bios and zoe.[78] What is politically interesting is that the masses, like the sovereign himself, as I examined in chapter 5, possess destructive power that needs to be normalized and regularized. To summarize my point, Ibn al-Muqaffaᶜ operates on the assumption that, as an individual touched by the divine, the sovereign is set free to dispense power in the way he desires. He is granted absolute power and ownership of the world not through the mediation of any religious dispensation but by God to satisfy the specific task of governing the world. Although the sovereign operates in a realm above or outside the law, he is the maker of the law that binds others. The question for Ibn al-Muqaffaᶜ is, of course, how to maintain social order under the authority of a sovereign who can dispense unpredictable, unmeasured, and unrestrained power? This is the fundamental point of departure in the text, and it is the driving premise of Ibn al-Muqaffaᶜ's other writings of which we know. As I have shown, the only way to bring the sovereign within the law is through techniques of management (politics, siyasa), including education, advice, and training to minimize his bare power, which is a task that falls on the shoulders of the sovereign's advisers and those who are assigned to his service. This view assumes that the sovereign has the moral and intellectual capacity to comprehend the instructions, manage his power, and deploy it properly.

The masses, on the other hand, are by constitution devoid of the capacity to organize life on their own and thus fall beneath the law. Ibn al-Muqaffaʿ reminds the caliph that they "have learned something certain, about which there can be no doubt, namely, that the masses have never improved their welfare by themselves, and that prosperity can come to them only through their imam."[79] As a political question for Ibn al-Muqaffaʿ, the *ʿāmma* in their usual existence reside therefore in the realm of bare life, the naked life of an animal, which is unpolitical. "This is because of the number of weak and ignorant people among them, who cannot exploit their own opinions, do not possess any knowledge, and do not stand out in managing affairs."[80] Because the natural state of the masses is bare life, they always retain the potential to unleash chaos and destruction, which necessitates constant control and restraint. They need to be treated as such because, as a starting point, they are barely at the threshold of being subject to the law, to which level they need to be raised first. They are the subject of the law only when they become the subjects of a sovereign. This is the level of proper social life, bio-life, which is utterly political.

Even though the masses do not possess agency, they must still be elevated to the level of governance if the sovereign desires to establish a social order. They would "need to have their conduct (*ādāb*) and ways corrected more than they need food for sustenance."[81] In other words, they need to be treated as political objects and governed with methodical skills, which include the bare-bones utilitarian deployment of religious piety. As Ibn al-Muqaffaʿ reminds the caliph, "the people of each metropolis, military district, and frontier zone are in dire need of people who have knowledge of religious jurisprudence (*fiqh*), tradition (*sunna*), pious practices (*siyar*), and good advice (*naṣīḥa*), who educate, correct, remind them of, and show them, their errors, preach against ignorance, prevent heretical falsities, caution against sedition, and scrutinize the affairs of the common people in their midst, so that nothing important can be concealed from them."[82]

The natural order entails that the ruler governs his flock not by oppressing them but by "training" and "educating" them through the elite and by instituting justice to arbitrate their conflicts and keep them in order. Being skillful in associating with the common people, the elite functions thus not only as the educators of the masses but also as their mentors and role models, tools of surveillance and control, and the engineers of orderly conduct in harmony with the sovereign's rule. Ibn al-Muqaffaʿ explains in the following statement how the masses can be controlled and their lives ordered by the elite, who possess the skills and techniques of management: "They [the elite] can then seek to correct the situation and address what they find disagreeable with their good judgment, kindness, and sincerity and submit the difficult cases to persons judged capable of resolving them, being confident that these capable persons will follow up on and fortify that concern, be able to perceive sound judgment as soon as it appears, and be competent physicians in extirpating what is disagreeable before it sets in."[83]

Combined with the other remarks about them in the "Epistle," one notices how the masses become the object of politics. They cannot act and speak for themselves but are spoken for by the elite. They must be mentored, coached, controlled, and disciplined, which are tasks left for the elites. Ibn al-Muqaffaʿ explains this situation to his patron as the order of life: "God places in their midst an elite of men of religion and reason (*dīn wa ʿaql*), whom they observe and listen to, and if their elite concern themselves with the affairs of the masses and approach them with seriousness, sincerity, perseverance, and vigor," he reminds the caliph, "God will make that an advantage for their community, the cause of blessing for their virtuous elite, an increase of what God has graciously bestowed upon them, and a way of achieving pure and total good."[84]

Taxpaying Subjects Versus Nonentities

Looking at how Ibn al-Muqaffaʿ discusses the "flock," I want to make two further points about the difference between tax and tribute to support my initial contention. On the one hand, the power to administer and tax a territory is evidence of regularized exercise of authority in the realm. Tribute, on the other hand, suggests the more arbitrary imposition of obligations, which can be punitive on a region, locality, or people by the right of conquest. Likewise, the recognition of people with legal standing and as taxpaying entities is evidence of sovereign authority, which suggests a functioning political order with the corollary rationalized and regulated tax obligations. It follows that being subject to tax obligations marks a crucial difference in the legal status of the individual, in the sense that it determines whether the subject is a "legal entity" governed by legitimate political power or a "nonentity" and therefore a dispensable person subject to arbitrary violence.[85]

Much of Ibn al-Muqaffaʿ's recommendations in the "Epistle" are connected to financial matters. One may venture to say that he seems to recognize that taxes and tax collection, calculating revenues, expenditures, balancing budgets, and the relationship of prices to production and market volatility form part of a much larger phenomenon (what we call the economy today), although he cannot quite put his finger on it as a process. Ibn al-Muqaffaʿ appreciates the economy not as a theoretical question but as a practical matter related to good governance, such as his calculation of the balance between agricultural production on the one hand and taxation and governance on the other. In the passages on the land tax where he expounds on the practical principles of fiscal administration and related issues, he aims to rationalize taxation as a function of good governance by establishing bearable tax obligations, instituting predictable administrative regulations, and employing trustworthy and knowledgeable tax agents to execute laws. By pondering taxation as part of the other functions of government, he connects politics to the economy not just to secure the ruler in his place but also to build a climate of welfare and contentment.

To reflect on the dialogic context of the text, a brief explanation is in order. In hindsight, one notices in the practices since the 630s the emergence of a distinction in terms of tax obligations between the Arabian Peninsula and its people and the regions beyond it, which are described as the conquered lands. The caliphs appreciated local traditions (Sasanian, Byzantine, Visigoth)[86] in their tax practices, including the poll tax and land tax. Muslims paid *ṣadaqa* tax (or *zakāt*) on their total wealth (about 2.5 percent) and *ʿushr* (10 percent, but not consistent) on farmland. While *ṣadaqa* was sometimes regulated and sometimes not, *ʿushr* and *jizya* were imposed and collected by tax agents. Non-Muslim subjects paid the poll tax (*jizya*) per individual (excluding women, children, and priests), the amount of which changed from time to time and location to location. Farmers cultivating the conquered lands outside the Arabian Peninsula (in the beginning non-Muslims, but from the reign of ʿUmar II in the second decade of the eighth century, Muslims cultivated such lands too) paid *kharāj* on their produce. After ʿUmar II's tax reforms, and with the growing number of non-Arab native converts in the conquered lands, *kharāj* came to denote the tax levied on the people cultivating farmlands in the conquered territories regardless of their faith.[87]

The question regarding non-Muslims (and non-Arab Muslims) during the Umayyad period was the overlap and confusion between *jizya* and *kharāj*, whether they were one or two obligations. There was also the problem among Muslims of the distinction between war spoils (*ghanīma* and its regulated form *fay'*, a trust for disbursement of revenue from spoils in perpetuity) and *kharāj*, and what actually constituted *kharāj*. Such questions related to fiscal management of the conquered lands and to taxation remained at the forefront of major controversies leading up ʿUmar II's tax reforms at the beginning of the eighth century. Indeed, they continued after him, contributing to the Abbasid revolt, and well into the struggles of empire building after the establishment of the Abbasid caliphate. A big part of these issues had to do with the terminology, the proper use of related vocabulary to identify the difference between various obligations, the status of taxpayers, and the classification of imperial subjects.

The debates and conflicts about them resulted in new practices, but taxation policies remained provisional for much of the eighth century.[88]

By the Abbasid revolution, the idea that converts should no longer pay *jizya* and that *kharāj* simply meant land tax was growing but not yet established. On the one hand, these taxes still indicated being non-Muslim and non-Arab Muslim in the conquered regions—those who lacked the privilege of entitlements, which was a sign of inferior and even slave status.[89] It had already been the practice that Muslims and non-Muslims paid different taxes, by which their social status and membership in the community were identified. *Jizya* and *kharāj* signified the subjection of one people by another, and of the native to the master or overlord by the right of conquest.

On the other hand, taking advantage of farmers and discrimination against them must have been widespread. An anecdotal but suggestive report in al-Ṭabarī cites that Shurayk, a legal scholar of the late Umayyad period, argued that "the people of the *sawād* lands [cultivated lands of lower Iraq] are slaves." Al-Ṭabarī also notes that the same scholar used to assert that "the *jizya* taken from the people of the *sawād* is a *kharāj* [tribute], like the *kharāj* taken from a slave. Their conversion to Islam does not nullify it."[90] In a similar vein, Ibn ʿAbd al-Ḥakam narrates a story about a man in Egypt who wanted to travel to Alexandria by boat. When he needed someone to row, he compelled a Copt to do it and declared openly that "they [the Copts] are in the status of slaves if we need them."[91]

The ulema engaged the problem of taxation and treatment of conquered peoples piecemeal as questions of religious obligations to be satisfied by the caliphs and individuals; of wealth distribution; and of piety, fairness, and justice in managing the native peoples. Yet no major work seems to have been composed about this subject until Abū Yūsuf's *Kitāb al-Kharāj* in the late eighth century, which recommended proportional tax instead of fixed percentage to alleviate the burden of overtaxation.[92] That al-ʿAnbarī raised the issue but did not address it satisfactorily and that Hārūn al-Rashīd later asked Abū Yūsuf to detail the matter for him to guide his practice suggest that the absence of any systematic intellectual input guiding the practice had rendered the administration's policies an ad hoc process. In this respect, Ibn al-Muqaffaʿ's assessment of the existing practice, its breakdown, and its reform after the revolt in writing as a theme worthy of theoretical analysis anticipated al-ʿAnbarī's discussion of it and Abū Yūsuf's study. Abū Yūsuf raised the discussion to a new level by dedicating a complete volume to it, which inaugurated the new field of "*kharāj* studies."

It should be plain enough that, although Ibn al-Muqaffaʿ deliberated the broad consequences of the revolt, he was addressing an ongoing problem. He apprised the caliph that Abbasid practices failed to alleviate the burden on farmers or made it worse. He addressed the main question head-on: "Among the things of which the Commander of the Faithful is reminded is the subject of the land and the land tax. It [the land] is the greatest, most significant, and most demanding thing to make productive, and closer to being lost from productivity. This includes in the area between the plain and the mountain, and which qualifies as neither rural districts (*rasātīq*) nor as villages."[93] Ibn al-Muqaffaʿ describes the maladministration of the land, pointing out that "the tax agents have no regulations to which they can refer, by which they can be held responsible, and which prevent them from committing extortionist practices against the peasants (*ahl al-arḍ*, the people of the land) after they have improved (*ʿimāra*) the land with care, hoping to derive a surplus (*faḍl*) from the work of their hands."[94]

Ibn al-Muqaffaʿ cites examples of maladministration and extortion to illustrate the severity of the situation, pointing out that "the treatment by the tax agents of these peasants takes one of two forms: either a person exacts dues by the threat of fear and violence wherever he finds something to take and tracks down individuals in rural districts to levy excessive taxes on whomever can be found; or another person, by surveying the land, levies tax on whomever has planted crops and exempts those who have not, so that those who have improved the land incur the burden of tax while those who have left it in ruin get away with it."[95] He then reminds the caliph that because of such practices, the method of tax collection has become unmoored: "Moreover, the principles of the assessment of obligations imposed on administrative districts were neither fixed nor known (*ʿilm*). There is not a district whose assessment of tax obligation has not been changed several times. The assessments of some have disappeared while those of others have continued to exist."[96] In his assessment, bad practices (absence of regulations, inaccurate land surveys, neglect of record keeping, lack of instruction manuals for administrators to follow, and arbitrariness in tax imposition and collection) contrast with an ideally efficient tax regime that ensures prosperity and order, which is what Ibn al-Muqaffaʿ hopes to convey.

After explaining the situation, Ibn al-Muqaffaʿ proceeds with his recommendation. "If the Commander of the Faithful would put into practice his judgment by assigning familiar fixed tax obligations on rural districts, villages and lands; having records kept in registers; and officially establishing basic tax collection principles, then a man can only be obliged to pay a tax about which he knows and which he can pay, and devote his energies to improving land, which will happen only if he can derive a surplus and benefit from it."[97] After having acted, he concludes, "we could then hope that these measures would be good for his [the caliph's] subjects and the improvement of the land and would close the doors of treason and wrongfulness of tax agents."[98] He warns his patron, however, that "this is an opinion that is extremely burdensome to put into practice, the men supporting it are few, and its benefits are slow in coming."[99] Ibn al-Muqaffaʿ concludes with a final suggestion about monitoring tax agents. "Other than that suggestion, the only idea regarding the land tax is the one that we have observed the Commander of the Faithful to have espoused, and we have not observed anyone else to have espoused it before him, concerning the careful selection of tax agents, and controlling, reprimanding, and replacing them."[100]

There are some empire-wide issues in this laconic discourse on taxes. For the system of obligations and the social hierarchies to work as desired, the sovereign would need to do more than deploy fair tax agents. Ibn al-Muqaffaʿ's most important recommendation is assigning a fixed tax amount on specified farming tracts so that revenue could be predicted by administrators and the tax would be known in advance by the farmers. Beyond that he aims at reducing the friction between tax collectors and farmers, increasing revenue by encouraging the cultivation of agricultural tracts that can be cultivated only with hard labor, rationalizing tax administration by setting rules and regulations for tax collectors, and by record keeping. The caliph must determine the assessment on the agricultural surplus fairly and ensure its efficient collection so that farmers were not oppressed. Organizing the tax system and administering it efficiently, which is the summation of his advice, ensures regularity of income, the contentment of farmers, and fair treatment of the empire's subjects as the sovereign's main charges to establish justice. It also inspires good practices in the empire by the fact of observing reasoned procedures and processes.

Bearing this discussion in mind, a few points may be made here. Ibn al-Muqaffaʿ wrote the "Epistle" against a background of contradictory practices and serious debates among the ulema about taxes, some of which normalized treating people as property to be exploited at will. Without suggesting that the jurists of the time were oblivious to these issues or, worse yet, complicit in oppression or unconcerned with grievances, I read Ibn al-Muqaffaʿ's advice on taxation as an attempt to move the discussion of governance toward constructing a notion of "imperial subjectivity," in which the totality of the people in the empire are reconstituted as "tax-paying subjects" instead of "tribute-paying nonentities," who exist but can be dispensed with at will.

Given the discursive context of the era before Abū Yūsuf, Ibn al-Muqaffaʿ seems to advance an argument that differentiates tribute from tax to distinguish between faith subject and imperial subject. By arguing for regulating *kharāj* as a standard tax levied on imperial subjects, Muslim and non-Muslim, rather than as a tribute imposed on a subjugated people, he suggests a practice in which the non-Muslim (and non-Arab Muslim) inhabitants of the caliphate obtain a taxpaying subject status like the other subjects of the empire. In this view, the differentiation among the people as imperial subjects would not rest on confessional identity but on "social class" (elite or common folk) and practices (differential treatment depending on context), which ensures an umbrella of protection for imperial subjects regardless of their faith affiliation.

We have already noted the reference to the non-Muslim inhabitants of the empire as the caliph's subjects with genuine rights and responsibilities by Ibn al-Muqaffaʿ's younger colleague al-ʿAnbarī. Abū Yūsuf also expands on this theme and discusses their status vis-à-vis the law and the caliph. Their attention to the topic suggests a scholarly and legal agency in pursuing the question of how to organize and normalize the non-Muslim peoples of the empire as taxpaying but differential subjects administered by specific regulations. Under the circumstances, enshrining these populations as legal entities entitled to justice was a moral and legal step forward taken to protect them within the caliphate. It was also an act of organizing and circumscribing them according to the values of the social order envisioned by the ulema.

There is another curious difference between Ibn al-Muqaffaʿ and al-ʿAnbarī and Abū Yūsuf. Unlike his younger contemporaries, who would deal with this issue—in the latter's case, at length—Ibn al-Muqaffaʿ did not even mention *ṣadaqa* tax (*zakāt*) and *jizya* or the customary charitable obligations among other faith groups in any form. He was not interested in them as a matter of fiscal administration. Pondering the implication of this differing position, I do not mean to suggest that Ibn al-Muqaffaʿ empties imperial subjectivity of its religious content. On the contrary, we know that he recognizes Islamic piety, in its varying forms, as a force that undergirded public morality and culture, inspired imperial ambitions, and shaped laws and policies. My suggestion is that his inattention to the *ṣadaqa* tax might have been, if not deliberate, a logical outcome of his broader vision of empire. By foregrounding the "political" status rather than the religious identity of the subjects in their interactions with the caliph, he seems to calculate that the political subject would act differently from the religious one, who is, theoretically, always subject to sacred law and for this reason potentially a hindrance to the sovereign's ability to rule.

What was Ibn al-Muqaffaʿ's objective? We need to keep in mind that what undergirds the "Epistle on the Caliph's Privy" is a vision of ideal monarchy. When one focuses on the performative function of his language, one notices a move against several rising groups and practices in the postrevolt Abbasid political scene. Ibn al-Muqaffaʿ's advice flies in the face of the bottom-up character of the revolt. He is unsparing, for instance, concerning the revolutionary enthusiasts who took part in the revolt and whom he portrayed as inept and greedy opportunists busy catching the bandwagon because they happened to have taken part in the Abbasid revolt or given the impression they had done so. Ibn al-Muqaffaʿ also rejects the ulema's practices. The ulema constituted a broad-based, expert collectivity active in the judiciary, religious practice, and scholarship with growing social power. Yet their pious exhortations and scholarship on the revealed law had hardly touched policy matters outside the judiciary, which Ibn al-Muqaffaʿ addressed and roundly rejected. For instance, he dismisses their knowledge in matters of governance and challenges their work. In his discussion of the law, he mocks them as a self-righteous and self-centered group who seem to operate with impunity.

Ibn al-Muqaffaʿ is also against the more egalitarian stance of the ulema. The elite whom he envisioned were not only morally distinct from the class of the ulema but also opposed the idea advocated by the jurists and the theologians. Not dependent on or restricted by an "originalist" religiosity and pious practice, the ruler and the elite, in his view, were more than just a faith community gathering around the sacred law as formulated by the ulema. He advocated a vision that confronted the idea of conceiving the empire as equal to the faith community where subjects are reconstituted as disciples of the ruler. In fact, the new ruling elite suggested by Ibn al-Muqaffaʿ promised to be damaging to the position of the ulema because the sociocultural ethos fostered by the new elite would not intersect with the concerns and interests of the ulema substantially.

In conclusion, who then did Ibn al-Muqaffaʿ promote? One possibility is that he attempted to advance his own personal career and his wish to be appointed to a prominent position with the caliph. It was indeed a time when old and new nobility, high-level administrators, and provincial functionaries were being shuffled and replaced as the Abbasids devoted their attention to controlling the provinces. Because he wrote the "Epistle" after the intra-Abbasid rivalry between al-Manṣūr and his uncle ʿAbdallāh b. ʿAlī had ended, he might have seen an opportunity to hope for an upward change in his career. However, this would not be a productive way of examining his proposal.

What one notices here is the defense of his social group and the promotion of its interests regardless of the diversity of their "big" ethnic, linguistic, and cultural identities. He defended his colleagues, the scribal professionals in the empire, against the growing power of the ulema and the revolutionary enthusiasts in the corridors of the Abbasid administrative establishment. I contend that Ibn al-Muqaffaʿ wrote about and tried to bring into reality a class of professionals in the company of the caliph and in his administration who would serve as experts in the empire. He endeavored to convince the caliph to identify functionaries and assistants with the necessary professional skills who would work like artisans in the imperial machinery following established administrative practices. Considering his proposal about positioning the empire on the

Iraq-Khurasan geopolitical axis, he had in fact a particular cadre of professionals in mind for the caliph to draw on to fill civil and military positions: the Iraqi nobility and experts, of whom he was one, as he stated. In the body of the text he wrote, Ibn al-Muqaffaᶜ assures the caliph that "among the people of Iraq is an elite who possess discernment (*fiqh*), integrity, insightfulness, and eloquence. One can almost doubt that there exists a group like them—or even like half their number—among all other people of the Qibla [Muslims]." Thus, if the caliph desires "to be content with all that he seeks in this class of people (*ṭabaqa min al-nās*)," Ibn al-Muqaffaᶜ promises, "he will find this in them."[101]

As he repeatedly notes, the elite have been long overlooked as the sovereign's most appropriate collaborators. For a professional who promoted the idea of monarchy, coherence in political practice was a priority. Ibn al-Muqaffaᶜ warns the caliph that "the elite's need for the imam by whom God corrects them is like the masses' need for the elite, if not more." He knew that imperial functionaries had come from diverse backgrounds, pursued conflicting interests, and had variable degrees of ability and expertise, which led them to take discordant positions and develop differing loyalties and aspirations. He reminds the caliph that, despite their talents, the elite still rely on the sovereign for inspiration, to set an example, and for guidance. They learn and inhabit the manners of nobility; have edifying conduct; grasp how to represent the sovereign; and, with his guidance, can show his subjects the way to a good life. He goes on to explain why the sovereign is the nexus of this collaboration and cooperation: "For, through the imams, God unites their [the elite's] affairs, restrains the people who would discredit them, unifies their opinions and their words, and shows them their status among the masses. He makes for them [the elite] the proof and the staunch support in the words they use against those who deviate from the path of their obligations toward them."[102]

In this model of politics, and following al-Fārābī's Aristotelian argument that different cities produce value according to their own constitutions, Ibn al-Muqaffaᶜ's arguments on "imperial estates" (subjects, army, elite, caliph's privy, common folk) worked against the notions of tyranny and oligarchy (the corrupted forms of monarchy and aristocracy) and the emerging notion of the imamate among the ulema. They did, however, more than destabilize the imamate as the only language of politics or generate a social structure that intersected with the *longue-durée* imperial practices in the region. Considering the content and direction of his discursive practice, Ibn al-Muqaffaᶜ also described a caliphate that was relatable to other "lay humanists," which opened an intellectual and moral space for new imaginaries of statecraft where various forms of reasoned social order could be elaborated.

Conclusion

Releasing Siyasa from the Imamate

A central focus of the study in this book has been to establish that siyasa presented a critical turn in the region's political thought tradition that disrupted the ulema's notion of religious governance, the imamate, with which the actors had always made sense of their political reality. It is important to reiterate that siyasa did not mean just another literary or textual supplement to an ongoing intellectual tradition. On the contrary, it emerged as a destabilizing intervention in the ulema-centric epistemic and moral universe, and established a new foundation or frame of reference for political thinking. The pioneers of this new intellectual venture did more than help shape structures and institutions to marshal new imperial subjectivities responsive to the emerging postrevolutionary Abbasid rule; they also reflected deliberately on politics and on the "rules of the game," so to speak. On the one hand, their work marked the difference between pre-politics, when ad hoc spontaneous and expedient responses to developments had constituted the bulk of political imagination, and politics proper, in which the consequence of a particular position or action is causally calculated or forecast in the exercise of power. On the other hand, they elaborated monarchical rule or royal authority (*mulk*) as a form of divine grace or blessing bestowed exclusively upon the ruler to maintain earthly order rather than as another iteration of tyranny, as religious scholars argued. Whereas the imamate necessarily bound governance to prophecy, religious community, and the sacred laws of the ulema, siyasa grounded governance in human nature and as a divine bestowal, independent of any specific prophetic dispensation. Aimed at constructing rule based on reasoned discourse, adab-siyasa conveyed a sense of governance that intended to direct the caliphate away from being a confessional entity and toward rule that recognized and managed faith but did not aim to subordinate itself to it, as the ulema wished. With this shift of assumptions, siyasa expanded the semantic range of the concept of the caliphate to royal notions of authority in the histories of Afro-Eurasia.

This book has set forth two major points to substantiate its main argument. One concerns siyasa as a particular form of governmentalizing sovereignty. Taking my cue from the concept of "governmentality," and thinking critically on the practices of state building, I explicated how the notions of siyasa and *tadbīr* were envisioned to function as a craft of governing, which demanded an application of knowledge and skills to the administration of peoples and affairs to produce social good. In the late Umayyad and early Abbasid intellectual milieu, when the transcendental normative language of imamate, which assumed an incompatibility between ruling and moral values, stood as the only language of politics, the language of siyasa opened a window on politics as the art of mitigating contingency and the technique of managing affairs to ensure a satisfactory result rather than a theological question or a subset of religious jurisprudence. When one considers its popularity in the following decades and centuries, the idea of siyasa continued to inspire intellectuals and administrators to think about politics in creative ways.

My second point is about temporality. Drawing on the theoretical insights of recent "postsecular" and postcolonial theories in the field, I have shown how siyasa rationality intersected with new ways of thinking and of living, which the Abbasid intellectual tradition expressed in the concepts of urbane conduct or civility or the art of good living (adab and *ẓarf*) and the associated term worldliness (*dunyawī*). As we have seen, the correlation of siyasa with temporal morality generated a new imagination of empire that epitomized a departure from the ethical horizon of the imamate and its central concepts of religious righteousness and religious community. This new worldly orientation evident in the adab-siyasa practices gave shape to a culture of moral self-formation and of social conduct that distinguished itself from pious practice (*waraʿ*, *taqwā*, and their cognates) espoused by the ulema. A long-term outcome of this development may be observed in the emergence of a new direction of political reflection that prioritized the calculated prudence of good governance over the abstract and universal principles of political piety.

Before siyasa, political reflection remained a spontaneous part of a century-long dialectic between the moral force of the Islamic faith and the caliphal practice in an empire extending from the Indus Valley through the Mediterranean to the Straits of Gibraltar. As in Judaism and Christianity, Islam also introduced a particular monotheistic imaginary, an episteme, which defined the framework of life for its followers. As a transcendental "enchantment," it grounded truth, inspired a new thinking about being in the world, generated a social practice, and inspired a moral position in life. One dynamic that spurred political reflection had to do with the militarization and imperialization of the faith community that entangled faith with politics, which led to substantial theological divisions that tore the faith community apart. Faith became intertwined with imperial affairs to the degree that one could not speak about a substantial faith group or a religious position without an associated political question. The other concerned the formation of the empire, with its complex structures and practices that prompted political reflection dedicated to improving administrative efficiency and political control. Because these two dynamics were not always complementary, they generated contending visions of governance.

The fast success of Islam revolutionized its environment. For its believers, it communicated a new understanding of life and enabled a language that made sense of politics in undeniably religious idioms throughout the first century of the caliphate. I have argued that the discourse on imamate (both the idea of contractual caliphate and the Shiite notion of designated imam) emerged from the late seventh century onward as the political language of the ulema, who defined and guided the caliphate as "pastoral" authority. For much of the eighth century, the idea of the imamate remained pre-political in content and pre-prose in form. We observe it as part of theological and sectarian controversies or as brief maxims and exhortations intended either as a defense or as critiques of the Umayyads, without sustained written investment until the late eighth century. Despite its incipient and abstract character typically disconnected from the details of actual governance, imamate in its various versions remained dominant until the mid-eighth century.

As a rationality of governance or a form of governmentalizing religion, the imamate evolved through the religious scholars' relentless labor operating in the eighth century (pre-Sunnite, Muʿtazilite, Shiite, Kharijite, and other groups). What seems to have happened is that soon after its rise as a discursive practice, siyasa compelled the ulema to respond to new questions in a literary style beyond the sectarian arguments that they had used before the mid-eighth century. My argument has been that only in the context of and with the compelling language of siyasa did the imamate gain self-awareness in the writing of ulema like al-ʿAnbarī and Abū Yūsuf. To make my point, I examined the difference between the early imamate texts and the later ones as a development that should be attributed to the impact of siyasa on the ulema, who could not remain impervious to the world of possibilities that siyasa created. In a sense, siyasa shaped in substantial ways the terms of discussion on political practice.

I have connected the emergence of siyasa to the efforts of several late Umayyad and early Abbasid lay bureaucrats who launched a debate on politics in the emerging literary prose writing in the eighth century. These professionals, who are often glorified as "realists," did work in the central administration near the rulers and helped Umayyad and Abbasid empire building. Having no choice but to operate under the structuring circumstances of the elementary language of imamate, this cadre of bureaucrats pushed back against the ulema's hitherto abstract, universal, and normative language by articulating incongruent political ideas that reoriented the empire in a new direction. Apprehensive about the ulema's language and concerned with the day-to-day matters of governance, these professionals reached out to the *longue-durée* imperial practices in the region to develop a new frame of thinking, reflecting the precarity of their social standing and the hybridity of their vision of governance. It is timely, therefore, to recognize their contributions as an intervention in an already occupied sociopolitical space that created, by necessity, an effect. As *mawālī*, many of these lay scholars led lives simultaneously as the elite and the other, which gave them a distinct vantage point to address political issues in new ways, criticize common views and practices about governance among the ulema, and suggest new directions.

Whether translating from Persian or writing in Arabic, the lay bureaucrat literati produced a cosmopolitan discourse and a hybrid cultural outlook away from reactionary nativism and assimilation. They embraced the sociocultural manifestations of Islam but were critical of the "Arabic" cultural hegemony and did not shy away from being deferential to the *longue-durée* political traditions of the region. Their pioneering work mobilized the political reflection in two directions. One of them excavated Greek political philosophy and the other one tapped into Persian political advice as venues to apprehend and inform Abbasid political practice. In hindsight, one gathers from the literary references to and reproduction of their work during later decades and centuries that this cadre of lay bureaucrats launched an intellectual tradition that enabled a space of exploration for non-Arabic Muslim dynasties in Afro-Eurasia, including those of the Seljuk and the Ottoman Turks, the Mongols, and the Mughals.

To explicate the tone-setting and structuring role of siyasa, I have focused my attention on Ibn al-Muqaffaʿ's discursive practice in his "Epistle" and his other writings. I have assessed the "Epistle" as a political manifesto exemplifying a discourse of deliberative state building, when the imamate texts imagined social organization as an affair of the religious community practicing the revealed laws. In a discursive universe where the caliphate (historical or ideal) existed as a question of pious practice, doctrinal truth claims, and religious obligation, this significant work shifted the language on caliphal practice from its current religious underpinnings to the context of rational ordering of society based on the idea of good governance.

As we have seen, the ulema were interested in the caliph's faith status and his pious credentials as a condition of his legitimacy. They interrogated the caliph's conduct for compliance with the religious requirements. They also discussed obeying or disobeying the caliph as a question of faith, the community of the faithful and membership to it, and the status of the first four caliphs. Their frequent references to fairness and justice were phrased in religious terms. In contrast, the "Epistle" underlined the sovereign and the mechanism of dispensing his power. Instead of pious submission to theological norms regardless of outcome, as advocated by the ulema, the work is stubbornly concerned with the empire, its political constitution and outcome—the knowledge of political practice and the tested techniques of administration needed for effective governance. In addition to its content, the "Epistle" created a new conceptual space in which a vision of an empire that concerned itself with the political reality as distinct from the religious community could be deliberated.

I have also discussed how the new discourse of politics intersected with the notions and practices of secularity and the associated concepts of urbane conduct and civility. The avant garde language and terminology of the "Epistle" highlighted a particular social practice associated with a rationality of governance not circumscribed by the dominant forms of religious practice. I have pointed out how the texts suggested a distinction between the demands of religious piety (*taqwā*) and the aspirations of adab, where one was aligned with religious morality and guided by the expert knowledge of the ulema and the other underlined civil manners and worldly attitudes and was inspired by the knowledge of non-ulema intellectuals.

Siyasa presented a notion of caliph that was distinct from the caliph of the imamate. I observed how, on the one hand, siyasa came to mean a craft of bringing the sovereign under the law through a regime of moral cultivation, adab, which included disciplining the ruler in right conduct, inculcating the codes of propriety and ethics, and encouraging him to nurture the practical skills necessary to be an effective ruler. On the other hand, siyasa signified the art of practicing governance through alleviating problems by normalized and agreeable means and aspiring to foster a climate of welfare among the subjects to keep a functioning social order.

Given that royal authority or kingship (*mulk*) represented a form of divine grace or blessing (*niʿma*), the agency of the ruler posed a question: How could the ruler be virtuous or acquire virtue? I have argued that, insofar as the ruler was a subject of adab, the mitigative capacity of siyasa situated political virtue in political effort rather than in self-cultivation alone through pious conduct. In this view, as the sovereign exerted himself to maintain his rule by practicing good governance through a prudent calculation of circumstances and rational judgment, he acquired virtue. Assessed in the light of Louis Althusser's analysis of the dialectic between contingency and agency, siyasa's political virtue developed as an outcome of agency or independence of the ruler, which enabled him to govern in view of the challenges he faced and make decisions not by the brute force of suppression but by strategizing and seeking consent to ensure satisfaction. Seen this way, political virtue in siyasa differentiated itself from religious virtue (pious abstention and dutifulness, *taqwâ* and *wara*ᶜ), which prioritized observing religious obligations regardless of the temporal outcome.

I have argued that the law of the empire no longer meant the cumulative jurisprudential judgments of the ulema nor did their legal morality remain the foundation of legal thinking. It encapsulated a vision of a code (or a collection of codes) with the capacity to translate the absolute power of the ruler into legitimate routine authority. It allowed various legal codes to function as a modality to normalize control of the people in the realm and shape existing power relations by channeling loyalty in public matters from the sacred law of the ulema to the sovereign's authority. This legal discourse aimed at rationalizing the process of legislation so that it made neither the ulema nor even the sovereign the sole authority of legislation but the "procedure" itself. Ibn al-Muqaffaᶜ's proposal came as no less than a game-changing epistemological intervention that targeted creating a law that was imperial rather than religious in a social order functioning according to the ethos of a monarchy.

Another related shift in political thought was the notion of territory in siyasa discourse. Moving away from the enthusiasm of the Abbasid revolt and the abstract ideal of the imamate, Ibn al-Muqaffaᶜ conceived the empire territorially as an administrable geopolitical entity. He identified a new core for the empire (the Iraq-Khurasan region), linking to this core other regions (Syria, the Arabian Peninsula, Egypt) according to their functions. He pursued the territorialization of the realm even if it meant severing certain limbs from the caliphate, such as North Africa and the Iberian Peninsula. I clarified how this intentional cognitive map of the empire created an imaginary of sociopolitical life within the framework of a territorialized realm otherwise imagined only in the idioms of religious community and faith. This territorial calculation made the empire more than a "community of faith," a bequest of the believers, or a collection of cities and villages simply inherited from the Umayyads. In this view, the realm became an organization, with its own rationally conceived territory, structures, and institutions, and an association, which was constituted rather than received, cultural rather than natural.

Under the supreme authority of the caliph, a distinct imperial elite rather than the ulema or de facto unregulated power brokers and nobility would govern this territorialized empire. In siyasa, the caliph was represented as an individual who was given the fortune of ruling the world, which elevated him to an ontological category above the rest of his subjects. His subjects were divided into two broad classes: the ruling class (the military, administrative elite, and empire-wide nobility, *al-khāṣṣa*, the elite), which held the privilege of governing, and the ruled (the common folk, *al-ʿāmma*). The significance of this is that siyasa texts generated from mundane imperial functionaries a "ruling class" by the fact of naming them and by refocusing the lens of anyone observing the operation of the caliphate on their function. This notion of siyasa also shaped the idea of a common folk by envisioning them as both the object of the elite's power and a naturalized social entity with distinct features and patterns of behaviors that must be controlled. Unlike the egalitarian notion of the religious community (*umma*) siyasa acknowledged, in fact, advocated, socially distinct classes as a constitutive part of the imperial domain. The elite in this setting functioned as a conduit that transferred the absolute power of the sovereign to the routine operation of governance. They functioned as a role model for the common folk, who always existed in the in-betweenness of "bios" and "zoe." Such a vision of the population communicates a notion of "imperial subject" as opposed to "faith subject" of the ulema, each of which demands different treatment.

Considering how Ibn al-Muqaffaʿ imagined his empire as a more inclusive and deconfessionalized category, one may justifiably ask *whose* empire was the Abbasid caliphate? What may be discerned from the foregoing analysis is a pathway to reimagine the Abbasid caliphate as an empire of not just the faith community of the ulema but the totality of its inhabitants, who shared the empire under a ruling dynasty despite their social and cultural diversity. Along the same lines and on the question of religion, I wish to encourage readers to reflect on how the over-religionization of the caliphate by modern (both "Western" and self-acknowledged Muslim) scholarship has distorted the image of the institution as the perpetual other. I reckon that if the current tenacious devotion to the ulema-centric perspective on the caliphate has some credibility, it cannot be by marginalizing the discursive value of the adab-siyasa tradition, despite the fact that the volume of surviving work in the siyasa tradition (statecraft, advice, mirror for princes, philosophical, ethical writings) seems to far exceed the work from the imamate tradition (Sunnite, Shiite, Muʿtazilite, Kharijite, legal, theological, Sufi writings).[1] And to those who wonder about how much impact a lone voice could exercise, I suggest they consider that Ibn al-Muqaffaʿ was not a lone voice but a window onto the larger world of adab-siyasa tradition, in which numerous professionals produced ideas and practices that defined the terms of political reflection in the following centuries. I hope my argument encourages a new historiographical possibility, one in which the non-ulema-centric histories of good governance can be told in more productive and constructive ways. After all, the most renown theoretician of the imamate, al-Māwardī, himself acknowledges the distinction between the two moralities of governance in the very title of his magnum opus, *Sultanic Ordinances and Religious Deputations* (*al-aḥkām al-sulṭāniyya wa al-wilāyāt al-dīniyya*).

Conventions and Spelling

I have followed the *International Journal of Middle East Studies* (*IJMES*) transliteration convention for the Latinization of the non-Latin script. Occasional differences in transliterated words indicate their varying pronunciations in the source language. I have tried to avoid gendered pronouns whenever I could but did not question the exclusive language of the primary sources. Considering the target audience, I translated quotations *ad sensum* and integrated in the sentence the explanatory words and phrases conventionally provided in brackets. I have, however, provided certain key terms in parentheses to avoid ambiguity and allow readers who are familiar with the source language to ground their understanding of the quotation. I have followed *Merriam-Webster's Collegiate Dictionary*, 11th Edition, for common Anglicized words (e.g., ulema, Sunnite, imamate). Common geographic terms (such as Khurasan) and proper names (such as Muhammad), frequently occurring terms (such as siyasa, shariʿa) are only minimally transliterated or not at all. In the alphabetical ordering of names, the Arabic definite article *al-* is ignored. "Ibn" (son of) in proper names is spelled out when it is part of the commonly known name, otherwise it is abbreviated as "b." when the name is fully spelled out. Thus, ʿAbd al-Malik b. Hishām is rendered Ibn Hishām. Bibliographic entries follow the order of the most commonly known names, as in Ibn Hishām, ʿAbd al-Malik. For dating, only the common era is used.

Journal titles, frequently cited sources, and general reference works are abbreviated as follows:

A1: Ibn Abī Ṭāhir Ṭayfūr, *Kitāb al-Manthūr wa al-Manẓūm*, Cairo al-Azhar Library, no. 464.

A2: Ibn Abī Ṭāhir Ṭayfūr, *Kitāb al-Manthūr wa al-Manẓūm*, Cairo al-Azhar Library, no. 1752.

AHR: ʿAbbas, *ʿAbd al-Ḥamīd b. Yaḥyā al-Kātib wa mā Tabaqqā min Rasāʾilihi wa Rasāʾil Sālim Abī al-ʿAlāʾ*.

AJSLL: *American Journal of Semitic Languages and Literatures*.

ALC: Cooperson and Toorawa. *Arabic Literary Culture* (Dictionary of Literary Biography).

b.: Ibn.

BJMES: *British Journal of Middle Eastern Studies*.

BJS: *British Journal of Sociology*.

BL: Ibn Abī Ṭāhir Ṭayfūr, *Kitāb al-Manthūr wa al-Manẓūm*, British Library, no. 18532.

BSOAS: *Bulletin of the School of Oriental and African Studies*.

C&ZES: Crone and Zimmermann, *The Epistle of Sālim*.

CH: *Critical Horizons*.

DDÇD: *Divan Disiplinlerarası Çalışmalar Dergisi*.

DI: *Der Islam*.

DKM1: Ibn Abī Ṭāhir Ṭayfūr, *Kitāb al-Manthūr wa al-Manẓūm*, Dār al-Kutub al-Miṣriyya, no. 1860.

DKM2: Ibn Abī Ṭāhir Ṭayfūr, *Kitāb al-Manthūr wa al-Manẓūm*, Dār al-Kutub al-Miṣriyya, no. 581.

EI$^{(1)}$: *Encyclopaedia of Islam*, 1st ed.

EI$^{(2)}$: *Encyclopaedia of Islam*, 2nd ed.

EI$^{(3)}$: *Encyclopaedia of Islam*, 3rd ed.

EI$^{(r)}$: *Encyclopaedia Iranica*.

IC: *Islamic Culture*.

IJMES: *International Journal of Middle East Studies*.

IJPS: *Indian Journal of Political Science*.

IS: *Iranian Studies*.

JAL: *Journal of Arabic Literature*.

JAOS: *Journal of the American Oriental Society*.

JAsH: *Journal of Asian History*.

JCR: *Journal of Consumer Research*.

JCS: *Journal of Church and State*.

JESHO: *Journal of the Economic and Social History of the Orient*.

JGH: *Journal of Global History*.

JHI: *Journal of the History of Ideas*.

JIS: *Journal of Islamic Studies*.

JNES: *Journal of Near Eastern Studies*.

JOS: *Journal of Ottoman Studies*.

JP: *Journal of Politics.*
JPS: *Journal of Persianate Studies.*
JSAI: *Jerusalem Studies in Arabic and Islam.*
JWH: *Journal of World History.*
KAR: Kurd ʿAlī. *Rasāʾil al-Bulaghāʾ.*
LIM: Lampe, *Ibn al-Muqaffaʿ.*
MEJ: *Middle East Journal.*
MW: *The Muslim World.*
PC: Pellat, *Conseilleur du calife.*
PEIPT: Böwering et al., *The Princeton Encyclopedia of Islamic Political Thought.*
PMLA: Publication of the Modern Language Association of America.
Q: *The Qurʾan.*
RJLR: *Rutgers Journal of Law and Religion.*
SI: *Studia Islamica.*
SJ: Ṣafwat, *Jamharat Rasāʾil al-ʿArab.*
SR: *Sociological Review.*
TDVIA: *Türkiye Diyanet Vakfı İslâm Ansiklopedisi.*
WA: Wakīʿ, *Akhbār al-Quḍāt.*

Notes

Preface

1. I use "disenchantment" in this book not in the sense of rejecting religion or the unidirectional demagicification of the world, as Weber seems to indicate. I refer to dismantling the ulema-centric understanding of political cosmology and the associated politics to explicate a new causality and rationality for political practice. For the notion of enchantment and disenchantment, see Charles Taylor, *Dilemmas and Connections: Selected Essays* (Cambridge, MA: Belknap Press of Harvard University, 2014), especially chap. 12. See also Max Weber, *The Vocation Lectures: "Science as a Vocation," "Politics as a Vocation,"* ed. David Owen and Tracy B. Strong, trans. Rodney Livingstone (Indianapolis, IN: Hachette, 2004), 12*ff*; Max Weber, *The Sociology of Religion*, trans. Ephraim Fischoff (London: Beacon, 1963), 1–19, 269–70. For a critique and evaluation, see Richard Jenkins, "Disenchantment, Enchantment, and Re-Enchantment: Max Weber at the Millennium," *Max Weber Studies* 1 (2000): 11–32.
2. For an overview of the idea of "confessionalization," see Susan R. Boettcher, "Confessionalization: Reformation, Religion, Absolutism, and Modernity," *History Compass* 2 (2004): 1–10, https://doi.org/10.1111/j.1478-0542.2004.00100.x. I am using this terminology here to get a point across rather than ascribe to the constitutive elements of the argument in explicating the emergence of the modern state. Nonetheless, the difference between the Byzantine Empire's caesaropapism or later European monarchies' *cuius regio, eius religio* and the Abbasid "religious plurality" must be noted.
3. Ludwig Wittgenstein, *Philosophical Investigations*, trans. G. E. M. Anscombe (Oxford: Basil Blackwell, 1972), 174*ff*, especially 178.
4. J. G. A. Pocock, *Politics, Language and Time: Essays on Political Thought and History* (Chicago: University of Chicago Press, 1989), 3*ff*.
5. Quentin Skinner, *Visions of Politics: Regarding Method* (Cambridge: Cambridge University Press, 2006), 1, chaps. 2, 6, 7.
6. John L. Austin, *How to Do Things with Words: The William James Lectures Delivered at Harvard University in 1955* (Oxford: Clarendon, 1962).

7. Mikhail Bakhtin, *The Dialogic Imagination: Four Essays*, ed. and trans. Michael Holquist and Caryl Emerson (Austin: University of Texas Press, 2008), 259*ff*.
8. Carol Bacchi and Jennifer Bonham, "Reclaiming Discursive Practices as an Analytic Focus: Political Implications," *Foucault Studies* 17 (2014): 174, 184, 190.
9. Pierre Bourdieu, *Language and Symbolic Power*, trans. Gino Raymond and Matthew Adamson (Cambridge, UK: Polity, 1991), 107*ff*.

Introduction: Critical Reflections on "Islamic Political Thought"

1. I use the concept of "tradition" as a dynamic and always updating sociopolitical and discursive orientation. For a critical engagement with the modernist devaluation of the term, see Kwame Gyekye, *Tradition and Modernity: Philosophical Reflections on the African Experience* (Oxford: Oxford University Press, 2011), especially chaps. 8 and 9; Alasdair C. MacIntyre, *Whose Justice? Which Rationality?* (Notre Dame, IN: University of Notre Dame Press, 2003), especially chaps. 17–19.
2. I use the terms "imamate" ("imam-governance") and "siyasa" to mean the discourse on and the technique of governance but not to refer either to the historical caliphate itself, which I always signify with the word caliphate/caliphs, or to politics as commonly used. The terms "imamate politics" and "siyasa politics" refer to different conceptualizations and modes of governing, as in "democratic politics" or "liberal politics," and so on. The term "imamate" appears in religious and mundane literature from the eighth century onward to signify political leadership. It is occasionally referred to as the "greater imamate," as opposed to the "lesser imamate," which denoted leadership in prayer or prominence in a specific branch of knowledge or profession (*al-imāma al-ʿuẓmā* versus *al-imāma al-ṣughrā*). It was used for later Umayyad caliphs alongside other caliphal appellations, each of which accentuated a different aspect of the caliph's authority. It signified the "ruling-imam" in reference to the governing caliph. Theoretically, the caliph was considered entitled to and in possession of it. It was also used for the Shiite imam, regardless of whether he wielded actual political power. The Shiite imam's case may be marked as "presumed" ruling-imam to indicate this crucial difference. On the idea of the imamate and the caliphate, see Hayrettin Yücesoy, "Imamate," in *The Princeton Encyclopedia of Islamic Political Thought* (*PEIPT*), ed. Gerhard Böwering, Patricia Crone, and Mahan Mirza (Princeton, NJ: Princeton University Press, 2013), 247*ff*; Wilferd Madelung, "Imāma," in *The Encyclopaedia of Islam*, 2nd ed. (*EI*$^{(2)}$), ed. P. J. Bearman, Thierry Bianquis, Clifford Edmund Bosworth, E. J. van Donzel, and Wolfhart Heinrichs (Leiden: Brill, 1960–2007), first published online in 2012; Hayrettin Yücesoy, "Caliph and Caliphate up to 923/1517," in *The Encyclopaedia of Islam*, 3rd ed. (*EI*$^{(3)}$), ed. Gudrun Krämer, Roger Allen, and Kate Fleet (Leiden: Brill, 2014–); Wadad al-Qadi (various appearances of the name in publications include, Qadi, al-Qāḍī, Kadi) and Aram Shahin, "Caliph, Caliphate," in *PEIPT*, 81*ff*; Patricia Crone, *Medieval Islamic Political Thought* (Edinburgh: Edinburgh University Press, 2004), also published as *God's Rule: Government and Islam* (New York: Columbia University Press, 2006); Ann K. S. Lambton, *State and Government in Medieval Islam: An Introduction to the Study of Islamic Political Theory: The Jurists* (Oxford: Oxford University Press, 1981); Ann K. S. Lambton, *Theory and Practice in Medieval Persian Government* (London: Variorum Reprints, 1980); Muhsin Mahdi, *Alfarabi and the Foundation of Islamic Political Philosophy* (Chicago: University of Chicago Press, 2001); Erwin Isak Jakob Rosenthal, *Political Thought in Medieval Islam* (Cambridge: Cambridge University Press, 1962); William M. Watt,

Islamic Political Thought (Edinburgh: Edinburgh University Press, 1998); Anthony Black, *The History of Islamic Political Thought: From the Prophet to the Present* (New York: Routledge, 2001).

3. *Ḥirāsat al-dīn wa siyāsat al-dunyā*. See Abū al-Ḥasan ʿAlī b. Muḥammad b. Ḥabīb al-Baṣrī al-Māwardī, *al-Aḥkām al-Sulṭāniyya wa al-Wilāyāt al-Dīniyya*, ed. Aḥmad al-Mubārak al-Baghdādī (Kuwait: Maktabat Dār Ibn Qutayba, 1989), 3; Abū al-Ḥasan ʿAlī b. Muḥammad b. Ḥabīb al-Baṣrī al-Māwardī, *The Ordinances of Government (al-Aḥkām al-Sulṭāniyya wa al-Wilāyāt al-Dīniyya)*, trans. Wafaa H. Wahba (Reading, UK: Garnet Publishing, 1996), 3.
4. I use this phrase in reference to articulating political ideas in the language of a religious discipline (*kalām*, *fiqh*, *ḥadīth*), which corresponded, from the mid-eighth century onward, to the discourse of imamate, in contradistinction to the statecraft and political philosophy envisaged in siyasa. Julian Obermann uses it in the former sense to describe political argumentation in the early *kalām* theology. See Julian Obermann, "Political Theology in Early Islam: Ḥasan al-Baṣrī's Treatise on Qadar," *JAOS*, 55 (1935): 138–62, doi:10.2307/594438. This is also how Josef van Ess discusses theology. See Josef van Ess, "Political Ideas in Early Islamic Religious Thought," *BJMES*, 28 (2001): 151–64, http://www.jstor.org/stable/826122; Josef van Ess, "The Beginnings of Islamic Theology," in *The Cultural Context of Medieval Learning*, ed. J. E. Murdoch and E. D. Sylla, Boston Studies in the Philosophy of Science, vol. 26 (Dordrecht: Springer, 1975), doi.org/10.1007/978-94-010-1781-7_4. I refrain from using it as a broad net to catch what is called "Islamic political thought" to avoid muddying the difference between distinct discourses of politics in caliphal and sultanic histories. It is inconceivable to lump together under one umbrella the Fārābīan politics with al-Māwardī's imamate.
5. Marshall Hodgson uses "piety minded." I prefer "piety oriented" because piety is not merely a question of intellectual reflection but also emotion and practice. See Marshall Hodgson, *The Venture of Islam: Conscience and History in a World Civilization: Classical Age of Islam* (Chicago: University of Chicago Press, 1974), vol 1.
6. For the concept of "counterpoint," see Edward Said, *Culture and Imperialism* (New York: Knopf, 1994), 32, 51*ff*, 66*ff*.
7. Part of Cornell Fleischer's book title, *Bureaucrat and Intellectual*, may be recalled here in a productive way to describe the craft of such professionals. See Cornell H. Fleischer, *Bureaucrat and Intellectual in the Ottoman Empire: The Historian Mustafa Âli (1541–1600)* (Princeton, NJ: Princeton University Press, 1986).
8. Abū Yaʿlā al-Farrā' and others seem to qualify the caliphate in this sense in the phrase *imāmat al-khilāfa*, the caliphate's imamate. See Muḥammad b. al-Ḥusayn b. Muḥammad Abū Yaʿlā al-Farrā', *al-Aḥkām al-Sulṭāniyya*, ed. Muḥammad Ḥāmid al-Faqī (Beirut: Dār al-Kutub al-ʿIlmiyya, 2000), 65 (from *al-Maktaba al-Shāmila* database online, https://islaamiclibrary.wordpress.com/2009/03/01/thecomprehensivelibrary/).
9. Saba Mahmood, *Politics of Piety: The Islamic Revival and the Feminist Subject* (Princeton, NJ: Princeton University Press, 2012), xi–xii.
10. Possibly Jaʿfar b. Ḥarb (d. 850). For its attribution to him, see Wilferd Madelung, "Frühe muʿtazilitische Häresiographie: Das Kitāb al-Uṣūl des Ġaʿfar ibn Ḥarb," *DI*, 57 (1980): 220*ff*. On Jaʿfar b. Harb, see "Jaʿfar b. Mohammad b. Harb" (Joseph van Ess), in *Encyclopaedia Iranica* (*EI*[(r)]), ed. Ehsan Yar-Shater (London: Routledge & Kegan Paul, 1985–2008), https://www.iranicaonline.org/.
11. ʿAbdallāh b. Muslim b. Qutayba, *ʿUyūn al-Akhbār* (Cairo: Dār al-Kutub al-Miṣriyya, 1996).
12. The word does not appear in al-Bāqillānī's (d. 1013) and al-Baghdādī's (d. 1037) texts on the imamate. See Abū Bakr b. al-Ṭayyib al-Bāqillānī, *al-Tamhīd fī al-Radd ʿala al-Mulḥida wa al-Muʿaṭṭila*

wa al-Rāfiḍa wa al-Khawārij wa al-Muʿtazila, ed. Maḥmūd Muḥammad al-Khuḍayrī and Muḥammad ʿAbd al-Hādī Abū Rayda (Cairo: Dār al-Fikr al-ʿArabī, 1947); ʿAbd al-Qāhir b. Ṭāhir al-Baghdādī, *Uṣūl al-Dīn* (Istanbul: Devlet Matbaası, 1928). For several examples of the citation of the word in various sources, see Bernard Lewis, "*Siyāsa*," in *In Quest of an Islamic Humanism: Arabic and Islamic Studies in Memory of Mohamed Al-Nowaihi*, ed. Mohamed Al-Nowaihi and Arnold H. Green (Cairo: American University in Cairo Press, 1986), 3*ff*.

13. The phrase's slow emergence as a concept in Ibn Taymiyya's writing deserves another genealogical study, which I cannot attempt here. On the use of *al-siyāsa al-sharʿiyya* in current political debates, as a resource for integrating secular laws into governance as an alternative to the modern state's legal monism, see Asifa Quraishi-Landes, "Islamic Constitutionalism: Not Secular. Not Theocratic. Not Impossible," *RJLR* 16 (2015): 553*ff*.
14. Nikolas Rose and Peter Miller, "Political Power Beyond the State: Problematics of Government," *BJS*, 43 (1992): 174, doi:10.2307/591464.
15. Rose and Miller, "Political Power," 174–75.
16. See Michel Foucault, "Technologies of the Self," in *Technologies of the Self: Seminar: Selected Papers*, ed. Michel Foucault, Luther H. Martin, Huck Gutman, and Patrick H. Hutton (Amherst: University of Massachusetts Press, 1988), 16*ff*; Colin Gordon, "Government Rationality: An Introduction," in *The Foucault Effect: Studies in Governmentality: With Two Lectures by and an Interview with Michel Foucault*, ed. Graham Burchell, Colin Gordon, and Peter M. Miller (London: Harvester Wheatsheaf, 1991), 1*ff*.
17. Michel Foucault, "Governmentality," in *The Foucault Effect: Studies in Governmentality: With Two Lectures by and an Interview with Michel Foucault*, ed. Graham Burchell, Colin Gordon, and Peter M. Miller (London: Harvester Wheatsheaf, 1991), 87*ff*. For "governmentalization," see Rose and Miller, "Political Power," 173–205; Gordon, "Government Rationality," 1*ff*.
18. Gordon makes this point concerning Machiavelli. See Gordon, "Government Rationality," 9.
19. The earliest copy of the "Epistle on the Caliph's Privy" has been preserved in the twelfth volume of a ninth-century anthology, the celebrated—but mostly still in manuscript—*Kitāb al-Manthūr wa al-Manẓūm* by the polymath Aḥmad b. Abī Ṭāhir Ṭayfūr. Various copies of the extant volumes of this work are housed in libraries in Cairo, London, Baghdad, and Medina. See Shawkat M. Toorawa, *Ibn Abī Ṭāhir Ṭayfūr and Arabic Writerly Culture: A Ninth Century Bookman in Baghdad* (London: Routledge, 2010), 4*ff*. As is mostly the case with older manuscripts, the *Kitāb al-Manthūr* itself survives only partially (volumes 11, 12, 13) and in much later copies. The earliest copy of the surviving volumes of *Kitāb al-Manthūr* dates to the late seventeenth century and the most recent one to the early twentieth. The "Epistle on the Caliph's Privy" has been edited by Muḥammad Kurd ʿAlī, *Rasāʾil al-Bulaghā*ʾ (Cairo: Maṭbaʿat Lajnat al-Taʾlīf wa al-Tarjuma wa al-Nashr, 1946) (earlier editions 1908, 1913); Aḥmad Zakī Ṣafwat, *Jamharat Rasāʾil al-ʿArab fī al-ʿUṣūr al-ʿArabiyya al-Zāhira* (Beirut: al-Maktaba al-ʿIlmiyya, 1937); Charles Pellat, *Conseilleur du calife* (Paris: G.-P. Maisonneuve et Larose, 1976). Kurd ʿAlī's 1946 edition is based on two copies of Ṭayfūr's *al-Manthūr* in Dār al-Kutub al-Miṣriyya, no. 1860 adab (DKM1), and Dār al-Kutub al-Miṣriyya, no. 581 adab (DKM2). DKM2, according to his assessment, was a copy of an earlier manuscript in one of the libraries in Medina to which he did not have access. Aḥmad Zaki Ṣafwat's edition appeared in his *Jamharat Rasāʾil al-ʿArab* based on Ṭayfūr's DKM1 (he also consulted DKM2), which improved on Kurd ʿAlī's work in *Rasāʾil al-Bulaghā*"s first and second editions. Charles Pellat copied his own version from the DKM2 and compared it with Kurd ʿAlī's 1946 edition. He translated the "Epistle" into French and supplemented it with an index, glossary, commentary, corrections, and editorial assessment. The work has been

translated into numerous languages. Its English translation appears in Gerald E. Lampe, "Ibn al-Muqaffaʿ: Political and Legal Theorist and Reformer" (PhD diss., Johns Hopkins University, 1986). I have used Lampe's translation with much discretion as the basis of my quotations. I have identified three additional copies of the "Epistle" that are also included in Ṭayfūr's *Kitāb al-Manthūr*. With the two copies that are already known, we now possess five different copies of the "Epistle." The British Library no. 18532 (marked BL) is dated 30 Shawwāl 1092/November 12, 1681. This is the earliest dated copy known so far. The Cairo Dār al-Kutub al-Miṣriyya no. 581 adab (DKM2), to which I did not have access until recently after the completion of this study but know from the multiple critical editions noted here, is dated 1880. The Cairo al-Azhar no. 464 adab seems to be dated (Jumāda Ūlā?) 1302/1885. The manuscript was donated to the al-Azhar Mosque Library in 1316/1898 (A1). The Cairo Dār al-Kutub al-Miṣriyya no. 1860 adab (DKM1) is dated 3 Shawwāl 1307/ May 23, 1890. The Cairo al-Azhar no. 1752 adab (A2) dates to 3 Muḥarram 1331/ December 13, 1912. The Baghdad manuscript (Maktabat Jāmiʿat al-Ḥikma no. 58 adab), which could be the earliest copy, remains inaccessible to me. The differences in the extant copies of the manuscript seem to indicate that they might have derived from multiple, now-lost earlier copies and not from a single *ur*-text. Although there are numerous differences, occasionally significant, among the available versions, the structure of the "Epistle" appears felicitously intact. The script is smooth and legible with minimal ambiguities, gaps, and scribal discretions. I am indebted to Shawkat Toorawa for sharing with me the digital copies of Ṭayfūr's *Kitāb al-Manthūr*. I am currently completing a critical edition of the Arabic text of the "Epistle," based on the available copies of the manuscripts, including three more manuscripts not known, with an updated English translation for easier access to its content. For more information about the "Epistle," see chap. 4 in this book.

20. Foucault deals with the problem of "maintaining power" in his "Governmentality," 90–91. Quentin Skinner sees it as the main question for Machiavelli. See Quentin Skinner, *Machiavelli: A Very Short Introduction* (New York: Oxford University Press, 1981), 25–26, 37–38*ff.*
21. Foucault, "Governmentality," 94–95.
22. Jacques Derrida, *The Beast and the Sovereign* (Chicago: University of Chicago Press, 2011), 2: 45.
23. See Daniel Philpott, "Sovereignty," in *The Stanford Encyclopedia of Philosophy* (Fall 2020 Edition), ed. Edward N. Zalta, https://plato.stanford.edu/archives/fall2020/entries/sovereignty/; Eli B. Lichtenstein, "Foucault's Analytics of Sovereignty," *CH* 22, no. 3 (2021): 287–305, doi:10.1080/14409917.2021.1953750; Leonard Lawlor and John Nale, eds., "Sovereignty," in *The Cambridge Foucault Lexicon* (Cambridge: Cambridge University Press, 2014), 456–65; Dean Hammer, "Foucault, Sovereignty, and Governmentality in the Roman Republic," *Foucault Studies*, 22 (2017): 49–71, http://dx.doi.org/10.22439/fs.v0i0.5243.
24. For an erudite assessment of the problems involved in using the terms "religion" and "religiosity," see Tomoko Masuzawa, *The Invention of World Religions or How European Universalism Was Preserved in the Language of Pluralism* (Chicago: University of Chicago Press, 2007); see also Jason Ananda Josephson, *The Invention of Religion in Japan* (Chicago: University of Chicago Press, 2012); Timothy Fitzgerald, *The Ideology of Religious Studies* (New York: Oxford University Press, 2013); Talal Asad, *Formations of the Secular: Christianity, Islam, Modernity* (Stanford, CA: Stanford University Press, 2003); Talal Asad, *Genealogies of Religion: Discipline and Reasons of Power in Christianity and Islam* (Baltimore, MD: Johns Hopkins University Press, 2009); Jonathan Z. Smith, "Religion, Religions, Religious," in *Critical Terms for Religious Studies*, ed. Mark C. Taylor (Chicago: University of Chicago Press, 1998), 269–84.
25. One may operate with metaphors such as Taylor's "enchantment" or Foucault's "episteme" to imagine the broad contours of thinking and feeling that inspire but do not overdetermine

aspects of life. See Taylor, *Dilemmas and Connections*, chap. 12; Michel Foucault, *The Order of Things* (Boca Raton, FL: Taylor and Francis, 2018), especially chap. 2, https://www.taylorfrancis.com/books/e/9781317336686.

26. It occurs in various forms in the eighth-century texts I have used in this study, such as *al-ḥudūd wa al-aḥkām*, *aḥkām al-dīn*, and other similar ways. For Ibn al-Muqaffaʿ, BL 70b; A2 174a; A1 199b; DKM1 184a–b; SJ 34–35; KAR 121; PC 27, 29; Muḥammad b. Khalaf b. Ḥayyān Wakīʿ, *Akhbār al-Quḍāt*, ed. ʿAbd al-ʿAzīz Muṣṭafā al-Marāghī (Cairo: Maktabat al-Istiqāma, 1947), 2: 98, 100, 101.
27. Its formal usage as a concept denoting the rules and regulations guiding the believer's conduct began in the second half of the eighth century (often as *sharʿ* rather than *sharīʿa*), but became more established in the ninth century. It appears in Ibn al-Muqaffaʿ's "Epistle on the Caliph's Privy" as a verb, following the qur'anic usage in the sense of "ordaining" revealed law for humans (*bi al-dīn alladhī sharaʿa lahum*). See BL 70b–71a; A2 174a–174b; A1 199b–200a; DKM1 184b–185a; SJ 35–36; KAR 121–22; PC 29, 31. For the term and its history, see *EI*[(2)], "Sharīʿa," (N. Calder). I use the term "sacred law" in this study not in its formal, established sense, but to signify the totality of the ordinances and ethical norms the piety-oriented scholars continued to promulgate and enforce so as to control the faith and guide the conduct of the believer. Sacred law therefore included more than merely legal rules. It is rarely noticed that Ibn al-Rushd's (d. 1198) celebrated treatise *Faṣl al-Maqāl fī mā bayn al-Ḥikma wa al-Sharīʿa min Ittiṣāl*, *The Decisive Treatise Determining the Connection Between Philosophical Wisdom and the Sacred Law*, discusses *sharīʿa*, rather than *dīn*.
28. For the pitfalls, indeed the impossibility and violence, of translating such terms to modern languages, and not just to English, see the eye-opening article by Wael B. Hallaq, "What Is Shariʿa?," *Yearbook of Islamic and Middle Eastern Law Online*, 12 (2005): 151–80, https://doi.org/10.1163/22112987-91000130; Wael B. Hallaq, *Sharīʿa: Theory, Practice and Modern Transformations* (Cambridge: Cambridge University Press, 2009), especially "introduction."
29. Ibn al-Muqaffaʿ, *Al-Adab al-Kabīr*, in KAR 40, 42, 45, 89.
30. Ibn al-Muqaffaʿ, *Al-Adab al-Kabīr*, 42: *aṣl al-amr fī al-dīn* and *aṣl al-amr fī iṣlāḥ al-jasad*, the basic principle of religion is and the basic principle of restoring the body is.
31. Later but nevertheless a remarkable text that exemplifies this distinction from the mundane life events is Ibn Sayyār al-Warrāq's *Kitāb al-Ṭabīkh*, in which the author expounds the Galenic humoral medicine and dietetics to undergird his discourse on the health of and care for the body. See Ibn Sayyār al-Warrāq, *Kitāb al-Ṭabīkh*, ed. Kaj Öhrnberg and Sahban Mroueh, Studia Orientalia 60 (Helsinki: Finnish Oriental Society, 1987). For the English translation, see Nawal Nasrallah, *The Annals of the Caliphs' Kitchens: Ibn Sayyār al-Warrāq's Tenth-Century Baghdadi Cookbook* (Leiden: Brill, 2014), 55*f*, 67*ff*, 71–78, 97*ff*.
32. For instance, the interrogation of the self by the early Sufis addresses this concern. See al-Ḥārith b. Asad al-Muḥāsibī, *Ādāb al-Nufūs*, ed. ʿAbd al-Qādir Aḥmad ʿAṭā (Beirut: Dār al-Jīl, 1984). Also see *EI*[(3)], "Asceticism" (Christopher Melchert); Ahmet T. Karamustafa, *Sufism: An Historical Introduction* (Edinburgh: Edinburgh University Press, 2007), 1*ff*; *EI*[(2)], "Al-Muḥāsibī" (Arnaldez, R.); Josef van Ess, *Die Gedankenwelt des Ḥārit al-Muḥāsibī* (Bonn: Orientalisches Seminar der University Bonn, 1961).
33. For a discussion of the theme of "taking care of oneself" versus "know yourself" in the context of Roman pagan and Christian history, see Foucault, "Technologies of the Self," 22. In this context, it is important to note Edward Said's discussion about self-awareness and worldliness in the sense of knowing others to appreciate the non-Eurocentric global forms of humanism.

See Edward W. Said, *Humanism and Democratic Criticism* (New York: Columbia University Press, 2004), especially chaps.1 and 3.

34. For social construction of taste, see Pierre Bourdieu, *Distinction: A Social Critique of the Judgment of Taste* (London: Routledge, 2015).
35. I employ "ethos" here as the character and authority of the discourse. Ethos emerges from both the illocutionary force of the language and the social position of the lay bureaucrats at the intersection of discursive and social dynamics. See James S. Baumlin and Craig A. Meyer, "Positioning Ethos in/for the Twenty-First Century: An Introduction to *Histories of Ethos*," *Humanities* 7, no. 3 (2018): 78, https://doi.org/10.3390/h7030078; Ruth Amossy, "Ethos at the Crossroads of Disciplines: Rhetoric, Pragmatics, Sociology," *Poetics Today: International Journal of Theory and Analysis of Literature and Communication* 22, no. 1 (2001): 1–23, https://doi.org/10.1215/03335372-22-1-1.
36. I should note in this context the intervention of Hamid Dabashi on the role of Persian literary humanism as a major current in Persianate history. See Hamid Dabashi, *The World of Persian Literary Humanism* (Cambridge, MA: Harvard University Press, 2012).
37. The paradigmatic text of the field in later centuries is *Tahdhīb al-Akhlāq* of Miskawayh. See Aḥmad b. Muḥammad b. Yaʿqūb Miskawayh, *Tahdhīb al-Akhlāq wa Taṭhīr al-Aʿrāq* (Cairo: al-Maktaba al-Ḥusayniyya, 1911). The point made above concerning moral self-cultivation comes into better view when one compares the technique of *tahdhīb* with that of *ḥadīth* and *fiqh*, or asceticism. For major figures of the ethics tradition, see *EI*[(3)], "Ethics in Philosophy" (Peter Adamson); and "Ethics in Ṣūfism" (Paul L. Heck).
38. Thus says al-Māwardī in *al-Aḥkām al-Sulṭāniyya*, 3: "The Imamate has been instituted as vicarate of the prophecy in upholding the faith and governing the affairs of the world." Al-Nasafī expands its scope even further to include royal authority: "The imamate, in addition to the affairs of the revealed law, contains the affairs of royal authority and siyasa" (*al-imāma maʿa amr al-dīn, fihā amr al-mulk wa al-siyāsa*). Abū Muʿīn Maymūn b. Muḥammad al-Nasafī, *Tabṣirat al-Adilla fī Uṣūl al-Dīn*, ed. Claude Salāme, Tome Deuxième (Damascus: Institut Français de Damas, 1993), 829. Ibn Taymiyya is even more assertive in expressing the "Islamization" of the term: *siyāsa sharʿiyya* appears as the title of his work on governance. Taqiy al-Dīn Aḥmad b. Taymiyya, *al-Siyāsa al-Sharʿiyya fī Iṣlāḥ al-Rāʿī wa al-Raʿiyya* (Beirut: Dār al-Kutub al-ʿIlmiyya, 2005).
39. See Talal Asad, "Thinking About Religion, Belief, and Politics," in *The Cambridge Companion to Religious Studies*, ed. R. Orsi (Cambridge Companions to Religion) (Cambridge: Cambridge University Press, 2011), 37*ff*.
40. Such as Jürgen Habermas, William Connolly, Charles Taylor, Talal Asad, José Casanova, Leon Wieseltier, and others. See Hent de Vries and Lawrence Eugene Sullivan, *Political Theologies: Public Religions in a Post-secular World* (New York: Fordham University Press, 2009); Charles Taylor, *A Secular Age* (Cambridge, MA: Belknap Press of Harvard University, 2018).
41. Asad, "Thinking About Religion," 39; Asad, *Genealogies of Religion*, especially 1*ff*, 27*ff*, 55*f*. For critical approaches to the framing of the discussion in modern and colonial discourses as it pertains to "early Islam" and "*sharīʿa* governance," see Hallaq, "Sharīʿa," 1*ff*, Wael B. Hallaq, *The Impossible State: Islam, Politics, and Modernity's Moral Predicament* (New York: Columbia University Press, 2014), 3*ff*, 19*ff*.
42. See Gauri Viswanathan, *Outside the Fold: Conversion, Modernity, and Belief* (Princeton, NJ: Princeton University Press, 1998), xiv–xv. The point, while directed at today's circumstances, can be productively made about the Abbasid period.

43. See Asad, *Formations of the Secular*, 4–5, where he discusses Taylor's argument. I should also note in this context the fine study of Omid Safi on the Selçuks. Safi does not deal with the question of secularity, but he recognizes how "premodern" governments did attempt to regulate their populations' lives through the deployments of "state apparatuses." See Omid Safi, *The Politics of Knowledge in Premodern Islam: Negotiating Ideology and Religious Inquiry* (Chapel Hill, NC: University of North Carolina Press, 2006), xxvi, 82*ff*, 100*ff*, 204*ff*.
44. For an insightful problematization of Europe and the European as a provincial rather than universal category, see Dipesh Chakrabarty, *Provincializing Europe: Postcolonial Thought and Historical Difference* (Princeton, NJ: Princeton University Press, 2000). For the idea of multiple secularities, see Marian Burchardt, Monika Wohlrab-Sahr, and Matthias Middell, *Multiple Secularities Beyond the West: Religion and Modernity in the Global Age* (Berlin: De Gruyter, 2015); and the research collective probing the theme online at https://www.multiple-secularities.de/. See also Markus Dressler, Armando Salvatore, and Monika Wohlrab-Sahr, "Islamicate Secularities: New Perspectives on a Contested Concept," *Historical Social Research/Historische Sozialforschung* 44, no. 3 (2019): 7–34.
45. Paul Slomkowski, *Aristotle's Topics* (Leiden: Brill, 1997), 164–65.
46. Gilles Deleuze, Félix Guattari, and Brian Massumi, *A Thousand Plateaus: Capitalism and Schizophrenia* (London: Bloomsbury, 2013), 3*ff*.
47. See Taylor, *A Secular Age*; Charles Taylor, "Secularism and Critique," *The Immanent Frame* (2008), https://tif.ssrc.org/2008/04/24/secularism-and-critique/. See also the insightful discussion among theorists on "Is Critic Secular?," *The Immanent Frame*, https://tif.ssrc.org/category/exchanges/is-critique-secular/.
48. Asad, "Thinking About Religion," 47; Asad, *Formations of the Secular*, 1*ff*, 21*ff*.
49. Asad, *Formations of the Secular*, 16–17, 24–25.
50. Leon Wieseltier, "Two Concepts of Secularism," in *Isaiah Berlin: A Celebration*, ed. Isaiah Berlin, Edna Ullmann-Margalit, and Avishai Margalit (Chicago: University of Chicago Press, 1991), 80*ff*.
51. See Armando Salvatore, "Secularity Through a 'Soft Distinction' in the Islamic Ecumene? Adab as Counterpoint to Sharīʿa," *Historical Social Research* 44 (2019): 36*ff*; Neguin Yavari, *Advice for the Sultan: Prophetic Voices and Secular Politics in Medieval Islam* (Oxford: Oxford University Press, 2014), 7–16; Neguin Yavari, "The Political Regard in Medieval Islamic Thought," *Historical Social Research/Historische Sozialforschung* 44 (2019): 52*ff*.
52. Already Ibn al-Muqaffaʿ uses this term on multiple occasions in the "Epistle on the Caliph's Privy" in various forms, including *iṣlāḥ* and *istiṣlāḥ*. Al-ʿAnbarī is aware of the dialectic between the two facets of life. See WA, 100, 101. See also ʿAmr b. Baḥr al-Jāḥiẓ, *Rasāʾil al-Jāḥiẓ*, ed. ʿAbd al-Salām Muḥammad Hārūn, (Cairo: Maktabat al-Khānjī, 1994), 4: 103, 207, 261, 288, where he uses the phrase *maṣāliḥ dīnihim wa dunyāhum* or *maṣāliḥ al-dunyā wa marāshid al-dīn*, which suggests a position on the relationality of the two in producing a desirable lifeworld.
53. I use it here both in a Bakhtinian sense and in music theory. See Mikhail M. Bakhtin, *Problems of Dostoevsky's Poetics* (Minneapolis: University of Minnesota Press, 1997), 5*ff*.
54. Muslim/Islamic political thought, Islamic/Muslim state, Islamic/Muslim society, Islamic /Muslim thought.
55. I have also contributed to it with the entry "imamate."
56. Unfortunately, Shahab Ahmed's phenomenological approach in his learned book *What Is Islam?* moves the needle in a direction that I must contest in this study. I am concerned that holding on to the term "Islam" as a universal analytical unit to discuss such a spectrum of people, ideas, practices, and histories as somehow a containable entity within this term is itself a

position that takes us back to the pre-Hodgson liberalist definition of Islam and the "Muslim world." Even though Ahmed challenges the Arabo-centrism and Sunnite or Shiite Orthodox normativity, his position nevertheless allows the reasoning that Islam, like race and color, somehow defines its subject no matter the circumstance and can therefore be referred to in the singular. Islam mutates, changes, develops various shades but can still be measured and treated. See Shahab Ahmed, *What Is Islam? The Importance of Being Islamic* (Princeton, NJ: Princeton University Press, 2015). See also the following reviews of the book: Alireza Doostdar, "*What Is Islam? The Importance of Being Islamic*, written by Shahab Ahmed," Shii Studies Review 1 (2017): 277–82, https://doi.org/10.1163/24682470-12340014; Michael E. Pregill, "I Hear Islam Singing: Shahab Ahmed's *What Is Islam? The Importance of Being Islamic*," *Harvard Theological Review* 110 (2017): 149–65. To understand the context Ahmed has missed, see Joseph Andoni Massad, *Islam in Liberalism* (Chicago: University of Chicago Press, 2016).

57. See Cemil Aydın, *The Idea of the Muslim World: A Global Intellectual History* (Cambridge, MA: Harvard University Press, 2017).
58. At this time, titles such as Islamic art, Islamic peoples, Islamic law, Islamic culture, and Islamic society were normalized and spread. See, for instance, the tables of contents in the first few volumes in *Der Islam* and *the Muslim World*, https://www.degruyter.com/journal/key/ISLM/html and https://onlinelibrary.wiley.com/loi/14781913.
59. The appearance of journals with the titles such as *Islam, the Muslim World*, and their variations (*Der Islam, Die Welt des Islams, Islamic Culture, Revue du Monde Musulman*) is part of this development. Early issues of these journals include articles about the imamate/caliphate according to various Muslim thinkers and sects.
60. Perhaps the most thorough examination of the nineteenth- to twentieth-century intellectual reflection on the "Islamic state" and the caliphate in the Ottoman and the modern Turkish context is İsmail Kara, "Hilafetten İslam Devletine Çağdaş İslam Siyasi Düşüncesinin Ana İstikametleri ve Problemleri," *DDÇD* 24/47 (2019): 1–109. For a remarkable world-historical contextualization of this debate, see Aydın, *The Idea of the Muslim World*, introduction, chaps. 2–3.
61. On Oriental despotism, see Franco Venturi, "Oriental Despotism," *JHI* 24 (1963): 133–42.
62. Edward Gibbon, *The History of the Decline and Fall of the Roman Empire (with Variorum Notes)* (London: Henry G. Bohn, 1853), 1: 183.
63. See Bryan S. Turner, *Marx and the End of Orientalism* (London: Allen and Unwin, 1978); Ian Almond, *The History of Islam: From Leibniz to Nietzsche* (New York: Routledge, 2010), 108*ff*; James Morris Blaut, *Eight Eurocentric Historians* (New York: Guilford, 2000), 19*ff*.
64. Max Weber, *Economy and Society*, ed. Guenther Roth and Claus Wittich (Berkeley: University of California Press, 1978), 2: 1010*ff*. For an analysis of Weber's views on Islam and Muslim societies, see Toby E. Huff and Wolfgang Schluchter, eds. *Max Weber and Islam* (New Brunswick, NJ: Transaction, 1999). Perhaps Karl August Wittfogel is the best example of more recent overt proponents of this line of thought. Karl August Wittfogel, *Oriental Despotism: A Comparative Study of Total Power* (New Haven, CT: Yale University Press, 1957), 167, 214.
65. Alfred von Kremer, *Geschichte des herrschenden Ideen des Islams: Der Gottesbegriff, die Prophetie und Staatsidee* (Leipzig: Brockhaus, 1868). I must note the difference between German Orientalism and that of the British and the French. See Suzanne Marchand, "German Orientalism and the Decline of the West," *Proceedings of the American Philosophical Society* 145, no. 4 (2001): 465–73.
66. Wilfrid Scawen Blunt, *The Future of Islam* (London: Kegan & Paul, 1882). On Blunt, see Massad, *Islam in Liberalism*, 64–67.

67. Duncan B. MacDonald, *Development of Muslim Theology, Jurisprudence and Constitutional Theory* (New York: Charles Scribner, 1903), 55–56.
68. J. H. Kramers, *Analecta Orientalia Posthumous Writings and Selected Minor Works* (Leiden: Brill, 1954), 279–80*ff*; Reynold A. Nicholson, *A Literary History of the Arabs* (New York: Charles Scribner, 1907), 256–57.
69. Thomas W. Arnold, *The Caliphate* (Oxford: Clarendon, 1924). In the intervening period, short publications resumed but seemed to be disrupted by the escalation of warfare. See Stanley Lane-Poole, "The Caliphate," *Quarterly Review* 224 (1915): 162–77.
70. Arnold acknowledges in the preface that he has not "done much more than present the results of their research to English readers." Arnold, *The Caliphate*, 5.
71. Arnold, *The Caliphate*, 17–18, 182–83.
72. Arnold, *The Caliphate*, 180.
73. Arnold, *The Caliphate*, 183.
74. For detailed information on this point, see Aydın, *The Idea of the Muslim World*, especially chaps. 3–5. For related writings in the late 1800s and early 1900s, see İsmail Kara, *Hilafet Risâleleri: İslam Siyasî Düşüncesinde Değişme ve Süreklilik*, vols. 1–6 (Istanbul: Klasik, 2003–2014). See also H. Yılmaz, "Containing Sultanic Authority: Constitutionalism in the Ottoman Empire before Modernity," *Osmanlı Araştırmaları* 45 (2015): 231–64.
75. See Kara, "Hilafetten İslam Devletine," 32*ff*. Said Halim Paşa titles his work *Les Institutions Politiques dans la Société Musulmane* in 1921. As Kara notes, this work may be the initial discursive turn toward the notion of the Islamic state. See Kara, "Hilafetten İslam Devletine," 55–62. Phillip K. Hitti, titled in 1919 his translation of al-Balādhurī's *Futūḥ al-Buldān* (*The Conquest of Regions*), *The Origins of the Islamic State*. See Aḥmad ibn Yaḥyā b. al-Jābir al-Balādhurī, Philip K. Hitti, Francis Clark Murgotten, and Michael Zwettler, *The Origins of the Islamic State: Being a Translation from the Arabic, Accompanied with Annotations, Geographic and Historic Notes of the Kitāb Futūḥ al-Buldān of al-Imām Abū-l ʿAbbās, Aḥmad Ibn Jābir al-Balādhurī* (New York: Columbia University Press, 1916).
76. For further discussion of the issue and examples, see Kara, "Hilafetten İslam Devletine," 31.
77. See Aydın, *The Idea of the Muslim World*, especially chap. 5; Mahmoud Haddad, "Arab Religious Nationalism in the Colonial Era: Rereading Rashīd Riḍā's Ideas on the Caliphate," *JAOS*, 117/2 (1997): 253–77; Kara, "Hilafetten İslam Devletine," 62–67. Kara cites Seyyid Bey, Sanhuri, ʿAlī ʿAbd al-Rāziq, and others as part of this trend.
78. 'Alī ʿAbd al-Rāziq, *Al-Islām wa Uṣūl al-Ḥukm* (Cairo: Al-Hay'a al-ʿĀmma al-Miṣriyya li-al-Kitāb, 1993).
79. For recent scholarship on the caliphate in the first half of the twentieth century, see the following studies: Mim Kemal Öke, *The Turkish War of Independence and the Independence Struggle of the South Asian Muslims: "The Khilafat Movement" 1919–1924* (Ankara: Ministry of Culture, 1991); Azmi Özcan, *Pan-Islamism: Indian Muslims, the Ottomans and Britain (1877–1924)* (Leiden: Brill, 1997); ʿAbd al-Ilāh Balqazīz, *The State in Contemporary Islamic Thought: A Historical Survey of the Major Muslim Political Thinkers of the Modern Era* (London: I. B. Tauris, 2009); Hamid Enayat, *Modern Islamic Political Thought* (New York: Palgrave, 2005); Nurullah Ardıç, *Islam and the Politics of Secularism: The Caliphate and Middle Eastern Modernization in the Early 20th Century* (New York: Routledge, 2012); Bobby S. Sayyid, *Recalling the Caliphate: Decolonisation and World Order* (London: Hurst, 2014).
80. Robert Adcock and Mark Bevir, "The History of Political Science," *Political Studies Review* 3, no. 1 (January 2005): 1–16, https://doi.org/10.1111/j.1478-9299.2005.00016.x; Baynes T. Spencer, ed.,

"Political Science," in *The Encyclopaedia Britannica: A Dictionary of Arts Sciences and General Literature* (Akron, OH: Werner, 1904–1905), accessed the online edition, May 4, 2022, https://www.britannica.com/topic/political-science.

81. Sir Muḥammad Iqbal, "Political Thought in Islam," *SR* 1, no. 3 (1908): 249–61. On Iqbal's political thought, see Iqbal Singh Sevea, *The Political Philosophy of Muhammad Iqbal: Islam and Nationalism in Late Colonial India* (Cambridge: Cambridge University Press, 2012).
82. Iqbal, "Political Thought in Islam," 252–53.
83. R. Strothmann, *Das Staatsrecht der Zaiditen* (Strasburg: Verlag von Karl J. Trübner, 1912), 1–3. Articles adopting the phrase "political thought" in their titles appear more frequently in the 1920s and 1930s.
84. See, for instance, Hamilton A. R. Gibb, "The Islamic Background of Ibn Khaldūn's Political Theory," *BSOAS* 7, no. 1 (1933): 23–31. His other articles on the subject from the 1930s onward are collected in Hamilton Alexander Rosskeen Gibb, *Studies on the Civilization of Islam*, ed. Stanford J. Shaw and William R. Polk (Princeton, NJ: Princeton University Press, 1962).
85. Haroon Khan Sherwani, *Studies in the History of Early Muslim Political Thought and Administration* (Lahore: Sh. M. Ashraf, 1942). He also penned articles and longer pieces, including *The Origin of Islamic Polity: The Qur'anic State* in 1936, "*A Muslim Political Thinker of the 9th Century, A.C.-Ibn Abi'r-Rabi*" in 1942, and *The Islamic Conception of Sovereignty* in 1957. Sherwani was appointed the chair of the department of history and political science at Osmania University after his return from Europe. I thank Cemil Aydın for alerting me to the details of his biography.
86. Sherwani, *Studies in the History*, 254–55.
87. His contemporary, Sachin Sen, was interested in "Muslim political thought" too, in the context of India's independence, Hindu-Muslim relations, and the question of partition. Sen's article in *The Indian Journal of Political Science* deals with the Indian Muslims' political claims about establishing a caliphate and briefly assesses the activities of the Wahhābī movement in India, dwelling on Sayyid Ahmad Khan's and Mohammed Iqbal's writings. The article was based on a lecture he had given in 1943. See Sachin Sen, "Moslem Political Thought since 1858," *IJPS* 6, no. 2 (1944): 97–108.
88. Erwin I. J. Rosenthal must not have seen Iqbal's or Sherwani's publications, although this is hard to imagine. He does mention Strothmann's pioneering study. See Erwin I. J. Rosenthal, "Some Aspects of Islamic Political Thought," *IC* 22 (1948): 1–17.
89. Rosenthal, *Political Thought in Medieval Islam*, 5, 69, 113, 131, 207, 211 (the label worded as "political thought in Islam," 58 and "Muslim political thought"). It appears also in Hans Kohn's published lecture in 1954, where he uses the label literally to mean "the general motivation behind the actions of the Mohammedan peoples in the world today." Hans Kohn, "Bases of Islamic Political Thought," *Naval War College Review* 7 (1954): 27–42. Leonard Binder's and Richard Walzer's articles in 1958 and 1963, respectively, continue to use the label without any critical engagement. See Leonard Binder, "Problems of Islamic Political Thought in the Light of Recent Developments in Pakistan," *JP* 22 (1958): 655–75; Richard Walzer, "Aspects of Islamic Political Thought: Al-Fārābī and Ibn Khaldūn," *Oriens* 16 (1963): 40–60.
90. Watt, *Islamic Political Thought*. See Rosenthal's review of the work, Erwin Isak Jakob Rosenthal, "Islamic Political Thought: The Basic Concepts by W. Montgomery Watt," *Middle East Journal* 23 (1969): 551–52.
91. See Lambton, *Theory and Practice;* Lambton, *State and Government*; Bernard Lewis, *The Political Language of Islam* (Chicago: University of Chicago Press, 1988).

92. For a few representative studies, see Black, *The History of Islamic Political Thought*, especially p. 349*ff*, where he summarizes the difference between "European" and "Islamic" political thought traditions (overdetermining power of religion, neotribalism, patrimonialism); Crone, *Medieval Islamic Political Thought*; Hugh Kennedy, *Caliphate: The History of an Idea* (New York: Basic Books, 2016); Gerhard Böwering, ed. *Islamic Political Thought: An Introduction* (Princeton, NJ: Princeton University Press, 2017).
93. For a critical discussion of this generation of scholarship, see Aziz Al-Azmeh, "God's Caravan: Topoi and Schemata in the History of Muslim Political Thought," in *Mirror for the Muslim Prince: Islam and the Theory of Statecraft*, ed. Mehrzad Boroujerdi (Syracuse, NY: Syracuse University Press, 2013), 326*ff*. Brief but valuable contributions are in Said Amir Arjomand, "Persianate Islam and the Secularity of Kingship," in *Companion to the Study of Secularity*, ed. HCAS "Multiple Secularities—Beyond the West, Beyond Modernities" (Leipzig University, 2019), www.multiple-secularities.de/publications/companion/css_arjomand_persianatekingship.pdf; Said Amir Arjomand, "Perso-Islamicate Political Ethic in Relation to the Sources of Islamic Law," in *Mirror for the Muslim Prince: Islam and the Theory of Statecraft*, ed. Mehrzad Boroujerdi (Syracuse, NY: Syracuse University Press, 2013), 82–84; and Javad Tabatabai, "An Anomaly in the History of Persian Political Thought," in *Mirror for the Muslim Prince: Islam and the Theory of Statecraft*, ed. Mehrzad Boroujerdi (Syracuse, NY: Syracuse University Press, 2013), 107*ff*.
94. Aziz Al-Azmeh, *Muslim Kingship: Power and the Sacred in Muslim, Christian, and Pagan Polities* (New York: I. B. Tauris, 2001).
95. Hallaq, *The Impossible State*.
96. See Ovamir Anjum, *Politics, Law, and Community in Islamic Thought: The Taymiyyan Moment* (Cambridge: Cambridge University Press, 2012); Mona Hassan, *Loss of Caliphate: The Trauma and Aftermath of 1258 and 1924* (Princeton, NJ: Princeton University Press, 2016); Hüseyin Yılmaz, *Caliphate Redefined: The Mystical Turn in Ottoman Political Thought* (Princeton, NJ: Princeton University Press, 2018).
97. Muhammad Qasim Zaman, *Religion and Politics Under the Early ʿAbbāsids* (Leiden: Brill, 1997); Sohaira Z. M. Siddiqui, *Law and Politics Under the ʿAbbāsids: An Intellectual Portrait of al-Juwaynī* (New York: Cambridge University Press, 2019). Watt, Lambton, Lewis, and others have already discussed siyasa, the Umayyad and Abbasid bureaucrats, and the conflict between the ulema and the scribal class. However, they do so in a manner and language that I have described above as ulema-centric.
98. For instance, Ira M. Lapidus perceptively points out how religious authority (the ulema) was separated from political authority (the caliphs) in the events of the *Miḥna* in the early ninth century onward. However, because Lapidus assumes Islamic normative law to be the foundation of political practice, the separation in his analysis merely means a struggle over who would be controlling power. See Ira M. Lapidus, "Separation of State and Religion in the Early Islamic Society," *IJMES* 6 (1975): 363–85. In a recent study Lapidus appears more critical of the alleged distinction between European and Islamic societies. See Ira M. Lapidus, "State and Religion in Islamic Societies," *Past and Present* 151 (1996): 3–27. See also the brief but welcome remark concerning *adab* and secularity by Devin Stewart, "Developments with Religious Sciences During the Rise and Decline of Empire," in Armando Salvatore et al., *The Wiley Blackwell History of Islam* (Hoboken, NJ: John Wiley, 2018), 140*ff*. For a useful study on political secularity focusing on India, see Muzaffar Alam, *The Languages of Political Islam: India 1200–1800* (Chicago: University of Chicago Press, 2004), 26*ff*, on adab and sharīʿa.

99. Louise Marlow, *Counsel for Kings: Wisdom and Politics in Tenth-Century Iran: The Naṣīḥat al-Mulūk of Pseudo-Mawardi: Contexts and Themes*, 2 volumes (Edinburgh: Edinburgh University Press, 2016).
100. See Yavari, *Advice for the Sultan*; Yavari, "The Political Regard." See also Alam, *The Languages of Political Islam*. Likewise, using "theory," Safi underlines the "premodern" scholar's predicament of dealing with government beyond the question of secularity. Safi, *The Politics of Knowledge*, 55, 110*ff*, 129*ff*, 139*ff*, 182*ff*, 202*ff*.
101. Linda T. Darling, *A History of Social Justice and Political Power in the Middle East: The Circle of Justice from Mesopotamia to Globalization* (London: Routledge, 2013). Malik Mufti's work from a political science perspective makes a case for a "realist" political thought tradition to address some of the political challenges the "Muslim world" faces today. His work's passing attention to the Abbasids and its thorough reliance on secondary material lessens its usefulness. See Malik Mufti, *The Art of Jihad: Realism in Islamic Political Thought* (Albany, NY: SUNY Press, 2019).
102. See Hodgson, *The Venture of Islam*, 1: 22*ff*. Said, *Humanism and Democratic Criticism*; Edward W. Said, *Orientalism* (New York: Vintage Books, 2003). For another recent critical perspective on the modern representations of Islam, see Massad, *Islam in Liberalism*. I should also cite the efforts in the "World Studies Interdisciplinary Project," particularly the work of Laura Doyle, *Inter-Imperiality: The Long Dialectics of Power and Culture in Gendered Political Economy* (Durham, NC: Duke University Press, 2020).

1. Caliphal Practice

1. For the concept, see Benedict Anderson, *Imagined Communities: Reflections on the Origin and Spread of Nationalism* (London: Verso, 2006); Charles Taylor, *Modern Social Imaginaries* (Durham, NC: Duke University Press, 2005).
2. See Fred McGraw Donner, *The Early Islamic Conquests* (Princeton, NJ: Princeton University Press, 1981), 51*ff*; Fred McGraw Donner, *Muhammad and the Believers: At the Origins of Islam* (Cambridge, MA: Belknap Press of Harvard University, 2010), 39*ff*. For another view on community formation and the early notion of jihad, see Asma Afsaruddin, *Striving in the Path of God: Jihād and Martyrdom in Islamic Thought* (Oxford: Oxford University Press, 2013), especially chaps. 1–3.
3. Muḥammad b. Isḥāq (henceforth Ibn Isḥāq), ʿAbd al-Malik b. Hishām, and Alfred Guillaume, *The Life of Muhammad: A Translation of Ibn Isḥāq's Sīrat Rasūl Allāh* (Oxford: Oxford University Press, 1967), 231*ff*. (Translations, where applicable from *Sīrat Rasūl Allāh*, are based on Guillaume's translation, but with modifications.) ʿAbd al-Malik b. Hishām (henceforth Ibn Hishām), *al-Sīra al-Nabawiyya*, ed. ʿUmar ʿAbd al-Salām Tadmūrī (Beirut: Dār al-Kitāb al-ʿArabī, 1990), 2: 143–46; Muhammad Hamidullah, *The First Written Constitution in the World: An Important Document of the Time of the Holy Prophet* (Lahore, Pakistan: Ashraf, 1975); Michael Lecker, *The Constitution of Medina: Muhammad's First Legal Document* (Princeton, NJ: Darwin, 2004); Frederick M. Denny, "*Ummah* in the Constitution of Medina," *JNES* 36 (1977): 39–47; Harald Suermann, *Die konstitution von medina erinnerung an ein anderes modell des zusammenlebens* (Piscataway, NJ: Gorgias, 2012); Robert B. Serjeant, "The Constitution of Medina," Islamic Quarterly 8 (1964): 3–16; Said A. Arjomand, "The Constitution of Medina: A Sociolegal Interpretation of Muhammad's Acts of Foundation of the Umma," *IJMES*, 41 (2009): 555–75; Moshe Gil, "The Constitution of Medina: A Reconsideration," *Israel Oriental Studies* 4 (1974): 44–66; Akira Goto, "The Constitution of Medina," *Orient: Report of the Society for Near Eastern Studies in Japan* 18 (1982): 1–17.

4. See Francis E. Peters, *Muhammad and the Origins of Islam* (Albany, NY: SUNY Press, 1994); Jonathan E. Brockopp, *The Cambridge Companion to Muhammad* (New York: Cambridge University Press, 2010); Donner, *Muhammad and the Believers*; Asma Afsaruddin, *The First Muslims: History and Memory* (London: One World, 2017); William Montgomery Watt, *Muhammad at Medina* (Oxford: Clarendon, 1968).
5. Q, 106: 1–4; 9: 101, 120. The citations and quotations are from M. A. Abdel Haleem, *The Qur'an: English Translation and Parallel Arabic Text* (Oxford: Oxford University Press, 2016).
6. For pre-Islamic Arabian sociopolitical setting, see George Hatke, "Agrarian, Commercial, and Pastoralist Dynamics in the Pre-Islamic Irano-Semitic Civilizational Area," in Armando Salvatore et al., *The Wiley Blackwell History of Islam* (Hoboken, NJ: John Wiley, 2018), 37*ff*; Hugh Kennedy, *The Prophet and the Age of the Caliphates: The Islamic Near East from the Sixth to the Eleventh Century* (London: Longman, 1986), 15–22. See also Donner, *The Early Islamic Conquests*, 11*ff*; Chase F. Robinson et al., *The New Cambridge History of Islam*, vol. 1 (Cambridge: Cambridge University Press, 2010), chaps. 1–4; Donner, *Muhammad and the Believers*, 27*ff*. For the most recent overview of pre-Islamic Arabia and its imperial context, see Greg Fisher, ed., *Arabs and Empires Before Islam* (Oxford: Oxford University Press, 2017); *EI*(2), "Ayyām al-ʿArab," (E. Mittwoch). For an early tenth-century representation of the imperial context in the seventh century, see Muḥammad b. Jarīr al-Ṭabarī, *Tārīkh al-Rusul wa al-Mulūk*, ed. Muḥammad Abū al-Faḍl Muḥammad Ibrāhīm (Cairo: Dār al-Maʿārif, 1968). English translation in thirty-nine volumes, Muḥammad b. Jarīr al-Ṭabarī, *The History of al-Ṭabarī*, ed. Ihsan Yarshater (Albany, NY: SUNY Press, 1985–1999, index 2007), 1: 571*ff*, 2: 37*ff*.
7. The assumption in modern-day scholarship has been that the idea of governance must have been rooted in the scripture and Muḥammad's message, whether it was actualized in his lifetime or evolved over the course of half a century. See Patricia Crone, *God's Rule: Government and Islam* (New York: Columbia University Press, 2006), 3*ff*. While I see the point of this argument, which is also true for other faith traditions before the "secular age," celestial politics does not predicate political consciousness.
8. See Fazlurrahman, *Major Themes in the Qur'ān* (Minneapolis, MN: Bibliotheca Islamica, 1994), 37*ff*; Frederick M. Denny, "The Meaning of the Umma in the Qur'ān," *History of Religions* 15 (1975): 34*ff*; Hayrettin Yücesoy, "Justification of Political Authority in Medieval Sunni Thought," in *Islam, the State, and Political Authority: Medieval Issues and Modern Concerns*, ed. Asma Afsaruddin (New York: Palgrave Macmillan, 2011), 11–12; Muḥammad ʿĀbid al-Jābrī, *al-Dīn wa al-Dawla wa Taṭbīq al-Sharīʿa* (Beirut: Markaz al-Dirāsāt al-Waḥda al-ʿArabiyya, 1996), 17–18.
9. See al-Qadi and Shahin, "Caliph, Caliphate," *PEIPT*, 81*ff*; Wadad al-Qadi, "The Term 'Khalīfa' in Early Exegetical Literature," *Die Welt des Islams* 28 (1988): 392–411.
10. For Saʿd b. ʿUbāda, see al-Ṭabarī, *The History of al- Ṭabarī*, 10: 8–11, *EI*(2), Saʿd b. ʿUbāda" (Montgomery Watt).
11. For the Ridda and such positions, see Elias S. Shoufani, *Al-Riddah and the Muslim Conquest of Arabia* (Toronto: University of Toronto Press, 1973); Donner, *The Early Islamic Conquests*, 82*ff*. For a primary source account of events in English, see Aḥmad ibn Yaḥyā b. al-Jābir al-Balādhurī, Philip K. Hitti, Francis Clark Murgotten, and Michael Zwettler, *The Origins of the Islamic State: Being a Translation from the Arabic, Accompanied with Annotations, Geographic and Historic Notes of the Kitāb Futūḥ al-Buldān of al-Imām Abū-l ʿAbbās, Aḥmad Ibn Jābir al-Balādhurī* (New York: Columbia University Press, 1916), 143*ff*; Muḥammad b. ʿUmar al-Wāqidī, *Kitāb al-Ridda*, ed. Muhammad Hamidullah (Paris: Editions Tougui, 1989), 37*ff*.

12. In his discussion of "love," the thirteenth-century scholar Nāṣir al-Dīn al-Ṭūsī would have summed up the crisis after the prophet's death this way. Naṣīr-ad-Dīn Muḥammad b. Muḥammad al-Ṭūsī and George M. Wickens, *The Nasirean Ethics* (London: George Allen & Unwin, 1964), 195–96.
13. Ibn Hishām, *al-Sīra al-Nabawiyya*, 4: 312; Ibn Isḥāq, *The Life of Muhammad*, 687. For the conquest movement, see Donner, *The Early Islamic Conquests*, 82*ff.* For a brief account of the conquests from a primary source, see al-Balādhurī et., *The Origins of the Islamic State*, 165*ff.*
14. For more information on this issue and period, see Marshall Hodgson, *The Venture of Islam: Conscience and History in a World Civilization: Classical Age of Islam* (Chicago: University of Chicago Press, 1974), vol. 1. For a shorter solid survey, see Kennedy, *The Prophet and the Age of the Caliphates*. See also Hayrettin Yücesoy, *Taṭawwur al-Fikr al-Siyāsī ʿinda Ahl al-Sunna: Fatrat al-Takwīn: Min Bidāyatihi ḥatta al-Thulth al-Awwal min al-Qarn al-Rābiʿ al-Hijrī* (Amman: Dār al-Bashīr, 1993), chap. 1; and Hayrettin Yücesoy, *Messianic Beliefs and Imperial Politics in Medieval Islam* (Columbia: University of South Carolina Press, 2009), 18*ff.*
15. For a short sensible analysis of the political and military arrangements, see ʿAbd al-ʿAzīz al-Dūrī, *Muqaddima fī Tārīkh Ṣadr al-Islām* (Beirut: Dār al-Mashriq, 1984), 26*ff*; Fred Donner, "The Formation of the Islamic State," *JAOS* 106 (1986): 283–96.
16. On empire building, see Chase F. Robinson, ed., *The New Cambridge History of Islam* (Cambridge: Cambridge University Press, 2011), vol. 1; Alain George and Andrew Marsham, *Power, Patronage, and Memory in Early Islam: Perspectives on Umayyad Elites* (New York: Oxford University Press, 2018). For the Umayyad empire building, social transformation, and related developments, see Patricia Crone, *Arabian Tribes to Islamic Empire* (Burlington, VT: Ashgate, 2008).
17. For instance, on ʿUmar I's legal attempts and reaction to them, see *EI*⁽²⁾, "Mutʿa," (Heffening). For a report of ʿUthmān's effort, see Muḥammad b. Ismāʿīl al-Bukhārī, *Saḥīḥ al-Bukhārī*, ed. Khalīl Ma'mūn Shayḥa (Beirut: Dār al-Maʿrifa, 2010), book 66, ḥadīth #4986, 4987, pp. 1291–92 (*Bāb Jamʿ al-Qur'ān*); Taqiy al-Dīn Aḥmad b. Taymiyya, *Daqā'iq al-Tafsīr*, ed. Muḥammad al-Sayyid al-Julaynad (Damascus: Mu'assasat Um al-Qur'ān, 1984), 3: 349–51. For the conventional account of the codification of the Qur'an, see Theodor Nöldeke and Friedrich Schwally, *Geschichte des Qorāns. Mit einem literarhistorischen Anhang über die muhammedanischen Quellen und die neuere christliche Forschung, Teil. 1-2* (Leipzig: Dieterich'sche Verlagsbuchhandlung, 1919); William Montgomery Watt, *Bell's Introduction to the Qur'ān* (Edinburgh: Edinburgh University Press, 1970); *EI*⁽²⁾, "al-Ḳur'ān," (A. T. Welch and J. D. Pearson). For more recent and critical accounts, see Claude Gilliot, "Creation of a Fixed Text," in *The Cambridge Companion to the Qur'ān*, ed. Jane Dammen McAuliffe (Cambridge: Cambridge University Press, 2006), 41*ff.* In the same volume see Harald Motzki, "Alternative Accounts of the Qur'an's Formation," in *The Cambridge Companion to the Qur'an*, ed. Jane Dammen McAuliffe (Cambridge: Cambridge University Press, 2006), 59*ff*; and Fred McGraw Donner, "The Historical Context," in *The Cambridge Companion to the Qur'an*, ed. Jane Dammen McAuliffe (Cambridge: Cambridge University Press, 2006), 30–35.
18. For an account of the events of the civil war in a primary source, see al-Ṭabarī, *Tārīkh*, volumes 4 and 5. In English, see al-Ṭabarī, *The History of al-Ṭabarī*, vols. 15 and 16. For contemporary accounts, see Kennedy, *The Prophet and the Age of the Caliphates*, 69*ff.*
19. For an early ninth-century representation of the first divisions from a doctrinal point of view, see ʿAbdallāh b. Muḥammad al-Nāshī al-Akbar and Josef van Ess, *Frühe muʿtazilitische Häresiographie: zwei Werke des Nāshī' al-Akbar (gest. 293 H.)* (Weisbaden and Beirut: In Kommission bei Franz Steiner Verlag, 1971), 16–17*ff*; Pseudo ʿAbdallāh b. Muslim b. Qutayba, *al-Imāma wa al-Siyāsa*, ed. ʿAlī Shayrī (Beirut: Dār al-Aḍwā', 1990), 1: 234*ff.*

20. For the Early Kharijites, see al-Ṭabarī, *Tārīkh*, 4: 558*ff*; Naṣr b. Muzāḥim, *Waqʿat Ṣiffīn*, ed. ʿAbd al-Salām Muḥammad Hārūn (Cairo: al-Mu'assasa al-ʿArabiyya al-Ḥadītha wa Maktabat al-Khānjī bi-Miṣr, 1981), 115*ff*; Elie Adib Salem, *Political Theory and Institutions of the Khawārij* (Baltimore, MD: Johns Hopkins University Press, 1956); Crone, *God's Rule*, 17*ff*, 54*ff*; Jeffrey Thomas Kenney, *Muslim Rebels: Khārijites and the Politics of Extremism in Egypt* (Oxford: Oxford University Press, 2006); Keith Lewinstein, "The Azāriqa in Islamic Heresiography," *BSOAS* 54 (1991): 251–68. For a Kharijite view on the first civil war, see Patricia Crone and Friedrich Zimmermann, *The Epistle of Sālim Ibn Dhakwān*. Oxford Oriental Monographs (Oxford: Oxford University Press, 2001).
21. Elton L. Daniel, *The Political and Social History of Khurāsān Under ʿAbbāsid Rule, 747–820* (Minneapolis, MN: Bibliotheca Islamica, 1979), 29–30; Moshe Sharon, *Black Banners from the East* (Leiden: Brill, 1983), 51*ff*; ʿAbd al-ʿAzīz Al-Dūrī, *Al-ʿAṣr al-ʿAbbāsī al-Awwal* (Beirut: Markaz Dirāsāt al-Waḥda al-ʿArabiyya, 2009), 31*ff*.
22. Aḥmad b. Abī Yaʿqūb al-Yaʿqūbī, *Tārīkh al-Yaʿqūbī*, ed. M. Th. Houtsama (Leiden: Brill, 1969), 2: 311*ff*; Yücesoy, *Taṭawwur*, 49–50, 57–58; Muḥammad ibn ʿAlī b. al-Ṭiqṭaqā and Ṭalāl Sālim Ḥadīthī, *Al-Fakhrī fī al-Ādāb al-Sulṭāniyya wa al-Duwal al-Islāmiyya*, ed. Hartwig Derenbourg (Paris: Emile Bouillon, 1895), 165–66; Pseudo Ibn Qutayba, *al-Imāma wa al-Siyāsa*, 2: 7*ff*.
23. Al-Yaʿqūbī, *Tārīkh*, 2: 276; al-Ṭabarī, *Tārīkh*, 5: 530; Paul Cobb, "The Empire in Syria, 705–763," in *The New Cambridge History of Islam*, ed. Chase F. Robinson (Cambridge: Cambridge University Press, 2011), 1: 255–56. On the *ʿaṣabiyya* in early Islam, see ʿAbd al-Raḥmān b. Muḥammad b. Khaldūn, *Kitāb al-ʿIbar wa Diwān al-Mubtada' wa al-Khabar*, ed. Ibrāhīm Shabbūḥ and Iḥsān ʿAbbās (Tunis: al-Dār al-ʿArabiyya li-al-Kitāb, 2006), 1: 215*ff*, 229.
24. Yücesoy, *Taṭawwur*, 56–58; Daniel, *The Political and Social History*, 43; Al-Yaʿqūbī, *Tārīkh*, 2: 383, 391*ff*; Carl Wurtzel, "The Coinage of the Revolutionaries in the Late Umayyad Period," *Museum Notes (American Numismatic Society)* 23 (1978): 161–99; Jamal Jawdah, *al-Awḍāʿ al-Ijtimāʿiyya wa al-Iqtiṣādiyya li-al-Mawālī fī Ṣadr al-Islām* (Amman: Dār al-Bashīr, 1989); Chase F. Robinson, "Neck-Sealing in Early Islam," *JESHO* 48 (2005): 401–41; Gerald. R. Hawting, *The First Dynasty of Islam: The Umayyad Caliphate AD 661–750* (London: Routledge, 2000), 104*ff*; *EI*(2), "Mawlā" (A. J. Wensinck, Patricia Crone); Al-Dūrī, *Muqaddima*, 77*ff*.
25. Pseudo Ibn Qutayba, *al-Imāma wa al-Siyāsa*, 1: 195–96. One of the best satirical critiques of the idea of family succession is provided by ʿAbd al-Raḥmān al-Salūlī: "If you come up with Ramla and Hind (female names), we would pledge allegiance to them as *amīrāt al-mu'minīna* ([female] commanders of the faithful), for, when Khusrau dies, a new Khusrau takes his place, we count three of them one after the other." ʿAlī b. al-Ḥusayn al-Masʿūdī, *Murūj al-Dhahab wa Maʿādin al-Jawhar*, ed. Charles Barbier de Meynard, Abel Pavet de Courteille, and Charles Pellat (Paris: Societe Asiatique, 1962), 5: 71.
26. Ismaʿīl b. al-Qāsim Abū ʿAlī al-Qālī, *Kitāb Dhayl al-Amālī wa al-Nawādir* (Beirut: Dār al-Āfāq al-Jadīda, 1980), 175.
27. See Yücesoy, *Taṭawwur*, 35*ff*, 83*ff*; Crone, *God's Rule*, 33*ff*, 259*ff*. See also Fred M. Donner, "Umayyad Efforts at Legitimation: The Umayyads' Silent Heritage," in *Umayyad Legacies: Medieval Memories from Syria to Spain*, ed. Antoine Borrut and Paul M. Cobb (Leiden: Brill, 2010), 187*ff*.
28. For the Abbasid revolt and the events leading up to it, see Stephen R. Humphreys, *Islamic History: A Framework for Inquiry—Revised Edition* (Princeton, NJ: Princeton University Press, 1991), 104–27; Muhammad Qasim Zaman, "The ʿAbbāsid Revolution: A Study of the Nature and Role of Religious Dynamics," *JAsH* 21, no. 2 (1987): 119–49; Muhammad Qasim Zaman, *Religion and Politics Under the Early ʿAbbāsids* (Leiden: Brill, 1997), 33*ff*; Said A. Arjomand, "ʿAbdallāh Ibn al-Muqaffaʿ and the ʿAbbāsid Revolution," *IS* 27 (1994): 9–12. For the organization

and deployment of the revolt in Khurāsān, see Salih Said Agha, *The Revolution Which Toppled the Umayyads: Neither Arab nor ʿAbbasid* (Leiden: Brill, 2003); Hawting, *The First Dynasty of Islam*, 105*ff*; Yücesoy, *Messianic Beliefs and Imperial Politics*, 18*ff*, 40*ff*; Crone, *God's Rule*, 77; Wilferd Madelung, "ʿAbdallāh b. al-Zubayr and the Mahdī," *JNES* 40 (1981): 291*ff*.

29. See ʿAbd al-Razzāq b. Hammām Al-Ṣanʿānī, *Al-Muṣannaf*, ed. Ḥabīb al-Raḥmān al-Aʿẓamī (Beirut: Al-Majlis al-ʿIlmī, 1970), 11: 366; Nuʿaym b. Ḥammād al-Khuzāʿī, *Kitāb al-Fitan*, ed. Suhayl Zakkār (Beirut: Dār al-Fikr, 1993), 110–14, 118, 121; Abū Muḥammad Aḥmad b. Aʿtham al-Kūfī, *Kitāb al-Futūḥ*, ed. Muḥammad ʿAbd al-Muʿīd Khān et al. (Hyderabad: Osmania Oriental Publications Bureau, 1968–1975), 8: 159.
30. Abū ʿAbdallāh Muḥammad b. Saʿd, *Kitāb al-Ṭabaqāt al-Kabīr*, ed. Eduard Sachau et al. (Leiden: Brill, 1912–1940), 5: 101, 117, 162; Abū Ḥasan ʿAlī b. al-Ḥusayn al-Ashʿarī, *Maqālāt al-Islamiyyīn*, ed. Helmut Ritter (Istanbul: Istanbul Darülfünun, Devlet Matbaası, 1927), 1: 17; Al-Nāshī al-Akbar, *Frühe muʿtazilitische Häresiographie*, 26–27; Wadād al-Qāḍī, *al-Kaysāniyya fī al-Tārīkh wa al-Adab* (Beirut: Dār al-Thaqāfa, 1974), 168*ff*; Jan-Olaf Blichfeldt, *Early Mahdīsm: Politics and Religion in the Formative Period of Islam* (Leiden: Brill, 1985), 105*ff*.
31. For a thorough treatment of the sect and its development, see al-Qāḍī, *al-Kaysāniyya*, 168*ff*. See also al-Ashʿarī, *Maqālāt*, 1: 5–6, 16, 20; *EI*(2), Kaysāniyya (Madelung); *EI*(2), Khidāsh (M. Sharon). For Khidāsh and his movement, see also Sharon, *Black Banners*, 165–73, 183–86; Zaman, *Religion and Politics*, 38–40; William F. Tucker, "ʿAbdallāh b. Muʿāwiya and the Janāḥiyya: Rebels and Ideologues of the Late Umayyad Period," *SI* 51 (1980): 39–57.
32. For a brief exposition of how some of the branches of the Kaysāniyya evolved into Imāmī Shiite messianic movements, see Abdulaziz A. Sachedina, *Islamic Messianism: The Idea of the Mahdī in Twelver Shīʿism* (Albany, NY: SUNY Press, 1981), 3*ff*.
33. Al-Dūrī, *Al-ʿAṣr al-ʿAbbāsī al-Awwal*, 19*ff*; Daniel, *The Political and Social History*, 19, 20; Gibb, *Studies on the Civilization of Islam*, 34–46; Philip Khuri Hitti, *History of the Arabs* (London: Macmillan, St. Martin's, 1970), 224*ff*; Cobb, "The Empire in Syria," 1: 244; *EI*(2), Irak (D. Sourdel, H. Laoust); Simon Gundelfinger and Peter Verkinderen, "The Governors of al-Shām and Fārs in the Early Islamic Empire—A Comparative Regional Perspective," in *Transregional and Regional Elites: Connecting the Early Islamic Empire*, ed. Hannah-Lena Hagemann and Stefan Heidemann (Berlin: de Gruyter, 2020), 275–80.
34. Sharon, *Black Banners*, 56, 57–58; Daniel, *The Political and Social History*, 19; Brian Ulrich, *Arabs in the Early Islamic Empire: Exploring Al-Azd Tribal Identity* (Edinburgh: Edinburgh University Press, 2019), 169–93. Agha estimates the size of the Dīwān enlisters at 50,000 and the Arab population in Khurāsān to be between 115,000 and 175,000. Saleh Said Agha, "The Arab Population in Khurāsān During the Umayyad Period," *Arabica* 46 (1999): 211–29.
35. Sharon, *Black Banners*, 204; Jacob Lassner, *The Shaping of ʿAbbāsid Rule* (Princeton, NJ: Princeton University Press, 1980), 139–62.
36. For the primary-source narratives of this shift, see Yazīd b. Muḥammad al-Azdī, *Tārīkh Mawsil*, ed. ʿAlī Ḥabība (Cairo: Lajnat al-Iḥyā' al-Turāth al-ʿArabī, 1967), 125 (al-Qā'im); Anonymous, *Akhbār al-Dawla al-ʿAbbāsiyya wa fīhi Akhbār al-ʿAbbās wa Wildihi*, ed. ʿAbd al-ʿAzīz al-Dūrī and A. J. al-Muṭṭalibī (Beirut: Dār al-Talīʿa, 1971), 139, 169, 201, 238 (al-Qā'im al-Mahdī); Abū Muḥammad Aḥmad b. Aʿtham al-Kūfī, *Kitāb al-Futūḥ*, ed. Muḥammad ʿAbd al-Muʿīd Khān et al. (Hyderabad: Osmania Oriental Publications Bureau, 1968–1975), 8: 197 (Mahdī); al-Yaʿqūbī, *Tārīkh*, 2: 297, 332, 342; Aḥmad b. Yaḥyā b. al-Jābir al-Balādhurī, *Ansāb al-Ashrāf*, ed. Al-Shaykh Muḥammad Bāqir al-Maḥmūdī (Beirut: Dār al-Taʿāruf li-al-Matbūʿāt, 1977), 3: 47, 82, 122, 162, 178; Nuʿaym b. Ḥammād, *Kitāb al-Fitan*, 64–65, 66, 230; al-Ṭabarī, *Tārīkh*, 7: 421. See also ʿAbd al-ʿAzīz al-Dūrī,

"Al-Fikra al-Mahdīyya bayna al-Daʿwa al-ʿAbbāsīyya wa al-ʿAṣr al-ʿAbbāsī al-Awwal," in *Studia Arabica and Islamica Festschrift for Iḥsān ʿAbbās*, ed. Wadād al-Qāḍī (Beirut: American University of Beirut, 1981), 124.

37. On ʿAlid-Abbasid competition and its sectarian dimension, see Sharon, *Black Banners*, 103*ff*. On Abū Hāshim and the Bayāniyya, see *EI*(2), Bayān b. Samʿān (Hodgson); William F. Tucker, "Bayān b. Samʿān and the Bayāniyya: Shīʿīte Extremists of Umayyad Iraq," *MW* 65 (1975): 241–53; al-Ashʿarī, *Maqālāt*, 1: 5, 19; Anonymous, *Akhbār al-Dawla al-ʿAbbāsiyya*, 184–85. Ibn Aʿtham also relates a report that depicts Muḥammad b. ʿAlī predicting the future of the Abbasids. Ibn Aʿtham al-Kūfī, *Kitāb al-Futūḥ*, 8: 154–55. See also *EI*(2), Kaysāniyya (Madelung); Wilferd Madelung, "The Hāshimiyyāt of al-Kumayt and the Hāshimī Shīʿīsm," *SI* 70 (1989): 5–26; *EI*(2), "ʿAlī b. ʿAbdallāh al-ʿAbbās" (K V Zetterstéen); Sachedina, *Islamic Messianism*, 9–11. For an analysis of the color yellow, see Maribel Fierro, "Al-Aṣfar," *SI* 77 (1993): 169*ff*; Daniel, *The Political and Social History*, 27, 29–30; Kennedy, *The Prophet and the Age of the Caliphates*, 124; Sharon, *Black Banners*, 54–55, 70, 75, 82*ff*; Cobb, "The Empire in Syria," 262; Al-Dūrī, *Al-ʿAṣr al-ʿAbbāsī al-Awwal*, 33–34.

38. Daniel, *The Political and Social History*, 60; Andrew Marsham, *Rituals of Islamic Monarchy: Accession and Succession in the First Muslim Empire* (Edinburgh: Edinburgh University Press, 2009), 192; Kennedy, *The Prophet and the Age of the Caliphates*, 123*ff*; Gundelfinger and Verkinderen, "The Governors," 266*ff*, 280*ff*.

39. For what has been termed "the Late Antiquity" and Islam, see Aziz Al-Azmeh, *Muslim Kingship: Power and the Sacred in Muslim, Christian, and Pagan Politics* (New York: I. B. Tauris, 2001); Garth Fowden, *Empire to Commonwealth: Consequence of Monotheism in Late Antiquity* (Princeton, NJ: Princeton University Press, 1994); Garth Fowden, *Before and After Muhammad: The First Millennium Refocused* (Princeton, NJ: Princeton University Press, 2017); Jack Tannous, *Making of the Medieval Middle East: Religion, Society, and Simple Believers* (Princeton, NJ: Princeton University Press, 2018).

40. For a thoughtful discussion of the universalistic aspirations of the Umayyads, see Fowden, *Empire to Commonwealth*; Garth Fowden, *Qusayr Amra: Art and Umayyad Elite in Late Antique Syria* (Berkeley: University of California Press, 2004); Guy G. Stroumsa, *The Making of the Abrahamic Religions in Late Antiquity* (Oxford: Oxford University Press, 2017); Tannous, *Making of the Medieval Middle East*; Garth Fowden, "Greek Myth and Arabic Poetry at Quṣayr ʿAmra," in *Islamic Crosspollinations: Interactions in the Medieval Middle East*, ed. A. Akasoy, J. E. Montgomery, and P. E. Pormann (Exeter: Gibb Memorial Trust, 2007), 29–45.

41. On the round city of al-Manṣūr, see Salih A. El-Ali, "The Foundation of Baghdad," in *The Islamic City*, ed. Albert H. Hourani and S. M. Stern (Oxford: Bruno Cassrier and University of Pennsylvania Press, 1970), 87–102; Guy Le Strange, *Baghdad During the ʿAbbāsid Caliphate* (Oxford: Clarendon, 1924), 15*ff*; Nezar Al-Sayyad, *Cities and Caliphs: On the Genesis of Arab Muslim Urbanism* (Westport, CT: Greenwood, 1991), 113–23; Charles Wendell, "Baghdad: Imago Mundi and Other Foundation Lore," *IJMES* 2 (1971): 99–128; Jacob Lassner, *The Topography of Baghdad in the Early Middle Ages* (Detroit, MI: Wayne State University Press, 1970), 25–42, 45–59.

42. See Al-Azmeh, *Muslim Kingship*; Hayrettin Yücesoy, "Ancient Imperial Heritage and Islamic Universal Historiography: Al-Dīnawarī's Secular Perspective," *JGH* 2, no. 2 (2007): 135–55. For a useful collection of studies on the Umayyad and Abbasid interest in the cultural and political history of the Persian-Sasanian history, see Shaul Shaked, *From Zoroastrian Iran to Islam: Studies in Religious History and Intercultural Contacts* (Farnham, VT: Ashgate, 2010), especially 31–67; Dimitri Gutas, "Classical Arabic Wisdom Literature: Nature and Scope," *JAOS* 101 (1981): 49–86.

43. *EI*(2), "Khalīfa" (D. Sourdel, A. K. S. Lambton); *EI*(3), "Caliph and Caliphate" (H. Yücesoy); al-Qadi and Shahin, "Caliphate," *PEIPT*; William M. Watt, *Islamic Political Thought* (Edinburgh: Edinburgh

University Press, 1998), 40*ff*, 59*ff*, 90*ff*; W. Montgomery Watt, "God's Caliph: Qur'ānic Interpretation and Umayyad Claims," in *Iran and Islam, in Memory of the Late Vladimir Minorsky*, ed. Clifford Edmund Bosworth (Edinburgh: Edinburgh University Press, 1971); Patricia Crone and Martin Hinds, *God's Caliph: Religious Authority in the First Centuries of Islam* (Cambridge: Cambridge University Press, 1986), 24*ff*.

44. For an extended source material information on the subject, see http://arabiclexicon.hawramani.com/%d8%ae%d9%84%d9%81/#8ae835.
45. *EI*(3), "Caliph and Caliphate" (Yücesoy). My discussion on the caliphate here is based on some of the material in this entry.
46. Al-Qadi, "The Term 'Khalīfa,' " 392–411.
47. See the discussion in Ernst H. Kantorowicz, *The King's Two Bodies: A Study in Mediaeval Political Theology* (Princeton, NJ: Princeton University Press, 2016), xv.
48. Abū Muḥammad al-Ḥasan b. Mūsā al-Nawbakhtī, *Kitāb Firaq al-Shīʿa*, ed. Helmut Ritter (Istanbul: German Oriental Society, Devlet Matbaası, 1931), 9; Saʿd b. ʿAbdallāh b. Khalaf al-Qummī, *Kitāb al-Maqālāt wa al-Firaq*, ed. Muḥammad Jawād Shakūr (Tehran: Mu'assasat-i Matbuʿāt-i Atanī, 1963), 132.
49. ʿAmr b. Baḥr al-Jāḥiẓ, "*Kitāb al-Futyā*," in ʿAmr b. Baḥr al-Jāḥiẓ, *Rasā'il al-Jāḥiẓ*, ed. ʿAbd al-Salām Muḥammad Hārūn (Cairo: Maktabat al-Khānjī, 1994), 1: 213–14; ʿAmr b. Baḥr al-Jāḥiẓ, *al-ʿUthmāniyya*, ed. ʿAbd al-Salām Hārūn (Cairo: Maktabat al-Khanjī bi-Miṣr and Maktabat al-Muthanna bi-Baghdād, 1955), 250, 256, 261–63; ʿAmr b. Baḥr al-Jāḥiẓ, "al-Jawābāt fī al-Imāma," in ʿAmr b. Baḥr al-Jāḥiẓ, *Rasā'il al-Jāḥiẓ*, ed. ʿAbd al-Salām Muḥammad Hārūn (Cairo: Maktabat al-Khānjī, 1994), 4: 285*ff*; Al-Balādhurī, *Ansāb al-Ashrāf* (ed. al-Maḥmūdī), 3: 270, 292, 294; Ibn Aʿtham al-Kūfī, *Kitāb al-Futūḥ*, 6: 273–74, 355; Al-Nawbakhtī, *Firaq al-Shīʿa*, 9–10; Ibn Saʿd, *Kitāb al-Ṭabaqāt*, 7: 18, 79, 82.
50. See Ibn Isḥāq, *The Life of Muhammad*, 686–87. For further sources, see Yücesoy, *Taṭawwur*, 70–71, 106*ff*.
51. For his reports, see ʿAbd al-Razzāq b. Hammām al-Ṣanʿānī, *al-Muṣannaf*, ed. Ḥabīb al-Raḥmān al-Aʿzamī (Beirut: Al-Majlis al-ʿIlmī, 1970), 5: 439*ff*, 448–50, 485*ff*; Ibn Hishām, *al-Sīra al-Nabawiyya*, 2: 661; Al-Zubayr b. Bakkār, *al-Akhbār al-Muwaffaqiyyāt*, ed. Sāmī Makkī al-ʿĀnī (Baghdad: Ri'āsat Dīwān al-Awqāf, 1972), 579.
52. Al-Nawbakhtī calls them the pioneer Ḥashwiyya, *awā'il al-ḥashwiyya*.
53. Al-Nawbakhtī, *Firaq al-Shīʿa*, 7. For the significance of the difference between *amr*/*umūr* and *mulk* after the death of Muhammad, see al-Jābrī, *al-Dīn wa al-Dawla*, 15–16.
54. Al-Nawbakhtī, *Firaq al-Shīʿa*, 7–8.
55. For the most detailed documentation of this title, see Crone and Hinds, *God's Caliph*, 4*ff*; John Walker, *A Catalogue of the Muḥammadan Coins in the British Museum*, vol. 2 (London: British Museum, 1956), 30–31.
56. Court poetry confers the appellation *al-mahdī* on later Umayyad rulers, most famously Sulaymān b. ʿAbd al-Malik (r. 96–99/715–717) and ʿUmar II (r. 99–101/717–720). Hammām b. Ghālib al-Farazdaq, *Diwān al-Farazdaq* (Beirut: Dār Ṣādir, 1970), 1: 264, 2: 9; Jarīr b. ʿAṭiyya, *Diwān Jarīr*, ed. Nuʿmān Muḥammad Amīn Ṭāha (Cairo: Dār al-Maʿārif, 1969), 1: 124–25; Ibn Saʿd, *Kitāb al-Ṭabaqāt*, 5: 333. See also Nuʿaym b. Ḥammād, *Kitāb al-Fitan*, 57–58, 67–68, 75, 222, 230; Yücesoy, *Messianic Beliefs and Imperial Politics*, 36*ff*.
57. While the title's textual attestation abounds, the earliest documentary evidence appears on a coin minted in Bukhara for the Abbasid caliph al-Mahdī in 768, when he was still the prince and heir apparent, and al-Manṣūr was the ruling caliph. Michael L. Bates, "Khurāsānī

Revolutionaries and al-Mahdī's Title," in *Culture and Memory in Medieval Islam: Essays in Honour of Wilferd Madelung*, ed. Wilferd Madelung, Farhad Daftary, and Josef W. Meri (London: I. B. Tauris, 2003), 279–317.

58. For an informed discussion of the consequences of the idea of seniority, precedence, and merit in the first two centuries of the caliphate, see Asma Afsaruddin, *Excellence and Precedence: Medieval Islamic Discourse on Legitimate Leadership* (Leiden: Brill, 2002).
59. I have dealt with the Umayyad and Abbasid succession practices in Yücesoy, *Taṭawwur*, 49*ff*.
60. Yücesoy, *Taṭawwur*, 50*ff*. See also Marsham, *Rituals of Islamic Monarchy*, 86*ff*, 113*ff*.
61. See Aziz Al-Azmeh, "Monotheistic Kingship," in *Monotheistic Kingship: The Medieval Variants*, ed. Aziz Al-Azmeh and János M. Bak (Budapest: Central European University Press, 2004), 10.
62. ʿAbd al-Raḥmān b. ʿAmr Abū Zurʿa al-Dimashqī, *Tārīkh Abī Zurʿa al-Dimashqī*, ed. Shukrallāh Niʿmat Allāh al-Qūjānī (n.p.: Majmaʿ al-Lugha al-ʿArabiyya bi-Dimashq, n.d.), 1: 601.
63. Abū Zurʿa, *Tārīkh*, 1: 202.
64. For the administration of justice during the Umayyad period, see Steven Judd, "The Jurisdictional Limits of 'Qāḍī' Courts During the Umayyad Period," *Bulletin d'études Orientales* 63 (2014): 43–56. Irit Bligh-Abramski, "The Judiciary (Qāḍīs) as a Governmental-Administrative Tool in Early Islam," *JESHO* 35 (1992): 40–71; Hawting, *The First Dynasty of Islam*, 34*ff*, 58*ff*; Hannah-Lena Hagemann, "Muslim Elites in the Early Islamic Jazīra: The Qāḍīs of Ḥarrān, al-Raqqa, and al-Mawṣil" in *Transregional and Regional Elites: Connecting the Early Islamic Empire*, ed. Hannah-Lena Hagemann and Stefan Heidemann (Berlin: de Gruyter, 2020), 331*ff*; Steven Judd, *Religious Scholars and the Umayyads: Piety-Minded Supporters of the Marwānid Caliphate* (New York: Routledge, 2019), 91*ff*, 131*ff*.
65. For the topic of insignia, see Hilāl b. al-Muḥassin al-Ṣābī and Elie A. Salem, *Rusūm Dār al-Khilāfah: The Rules and Regulations of the ʿAbbāsid Court* (Beirut: Lebanese Commission for the Translation of Great Works, 1977); *EI*(3), "Caliph and Caliphate" (Yücesoy).
66. For details and issues, see Hugh Kennedy, *The Great Arab Conquests: How the Spread of Islam Changed the World We Live in* (Philadelphia: De Capo, 2007); Fred McGraw Donner, *The Expansion of the Early Islamic State* (Aldershot, UK: Ashgate/Variorum, 2008).
67. See Donner, *The Early Islamic Conquests*, 267*ff*; Kennedy, *The Great Arab Conquests*, 34*ff*, 363*ff*.
68. For a succinct but useful overview of the imperial administrative-military division, see Cobb, "The Empire in Syria." See also Travis Zadeh, *Mapping Frontiers Across Medieval Islam: Geography, Translation and the ʿAbbāsid Empire* (London: I. B. Tauris, 2011); Guy Le Strange, *The Lands of the Eastern Caliphate: Mesopotamia, Persia, and Central Asia from the Moslem Conquest to the Time of Timur* (New York: Barnes and Noble, 1873).
69. ʿAbd al-ʿAzīz al-Dūrī, *Early Islamic Institutions Administration and Taxation from the Caliphate to the Umayyads and ʿAbbāsids* (London: I. B. Tauris, 2011); Daniel, *The Political and Social History*; Gibb, *Studies on the Civilization of Islam*, 141*ff*.
70. The word initially meant "register" and later came to signify an office where scribes worked. See *EI*(2), "Dīwān" (A. A. Duri); *EI*(2), "Kharāj" (Claude Cahen); Hugh Kennedy, *The Armies of the Caliphs: Military and Society in the Early Islamic State* (London: Routledge, 2001), 60*ff*.
71. Hugh Kennedy, "Central Government and Provincial Elites in the Early ʿAbbāsid Caliphate," *BSOAS* 44 (1981): 26–38; Jacob Lassner, "Provincial Administration under the Early ʿAbbāsids: Abū Jaʿfar al-Manṣūr and the Governors of the Ḥaramayn," SI 49 (1979): 39–54; Chase F. Robinson, *Empire and Elites After the Muslim Conquest: The Transformation of Northern Mesopotamia* (New York: Cambridge University Press, 2000); Jürgen Paul, "Early Islamic History of Iran: From the Arab Conquest to the Mongol Invasion," *IS* 31 (1998): 463–71.

72. Hugh Kennedy, *The Court of the Caliphs* (London: Weidenfeld & Nicolson, 2004); Julia Ashtiany et al., *The Cambridge History of Arabic Literature: ʿAbbāsid Belles Lettres* (Cambridge: Cambridge University Press, 1990).
73. See Majid Khadduri, *War and Peace in the Law of Islam* (Baltimore, MD: Johns Hopkins University Press, 1955), 156.
74. Milka Levy-Rubin, *Non-Muslims in the Early Islamic Empire: From Surrender to Coexistence* (New York: Cambridge University Press, 2011); David M. Freidenreich and Miriam Bayla Goldstein, *Beyond Religious Borders: Interaction and Intellectual Exchange in the Medieval Islamic World* (Philadelphia: University of Pennsylvania Press, 2012); Jacob Lassner, *Jews, Christians, and the Abode of Islam: Modern Scholarship, Medieval Realities* (Chicago: University of Chicago Press, 2012); Khaled Abou El Fadl, "Islamic Law and Muslim Minorities: The Juristic Discourse on Muslim Minorities from the Second/Eighth to the Eleventh/Seventeenth Centuries," *Islamic Law and Society* 1, no. 2 (1994): 141–87. For a recent substantial study of non-Muslim subjects, see Anver M. Emon, *Religious Pluralism and Islamic Law: Dhimmīs and Others in the Empire of Law* (Oxford: Oxford University Press, 2014).
75. John Tomlinson, *Globalization and Culture* (Chicago: University of Chicago Press, 1999), 37*ff*.
76. Sidney Harrison Griffith, *The Church in the Shadow of the Mosque: Christians and Muslims in the World of Islam* (Princeton, NJ: Princeton University Press, 2008); Hawting, *The First Dynasty of Islam*, 72*ff*, 104*ff*; Jawdah, *al-Awḍāʿ*.
77. Muḥammad b. al-Ḥasan Shaybānī and Majid Khadduri, *The Islamic Law of Nations: Shaybānī's Siyar* (Baltimore, MD: Johns Hopkins Press, 1966); Khadduri, *War and Peace*.
78. George F. Hourani and John Carswell, *Arab Seafaring in the Indian Ocean in Ancient and Early Medieval Times* (Princeton, NJ: Princeton University Press, 1995); Abdul Sheriff, *Dhow Cultures of the Indian Ocean: Cosmopolitanism, Commerce and Islam* (New York: Columbia University Press, 2010); Andrew M. Watson, *Agricultural Innovation in the Early Islamic World: The Diffusion of Crops and Farming Techniques, 700–1100* (Cambridge: Cambridge University Press, 1983); Michael G. Morony, *Production and the Exploitation of Resources* (Aldershot, UK: Ashgate/Variorum, 2002). For several important articles on the Umayyad political economy and society, see John F. Haldon, *Money, Power and Politics in Early Islamic Syria: A Review of Current Debates* (London: Routledge, 2016).
79. For early caliphs' authority, see Crone and Hinds, *God's Caliph*, 4*ff*, 24*ff*; Crone, *God's Rule*, 33*ff*; Andrew Marsham, "God's Caliph Revisited: Umayyad Political Thought in Its Late Antique Context," in *Power, Patronage, and Memory in Early Islam: Perspectives on Umayyad Elites*, ed. Alain George and Andrew Marsham (New York: Oxford University Press, 2018), 3*ff*; Robert Hillenbrand, "Hishām's Balancing Act: The Case of Qaṣr al-Ḥayr al-Gharbī," in *Power, Patronage, and Memory in Early Islam: Perspectives on Umayyad Elites*, ed. Alain George and Andrew Marsham (New York: Oxford University Press, 2018), 83*ff*; Nadia Ali and Mattia Guidetti, "Umayyad Palace Iconography: On the Practical Aspects of Artistic Creation," in *Power, Patronage, and Memory in Early Islam: Perspectives on Umayyad Elites*, ed. Alain George and Andrew Marsham (New York: Oxford University Press, 2018), 175*ff*.
80. For the Arabization efforts, see M. Sprengling, "From Persian to Arabic," *AJSLL* 56 (1939): 175*ff* and 57 (1940): 302*ff*; *EI*(2), "Dīwān" (A. A. Duri).
81. For some examples of mediation, see Amir Harrak, *The Chronicle of Zuqnin* (Toronto: Pontifical Institute for Medieval Studies, 2000), 182–83, 230, 232–36, 241, 257.
82. Zaman, *Religion and Politics*, 1*ff*, 71*ff*; Crone, *God's Rule*, 125*ff*, 219*ff*.
83. They were neither non-Sunnite nor destined to become Sunnite, as implied in the anticipatory prefix "proto," but dynamic "formations" in which Sunnism emerged. One might therefore talk about potentiality rather than a nucleus or latency.

84. For the ulema and the caliphate, see Zaman, *Religion and Politics*. Wael B. Hallaq, *The Origins and Evolution of Islamic Law* (Cambridge: Cambridge University Press, 2011); Judd, *Religious Scholars and the Umayyads*, 39*ff*.
85. For the role of the ulema, see Suleiman Ali Mourad, *Early Islam Between Myth and History: Al-Ḥasan al-Baṣrī (D. 110 H = 728 CE) and the Formation of His Legacy in Classical Islamic Scholarship* (Leiden: Brill, 2006), 1*ff*. For an encyclopedic and critical account of the works and lives of the ulema in early Islam, see Josef van Ess, *Theologie und Gesellschaft im 2. Und 3. Jahrhundert Hidschra* (Berlin: de Gruyter, 1997), vols. 1–4, and its English translation, Josef van Ess and Gwendolin Goldbloom, *Theology and Society in the Second and Third Centuries of the Hijra: A History of Religious Thought in Early Islam* (Leiden: Brill, 2017–2019), vols. 1–4; Judd, *Religious Scholars and the Umayyads*, 39*ff*; Hagemann, "Muslim Elites in the Early Islamic Jazīra," 331*ff*.

2. The Language of Imamate

1. See Hayrettin Yücesoy, *Taṭawwur al-Fikr al-Siyāsī ʿinda Ahl al-Sunna: Fatrat al-Takwīn: Min Bidāyatihi ḥatta al-Thulth al-Awwal min al-Qarn al-Rābiʿ al-Hijrī* (Amman: Dār al-Bashīr, 1993), 35*ff*, 83*ff*; Patricia Crone, *God's Rule: Government and Islam* (New York: Columbia University Press, 2006), 33*ff*, 259*ff*.
2. "The inheritors of Muḥammad's authority (*sulṭān*) and his ring and the illuminated staff." See Aḥmad b. Yaḥyā b. al-Jābir al-Balādhurī, *Ansāb al-Ashrāf*, ed. S. D. F. Goitein (Jerusalem: Hebrew University, 1936), 5: 139. Also see Hammām b. Ghālib al-Farazdaq, *Dīwān al-Farazdaq* (Beirut: Dār Ṣādir, 1970), 2: 282–83: "You inherited the friend of God, every chest box and every scripture stand on the authority of messengership."
3. Al-Farazdaq, *Dīwān*, 1: 24.
4. For ʿAbd al-Malik b. Marwān's use of God's caliph on coins, see Yücesoy, *Taṭawwur*, 60–61, 62; John Walker, *A Catalogue of the Muhammadan Coins in the British Museum: A Catalogue of the Arab-Byzantine and Post-Reform Umaiyad Coins*, vol. 2 (Oxford: British Museum, 1956), 2: 30–31; al-Balādhurī, *Ansāb*, 5: 354; Patricia Crone and Martin Hinds, *God's Caliph: Religious Authority in the First Centuries of Islam* (Cambridge: Cambridge University Press, 1986), 4*ff*, 24*ff*. Marsham attempts to place this title in a wider context: Andrew Marsham, "'God's Caliph' Revisited: Umayyad Political Thought in Its Late Antique Context" in *Power, Patronage, and Memory in Early Islam: Perspectives on Umayyad Elites*, ed. Alain George and Andrew Marsham (New York: Oxford University Press, 2018), 3*ff*, 10*f*.
5. Muḥammad b. Jarīr al-Ṭabarī, *Tārīkh al-Rusul wa al-Mulūk*, ed. Muḥammad Abū al-Faḍl Muḥammad Ibrāhīm (Cairo: Dār al-Maʿārif, 1968), 7: 222–23.
6. Al-Ṭabarī, *Tārīkh*, 7: 218–24; Muḥammad b. Jarīr al-Ṭabarī, *The History of al-Tabarī*, ed. Ihsan Yarshater (Albany, NY: SUNY Press, 1985–2007), 26: 106–15. Crone and Hinds, *God's Caliph*, translation of the letter, 116–26. "Written by Samāl. Tuesday, 21 Rajab in the year 125 [=20 May, 743]." The name might be a typo of Sālim (s-m-a-l vs. s-a-l-m). See also Iḥsān ʿAbbās, *ʿAbd al-Ḥamīd b. Yaḥyā al-Kātib wa mā Tabaqqā min Rasāʾilihi wa Rasāʾil Sālim Abī al-ʿAlāʾ* (Amman: Dār al-Shurūq, 1988), 311–17. I will refer to the work as AHR. See also Marsham, "'God's Caliph' Revisited," 13*ff*.
7. The text of the letter is found in al-Ṭabarī, *Tārīkh*, 7: 275–77; Al-Ṭabarī, *The History of al-Ṭabarī*, 26: 204–7; Aḥmad Zakī Ṣafwat, *Jamharat Rasāʾil al-ʿArab fī al-ʿUṣūr al-ʿArabiyya al-Ẓāhira* (Beirut: al-Maktaba al-ʿIlmiyya, 1937), 2: 398–400. Translation of the letter is from Crone and Hinds,

God's Caliph, 126–28, with discretion. See also Josef Van Ess, *Theology and Society in the Second and Third Centuries of the Hijra: A History of Religious Thought in Early Islam*, trans. Gwendolin Goldbloom (Leiden: Brill, 2017–2019), vol. 1, 94*ff.*

8. Al-Ṭabarī, *Tārīkh*, 7: 275–76; Crone and Hinds, *God's Caliph*, 127.
9. Al-Ṭabarī, *Tārīkh*, 7: 276–77; Crone and Hinds, *God's Caliph*, 128.
10. Umayyad poetry is notable for allusions and explicit references to fate and destiny. See al-Farazdaq, *Dīwān*, 1: 24, 25, 79*ff*, 89, 286, 337; Al-Ṭabarī, *Tārīkh*, 7: 220, 222, 223; Aḥmad b. Muḥammad b. ʿAbd Rabbih, *al-ʿIqd al-Farīd*, ed. ʿAbd al-Majīd al-Tarḥīnī (Beirut: Dār al-Kutub al-ʿIlmiyya, 1983), 3: 309, 4: 89, 112, 424; Ghiyāth b. Ghawth al-Akhṭal, *Dīwān al-Akhṭal*, ed. Mahdī Muḥammad Nāṣir al-Dīn (Beirut: Dār al-Kutub al-ʿIlmiyya 1986), 27, 32, 33, 91*ff*; Jarīr b. ʿAṭiyya, *Dīwān Jarīr*, ed. Nuʿmān Muḥammad Amīn Ṭāha (Cairo: Dār al-Maʿārif, 1969), 1: 70, 94–95, 290*ff*; Muḥammad b. Saʿd, *Kitāb al-Ṭabaqāt al-Kabīr*, ed. Eduard Sachau et al. (Leiden: Brill, 1912–1940), 5: 245; AHR, 193, 207.
11. Abū Muḥammad ʿAbdallāh b. Muslim b. Qutayba, *al-Maʿārif*, ed. Tharwat ʿUkkāsha (Cairo: Dār al-Maʿārif, 1981), 441, 484, 625; Abū Muḥammad al-Ḥasan b. Mūsā al-Nawbakhtī, *Kitāb Firaq al-Shīʿa*, ed. Helmut Ritter (Istanbul: German Oriental Society, Devlet Matbaası, 1931), 9; Ibn Saʿd, *Kitāb al-Ṭabaqāt*, 7: 91*ff*, 122, 227. References in Yücesoy, *Taṭawwur*, 89–91. For early Qadarites, see Van Ess, *Theology and Society*, vol. 1, 82*ff.*
12. AHR, 207.
13. For early Kharijites, see Van Ess, *Theology and Society*, vol. 1, 473*ff.*
14. For early Murji'ites, see Van Ess, *Theology and Society*, vol. 1, 173*ff.* See also Saleh Said Agha, "A Viewpoint of the Murji'a in the Umayyad Period: Evolution Through Application," *JIS* 8 (1997): 1–42.
15. For early Muʿtazilites, see Van Ess, *Theology and Society*, vol. 2, 268*ff.*
16. See Patricia Crone and Fritz Zimmermann, *The Epistle of Sālim b. Dhakwān* (Oxford: Oxford University Press, 2001), 251*ff*, 261. The edited text of the *Kitāb al-Irjā'* is also found in Van Ess, *Theology and Society*, vol. 1, 199*ff*; Josef Van Ess, "Das 'Kitāb al-Irgā' des Ḥasan b. Muḥammad b. al-Ḥanafiyya," *Arabica* 21 (1974): 20–52*ff.*
17. For a more detailed analysis and summary, see Van Ess, "Das 'Kitāb al-Irga,'" 20*ff*; Van Ess, *Theology and Society*, vol. 1, 199*ff.*
18. For the sect, see Sean W. Anthony, *The Caliph and the Heretic: Ibn Saba' and the Origins of Shīʿism* (Leiden: Brill, 2012).
19. C&*ZES*, 186, 299–300; Van Ess, *Theology and Society*, vol. 1, 196–99. Sālim b. Dhakwān was possibly an Omani or Iranian provincial ʿIbādite sectarian who lived in the first half of the eighth century. Crone and Zimmermann summarize the dates of composition proposed for *Sīrat Sālim* in contemporary literature as 691 (Cook), ca. 701 (Madelung), ca. 718 (Van Ess), ca. 747 (Cook's second and preferred date), and the early Abbasid period (Calder). I have used Crone and Zimmermann's translation with modifications. I have referred to the edited Arabic text included in their study.
20. C&*ZES*, 23. For the text and its translation, see 38*ff.*
21. C&*ZES*, 23–24. Given my purpose in this study, I would refrain from describing it as a "pulpit manifesto" because of its length, complexity, and its sustained argumentative content and language. I agree that it fits the expectations of being a transitory text, but I still see it as a "peripatetic lecture" rather than a pulpit manifesto. It is a text that has departed from the rhetoric of orality and moved on to experimenting with prose writing without expecting "silent reading" and assuming an epistolary prose style. If one reads the *The Epistle of Sālim b.*

Dhakwān aloud with a stern tone, it may sound like a pulpit manifesto, but, of course, one does not have to read it that way. A "calm" reading of the text would make it sound closer to a reasoned lecture.

22. Sālim uses the word "caliph" twice as a verb (*istakhlafa*, appointed as deputy), once referring to David in a qur'anic citation, and once to Abū Bakr and ʿUmar I as being two caliphs after Muhammad.
23. The word "imam" appears on a regular basis as the principal signifier of a religiopolitical leader who, in ideal circumstances, would have the legitimate or rightful authority to legislate in religious matters besides governing.
24. He speaks in the first-person plural as "we," suggesting a collective identity of a like-minded group.
25. C&*ZES*, 15–19.
26. C&*ZES*, 135.
27. C&*ZES*, 26.
28. C&*ZES*, 30.
29. ʿAbd al-ʿAzīz al-Dūrī, *Awrāq fī al-Tārīkh wa al-Ḥaḍāra: Awrāq fī ʿIlm al-Tārīkh* (Beirut: Markaz al-Dirāsāt al-Waḥda al-ʿArabiyya, 2009), 55*ff.*
30. For Ibn Isḥāq's work and its textual history, see Muḥammad Ibn Isḥāq, ʿAbd al-Malik b. Hishām, and Alfred Guillaume, *The Life of Muhammad: A Translation of Ibn Isḥāq's Sīrat Rasūl Allāh* (Oxford: Oxford University Press, 1967); ʿAbd al-ʿAzīz al-Dūrī, *Nash'at ʿIlm al-Tārīkh ʿinda al-ʿArab* (Beirut: Markaz al-Dirāsāt al-Waḥda al-ʿArabiyya, 2007), 55*ff*; Harald Motzki, *Reconstruction of a Source of Ibn Isḥāq's Life of the Prophet and Early Qur'ān Exegesis: A Study of Early Ibn ʿAbbās Traditions* (Piscataway, NJ: Gorgias, 2017).
31. For various forms of historiographical representation, see Michel Foucault, *The Archaeology of Knowledge and the Discourse on Language*, trans. A. M. Sheridan Smith (New York: Pantheon, 1972), 5; Quentin Skinner, *Great Political Thinkers: Machiavelli* (Oxford: Oxford University Press, 1992), 2; Keith Jenkins, *On "What Is History?": From Carr and Elton to Rorty and White* (London: Routledge, 2005), chap. 1.
32. Here I mean the arguments justifying and defending the caliphate as it developed historically, regardless of varying positions on some caliphs. Juridical discourse is commonly associated with scholars (ulema) specializing in jurisprudential reasoning (*fuqahā'*) and *ḥadīth* collection and dissemination (*muḥaddithūn*) in ways that are recognizably different from, and often opposed to, the views of other established or emerging sects, such as the Kharijites and the Shiites.
33. ʿAbd al-Malik b. Hishām, *al-Sīra al-Nabawiyya*, ed. ʿUmar ʿAbd al-Salām Tadmūrī (Beirut: Dār al-Kitāb al-ʿArabī, 1990), 4: 304, 306–8, 309–11, 317; Ibn Isḥāq, *The Life of Muhammad*, 681–83, 685–86.
34. Ḥamad b. Muḥammad al-Khaṭabī al-Bustī, *Gharīb al-Ḥadīth*, ed. ʿAbd al-Karīm Ibrāhīm al-Gharbāwī (Mecca: Jāmiʿat Umm al-Qurā, 1982), 2: 128. The position taken by the Anṣār continued to unsettle the ulema. Al-Bustī (d. 998) explains their position (one *amīr* for the Anṣār and one *amīr* for the Muhājirūn) by making a reference to their kinship (*qabīla*, often rendered tribe) culture. He flags their suggestion as an out-of-place practice derived from the ancient tradition of the Bedouin, according to which no one could rule over a *qabīla* unless one belonged to it and that the verdict of Islam was contrary to that custom.
35. For the transformation of the faithful from kinship group solidarity to faith-based collectivity, see Toshihiko Izutsu, *Ethico-Religious Concepts in the Qur'ān* (Quebec: McGill-Queen's University Press, 2002), 55*ff.*

36. Ibn Hishām, *al-Sīra al-Nabawiyya*, 4: 309*ff*; Ibn Isḥāq, *The Life of Muhammad*, 686–87.
37. See al-Ṭabarī, *Tārīkh*, 3: 210; Ibn Qutayba, *al-Maᶜārif*, 170.
38. Khalīfa b. al-Khayyāṭ, *Tārīkh Khalīfa b. al-Khayyāṭ*, ed. Akram Ḍiyā' al-ᶜUmarī (Beirut: Dār al-Qalam-Mu'assasat al-Risāla, 1977), 213–14; Aḥmad b. Abī Yaᶜqūb al-Yaᶜqūbī, *Tārīkh al-Yaᶜqūbī*, ed. M. T. Houtsama (Leiden: Brill, 1969), 2: 271; al-Ṭabarī, *Tārīkh*, 5: 302–3; Yücesoy, *Taṭawwur*, 49–50.
39. Ibn Hishām, *al-Sīra al-Nabawiyya*, 4: 312; Ibn Isḥāq, *The Life of Muhammad*, 687.
40. ᶜAbdallāh b. ᶜAbd al-Raḥmān al-Dārimī, *Sunan al-Dārimī*, ed. Muḥammad Aḥmad Dahmān (Beirut: Dār al-Kutub al-ᶜIlmiyya, n.d.), 1: 79. ᶜUmar I remarks: "O crowd of Bedouin Arabs! Watch out for the land, the land. For there is no Islam without community, no community without leadership, no leadership without obedience."
41. Muḥammad b. Idrīs al-Shāfiᶜī, *al-Risāla*, ed. Aḥmad Muḥammad Shākir (Cairo: Maktabat Ibn Taymiyya, 1940), 79–80.
42. They were a small cluster of scholars and ascetics associated with the circle of Bishr b. al-Muᶜtamir (d. 825), Abū Mūsā ᶜĪsā b. Ṣabīḥ al-Murdār (d. ca. 840–841), and Ibrāhīm b. al-Sayyār al-Naẓẓām (d. ca. 836). See Ibn Ḥazm, *al-Faṣl fī al-Milal wa al-Ahwā' wa al-Niḥal*, ed. Muḥammad Ibrāhīm Naṣr and ᶜAbd al-Raḥmān ᶜUmayra (Jidda: Sharikat Maktabāt 'Ukāẓ, 1982), 5: 64–65; Florian Sobieroj, "The Muᶜtazila and Ṣūfism," in *Islamic Mysticism Contested: Thirteen Centuries of Controversies and Polemics*, ed. F. de Jong and Bernd Radtke (Leiden: Brill, 1999), 69–70; Toby Mayer, "Theology and Ṣūfism," in *The Cambridge Companion to Classical Islamic Theology*, ed. Tim Winter (Cambridge: Cambridge University Press, 2007), 261; Christopher Melchert, "The Ḥanābila and the Early Ṣūfis," *Arabica* 48 (2001): 355.
43. See ᶜAbdallāh b. Muḥammad al-Nāshī al-Akbar and Josef Van Ess, *Frühe muᶜtazilitische Häresiographie: zwei Werke des Nāshī' al-Akbar (gest. 293 H.)* (Weisbaden and Beirut: In Kommission bei Franz Steiner Verlag, 1971), 49–50; *EI*(r), "Jaᶜfar b. Mohammad b. Harb" (Joseph Van Ess).
44. For a treatment of this subject see Hayrettin Yücesoy, "Political Anarchism, Dissent, and Marginal Groups in the Early Ninth Century: The Ṣūfis of the Muᶜtazila Revisited," in *The Lineaments of Islam: Studies in Honor of Fred McGraw Donner*, ed. Paul Cobb (Leiden: Brill, 2012), 61*ff*; Patricia Crone, "Ninth-Century Muslim Anarchists," *Past and Present* 167 (2000): 3–28.
45. On this concept, see Eviatar Zerubavel, *Fine Line: Making Distinctions in Everyday Life* (Chicago: University of Chicago Press, 1993), 5*ff*.
46. On anarchism, see Harold Barclay, People Without Government: An Anthropology of Anarchism (London: Kahn & Averill, 1996), 17.
47. For al-ᶜAnbarī and the authenticity of the letter, see Mathieu Tillier, "Un traité politique du IIe/VIIIe siècle: L'épître de ᶜUbayd Allāh b. al-Ḥasan al-ᶜAnbarī au calife al-Mahdī," *Annales Islamologiques* 40 (2006): 139–70. I am indebted to Mathieu Tillier for making me aware of his article. Muhammad Qasim Zaman, *Religion and Politics Under the Early ᶜAbbāsids* (Leiden: Brill, 1997), 85–91.
48. Tillier, "Un traité politique," 145*ff*.
49. Unfortunately, the primary sources offer only scant information about his life. The most detailed account is given by Wakīᶜ himself, which is mostly anecdotal and nonbiographical. Muḥammad b. Khalaf b. Ḥayyān Wakīᶜ, *Akhbār al-Quḍāt* (WA), ed. ᶜAbd al-ᶜAzīz Muṣṭafā al-Marāghī (Cairo: al-Maktaba al-Istiqāma, 1947), vol. 2, 88*ff*. For his most complete biography, see Tillier, "Un traité politique," 140*ff*; and *EI*(3), "al-ᶜAnbarī, ᶜUbaydallāh b. al-Ḥasan" (Mathieu Tillier).
50. *EI*(3), "Al-ᶜAnbarī" (Matthew Tillier); Tillier, "Un traité politique," 140.

51. WA. The letter is recorded on pp. 97–107 of volume 2.
52. Contemporary scholars have studied al-ʿAnbarī's text to assess the relations between caliphs and jurists, which I cannot engage in this study. See Zaman, *Religion and Politics*, 85*ff*, 91. Concerning the early Abbasid period, see Zaman, *Religion and Politics*, 70*ff*, 119*ff*; Tillier, "Un traité politique," 152–54.
53. For a useful survey of advice literature, see *EI*(3), "Advice and Advice Literature" (Louise Marlow).
54. WA, 2: 97.
55. Qur'an (Q), 24: 55.
56. WA, 2: 97–99.
57. WA, 2: 99–100.
58. *Ṣadaqa*, more commonly known as *zakāt*, a kind of alms a Muslim reaching a certain threshold of wealth was obliged to pay. Its general principles, amount, limits, and disbursement are stipulated in the Qur'an. Whether it is collected and disbursed by the administration or left to individual discretion varied from time to time in the seventh and eighth centuries. See *EI*(2), "Ṣadaḳa" (T. H. Weir-A. Zysow).
59. Kennedy summarizes the key issues related to the distribution of the surplus revenue in the eighth century. Hugh Kennedy, *The Armies of the Caliphs: Military and Society in the Early Islamic State* (London: Routledge, 2001), 74*ff*, 78.
60. WA, 2: 100–1.
61. The termination of duty or retirement here.
62. WA, 2: 101–2.
63. WA, 2: 102.
64. Q, 59.
65. Q, 8: 1.
66. WA, 2: 102–4. The status of the lands and the tax implications of ownership were an important legal discussion among jurists in the eighth century. Al-ʿAnbarī seems to use *fay'* here in the sense of tax or wealth collected from the "conquered lands," barring other arrangements of allocation and ownership, and therefore inclusive of the land tax (*kharāj*). Abū Yūsuf deals with this question and the subject of *ṣadaqa* extensively in his *Kitāb al-Kharāj*. Yaʿqūb b. Ibrāhīm Abū Yūsuf, *Kitāb al-Kharāj* (Beirut: Dār al-Maʿrifa, 1979).
67. WA, 2: 104.
68. WA, 2: 105.
69. WA, 2: 105.
70. The other *ḥadīth*s include the following: "There is little time left of this world, like the time left of this day. The sun was touching the summit of the mountains, the end of that day." "How can I enjoy comfort, while the master of the Trumpet has already brought it to his mouth, tilted his forehead, stretched out his ear, advanced one foot and put back the other, and only waits to blow it as soon as the order to blow is given to him?" "My situation with the Hour is like a group of men sent a lookout guard to look out for their enemy. He saw the enemy and feared that they would precede him to attack his companions. And he began to scream: Alert." WA, 2: 105–6.
71. There may be a scribal interpolation here because the question can also be read as probing the veracity of the reports mentioned. The statement seems out of place, too, as the text abruptly turns to another subject.
72. WA, 2: 106–7.

73. Q, 3: 159. "Consult them on the affairs, but when you decide, place your trust in God. God loves those who trust Him."
74. Q, 42: 38. "Their affairs are done in consultation among them; and they spend charitably a portion of the goods we have given them."
75. WA, 2: 107.
76. WA, 2: 107; Tillier, "Un traité politique," 155–67.
77. Abū al-Ḥasan ʿAlī b. Muḥammad b. Ḥabīb al-Baṣrī al-Māwardī, *Al-Aḥkām al-Sulṭāniyya wa al-Wilāyāt al-Dīniyya*, ed. Aḥmad al-Mubārak al-Baghdādī (Kuwait: Maktabat Dār Ibn Qutayba, 1989), 22.
78. Wael B. Hallaq, *The Origins and Evolution of Islamic Law* (Cambridge: Cambridge University Press, 2011), 185; Zaman, *Religion and Politics*, 101–2*ff.*
79. Abū Yūsuf, *Kitāb al-Kharāj*; Aharon Ben Shemesh, *Taxation in Islam*, vol. 3: *Abū Yūsuf's Kitāb al-Kharāj* (Leiden: Bill, 1970).
80. *EI*(2), "Abū Yūsuf" (J. Schacht); Norman Calder, *Studies in Early Muslim Jurisprudence* (Oxford: Oxford University Press, 1993), 105–6; Paul Heck, "Abū Yūsuf," *PEIPT*, 15–16.
81. Muḥammad b. Isḥāq b. al-Nadīm, *al-Fihrist*, ed. Gustav Flugel (Beirut: Maktabat Khayyāṭ, 1966), 1: 203. See Calder, *Studies in Early Muslim Jurisprudence*, 106*ff*, who argues that the work dates to a later Abbasid period, in the middle of the ninth century. Zaman, *Religion and Politics*, 91–95, competently discusses the authenticity of the work. Three further works attributed to Abū Yūsuf may be authentic: *Kitāb al-Athar* is a collection of *ḥadīths* of Kufan origin; *Kitāb Ikhtilāf Abū Ḥanīfa wa Ibn Abī Laylā* is an exposition of the opinions and disagreements of two eminent Kufan scholars; *Kitāb al-Radd al-Siyar al-Awzāʿī* is a refutation of the opinions of the Syrian scholar *al-Awzāʿī* on the law of war. *EI*(2), "Abū Yūsuf" (J. Schacht); Heck, "Abū Yūsuf," *PEIPT*, 15–16.
82. *EI*(2), "Abū Yūsuf" (J. Schacht).
83. Zaman, *Religion and Politics*, 97–101, seems to argue that the *Kitāb al-Kharāj* advocated the Abbasid cause. On Abbasid loyalty, see also Calder, *Studies in Early Muslim Jurisprudence*, 106.
84. Abū Yūsuf, *Kitāb al-Kharāj*, introductory text, pp. 3–6, *ḥadīth* quotations, pp. 6–17, responses, 18*ff*; Shemesh, *Taxation in Islam*, 35.
85. Shemesh, *Taxation in Islam*, 38, with modification. See the Arabic text, Abū Yūsuf, *Kitāb al-Kharāj*, 3*ff.*
86. Shemesh, *Taxation in Islam*, 35–50.
87. The content of the *Kitāb al-Kharāj* includes: introduction; *ḥadīths* of exhortation; spoils; *fay'* and *kharāj*; existing practice in the Sawād; Syria and the Jazira, what should be done in the Sawād; the Hijaz, Mecca, Medina, the Yemen, and Arab lands; Arab lands in the status of non-Arab lands; Basra and Khurasan as the Sawād land; the conversion of people of the *ahl al-ḥarb* and the people of the desert; lands taken by force and by peace; apostates; the people of villages and lands, the cities and their people; definitions of *ʿushr* and *kharāj* land; *ṣadaqāt*; the renting of land; tax farming in the Sawād; the Christians of the Banū Taghlib; those who are subject to *jizya*, the dress of non-Muslims and their costumes; churches, religious buildings, and crosses; the Magians; tax administrators and judges; spies and spying; fighting the unbelievers and rebels. For further discussion see also Calder, *Studies in Early Muslim Jurisprudence*, 115, 152–53. On the concept and practice of "normal science," see Thomas S. Kuhn, *The Structure of Scientific Revolutions* (Chicago: University of Chicago Press, 1962), especially chaps. 2–4.
88. The abundance of *ḥadīth* reports in the works of both al-ʿAnbarī and Abū Yūsuf is remarkable.

3. Political Prose Revolution

1. The verbal noun *mawlā* was used for both client and master: sing. *mawlā*, pl. *mawālī*. The early practice suggests that the conquered peoples were considered clients whether or not they converted to Islam. Later, the term signified the non-Arab converts. The more systematic jurisprudential discourse about this question is a later canonization of various earlier practices.
2. It is useful to recall here the often overlooked practice of Marshall Hodgson about characterizing "Islamic civilization" as an heir to both the Greco-Roman and Irano-Semitic civilizations. See Marshall Hodgson, *The Venture of Islam: Conscience and History in a World Civilization: Classical Age of Islam* (Chicago: University of Chicago Press, 1974), 1: 103*ff.*
3. For the emergence of prose writing, see R. B. Serjeant, "Early Arabic Prose," in *The Cambridge History of Arabic Literature: Arabic Literature to the End of the Umayyad Period*, ed. A. F. L. Beeston (Cambridge: Cambridge University Press, 2012), 114*ff.*
4. On early secretarial work and its connection to political culture and *adab*, see also Said A. Arjomand, "ʿAbdallāh Ibn al-Muqaffaʿ and the ʿAbbāsid Revolution," *IS* 27 (1994), especially 14; Najm al-Din Yousefi, "Islam Without Fuqahāʾ: Ibn al-Muqaffaʿ and His Perso-Islamic Solution to the Caliphate's Crisis of Legitimacy (70–142 AH/690–760 CE)," *IS* (2017): 12*ff*; István T. Kristó-Nagy, "Conflict and Cooperation Between Arab Rulers and Persian Administrators in the Formative Period of Islamdom, c.600–c.950 CE," in *Empires and Bureaucracy in World History: From Late Antiquity to the Twentieth Century*, ed. Peter Crooks and Timothy Parson (Cambridge: Cambridge University Press, 2016), especially 69*ff*; István T. Kristó-Nagy, "Marriage After Rape: The Ambiguous Relationship Between Arab Lords and Iranian Intellectuals as Reflected in Ibn al-Muqaffaʿ's Oeuvre," in *Tradition and Reception in Arabic Literature: Essays Dedicated to Andras Hamori, Series: Mîzân. Studien zur Literatur in der islamischen Welt*, ed. Margaret Larkin and Jocelyn Sharlet (Wiesbaden: Harrassowitz Verlag, 2019), 165*ff.*
5. For ʿAbd al-Malik's reforms and their consequences, see M. Sprengling, "From Persian to Arabic," *AJSLL* 56 (1939): 175*ff*; M. Sprengling, "From Persian to Arabic," *AJSLL* 57 (1940): 325*ff*; *EI*(2), "Dīwān" (A. A. Duri); A. I. Sabra, "The Appropriation and Subsequent Naturalization of Greek Science in Medieval Islam: A Preliminary Statement," *History of Science* 25 (1987): 236–37. See also Dimitri Gutas, *Greek Thought, Arabic Culture: The Graeco-Arabic Translation Movement in Baghdad and Early ʿAbbasid Society (2nd–4th/5th–10th Centuries)* (New York: Routledge, 1998), 1*ff*, 43, 107*ff*; George Saliba, *Islamic Science and the Making of the European Renaissance* (Cambridge, MA: MIT Press, 2007), 1–25; Wadad al-Qadi, "The Names of Estates in State Registers Before and After the Arabization of the 'Dīwāns," in *Umayyad Legacies: Medieval Memories from Syria to Spain*, ed. Antoine Borrut and Paul M. Cobb (Leiden: Brill, 2010), 255*ff*; Arjomand, "ʿAbdallāh Ibn al-Muqaffaʿ," 12–14.
6. Hayrettin Yücesoy, "Language of Empire: Politics of Arabic and Persian in the Abbasid World," *PMLA* 130, no. 2 (2015): 385–86.
7. See Wadad al-Qadi, "Identity Formation of the Bureaucracy of the Early Islamic State: ʿAbd al-Ḥamīd's 'Letter to the Secretaries,'" in *Mediterranean Identities in the Premodern Era: Entrepôts, Islands, Empires*, ed. John Watkins, Kathryn L. Reyerson (London: Routledge Taylor & Francis, 2016), 143*ff.*
8. For early juristic writing, see Norman Calder, *Studies in Early Muslim Jurisprudence* (Oxford: Oxford University Press, 1993), 161–66.
9. For this dīwān, see *EI*(2), "Dīwān" (A. A. Duri).

10. Iḥsān ʿAbbās, *ʿAbd al-Ḥamīd b. Yaḥyā al-Kātib wa mā Tabaqqā min Rasāʾilihi wa Rasāʾil Sālim Abī al-ʿAlāʾ* (Amman: Dār al-Shurūq, 1988) (AHR), 50*ff*, 63*ff*, 130*ff*; *EI*^(r), "ʿAbd-Al-Ḥamīd b. Yaḥyā" (W. N. Brinner); Al-Thaʿālibī: "[Arabic] epistolary style began with ʿAbd-al-Ḥamīd and ended with Ibn al-ʿAmīd."
11. Abdul Aziz Duri, "Note on Taxation in Early Islam," *JESHO* 17, no. 2: (1974): 136–44; Kathryn Maurer Trinkaus, "Settlement of Highlands and Lowlands in Early Islamic Damghan," *Iran* 23 (1985): 129–41.
12. Albert Memmi, *The Colonizer and the Colonized: Introduction by Jean-Paul Sartre* (London: Earthscan, 2003), 150*ff*.
13. ʿAbd al-ʿAzīz Al-Dūrī, *Al-ʿAṣr al-ʿAbbāsī al-Awwal* (Beirut: Markaz Dirāsāt al-Waḥda al-ʿArabiyya, 2009), 10; Moshe Sharon, *Black Banners from the East* (Leiden: Brill, 1983), 65–66; Muḥammad b. Yazīd al-Mubarrad, *al-Kāmil fī al-Lugha wa al-Adab wa al-Naḥw wa al-Ṭaṣrīf*, ed. Muḥammad Aḥmad al-Dālī (Beirut: Mu'assasat al-Risāla, 1986), 2: 439.
14. See Antonio Gramsci, *Selections from the Prison Notebooks of Antonio Gramsci*, ed. and trans. Quentin Hoare and Geoffrey Nowell Smith (London: Elec, 1999), 20, 202*ff*. Gramsci sometimes uses "subordinate" or "instrumental" in addition to subaltern.
15. As one should expect, there were other non-Arab Muslim scholars, such as Ibn Isḥāq, who were fully assimilated into, and became ardent proponents of, the "Arabic" cultural hegemony, without leaving many traces of their own backgrounds in their writings. See Harald Motzki, "The Role of Non-Arab Converts in the Development of Early Islamic Law," *Islamic Law and Society* 6 (1999): 293*ff*.
16. We know ʿAbd al-Ḥamīd married Sālim's daughter or sister, but we have no information about Ibn al-Muqaffaʿ's marriage.
17. Frantz Fanon, *The Wretched of the Earth*, trans. Richard Philcox (New York: Grove, 2004), 158–59.
18. What he calls here "African culture," that is, an imagined, stereotyped, homogenized, racialized, and timeless culture supposedly seen throughout the continent, which may be captured in the statement, "I am from Africa."
19. Fanon, *The Wretched of the Earth*, 150–51, 154, 170*ff*.
20. For an excellent assessment of variegated issues of cultural identity with respect to Iran's Persian cultural elite's sense of belonging and loyalty, as reflected in written work from the ninth to the eleventh century, see Sarah Bowen Savant, *The New Muslims of Post-Conquest Iran: Tradition, Memory, and Conversion* (Cambridge: Cambridge University Press, 2013), 16*ff*. See also Patricia Crone's solid engagement with the question of empire and colonialism in "early Islam" in Patricia Crone, "Post-Colonialism in Tenth-Century Islam," *DI* 83 (2006): 2–38, doi:https://doi.org/10.1515/ISLAM.2006.002; and Patricia Crone, "Imperial Trauma: The Case of the Arabs," *Common Knowledge* 12 (2006): 107–16, doi:https://doi.org/10.1215/0961754X-12-1-107. I am grateful to Michael Cooperson for alerting me to these two articles.
21. Memmi, *The Colonizer and the Colonized*, 152–53; Kathryn Scott Kaufmann, *Subjectivity and Medieval Arabic Adab* (PhD diss., University of California, Berkeley, 1997), 63.
22. See Crone, "Post-Colonialism in Tenth-Century Islam," 11*ff*; Crone, "Imperial Trauma," 111*ff*; Hamid Dabashi, *The World of Persian Literary Humanism* (Cambridge, MA: Harvard University Press, 2012), 50*ff*.
23. For discourse and social position, see Pierre Bourdieu, *Language and Symbolic Power*, trans. Gino Raymond and Matthew Adamson (Cambridge: Polity, 1991), 109–10.
24. For a different view on this, see J. D. Latham, "The Beginnings of Arabic Prose Literature: The Epistolary Genre," in *The Cambridge History of Arabic Literature: Arabic Literature to the End of the*

Umayyad Period, ed. Alfred Felix Landon Beeston (Cambridge: Cambridge University Press, 2012), 163.

25. Latham, "The Beginnings of Arabic Prose Literature," 164.
26. AHR, 28–29; Muḥammad b. Jarīr Al-Ṭabarī, *The History of al-Tabarī*, ed. Ihsan Yarshater (Albany, NY: SUNY Press, 1985–2007), 2: 1731.
27. J. D. Latham persuasively corroborates the late Umayyad provenance of the composition. Shaul Shaked, J. D. Latham, and Kevin T. van Bladel make a convincing case about the Persian mediation of the original text. For the complex genealogy of this work, see Muḥammad b. Isḥāq b. al-Nadīm, *al-Fihrist*, ed. Gustav Flugel (Beirut: Maktabat Khayyāṭ, 1966), 1: 117; AHR, 30–31; Aḥmad b. Yūsuf b. Ibrāhīm and ʿAbd al-Raḥmān Badawī, *al-Uṣūl al-Yūnāniyya li-al-Naẓariyyāt al-Siyāsiyya fī al-Islām 1. 1* (Cairo: Maktabat al-Nahḍa al-Miṣriyya, 1954), 67*ff*; Mario Grignaschi, "Les 'Rasā'il 'Arisṭaṭalisa ilā-l-Iskandar' de Sālim Abī-l-ʿAlā' et l'activite culturelle a l'apoque omayyade," *Bulletin d'etudes Orientales* 19 (1965–1966): 7*ff*; Mario Grignaschi, "Le roman epistolaire classique conserve' dans la version de Sālim Abū-l-ʿAlā'," *Museon* 80 (1967): 211*ff*; Mario Grignaschi, "L'origine et les Métamorphoses du 'Sirr-al-Asrār,'" *Archives d'histoire doctrinale et littéraire du Moyen Age* 43 (1976): 7*ff*; Latham, "The Beginnings of Arabic Prose Literature," 154*ff*; Shaul Shaked, *From Zoroastrian Iran to Islam: Studies in Religious History and Intercultural Contacts* (Farnham, Surrey: Ashgate, 2010), section VI: 31*ff*; Kevin T. van Bladel, "The Iranian Characteristics and Forged Greek Attributions in the Arabic *Sirr al-Asrār* (Secret of Secrets)," *Mélanges de l'Université Saint-Joseph* 57 (2004): 151*ff*; Miklós Maróth, "The Correspondence Between Aristotle and Alexander the Great: An Anonymous Greek Novel in Letters in Arabic Translation," *Acta Antiqua* 45, no. 2–3 (2005): 231–315; Neguin Yavari, *Advice for the Sultan: Prophetic Voices and Secular Politics in Medieval Islam* (Oxford: Oxford University Press, 2014), 8–16; Jaakko Hämeen-Anttila, *Khwadāynāmag: The Middle Persian Book of Kings* (Leiden: Brill, 2018), https://www.doabooks.org/doab?func=fulltext&rid=45435, 45*ff*. The question of the connection between *The Book of Politics* and the celebrated *Sirr al-Asrār* should not concern us much here. According to Mario Grignaschi, the pseudo-Aristotelian corpus *Sirr al-Asrār*, *The Secret of Secrets* of the ninth century (known in precapitalist Europe as *Secretum secretorum*), might have derived from or at least been inspired by this work. Although Grignaschi connects both works—albeit through a mediation of another "Alexander Romance"—his evidence and reasoning about the authenticity of the existing text as an Umayyad-period work has been challenged in substantial ways. Mahmoud Manzalaoui demonstrates with persuasive evidence that, while it is still possible that *Sirr al-Asrār*'s initial pages and its "germinal notion" derived from an Umayyad period work attributed to Sālim and the scribes in his circle, the existing work is a later Abbasid compilation. The surviving *Sirr al-Asrār* tells a story of a different time, which is traceable to no earlier than the ninth century and to an unknown author, who might have attributed his translation to Yaḥyā b. Biṭrīq. For a detailed and careful study of the topic, see Mahmoud Manzalaoui, "The Pseudo-Aristotelian *Kitāb Sirr al-Asrār: Facts and Problems*," *Oriens* 23, no. 24 (1974): 147*ff*.
28. Latham, "The Beginnings of Arabic Prose Literature," 154*ff*.
29. J. D. Latham lauds ʿAbd al-Ḥamīd as "a graduate of his school" in a casual sense. Latham, "The Beginnings of Arabic Prose Literature," 164. I use the term here more intently to signify a certain level of discursive and methodological coherence.
30. Wadad al-Qadi, "ʿAbd al-Ḥamīd al-Kātib b. Yaḥyā al-Āmirī," *PEIPT*, 2–3; Wadad al-Qadi, "ʿAbd al-Ḥamīd al-Kātib," in *Arabic Literary Culture, 500–925* (Dictionary of Literary Biography, vol. 311), ed. Michael Cooperson and Shawkat M. Toorawa (Detroit, MI: Thomson Gale, 2005), 3*ff*.

31. AHR, 26–27.
32. See his "The Letter to the Crown Prince," AHR, 215*ff.*
33. *EI*(3), "ʿAbd al-Ḥamīd" (Al-Qadi); Wadad al-Qadi, "ʿAbd al-Ḥamīd al-Kātib," ALC, 3*ff.*
34. *EI*(r), "ʿAbd-Al-Ḥamīd b. Yaḥyā" (W. N. Brinner).
35. *EI*(3), "ʿAbd al-Ḥamīd al-Kātib" (Al-Qadi).
36. AHR, 61*ff.*
37. For a detailed examination of the letters, see Wadad al-Qadi, "Early Islamic State Letters: The Question of Authenticity," in *The Byzantine and Early Islamic Near East, I. Problems in the Literary Source Material*, ed. A. Cameron and L. Conrad (Princeton, NJ: Darwin,1999), 215–71.
38. Al-Qadi, "Identity Formation of the Bureaucracy," 145; *EI*(3), "ʿAbd al-Ḥamīd" (Al-Qadi).
39. AHR, 55–59.
40. The statement in Arabic reads, "*wa kāna ʿAbd al-Ḥamīd al-Kātib istakhraja amthilat al-kitāba allatī rasamahā min al-lisān al-Fārisī, fa ḥawwalahā ilā al-lisān al-ʿArabī.*" Abū Hilāl al-ʿAskarī, *Diwān al-Maʿānī*, ed. Aḥmad Ḥasan Basaj (Beirut: Dār al-Kutub al-ʿIlmiyya, 1994), 2: 436.
41. Wadad al-Qadi, "ʿAbd al-Ḥamīd al-Kātib," *PEIPT*, 2–3; *EI*(3), "ʿAbd al-Ḥamīd al-Kātib" (Al-Qadi).
42. The Arabic phrasing reads "*kāna ʿAbd al-Ḥamīd awwal man fataqa akmām al-balāgha, wa sahhala turūqihā wa fakka riqāb al-shiʿr.*" Aḥmad b. Muḥammad b. ʿAbd Rabbih, *Al-ʿIqd al-Farīd*, ed. ʿAbd al-Majīd al-Tarḥīnī (Beirut: Dār al-Kutub al-ʿIlmiyya, 1983), 4: 247. Latham, "The Beginnings of Arabic Prose Literature," 174; *EI*(1), "ʿAbd al-Ḥamīd al-Kātib" (H. A. R. Gibb).
43. See AHR, 51, where Iḥsān ʿAbbās portrays ʿAbd al-Ḥamīd as an example of a social subject who assimilates into the manners of his society.
44. See also Al-Qadi, "Identity Formation of the Bureaucracy," 150, 151–52.
45. See Wadad al-Qadi, "The Religious Foundation of Late Umayyad Ideology and Practice," in *Saber religioso y poder politico en el Islam: Actas del simposio international, Granada, 15–18 Ocotobre 1991*, ed. Manuela Marin and Mercedes García-Arenal (Madrid: Agencia Española de Cooperacion Internacional, 1994), especially 241*ff*; Wadad al-Qadi, "The Impact of the Qur'ān on the Epistolography of ʿAbd al-Ḥamīd," in *Approaches to the Qur'ān*, ed. Gerald R. Hawting and Abdul-Kader A. Shareef (London: Routledge, 1993), 285*ff.*
46. See his letters on civil discord and obedience, AHR, 209–15; his letter on behalf of Marwān b. Muḥammad to Naṣr b. Sayyār, AHR, 198–201; on the Qadarites, AHR, 207; in his "Testament to the Crown Prince," AHR, especially 215–22; and on the glory of Islam, AHR, 273–74.
47. This rhetoric surfaces in the entirety of his "political" letters. AHR, 209*ff.*
48. Al-Qadi, "The Religious Foundation of Late Umayyad Ideology," 242*ff.*
49. Poignant in his letter on obedience, AHR, 210–13.
50. AHR, 210, 214.
51. AHR, 198–201, 207, 209, 216; Al-Qadi, "The Religious Foundation of Late Umayyad Ideology," 241–42.
52. AHR, 207, in his letter to Hishām on the Qadariyya.
53. AHR, 211; Al-Qadi, "The Religious Foundation of Late Umayyad Ideology," 252.
54. AHR, especially 209, 210–13, 214; Al-Qadi, "Early Islamic State Letters"; Al-Qadi, "The Religious Foundation of Late Umayyad Ideology"; Wadad al-Qadi, "ʿAbd al-Ḥamīd al-Kātib," *PEIPT*, 2–3.
55. Comprises about forty pages in Iḥsān ʿAbbās' edition.
56. *EI*(3), "ʿAbd al-Ḥamīd" (Al-Qadi); Louise Marlow, *Counsel for Kings: Wisdom and Politics in Tenth-Century Iran: The Naṣīḥat Al-Mulūk of Pseudo-Mawardi: Contexts and Themes*, 2 vols. (Edinburgh: Edinburgh University Press, 2016), 2: 3*ff.*
57. See *EI*(2), "Naṣīḥat al-Mulūk" (C. E. Bosworth).

58. BL 75b–83b; A1 216b–230b (text resumes in a separate part with new cover and pagination, 1a–10a). The most up-to-date edition and publication of the "Testament" is provided by Iḥsān ʿAbbās. See AHR, 215–65.
59. Latham, "The Beginnings of Arabic Prose Literature," 168. ʿAbdallāh was not able to defeat the Kharijites. He retreated to Nisibis in upper Mesopotamia—today's Nusaybin in Turkey.
60. Latham, "The Beginnings of Arabic Prose Literature," 167–68; *EI*[(r)], "ʿAbd-Al-Ḥamīd b. Yaḥyā" (W. N. Brinner).
61. For another assessment of the "Testament," see Latham, "The Beginnings of Arabic Prose Literature," 167.
62. AHR, 215–16.
63. AHR, 216–22.
64. AHR, 219–20.
65. AHR, 222–27.
66. AHR, 226–27.
67. AHR, 227–34; Latham, "The Beginnings of Arabic Prose Literature," 170.
68. AHR, 227–30; Latham, "The Beginnings of Arabic Prose Literature," 170.
69. For a summary of the text in English, see Latham, "The Beginnings of Arabic Prose Literature," 167–72.
70. AHR, 234–65. Iḥsān ʿAbbās provides useful subheadings to clarify the structure and flow of the text.
71. AHR, 233–34.
72. AHR, 281.
73. AHR, 216–17.
74. Al-Qadi, "Identity Formation of the Bureaucracy," 151. For an extended discussion of the letter's authenticity and its variants, see Al-Qadi, "Early Islamic State Letters," 245*ff.*
75. Latham, "The Beginnings of Arabic Prose Literature," 177.
76. See also Al-Qadi, "Identity Formation of the Bureaucracy," 147; Latham, "The Beginnings of Arabic Prose Literature," 166–67.
77. AHR, 281–83.
78. AHR, 283.
79. AHR, 283–85.
80. AHR, 285–88.
81. One of the earliest uses of the word *siyāsa* occurs in ʿAbd al-Ḥamīd's letters. See AHR, 281.
82. AHR, 281–82; Ibn Khaldūn, *The Muqaddimah: An Introduction to History*, trans. Franz Rosenthal (London: Routledge and Kegan Paul, 1958), 2: 29–35.
83. Al-Qadi, "Identity Formation of the Bureaucracy," 147. Al-Qadi signifies with it "Islamic bureaucracy."
84. For a pensive discussion of agency, performativity, embodiment, and ethical formation, see Saba Mahmood, *Politics of Piety: The Islamic Revival and the Feminist Subject* (Princeton, NJ: Princeton University Press, 2012), especially chap. 5. While the study examines modern Egypt, I find its approach and conceptualization pertinent.
85. *Yā ahl hādhihi al-ṣināʿa*, "you who practice this craft," AHR, 281. See Al-Qadi, "Identity Formation of the Bureaucracy," 146*ff.*
86. AHR, 281. For the meaning of *al-sūqa*, see al-Ṣāḥib b. ʿAbbād, *al-Muḥīṭ fī al-Lugha*, http://arabiclexicon.hawramani.com/search/%D8%B3%D9%88%D9%82?cat=38: *Al-sūqa min al-nās, wa al-jamīʿ al-suwaq: mā dūna al-mulūk, dhakar wa untha wa al-wāḥid wa al-jamīʿ fīhi siwā*/common folk, plural

crowds of people: those who are under kings, they are the same whether male or female, singular or plural.

87. AHR, 281.
88. AHR, 281.
89. Patricia Crone traces the appearance of this idea to al-Jāḥiẓ in the early ninth century. See Patricia Crone, *God's Rule: Government and Islam* (New York: Columbia University Press, 2006), 260–61, where she also lists other thinkers citing this opinion from the ninth century onward.
90. AHR, 281.
91. AHR, 281; Ibn Khaldūn, *The Muqaddimah*, 2: 29; Latham, "The Beginnings of Arabic Prose Literature," 166–67.

4. The Disruptive Language of Siyasa

1. Muḥammad b. ʿAbdūs al-Jahshiyārī, *al-Wuzarāʾ wa al-Kuttāb*, ed. Muṣṭafā Saqqā, Ibrāhīm Ibyārī, and ʿAbd al-Ḥafīẓ Shalabī (Cairo: Maṭbaʿat Muṣṭafā al-Bābī al-Ḥalabī, 1938), 80.
2. The individual and political value of friendship features in the writings of both scribes.
3. For his biography, see Aḥmad b. Muḥammad Shams al-Dīn b. Khallikān, *Wafiyāt al-Aʿyān wa Anbāʾ Abnāʾ al-Zamān* (Beirut: Dār Ṣādir, 1978), 2: 151*ff*; Al-Jahshiyārī, *Kitāb al-Wuzarāʾ wa al-Kuttāb*, 103*ff*. The outline of his biography and his major activities are summarized efficiently based on available sources by Aḥmad Amīn, Shelomo D. Goitein, Francesco Gabrieli, Charles Pellat, Dominique Sourdel, John D. Latham, Gerald Lampe, William M. Brinner, Said A. Arjomand, Michael Cooperson, Najm al-Din Yousefi, Istvan Kristó-Nagy, İsmail Durmuş and İlhan Kutluer, Mustafa Demirci, and others. However, I must single out the following: *EI*[(r)], "Ebn al-Moqaffaʿ, Abū Moḥammad ʿAbd-allāh Rōzbeh" (J. D. Latham); J. D. Latham, "Ibn al-Muqaffaʿ and Early ʿAbbāsid Prose," in *The Cambridge History of Arabic Literature: ʿAbbasid Belles-Lettres*, ed. Julia Ashtiany et al. (Cambridge: Cambridge University Press, 1990), 48*ff*; Francesco Gabrieli, "L'opera di Ibn al-Muqaffaʿ," *Rivista degli studi orientali* 13 (1932): 197–247; Dominique Sourdel, "La Biographie D'Ibn Al-Muqaffaʿ D'Après Les Sources Anciennes," *Arabica* 1, no. 3 (1954): 307–23; Michael Cooperson, "Ibn al-Muqaffaʿ," in *Arabic Literary Culture, 500–925* (*Dictionary of Literary Biography*, vol. 311), ed. Michael Cooperson and Shawkat M. Toorawa (Detroit, MI: Thomson Gale, 2005), 150–63 (ALC); István T. Kristó-Nagy, *La Pensée d'Ibn al-Muqaffaʿ: Un Agent Double dans le Monde Persan et Arabe* (Paris: Editions de Paris, 2013); Josef Van Ess, *Theology and Society in the Second and Third Centuries of the Hijra: A History of Religious Thought in Early Islam*, trans. Gwendolin Goldbloom, 5 vols. (Leiden: Brill, 2017–2019), 2: 26*ff*.
4. He is rumored to have been struck by the Umayyad governor al-Ḥajjāj b. Yūsuf on his hand on account of embezzlement, a blow that caused a deformity, hence his son's derogatory epithet, "the son of the shriveled-handed," that is, Ibn al-Muqaffaʿ. In another version of the account, the name is an active, not passive, participle derived from the root related to basket weaving. It describes his father's profession as a weaver of palm-leaf baskets (Muqaffiʿ). "Ibnü-l-Mukaffaʿ" (Ismail Durmuş), *Türkiye Diyanet Vakfı İslam Ansiklopedisi* (TDVIA), (Istanbul: Türkiye Diyanet Vakfı, 2016); LIM, 9.
5. Aḥmad Amīn, *Ḍuḥā al-Islām* (Cairo: Maktabat al-Nahḍa, 1933), 1: 195*ff*; Sourdel, "La Biographie d'Ibn Al-Muqaffaʿ," 308; *EI*[(2)], "Ibn al-Muqaffaʿ" (Gabrieli); Said A. Arjomand, "ʿAbdallāh Ibn al-Muqaffaʿ and the ʿAbbāsid Revolution," *IS* 27 (1994): 12–14; Cooperson, "Ibn al-Muqaffaʿ,"

ALC, 151; Najm al-Din Yousefi, "Islam Without Fuqahā': Ibn al-Muqaffaᶜ and His Perso-Islamic Solution to the Caliphate's Crisis of Legitimacy (70–142 AH/690–760 CE)," *IS* (2017): 11*ff.*

6. See also Kristó-Nagy, *La Pensée d'Ibn al-Muqaffa*ᶜ, 51–52.
7. Cooperson, "Ibn al-Muqaffaᶜ," ALC, 151; Latham, "Ibn al-Muqaffaᶜ and Early ᶜAbbāsid Prose," 48; *EI*⁽ʳ⁾, "Ebn al-Moqaffaᶜ" (J.D. Latham); Kristó-Nagy, *La Pensée d'Ibn al-Muqaffa*ᶜ, 51.
8. Sourdel, "La Biographie d'Ibn Al-Muqaffaᶜ," 308; Latham, "Ibn al-Muqaffaᶜ and the Early ᶜAbbāsid Prose," 48; Cooperson, "Ibn al-Muqaffaᶜ," ALC, 151; Arjomand, "ᶜAbdallāh Ibn al-Muqaffaᶜ," 15*ff*; Yousefi, "Islam Without *Fuqahā*'," 11*ff.*
9. Sourdel, "La Biographie d'Ibn Al-Muqaffaᶜ," 309–10; *EI*⁽²⁾, "Ibn al-Muqaffaᶜ" (Gabrieli); Latham, "Ibn al-Muqaffaᶜ and the Early ᶜAbbāsid Prose," 48–49; Al-Jahshiyārī, *al-Wuzarā'*, 105; TDVIA, "Ibnü-l-Mukaffaᶜ" (Ismail Durmuş).
10. See Wadad al-Qadi, "Identity Formation of the Bureaucracy of the Early Islamic State: ᶜAbd al-Ḥamīd's 'Letter to the Secretaries,'" in *Mediterranean Identities in the Premodern Era: Entrepôts, Islands, Empires* (London: Routledge Taylor & Francis, 2016), 153, on citing a report from Aḥmad b. Yaḥyā b. al-Jābir al-Balādhurī, *Ansāb al-Ashrāf*, vol. 3., ed. ᶜAbd al-ᶜAzīz al-Dūrī (Beirut: Franz Steiner Verlag, 1978), 164. ᶜAbd al-Ḥamīd's alleged reprimand of the agents of the Abbasids who wanted to torture him was that a good scribe should be able to serve under any ruler.
11. Al-Jahshiyārī, *al-Wuzarā'*, 104, 105.
12. Ibn Khallikān, *Wafiyāt*, 2: 152–53; Al-Jahshiyārī, *al-Wuzarā'*, 103–5; Sourdel, "La Biographie d'Ibn Al-Muqaffaᶜ," 317*ff*; *EI*⁽²⁾, "Ibn al-Muqaffaᶜ" (Gabrieli); Latham, "Ibn al-Muqaffaᶜ and the Early ᶜAbbāsid Prose," 48; Cooperson, "Ibn al-Muqaffaᶜ," ALC, 161; Mustafa Demirci, "Emevilerden Abbasilere Geçiş Sürecinin bir Tanığı: Abdullah İbnü'l-Mukaffâ ve "Risâletü's-Sahâbesi," *DEU İlahiyat Fakultesi Dergisi* 21 (2005): 120–22.
13. Saᶜd b. ᶜAbdallāh al-Qummī, *al-Maqālāt wa al-Firaq*, ed. Muḥammad Jawād Mashkūr (Tehran: n.p., 1341H/1922), 67.
14. Van Ess, *Theology and Society*, 2: 28–29.
15. Ibn Khallikān, *Wafiyāt*, 2: 151.
16. For a perceptive reflection on Ibn al-Muqaffaᶜ's personal dilemma concerning his *mawlā* status and contributions, see Kristó-Nagy, *La Pensée d'Ibn al-Muqaffa*ᶜ, 34–36, 44, 66–72, 78, 104. István T. Kristó-Nagy, "Marriage After Rape: The Ambiguous Relationship Between Arab Lords and Iranian Intellectuals as Reflected in Ibn al-Muqaffaᶜ's Oeuvre," in *Tradition and Reception in Arabic Literature: Essays Dedicated to Andras Hamori*, ed. Margaret Larkin and Jocelyn Sharlet, Series: Mîzân. Studien zur Literatur in der islamischen Welt (Wiesbaden: Harrassowitz Verlag, 2019), 170; István T. Kristó-Nagy, "Conflict and Cooperation Between Arab Rulers and Persian Administrators in the Formative Period of Islamdom, c.600–c.950 CE," in *Empires and Bureaucracy in World History: From Late Antiquity to the Twentieth Century*, ed. Peter Crooks and Timothy Parsons (Cambridge: Cambridge University Press, 2016), 64–66.
17. Sources make the point that he liked dying his hair with saffron as a statement about his cultural identity.
18. One might go in several directions as to what the Shuᶜūbī/Shuᶜūbiyya denotes in this context. I prefer what Abū ᶜUbayd Qāsim b. Sallām suggests in his *Gharīb al-Ḥadīth*: "Al-Aṣmaᶜī said: it is said that man *shaᶜaba* his affair if he divided and separated it . . . Abū ᶜUbayd said, *yashᶜabū* in a different sense refers to improving a thing (*iṣlāḥ*) and unification (*ijtimā*ᶜ), and this variance (*ḥarf*) is from the antonyms." Abū ᶜUbayd al-Qāsim b. Sallām, *Kitāb Gharīb al-Ḥadīth*, ed. Ḥasan M. M. Sharaf and ᶜAbd al-Salām Hārūn (Cairo: al-Maṭābiᶜ al-Amīriyya, 1984), 5: 36. http://

arabiclexicon.hawramani.com/%d8%b4%d8%b9%d8%a8/#f25d71. The word later carried a more concrete meaning in the sense of rejecting the superiority of the Arabs over others. See al-Ṣāḥib b. ʿAbbād, *al-Muḥīṭ fī al-Lugha*: "The Shuʿūbī is the person who diminishes the value of the Arabs and does not see them superior in merit (*faḍlan*) over others." Al-Ṣāḥib Ismāʿīl b. ʿAbbād, *Al-Muḥīṭ fī al-Lugha*, ed. Muḥammad Ḥasan Āl Yāsīn (Beirut: ʿĀlam a-Kutub, 1994), 1: 294. http://arabiclexicon.hawramani.com/%d8%b4%d8%b9%d8%a8/#9f3391.

19. Sourdel, "La Biographie d'Ibn Al-Muqaffaʿ," 313*ff*; Shaul Shaked, "From Iran to Islam," *JSAI* 4 (1984): 50*ff*; LIM, 26–27; Josef Van Ess, "Some Fragments of the *Mu'araḍat al-Qur'ān* Attributed to Ibn al-Muqaffaʿ," in Wadād al-Qāḍī, *Studia Arabica et Islamica: Festschrift for Iḥsān ʿAbbās* (Beirut: American University of Beirut, 1981), 151*ff*; István T. Kristó-Nagy, "A Violent, Irrational and Unjust God: Antique and Medieval Criticism of Jehovah and Allāh," in *La morale au crible des religions, Collection: "Studia Arabica,"* vol. 21, ed. Marie-Thérèse Urvoy (Versailles: Éditions de Paris, 2013), 143*ff*.
20. For further information and another perspective, see István T. Kristó-Nagy, "Reason, Religion and Power in Ibn al-Muqaffaʿ," *Acta Orientalia Academiae Scientiarum Hungaricae* 62, no. 3 (2009): 285–301; Kristó-Nagy, *La Pensée d'Ibn al-Muqaffaʿ*, 75–79; Kristó-Nagy, "Marriage After Rape," 178–80.
21. Van Ess, "Some Fragments," 2: 160*ff*; Van Ess, *Theology and Society*, 2: 32–33. See also Gabrieli, "L'opera di Ibn al-Muqaffaʿ," 236*ff*; LIM, 31–32; István T. Kristó-Nagy, "Denouncing the Damned *Zindīq*! Struggle and Interaction Between Monotheism and Dualism," in *Accusations of Unbelief in Islam: A Diachronic Perspective on Takfir*, ed. Camilla Adang, Hassan Anṣāri, Maribel Fierro, and Sabine Schmidtke (Leiden: Brill, 2015), 59.
22. For a detailed treatment of the text, see Andrew Marsham and Chase F. Robinson, "The Safe-Conduct for the ʿAbbāsid ʿAbd Allāh b. ʿAlī (d. 764)," *BSOAS* 2 (2007): 247*ff*.
23. Ibn Khallikān, *Wafiyāt*, 2: 152–53; Al-Jahshiyārī, *al-Wuzarā'*, 103, 104, 105; Latham, "Ibn al-Muqaffaʿ and the Early ʿAbbāsid Prose," 49.
24. For a perspective on Ibn al-Muqaffaʿ's predicament of coming to terms with the Islamic rule, see Kristó-Nagy, "Marriage After Rape," 161*ff*.
25. See also Hamid Dabashi, *The World of Persian Literary Humanism* (Cambridge, MA: Harvard University Press, 2012), 70*ff*; Van Ess, *Theology and Society*, 2: 26; Kristó-Nagy, *La Pensée d'Ibn al-Muqaffaʿ*, 23, 44, 67; Anthony Black, *The History of Islamic Political Thought: From the Prophet to the Present* (New York: Routledge, 2001), 22.
26. For Ibn al-Muqaffaʿ's literary and scholarly contribution, see Gabrieli, "L'opera di Ibn al-Muqaffaʿ," 197*ff*; Kristó-Nagy, *La Pensée d'Ibn al-Muqaffaʿ*, 81*ff*; *EI*(2), "Adab" (Gabrieli). Cooperson, "Ibn al-Muqaffaʿ," ALC, 150–64; Latham, "Ibn al-Muqaffaʿ and Early ʿAbbāsid Prose," 48; Arjomand, "ʿAbdallāh Ibn al-Muqaffaʿ," 15*ff*; TDVIA, "Ibnü-l-Mukaffa'" (Ismail Durmuş and İlhan Kutluer). Mustafa Demirci, "Abdullah İbnü'l-Mukaffa'nın 'Risâletü's-Sahâbe'Adlı Risalesi: Takdim ve Tercüme,"İstem 12 (2008): 217ff; Louise Marlow, *Counsel for Kings: Wisdom and Politics in Tenth-Century Iran: The Naṣīḥat al-Mulūk of Pseudo-Māwardī: Contexts and Themes*, 2 vols. (Edinburgh: Edinburgh University Press, 2016), 2: 3ff, 35ff.
27. Latham, "Ibn al-Muqaffaʿ and the Early ʿAbbāsid Prose," 76–77.
28. *EI*(2), "Ibn al-Muqaffaʿ" (Gabrieli). Iyas Hassan, "Language nomade en cours impériale: L'arabe d'Ibn al-Muqaffaʿ, entre deux ères," *Bulletin d'études Orientales* 65 (2016): 221*ff*. The author underlines Ibn al-Muqaffaʿ's writing as a bridge between orality and prose writing.
29. *EI*(2), "Ibn al-Muqaffaʿ" (Gabrieli).
30. Ibn Khaldūn, *The Muqaddimah: An Introduction to History*, trans. Franz Rosenthal (London: Routledge and Kegan Paul, 1958), 1: 82–83.

31. Fable writing is different from narrating a single story in which an animal plays a role (pre-Islamic Arabic poetry and qur'anic stories involving animals fit this description), although both rest on the fundamental assumption about human-animal relations that animals, as creations of God, serve as lessons and examples for humans. Animals in these stories not only shared the same universe as humans but also were diverse, purposeful, and morally endowed.
32. ʿAbdallāh Ibn al-Muqaffaʿ, *Kalīlah and Dimnah: Fables or Virtue and Vice*, ed. Michael Fishbein, trans. Michael Fishbein and James E. Montgomery (New York: New York University Press, 2021). For further information and references see *EI*[2], "Kalīla Wa Dimna" (Carl Brockelmann); François de Blois and Burzūyah, *Burzōy's Voyage to India and the Origin of the Book of Kalīlah Wa Dimnah* (London: Royal Asiatic Society, 1990), 1*ff*, 12*ff*; *EI*[r] "Kalila wa Demna" (Dagmar Reidel), https://iranicaonline.org/articles/kalila-demna-index; Kristó-Nagy, *La Pensée d'Ibn al-Muqaffaʿ*, 90–91.
33. In addition to Borzoe's own introduction explaining the reason for his trip to India in search of "wisdom and truth," the work contains five stories coming from an earlier rendition of the Pancha-tantra, which make up the core of the book. Three tales come from book 12 of the Mahabharata, and one comes from the Buddhist legend of the king Chanda Pradyota. Some tales are of Indian origins, and others came from other sources during translation or adaptation into various languages over the course of several centuries. *EI*[2], "Ibn al-Muqaffaʿ" (Gabrieli). Gabrieli, "L'opera di Ibn al-Muqaffaʿ," 198*ff*; Cooperson, "Ibn al-Muqaffaʿ," ALC, 153*ff*; *EI*[r], "Kalila wa Demna" (Dagmar Reidel); Latham, "Ibn al-Muqaffaʿ and the Early ʿAbbāsid Prose," 51–53; István T. Kristó-Nagy, "Wild Lions and Wise Jackals: Killing Kings and Clever Counsellors in Kalīla wa Dimna," in *Prophets, Viziers and Philosophers: Wisdom and Authority in Early Arabic Literature*, ed. Emily J. Cottrell (Barkhuis: University Library, Groningen, 2020), 147*ff*. See the valuable project of Beatrice Gründler on *Kalīla and Dimna* at https://www.geschkult.fu-berlin.de/en/e/kalila-wa-dimna/topics/How-To-Use-A-Book.html. On the introduction of *Kalīla and Dimna*, see Beatrice Gründler, "Les versions de Kalīla wa-Dimna: und transmission et une circulation mouvantes," in *Énoncés sapientiels et littérature exemplaire: une intertextualité complexe*, ed. Marie-Sol Ortola (Nancy: Éditions Universitaires de Lorraine, 2013), 385–416.
34. Ibn al-Muqaffaʿ, *Kalīlah and Dimnah*, 23. To compare with an early nineteenth century translation of the work to English language, see ʿAbdallāh Ibn al-Muqaffaʿ and Wyndham Knatchbull, *Kalīla and Dimna or The Fables of Bidpai* (Oxford: W. Baxter, 1819), 29. http://catalog.hathitrust.org/api/volumes/oclc/4567613.html.
35. Ibn al-Muqaffaʿ, *Kalīlah and Dimnah*, 23; Ibn al-Muqaffaʿ, *Kalīla and Dimna*, 29.
36. Ibn al-Muqaffaʿ, *Kalīlah and Dimnah*, 25; Ibn al-Muqaffaʿ, *Kalīla and Dimna*, 47–48.
37. Ibn al-Muqaffaʿ, *Kalīlah and Dimnah*, 25; Ibn al-Muqaffaʿ, *Kalīla and Dimna*, 48. For the metaphoric and Aesopian language of the work see István T. Kristó-Nagy, "The Crow Who Aped the Partridge: Aesopian Language by Ibn al-Muqaffaʿ's in a Fable of Kalīla wa-Dimna," in *L'Adab toujours recommencé—origines, transmission et metamorphoses*, ed. Catherine Mayeur-Jaouen, Francesca Bellino, and Luca Patrizi (Leiden: Brill, forthcoming).
38. Ibn al-Muqaffaʿ, *Kalīlah and Dimnah*, 25; Ibn al-Muqaffaʿ, *Kalīla and Dimna*, 49–50.
39. The most authoritative work on the Khuday-nāma to date is Jaakko Hämeen-Anttila, *Khwadāynāmag: The Middle Persian Book of Kings* (Leiden: Brill, 2018), especially 59*ff*, 67*ff*, 89*ff*, 128*ff*, https://www.doabooks.org/doab?func=fulltext&rid=45435. I am grateful to Michael Cooperson for this reference. For andarz literature, see Shaul Shaked, "Andarz and Andarz Literature in Pre-Islamic Iran," in *Zoroastrianism: A Collection of Articles from Encyclopedia Iranica*, ed. Mahnaz Moazami (New York: Encyclopedia Iranica Foundation, 2016), 798*ff*; Marlow, *Counsel*

for Kings, 2: 35*ff*. The connection between *Arthaśāstra* and the early Arabic political prose needs further research, but it seems evident. See Kauṭilya and Patrick Olivelle, *King Governance and Law in Ancient India: Kauṭilya's Arthaśāstra: A New Annotated Translation* (Oxford: Oxford University Press, 2013), 1*ff*.

40. ʿAbdallāh b. Muslim b. Qutayba, *ʿUyūn al-Akhbār* (Cairo: Dār al-Kutub al-Miṣriyya, 1996), 3*ff*; Muḥammad b. Jarīr al-Ṭabarī, *Tārīkh al-Rusul wa al-Mulūk*, ed. Muḥammad Abū al-Faḍl Muḥammad Ibrāhīm (Cairo: Dār al-Maʿārif, 1968), 2: 37*ff*; Gabrieli, "L'opera di Ibn al-Muqaffaʿ," 208*ff*; *EI*[2], "Ibn al-Muqaffaʿ" (Gabrieli); Latham, "Ibn al-Muqaffaʿ and the Early ʿAbbāsid Prose," 53–54; Zeev Rubin, "Ibn al-Muqaffaʿ and the Account of Sasanian History in the Arabic Codex Sprenger 30," *JSAI* 30 (2005): 52–93.
41. *EI*[r], "Ibn al-Muqaffaʿ" (Latham); Latham, "Ibn al-Muqaffaʿ and Early ʿAbbāsid Prose," 54; Cooperson, "Ibn al-Muqaffaʿ," ALC, 156; *EI*[2], "Ibn al-Muqaffaʿ" (Gabrieli).
42. Gabrieli, "L'opera di Ibn al-Muqaffaʿ," 215; *EI*[2], "Ibn al-Muqaffaʿ" (Gabrieli); *EI*[3], "Advice and Advice Literature" (Marlow).
43. Muḥammad b. Isḥāq b. al-Nadīm, *Al-Fihrist*, ed. Gustav Flugel (Beirut: Maktabat Khayyāṭ, 1966), 1: 118 (on Ibn al-Muqaffaʿ as translator of the work), 305.
44. Hämeen-Anttila, *Khwadāynāmag*, 30–31. Cooperson, "Ibn al-Muqaffaʿ," ALC, 155.
45. The prose was deemed to be verbose and of inferior quality. Muḥammad ibn al-Ḥasan Ibn Isfandiyār, *Letter of Tansar*, ed. Mary Boyce (Roma: Istituto Italiano per il Medio ed Estremo Oriente, 1968), 7; Latham, "Ibn al-Muqaffaʿ and Early ʿAbbāsid Prose," 56; *EI*[2], "Ibn al-Muqaffaʿ" (Gabrieli); Gabrieli, "L'opera di Ibn al-Muqaffaʿ," 216–18.
46. Ibn Isfandiyār, *Letter of Tansar*, 34*ff*, 50*ff*. See also Kristó-Nagy, *La Pensée d'Ibn al-Muqaffaʿ*," 149–69; Kristó-Nagy, "Marriage After Rape," 171–75; Hämeen-Anttila, *Khwadāynāmag*, 34–35.
47. *Bilawhar and Yudasaf* may be considered authentic. It is a middle Persian compilation based on various ancient Indian stories about the life of Gautama Buddha. It is the tale of a childless king's miraculously born son, Yudasaf, who escapes the confines of his father's palace and embarks on a journey of self-discovery that leads him to Bilawhar. Bilawhar teaches him the ascetic manners that he pursues as a wanderer until his death. The early Arabic version of this work is lost. The earliest extant version comes from the tenth century and has later adaptations. Gabrieli, "L'opera di Ibn al-Muqaffaʿ," 216*ff*. We know *Kitāb Mazdak/Mardak* only by name. Contrary to what its title suggests, this work was neither a biography of Mazdak nor an account of his teachings but perhaps "a book of moral advice and anecdotes" in the line of *andarz* genre known as the *Book of Mardak*, variably written as Marwak, Mardak, and Mazdak. *EI*[2], "Bilawhar wa Yudasaf" (D. M. Lang); Ahmad Tafazzoli, "Observations sur le soi-disant Mazdak-nāmag," in *Orientalia J. Duchesne-Guillemin emerito oblata, Acta Iranica, Hommages et opera minora* 9 (Leiden: Brill, 1984), 507–10; Kristó-Nagy, *La Pensée d'Ibn al-Muqaffaʿ*, 88; Hämeen-Anttila, *Khwadāynāmag*, 35–36; Cooperson, "Ibn al-Muqaffaʿ," ALC, 156. See ʿAbd al-Salām Harūn's amendment of the name from Marwak to Mazdak: Al-Jāḥiẓ, *Rasā'il al-Jāḥiẓ*, ed. ʿAbd al-Salām Muḥammad Hārūn (Cairo: Maktabat al-Khānjī, 1994), 3: 192. Ibn al-Muqaffaʿ's name has been associated with numerous other writings on governance that date to later centuries, such as the following: *Risālat al-Akhlāq fī al-Siyāsa* is contained in *al-Majmūʿa al-Muʿtabara min al-Rasā'il wa al-Fawā'id*. Süleymaniye Kütüphanesi, Esad Efendi no. 3690, pp. 105b–119a. Also attributed to him is the *Risāla fī Makārim al-Akhlāq wa al-Siyāsa al-Madaniyya* in *Rasā'il fī al-Manṭiq*, Süleymaniye Kütüphanesi, Şehid Ali Paşa no. 2722, pp. 59a–90b. The following is attributed to his son Muḥammad: *al-Tibr al-Masbūk fīmā Yaḥtājūnā ilayhi al-Mulūk*, Süleymaniye Kütüphanesi, Molla Çelebi no. 113.

48. See Cooperson, "Ibn al-Muqaffaᶜ," ALC, 156; Hämeen-Anttila, *Khwadāynāmag*, 90–91; Eric Hermans, "A Persian Origin of the Arabic Aristotle? The Debate on the Circumstantial Evidence of the Manteq Revisited," *Journal of Persian Studies* 11 (2018): 72–88. Hermans argues that Ibn al-Muqaffaᶜ or his son must have translated the paraphrase of Aristotle's text from middle Persian sometime during the second half of the eighth century. For a similar view, see Istvan T. Kristó-Nagy and Abdessamad Belhaj, "Ancient Greek Philosophy and Islamic Political Advice Literature," in *Brill's Companion to the Reception of Ancient Philosophy in Islamic Political Thought*, ed. Vasileios Syros (Leiden: Brill, forthcoming).
49. As Iḥsān ᶜAbbās notes, misattribution does not disprove Ibn al-Muqaffaᶜ's familiarity with Greek and Aristotelian thought, which the reader detects in his *Al-Adab al-Kabīr*. Iḥsan ᶜAbbās, "Naḍra Jadīda fī Baᶜḍ al-Kutub al-Mansūba li-Ibn al-Muqaffaᶜ," *Majallat Majmaᶜ al-ᶜIlmī al-ᶜArabī* 3 (1977): 542*ff*; Andras Hamori, "Prudence, Virtue, and Self-Respect in Ibn al-Muqaffaᶜ," in *Reflections on Reflections: Near Eastern Writers Reading Literature: Dedicated to Renate Jacobi*, ed. Angelika Neuwirth and Andreas Christian Islebe (Wiesbaden: Reichert Verlag, 2006), 164–77.
50. Regarding this text, see Kristó-Nagy, *La Pensée d'Ibn al-Muqaffaᶜ*, 267–77, which also includes an edition and a French translation, 372–404, and Kristó-Nagy, "Marriage After Rape," 171–74. The remaining works credited to Ibn al-Muqaffaᶜ are of doubtful attribution, including *al-Adab al-Saghīr* and *Muᶜāraḍat al-Qur'ān*. See *EI*^(r), "Ibn Muqaffaᶜ" (Latham); Latham, "Ibn Muqaffaᶜ and Early ᶜAbbāsid Prose," 74–75; Cooperson, "Ibn Muqaffaᶜ," ALC, 159–60; ᶜAbbās, "Naḍra Jadīda," 539*ff*; Gabrieli, "L'opera di Ibn al-Muqaffaᶜ," 219*ff*, 239–40; Van Ess, "Some Fragments of the *Muᶜāraḍat al-Qur'ān* Attributed to Ibn al-Muqaffaᶜ," 151–63; Kristó-Nagy, *La Pensée d'Ibn al-Muqaffaᶜ*, 287–340, 438–61; Kristó-Nagy, "A Violent, Irrational and Unjust God," 150–60 (with an English translation of some of the fragments); and Eva-Maria Lika, *Proofs of Prophecy and the Refutation of the Ismāᶜīliyya: the Kitāb Ithbāt nubuwwat al-nabī of the Zaydī al-Mu'ayyad bi-llāh al-Hārūnī* (Berlin: de Gruyter, 2018), 147–50.
51. ᶜAbbās, "Naḍra Jadīda," 539*ff*, 555*ff*; Kristó-Nagy, *La Pensée d'Ibn al-Muqaffaᶜ*, 102, 187. On naming the work, see Istvan T. Kristo-Nagy, "On the Authenticity of *al-Adab al-Ṣaġīr* Attributed to Ibn al-Muqaffa and Problems Concerning Some of His Titles," *Acta Orientalia Academiae Scientiarum Hungaricae* 62 (2009): 199–218.
52. Latham, "Ibn al-Muqaffaᶜ and Early ᶜAbbāsid Prose," 63*ff*.
53. *EI*^(2), "Ibn al-Muqaffaᶜ" (Gabrieli); Cooperson, "Ibn al-Muqaffaᶜ," ALC, 158.
54. See Judith Josephson, "The Multicultural Background of the *Kitāb al-Adab al-Kabīr* by ᶜAbdallāh Ibn al-Muqaffaᶜ," in *Current Issues in the Analysis of Semitic Grammar and Lexicon I*, ed. Lutz Edzard and Jan Retsö (Weisbaden: Harrassowitz Verlag, 2005), 166*ff*.
55. Abū al-Ḥasan Muḥammad b. Yūsuf Al-ᶜĀmirī, *Al-Iᶜlām bi-Manāqib al-Islām*, ed. Aḥmad ᶜAbd al-Ḥamīd Ghurāb (Riyad: Dār al-Thaqāfa li-al-Nashr wa al-Iᶜlām, 1967), 159–60; ᶜAbbās, "Naḍra Jadīda," 542; Hans Daiber, "Das Kitāb al-Adab al-Kabīr des Ibn al-Muqaffaᶜ als Ausdruck griechischer Ethik, islamischer Ideologie und iranisch-sassanidischer Hofetikette," *Oriens* 43 (2015): 273*ff*.
56. ᶜAbdallāh b. al-Muqaffaᶜ, "*Al-Adab al-Kabīr*," in *Rasā'il al-Bulaghā'*, ed. Muḥammad Kurd ᶜAlī (Cairo: Maṭbaᶜat Lajnat al-Ta'līf wa al-Tarjuma wa al-Nashr, 1946), 40–106. See also Ibn al-Muqaffaᶜ, *Al-Adab al-Kabīr*, in Kathryn Scott Kaufmann, *Subjectivity and Medieval Arabic Adab* (PhD diss., University of California, Berkeley, 1997), 198*ff*.
57. The known manuscripts introduce the "Epistle on the Caliph's Privy" in the following way: "and among the writings is the epistle of Ibn al-Muqaffaᶜ on the companions (*wa minha risālat Ibn al-Muqaffaᶜ fī al-ṣaḥāba*)."

58. As readers must have noticed, I opted to use the word "privy" to render *al-ṣaḥaba* to avoid the apolitical and casual sense of the word "companion" in this context.
59. Only Said Amir Arjomand claimed that it was intended for the uncle of al-Manṣūr, ʿAbdallāh b. ʿAlī, during his bid for the caliphate after the death of al-Saffāḥ in 754. See Arjomand, "ʿAbd Allāh b. al-Muqaffaʿ," 24*ff*. It is an unconvincing argument. In fact, if anything, several phrases and references suggest clearly that the addressee was al-Manṣūr, but the subject does not require a treatment here. See also Kristó-Nagy, *La Pensée d'Ibn al-Muqaffaʿ*, 214–17; Yousefi, "Islam Without *Fuqahā'*," 17*ff*. Francesco Gabrieli argues that Ibn al-Muqaffaʿ's patrons ʿĪsā b. ʿAlī and Sulaymān b. ʿAlī might have suggested to him to write it for al-Manṣūr. See Gabrieli, "L'opera di Ibn al-Muqaffaʿ," 235.
60. Tilman Nagel argues that the caliph al-Manṣūr might have heeded his advice. See Tilman Nagel, *Staat und Glaubensgemeinschaft im Islam: Geschichte der politischen Ordnungsvorstellungen der Muslime* (Munich: Artemis Verlag, 1981), 170.
61. Shelomo D. Goitein, "A Turning Point in the History of Muslim State: Apropos of Ibn al-Muqaffaʿ's *Kitāb al-Ṣaḥāba*," *IC* 23 (1949): 128–29; Shaked, "From Iran to Islam," 32*ff*; Gabrieli, "L'opera di Ibn al-Muqaffaʿ," 231*ff*; Muḥammad ʿĀbid al-Jābrī, *al-ʿAql al-Siyāsī al-ʿArabī: Muḥaddātuhu wa Tajalliyātuhu* (Beirut: Markaz Dirāsāt al-Waḥda al-ʿArabiyya, 1990), 341*ff*; Patricia Springborg, *Western Republicanism and the Oriental Prince* (Cambridge: Polity, 1992), 265–68; Arjomand, "ʿAbd Allāh b. al-Muqaffaʿ," 31–33; Black, *The History of Islamic Political Thought*, 21–24; Yousefi, "Islam Without *Fuqahā'*," 9*ff*.
62. Direct policy recommendations between numbers 3 and 9 are indicated in the text with the phrase "among the matters that the commander of the faithful should be reminded" (*wa min al-umūr allatī yudhakkar bihā amīr al-mu'minīn*) and their subjections "among the matters to examine" as they appear under any of these seven categories (indicated with the phrase *mimma yunẓaru fīhi*) and further subcategories "among such matters" (*wa min dhālika*), and "also" (*immā/ammā*). For comparable but nevertheless differing arrangements of the epistle's content, see the learned article in legal thinking by Joseph E. Lowry, "The First Islamic Legal Theory: Ibn al-Muqaffaʿ on Interpretation, Authority, and the Structure of the Law," *JAOS* 128 (2008): 28*ff*, http://www.jstor.org/stable/25608305; and Yousefi, "Islam Without *Fuqahā'*," 21–22.
63. For a lucid survey of the idea of social justice and what is famously known as the "circle of justice" from the Sasanian to the contemporary era, see Linda T. Darling, *A History of Social Justice and Political Power in the Middle East: The Circle of Justice from Mesopotamia to Globalization* (London: Routledge, 2013). Also, for a brief account of the topic, see Jennifer A. London, "The 'Circle of Justice,'" *History of Political Thought* 32 (2011): 425*ff*. For a discussion of the idea concerning Ibn al-Muqaffaʿ, see Jennifer A. London, "The ʿAbbāsid 'Circle of Justice': Re-reading Ibn al-Muqaffaʿ's Letter on Companionship," in *Comparative Political Theory in Time and Place*, ed. Daniel Kapust and H. Kinsella (New York: Palgrave Macmillan, 2017), 25*ff*, especially 33*ff*; Kristó-Nagy, *La Pensée d'Ibn al-Muqaffaʿ*, 173, 225–27; and Kristó-Nagy, "Marriage After Rape," 175–76.
64. The ruler is supported by the military, which depends on finances, and the money is collected from the common folk, who rely on the ruler for their well-being.
65. Scholars since Kurd ʿAlī, Aḥmad Amīn, and Shelomo Goitein in the mid-twentieth century have recognized the significance of the "Epistle on the Caliph's Privy" as an original composition. For the economy of space, I will not list them here, as they are noted throughout the study.
66. See also Kristó-Nagy, *La Pensée d'Ibn al-Muqaffaʿ*, 215, where he describes the work as a postrevolutionary program of state building and stabilization.

67. ʿAbdallāh b. al-Muqaffaʿ, *Nāmah-i Tansar ba-Gushnasp*, ed. Mujtabá Mīnuvī (Tahran: Shirkati Sihāmī Intisharāt-i Khawārizmī, 1354 [1975 CE]), 52.
68. See Hayrettin Yücesoy, *Messianic Beliefs and Imperial Politics in Medieval Islam* (Columbia: University of South Carolina Press, 2009), 107–8; K. A. C. Creswell, *Early Muslim Architecture* (Oxford: Oxford University Press, 1969), 65; Oleg Grabar, *The Formation of Islamic Art* (New Haven, CT: Yale University Press, 1973), 59; and Myriam Rosen-Ayalon, *The Early Islamic Monuments of al-Haram al-Sharīf: An Iconographic Study* (Jerusalem: Hebrew University, 1989), 67.
69. Grabar, *The Formation of Islamic Art*, 53–56, 58*ff*; *EI*(2), "Ḳubbat al-Sakhra" (Oleg Grabar).
70. Grabar, *The Formation of Islamic Art*, 61; Oleg Grabar with contribution by Muhammad al-Asad, Abeer Audeh, and Said Nusseibeh, *The Shape of the Holy: Early Islamic Jerusalem* (Princeton, NJ: Princeton University Press, 1996), 162.
71. Rosen-Ayalon, *The Early Islamic Monuments*, 59*ff*; Shemuel Tamari, *Iconotextual Studies in the Muslim Vision of Paradise* (Weisbaden: Harrasovitz, 1999), especially 63*ff*.
72. Grabar, *The Formation of Islamic Art*, 46–48; Garth Fowden, *Qusayr Amra: Art and Umayyad Elite in Late Antique Syria* (Berkeley: University of California Press, 2004), 197*ff*. Garth Fowden, *Empire to Commonwealth: Consequence of Monotheism in Late Antiquity* (Princeton, NJ: Princeton University Press, 1994), 138*ff*. For artistic work and Umayyad power, see Alain George and Andrew Marsham, eds., *Power, Patronage, and Memory in Early Islam: Perspectives on Umayyad Elites* (New York: Oxford University Press, 2018), 83–254; Nancy A. Khalek, *Damascus After the Muslim Conquest Text and Image in Early Islam* (New York: Oxford University Press, 2011), 85*ff*.
73. See Ralph S. Hattox, *Coffee and Coffeehouses: The Origins of a Social Beverage in the Medieval Near East* (Seattle: University of Washington Press, 1985); Özlem Çaykent and Derya Gürses Tarbuck, "Coffeehouse Sociability: Themes, Problems, and Directions," *JOS* 49 (2017): 223*ff*; Eminegül Karababa and Güliz Ger, "Early Modern Coffeehouse Culture and the Formation of the Consumer Subject," *JCR* 37 (2011): 737*ff*.
74. *EI*(2), "Shurṭa" (J. S. Nielsen).
75. See *EI*(2), "Ḥisba" (Claude Cahen, M. Talbi).
76. BL 84a–85a; A1 10a–12a, Iḥsān ʿAbbās, *ʿAbd al-Ḥamīd b. Yaḥyā al-Kātib wa mā Tabaqqā min Rasā'il-ihi wa Rasā'il Sālim Abī al-ʿAlā'* (henceforth AHR) (Amman: Dār al-Shurūq, 1988), 198*ff*.
77. See Hamilton Alexander Rosskeen Gibb, *Studies on the Civilization of Islam*, ed. Stanford J. Shaw and William R. Polk (Princeton, NJ: Princeton University Press, 1962), 63*ff*. Gibb makes a similar argument in the context of his discussion on the origins of the Shuʿūbiyya, which need not concern us here. As S. A. Bonebaker notes, too, he places too much stress on the Shuʿūbī character of early adab, which I wish to deemphasize. The interrelations among various sociocultural collectivities were much more complex than a binary, as I have tried to explain earlier.
78. http://arabiclexicon.hawramani.com/%d8%a7%d8%af%d8%a8/#55cbd4.
79. See Mhammed F. Ghazi, "Un groupe social: 'Les Raffines' (Zurafa)," *Studia Islamica* 11 (1959): 39*ff*; Lois A. Giffen, "Ẓarf," in *The Routledge Encyclopedia of Arabic Literature*, ed. Julie Scott Meisami (London: Routledge, 2010), 281–82; *EI*(2), "Ẓarīf" (J. Montgomery). The most recognized record of "ẓarf culture" from a tenth-century prism is al-Washshā's (d. ca. 936) *Kitāb al-Muwashshā*, also known as *al-Ẓarf wa al-Ẓurafā'*. Muḥammad b. Isḥāq Al-Washshā and Rudolf-Ernst Brünnow, *Kitāb al-Muwashshā of Abū al-Ṭayyib Muḥammad ibn Isḥāq al-Washshā* (Leiden: Brill, 1886).
80. AHR, especially 230*ff*, 281*ff*.

81. On *ʿilm* and ways of knowing and the distinction between religious and secular knowledge, see the learned study of Franz Rosenthal, *Knowledge Triumphant: The Concept of Knowledge in Medieval Islam* (Leiden: Brill, 2007). On the translation movement, see Dimitri Gutas, *Greek Thought, Arabic Culture: The Graeco-Arabic Translation Movement in Baghdad and Early ʿAbbasid Society (2nd–4th/5th–10th Centuries)* (New York: Routledge, 1998); Abdelhamid I. Sabra, "The Appropriation and Subsequent Naturalization of Greek Science in Medieval Islam: A Preliminary Statement," *History of Science* 25 (1987): 223–43; Hayrettin Yücesoy, "Translation as Self-Consciousness: The Abbasid Translation Movement, Ancient Sciences, and Antediluvian Wisdom (ca. 750–850)," *JWH* 20 (2009): 523–57.
82. *EI*[(3)], "Adab" (Hämeen-Anttila); *EI*[(3)], "Adab" (Enderwitz); *EI*[(2)], "Adab" (F. Gabrieli); S. A. Bonebaker, "Adab and the Concept of Belles-Lettres," in *The Cambridge History of Arabic Literature: Abbasid Belles Lettres*, ed. Julia Ashtiany et al. (Cambridge: Cambridge University Press, 1990), 16*ff*, 19*ff*, 22–23; Cooperson, "Ibn al-Muqaffaʿ," ALC, 158.
83. The subject is much broader, of course, than merely the distinction between *ʿilm* and adab. See Rosenthal, *Knowledge Triumphant*, especially 19–47; *EI*[(2)], "ʿIlm" (the editor).
84. In the "Epistle on the Caliph's Privy," Ibn al-Muqaffaʿ uses several forms of the root *ʿi-l-m* in the sense of knowing, to learn, to comprehend, persons of knowledge as opposed to of ignorance (*ʿulamā'* versus *juhhāl*), knowledge based on proof, mundane knowledge, God's prior knowledge, religious knowledge, and person with vast knowledge (*ʿallāma*). Only in one place does the word come with the definitive article, as in "the people of knowledge" (*ahl al-ʿilm*), in the context of justifying obedience in religious terms. In several places he uses *fiqh, tafaqquh, faqīh* ("to discern," "to have insight into") to signify religious knowledge.
85. Ibn al-Muqaffaʿ, *Al-Adab al-Kabīr*, 83.
86. Abū Ḥāmid Muḥammad b. Muḥammad al-Ghazālī, *Iḥyā' ʿUlūm al-Dīn* (Beirut: Dār al-Jīl, 1992), 2 (Book of Knowledge, Section 2), http://www.alwaraq.net/Core/AlwaraqSrv/bookpage?book=1&session=ABBBVFAGFGFHAAWER&fkey=2&page=1&option=1. The fascinating debate about the use and meaning of "ilim" versus "bilim" in modern Turkey may be cited as another example of signification related to distinct moral and political positions in the public space.
87. For various uses of words to signify "this world" and "the next," time, and temporality, see BL 70a, 70b, 72b; A1 203a, 205a; A2 177a, 172a, 179a; DMK1 182a, 183ab, 184a, 188a, 189b; SJ 3: 31, 33, 40–41; KAR 118, 127; PC 19, 23, 45, 49, 53. Al-ʿAnbarī makes the distinction more precise and explicit to explain the importance of the frontiers in securing benefits and welfare for the community of believers: "so that they attain their benefits and welfare in their *dīn* and *dunyā*." WA, 101. For a treatment of the subject in various texts from different eras, see Rushain Abbasi, "Did Premodern Muslims Distinguish the Religious and Secular? The Dīn-Dunyā Binary in Medieval Islamic Thought," *JIS* 31 (2020): 185–225, https://doi.org/10.1093/jis/etz048. For a learned analysis of the theme concerning religion and the state, see Muḥammad ʿĀbid Al-Jābrī, *Al-Dīn wa al-Dawla wa Taṭbīq al-Sharīʿa* (Beirut: Markaz Dirāsāt al-Waḥda al-ʿArabiyya, 1996). Unfortunately, none of the studies address the conceptual and methodological confusion that the jargon "Islamic political thought" generates.
88. Ibn Ḥazm uses the word in a similar sense: "Then it becomes clear that all sciences are nothing but tools in the service of the knowledge, which is worthy of lifelong pursuit by a person seeking it because it guarantees salvation in the afterlife. That knowledge is the knowledge of the sacred law, *al-sharīʿa*, of Islam. It is a knowledge that is taken from none other than the owner of the shariʿa himself without the seeker having a worldly (*dunyawī*) goal of

attaining leadership or earning money." ʿAlī b. Aḥmad b. Ḥazm, *Rasāʾil Ibn Ḥazm al-Andalusī*, ed. Iḥsān ʿAbbās (Beirut: al-Muʾassasa al-ʿArabiyya li-al-Dirāsāt wa al-Nashr, 1981), 3: 30, http://www.alwaraq.net/Core/ExLib/booksearch?book=3085&option=1&offset=1&searchtext=2K/ZhtmK2YjZig==&fkey=1&RangeOp=1&WordForm=1&totalpages=1.

89. The term has been used to signify temporal duration, earthly time, being conditioned on circumstance. See http://arabiclexicon.hawramani.com/%d9%88%d9%82%d8%aa/#c2a9df, http://arabiclexicon.hawramani.com/%d9%88%d9%82%d8%aa/#215f31.
90. http://arabiclexicon.hawramani.com/%d8%af%d9%86%d9%88/.
91. Ibn al-Muqaffaʿ, *Al-Adab al-Kabīr*, 40. For an English translation of the text see Kaufmann, *Subjectivity and Medieval Arabic Adab*, 198 (with modification).
92. http://www.alwaraq.net/Core/SearchServlet/searchone?docid=91&searchtext=2KfZhNiq2K/ZitmG&option=1&offset=1&WordForm=1&exactpage=30&totalpages=1&AllOffset=1. Al-Ghazālī is keenly aware of the distinction, and he is clear about his own position: "As for what is desired (by traveling), it is either worldly (*dunyawī*) benefit, such as wealth and prestige, or religious (*dīnī*) gain. The religious is either knowledge or practice." Al-Ghazālī, *Iḥyāʾ ʿUlūm al-Dīn* (book 17 on the etiquette of travel), http://www.alwaraq.net/Core/SearchServlet/searchone?docid=1&searchtext=2K/ZhtmK2YjZig==&option=1&offset=1&WordForm=1&exactpage=586&totalpages=3&AllOffset=1.
93. Ibn al-Muqaffaʿ, *Al-Adab al-Kabīr*, 42; Kaufmann, *Subjectivity and Medieval Arabic Adab*, 199–200.
94. Abū al-Ḥasan ʿAlī b. Muḥammad b. Ḥabīb al-Baṣrī al-Māwardī, *Adab al-Dunyā wa al-Dīn* (Beirut: Dār al-Minhāj, 2013), 218. In another attributed treatise, al-Māwardī discusses the virtuous sultanic governance, "*adab al-salṭana*." See *al-Majmūʿa al-Muʿtabara min al-Rasāʾil wa al-Fawāʾid* in Esad Efendi, manuscript no. 3690, 41*ff*.
95. Muḥammad b. Manṣūr b. al-Ḥaddād, *al-Jawhar al-Nafīs fī Siyāsat al-Raʾīs*, ed. Riḍwān al-Sayyid (Mecca: Maktabat Niẓār al-Bāz, 1996), 118–19.
96. Al-Jāḥiẓ, *Rasāʾil*, 3: 187–209; ʿAmr b. Baḥr Al-Ǧāḥiẓ and William M. Hutchins, *Nine Essays of al-Ǧāḥiẓ* (New York: Peter Lang, 1989), 55–66.
97. Al-Jāḥiẓ, *Rasāʾil*, 2: 193–94; Ǧāḥiẓ and Hutchins, *Nine Essays*, 58. *Amthāl Buzurjmihr, ʿAhd Ardashīr, Adab of Ibn al-Muqaffaʿ, Kitāb Marwak, Kalīla wa Dimna, Siyāsat Ardashīr Bābākān, Tadbīr Anūshirwān, Istiqāmat al-Bilād li-Āl Sāsān.*
98. Al-Shurayḥ b. al-Ḥārith, an early judge (d. ca. between 691 and 718). *EI*(2), "Shurayḥ b. al-Ḥārith" (Bosworth).
99. Al-Ḥasan al-Baṣrī, a celebrated early ascetic, theologian, legal scholar, and exegete (d. 728).
100. ʿĀmir b. Sharaḥbīl al-Shaʿbī, legal scholar, *ḥadīth* transmitter (d. ca. between 721 and 728). *EI*(2), "Shaʿbī" (Juynboll).
101. Saʿīd b. Jubayr, legal scholar (d. 714).
102. Ibrāhīm b. Yazīd al-Nakhāʿī, legal scholar, theologian (d. ca. 717).
103. Al-Jāḥiẓ, *Rasāʾil*, 2: 194; Ǧāḥiẓ and Hutchins, *Nine Essays*, 58.
104. Persian sage and minister to the Sasanian king Khusrau I Anūshirvan (sixth century CE). See *EI*(2), "Buzurgmihr" (H. Massé).
105. Al-Jāḥiẓ, *Rasāʾil*, 2: 191–92; Ǧāḥiẓ and Hutchins, *Nine Essays*, 57.
106. Al-Jāḥiẓ, *Rasāʾil*, 2: 196–97; Ǧāḥiẓ and Hutchins, *Nine Essays*, 59.
107. Al-Jāḥiẓ, *Rasāʾil*, 2: 191–92, 192–93; Ǧāḥiẓ and Hutchins, *Nine Essays*, 58 (quotations with modification).
108. Elegantly stated by Skinner concerning Machiavelli. See Quentin Skinner, *Great Political Thinkers: Machiavelli* (Oxford: Oxford University Press, 1992), 2.

5. Deconfessionalizing the Caliph

1. Carl Schmitt, *Political Theology: Four Chapters on the Concept of Sovereignty*, trans. George Schwab (Chicago: University of Chicago Press, 2005), 5. "Sovereign is he who decides on the exception."
2. Q, 43: 51; 12: 43, 50, 54, 72.
3. Q, 2: 246.
4. Q, 2: 251.
5. Q, 5: 20.
6. Q, 27: 34.
7. See Hayrettin Yücesoy, "Islamic Political Theory," in *Medieval Islamic Civilization: An Encyclopedia*, ed. Yousef Meri (London: Routledge, 2006), 624; Asma Afsaruddin, "The 'Islamic State': Genealogy, Facts, and Myths," *JCS* 48 (2006): 161–62, 163.
8. See Patricia Crone, *God's Rule: Government and Islam* (New York: Columbia University Press, 2006), 33*ff*, 44*ff*.
9. BL 70a; PC 17.
10. BL *ānāhu*, which is a corruption.
11. A1 and A2 *mulkuhu* instead of *mulkahā*.
12. BL 70a; PC 17.
13. Iḥsān ʿAbbās, *ʿAbd al-Ḥamīd b. Yaḥyā al-Kātib wa mā Tabaqqā min Rasāʾilihi wa Rasāʾil Sālim Abī al-ʿAlāʾ*, ed. Iḥsan ʿAbbās (henceforth AHR), (Amman: Dār al-Shurūq, 1988), 281.
14. BL 70a; PC 17.
15. BL 70a, 71b; PC 23, 41.
16. Deborah Tor, "Sulṭān," in *The Princeton Encyclopedia of Islamic Political Thought*, ed. Gerhard Böwering, Patricia Crone, and Mahan Mirza (*PEIPT*) (Princeton, NJ: Princeton University Press, 2013), 532.
17. BL 70a, 71b; PC 23, 41.
18. For various uses of the word *ṣalāḥ*, see BL 70a, 70b, 72a, 72b, 73a–73b. It is used in the sense of being or bringing something and/or someone into a virtuous, proper, orderly, good, and desirable state. In one place, he seems to use the word *saʿāda* ("one of the most obvious marks of felicity") for the caliph al-Manṣūr in the context of being honored with the caliphate and thus having the virtue of not preoccupying himself with pride, vanity, riches, or seeking to satisfy a personal desire).
19. Tansar warns of the dangers of oppression and tyranny as the binary opposite of order. ʿAbdallāh b. al-Muqaffaʿ, *Nāmah-i Tansar ba-Gushnasp*, ed. Mujtabá Mīnuvī (Tehran: Shirkati Sihāmī Intisharāt-i Khawārizmī, 1354 [1975 CE]), 61*ff*.
20. The concept I am referring to here is the mundane use of the words *ṣulḥ*, *ṣalāḥ*, *iṣlāḥ*, *maṣlaḥa*, being whole, good, proper, well, incorrupt, righteous as opposed to vulgar, impetuous, corrupt, vile. I suppose the semiotic affinity of this concept to the Aristotelian "*saʿāda*," or virtue cannot be dismissed.
21. See Abū Nasr Alfarabi and Charles E. Butterworth, *The Political Writings: Selected Aphorisms and Other Texts* (Ithaca, NY: Cornell University Press, 2016); Abū Nasr Alfarabi and Charles E. Butterworth, *Alfārābī: The Political Writings, Volume II* (Ithaca, NY: Cornell University Press, 2015).
22. For a learned exposition of the notion of the sultanate in the Ottoman context see Hüseyin Yılmaz, *Caliphate Redefined: The Mystical Turn in Ottoman Political Thought* (Princeton, NJ: Princeton University Press, 2018), chap. 3.

23. AHR, 285. Translation from Wadad al-Qadi, "Identity Formation of the Bureaucracy of the Early Islamic State: ʿAbd al-Ḥamīd's 'Letter to the Secretaries,'" in *Mediterranean Identities in the Premodern Era: Entrepôts, Islands, Empires* (London: Routledge Taylor & Francis, 2016), 149–50, with modification. Al-Qadi approaches the passage as an illustration of the difference of expertise and knowledge between the scribe and the ruler, where the ruler comes to power without expertise, while the scribe works hard to cultivate skills but has no power, which skews their relationship. While correct, this explanation does not compute the ontological difference between the scribe and the ruler, which sets the terms of power relations.
24. BL 70a–70b, 71b, 72b; PC 23, 25, 29, 41.
25. BL 70b, 72b; PC 27, 55.
26. Jacques Derrida, *The Beast and the Sovereign* (Chicago: University of Chicago Press, 2011), 2: 45.
27. ʿAbdallāh Ibn al-Muqaffaʿ, *Kalīlah and Dimnah: Fables or Virtue and Vice*, ed. Michael Fishbein, trans. Michael Fishbein and James E. Montgomery (New York: New York University Press, 2021), 62*ff*.
28. ʿAbdallāh b. al-Muqaffaʿ, *Al-Adab al-Kabīr*, in *Rasā'il al-Bulaghā'*, ed. Muḥammad Kurd ʿAlī (Cairo: Maṭbaʿat Lajnat al-Ta'līf wa al-Tarjuma wa al-Nashr, 1946), 55.
29. Ibn al-Muqaffaʿ, *Al-Adab al-Kabīr*, 51; Kathryn Scott Kaufmann, *Subjectivity and Medieval Arabic Adab* (PhD diss., University of California, Berkeley, 1997), 205.
30. Ibn al-Muqaffaʿ, *Al-Adab al-Kabīr*, 54; Kaufmann, *Subjectivity and Medieval Arabic Adab*, 207.
31. Ibn al Muqaffaʿ, *Al Adab al Kabīr*, 49; Kaufmann, *Subjectivity and Medieval Arabic Adab*, 204; Ibn al-Muqaffaʿ, *Nāmah-i Tansar*, 52, warns about whimsical rule.
32. BL 72b; A1 205a; A2 178a; DKM1 189a; SJ 42; KAR 129; PC 51.
33. Ibn al-Muqaffaʿ uses "siyasa" only once, and *dabbara/tadbīr* multiple times in the "Epistle on the Caliph's Privy."
34. William E. Lane, *An Arabic-English Lexicon* (New York: Frederick Ungar, 1863), http://arabiclexicon.hawramani.com/william-edward-lane-arabic-english-lexicon/; *EI*(2), "Tadbīr" (W. Heffening [G. Endress]).
35. Q, 10: 31, 32: 5, 13: 2, 10: 3.
36. Q, 47: 24.
37. BL 70b; LIM, 94.
38. BL 70b–71a; A2 174a–174b; A1 199b–200a; DKM1 184b–185a; SJ 35–36; KAR 121–22; PC 29, 31.
39. BL 73b; A1 207b; A2 181a; DKM1 192b; SJ 67; KAR 134; PC 65; LIM, 124.
40. BL 72a; A1 203a–203b; A2 177a–177b; DMK1 188a; SJ 40–41; KAR 127; PC 45, 47.
41. For relationality and sovereignty see the insightful theorization of inter-imperiality by Laura Doyle, *Inter-Imperiality: The Long Dialectics of Power and Culture in Gendered Political Economy* (Durham, NC: Duke University Press, 2020), 3–4.
42. Lane, *An Arabic-English Lexicon*, http://arabiclexicon.hawramani.com/%d8%b3%d9%88%d8%b3/?book=50#7502e4; *EI*(2), "*Siyāsa*" (C.E. Bosworth). Fauzi M. Najjar, "*Siyāsa* in Islamic Political Philosophy," in *Islamic Theology and Philosophy: Studies in Honor of G. F. Hourani*, ed. Michael E. Marmura (Albany: SUNY Press, 1984), 92*ff*, 295*ff*; Ann K. S. Lambton, "Justice in the Medieval Persian Theory of Kingship," *SI* 17 (1962), 91*ff*. From historiographical perspective, Tarif Khalidi, *Arabic Historical Thought in the Classical Period* (Cambridge: Cambridge University Press, 1994), chap. 3, 83*ff*; Bernard Lewis, "*Siyāsa*," in *In Quest of an Islamic Humanism: Arabic and Islamic Studies in Memory of Mohamed Al-Nowaihi*, ed. Mohamed Al-Nowaihi and Arnold H. Green (Cairo: American University in Cairo Press, 1986), 3*ff*.
43. BL 72b; A1 204a; A2 178a; DKM1 189a; SJ 42; KAR 129; PC 51; LIM 112–13.

44. For various uses of the term see Lewis, "*Siyāsa*," 5*ff.* As a technique of self-governance, see Louise Marlow, *Counsel for Kings: Wisdom and Politics in Tenth-Century Iran: The Naṣīḥat al-Mulūk of Pseudo-Māwardī: Contexts and Themes*, 2 vols. (Edinburgh: Edinburgh University Press, 2016), 2: 73*ff.*
45. Maintaining power was a common topic in advice literature through the sixteenth century. See, for instance, the Ottoman Celalzade Koca Nişancı Mustafa (d. 1567), *Mevâhib ül-Hallâk fî Merâtib il-Ahlâk*, Süleymaniye-Fatih, catalogue no. 3521, 350a, where he notes that the stability of the reign of kings and the estates of sultans depends on comport and affection between the military and the subjects: "*padişahların sebat-ı saltanatları sultanların devam-ı devletleri sipah ile ra'iyyet ortasında muvafakat ve muhabbet olmağladır, gammazların gamzı sebebi ile ol muvafakat ve ittihad bozulur.*" I thank Hüseyin Yılmaz for sharing this reference.
46. Louis Althusser, "Ideology and Ideological State Apparatuses (Notes Towards an Investigation)," in *Lenin and Philosophy and Other Essays*, trans. Ben Brewster (New York: Monthly Review, 1971), 79*ff.*
47. BL 72b; DKM1 189a; A2 178ab; A1 204b; PC 51; LIM 112.
48. BL 72b; A1 205a; A2 179a; DKM1 189b–190a; PC 53; LIM 114. By "the Arabs" he refers to non-Qurashi Arabic speaking kinship groups, the Bedouins, the "tribal" Arabia, not so much what one considers a nation or even an ethnicity today.
49. BL 72b; A1 205a–205b; A2 179a; DKM1 189b–190a; PC 55; LIM 115–16.
50. See Jane Burbank and Frederick Cooper, *Empires in World History: Power and the Politics of Difference* (Princeton, NJ: Princeton University Press, 2011), 8*ff*, 16*ff*, 31*ff*, and other sections.
51. See Fred McGraw Donner, *The Early Islamic Conquests* (Princeton, NJ: Princeton University Press, 1981), 267*ff*; Hugh Kennedy, *The Great Arab Conquests: How the Spread of Islam Changed the World We Live in* (Philadelphia: De Capo, 2007), 34*ff*, 363*ff.*
52. See Kennedy, *The Great Arab Conquests*; Fred McGraw Donner, *The Expansion of the Early Islamic State* (Aldershot, UK: Ashgate/Variorum, 2008); Fred McGraw Donner, "Qur'ānicization of Religio-Political Discourse in the Umayyad Period," *Revue des mondes musulmans et de la Méditerranée* 129 (2011): 79–92.
53. See Fred McGraw Donner, *Muhammad and the Believers: At the Origins of Islam* (Cambridge, MA: Belknap Press of Harvard University, 2010), 57*ff*, 195*ff*; Donner, "Qur'ānicization of Religio-Political Discourse," 82–83*ff.*
54. For references to titles in correspondence see al-Ḥusayn b. Muḥammad Ibn al-Farrā', *Rusul al-Mulūk*, ed. Ṣalāḥ al-Dīn al-Munajjid (Beirut: Dār al-Kutub al-Jadīd, 1993); Maria Vaiou, *Diplomacy in the Early Islamic World* (London: I. B. Tauris, 2015); Donner, "Qur'ānicization of Religio-Political Discourse," 82–83.
55. BL 70b; PC 25.
56. BL 70b; A1 198b–199a; A2 17a; DKM1 183a; PC 25.
57. BL 70b; LIM 91–92.
58. BL 70b–71b; A1 200a–200b; A2 174b–175a; DKM1 185a–185b; PC 35.
59. BL 70b; PC 25.
60. In his *Al-Adab al-Kabīr*, he emphasizes the importance of diligence in taking administrative responsibilities and the supervision of administrators. See Ibn al-Muqaffaʿ, *Al-Adab al-Kabīr*, 47–48, 50–54, and other places. Diligence plays a key role in assuring success in Pseudo al-Māwardī as well. See Marlow, *Counsel for Kings*, I: especially chaps. 3, 4, 7, 8, II: especially chaps. 3, 4, 5.
61. BL 71b; PC 43.
62. BL 70b–71a.
63. BL 70b; LIM 94.

64. BL 70b–71a.
65. BL 70b–71a, 71b–72a; PC 43, 59.
66. Michel Foucault discusses this aspect of power as related to political discourses after Machiavelli. See Michel Foucault, "Governmentality," in *The Foucault Effect: Studies in Governmental Rationality, with Two Lectures by and an Interview with Michel Foucault*, ed. Graham Burchell, Colin Gordon, and Peter M. Miller (London: Harvester Wheatsheaf, 1991), 87–104.
67. *EI*(2), "Raʿiyya" (Bosworth).
68. BL 73b; PC 65.
69. ALC, 281. The theme of divine privilege of prophets and kings as ontologically distinguished classes from the rest of the humans would become a major point in later siyasa genre of all kinds. See, for instance, Niẓām al-Mulk, *The Book of Government or Rules for Kings: The Siyar al-Mulūk or Siyāsat Nāma*, ed. and trans. Hubert Darke (New Haven, CT: Yale University Press, 1960), 9: "In every age and time God (be He exalted) chooses one member of the human race and, having adorned and endowed him with kingly virtues, entrusts him with the interests of the world and the well-being of His servants; He charges that person to close the doors of corruption, confusion and discord, and He imparts to him such dignity and majesty in the eyes and hearts of men, that under his just rule they may live their lives in constant security and ever wish for his reign to continue." See also Abū Ḥāmid Muḥammad b. Muḥammad al-Ghazālī, *Ghazālī's Book of Counsel for Kings (Naṣīḥat Al-Mulūk)*, trans. F. R. C. Bagley (London: Oxford University Press, 1964), 45. Marlow elaborates on how the author of the *Counsel for Kings* articulates a similar view. Marlow, *Counsel for Kings*, I: 95*ff*.
70. BL 73b.
71. BL 70a; PC 17, 19.
72. BL 73b; LIM 124.
73. Hugh Kennedy, *The Prophet and the Age of the Caliphates: The Islamic Near East from the Sixth to the Eleventh Century* (London: Longman, 1986), 129.
74. A2 and BL *ʿirfān*, the other manuscripts give *ʿarafa*.
75. BL 70a; PC 17; LIM 85–86.
76. Al-Ṣāḥib b. ʿAbbād, *al-Muḥīṭ fī al-Lugha*, http://arabiclexicon.hawramani.com/%d9%86%d8%b9%d9%85/#14acd5.
77. See Aḥmad b. Fāris, *Muʿjam Maqāyīs al-Lugha*, ed. ʿAbd al-Salām Muḥammad Hārūn (Cairo: Dār al-Fikr, 1979). http://arabiclexicon.hawramani.com/%d9%86%d9%8e%d8%b9%d9%90%d9%85%d9%8e/#b05069.
78. For divine favor, see R. N. Frye, "The Charisma of Kingship in Ancient Iran," *Iranica Antiqua* 4 (1964): 36*ff*; Seyed Sadegh Haghighat, "Persian Mirrors for Princes: Pre-Islamic and Islamic Mirrors Compared," in *Global Medieval: Mirrors for Princes Reconsidered*, ed. Regula Forster and Neguin Yavari (Boston: Ilex Foundation, 2015), 88; Marlow, *Counsel for Kings*, I: 196*ff*, 202*ff*, 214*ff*; Mary Boyce, *A History of Zoroastrianism* (Leiden: Brill, 1975), 1: 66–68.
79. Quentin Skinner, *Great Political Thinkers: Machiavelli* (Oxford: Oxford University Press, 1992), 26*ff*; Louis Althusser, *Machiavelli and Us*, ed. Francois Matheron, trans. Gregory Elliot (London: Verso, 1999), 74*ff*; Louis Althusser, "Machiavelli's Solitude," in *Machiavelli and Us*, ed. Francois Matheron, trans. Gregory Elliot (London: Verso, 1999), 120, 121–22.
80. Boyce, *A History of Zoroastrianism*, 1: 66.
81. Boyce, *A History of Zoroastrianism*, 1: 67.
82. Nasser O. Rabbat, "The Ideological Significance of the *Dār al-ʿAdl* in the Medieval Islamic Orient," *IJMES* 27 (1995): 3–28.

83. See Patricia Crone and Martin Hinds, *God's Caliph: Religious Authority in the First Centuries of Islam* (Cambridge: Cambridge University Press, 1986), 4*ff*, 24*ff*; Andrew Marsham, "'God's Caliph' Revisited: Umayyad Political Thought in Its Late Antique Context," in *Power, Patronage, and Memory in Early Islam: Perspectives on Umayyad Elites*, ed. Alain George and Andrew Marsham (New York: Oxford University Press, 2018), 3*ff*, 10*ff*; Hayrettin Yücesoy, *Taṭawwur al-Fikr al-Siyāsī ʿinda Ahl al-Sunna: Fatrat al-Takwīn: Min Bidāyatihi ḥatta al-Thulth al-Awwal min al-Qarn al-Rābiʿ al-Hijrī* (Amman: Dār al-Bashīr, 1993), 61*ff*.
84. See Ibn al-Muqaffaʿ's discussion of religion and reason in the "Epistle on the Caliph's Privy," BL 71a. For a detailed discussion of the ruler's relations with religion and religious scholars in Pseudo-Māwardī's *Counsel for Kings*, see Marlow, *Counsel for Kings*, I: 143*ff*, 180*ff*, 202*ff*, 228*ff*.
85. See BL 70a, 71a.
86. BL 71b; PC 39.
87. DKM1: *yubtala*; BL, A1, A2: *yanīl*.
88. A1, A2: *intaqaẓa* instead of *intaqaṣa*.
89. BL 70a; PC 21; LIM 87.
90. BL 72b; PC 49; LIM 111. In Ibn al-Muqaffaʿ, *Nāmah-i Tansar*, 54, kings are given *iqbāl wa bakht* (success and good fortune).
91. For the text of "Yatīma," see BL 62a–62b; A1 176a–176b; KAR 109–110.
92. Although one may not be able to attribute the wording itself to Ibn al-Muqaffaʿ, one can assume the presence of the theme itself in the tales. For the notion of fortune in Ibn al-Muqaffaʿ's other writing, see Paule Charles-Dominique, "Le systeme ethhique d'Ibn al-Muqaffaʿ d'apres ses deux epitres dites al-saghir et al-kabir," *Arabica* 12 (1965): 47–50.
93. BL 70a; PC 17.
94. BL 70a; PC 17.
95. See Althusser, *Machiavelli and Us*, 18–19*ff*, 44, 57, 74–75; Neguin Yavari, *Advice for the Sultan: Prophetic Voices and Secular Politics in Medieval Islam* (Oxford: Oxford University Press, 2014), 7–16, 38, 43–44, 81; Neguin Yavari, "Secularity in the Premodern Islamic World," in *Companion of the Study of Secularity*, ed. The Humanities Center for Advanced Studies (HCAS), "Multiple Secularities: Beyond the West, Beyond Modernities" (Leipzig: Leipzig University, 2019), https://www.multiple-secularities.de/publications/companion/secularity-in-the-premodern-islamic-world/.
96. Althusser, *Machiavelli and Us*, 74–75.
97. BL 73a. Afsaruddin fittingly makes the note of how Ibn al-Muqaffaʿ uses the words *istiṣlāḥ* and *iṣlāḥ* in a political sense to signify public interest or utility. Asma Afsaruddin, "Maslahah as a Political Concept," in *Mirror for the Muslim Prince: Islam and the Theory of Statecraft*, ed. Mehrzad Boroujerdi (Syracuse, NY: Syracuse University Press, 2013), 16*ff*.
98. BL 70a–70b; PC 67*ff*. For the complex semantic range of the words in primary source dictionaries and in English, see http://arabiclexicon.hawramani.com/.
99. BL 73a.
100. BL 70a; A1 167a–167b; A2 172a, 182a–182b; SJ 31–32; KAR 118; PC 19; LIM 86–87.
101. Discrepancy in the spelling of "khabar." BL, A1 *bi al-khayra*; A2 *al-khibra*; DKM1 *al-khabar*.
102. BL 72a.
103. BL 70b
104. Different wording in the phrase, *fa-fī al-ilḥān lahu shahīd* (BL, DKM1) and *fa-fī al-līn lahu shahīd* (A1, A2), which I excluded here.
105. BL 70a; A1 168a; A2 172b–173a; DKM1 183a; SJ 32–33; KAR 119; PC 21; LIM 88–89.
106. BL 7b; PC 29.

107. BL 70a; A1 168a; A2 172b–173a; DKM1 183a; SJ 32–33; KAR 119; PC 23.
108. A1 197a; A2 171b; PC 17, 19; LIM 84; BL 70a; DKM1 182a; and what follows: "Surely, the Commander of the Faithful, may God protect him, combines with his knowledge, the merit of inquiry and readiness to listen to others . . . and he reinforces his opinion with evidence, which he takes as a measure to treat his subjects with the grace of inquiring into their affairs."
109. BL 70a–70b; PC 19.
110. For the notion of justice, see J. Sadan, "Community and Extra-Community as a Legal and Literary Problem: Strict Community Doctrines Versus Justice in Mediaeval Arabic Moral-Political Literature (Following A. K. S. Lambton's Studies on Persian Specula Regis)," *Israel Oriental Studies* 10 (1980): 102*ff*; Franz Rosenthal, "Political Justice and the Just Ruler," *Israel Oriental Studies* 10 (1980): 92*ff*; Majid Khadduri, *The Islamic Conception of Justice* (Baltimore, MD: John Hopkins University Press, 1984).
111. The word here is not clear, and there does not seem to be agreement on how one should read it. I prefer BL *al-qunūt*. A1 and A2 give *al-fuṭūr*, DMK1 has *al-ʿuyūb* and *al-quʿūd*.
112. BL 70a; A1 167a–167b; A2 172a; DKM1 182a–182b; SJ 31–32; KAR 118; PC 19; LIM 86–87. BL has the word *ḥazm* as *jazm*.
113. BL 70a; A1 168a; A2 172b–173a; DKM1 183a; SJ 32–33; KAR 119; PC 21; LIM 88–89. I left out the awkward parenthetical phrasing "in [showing] leniency he has witnesses" and "his [acts of] pardon testify to it."
114. BL 70a.
115. BL 70a,72b; PC 49.
116. BL 70a.
117. BL 70a–70b; PC 19.
118. Following BL *fa-mā* instead of *fī-mā* in DKM1.
119. BL 70a; A1 168a; A2 172b–173a; DKM1 183a; SJ 32–33; KAR 119; PC 23; LIM 88–89.
120. BL 70a; PC 17; LIM 84–85.
121. BL 70a; A1 168a; A2 172b–173a; DKM1 183a; SJ 32–33; KAR 119; PC 23; LIM 88–89.
122. Following DKM1 *yaṣluḥ*. Note that *lā* is erased with ink. BL, A1, and A2 have it *lā yaṣluḥ*, which is also possible, but this would alter the tone if not the broad meaning.
123. BL 70a; A1 168a; A2 172b–173a; DKM1 183a; SJ 32–33; KAR 119; PC 23.
124. For an extended and informed discussion of the supporters of free will and their opponents, see Josef Van Ess, *Theology and Society in the Second and Third Centuries of the Hijra: A History of Religious Thought in Early Islam*, trans. Gwendolin Goldbloom, 5 vols. (Leiden: Brill, 2017–2019), 1: 69*ff*, 433*ff*, 463*ff*, 2: 57*ff*, 23*ff*, 269*ff*, 316*ff*. See also Yücesoy, *Taṭawwur*, 88*ff*.
125. His mentor ʿAbd al-Ḥamīd, also had emphasized the necessity of obedience to the ruler in multiple letters against the opponents of the Umayyad caliphs. See AHR, 210*ff*, 214*ff*.
126. BL 72b; PC 49; LIM 111–12.

6. A Theory of Imperial Law

1. See Jürgen Habermas, "The Political: The Rational Meaning of a Questionable Inheritance of Political Theology," in *The Power of Religion in the Public Sphere*, ed. Judith Butler and Eduardo Mendieta (New York: Columbia University Press, 2011), 17–18.

2. For an overview of the emergence of Islamic law, see Wael B. Hallaq, *The Origins and Evolution of Islamic Law* (Cambridge: Cambridge University Press, 2011), 57*ff*; Ahmed El Shamsy, *The Canonization of Islamic Law: A Social and Intellectual History* (Cambridge: Cambridge University Press, 2015), 22*ff*; Josef Schacht, "Pre-Islamic Background and Early Development of Jurisprudence," in *The Formation of Islamic Law*, ed. Wael Hallaq (Burlington, VT: Ashgate Variorum, 2004), 29–57; Zafar Ishaq Ansari, "Islamic Juristic Terminology Before Shāfiʿī: A Symantic Analysis with Special Reference to Kufa," in *The Formation of Islamic Law*, ed. Wael Hallaq (Burlington, VT: Ashgate Variorum, 2004), 211–56.
3. Hallaq, *The Origins and Evolution of Islamic Law*, 57*ff*; Schacht, "Pre-Islamic Background," 29*ff*; Ansari, "Islamic Juristic Terminology," 211*ff*.
4. Aḥmad Amīn, *Ḍuḥā al-Islām* (Cairo: Maktabat al-Nahḍa, 1933), 209–11; Shelomo D. Goitein, "A Turning Point in the History of the Muslim State," *IC* 23 (1949): 128, 129, 130; Josef Schacht, *The Origins of the Muhammedan Jurisprudence* (Oxford: Oxford University Press, 1950), 95, 102–103; Josef Schacht, *Introduction to Islamic Law* (Oxford: Oxford University Press, 1982), 52–56; PC 9–10; LIM 54–55, 65, 66–67; J. D. Latham, "Ibn al-Muqaffaʿ and Early ʿAbbāsid Prose," in *The Cambridge History of Arabic Literature: Abbasid Belles Lettres*, ed. Julia Ashtiany et al. (Cambridge: Cambridge University Press, 1990), 68–69; Shaul Shaked, "From Iran to Islam: Notes on Some Themes in Transmission, 1. 'Religion and Sovereignty are Twins' in Ibn al-Muqaffaʿ's Theory of Government. 2. The Four Sages," *JSAI* 4 (1984): 37; Patricia Crone, *Slaves on Horses: The Evolution of the Islamic Polity* (Cambridge: Cambridge University Press, 2003), 69–70; Patricia Crone and Martin Hinds, *God's Caliph: Religious Authority in the First Centuries of Islam* (Cambridge: Cambridge University Press, 1986), 43*ff*, 92; Said A. Arjomand, "ʿAbdallāh Ibn al-Muqaffaʿ and the ʿAbbāsid Revolution," *IS* 27 (1994): 32–33; Muhammad Qasim Zaman, *Religion and Politics Under the Early ʿAbbāsids* (Leiden: Brill, 1997), 82–85; Muḥammad ʿĀbid Al-Jābrī, *Al-ʿAql al-Siyāsī al-ʿArabī: Muḥaddātuhu wa Tajalliyātuhu* (Beirut: Markaz Dirāsāt al-Waḥda al-ʿArabiyya, 1990), 348*ff*; Hallaq, *The Origins and Evolution of Islamic Law*, 57*ff*; István T. Kristó-Nagy, *La Pensée d'Ibn al-Muqaffaʿ: Un Agent Double dans le Monde Persan et Arabe* (Paris: Editions de Paris, 2013), 213*ff*; Istvan Kristó-Nagy, "Reason, Religion, and Power in Ibn al-Muqaffaʿ," *Acta Orientalia Academiae Scientiarum Hungaricae* 62 (2009): 285*ff*; Anthony Black, *The History of Islamic Political Thought: From the Prophet to the Present* (New York: Routledge, 2001), 22–24; Joseph E. Lowry, "The First Islamic Legal Theory: Ibn Al-Muqaffaʿ on Interpretation, Authority, and the Structure of the Law," *JAOS* 128 (2008): 25*ff*; Najm al-Din Yousefi, "Islam Without *Fuqahā'*: Ibn al-Muqaffaʿ and His Perso-Islamic Solution to the Caliphate's Crisis of Legitimacy (70–142 AH/690–760 CE)," *IS* (2017): 10–11, 18–19, 22. Muhammad Khalid Masud, "The Doctrine of the *Siyāsa* in Islamic Law," *Recht van de Islam* 18 (2001): 1–29, probes the distinction between *siyāsa* and *sharīʿa* with respect to the administration of law.
5. This terminology is a token of the colonial language in the study of the Other, which has created its own reality. For an argument for a "Christian Society," see Thomas Stearns Eliot, *Christianity and Culture: The Idea of a Christian Society and Notes Towards the Definition of Culture* (New York: Harcourt Brace Jovanovich, 1968). The contrast is stark here: while almost no one takes seriously such a suggestion as a blanket definition of "European civilization," there has been almost no objection to using its counterpart, "Islamic society," for larger regions and groups of people in the world until recently.
6. Neguin Yavari, *Advice for the Sultan: Prophetic Voices and Secular Politics in Medieval Islam* (Oxford: Oxford University Press, 2014), 41–44, where she makes a brief but insightful remark on Ibn al-Muqaffaʿ's discourse on religion. She describes Ibn al-Muqaffaʿ as an early strong voice who

proposes nothing short of "domestication of religion" and "subordination of religion to kingship." This is a point that I find perceptive, but it is only an assertion made in passing regarding Ibn al-Muqaffaʿ's legal proposal to the caliph al-Manṣūr.

7. The "verse of obedience," 4: 59, reads as follows: "You who believe, obey God and the Messenger, and those in authority among you. If you are in dispute over any matter, refer it to God and the Messenger, if you truly believe in God and the Last Day: that is better and fairer in the end" (Abdel Haleem). In its phrased form, the statement is also attributed to the Prophet Muhammad in multiple *ḥadīth* sources.
8. BL 70b supplies *ghayr*, "other than," which is omitted in the other manuscripts. See Kurd ʿAlī (adds *ghayr*), 120; SJ 34; PC 27 (adds *ghayr*).
9. There is much discrepancy in the structure of the paragraph in the available manuscript versions. BL and A2 miss a line and confuse sentences. DKM1 offers a more coherent wording. See also SJ 34; KAR 120–21; PC 27–28; LIM 92–93.
10. Following the wording in the margin of DKM1 183b–184a in using *al-shayṭān* (the devil) rather than *al-sulṭān* (ruler), which makes better sense in this context.
11. Following DKM1 *li-kay*.
12. Following BL, A1, A2 *tahjīn*.
13. Following BL, A1 *al-faẓīʿ*.
14. BL 70b; A2 173b–174a; A1 199a; DKM1 183b–184a; SJ 34; KAR 120–21; PC 27–28; LIM 92–93.
15. In most cases, the reference in, for instance, "obedience to God" is to the cumulative divine message, which is inclusive of, but not reducible to, the qur'anic text alone. It may include the scripture and the agreed-on traditions or practices that became commonplace by his time. Ibn al-Muqaffaʿ uses "the book" when he refers to the scripture, although some of his references to the law, such as in his statement on "firm divine obligations and legal sanctions," may still suggest what is articulated in the qur'anic text rather than the broader tradition.
16. *Taskhīfihim*, following Kurd ʿAlī. The spelling in each version makes little sense otherwise.
17. Pellat reads *abhamūhu*. All versions and Kurd ʿAlī and Ṣafwat have *abhamū*, which I also prefer.
18. DKM1 correction on the manuscript, *bi-annahu*.
19. BL has *muwādaʿatihi*, "taking leave from," which I follow. The rest have *mukhādaʿatihi*, "deceiving."
20. Awkward phrasing in all versions: *wa al-akhdh li-al-muslimīn wa al-iʿṭāʾi ʿalayhim*, "taking for Muslims and giving out for/on behalf of them." Kurd ʿAlī renders it *ʿanhum* to improve phrasing, although the propositions *li* and *ʿalā* do go together.
21. BL 70b; A2 174a; A1 199b; DKM1 184a–184b; SJ 34–35; KAR 121; PC 27, 29; LIM 93–95.
22. Lowry assesses Ibn al-Muqaffaʿ's suggestion from the perspective of legal epistemology and points out that the scribe's primary intervention was that he distinguished what was interpretable in the scripture from what was not, which made a pioneering contribution to legal epistemology and legal interpretation before al-Shāfiʿī. See Lowry, "The First Islamic Legal Theory," 28*ff*. On Islamic criminal law and divine legislation, see Intisar A. Rabb, *Doubt in Islamic Law: A History of Legal Maxims, Interpretation, and Islamic Criminal Law* (Cambridge: Cambridge University Press, 2017), especially 29*ff*; El Shamsy, *The Canonization of Islamic Law*, 31–34.
23. For a mirror for princes' perspective on the administration of justice, see Louise Marlow, "Justice, Judges, and Law in Three Arabic Mirrors for Princes, 8th–11th Centuries," in *Justice and Leadership in Early Islamic Courts*, ed. Intisar A. Rabb and Abigail Krasner Balbale (Cambridge, MA: Harvard University Press, 2017), 109*ff*.
24. Compare with Andras Hamori, *PEIPT*, 232–33; Yavari, *Advice for the Sultan*, 45*ff*, where the role of reason in political practice is discussed in the context of *Kalīla and Dimna*; Black, *The History of Islamic Political Thought*, 23–24; Crone and Hinds, *God's Caliph*, 58*ff*, 85–88. For another

perspective on Ibn al-Muqaffaʿ's political uses of reason and religion, see Kristó-Nagy, "Reason, Religion and Power," 286*ff.*

25. BL 70b; A2 174a; A1 199b; DKM1 184b; SJ 35; KAR 121; PC 27, 29.
26. BL 72a; A1 203a–203b; A2 177a–177b; DKM1 188a; SJ 40–41; KAR 127; PC 45, 47; LIM 107–108.
27. For another evaluation, see Lowry, "The First Islamic Legal Theory," 25*ff.* Yousefi, "Islam Without *Fuqahā*'," 9*ff.* To my knowledge, the only involved analysis of Ibn al-Muqaffaʿ's legal proposal recently has appeared in Lowry's article, which underscores critical legal epistemological aspects of the "Epistle on the Caliph's Privy." While I see the value of Lowry's reasoning and argument concerning Ibn al-Muqaffaʿ's legal epistemology, he seems to assume that Ibn al-Muqaffaʿ referred to the scripture (the Qur'an) in his discussion of what could be interpreted and what could not, which may not be the case. Because Ibn al-Muqaffaʿ's language is not precise, and because he refers to "the book and the sunna" and *athar* rather than the "scripture" alone, I contend that Ibn al-Muqaffaʿ alludes to more than the mere scripture to include the higher category of revealed law (*dīn*) as a way of knowing, whose constitutive parts included the scripture (the Qur'an), prophetic practice (Sunna), and the trace of established precedent (*athar*), which he discusses in the same section.
28. BL 71a; A2 174b; A1 200a; DKM1 185a; SJ 36; KAR 122; PC 31; LIM 96.
29. All manuscript versions read *yaʿlamūnahā*. I follow the reading by Ṣafwat and Kurd ʿAlī, *yuʿmilūnahā*, which fits the meaning of the sentence better.
30. BL *lam yasaʿhu*; DKM1, A1, A2 *lam yakun yasaʿhu.*
31. A paraphrase of Q, 7: 43.
32. Reading *al-naṣīḥa bi-ẓahr al-ghayb.*
33. Awkward sentence, *minman huwa fī maʿna dhālika.* Ṣafwat and Kurd ʿAlī prefer *mimma*, which makes better sense.
34. BL 70b–71a; A2 174a–174b; A1 199b–200a; DKM1 184b–185a; SJ 35–36; KAR 121–22; PC 29, 31; LIM 95–96. Knowledge and prudent reasoning is a subject of frequent discussion in *Kalīla and Dimna*, where Buzurgmihr begins his advice on the value of human reason. See ʿAbdallāh Ibn al-Muqaffaʿ, *Kitāb Kalīlah wa-Dimnah*, ed. Michael Fishbein, trans. Michael Fishbein and James E. Montgomery (New York: New York University Press, 2021), 27, 29, 33, 49.
35. In his *Al-Adab al-Kabīr*, the term *dīn* signifies inner faculty or quality of a person, a person's spiritual self, honor and dignity, and moral position, revealed law, in addition to the generic sense "religion." For a succinct but a useful treatment of this subject, see Judith Josephson, "The Multicultural Background of the *Kitāb al-Adab al-Kabīr* by ʿAbdallāh Ibn al-Muqaffaʿ," in *Current Issues in the Analysis of Semitic Grammar and Lexicon I*, ed. Lutz Edzard and Jan Retsö (Wiesbaden: Harrassowitz Verlag, 2005), 181–83.
36. BL 71b–72a.
37. For various uses in context, see BL 70a–70b.
38. Hallaq, *The Origins and Evolution of Islamic Law*, 70–71, 75–76. See also Schacht, *Introduction to Islamic Law*, 29, 33; Crone and Hinds, *God's Caliph*, 58*ff.*
39. Hallaq, *The Origins and Evolution of Islamic Law*, 73; Schacht, *Introduction to Islamic Law*, 37–40; *EI*⁽²⁾, "Ra'y" (Jeanette Wakin and A. Zysow).
40. Hallaq, *The Origins and Evolution of Islamic Law*, 74–76; Schacht, *Introduction to Islamic Law*, 34–35, 40; El Shamsy, *The Canonization of Islamic Law*, 45*ff*, 52*ff.*
41. Grammatical error in the original is corrected by Ṣafwat and Kurd ʿAlī.
42. Following DKM1's marginal note of correction, which Ṣafwat and Kurd ʿAlī use.
43. BL 71b; A1 202a–202b; A2 176b; DKM1 187a; SJ 39; KAR 126; PC 41, 43; LIM 104–105. ʿAbdallāh b. al-Muqaffaʿ, *Nāmah-i Tansar ba-Gushnasp*, ed. Mujtabá Mīnuvī (Tehran: Shirkati Sihāmī

Intisharāt-i Khawārizmī, 1354 [1975 CE]), 67–68, defends the king of king's reform activities as justified because the ruler found the practice of revealed law in disarray, corrupt, and full of falsehood and heresy. For how Pseudo-Māwardī deals with a similar question, see Louise Marlow, *Counsel for Kings: Wisdom and Politics in Tenth-Century Iran: The Naṣīḥat al-Mulūk of Pseudo-Māwardī: Contexts and Themes*. 2 vols. (Edinburgh: Edinburgh University Press, 2016), I: 143*ff*, 151*ff*, 180*ff*.

44. "and his family" in BL 72a. The other versions drop this phrase.
45. BL 72a; A1 202b; A2 176b–177a; DKM1 187a–187b; SJ 39; KAR 126; PC 43; LIM 105–6.
46. For the debate on matters of interpretation and legislation, see Rabb, *Doubt in Islamic Law*, 30*ff*, especially 48*ff*; El Shamsy, *The Canonization of Islamic Law*, 71*ff*.
47. BL 72a adds *al-aqḍiya wa al-siyar wa al-sunan*; DKM1 *al-aqḍiya wa al-siyar*; A1, A2 *al-aqḍiya wa al-sunan*.
48. The original wording in DKM1, A1, A2, BL is *mukhtalifa*. However, Kurd ʿAlī's suggestion to read it as *al-mukhtaliṭa* makes better sense.
49. BL 72a; A1 202b–203a; A2 177a; DKM1 187b; SJ 40; KAR 126–27; PC 43, 45; LIM 106–7.
50. Ibn Khaldūn uses inspiration in this sense. "We, on the other hand, were inspired by God. He led us to a science whose truth we ruthlessly set forth." ʿAbd al-Raḥmān b. Muḥammad b. Khaldūn, *The Muqaddimah: An Introduction to History*, trans. Franz Rosenthal (London: Routledge and Kegan Paul, 1958), 1: 83.
51. Scribal omission of a sentence in the body of the text, which is added in the margin in DKM1.
52. DKM1, A1, A2, BL has it *ghayr*, which is a clear scribal error. Ṣafwat corrected it to *ʿayn*.
53. BL has different wording that disturbs the meaning.
54. Part of the sentence is in the margin in DKM1.
55. I follow the wording in DKM1: "do I tell?"
56. BL 72a; A1 203a–203b; A2 177a–177b; DKM1 188a; SJ 40–41; KAR 127; PC 45, 47; LIM 107–108.
57. See Hallaq, *The Origins and Evolution of Islamic Law*, 114–15.
58. Habermas, "The Political," 17–19.
59. Abū Muḥammad ʿAbdallāh b. Muslim b. Qutayba, *Al-Maʿārif*, ed. Tharwat ʿUkkāsha (Cairo: Dār al-Maʿārif, 1981), 384; ʿAbdallāh b. Muslim b. Qutayba, *Al-Imāma* wa al-*Siyāsa*, ed. ʿAlī Shayrī (Beirut: Dār al-Aḍwā', 1990), 2: 193, 201–202. For a brief discussion, see Crone and Hinds, *God's Caliph*, 86–87.
60. BL 70b–71a; A2 174a–174b; A1 199b–200a; DKM1 184b–185a; SJ 35–36; KAR 121–22; PC 29, 31; LIM 95–96.
61. Ibn al-Muqaffaʿ, *Nāmah-i Tansar*, 55–56, includes a remarkable discussion about reforming existing laws and the revealed law to suit current circumstances.

7. Territorial Consciousness

1. See Hugh Kennedy, *The Armies of the Caliphs: Military and Society in the Early Islamic State* (London: Routledge, 2001), 97–98, where he estimates some 100,000 salaried troops were maintained by the Abbasids at the time of the rebellion of Muḥammad the Pure Soul and his brother Ibrāhīm in 762.
2. Kennedy, *The Armies of the Caliphs*, 78–88, offers a brief informative discussion of military pensions and salaries in the early Abbasid period.

3. BL 70b; DKM1 183ab–184a; PC 23; SJ 3: 33; LIM 90. In BL "shadow," ẓill; the rest "humility," *dhull.*
4. All manuscripts, *al-yawm*, "today," "at present." KAR *al-qawm*, "the people," "group," "community."
5. All manuscripts, *ikhtilāṭ*, KAR *akhlāṭ*.
6. Correcting their hands, opinion, and speech (*aydīhim, ra'yahum, kalāmahum*).
7. BL 70b; DKM1 183ab–184a; PC 23, 25; SJ 3: 33; LIM 90. He uses the same metaphor in ʿAbdallāh b. al-Muqaffaʿ, "*Al-Adab al-Kabīr*," in *Rasā'il al-Bulaghā'*, ed. Muḥammad Kurd ʿAlī (Cairo: Maṭbaʿat Lajnat al-Ta'līf wa al-Tarjuma wa al-Nashr, 1946), 51. S. Goitein considers Ibn al-Muqaffaʿ's discussion of the army as an attempt to create a religious bond between the Abbasids and the military. S. Goitein, "A Turning Point in the History of the Muslim State," *IC* 23 (1949): 122*ff.*
8. Patricia Crone counts them as "religious disputants and propagandists" among the "theologians" used by the Abbasids. See Patricia Crone, *Slaves on Horses: The Evolution of the Islamic Polity* (Cambridge: Cambridge University Press, 2003), 64. J. D. Latham prefers "religious instructors." See J. D. Latham, "Ibn al-Muqaffaʿ and Early ʿAbbāsid Prose," in *The Cambridge History of Arabic Literature: Abbasid Belles Lettres*, ed. Julia Ashstiany et al. (Cambridge: Cambridge University Press, 1990), 67. While this group of people were opinionated Abbasid enthusiasts and propagandists, they were by no means theologians or instructors.
9. Following BL and Kurd ʿAlī's reading (*fī-mā ya'mur al-āmir wa yazʿam al-zāʿim*). The wording in A1, A2 is slightly different but still possible grammatically.
10. Muslim worshippers turn their faces toward the Kaʿba when performing their daily ritual prayer, which is called the *qibla* (from "to face," "to turn in the direction of").
11. DKM1 184a; BL 70b; PC 25; SJ 3: 33–34; LIM 91–92.
12. "Listened to" added later in DKM1, "accepted by" in BL, blank (with annotation, "this is in the original") in A1 and A2.
13. Elton L. Daniel, *The Political and Social History of Khurāsān Under ʿAbbāsid Rule, 747–820* (Minneapolis, MN: Bibliotheca Islamica, 1979), 105. For what follows, see also Hayrettin Yücesoy, *Messianic Beliefs and Imperial Politics in Medieval Islam* (Columbia: University of South Carolina Press, 2009), 22*ff.*
14. Abū Ḥasan ʿAlī b. al-Ḥusayn al-Ashʿarī, *Maqālāt al-Islamiyyīn*, ed. Helmut Ritter (Istanbul: Istanbul Darülfünun, Devlet Matbaası, 1927), 1: 20; ʿAbdallāh b. Muḥammad al-Nāshī al-Akbar and Josef Van Ess, *Frühe muʿtazilitische Häresiographie: zwei Werke des Nāshī' al-Akbar (gest. 293 H.)* (Weisbaden and Beirut: In Kommission bei Franz Steiner Verlag, 1971), 32.
15. See *EI*(2), "Sunbadh" (Madelung).
16. *EI*(2), "Mukanna" (editor).
17. Al-Ashʿarī, *Maqālāt al-Islamiyyīn*, 1: 19.
18. Muḥammad b. Jarīr al-Ṭabarī, *Tārīkh al-Rusul wa al-Mulūk*, ed. Muḥammad Abū al-Faḍl Muḥammad Ibrāhīm (Cairo: Dār al-Maʿārif, 1968), 8: 505–8.
19. Aḥmad b. Yaḥyā b. al-Jābir al-Balādhurī, *Ansāb al-Ashrāf*, ed. S. D. F. Goitein (Jerusalem: Hebrew University, 1936), 3: 198.
20. DKM1 184a; BL 70b; PC 25; SJ 3: 33–34; LIM 91–92.
21. BL 71a; A2 175a; A1 200b; DKM1 185b–186a; PC 33; SJ 3: 36; LIM 98.
22. He uses *al-nās* ("people") here.
23. DKM1 184a; BL 70b; SJ 3: 33; PC 25; LIM 91.
24. Following DKM1.
25. A2 175a; A1 200b; DKM1 186a; PC 35; SJ 3: 36; LIM 98–99. Part of this statement is missing in BL 71a: *wa man akhadha bihimā ḥatta yaʿlamū anna maʿrūf amīr al-mu'minīn* ("and whoever has

followed them until they know that the approval of the Commander of the faithful"), which occurs some lines later in another version, is given here.

26. BL 71a–71b; A2 175a–175b; A1 201a; DKM1 186b; PC 37; SJ 3: 37.
27. BL 71a–71b; A2 175a–175b; A1 201a; DKM1 186b.
28. BL 71a; A2 174b–175a; A1 200b–201a; DKM1 185b; PC 33; SJ 3: 36; LIM 97–98.
29. *Kullu amrihim*, following Kurd ʿAlī; *kullu amr* in DKM1, A1, A2, BL.
30. *Naṣīḥatuhum wa ṭāʿatuhum*, following Kurd ʿAlī; *naṣīḥatuhu wa ṭāʿatuhu* in DKM1, BL, A1, A2.
31. The statement here is not clear. Only by approximation and interpretation can one render it a sound sentence with the meaning indicated here. BL, A1, A2: *fa-in juʿila baynahu wa bayna rabʿayhi/rafʿatihi amraḍathu al-ḥamiyya.*
32. Both ʿ*aṭā*' and *rizq* are common terms referring to compensation in kind or cash, be it ration, salary, or pension. Because their use in textual sources is not consistent (for instance, Ibn al-Muqaffaʿ's use is different from al-ʿAnbarī's), my rendering of these terms also differs in various texts.
33. Kennedy, *The Armies of the Caliphs*, 59*ff*, 71*ff*.
34. BL 71a; A1 175a; A2 200b; DKM1 186a; PC 35; SJ 3: 36; LIM 99–100.
35. BL misses most of the last two sentences here.
36. Following BL which makes better sense and complements the other versions with the addition of *amara bi-arzāqihim*.
37. Following DKM1 and Kurd ʿAlī.
38. BL 71a–71b; A2 175a–175b; A1 201a; DKM1 186a–186b; PC 35, 37; SJ 3: 37; LIM 100–102.
39. See Yassine Essid, *A Critique of the Origins of Islamic Economic Thought* (Leiden: Brill, 1995), 101.
40. For empires in world history and their broad characteristics, see Jane Burbank and Frederick Cooper, *Empires in World History: Power and the Politics of Difference* (Princeton, NJ: Princeton University Press, 2011), 1–23.
41. ʿAbd al-ʿAzīz Al-Dūrī, *Al-ʿAṣr al-ʿAbbāsī al-Awwal* (Beirut: Markaz Dirāsāt al-Waḥda al-ʿArabiyya, 2009), 19*ff*; Daniel, *The Political and Social History*, 19, 20; Hamilton Alexander Rosskeen Gibb, *Studies on the Civilization of Islam*, ed. Stanford J. Shaw and William R. Polk (Princeton, NJ: Princeton University Press, 1962), 34–46; Simon Gundelfinger and Peter Verkinderen, "The Governors of al-Shām and Fārs in the Early Islamic Empire—A Comparative Regional Perspective," in *Transregional and Regional Elites: Connecting the Early Islamic Empire*, ed. Hannah-Lena Hagemann and Stefan Heidemann (Berlin: de Gruyter, 2020), 275–80.
42. Philip Khuri Hitti, *History of the Arabs* (London: Macmillan and St. Martin's, 1970), 224*ff*; Paul Cobb, "The Empire in Syria, 705–763," in *The New Cambridge History of Islam*, ed. Chase F. Robinson (Cambridge: Cambridge University Press, 2011), 1: 244; *EI*(2), "Irāḳ" (D. Sourdel, H. Laoust); Gundelfinger and Verkinderen, "The Governors," 275–80.
43. Brian Ulrich, *Arabs in the Early Islamic Empire: Exploring Al-Azd Tribal Identity* (Edinburgh: Edinburgh University Press, 2019), 169–93; Daniel, *The Political and Social History*, 19.
44. Moshe Sharon, *Black Banners from the East* (Leiden: Brill, 1983), 57–58; Saleh Said Agha, "The Arab Population of Ḥurasan During the Umayyad Period: Some Demographic Computations," *Arabica* 46 (1999): 211–29.
45. Daniel, *The Political and Social History*, 22; Roberto Marín-Guzmán, "The ʿAbbāsid Revolution in Central Asia and Khurāsān: An Analytical Study of the Role of Taxation, Conversion, and Religious Groups in its Genesis," *JIS* 33 (1994): 227–52.
46. Daniel, *The Political and Social History*, 20–22; Rafia Riaz, "The Role of State in Regulating Migration: A Study of the Arab Migration to Iraq 632–750 CE," *JIS* 51 (2012): 423–44.

47. Sharon, *Black Banners*, 56.
48. Khalid Yahya Blankinship, "The Tribal Factor in the ʿAbbāsid Revolution: The Betrayal of the Imām Ibrāhīm b. Muḥammad," *JAOS* 108 (1988): 589–603.
49. Cobb, "The Empire in Syria," 1: 253.
50. Ulrich, *Arabs in the Early Islamic Empire*, 169*ff*; Agha, "The Arab Population of Ḫurasan," 211*ff*; Sharon, *Black Banners*, 20–21.
51. Sharon, *Black Banners*, 57–58.
52. Anonymous, *Akhbār al-Dawla al-ʿAbbāsiyya wa fīhi Akhbār al-ʿAbbās wa Wildihi*, ed. ʿAbd al-ʿAzīz al-Dūrī and A. J. al-Muṭṭalibī (Beirut: Dār al-Talīʿa, 1971), 204–205; Daniel, *The Political and Social History*, 30.
53. Even though the "two metropolises" are not spelled out, the occurrence of the phrase "al-Kufa and al-Hira" and the relative sociopolitical significance of both towns at the time make it more likely that Ibn al-Muqaffaʿ meant Kufa and Hira. The editors of the "Epistle on the Caliph's Privy" prefer Kufa and Basra, which is not my operating assumption, yet Basra and Kufa cannot be ruled out.
54. *Maʿiyyatuhu* in A2 and A1.
55. "Hāmmatuhum" in all manuscripts, compare to SJ; KAR; and Charles Pellat, *Ibn al-Muqaffaʿ mort vers 140/757, "Conseilleur" du calife* (Paris: G.-P. Maisonneuve et Larose, 1976), where it is rendered "ʿāmmatuhum."
56. BL 71b; A2 176a; A1 201b; DKM1 186b.
57. Break in text, awkward phrasing. BL 71b; A2 176; A1 201b; DKM1 186a. I follow Ṣafwat's editorial discretion here; see SJ 38.
58. Much confusion in text. Kurd ʿAlī and Ṣafwat disagree. Both readings and editorial additions seem pertinent. Kurd ʿAlī's reading fits my own reading here. See SJ 38; KAR 125.
59. Different lettering in each manuscript. *Ḥimāl/ḥamāl? Jimāl/Jamāl? Ḥalāl?* Kurd ʿAlī prefers *Khabāl*, Ṣafwat *Jimāl*. *Ḥimāl/Ḥamāl* appears to work better in my reading. It is the lettering of DKM1 186b.
60. BL 71b; A2 175a–175b; A1 201a; DKM1 186b–187a; PC 37, 39; LIM 102.
61. As Ibn Qutayba quotes in his *Kitāb Faḍl al-ʿArab*, an Abbasid Persian dignitary remarked to an Arab peer, "nobility is inherited and the noble from each people is a relative of the noble of any people." KAR 345.
62. See Cobb, "The Empire in Syria," 1: 244; Mattia Guidetti, "Sacred Topography in Medieval Syria and Its Roots Between the Umayyads and Late Antiquity," in *Umayyad Legacies: Medieval Memories from Syria to Spain*, ed. Antoine Borrut and Paul M. Cobb (Leiden: Brill, 2010), 339*ff*; Donald Whitcomb, "An Umayyad Legacy for the Early Islamic City: Fusṭāṭ, and the Experience of Egypt," in *Umayyad Legacies: Medieval Memories from Syria to Spain*, ed. Antoine Borrut and Paul M. Cobb (Leiden: Brill, 2010), 403*ff*.
63. BL 73a; A2 180a; A1 206b; DKM1 191b; SJ 46; KAR 132–33; PC 61; LIM 120.
64. BL 73a; A2 180a; A1 206b; DKM1 191b; SJ 46; KAR 132–33; PC 61; LIM 120.
65. BL 72a; A2 178a; A1 203b; DKM1 188b; SJ 41; KAR 128; PC 47.
66. Aḥmad b. Abī Yaʿqūb al-Yaʿqūbī, *Tārīkh al-Yaʿqūbī*, ed. M. T. Houtsama (Leiden: Brill, 1969), 2: 419–20; Hayrettin Yücesoy, *Taṭawwur al-Fikr al-Siyāsī ʿinda Ahl al-Sunna: Fatrat al-Takwīn: Min Bidāyatihi ḥatta al-Thulth al-Awwal min al-Qarn al-Rābiʿ al-Hijrī* (Amman: Dār al-Bashīr, 1993), 65, 73; Aḥmad b. Yaḥyā b. al-Jābir al-Balādhurī, *Ansāb al-Ashrāf*, III, ed. ʿAbd al-ʿAzīz al-Dūrī (Beirut and Wiesbaden: Franz Steiner Verlag, 1978), 3: 268; Al-Ṭabarī, *Tārīkh*, 8: 89–90; Nuʿaym b. Ḥammād al-Khuzāʿī, *Kitāb al-Fitan*, ed. Suhayl Zakkār (Beirut: Dār al-Fikr, 1993), 52, 64, 67,

247–48, 271; ʿAbdallāh b. Muḥammad b. Abī Shayba, *Kitāb al-Muṣannaf fī al-Aḥādīth wa al-Āthār*, ed. Kamāl Yūsuf al-Ḥūt (Beirut: Dār al-Tāj, 1989), 7: 513; Al-Balādhurī, *Ansāb*, 3: 47, 48; *EI*(2), "Mahdī" (Madelung).

67. The passage in BL 71a; A2 174b; A1 200a; DKM1 185a; SJ 36; KAR 122; PC 31; LIM 96, might be a scribal misplacement in the urtext, which the later copies repeated. I suspect that it belongs to the end of the passage several lines above.
68. BL 71a; A2 174b; A1 200a; DKM1 185a; SJ 36; KAR 122; PC 33; LIM 97.
69. Al-Dūrī, *Al-ʿĀṣr al-ʿAbbāsī al-Awwal*, 52, 78–79; Hitti, *History of the Arabs*, 288*ff*, 317*ff*; Hugh Kennedy, "Central Government and Provincial Elites in the Early ʿAbbāsid Caliphate," *BSOAS* 44 (1981): 26–38.
70. Al-Dūrī, *Al-ʿĀṣr al-ʿAbbāsī al-Awwal*, 52, 78–79; Hitti, *History of the Arabs*, 288*ff*, 317*ff*; Kennedy, "Central Government and Provincial Elites," 26–38.
71. Al-Yaʿqūbī, *Tārīkh*, 2: 419–20; Al-Balādhurī, *Ansāb*, 3: 140–43; Al-Ṭabarī, *Tārīkh*, 7: 425–28; Abū al-Ḥasan ʿAlī b. al-Ḥusayn al-Masʿūdī, *Murūj al-Dhahab wa Maʿādin al-Jawhar*, ed. Charles Barbier de Meynard, Abel Pavet de Courteille, and Charles Pellat (Paris: Société Asiatique, 1962), 3: 270; Abū Muḥammad Aḥmad b. Aʿtham al-Kūfī, *Kitāb al-Futūḥ*, ed. Muḥammad ʿAbd al-Muʿīd Khān et al. (Hyderabad: Osmania Oriental Publications Bureau, 1968–1975), 8: 358–59; Yücesoy, *Taṭawwur*, 72.
72. Cobb, "The Empire in Syria," 705–63, 264; Muhammad Qasim Zaman, *Religion and Politics Under the Early ʿAbbāsids* (Leiden: Brill, 1997), 33*ff*.
73. Al-Balādhurī, *Ansāb*, 3: 141–43; Al-Ṭabarī, *Tārīkh*, 7: 425–26; Ibn Aʿtham, *al-Futūḥ*, 8: 358–59; Yücesoy, *Taṭawwur*, 72, n136.
74. Hugh Kennedy, *The Prophet and the Age of the Caliphates: The Islamic Near East from the Sixth to the Eleventh Century* (London: Longman, 1986), 130.
75. On him and his movement, see Yazīd b. Muḥammad al-Azdī, *Tārīkh Mawsil*, ed. ʿAlī Ḥabība (Cairo: Lajnat al-Iḥyā' al-Turāth al-ʿArabī, 1967), 182; *EI*(2), "al-Mahdī" (Madelung); Farouk Omar, *The ʿAbbāsid Caliphate: 132/750–170/786* (Baghdad: n.p., 1969), 223*ff*; Abū al-Faraj ʿAlī b. Al-Ḥusayn Iṣfahānī, *Maqātil al-Ṭālibiyyīn*, ed. Kāẓim al-Muẓaffar (Najaf: Maktabat al-Ḥaydariyya, 1965), 162; for controversial views about him, 160–65, 166*ff*; Al-Ashʿarī, *Maqālāt al-Islāmiyyīn*, 1: 6–8, 21. See also Steven Wasserstrom, "The Moving Finger Writes: Mughīra b. Saʿīd's Islamic Gnosis and the Myths of its Rejection," *History of Religions* 25 (1985–1986): 1–29; William F. Tucker, "Rebels and Gnostics: Al-Mughīra ibn Saʿīd and the Mughīriyya," *Arabica* 22 (1975): 33–47; *EI*(2), "Mughīriyya" (Madelung). See also ʿAbd al-Qāhir b. Ṭāhir Al-Baghdādī, *Al-Farq bayna al-Firaq*, ed. Muḥammad ʿUthmān al-Khisht (Cairo: Maktabat Ibn Sīnā, 1988), 42, 58.
76. See ʿAbd al-ʿAzīz Al-Dūrī, "Al-Fikra al-Mahdīyya bayna al-Daʿwa al-ʿAbbāsīyya wa al-ʿAṣr al-ʿAbbāsī al-Awwal," in *Studia Arabica and Islamica Festschrift for Iḥsān ʿAbbās*, ed. Wadād al-Qāḍī (Beirut: American University of Beirut, 1981), 131–32; Jere L. Bacharach, "Laqab for a Future Caliph: The Case of the ʿAbbāsid Mahdī," *JAOS* 113 (1993): 271–74. See also Fārūq ʿUmar (Farouk Omar), *Buḥūth fī al-Tārīkh al-ʿAbbāsī* (Beirut-Baghdad: Dār al-Qalam and Maktabat al-Nahḍa, 1977), 213–14; *EI*(2), "al-Mahdī" (Madelung).
77. Ibn al-Muqaffaʿ supported al-Manṣūr's uncle ʿAbdallāh b. ʿAlī in his bid against the caliph, wrote a letter of good conduct on behalf of ʿAbdallāh b. ʿAlī, and now was pivoting, only few years after ʿAbdallāh b. ʿAlī's defeat, toward the caliph al-Manṣūr. His statement in the "Epistle on the Caliph's Privy" concerning the family and the sovereign might have been perceived as too much interference of a scribe in the ruling family's internal business and caliphal matters, exceeding the threshold of assertive advice.

78. BL 73a; PC 57; LIM 117–18.
79. BL 73a; LIM 117–18.
80. See Yücesoy, *Messianic Beliefs and Imperial Politics*, 91*ff* (and for further references).
81. BL 70a; PC 33.
82. Sheldon Pollock, "Axialism and Empire," in *Axial Civilizations and World History*, ed. J. P. Arnason, S. N. Eisenstadt, and B. Wittrock (Leiden: Brill, 2005): 397–450.
83. Cobb, "The Empire in Syria," 1: 242–43; Gundelfinger and Verkinderen, "The Governors," 261*ff*, 266*ff*.
84. BL 72a; A2 177b; A1 203b; DKM1 188b; SJ 41–42; KAR 128–29; PC 47; LIM 109–110. BL is missing parts of the sentence.
85. Awkward sentence that does not make much sense in context, as Kurd ʿAlī and Ṣafwat note. I follow their rendition (*wa lākin ukhidha fī amr ahl al-shām ʿalā al-qiṣaṣ*), but the extant manuscripts have the following identical phrasing: *wa laysa aḥad fī amr ahl al-silm ʿalā al-qiyās*.
86. BL 72a; A2 177b; A1 203b; DKM1 188b; SJ 41–42; KAR 128–29; PC 47; LIM 109–10.
87. BL 72a; A2 177b; A1 203b; DKM1 188b; SJ 41–42; KAR 128–29; PC 47; LIM 109–10.
88. BL 72a; A2 177b; A1 203b; DKM1 188b; SJ 41–42; KAR 128–29; PC 47; LIM 109.
89. BL 72a; A2 178a; A1 203b–204a; DKM1 188b–189a; SJ 41–42; KAR 128–29; PC 47–48; LIM 110–11.
90. BL 72a; A2 177b; A1 203b; DKM1 188b; SJ 41–42; KAR 128–29; PC 47; LIM 109.
91. BL 72a; A2 178a; A1 203b; DKM1 188b; SJ 41–42; KAR 128; PC 47; LIM 110.
92. BL 72a; A2 178a; A1 203b; DKM1 188b; SJ 41–42; KAR 128; PC 47; LIM 110.
93. BL 72a; A2 178a; A1 203b–204a; DKM1 188b–189a; SJ 41–42; KAR 128–29; PC 47–48; LIM 110–11.
94. Cobb, "The Empire in Syria," 1: 266–67.
95. BL 72a; SJ 42; KAR 129; PC 49–51; LIM 111–12. I have rendered "their uproot and sedation," suppression. For a learned discussion on "attachment to past empire" and "imperial affect" in the context of multiple instances in world history, see Laura Doyle, *Inter-Imperiality: The Long Dialectics of Power and Culture in Gendered Political Economy* (Durham, NC: Duke University Press, 2020), chaps. 4 and 5. See also Pradip Kumar Datta, "The Interlocking Worlds of the Anglo-Boer War in South Africa/India," *South African Historical Journal* 57 (2007): 35–59, doi:10.1080/02582470709464708.
96. On emotions and sociopolitical life, see Barbara H. Rosenwein, *Generations of Feeling: A History of Emotions, 600–1700* (Cambridge: Cambridge University Press, 2016), 3. I thank Laura Doyle for alerting me that an investment of this kind may be characterized as masculine. This is a matter I cannot indulge here but recognize it as a question for future work.
97. BL 72a; SJ 42; KAR 129; PC 49–51; LIM 111–12.
98. For the transformation of northern Mesopotamia into an Umayyad and early Abbasid province, see Chase F. Robinson, *Empire and Elites After the Muslim Conquest: The Transformation of Northern Mesopotamia* (New York: Cambridge University Press, 2000), especially chaps. 2, 3, 5, and 6. For the methods of control and administration in the Umayyad and early Abbasid countryside, see Alain Delattre, Marie Legendre, and Petra Sijpesteijn, eds., *Authority and Control in the Countryside: From Antiquity to Islam in the Mediterranean and Near East (Sixth–Tenth Century)* (Leiden: Brill, 2019).
99. Also known as *The Chronicle of Joshua the Stylite of Zuqnin*, *The Chronicle of Pseudo-Joshua the Stylite*, or *The Chronicle of Pseudo-Dionysius of Tel-Mahre*.
100. Amir Harrak, "Zuqnin, Chronicle of," in *Gorgias Encyclopedic Dictionary of the Syriac Heritage: Electronic Edition*, ed. Sebastian P. Brock, Aaron M. Butts, George A. Kiraz, and Lucas Van Rompay (Piscataway, NJ: Gorgias, 2011; online ed. Beth Mardutho, 2018), https://gedsh.bethmardutho

.org/Zuqnin-Chronicle-of. Parts 3 and 4 have been edited and translated by A. Harrak, *The Chronicle of Zuqnin, Parts III and IV: A.D. 488–775* (Toronto: Pontifical Institute of Mediaeval Studies, 1999).

101. The Syriac designation is Tayyoye, Tayy people, in reference perhaps to the Tayy tribe.
102. Amir Harrak, *The Chronicle of Zuqnin* (Toronto: Pontifical Institute for Medieval Studies, 2000), 174, 178–80.
103. Harrak, *The Chronicle of Zuqnin*, 179–80.
104. Harrak, *The Chronicle of Zuqnin*, 180.
105. Harrak, *The Chronicle of Zuqnin*, 239. See also Amir Harrak, "The Jazirah During the Islamic Period," in *Annual Symposium of the Canadian Society for Mesopotamian Studies*, ed. Michel Fortin, *Bulletin of the Canadian Society for Mesopotamian Studies* 36 (2001): 2: 227–33.
106. Harrak, *The Chronicle of Zuqnin*, 241.
107. Harrak, *The Chronicle of Zuqnin*, 257.
108. Harrak, *The Chronicle of Zuqnin*, 254–55.
109. ʿAbd al-ʿAziz Al-Dūrī, *Early Islamic Institutions Administration and Taxation from the Caliphate to the Umayyads and Abbasids* (London: I. B. Tauris, 2011), 116; Harrak, "The Jazirah During the Islamic Period," 229*ff.*
110. Harrak, *The Chronicle of Zuqnin*, 292–93.
111. Harrak, *The Chronicle of Zuqnin*, 232, 259–61.
112. Harrak, *The Chronicle of Zuqnin*, 239, 245, 259.
113. Harrak, *The Chronicle of Zuqnin*, 255.
114. Harrak, *The Chronicle of Zuqnin*, 247, 256–57.
115. Harrak, *The Chronicle of Zuqnin*, 236.
116. Harrak, *The Chronicle of Zuqnin*, 193, 219–20, 222.
117. See Yücesoy, *Messianic Beliefs and Imperial Politics*, 74*ff.*
118. See Cobb, "The Empire in Syria," 1: 267–68.
119. For the conquest of North Africa and the Iberan Peninsula, see Walter Emil Kaegi, *Muslim Expansion and Byzantine Collapse in North Africa* (Cambridge: Cambridge University Press, 2015), 200*ff*; Hugh Kennedy, *Muslim Spain and Portugal: A Political History of Al-Andalus* (New York: Routledge, 2016), 3*ff.*
120. Al-Dūrī, *Al-Aṣr al-ʿAbbāsī al-Awwal*, 74–75; Roger Collins, *The Arab Conquest of Spain: 710-797* (Oxford: Blackwell, 2012), 135*ff*; Kennedy, *Muslim Spain and Portugal*, 34–35.
121. See WA, 98, 99–100, 101, and 104 in the section on al-ʿAnbarī: "if the foreign merchants, *tujjār al-ḥarb*, visit the Muslims," also the words *bayḍa, ahl al-ḥarb, ḥarbī, arḍ, bilād*. In Yaʿqūb b. Ibrāhīm Abū Yūsuf, *Kitāb al-Kharāj* (Beirut: Dār al-Maʿrifa 1979), 21: lands of the Arabs and the lands of the foreigners, *arḍ al-ʿarab, arḍ al-ʿajam*, 22: (*dār al-islām, dār al-ḥarb*).
122. He also juxtaposes Hijaz (Mecca in particular) and Iraqi and Iranian territories. While both are given credit for their own legacies, Iraq and Iran are glorified as the "hearth of kingship." See Abū Ḥanīfa Aḥmad b. Dāwūd al-Dīnawarī, *Al-Akhbār al-Ṭiwāl*, ed. ʿAbd al-Munʿim ʿĀmir and Jamāl al-Dīn al-Shayyāl (Cairo: Dar Iḥyā al-Kutub al-ʿArabiyya, 1960), 1. He makes Alexander visit Mecca for the pilgrimage, 34. See Hayrettin Yücesoy, "Ancient Imperial Heritage and Islamic Universal Historiography: Al-Dīnawarī's Secular Perspective," *Journal of Global History* 2 (2007): 135–55.
123. Abū Isḥāq Ibrāhīm b. Muḥammad al-Fārisī al-Iṣṭakhrī, *Masālik al-Mamālik*, ed. M. J. De Goeje, Biblioteca Geographorum Arabicorum, Lugduni Batavorum (Leiden: Brill, 1927), 1, 3–4; *EI*$^{(2)}$, "Iḳlīm" (A. Miquel); Aziz Al-Azmeh, "Barbarians in Arab Eyes," *Past and Present* 134 (1992): 3*ff*;

Caroline Janssen, *Babil, the City of Witchcraft and Wine: The Name and Fame of Babylon in Medieval Arabic Geographical Texts*, Mesopotamian History and Environment, Memoirs (Ghent: University of Ghent, 1995), 114–15; Yücesoy, "Ancient Imperial Heritage and Islamic Universal Historiography," 149*ff*; J. T. Olsson, "The World in Arab Eyes: A Reassessment of the Climes in Medieval Islamic Scholarship," *BSOAS* 77 (2014): 487*ff*, doi:10.1017/S0041977X14000512. The narrator in the *Nāmah-i Tansar* offers a geopolitical division of the world; see ʿAbdallāh b. al-Muqaffaʿ, *Nāmah-i Tansar ba-Gushnasp*, ed. Mujtabá Mīnuvī (Tehran: Shirkati Sihāmī Intisharāt-i Khawārizmī, 1354 [1975 CE]), 89–90.

8. Reimagining the People of the Empire

1. *Tansar* outlines four "organs," at the head of which is the king as distinct from the rest. ʿAbdallāh b. al-Muqaffaʿ, *Nāmah-i Tansar ba-Gushnasp*, ed. Mujtabá Mīnuvī (Tehran: Shirkati Sihāmī Intisharāt-i Khawārizmī, 1354 [1975 CE]), 57: clergy, soldiers, scribes, craftspeople, who all must cooperate to ensure welfare. For the role of the learned elite in Ibn al-Muqaffaʿ's work, see István T. Kristó-Nagy, "Who Shall Educate Whom? The Official and the Sincere Views of Ibn al-Muqaffaʿ About Intellectual Hierarchy," in *Synoptikos: Mélanges offerts à Dominique Urvoy*, ed. Nicole Koulayan and Mansour Sayah (Toulouse: Presses Universitaires du Mirail, 2011), 279–93. For a detailed study of the notions of the elite and the common folk see Louise Marlow, *Counsel for Kings: Wisdom and Politics in Tenth-Century Iran: The Naṣīḥat al-Mulūk of Pseudo-Māwardī: Contexts and Themes*, 2 vols. (Edinburgh: Edinburgh University Press, 2016), I: 95*ff*, 129*ff*, II: 139*ff*, 197*ff*.
2. For earlier uses of the word, see Frederick Mathewson Denny, "The Meaning of 'Ummah' in the Qur'an," *History of Religions* 15 (1975): 34–70, https://doi.org/10.1086/462733. In the "Constitution of Medina," denoting a "nation" of diverse faith groups united under the authority of Muhammad, see ʿAbd al-Malik b. Hishām, *Al-Sīra al-Nabawiyya*, ed. ʿUmar ʿAbd al-Salām Tadmūrī (Beirut: Dār al-Kitāb al-ʿArabī, 1990), 2: 143–46. For further references see chap. 2 of this study.
3. BL 70a; A1 197a–197b; A2 172a; DKM1 182a–182b; SJ 31–32; KAR 118; PC 19; LIM 86–87.
4. BL 70a; A1 168a; A2 172b–173a; DKM1 183a; SJ 32–33; KAR 119; PC 23; LIM 88–89.
5. See for instance Abū al-Ḥasan ʿAlī b. al-Ḥusayn al-Masʿūdī, *Kitāb al-Tanbīh wa al-Ishrāf* (Leiden: Brill, 1893), 76–79. Al-Fārābī uses the word *umma* in the sense of a large "culture zone." See Abū Naṣr Muḥammad b. Muḥammad al-Fārābī and Richard Walzer, *al-Fārābī on the Perfect State: Mabādi' Ārā' Ahl al-Madīna al-Fāḍila* (Oxford: Clarendon, 1985), 228–31; Abū Naṣr Muḥammad b. Muḥammad al-Fārābī, *Kitāb Arā' Ahl al-Madīna al-Fāḍila*, ed. Albert Nasri Nadir (Beirut: Dār al-Mashriq, 1986), 117–19; Abū Naṣr Muḥammad b. Muḥammad al-Fārābī, *Kitāb al-Siyāsa al-Madaniyya al-Mulaqqab bi-Mabādi' al-Mawjūdāt*, ed. Fauzi M. Najjar (Beirut: Imprimerie Catholique, 1964), 69–70.
6. BL 73b; A1 207b; A2 181a; DKM1 192b; SJ 67; KAR 134; PC 65; LIM 124.
7. For another perspective on the role of the elite and the common folk in the "Epistle on the Caliph's Privy," see Muḥammad ʿĀbid al-Jābrī, *Al-ʿAql al-Siyāsī al-ʿArabī: Muḥaddātuhu wa Tajalliyātuhu* (Beirut: Markaz Dirāsāt al-Waḥda al-ʿArabiyya, 1990), 341*ff*. Also see Marlow, *Counsel for Kings*, II: 139*ff*, 197*ff*.
8. He devotes a chapter to "On Companionship of the Ruler" in his *Al-Adab al-Kabīr* to offer timeless wisdom on the subject to those who accompany the ruler. The chapter reads in its totality

like the protocol or etiquette of engagement with the ruler in his court. The intertextual and dialogic connection between the two texts is evident in the discourse. See ʿAbdallāh b. al-Muqaffaʿ, "*Al-Adab al-Kabīr*," in *Rasā'il al-Bulaghā'*, ed. Muḥammad Kurd ʿAlī (Cairo: Maṭbaʿat Lajnat al-Ta'līf wa al-Tarjuma wa al-Nashr, 1946), 54*ff.*

9. Ibn al-Muqaffaʿ, *Nāmah-i Tansar*, 46–47; Mary Boyce and Muḥammad b. al-Ḥasan b. Isfandiyār, *The Letter of Tansar* (Roma: Istituto Italiano per il Medio ed Estremo Oriente, 1968), 27–28.
10. BL 70a; A1 168a; A2 172b–173a; DKM1 183a; SJ 31; KAR 117; PC 17.
11. BL 72b; A1 205a; A2 178a; DKM1 189a; SJ 42; KAR 129; PC 51.
12. BL 72b; PC 51, 55–57.
13. BL 73a–73b; PC 61.
14. See Alasdair Macintyre, *A Short History of Ethics: A History of Moral Philosophy from the Homeric Age to the Twentieth Century* (Notre Dame, IN: University of Notre Dame Press, 2022), 57*ff.*
15. In *The Letter of Tansar*, wisdom in addition to knowledge seems to be an ideal form of advice. The king should associate with the people of wisdom and avoid the fool. See Ibn al-Muqaffaʿ, *Nāmah-i Tansar*, 51; Ibn Isfandiyār, *The Letter of Tansar*, 32–33.
16. The discrepancy in wording present here does not drastically alter the meaning in the sentence. I prefer BL, *fīmā yalṭufu Allāh lahu* (A1, A2, and DKM1 without the word Allāh) instead of *fīmā yultafu lahu*.
17. BL 70b; LIM 85, see also, 86, 87, 88; PC 17, 19. Corrupt text at the end of the sentence. BL: *taslīṭ al-fajara wa taslīṭ al-diyāt*, A1: *taslīṭ al-dhi'āb*, A2: *taslīṭ al-dhināb*, DKM1: *taslīṭ al-diyān* and correction in margin, *al-dhi'āb*. SJ: *taslīṭ al-dhi'āb*; KAR: *tasalluṭ al-diyān*; Pellat: *tasalluṭ al-diyān*. In A1 and A2: *khayr* instead of *khabar*.
18. Discrepancy of wording. BL, A1, A2, and DKM1 have it *tanāwuluhu bi al-khibra* (typo two dots under "ba" in BL and A2), DKM1 *tanāwuluhu bi al-khabar* or *khayr*. Ṣafwat reads it *tanāwuluhu bi al-khabar*. Kurd ʿAlī replaces the wording with *mubādaratihi bi al-khabar*. Ṣafwat's reading seems sufficiently correct to keep.
19. BL 70a; A1 167a–167b; A2 172a; DKM1 182a–182b; SJ 31–32; KAR 118; PC 19; LIM 86–87. BL has the word "*taʿālā*."
20. In A1: *Mukhayyaran*, instead of *mukhbiran*.
21. BL 70a; A1 167a–167b; A2 172a; DKM1 182a–182b; SJ 31–32; KAR 118; PC 19; LIM 86–87.
22. DMK1: *annahu mimmā*. Other versions show *a'inna mimmā* without the pronoun, which ruins the grammatical accuracy.
23. BL 70a; A1 167a–167b; A2 172a; DKM1 182a–182b; SJ 31–32; KAR 118; PC 19; LIM 86–87.
24. BL 72b; PC 51, 55–57; LIM 112–13, 116–17.
25. BL 73a; A1 207b; A2 181a; DKM1 192b; SJ 47; KAR 134; PC 65; LIM 122.
26. BL 73a; A1 207b; A2 181a; DKM1 192b; SJ 47; KAR 134; PC 65; LIM 122.
27. For an account of imperial protocol and etiquette, see Hilāl b. al-Muḥassin al-Ṣābī and Elie A. Salem, *Rusūm Dār al-Khilāfah: The Rules and Regulations of the ʿAbbasid Court* (Beirut: Lebanese Commission for the Translation of Great Works, 1977), 13*ff.*
28. See Aziz Al-Azmeh, *Muslim Kingship: Power and the Sacred in Muslim, Christian, and Pagan Polities* (New York: I. B. Tauris, 2001), 11*ff*, 17*ff*, 93*ff*, 131*ff*; Stefan Sperl, "Islamic Kingship and Arabic Panegyric Poetry in the Early 9th Century," *JAL* 8 (1977): 20–35.
29. BL 73b; A1 1207b; A2 181a; DKM1 192b; SJ 47; KAR 134; PC 65; LIM 124.
30. BL 73a; A1 207b; A2 181a; DKM1 192b; SJ 46–47; KAR 134; PC 65; LIM 122.
31. Following DKM1: *fa-taʿawhu*.
32. BL 71b; A2 176a; A1 201b; DKM1 186b; PC 39; LIM 102–3.

33. Grammatical discrepancy. I follow DKM1 and Kurd ʿAlī, *fīhā khilālan taqṭaʿu al-ra'y wa tumsik al-afwāh.*
34. Translation: shocking, jaw dropping. BL 70a; A1 167a–167b; A2 172a; DKM1 182a–182b; SJ 31–32; KAR 118; PC 19; LIM 87–88.
35. Following DKM1: *aw hammahu.*
36. BL differs in wording: *bi ṣarāmati ḥurmin aw ḥurmatin* instead of *bi-ṣarāmatin aw ḥazmin* in other versions.
37. Discrepancy in wording. It is not clear if the word is *nabth* or *nashab* or something else. I prefer *nabth*, following DKM1's marginal note.
38. BL 70a; A1 167a–167b; A2 172a; DKM1 182a–182b; SJ 31–32; KAR 118; PC 19; LIM 87–88. Following DMK1: *yujmaʿ aw yuqassam.*
39. Following DKM1: *tubtalā.*
40. BL 70a; A1 167a–167b; A2 172a; DKM1 182a–182b; SJ 31–32; KAR 118; PC 19; LIM 87–88.
41. Following DKM1.
42. BL 70a; A1 167a–167b; A2 172a; DKM1 182a–182b; SJ 31–32; KAR 118; PC 19; LIM 87–88.
43. The tone is eerily similar to the one in Ibn al-Muqaffaʿ's letter of safe conduct he wrote on behalf of his then patron ʿAbdallāh b. ʿAlī to al-Manṣūr. See Andrew Marsham and C. F. Robinson, "The Safe-Conduct for the ʿAbbāsid ʿAbd Allāh b. ʿAlī (d. 764)," *BSOAS* 2 (2007): 247*ff.*
44. BL 71b; A2 176a; A1 202a; DKM1 186b; PC 39; KAR 125; SJ 38; LIM 103.
45. BL 71b; A2 176a; A1 202a; DKM1 186b; PC 39; KAR 125; SJ 38; LIM 103.
46. BL 71b; A2 176a–176b; A1 202a; DKM1 186b–187a; PC 39, 40, 41; KAR 125–26; SJ 38–39; LIM 103–4.
47. He addresses the same concern with similar phrasing in his *Al-Adab al-Kabīr* as well. See Ibn al-Muqaffaʿ, *Al-Adab al-Kabīr*, 55–56.
48. BL 71b; A2 176a–176b; A1 202a; DKM1 186b–187a; PC 39, 40, 41; KAR 125–26; SJ 38–39; LIM 103–4.
49. BL 71b; A2 176a–176b; A1 202a; DKM1 186b–187a; PC 39, 40, 41; KAR 125–26; SJ 38–39; LIM 103–4.
50. BL 71b; A2 176a–176b; A1 202a; DKM1 186b–187a; PC 39, 40, 41; KAR 125–26; SJ 38–39; LIM 103–4.
51. BL 72b; A1 204a; A2 178a; DKM1 189a; SJ 42; KAR 129; PC 51.
52. See Muhammad Qasim Zaman, *Religion and Politics Under the Early ʿAbbāsids* (Leiden: Brill, 1997), 83.
53. S. Goitein, "A Turning Point in the History of the Muslim State," *IC* 23 (1949): 134, n27, sees the term "companions" within the boundaries of the canon established in Hellenic and Hellenistic thought for the royal *philos* ("companion," "friend"), which itself had originated in the ancient Middle East, such as the Hebrew "the friend of the king." See also Patricia Springborg, *Western Republicanism and the Oriental Prince* (Cambridge: Polity, 1992), 266–67.
54. I follow Ṣafwat's reading (*bahā'u finā'ihi*) which seems more compatible with the phrasing in the sentence and closer to the script in BL and DKM1.
55. Following A1, A2, BL, and DKM1 have it *alsinatuhu wa raʿiyyatuhu.*
56. BL 72b; A1 204a; A2 178a; DKM1 189a; SJ 42; KAR 129; PC 51; LIM 112.
57. Following BL *al-wuzarā'* instead of *al-wizāra* in DKM1, A1, and A2.
58. The four manuscripts have it *ṣuḥbat al-khalīṭ*. Kurd ʿAlī reads it *ṣuḥbat al-khalīfa*, which also works quite nicely in the sentence.
59. The word seems closer to "s-f-r" but could also be read "y-n-f-r," which I prefer, following Kurd ʿAlī.
60. BL 72b; A1 204a; A2 178a; DKM1 189a; SJ 42; KAR 129; PC 51; LIM 112–13.
61. BL 72b; LIM 114.
62. BL 72b; A1 204a; A2 178a; DKM1 189a; SJ 42; KAR 129; PC 51; LIM 113–14.

63. The verse is attributed to the Yemeni Jāhilī poet Ṣalā' b. ʿAmr b. Mālik, also known as al-Afwah al-ʿAwdī. Abū al-Ḥasan ʿAlī bin Muḥammad bin Ḥabīb al-Baṣrī al-Māwardī quotes the same verse in his *Al-Aḥkām al-Sulṭāniyya wa al-Wilāyāt al-Dīniyya*, ed. Aḥmad al-Mubārak al-Baghdādī (Kuwait: Maktabat Dār Ibn Qutayba, 1989), 3.
64. The last Umayyad governor of Khurasan (governorship, 738–748 CE), who is being denigrated here.
65. BL 72b; A1 204a; A2 178a; DKM1 189a; SJ 42; KAR 129; PC 51; LIM 113–14.
66. Ibn al-Muqaffaʿ, *Nāmah-i Tansar*, 64–65, discusses the critical importance of keeping prominent families, people of rank, and nobility satisfied.
67. BL 72b; LIM 114–15. Ibn al-Muqaffaʿ, *Nāmah-i Tansar*, 64–67, points out the importance of being careful when promoting and demoting servants to avoid upsetting the order.
68. BL 72b; LIM 115–16.
69. BL 72b; LIM 115–16.
70. BL 72b; LIM 115–16.
71. BL 72b; LIM 115–16.
72. BL 70b; A2 173b–174a; A1 199a; DKM1 183b–184a; SJ 34; KAR 120–21; PC 27–28.
73. BL 72b–173a; LIM 116–17.
74. In his *Al-Adab al-Kabīr* Ibn al-Muqaffaʿ discusses at some length the privy of the caliph to offer general counsel about their conduct, and here too he frames this group as a collectivity consisting of individuals from a cross-section of the nobility, skilled individuals, experts, and talented people. See Ibn al-Muqaffaʿ, *Al-Adab al-Kabīr*, 54*ff*.
75. BL 72b; A1 205a; A2 178a; DKM1 189a; SJ 42; KAR 129; PC 51.
76. BL 73a; A1 207b; A2 181a; DKM1 192b; SJ 47; KAR 133; PC 65; LIM 121–22.
77. BL 70a; A1 167a–167b; A2 172a; DKM1 182b; SJ 32; KAR 118; PC 21.
78. See Giorgio Agamben, *Sovereign Power and Bare Life* (Stanford, CA: Stanford University Press, 1998), 30*ff*.
79. BL 73b; A1 207b; A2 181a; DKM1 192b; SJ 47; KAR 133–34; PC 63; LIM 123.
80. BL 73b; A1 207b; A2 181a; DKM1 192b; SJ 47; KAR 133–34; PC 63; LIM 123.
81. BL 73a; A1 207b; A2 181a; DKM1 192b; SJ 47; KAR 133; PC 65; LIM 121–22.
82. BL 73a; A1 207b; A2 181a; DKM1 192b; SJ 47; KAR 133; PC 65; LIM 121–22.
83. BL 73a; A1 207b; A2 181a; DKM1 192b; SJ 47; KAR 133; PC 61–63; LIM 121–22.
84. BL 73b; A1 207b; A2 181a; DKM1 192b; SJ 47; KAR 133–34; PC 65; LIM 123.
85. See his discussion on the land tax: BL 70b–71a; PC 59.
86. For the Visigoth practices and developments, see Javier Martínez Jiménez, "The Rural Hinterland of the Visigoth Capitals of Toledo and Reccopolis, Between the Years 400–800 CE," in *Authority and Control in the Countryside*, ed. A. Delattre, M. Legendre, and P. Sijpesteijn (Leiden: Brill, 2018), 97–127, doi:https://doi.org/10.1163/9789004386549_005.
87. For *kharāj* and its historical development in various provinces, see ʿAbd al-ʿAzīz al-Dūrī, *Al-Nuẓum al-Islāmiyya* (Baghdad: Bayt al-Ḥikma, 1988), 68*f*; *EI*[(2)], "Kharāj" (C. Cahen).
88. Al-Dūrī, *Al-Nuẓum al-Islāmiyya*, 68*ff*, 82, 91*ff*; *EI*[(2)], "Kharāj" (C. Cahen).
89. The Protected People, *ahl al-dhimma*, were excluded from the community of believers by the payment of *jizya*, did not have equal protection in criminal justice, and were not entitled to *fay'*, *ghanīma*, and other payments like their Muslim counterparts. Legal scholars' discourse codified such practices as legal rules and regulations.
90. Muḥammad b. Jarīr al-Ṭabarī, *Kitāb Ikhtilāf al-Fuqahā'*, ed. Joseph Schacht (Leiden: Brill, 1933), 225; Al-Dūrī, *Al-Nuẓum*, 82, 101.

91. Ibn ʿAbd al-Ḥakam, *Futūḥ Miṣr wa Akhbāruha*, ed. Charles C. Torrey (Leiden: Brill, 1920), 90; Al-Dūrī, *Al-Nuẓum*, 101.
92. Goitein, "A Turning Point," 128–29.
93. BL 73a; A2 179b; A1 206a; DKM1 191a; PC 57, 59; LIM 118–19.
94. BL 73a; A2 179b; A1 206a; DKM1 191a; PC 57, 59; LIM 118–19.
95. BL 73a; A2 179b; A1 206a; DKM1 191a; PC 57, 59; LIM 118–19.
96. BL 73a; A2 179b; A1 206a; DKM1 191a; PC 57, 59; LIM 118–19.
97. BL 73a; A2 179b–180a; A1 206a; DKM1 191a; PC 59; LIM 119–20.
98. BL 73a; A2 179b–180a; A1 206a; DKM1 191a; PC 59; LIM 119–20.
99. BL 73a; A2 180a; A1 206b; DKM1 191a–191b; SJ 45–46; KAR 132; PC 60–61; LIM 120.
100. BL 73a; A2 180a; A1 206b; DKM1 191a–191b; SJ 45–46; KAR 132; PC 60–61; LIM 120.
101. Awkward sentence. I follow DKM1 and Kurd ʿAlī and Ṣafwat here. BL 71b; A2 176a; A1 201b; DKM1 186b; PC 39; LIM 102–3.
102. BL 73a; A1 207b; A2 181a; DKM1 192b; SJ 47; KAR 134; PC 65; LIM 123.

Conclusion: Releasing Siyasa from the Imamate

1. A cursory library catalogue search suggests that the work on the imamate/caliphate constitutes only about 30 percent of the total number of manuscripts on governance in the Turkish Manuscripts Directorate's collections. I suspect that the Egyptian National Library's collection would yield a similar count.

Bibliography

Primary Sources

Abū ʿUbayd al-Qāsim b. Sallām. *Kitāb Gharīb al-Ḥadīth*. Ed. Ḥasan M. M. Sharaf and ʿAbd al-Salām Hārūn. Cairo: al-Maṭābiʿ al-Amīriyya, 1984. http://arabiclexicon.hawramani.com/%d8%b4%d8%b9%d8%a8/#f25d71.

Abū Yūsuf, Ya'qūb b. Ibrāhīm. *Kitāb al-Kharāj*. Beirut: Dār al-Maʿrifa, 1979.

Abū Zurʿa al-Dimashqī, ʿAbd al-Raḥmān b. ʿAmr. *Tārīkh Abī Zurʿa al-Dimashqī*. Ed. Shukrallāh Niʿmat Allāh al-Qūjānī. n.p.: Majmaʿ al-Lugha al-ʿArabiyya bi-Dimashq, n.d.

Anonymous. *Akhbār al-Dawla al-ʿAbbāsiyya wa fīhi Akhbār al-ʿAbbās wa Wildihi*. Ed. ʿAbd al-ʿAzīz al-Dūrī and A. J. al-Muṭṭalibī. Beirut: Dār al-Talīʿa, 1971.

Al-Azdī, Yazīd b. Muḥammad, *Tārīkh Mawsil*. Ed. ʿAlī Ḥabība. Cairo: Lajnat al-Iḥyā' al-Turāth al-ʿArabī. 1967.

Al-Baghdādī, ʿAbd al-Qāhir b. Ṭāhir. *Al-Farq bayna al-Firaq*. Ed. Muḥammad ʿUthmān al-Khisht. Cairo: Maktabat Ibn Sīnā, 1988.

——. *Uṣūl al-Dīn*. Istanbul: Devlet Matbaası, 1928.

Al-Balādhurī, Aḥmad b. Yaḥyā b. al-Jābir. *Ansāb al-Ashrāf*. Ed. Al-Shaykh Muḥammad Bāqir al-Maḥmūdī. Beirut: Dār al-Taʿāruf li-al-Matbūʿāt, 1977.

——. *Ansāb al-Ashrāf*, III. Ed. ʿAbd al-ʿAzīz al-Dūrī. Beirut and Wiesbaden: Franz Steiner Verlag, 1978.

——. *Ansāb al-Ashrāf*. Ed. S. D. F. Goitein. Jerusalem: The Hebrew University, 1936.

——. *The Origins of the Islamic State: Being a Translation from the Arabic, Accompanied with Annotations, Geographic and Historic Notes of the Kitāb Futūḥ al-Buldān of al-Imām Abū-l ʿAbbās, Aḥmad Ibn Jābir al-Balādhurī*. Trans. Philip K. Hitti, Francis Clark Murgotten, and Michael Zwettler. New York: Columbia University Press, 1916.

Al-Bāqillānī, Abū Bakr b. al-Ṭayyib. *Al-Tamhīd fī al-Radd ʿala al-Mulḥida wa al-Muʿaṭṭila wa al-Rāfiḍa wa al-Khawārij wa al-Muʿtazila*. Ed. Maḥmūd Muḥammad al-Khuḍayrī and Muḥammad ʿAbd al-Hādī Abū Rayda. Cairo: Dār al-Fikr al-ʿArabī, 1947.

Al-Bukhārī, Muḥammad b. Ismāʿīl. *Saḥīḥ al-Bukhārī*. Ed. Khalīl Ma'mūn Shayḥa. Beirut: Dār al-Maʿrifa, 2010.

Al-Bustī, Ḥamad b. Muḥammad al-Khaṭabī. *Gharīb al-Ḥadīth*. Ed. ʿAbd al-Karīm Ibrāhīm al-Gharbāwī. Mecca: Jāmiʿat Umm al-Qurā, 1982.

Celalzade Koca Nişancı, Mustafa. *Mevâhib ül-Hallâk fi Merâtib il-Ahlâk*. Süleymaniye-Fatih. Manuscript access no. 3521.

Al-Dārimī, ʿAbdallāh b. ʿAbd al-Raḥmān. *Sunan al-Dārimī*. Ed. Muḥammad Aḥmad Dahmān. Beirut: Dār al-Kutub al-ʿIlmiyya, n.d.

Al-Dīnawarī, Abū Ḥanīfa Aḥmad b. Dāwūd. *Al-Akhbār al-Ṭiwāl*. Ed. ʿAbd al-Munʿim ʿĀmir and Jamāl al-Dīn al-Shayyāl. Cairo: Dar Iḥyā al-Kutub al-ʿArabiyya, 1960.

Al-Fārābī, Abū Naṣr Muḥammad b. Muḥammad. *Kitāb Arā' Ahl al-Madīna al-Fāḍila*. Ed. Albert Nasri Nadir, Beirut: Dār al-Mashriq, 1986.

——. *Kitāb al-Siyāsa al-Madaniyya al-Mulaqqab bi-Mabādi' al-Mawjūdāt*. Ed. Fauzi M. Najjar. Beirut: Imprimerie Catholique, 1964.

Al-Fārābī, Abū Naṣr Muḥammad b. Muḥammad, and Richard Walzer. *Al-Fārābī on the Perfect State: Mabādi' Ārā' Ahl al-Madīna al-Fāḍila*. Oxford: Clarendon, 1985.

Al-Farazdaq, Hammām b. Ghālib. *Diwān al-Farazdaq*. Beirut: Dār Ṣādir, 1970.

Al-Ghazālī, Abū Ḥāmid Muḥammad b. Muḥammad. *Iḥyā' ʿUlūm al-Dīn*. Beirut: Dār al-Jīl, 1992.

Al-Ghazālī, Abū Ḥāmid Muḥammad b. Muḥammad, and F. R. C. Bagley. *Ghazālī's Book of Counsel for Kings (Naṣīḥat Al-Mulūk)*. London: Oxford University Press, 1964.

Ibn ʿAbd Rabbih, Aḥmad b. Muḥammad. *Al-ʿIqd al-Farīd*. Ed. ʿAbd al-Majīd al-Tarḥīnī. Beirut: Dār al-Kutub al-ʿIlmiyya, 1983.

Ibn Abī Shayba, Abū Bakr ʿAbd Allāh b. Muḥammad. *Kitāb al-Muṣannaf fī al-Aḥādīth wa al-Āthār*. Ed. Kamāl Yūsuf al-Ḥūt. Beirut: Dār al-Tāj, 1989.

Ibn Abī Ṭāhir Ṭayfūr, Aḥmad. *Kitāb al-Manthūr wa al-Manẓūm*. Cairo al-Azhar Library. Manuscript access no. 464 adab.

——. *Kitāb al-Manthūr wa al-Manẓūm*. Cairo al-Azhar Library. Manuscript access no. 1752 adab.

——. *Kitāb al-Manthūr wa al-Manẓūm*. Dār al-Kutub al-Miṣriyya. Manuscript access no. 1860 adab.

——. *Kitāb al-Manthūr wa al-Manẓūm*. British Library. Manuscript access no. 18532.

Ibn Aʿtham al-Kūfī, Abū Muḥammad Aḥmad. *Kitāb al-Futūḥ*. Ed. Muḥammad ʿAbd al-Muʿīd Khān et al. Hyderabad: Osmania Oriental Publications Bureau, 1968–1975.

Ibn Fāris, Aḥmad. *Muʿjam Maqāyīs al-Lugha*. Ed. ʿAbd al-Salām Muḥammad Hārūn. Cairo: Dār al-Fikr, 1979.

Ibn al-Farrā', al-Ḥusayn b. Muḥammad. *Rusul al-Mulūk*. Ed. Ṣalāḥ al-Dīn al-Munajjid. Beirut: Dār al-Kutub al-Jadīd, 1993.

Ibn al-Ḥaddād, Muḥammad b. Manṣūr. *Al-Jawhar al-Nafīs fī Siyāsat al-Ra'īs*. Ed. Riḍwān al-Sayyid. Mecca: Maktabat Nizār al-Bāz, 1996.

Ibn Ḥazm, ʿAlī b. Aḥmad b. Saʿīd. *Rasā'il Ibn Ḥazm al-Andalusī*. Ed. Iḥsān ʿAbbās. Beirut: al-Mu'assasa al-ʿArabiyya li-al-Dirāsāt wa al-Nashr, 1981.

——. *Al-Faṣl fī al-Milal wa al-Ahwā' wa al-Niḥal*. Ed. Muḥammad Ibrāhīm Naṣr and ʿAbd al-Raḥmān ʿUmayra. Jiddah: Sharikat Maktabāt 'Ukāẓ, 1982.

Ibn Hishām, ʿAbd al-Malik. *Al-Sīra al-Nabawiyya*. Ed. ʿUmar ʿAbd al-Salām Tadmūrī. Beirut: Dār al-Kitāb al-ʿArabī, 1990.

Ibn Isḥāq, Muḥammad, ʿAbd al-Malik b. Hishām, and Alfred Guillaume. *The Life of Muhammad: A Translation of Ibn Isḥāq's Sīrat Rasūl Allāh*. Oxford: Oxford University Press, 1967.

Ibn Khaldūn, ʿAbd al-Raḥmān b. Muḥammad. *The Muqaddimah: An Introduction to History*. Trans. Franz Rosenthal. London: Routledge and Kegan Paul, 1958.

——. *Kitāb al-ʿIbar wa Diwān al-Mubtada' wa al-Khabar*, vol. 1. Ed. Ibrāhīm Shabbūḥ and Iḥsān ʿAbbās. Tunis: al-Dār al-ʿArabiyya li-al-Kitāb, 2006.

Ibn Khallikān, Aḥmad b. Muḥammad Shams al-Dīn. *Wafiyāt al-Aʿyān wa Anbāʾ Abnāʾ al-Zamān*. Beirut: Dār Ṣādir, 1978.

Ibn al-Muqaffaʿ, ʿAbdallāh. *Nāmah-i Tansar ba-Gushnasp*. Ed. Mujtabá Mīnuvī. Tahran: Shirkati Sihāmī Intisharāt-i Khawārizmī, 1354 (1975 CE).

——. "Risāla fī al-Ṣaḥāba." In Aḥmad b. Abī Ṭāhir Ṭayfūr. *Kitāb al-Manthūr wa al-Manẓūm*. The British Library. Manuscript access no. 18532 (BL).

——. "Risāla fī al-Ṣaḥāba." In Aḥmad b. Abī Ṭāhir Ṭayfūr. *Kitāb al-Manthūr wa al-Manẓūm*. Cairo al-Azhar Library. Manuscript access no. 464 adab (A1).

——. "Risāla fī al-Ṣaḥāba." In Aḥmad b. Abī Ṭāhir Ṭayfūr. *Kitāb al-Manthūr wa al-Manẓūm*. Cairo al-Azhar Library. Manuscript access no. 1752 adab (A2).

——. "Risāla fī al-Ṣaḥāba." In Aḥmad b. Abī Ṭāhir Ṭayfūr. *Kitāb al-Manthūr wa al-Manẓūm*. Cairo Dār al-Kutub al-Miṣriyya. Manuscript access no. 1860 adab (DKM1).

——. "*Al-Adab al-Kabīr*." In *Rasāʾil al-Bulaghāʾ*. Ed. Muḥammad Kurd ʿAlī. Cairo: Maṭbaʿat Lajnat al-Taʾlīf wa al-Tarjuma wa al-Nashr, 1946.

——. "Risālat al-Akhlāq fī al-Siyāsa." In *al-Majmūʿa al-Muʿtabara min al-Rasāʾil wa al-Fawāʾid*. Süleymaniye, Esad Efendi. Manuscript access no. 3690.

——. "Risāla fī Makārim al-Akhlāq wa al-Siyāsa al-Madaniyya." In *Rasāʾil fī al-Manṭiq*. Süleymaniye, Şehid Ali Paşa. Manuscript access no. 2722.

——. *Al-Tibr al-Masbūk fīmā Yaḥtājūnā Ilayhi al-Mulūk*. Süleymaniye, Molla Çelebi. Manuscript access no. 113.

Ibn al-Muqaffaʿ, ʿAbdallāh. *Kalīlah and Dimnah: Fables of Virtue and Vice*. Ed. Michael Fishbein. Trans. Michael Fishbein and James E. Montgomery. New York: New York University Press, 2021.

Ibn Muqaffaʿ, ʿAbdallāh, and Wyndham Knatchbull. *Kalīla and Dimna, or The Fables of Bidpai*. Oxford: W. Baxter for J. Parker, 1819. http://catalog.hathitrust.org/api/volumes/oclc/4567613.html.

Ibn al-Nadīm, Muḥammad b. Isḥāq. *Al-Fihrist*. Ed. Gustav Flugel. Beirut: Maktabat Khayyāṭ, 1966.

Ibn Qutayba, Abū Muḥammad ʿAbdallāh b. Muslim. *ʿUyūn al-Akhbār*. Cairo: Dār al-Kutub al-Miṣriyya, 1996.

——. *Al-Maʿārif*. Ed. Tharwat ʿUkkāsha. Cairo: Dār al-Maʿārif, 1981.

Ibn Saʿd, Muḥammad. *Kitāb al-Ṭabaqāt al-Kabīr*. Ed. Eduard Sachau et al. Leiden: Brill, 1912–1940.

Ibn Taymiyya, Taqīy al-Dīn Aḥmad. *Al-Siyāsa al-Sharʿiyya fī Iṣlāḥ al-Rāʿī wa al-Raʿiyya*. Beirut: Dār al-Kutub al-ʿīlmiyya, 2005.

——. *Daqāʾiq al-Tafsīr*. Ed. Muḥammad al-Sayyid al-Julaynad. Damascus: Muʾassasat Um al-Qurʾān, 1984.

Ibn al-Ṭiqṭaqā, Muḥammad b. ʿAlī, and Ṭalāl Sālim. *Al-Fakhrī fī al-Ādāb al-Sulṭāniyya wa al-Duwal al-Islāmīyya*. Ed. Hartwig Derenbourg. Paris: Emile Bouillon, 1895.

Iṣfahānī, Abū al-Faraj ʿAlī b. al-Ḥusayn. *Maqātil al-Ṭālibiyyīn*. Ed. Kāẓim al-Muẓaffar. Najaf: Maktabat al-Ḥaydariyya, 1965.

Al-Iṣṭakhrī, Abū Isḥāq Ibrāhīm b. Muḥammad al-Fārisī. *Masālik al-Mamālik*. Ed. M. J. De Goeje, Bibliotheca Geographorum Arabicorum, and Lugduni Batavorum. Leiden: Brill, 1927.

Al-Jāḥiẓ, ʿAmr b. Baḥr. *Rasāʾil al-Jāḥiẓ*. Ed. ʿAbd al-Salām Muḥammad Hārūn. Cairo: Maktabat al-Khānjī, 1994.

Al-Jāḥiẓ (Al-Gāḥiẓ), ʿAmr b. Baḥr and William M. Hutchins. *Nine Essays of al-Gāḥiẓ*. New York: Peter Lang, 1989.

Al-Jahshiyārī, Muḥammad b. ʿAbdūs. *Al-Wuzarāʾ wa al-Kuttāb*. Ed. Muṣṭafā Saqqā, Ibrāhīm Abyārī, and ʿAbd al-Ḥafīẓ Shalabī. Cairo: Maṭbaʿat Muṣṭafā al-Bābī al-Ḥalabī, 1938.

Jarīr b. ʿAṭiyya. *Diwān Jarīr*. Ed. Nuʿmān Muḥammad Amīn Ṭāha. Cairo: Dār al-Maʿārif, 1969.

Kauṭilya, and Patrick Olivelle. *King, Governance, and Law in Ancient India: Kauṭilya's Arthaśāstra: A New Annotated Translation*. Oxford: Oxford University Press, 2013.

Khalīfa b. al-Khayyāṭ. *Tārīkh Khalīfa b. al-Khayyāṭ*. Ed. Akram Ḍiyā' al-ʿUmarī. Beirut: Dār al-Qalam-Mu'assasat al-Risāla, 1977.

Al-Masʿūdī, Abū al-Ḥasan ʿAlī b. al-Ḥusayn. *Murūj al-Dhahab wa Maʿādin al-Jawhar*. Ed. Charles Barbier de Meynard, Abel Pavet de Courteille, and Charles Pellat. Paris: Société Asiatique, 1962.

——. *Kitāb al-Tanbīh wa al-Ishrāf*. Ed. M. J. de Goeje. Leiden: Brill, 1893.

Al-Māwardī, Abū al-Ḥasan ʿAlī b. Muḥammad. *Al-Aḥkām al-Sulṭāniyya wa al-Wilāyāt al-Dīniyya*. Ed. Aḥmad al-Mubārak al-Baghdādī. Kuwait: Maktabat Dār Ibn Qutayba, 1989.

——. *Adab al-Dunyā wa al-Dīn*. Beirut: Dār al-Minhāj, 2013.

——. "Adab al-Salṭana." In *al-Majmūʿa al-Muʿtabara min al-Rasā'il wa al-Fawā'id*. Süleymaniye, Esad Efendi. Manuscript access no. 3690.

——. *The Ordinances of Government (al-Aḥkām al-Sulṭāniyya wa al-Wilāyāt al-Dīniyya)*. Trans. Wafaa H. Wahba. Reading, UK: Garnet, 1996.

Miskawayh, Aḥmad b. Muḥammad b. Yaʿqūb. *Tahdhīb al-Akhlāq wa Taṭhīr al-Aʿrāq*. Cairo: al-Maktaba al-Ḥusayniyya, 1911.

Mubarrad, Muḥammad b. Yazīd. *Al-Kāmil fī al-Lugha wa al-Adab wa al-Naḥw wa al-Taṣrīf*. Ed. Muḥammad Aḥmad al-Dālī. Beirut: Mu'assasat al-Risāla, 1986.

Al-Muḥāsibī, al-Ḥārith b. Asad. *Ādāb al-Nufūs*. Ed. ʿAbd al-Qādir Aḥmad ʿAṭā. Beirut: Dār al-Jīl, 1984.

Al-Nasafī, Abū Muʿīn Maymūn b. Muḥammad. *Tabṣirat al Adilla fī Uṣūl al-Dīn*. Ed. Claude Salame. Tome Deuxième. Damascus: Institut Français de Damas, 1993.

Al-Nāshī al-Akbar, ʿAbdallāh b. Muḥammad, and Josef van Ess. *Frühe muʿtazilitische Häresiographie: zwei Werke des Nāshī' al-Akbar (gest. 293 H.)*. Weisbaden and Beirut: In Kommission bei Franz Steiner Verlag, 1971.

Naṣr b. Muzāḥim, *Waqʿat Ṣiffīn*. Ed. ʿAbd al-Salām Muḥammad Hārūn. Cairo: al-Mu'assasa al-ʿArabiyya al-Ḥadītha wa Maktabat al-Khānjī bi-Miṣr, 1981.

Al-Nawbakhtī, Abū Muḥammad al-Ḥasan b. Mūsā. *Kitāb Firaq al-Shīʿa*. Ed. Helmut Ritter. Istanbul: German Oriental Society, Devlet Matbaası, 1931.

Niẓām al-Mulk. *The Book of Government or Rules for Kings: The Siyar al-Mulūk or Siyāsat Nāma*. Trans. H. Darke. New Haven, CT: Yale University Press, 1960.

Nuʿaym b. Ḥammād al-Khuzāʿī. *Kitāb al-Fitan*. Ed. Suhayl Zakkār. Beirut: Dār al-Fikr, 1993.

Pseudo Ibn Qutayba, ʿAbdallāh b. Muslim. *Al-Imāma wa al-Siyāsa*. Ed. ʿAlī Shayrī, Beirut: Dār al-Aḍwā', 1990.

Al-Qālī, Abū ʿAlī Ismāʿīl b. al-Qāsim. *Kitāb Dhayl al-Amālī wa al-Nawādir*. Beirut: Dār al-Āfāq al-Jadīda, 1980.

Al-Qummī, Saʿd b. ʿAbdallāh b. Khalaf. *Kitāb al-Maqālāt wa al-Firaq*. Ed. Muḥammad Jawād Shakūr. Tehran: Mu'assasat-i Matbuʿāt-i Atanī, 1963.

Al-Ṣābī, Hilāl b. al-Muḥassin, and Elie A. Salem. *Rusūm Dār al-Khilāfah: The Rules and Regulations of the ʿAbbasid Court*. Beirut: Lebanese Commission for the Translation of Great Works, 1977.

Al-Ṣāḥib Ismāʿīl b. ʿAbbād. *Al-Muḥīṭ fī al-Lugha*. Ed. Muḥammad Ḥasan Āl Yāsīn. Beirut: ʿĀlam al-Kutub, 1994. http://arabiclexicon.hawramani.com.

Al-Ṣanʿānī, ʿAbd al-Razzāq b. Hammām. *Al-Muṣannaf*. Ed. Ḥabīb al-Raḥmān al-Aʿẓamī. Beirut: Al-Majlis al-ʿIlmī, 1970.

Al-Shāfiʿī, Muḥammad b. Idrīs. *Al-Risāla*. Ed. Aḥmad Muḥammad Shākir. Cairo: Maktabat Ibn Taymiyya, 1940.

Al-Ṭabarī, Muḥammad b. Jarīr. *The History of al-Tabarī*. 40 vols. Ed. Ihsan Yarshater. Albany, NY: SUNY Press, 1985–2007.

——. *Kitāb Ikhtilāf al-Fuqahā'*. Ed. Joseph Schacht. Leiden: Brill, 1933.

——. *Tārīkh al-Rusul wa al-Mulūk*. Ed. Muḥammad Abū al-Faḍl Muḥammad Ibrāhīm. Cairo: Dār al-Maʿārif, 1968.

Al-Ṭūsī, Naṣīr al-Dīn Muḥammad b. Muḥammad, and George M. Wickens. *The Nasirean Ethics*. London: George Allen & Unwin, 1964.

Wakīʿ, Muḥammad b. Khalaf b. Ḥayyān. *Akhbār al-Quḍāt*. Ed. ʿAbd al-ʿAzīz Muṣṭafā al-Marāghī. Cairo: Maktabat al-Istiqāma, 1947.

Al-Wāqidī, Muḥammad b. ʿUmar. *Kitāb al-Ridda*. Ed. Muhammad Hamidullah, Paris: Editions Tougui, 1989.

Al-Warrāq, Abū Muḥammad al-Muẓaffar b. Sayyār. *Kitāb al-Ṭabīkh*. Ed. Kaj Öhrnberg and Sahban Mroueh. Studia Orientalia 60. Helsinki: The Finnish Oriental Society, 1987.

Al-Washshā, Muḥammad b. Isḥāq, and Rudolf-Ernst Brünnow. *Kitāb al-Muwashshā of Abū al-Ṭayyib Muḥammad ibn Isḥāq al-Washshā*. Leiden: Brill, 1886.

Al-Yaʿqūbī, Aḥmad b. Abī Yaʿqūb. *Tārīkh al-Yaʿqūbī*. Ed. M. T. Houtsama. Leiden: Brill, 1969.

Al-Zubayr b. Bakkār. *Al-Akhbār al-Muwaffaqiyyāt*. Ed. Sāmī Makkī al-ʿĀnī. Baghdad: Ri'āsat Dīwān al-Awqāf, 1972.

Scholarship

ʿAbbās, Iḥsān. *ʿAbd al-Ḥamīd b. Yaḥyā al-Kātib wa mā Tabaqqā min Rasā'ilihi wa Rasā'il Sālim Abī al-ʿAlā'*, ed. Iḥsan ʿAbbās. Amman: Dār al-Shurūq, 1988.

——. "Naḍra Jadīda fī Baʿḍ al-Kutub al-Mansūba li-Ibn al-Muqaffaʿ." *Majallat Majmaʿ al-ʿIlmī al-ʿArabī* 3 (1977): 538–80.

Abbasi, Rushain. "Did Premodern Muslims Distinguish the Religious and Secular? The Dīn-Dunyā Binary in Medieval Islamic Thought." *Journal of Islamic Studies* 31 (2020): 185–225. https://doi.org/10.1093/jis/etz048.

Abbès, Makram. Islam et politique à l'âge classique. Paris: Presses Universitaires de France, 2009. (I was not able to engage this fine study as I came across it only in the proofreading stage of my book.)

ʿAbd al-Rāziq, ʿAlī. *Al-Islām wa Uṣūl al-Ḥukm*. Cairo: Al-Hay'a al-ʿĀmma al-Miṣriyya li-al-Kitāb, 1993.

Abdel Haleem, M. A. *The Qur'an: English Translation and Parallel Arabic Text*. Oxford: Oxford University Press, 2016.

Adcock, Robert, and Mark Bevir. "The History of Political Science." *Political Studies Review* 3 (2005): 1–16. https://doi.org/10.1111/j.1478-9299.2005.00016.x.

Afsaruddin, Asma. *Excellence and Precedence: Medieval Islamic Discourse on Legitimate Leadership*. Leiden: Brill, 2002.

——. *The First Muslims: History and Memory*. London: One World, 2017.

——. "The 'Islamic State' Genealogy, Facts, and Myths." *Journal of Church and State* 48 (2006): 153–73.

——, ed. *Islam, the State, and Political Authority: Medieval Issues and Modern Concerns*. New York: Palgrave Macmillan, 2011.

——. "Maslahah as a Political Concept." In *Mirror for the Muslim Prince: Islam and the Theory of Statecraft*, ed. Mehrzad Boroujerdi, 16–44. Syracuse, NY: Syracuse University Press, 2013.

——. *Striving in the Path of God: Jihād and Martyrdom in Islamic Thought*. Oxford: Oxford University Press, 2013.

Agamben, Giorgio. *Sovereign Power and Bare Life*. Stanford, CA: Stanford University Press, 1998.

Agha, Saleh Said. "The Arab Population of Ḥurasan During the Umayyad Period: Some Demographic Computations." *Arabica* 46 (1999): 211–29.

——. *The Revolution Which Toppled the Umayyads: Neither Arab nor ʿAbbasid*. Leiden: Brill, 2003.

——. "A Viewpoint of the Murji'a in the Umayyad Period: Evolution Through Application." *Journal of Islamic Studies* 8 (1997): 1–42.

Ahmed, Shahab. *What Is Islam? The Importance of Being Islamic*. Princeton, NJ: Princeton University Press, 2015.

Alam, Muzaffar. *The Languages of Political Islam: India 1200–1800*. Chicago: University of Chicago Press, 2004.

Ali, Nadia, and Mattia Guidetti. "Umayyad Palace Iconography: On the Practical Aspects of Artistic Creation." In *Power, Patronage, and Memory in Early Islam: Perspectives on Umayyad Elites*, ed. Alain George and Andrew Marsham, 175–251. New York: Oxford University Press, 2018.

Almond, Ian. *The History of Islam: from Leibniz to Nietzsche*. New York: Routledge, 2010.

Althusser, Louis. "Ideology and Ideological State Apparatuses (Notes Towards an Investigation)." In *Lenin and Philosophy and Other Essays*. Trans. Ben Brewster, 121–76. New York: Monthly Review Press, 1971.

——. "Machiavelli's Solitude." In *Machiavelli and Us*, ed. Francois Matheron, trans. Gregory Elliot, 115–30. London: Verso, 1999.

Amīn, Aḥmad. *Ḍuḥā al-Islām*. Cairo: Maktabat al-Nahḍa, 1933.

Amossy, Ruth. "Ethos at the Crossroads of Disciplines: Rhetoric, Pragmatics, Sociology." *Poetics Today: International Journal of Theory and Analysis of Literature and Communication* 21 (2001): 1–23. https://doi.org/10.1215/03335372-22-1-1.

Anderson, Benedict. *Imagined Communities: Reflections on the Origin and Spread of Nationalism*. London: Verso, 2006.

Anjum, Ovamir. *Politics, Law, and Community in Islamic Thought: The Taymiyyan Moment*. Cambridge: Cambridge University Press, 2014.

Ansari, Zafar Ishaq. "Islamic Juristic Terminology Before Shāfiʿī: A Symantic Analysis with Special Reference to Kufa." In *The Formation of Islamic Law*, ed. Wael Hallaq, 211–56. Burlington, VT: Ashgate Variorum, 2004.

Anthony, Sean W. *The Caliph and the Heretic: Ibn Saba' and the Origins of Shīʿism*. Leiden: Brill, 2012.

Ardıç, Nurullah. *Islam and the Politics of Secularim: The Caliphate and Middle Eastern Modernization in the Early 20th Century*. New York: Routledge, 2012.

Arjomand, Said A. "ʿAbdallāh Ibn al-Muqaffaʿ and the ʿAbbāsid Revolution." *Iranian Studies* 27 (1994): 9–36.

——. "The Constitution of Medina: A Sociolegal Interpretation of Muhammad's Acts of Foundation of the Umma." *International Journal of Middle East Studies* 41 (2009): 555–75.

——. "Persianate Islam and the Secularity of Kingship." In *Companion to the Study of Secularity*, ed. The Humanities Center for Advanced Studies (HCAS), "Multiple Secularities—Beyond the West, Beyond Modernities," 1–13. Leipzig: Leipzig University, 2019. www.multiple-secularities.de/publications/companion/css_arjomand_persianatekingship.pdf.

——. "Persianate Political Thought and Islam." *Journal of Persianate Studies* 12 (2019): 167–74. doi:https://doi.org/10.1163/18747167-12341332.

——. "Perso-Islamicate Political Ethic in Relation to the Sources of Islamic Law." In *Mirror for the Muslim Prince: Islam and the Theory of Statecraft*, ed. Mehrzad Boroujerdi, 82–106. Syracuse, NY: Syracuse University Press, 2013.

Arnold, Thomas W. *The Caliphate*. Oxford: Clarendon, 1924.

Asad, Talal. *Formations of the Secular: Christianity, Islam, Modernity*. Stanford, CA: Stanford University Press, 2003.

——. *Genealogies of Religion: Discipline and Reasons of Power in Christianity and Islam*. Baltimore, MD: Johns Hopkins University Press, 2009.

——. "Thinking About Religion, Belief, and Politics." In *The Cambridge Companion to Religious Studies (Cambridge Companions to Religion)*, ed. R. Orsi, 36–57. Cambridge: Cambridge University Press, 2011.

Ashtiany, Julia, et al. *The Cambridge History of Arabic Literature: Abbasid Belles Lettres*. Cambridge: Cambridge University Press, 1990.

Austin, John L. *How to Do Things with Words: The William James Lectures Delivered at Harvard University in 1955*. Oxford: Clarendon, 1962.

Aydın, Cemil. *The Idea of the Muslim World: A Global Intellectual History*. Cambridge, MA: Harvard University Press, 2017.

Al-Azmeh, Aziz. "Barbarians in Arab Eyes." *Past and Present* 134 (1992): 3–18.

——. "God's Caravan: Topoi and Schemata in the History of Muslim Political Thought." In *Mirror for the Muslim Prince: Islam and the Theory of Statecraft*, ed. Mehrzad Boroujerdi, 326–99. Syracuse, NY: Syracuse University Press, 2013.

——. "Monotheisctic Kingship." In *Monotheistic Kingship: The Medieval Variants*, ed. Aziz Al-Azmeh and János M. Bak, 9–29. Budapest: Central European University Press, 2004.

——. *Muslim Kingship: Power and the Sacred in Muslim, Christian and Pagan Polities*. New York: I. B. Tauris, 2001.

Bacchi, Carol, and Jennifer Bonham. "Reclaiming Discursive Practices as an Analytic Focus: Political Implications." *Foucault Studies* 17 (2014): 173–92.

Bacharach, Jere L. "Laqab for a Future Caliph: The Case of the ʿAbbāsid Mahdī." *Journal of the American Oriental Society* 113 (1993): 271–74.

Badawī, ʿAbd al-Raḥmān, and Aḥmad b. Yūsuf b. Ibrāhīm. *Al-Uṣūl al-Yūnāniyya li-al-Naẓariyyāt al-Siyāsiyya fī al-Islām*. Cairo: Maktabat al-Nahḍa al-Miṣriyya, 1954.

Bakhtin, Mikhail M. *The Dialogic Imagination: Four Essays*, ed. and trans. Michael Holquist and Caryl Emerson. Austin: University of Texas Press, 2008.

——. *Problems of Dostoevsky's Poetics*. Minneapolis: University of Minnesota Press, 1997.

Balqazīz, ʿAbd al-Ilāh. *The State in Contemporary Islamic Thought: A Historical Survey of the Major Muslim Political Thinkers of the Modern Era*. London: I. B. Tauris, 2009.

Barclay, Harold. People Without Government: An Anthropology of Anarchism. London: Kahn & Averill, 1996.

Bates, Michael L. "Khurāsānī Revolutionaries and al-Mahdī's Title." In *Culture and Memory in Medieval Islam: Essays in Honour of Wilferd Madelung*, ed. Wilferd Madelung, Farhad Daftary, and Josef W. Meri, 279–317. London: I. B. Tauris, 2003.

Baumlin, James S., and Craig A. Meyer. "Positioning Ethos in/for the Twenty-First Century: An Introduction to *Histories of Ethos*." *Humanities* 7, no. 3 (2018): 78. https://doi.org/10.3390/h7030078.

Beeston, Alfred Felix Landon. *The Cambridge History of Arabic Literature: Arabic Literature to the End of the Umayyad Period*. Cambridge: Cambridge University Press, 2012.

Binder, Leonard. "Problems of Islamic Political Thought in the Light of Recent Developments in Pakistan." *Journal of Politics* 22 (1958): 655–75.

Black, Anthony. *The History of Islamic Political Thought: From the Prophet to the Present*. New York: Routledge, 2001.

Blankinship, Khalid Yahya. "The Tribal Factor in the ʿAbbāsid Revolution: The Betrayal of the Imām Ibrāhīm b. Muḥammad." *Journal of the American Oriental Society* 108 (1988): 589–603.

Blaut, James Morris. *Eight Eurocentric Historians*. New York: Guilford, 2000.

Blichfeldt, Jan-Olaf. *Early Mahdīsm: Politics and Religion in the Formative Period of Islam*. Leiden: Brill, 1985.

Bligh-Abramski, Irit. "The Judiciary (Qāḍīs) as a Governmental-Administrative Tool in Early Islam." *Journal of the Economic and Social History of the Orient* 35 (1992): 40–71.

Blunt, Wilfrid Scawen. *The Future of Islam*. London: Kegan & Paul, 1882.

Boettcher, Susan R. "Confessionalization: Reformation, Religion, Absolutism, and Modernity." *History Compass* 2 (2004): 1–10. https://doi.org/10.1111/j.1478-0542.2004.00100.x.

Bonebaker, S. A. "*Adab* and the Concept of Belles-Lettres." In *The Cambridge History of Arabic Literature: Abbasid Belles Lettres*, ed. Julia Ashtiany et al., 16–30. Cambridge: Cambridge University Press, 1990.

Borrut, Antoine, and Paul Cobb. *Umayyad Legacies: Medieval Memories from Syria to Spain*. Leiden: Brill, 2010.

Bourdieu, Pierre. *Distinction: A Social Critique of the Judgment of Taste*. London: Routledge, Taylor & Francis, 2015.

——. *Language and Symbolic Power*. Trans. Gino Raymond and Matthew Adamson. Cambridge: Polity, 1991.

Böwering, Gerhard, ed. *Islamic Political Thought: An Introduction*. Princeton, NJ: Princeton University Press, 2017.

Böwering, Gerhard, Patricia Crone, and Mahan Mirza. *The Princeton Encyclopedia of Islamic Political Thought*. Princeton, NJ: Princeton University Press, 2013.

Boyce, Mary, and Muḥammad ibn al-Ḥasan Ibn Isfandiyār. *A History of Zoroastrianism: The Early Period*. Leiden: Brill, 1975.

——. *The Letter of Tansar*. Roma: Istituto Italiano per il Medio ed Estremo Oriente, 1968.

Brockopp, Jonathan E. *The Cambridge Companion to Muhammad*. New York: Cambridge University Press, 2010.

Burbank, Jane, and Frederick Cooper. *Empires in World History: Power and the Politics of Difference*. Princeton, NJ: Princeton University Press, 2011.

Burchardt, Marian, Monika Wohlrab-Sahr, and Matthias Middell. *Multiple Secularities Beyond the West: Religion and Modernity in the Global Age*. Berlin: De Gruyter, 2016. https://www.multiple-secularities.de/.

Burchell, Graham, Colin Gordon, and Peter M. Miller. *The Foucault Effect: Studies in Governmentality, with Two Lectures by and an Interview with Michel Foucault*. London: Harvester Wheatsheaf, 1991.

Burke, Edmund. "Islam at the Center: Technological Complexes and the Roots of Modernity." *Journal of World History* 20 (2009): 165–86.

Büyükkara, M. Ali. "The Schism in the Party of Mūsa al-Kāẓim and the Emergence of the Wāqifa." *Arabica* 47 (2000): 78–99.

Calder, Norman. *Studies in Early Muslim Jurisprudence*. Oxford: Oxford University Press, 1993.

Çaykent, Özlem, and Derya Gürses Tarbuck. "Coffeehouse Sociability: Themes, Problems, and Directions." *Journal of Ottoman Studies* 49 (2017): 223–39.

Chakrabarty, Dipesh. *Provincializing Europe: Postcolonial Thought and Historical Difference*. Princeton, NJ: Princeton University Press, 2000.

Charles-Dominique, Paule. "Le systeme ethhique d'Ibn al-Muqaffa d'apres ses deux epitres dites al-saghir et al-kabir." *Arabica* 12 (1965): 45–66.

Cobb, Paul. "The Empire in Syria, 705–763." In *The New Cambridge History of Islam*, vol. 1, ed. Chase F. Robinson, 226–68. Cambridge: Cambridge University Press, 2011.

Collins, Roger. *The Arab Conquest of Spain: 710–797*. Oxford: Blackwell, 2012.

Connolly, William E. *Political Theory and Modernity: With a New Epilogue*. Ithaca, NY: Cornell University Press, 1994.

Cooperson, Michael. "Ibn al-Muqaffaʿ." In *Arabic Literary Culture, 500–925 (Dictionary of Literary Biography*, vol. 311), ed. Michael Cooperson and Shawkat M. Toorawa, 149–63. Detroit, MI: Thomson Gale, 2005.

Cooperson, Michael, and Shawkat M. Toorawa, ed. *Arabic Literary Culture, 500–925* (*Dictionary of Literary Biography*, vol. 311). Detroit, MI: Thomson Gale, 2005.

Creswell, K. A. C. *Early Muslim Architecture*. Oxford: Oxford University Press, 1969.

Crone, Patricia. *From Arabian Tribes to Islamic Empire: Army, State and Society in the Near East C. 600–850*. Burlington, VT: Ashgate, 2008.

——. *God's Rule: Government and Islam*. New York: Columbia University Press, 2006.

——. "Imperial Trauma: The Case of the Arabs." *Common Knowledge* 12 (2006): 107–16. doi:https://doi.org/10.1215/0961754X-12-1-107.

——. *Medieval Islamic Political Thought*. Edinburgh: Edinburgh University Press, 2004.

——. "Ninth-Century Muslim Anarchists." *Past and Present* 167 (2000): 3–28.

——. "Post-Colonialism in Tenth-Century Islam." *Der Islam* 83 (2006): 2–38. doi:https://doi.org/10.1515/ISLAM.2006.002.

——. *Slaves on Horses: The Evolution of the Islamic Polity*. Cambridge: Cambridge University Press, 2003.

Crone, Patricia, and Martin Hinds. *God's Caliph: Religious Authority in the First Centuries of Islam*. Cambridge: Cambridge University Press, 1986.

Crone, Patricia, and Fritz Zimmermann. *The Epistle of Sālim b. Dhakwān*. Oxford: Oxford University Press, 2001.

Dabashi, Hamid. *The World of Persian Literary Humanism*. Cambridge, MA: Harvard University Press, 2012.

Daiber, Hans. "Das Kitāb al-Adab al-Kabīr des Ibn al-Muqaffaʿ als Ausdruck griechischer Ethik, islamischer Ideologie und iranisch-sassanidischer Hofetikette." *Oriens* 43 (2015): 273–92.

Daniel, Elton L. *The Political and Social History of Khurāsān Under Abbasid Rule, 747–820*. Minneapolis: Bibliotheca Islamica, 1979.

Darling, Linda T. *A History of Social Justice and Political Power in the Middle East: The Circle of Justice from Mesopotamia to Globalization*. London: Routledge, 2013.

Datta, Pradip Kumar. "The Interlocking Worlds of the Anglo-Boer War in South Africa/India." *South African Historical Journal* 57 (2007): 35–59. doi:10.1080/02582470709464708.

De Blois, François, and Burzūyah. *Burzōy's Voyage to India and the Origin of the Book of Kalīlah wa Dimnah*. London: Routledge, 2011.

Delattre, Alain, Marie Legendre, and Petra Sijpesteijn. *Authority and Control in the Countryside: From Antiquity to Islam in the Mediterranean and Near East (Sixth–Tenth Century)*. Leiden: Brill, 2019.

Deleuze, Gilles, Félix Guattari, and Brian Massumi. *A Thousand Plateaus: Capitalism and Schizophrenia*. London: Bloomsbury, 2013.

Demirci, Mustafa. "Abdullah İbnü'l-Mukaffâ'nın '*Risâletü's-Sahâbe*' Adlı *Risâlesi*: Takdim ve Tercüme." *Istem* 12 (2008): 217–40.

——. "Emevilerden Abbasilere Geçiş Sürecinin bir Tanığı: Abdullah İbnü'l-Mukaffâ ve 'Risâletü's-Sahâbesi.'" *Dokuz Eylül Üniversitesi İlahiyat Fakültesi* Dergisi 21 (2005): 117–48.

Denny, Frederick Mathewson. "The Meaning of 'Ummah' in the Qur'an." *History of Religions* 15 (1975): 34–70. https://doi.org/10.1086/462733.

Denny, F. M. "Ummah in the Constitution of Medina." *Journal of Near Eastern Studies* 36 (1977): 39–47.

Donner, Fred McGraw. *The Early Islamic Conquests*. Princeton, NJ: Princeton University Press, 1981.

——, ed. *The Expansion of the Early Islamic State*. Aldershot, UK: Ashgate Variorum, 2008.

——. "The Formation of the Islamic State." *Journal of the American Oriental Society* 106, no. 2 (1986): 283–96.

——. "The Historical Context." In *The Cambridge Companion to the Qur'an*, ed. Jane Dammen McAuliffe, 23–40. Cambridge: Cambridge University Press, 2006.

——. *Muhammad and the Believers: At the Origins of Islam*. Cambridge, MA: Belknap Press of Harvard University, 2010.

——. "Qur'anicization of Religio-Political Discourse in the Umayyad Period." *Revue des mondes musulmans et de la Mediterranee* 129 (2011): 79–92.

Doostdar, Alireza. "*What Is Islam? The Importance of Being Islamic*, written by Shahab Ahmed." *Shii Studies Review* 1, no. 1–2 (2017): 277–82. doi:https://doi.org/10.1163/24682470-12340014.

Doyle, Laura. *Inter-Imperiality: The Long Dialectics of Power and Culture in Gendered Political Economy*. Durham, NC: Duke University Press, 2020.

Dressler, Markus, Armando Salvatore, and Monika Wohlrab-Sahr. "Islamicate Secularities: New Perspectives on a Contested Concept." *Historical Social Research/Historische Sozialforschung* 44, no. 3 (2019).

Duncan, B. MacDonald. *Development of Muslim Theology, Jurisprudence and Constitutional Theory*. New York: Charles Scribner, 1903.

Al-Dūrī, ʿAbd al-ʿAzīz. *Early Islamic Institutions Administration and Taxation from the Caliphate to the Umayyads and Abbasids*. London: I. B. Tauris, 2011.

——. *Al-Nuẓum al-Islāmiyya*. Baghdad: Bayt al-Ḥikma, 1988.

——. *Awrāq fī al-Tārīkh wa al-Ḥaḍāra: Awrāq fī ʿIlm al-Tārīkh*. Beirut: Markaz al-Dirāsāt al-Waḥda al-ʿArabiyya, 2009.

——. *Al-ʿAṣr al-ʿAbbāsī al-Awwal*. Beirut: Markaz Dirāsāt al-Waḥda al-ʿArabiyya, 2009.

——. "Al-Fikra al-Mahdīyya bayna al-Daʿwa al-ʿAbbāsīyya wa al-ʿAṣr al-ʿAbbāsī al-Awwal." In *Studia Arabica and Islamica Festschrift for Iḥsān ʿAbbās*, ed. Wadād al-Qāḍī, 123–32. Beirut: American University of Beirut, 1981.

——. *Muqaddima fī Tārīkh Ṣadr al-Islām*. Beirut: Dār al-Mashriq, 1984.

——. *Nash'at ʿIlm al-Tārīkh ʿinda al-ʿArab*. Beirut: Markaz al-Dirāsāt al-Waḥda al-ʿArabiyya, 2007.

——. "Note on Taxation in Early Islam." *Journal of Economic and Social History of the Orient* 17 (1974): 136–44.

Durmuş, Ismail, and İlhan Kutluer. "Ibnü-l-Mukaffa'." In *Türkiye Diyanet Vakfi İslam Ansiklopedisi*. Istanbul: Türkiye Diyanet Vakfı, 2016.

El-Ali, Salih A. "The Foundation of Baghdad." In *The Islamic City*, ed. Albert Hourani and S. M. Stern, 87–101. Oxford: Bruno Cassrier, 1970.

Eliot, Thomas Stearns. *Christianity and Culture: The Idea of a Christian Society and Notes Towards the Definition of Culture*. New York: Harcourt Brace Jovanovitch, 1968.

El Shamsy, Ahmed. *The Canonization of Islamic Law: A Social and Intellectual History*. Cambridge: Cambridge University Press, 2015.

Emon, Anver M. *Religious Pluralism and Islamic Law: Dhimmīs and Others in the Empire of Law*. Oxford: Oxford University Press, 2014.

Enayat, Hamid. *Modern Islamic Political Thought*. New York: Palgrave, 2005.

The Encyclopaedia Britannica: A Dictionary of Arts Sciences and General Literature, ed. Baynes T. Spencer. Akron, OH: Werner, 1904–1905. https://www.britannica.com/topic/political-science.

Encyclopaedia Iranica, ed. Ehsan Yar-Shater. London: Routledge & Kegan Paul, 1985–2008. https://www.iranicaonline.org/.

The Encyclopaedia of Islam, First Edition (1913–1936), ed. M. Th. Houtsma, T. W. Arnold, R. Basset, and R. Hartmann. Leiden: Brill, 2011.

The Encyclopaedia of Islam, Second Edition, ed. P. J. Bearman, Thierry Bianquis, Clifford Edmund Bosworth, E. J. van Donzel, and Wolfhart Heinrichs. Leiden: Brill, 2012.

The Encyclopaedia of Islam, Third Edition, ed. Kate Fleet, Gudrun Krämer, Denis Matringe, John Nawas, and Everett Rowson. Leiden: Brill, 2014. http://dx.doi.org/10.1163/1573-3912_ei3_COM_27754.

Fanon, Frantz. *The Wretched of the Earth*. Trans. Richard Philcox with commentary by Jean-Paul Sartre and Homi K Bhabha. New York: Gove, 2004.

Fierro, Maribel. "Al-Aṣfar." *Studia Islamica* 77 (1993): 169–81.

Fisher, Greg, ed. *Arabs and Empires Before Islam*. Oxford: Oxford University Press, 2017.

Fitzgerald, Timothy. *The Ideology of Religious Studies*. New York: Oxford University Press, 2013.

Fleischer, Cornell H. *Bureaucrat and Intellectual in the Ottoman Empire: The Historian Mustafa Âli (1541-1600)*. Princeton, NJ: Princeton University Press, 1986.

Foucault, Michel. *The Archaeology of Knowledge and the Discourse on Language*. Trans. A. M. Sheridan Smith. New York: Pantheon, 1972.

——. "Governmentality." In *The Foucault Effect: Studies in Governmental Rationality, with Two Lectures by and an Interview with Michel Foucault*, ed. Graham Burchell, Colin Gordon, and Peter M. Miller, 87–104. London: Harvester Wheatsheaf, 1991.

——. *The Order of Things*. Boca Raton, FL: Taylor & Francis, 2018. https://www.taylorfrancis.com/books/e/9781317336686.

——. "Technologies of the Self." In *Technologies of the Self: Seminar: Selected Papers*, ed. Michel Foucault, Luther H. Martin, Huck Gutman, and Patrick H. Hutton, 16–49. Amherst: University of Massachusetts Press, 1988.

Fowden, Garth. *Before and After Muhammad: The First Millennium Refocused*. Princeton, NJ: Princeton University Press, 2017.

——. *Empire to Commonwealth: Consequence of Monotheism in Late Antiquity*. Princeton, NJ: Princeton University Press, 1994.

——. "Greek Myth and Arabic Poetry at Quṣayr ʿAmra." In *Islamic Crosspollinations: Interactions in the Medieval Middle East*, ed. A. Akasoy, J. E. Montgomery, and P. E. Portmann, 29–46. Exeter: Gibb Memorial Trust, 2007.

——. *Qusayr Amra: Art and Umayyad Elite in Late Antique Syria*. Berkeley: University of California Press, 2004.

Freidenreich, David M., and Miriam Bayla Goldstein. *Beyond Religious Borders: Interaction and Intellectual Exchange in the Medieval Islamic World*. Philadelphia: University of Pennsylvania Press, 2012.

Frye, R. N. "The Charisma of Kingship in Ancient Iran." *Iranica Antiqua* 4 (1964): 36–53.

Gabrieli, Francesco. "L'opera di Ibn al-Muqaffaʿ." *Rivista degli studi orientali* 13 (1932): 197–247.

George, Alain, and Andrew Marsham. *Power, Patronage, and Memory in Early Islam: Perspectives on Umayyad Elites*. New York: Oxford University Press, 2018.

Ghazi, Mhammed F. "Un groupe social: 'Les Raffines' (Ẓurafā)." *Studia Islamica* 11 (1959): 39–71.

Gibb, Hamilton Alexander Rosskeen. "The Islamic Background of Ibn Khaldūn's Political Theory." *Bulletin of the School of Oriental Studies, University of London* 7 (1933): 23–31.

——. *Studies on the Civilization of Islam*, ed. Stanford J. Shaw and William R. Polk. Princeton, NJ: Princeton University Press, 1962.

Gibbon, Edward. *The History of the Decline and Fall of the Roman Empire with Variorum Notes*. London: Bohn, 1853.

Giffen, Lois A. "Ẓarf." In *The Routledge Encyclopedia of Arabic Literature*, ed. Julie Scott Meisami. London: Routledge, 2010.

Gikandi, Simon E. *Maps of Englishness: Writing Identity in the Culture of Colonialism*. New York: Columbia University Press, 1997.

——. *Slavery and the Culture of Taste*. Princeton, NJ: Princeton University Press, 2014.

Gil, Moshe. "The Constitution of Medina: A Reconsideration." *Israel Oriental Studies* 4 (1974): 44–66.

Gilliot, Claude. "Creation of a Fixed Text." In *The Cambridge Companion to the Qur'an*, ed. Jane Dammen McAuliffe, 41–58. Cambridge: Cambridge University Press, 2006.

Goitein, Shelomo D. "A Turning Point in the History of the Muslim State." *Islamic Culture* 23 (1949): 120–35.

Gordon, Colin. "Government Rationality: An Introduction." In *The Foucault Effect: Studies in Governmental Rationality, with Two Lectures by and an Interview with Michel Foucault*, ed. Graham Burchell, Colin Gordon, and Peter M. Miller, 1–51. London: Harvester Wheatsheaf, 1991.

Goto, A. "The Constitution of Medina." *Orient: Report of the Society for Near Eastern Studies in Japan* 18 (1982): 1–17.

Grabar, Oleg. *The Formation of Islamic Art*. New Haven, CT: Yale University Press, 1973.

Grabar, Oleg, with contribution by Muhammad al-Asad, Abeer Audeh, and Said Nusseibeh. *The Shape of the Holy: Early Islamic Jerusalem*. Princeton, NJ: Princeton University Press, 1996.

Gramsci, Antonio. *Selections from the Prison Notebooks of Antonio Gramsci*, ed. and trans. Quentin Hoare and Geoffrey Nowell Smith. London: ElecBooks, 1999.

Griffith, Sidney Harrison. *The Church in the Shadow of the Mosque: Christians and Muslims in the World of Islam*. Princeton, NJ: Princeton University Press, 2008.

Grignaschi, Mario. "Le roman epistolaire classique conserve 'dans la version de Sālim Abū-l-ʿAlā.'" *Museon 80* (1967): 211–64.

——. "Les 'Rasā'il Arisṭaṭalisa ila-l-Iskandar' de Sālim Abi-l-ʿAlā' et l'activite culturellé a l'époque omayyade." *Bulletin d'etudes Orientales* 19 (1965–1966): 7–83.

——. "L'origine et les Métamorphoses du 'Sirr-al-Asrār.'" *Archives d'histoire doctrinale et littéraire du Moyen Age* 43 (1976): 7–112.

Gründler, Beatrice. "How to Use a Book." https://www.geschkult.fu-berlin.de/en/e/kalila-wa-dimna/topics/How-To-Use-A-Book.html.

——. "Les versions de Kalīla wa-Dimna: und transmission et une circulation mouvantes." In *Énoncés sapientiels et littérature exemplaire: une intertextualité complexe*, ed. Hg. Marie-Sol Ortola, 385–416. Nancy: Éditions Universitaires de Lorraine, 2013.

Guidetti, Mattia. "Sacred Topography in Medieval Syria and Its Roots Between the Umayyads and Late Antiquity." In *Umayyad Legacies: Medieval Memories from Syria to Spain*, ed. Antoine Borrut and Paul M. Cobb, 337–63. Leiden: Brill, 2010.

Gundelfinger, Simon, and Peter Verkinderen. "The Governors of al-Shām and Fārs in the Early Islamic Empire—A Comparative Regional Perspective." In *Transregional and Regional Elites: Connecting the Early Islamic Empire*, ed. Hannah-Lena Hagemann and Stefan Heidemann, 255–329. Berlin: De Gruyter, 2020.

Gutas, Dimitri. "Classical Arabic Wisdom Literature: Nature and Scope." *Journal of American Oriental Society* 101 (1981): 49–86.

——. *Greek Thought, Arabic Culture: The Graeco-Arabic Translation Movement in Baghdad and Early 'Abbasid Society (2nd–4th/5th–10th Centuries)*. New York: Routledge, 1998.

Gyekye, Kwame. *Tradition and Modernity: Philosophical Reflections on the African Experience*. Oxford: Oxford University Press, 2011.

Habermas, Jürgen. "'The Political:' The Rational Meaning of a Questionable Inheritance of Political Theology." In *The Power of Religion in the Public Sphere*, ed. Judith Butler and Eduardo Mendieta, 15–33. New York: Columbia University Press, 2011.

——. *Toward a Rational Society*. New York: John Wiley, 2014.

Haddad, Mahmoud. "Arab Religious Nationalism in the Colonial Era: Rereading Rashīd Riḍā's Ideas on the Caliphate." *Journal of the American Oriental Society* 117 (1997): 253–77.

Hagemann, Hannah-Lena. "Muslim Elites in the Early Islamic Jazīra: The Qāḍīs of Ḥarrān, al-Raqqa, and al-Mawṣil." In *Transregional and Regional Elites: Connecting the Early Islamic Empire*, ed. Hannah-Lena Hagemann and Stefan Heidemann, 331–58. Berlin: De Gruyter, 2020.

Haldon, John F. *Money, Power and Politics in Early Islamic Syria: A Review of Current Debates*. London: Routledge, 2016.

Hallaq, Wael B. *The Impossible State: Islam, Politics, and Modernity's Moral Predicament*. New York: Columbia University Press, 2014.

——. *The Origins and Evolution of Islamic Law*. Cambridge: Cambridge University Press, 2011.

——. *Shariʿa: Theory, Practice and Modern Transformations*. Cambridge: Cambridge University Press, 2009.

——. "What Is Shariʿa?" *Yearbook of Islamic and Middle Eastern Law Online* 12 (2005): 151–80. doi:https://doi.org/10.1163/22112987-91000130.

Hämeen-Anttila, Jaakko. *Khwadāynāmag: The Middle Persian Book of Kings*. Leiden: Brill, 2018. https://www.doabooks.org/doab?func=fulltext&rid=45435.

Hamidullah, Muhammad. *The First Written Constitution in the World: An Important Document of the Time of the Holy Prophet*. Lahore, Pakistan: Ashraf, 1975.

Hammer, Dean. "Foucault, Sovereignty, and Governmentality in the Roman Republic." *Foucault Studies* 22 (2017): 49–71.

Hamori, Andras. "Prudence, Virtue, and Self-Respect in Ibn al-Muqaffaʿ." In *Reflections on Reflections: Near Eastern Writers Reading Literature*, ed. Angelika Neuwirth and Andreas Christian Islebe, 164–77. Wiesbaden: Reichert Verlag, 2006.

Harrak, Amir. *The Chronicle of Zuqnin*. Toronto: Pontifical Institute for Medieval Studies, 2000.

——. "The Jazirah During the Islamic Period." *Annual Symposium of the Canadian Society for Mesopotamian Studies, Bulletin of the Canadian Society for Mesopotamian Studies* 36 (2001): 227–33.

Hassan, Iyas. "Language nomade en cours impériale: L'arabe d'Ibn al-Muqaffa, entre deux ères." *Bulletin d'études Orientales* 65 (2016): 221–46.

Hassan, Mona. *Loss of Caliphate: The Trauma and Aftermath of 1258 and 1924*. Princeton, NJ: Princeton University Press, 2016.

Hatke, George. "Agrarian, Commercial, and Pastoralist Dynamics in the Pre-Islamic Irano-Semitic Civilizational Area." In *The Wiley Blackwell History of Islam*, ed. Armando Salvatore et al., 37–57. Hoboken, NJ: John Wiley, 2018.

Hattox, Ralph S. *Coffee and Coffeehouses: The Origins of a Social Beverage in the Medieval Near East*. Seattle: University of Washington Press, 1985.

Hawting, Gerald R. *The First Dynasty of Islam: The Umayyad Caliphate AD 661–750*. London: Routledge, 2000.

Heck, Paul. "Abū Yūsuf." In *The Princeton Encyclopedia of Islamic Political Thought*, ed. Gerhard Böwering, Patricia Crone, and Mahan Mirza. Princeton, NJ: Princeton University Press, 2013.

Hermans, Eric. "A Persian Origin of the Arabic Aristotle? The Debate on the Circumstantial Evidence of the Manteq Revisited." *Journal of Persian Studies* 11 (2018): 72–88.

Hillenbrand, Robert. "Hisham's Balancing Act: The Case of Qaṣr al-Ḥayr al-Gharbī." In *Power, Patronage, and Memory in Early Islam: Perspectives on Umayyad Elites*, ed. Alain George and Andrew Marsham, 83–132. New York: Oxford University Press, 2018.

Hitti, Philip Khuri. *History of the Arabs*. London: Macmillan and St. Martin's, 1970. https://www.britannica.com/topic/governmentality.

Hodgson, Marshall. *The Venture of Islam*. Chicago: University of Chicago Press, 1974.

Hourani, George F., and John Carswell. *Arab Seafaring in the Indian Ocean in Ancient and Early Medieval Times*. Princeton, NJ: Princeton University Press, 1995.

Huff, Toby E., and Wolfgang Schluchter, eds. *Max Weber and Islam*. New Brunswick, NJ: Transaction, 1999.

Humphreys, R. Stephen. *Islamic History: A Framework for Inquiry*, rev. ed. Princeton, NJ: Princeton University Press, 1991.

Iqbal Academy Pakistan. https://www.allamaiqbal.com/biography/en/chronology.php.

Iqbal, S. M. "Political Thought in Islam." *Sociological Review* 1 (1908): 249–61.

Izutsu, Toshihiko. *Ethico-Religious Concepts in the Qur'an*. Quebec: McGill-Queen's University Press, 2002.

Al-Jābrī, Muḥammad ʿĀbid. *Al-ʿAql al-Siyāsī al-ʿArabī: Maḥaddātuhu wa Tajalliyātuhu*. Beirut: Markaz Dirāsāt al-Waḥda al-ʿArabiyya, 1990.

——. *Al-Dīn wa al-Dawla wa Taṭbīq al-Sharīʿa*. Beirut: Markaz Dirāsāt al-Waḥda al-ʿArabiyya, 1996.

Janssen, Caroline. *Babil, the City of Witchcraft and Wine: The Name and Fame of Babylon in Medieval Arabic Geographical Texts. Mesopotamian History and Environment. Memoirs*. Ghent: University of Ghent, 1995.

Jawda, Jamal. *Al-Awḍāʿ al-Ijtimāʿiyya wa al-Iqtiṣādiyya li-al-Mawālī fī Ṣadr al-Islām*. Amman: Dār al-Bashīr, 1989.

Jenkins, Keith. *On "What Is History?": From Carr and Elton to Rorty and White*. London: Routledge, 2005.

Jenkins, Richard. "Disenchantment, Enchantment, and Re-Enchantment: Max Weber at the Millennium." *Max Weber Studies* 1 (2000): 11–32.

Josephson, Jason Ananda. *The Invention of Religion in Japan*. Chicago: University of Chicago Press, 2012.

Josephson, Judith. "The Multicultural Background of the Kitāb al-Adab al-Kabīr by ʿAbdallāh Ibn al-Muqaffaʿ." In *Current Issues in the Analysis of Semitic Grammar and Lexicon I*, ed. Lutz Edzard and Jan Retsö, 166–92. Weisbaden: Harrassowitz Verlag, 2005.

Judd, Steven. "The Jurisdictional Limits of 'Qāḍī' Courts During the Umayyad Period." *Bulletin d'études Orientales* 63 (2014): 43–56.

——. *Religious Scholars and the Umayyads: Piety-Minded Supporters of the Marwanid Caliphate*. New York: Routledge, 2019.

Kaegi, Walter Emil. *Muslim Expansion and Byzantine Collapse in North Africa*. Cambridge: Cambridge University Press, 2015.

Kantorowicz, Ernst H. *The King's Two Bodies: A Study in Mediaeval Political Theology*. Princeton, NJ: Princeton University Press, 2016.

Kara, İsmail. *Hilafet Risâleleri: İslam Siyasi Düşüncesinde Değişme ve Süreklilik*, vols. 1–6. Istanbul: Klasik, 2003–2014.

——. "Hilafetten İslam Devletine Çağdaş İslam Siyasi Düşüncesinin Ana İstikametleri ve Problemleri." *Divan Disiplinlerarası Çalışmalar Dergisi* 24 (2019): 1–108.

Karababa, Eminegül, and Güliz Ger. "Early Modern Coffeehouse Culture and the Formation of the Consumer Subject." *Journal of Consumer Research* 37 (2011): 737–60.

Karamustafa, Ahmet T. *Sufism: An Historical Introduction*. Edinburgh: Edinburgh University Press, 2007.

Kaufmann, Kathryn Scott. *Subjectivity and Medieval Arabic Adab*. PhD diss., University of California at Berkeley, 1997.

Kennedy, Hugh. *The Armies of the Caliphs: Military and Society in the Early Islamic State*. London: Routledge, 2001.

——. *Caliphate: The History of an Idea*. New York: Basic Books, 2016.

——. "Central Government and Provincial Elites in the Early ʿAbbāsid Caliphate." *Bulletin of the School of Oriental and African Studies* 44 (1981): 26–38.

——. *The Court of the Caliphs*. London: Weidenfeld & Nicolson, 2004.

——. *The Early Abbasid Caliphate: A Political History*. New York: Routledge, 1981.

——. *The Great Arab Conquests: How the Spread of Islam Changed the World We Live in*. Philadelphia: De Capo, 2007.

——. *Muslim Spain and Portugal: A Political History of Al-Andalus*. London: Routledge, 2016.

——. *The Prophet and the Age of the Caliphates: The Islamic Near East from the Sixth to the Eleventh Century*. New York: Pearson, 2004.

Kenney, Jeffrey Thomas. *Muslim Rebels: Kharijites and the Politics of Extremism in Egypt*. Oxford: Oxford University Press, 2006.

Khadduri, Majid. *War and Peace in the Law of Islam*. Baltimore, MD: Johns Hopkins Press, 1955.

Khadduri, Majid, and Muḥammad b. al-Ḥasan al-Shaybānī. *The Islamic Law of Nations: Shaybānī's Siyar*. Baltimore, MD: Johns Hopkins Press, 1966.

Khaled Abou El Fadl. "Islamic Law and Muslim Minorities: The Juristic Discourse on Muslim Minorities from the Second/Eighth to the Eleventh/Seventeenth Centuries." *Islamic Law and Society* 1, no. 2 (1994): 141–87.

Khalek, Nancy A. *Damascus After the Muslim Conquest: Text and Image in Early Islam*. New York: Oxford University Press, 2011.

Khalidi, Tarif. *Arabic Historical Thought in the Classical Period*. Cambridge: Cambridge University Press, 1994.

Khazanov, Anatoly M. "Muhammad and Jenghiz Khan Compared: The Religious Factor in World Empire Building." *Comparative Studies in Society and History* 35, no. 3 (1993): 461–79.

——. *Nomads and the Outside World*. Madison: University of Wisconsin Press, 1994.

Kohn, Hans. "Bases of Islamic Political Thought." *Naval War College Review* 7 (1954): 27–42.

Kramers, J. H. *Analecta Orientalia Posthumous Writings and Selected Minor Works*. Leiden: Brill, 1954.

Kremer, Alfred von. *Geschichte des herrschenden Ideen des Islams: Der Gottesbegriff, die Prophetie und Staatsidee*. Leipzig: Brockhaus, 1868.

Kristo-Nagy, I. "Conflict and Cooperation Between Arab Rulers and Persian Administrators in the Formative Period of Islamdom, c.600–c.950 CE." In *Empires and Bureaucracy in World History: From Late Antiquity to the Twentieth Century*, ed. Peter Crooks and Timothy Parson, 54–80. Cambridge: Cambridge University Press, 2016.

——. "The Crow Who Aped the Partridge: Aesopian Language by Ibn al-Muqaffaʿ's in a Fable of Kalīla wa-Dimna." In *L'Adab toujours recommencé—origines, transmission et metamorphoses*, ed. Catherine Mayeur-Jaouen, Francesca Bellino, and Luca Patrizi. Leiden: Brill, forthcoming.

——. "Denouncing the Damned Zindīq! Struggle and Interaction Between Monotheism and Dualism." In *Accusations of Unbelief in Islam: A Diachronic Perspective on Takfīr*, ed. Camilla Adang, Hassan Ansari, Maribel Fierro, and Sabine Schmidtke, 56–81. Leiden: Brill, 2015.

——. *La Pensée d'Ibn al-Muqaffaʿ: Un "agent double" dans le monde persan et arabe*. Paris: Éditions de Paris, 2013.

——. "Marriage After Rape: The Ambiguous Relationship Between Arab Lords and Iranian Intellectuals as Reflected in Ibn al-Muqaffaʿ's Oeuvre." In *Tradition and Reception in Arabic Literature: Essays Dedicated to Andras Hamori*, ed. Margaret Larkin and Jocelyn Sharlet, 161–88. Series: Mîzân. Studien zur Literatur in der islamischen Welt. Wiesbaden: Harrassowitz Verlag, 2019.

——. "On the Authenticity of al-Adab al-Saghīr Attributed to Ibn al-Muqaffaʿ and Problems Concerning Some of His Titles." *Acta Orientalia Academiae Scientiarum Hungaricae* 62 (2009): 199–218.

——. "Reason, Religion and Power in Ibn al-Muqaffaʿ." *Acta Orientalia Academiae Scientiarum Hungaricae* 62 (2009): 285–301.

——. "A Violent, Irrational and Unjust God: Antique and Medieval Criticism of Jehovah and Allāh." In *La morale au crible des religions*, Collection: "Studia Arabica," vol. 21, ed. Marie-Thérèse Urvoy, 143–64. Versailles: Éditions de Paris, 2013.

——. "Who Shall Educate Whom? The Official and the Sincere Views of Ibn al-Muqaffaʿ About Intellectual Hierarchy." In *Synoptikos: Mélanges offerts à Dominique Urvoy*, ed. Nicole Koulayan and Mansour Sayah, 279–93. Toulouse: Presses Universitaires du Mirail, 2011.

——. "Wild Lions and Wise Jackals: Killing Kings and Clever Counsellors in Kalīla wa Dimna." In *Prophets, Viziers and Philosophers: Wisdom and Authority in Early Arabic Literature*, ed. Emily J. Cottrell, 147–209. Groningen: Barkhuis & Groningen University Library, 2020.

Kristo-Nagy, Istvan T., and Abdessamad Belhaj, "Ancient Greek Philosophy and Islamic Political Advice Literature." In *Brill's Companion to the Reception of Ancient Philosophy in Islamic Political Thought*, ed. Vasileios Syros. Leiden: Brill, forthcoming.

Kuhn, Thomas S. *The Structure of Scientific Revolutions*. Chicago: University of Chicago Press, 1962.

Kurd ʿAlī, Muḥammad. *Rasā'il al-Bulaghā'*. Cairo: Maṭbaʿat Lajnat al-Ta'līf wa al-Tarjuma wa al-Nashr, 1946.

Lambton, Ann K. S. "Justice in the Medieval Persian Theory of Kingship." *Studia Islamica* 17 (1962): 91–119.

——. *State and Government in Medieval Islam: An Introduction to the Study of Islamic Political Theory: The Jurists*. Oxford: Oxford University Press, 1981.

——. *Theory and Practice in Medieval Persian Government*. London: Variorum Reprints, 1980.

Lampe, Gerald E. *Ibn al-Muqaffaʿ: Political and Legal Theorist and Reformer*. PhD diss., Johns Hopkins University, 1986.

Lane, William E. *An Arabic-English Lexicon*. New York: Frederick Ungar, 1863.

Lane-Poole, Stanley. "The Caliphate." *Quarterly Review* 224 (1915): 162–77.

Lapidus, Ira M. "Separation of State and Religion in the Early Islamic Society." *International Journal of Middle East Studies* 6 (1975): 363–85.

——. "State and Religion in Islamic Societies." *Past and Present* 151 (1996): 3–27.

Lassner, Jacob. *Jews, Christians, and the Abode of Islam: Modern Scholarship, Medieval Realities*. Chicago: University of Chicago Press, 2012.

——. "Provincial Administration Under the Early ʿAbbāsids: Abū Jaʿfar al-Manṣūr and the Governors of the Ḥaramayn." *Studia Islamica* 49 (1979): 39–54.

——. *The Shaping of Abbasid Rule*. Princeton, NJ: Princeton University Press, 1980.

——. *The Topography of Baghdad in the Early Middle Ages*. Detroit, MI: Wayne State University Press, 1970.

Latham, John D. "The Beginnings of Arabic Prose Literature: The Epistolary Genre." In *The Cambridge History of Arabic Literature: Arabic Literature to the End of the Umayyad Period*, ed. Alfred Felix Landon Beeston, 154–79. Cambridge: Cambridge University Press, 2012.

——. "Ibn al-Muqaffaʿ and Early ʿAbbāsid Prose." In *The Cambridge History of Arabic Literature: Abbasid Belles Lettres*, ed. Julia Ashstiany et al., 48–77. Cambridge: Cambridge University Press, 1990.

Lawlor, Leonard, and John Nale, eds. "Sovereignty." In *The Cambridge Foucault Lexicon*, 456–65. Cambridge: Cambridge University Press, 2014.

Lecker, Michael. *The Constitution of Medina: Muḥammad's First Legal Document*. Princeton, NJ: Darwin, 2004.

Le Strange, Guy. *Baghdad During the Abbasid Caliphate*. Oxford: Clarendon, 1924.

——. *The Lands of the Eastern Caliphate: Mesopotamia, Persia, and Central Asia from the Moslem Conquest to the Time of Timur*. New York: Barnes and Noble, 1873.

Levy-Rubin, Milka. *Non-Muslims in the Early Islamic Empire: From Surrender to Coexistence*. New York: Cambridge University Press, 2011.

Lewinstein, Keith. "The Azāriqa in Islamic Heresiography." *Bulletin of the School of Oriental and African Studies* 54 (1991): 251–68.

Lewis, Bernard. *The Political Language of Islam*. Chicago: University of Chicago Press, 1988.

——. "*Siyāsa*." In *In Quest of an Islamic Humanism: Arabic and Islamic Studies in Memory of Mohamed Al-Nowaihi*, ed. Mohamed Al-Nowaihi and Arnold H. Green, 3–24. Cairo: American University in Cairo Press, 1986.

Lichtenstein, Eli B. "Foucault's Analytics of Sovereignty." *Critical Horizons* 22 (2021): 287–305. doi:10.1080/14409917.2021.1953750.

Lika, Eva-Maria. *Proofs of Prophecy and the Refutation of the Ismāʿīliyya: The Kitāb Ithbāt Nubuwwat al-Nabī of the Zaydī al-Muʾayyad bi-llāh al-Hārūnī*. Berlin: de Gruyter, 2018.

London, Jennifer A. "The Abbasid 'Circle of Justice': Re-reading Ibn al-Muqaffaʿ's Letter on Companionship." In *Comparative Political Theory in Time and Place*, ed. Daniel Kapust and H. Kinsella, 25–50. New York: Palgrave McMillan, 2017.

——. "The 'Circle of Justice.'" *History of Political Thought* 32 (2011): 445–47.

Lowry, Joseph E. "The First Islamic Legal Theory: Ibn Al-Muqaffaʿ on Interpretation, Authority, and the Structure of the Law." *Journal of the American Oriental Society* 128 (2008): 25–40. http://www.jstor.org/stable/25608305.

MacDonald, Duncan B. *Development of Muslim Theology, Jurisprudence and Constitutional Theory*. New York: Charles Scribner, 1903.

Macintyre, Alasdair. *A Short History of Ethics: A History of Moral Philosophy from the Homeric Age to the Twentieth Century*. Notre Dame, IN: University of Notre Dame Press, 2022.

——. *Whose Justice? Which Rationality?* Notre Dame, IN: University of Notre Dame Press, 2003.

Madelung, Wilferd. "ʿAbdallāh b. al-Zubayr and the Mahdī." *Journal of Near Eastern Studies* 40 (1981): 291–305.

——. "Frühe muʿtazilitische Häresiographie: Das Kitāb al-Uṣūl des Ġaʿfar ibn Ḥarb." *Der Islam* 57 (1980): 220–36.

——. "The Hāshimiyyāt of al-Kumayt and the Hāshimī Shīʿism." *Studia Islamica* 70 (1989): 5–26.

Mahdi, Muhsin. *Alfarabi and the Foundation of Islamic Political Philosophy*. Chicago: University of Chicago Press, 2001.

Mahmood, Saba. *Politics of Piety: The Islamic Revival and the Feminist Subject*. Princeton, NJ: Princeton University Press, 2012

Manzalaoui, Mahmoud. "The Pseudo-Aristotelian Kitāb Sirr al-Asrār: Facts and Problems." *Oriens* 23, no. 24 (1974): 147–257.

Marchand, Suzanne. "German Orientalism and the Decline of the West." *Proceedings of the American Philosophical Society* 145, no. 4 (2001): 465–73.

Marín-Guzmán, Roberto. "The ʿAbbasid Revolution in Central Asia and Khurāsān: An Analytical Study of the Role of Taxation, Conversion, and Religious Groups in Its Genesis." *Islamic Studies* 33 (1994): 227–52.

Marlow, Louise. *Counsel for Kings: Wisdom and Politics in Tenth-Century Iran: The Naṣīḥat al-Mulūk of Pseudo-Māwardī: Contexts and Themes*. 2 vols. Edinburgh: Edinburgh University Press, 2016.

——. "Justice, Judges, and Law in Three Arabic Mirrors for Princes, 8th–11th Centuries." In *Justice and Leadership in Early Islamic Courts*, ed. Intisar A. Rabb and Abigail Krasner Balbale, 109–27. Cambridge, MA: Harvard University Press, 2017.

——. "Kings, Prophets and the 'Ulamā' in Mediaeval Islamic Advice Literature." *Studia Islamica* 81 (1995): 101–20.

Maróth, Miklós. "The Correspondence Between Aristotle and Alexander the Great: An Anonymous Greek Novel in Letters in Arabic Translation." *Acta Antiqua* 45, no. 2–3 (2005): 231–315.

Marsham, Andrew. "God's Caliph Revisited: Umayyad Political Thought in Its Late Antique Context." In *Power, Patronage, and Memory in Early Islam: Perspectives on Umayyad Elites*, ed. Alain George and Andrew Marsham, 3–38. New York: Oxford University Press, 2018.

——. *Rituals of Islamic Monarchy: Accession and Succession in the First Muslim Empire*. Edinburgh: Edinburgh University Press, 2009.

Marsham, Andrew, and Chase F. Robinson. "The Safe-Conduct for the ʿAbbāsid ʿAbd Allāh b. ʿAlī (d. 764)." *Bulletin of the School of Oriental and African Studies* 2 (2007): 247–81.

Martínez Jiménez, Javier. "The Rural Hinterland of the Visigothic Capitals of Toledo and Reccopolis, Between the Years 400–800 CE." In *Authority and Control in the Countryside*, ed. A. Delattre, M. Legendre, and P. Sijpesteijn, 97–127. Leiden: Brill, 2018. doi:https://doi.org/10.1163/9789004386549_005.

Massad, Joseph Andoni. *Islam in Liberalism*. Chicago: University of Chicago Press, 2016.

Masud, Muhammad Khalid. "The Doctrine of the *Siyāsa* in Islamic Law." *Recht van de Islam* 18 (2001): 1–29.

Masuzawa, Tomoko. *The Invention of World Religions or, How European Universalism Was Preserved in the Language of Pluralism*. Chicago: University of Chicago Press, 2007.

Matheron, Francois, ed. *Machiavelli and Us*. Trans. Gregory Elliot. London: Verso, 1999.

Mayer, Toby. "Theology and Ṣūfism." In *The Cambridge Companion to Classical Islamic Theology*, ed. Tim Winter, 258–87. Cambridge: Cambridge University Press, 2007.

Melchert, Christopher. "The Ḥanābila and the Early Ṣūfīs." *Arabica* 48 (2001): 352–67.

Memmi, Albert. *The Colonizer and the Colonized*. London: Earthscan, 2003.

Morony, Michael G., ed. *Production and the Exploitation of Resources*. Aldershot, UK: Ashgate/Variorum, 2002.

Motzki, Harald. "Alternative Accounts of the Qur'an's Formation." In *The Cambridge Companion to the Qur'an*, ed. Jane Dammen McAuliffe, 59–76. Cambridge: Cambridge University Press, 2006.

——. *Reconstruction of a Source of Ibn Isḥāq's Life of the Prophet and Early Qur'an Exegesis: A Study of Early Ibn ʿAbbās Traditions*. Piscataway, NJ: Gorgias, 2017.

——. "The Role of Non-Arab Converts in the Development of Early Islamic Law." *Islamic Law and Society* 6 (1999): 293–317.

Mourad, Suleiman Ali. *Early Islam Between Myth and History: Al-Ḥasan Al-Baṣrī (D. 110 H = 728 CE) and the Formation of His Legacy in Classical Islamic Scholarship*. Leiden: Brill, 2006.

Mufti, Malik. *The Art of Jihad: Realism in Islamic Political Thought*. Albany, NY: SUNY Press, 2019.

Nagel, Tilman. *Staat und Glaubensgemeinschaft im Islam: Geschichte der politischen Ordnungsvorstellungen der Muslime*. Munich: Artemis Verlag, 1981.

Najjar, Fauzi M. "*Siyāsa* in Islamic Political Philosophy." In *Islamic Theology and Philosophy: Studies in Honor of G. F. Hourani*, ed. Michael E. Marmura, 92–110. Albany, NY: SUNY Press, 1984.

Nasrallah, Nawal. *The Annals of the Caliphs' Kitchens: Ibn Sayyār al-Warrāq's Tenth-Century Baghdadi Cookbook*. Leiden: Brill, 2014.

Nicholson, Reynold A. *A Literary History of the Arabs*. New York: Charles Scribner, 1907.

Nöldeke, Theodor, and Friedrich Schwally. *Geschichte des Qorāns. mit einem literarhistorischen Anhang über die muhammedanischen Quellen und die neuere christliche Forschung*, vol. 2. Leipzig: Dieterich'sche Verlagsbuchhandlung, 1919.

Obermann, Julian. "Political Theology in Early Islam: Ḥasan Al-Baṣrī's Treatise on Qadar." *Journal of the American Oriental Society* 55 (1935): 138–62. doi:10.2307/594438.

Öke, Mim Kemal. *The Turkish War of Independence and the Independence Struggle of the South Asian Muslims: "The Khilafat Movement" 1919–1924*. Ankara: Ministry of Culture, 1991.

Olsson, J. T. "The World in Arab Eyes: A Reassessment of the Climes in Medieval Islamic Scholarship." *Bulletin of the School of Oriental and African Studies* 77 (2014): 487–508. doi:10.1017/S0041977X14000512.

Omar, Farouk. *The ʿAbbāsid Caliphate: 132/750–170/786*. Baghdad: n.p., 1969.

Özcan, Azmi. *Pan-Islamism: Indian Muslims, the Ottomans and Britain (1877–1924)*. Leiden: Brill, 1997.

Paul, Jürgen. "Early Islamic History of Iran: From the Arab Conquest to the Mongol Invasion." *Iranian Studies* 31 (1998): 463–71.

Pellat, Charles. *Ibn al-Muqaffaʿ mort vers 140/757, "Conseilleur" du calife*." Paris: G.-P. Maisonneuve et Larose, 1976.

Perret, Noëlle-Laetitia, and Stéphane Péquignot. *A Critical Companion to the "Mirrors for Princes" Literature*. Leiden: Brill, 2022.

Peters, F. E. *Muhammad and the Origins of Islam*. Albany, NY: SUNY Press, 1994.

Philpott, Daniel. "Sovereignty." In *The Stanford Encyclopedia of Philosophy*, ed. Edward N. Zalta. Fall 2020 Edition. https://plato.stanford.edu/archives/fall2020/entries/sovereignty.

Pocock, J. G. A. *Politics, Language and Time: Essays on Political Thought and History*. Chicago: University of Chicago Press, 1989.

Pollock, Sheldon. "Axialism and Empire." In *Axial Civilizations and World History*, ed. J. P. Arnason, S. N. Eisenstadt, and B. Wittrock, 175–88. Leiden: Brill, 2005.

——. "Empire and Imitation." In *Lesssons of Empire: Imperial Histories and American Power*, ed. Craig Calhoun. New York: New Press, 2006.

Pregill, Michael E. "I Hear Islam Singing: Shahab Ahmed's *What Is Islam? The Importance of Being Islamic*." *Harvard Theological Review* 110, no. 1 (2017): 149–65.

Al-Qadi (Qadi, al-Qāḍī, Kadi), Wadad. "ʿAbd al-Ḥamīd al-Kātib." In *Arabic Literary Culture (Dictionary of Literary Biography)*, ed. Michael Cooperson and Shawkat M. Toorawa, 3–11. Detroit, MI: Thomson Gale, 2005.

——. "ʿAbdulḥamīd al-Kātib b. Yaḥyā al-Āmirī." In *The Princeton Encyclopedia of Islamic Political Thought*, ed. Gerhard Böwering, Patricia Crone, and Mahan Mirza. Princeton, NJ: Princeton University Press, 2013.

——. *Al-Kaysāniyya fī al-Tārīkh wa al-Adab*. Beirut: Dār al-Thaqāfa, 1974.

——. "Identity Formation of the Bureaucracy of the Early Islamic State: ʿAbd al-Ḥamīd's 'Letter to the Secretaries.'" In *Mediterranean Identities in the Premodern Era: Entrepôts, Islands, Empires*, ed. John Watkins and Kathryn L. Reyerson, 141–54. London: Routledge Taylor & Francis, 2016.

——. "The Impact of the Qur'an on the Epistolography of ʿAbd al-Ḥamīd." In *Approaches to the Qur'an*, ed. G. R. Hawting and Abdul-Kader A. Shareef, 285–313. London: Routledge, 1993.

——. "The Religious Foundation of Late Umayyad Ideology and Practice." In *Saber religioso y poder politico en el Islam: Actas del simposio international, Granada, 15–18 Ocotobre 1991*, ed. Manuela Marin and Mercedes García-Arenal, 37–80. Madrid: Agencia Española de Cooperacion Internacional, 1994.

——. "The Term 'Khalīfa' in Early Exegetical Literature." *Die Welt des Islams* 28 (1988): 392–411.

Al-Qadi, Wadad, and Aram Shahin. "Caliph, Caliphate." In *The Princeton Encyclopedia of Islamic Political Thought*, ed. Gerhard Böwering, Patricia Crone, and Mahan Mirza. Princeton, NJ: Princeton University Press, 2013.

Quraishi-Landes, Asifa. "Islamic Constitutionalism: Not Secular. Not Theocratic. Not Impossible." *Rutgers Journal of Law and Religion* 16 (2015): 553–79.

Rabb, Intisar A. *Doubt in Islamic Law: A History of Legal Maxims, Interpretation, and Islamic Criminal Law.* Cambridge: Cambridge University Press, 2017.

Rabbat, Nasser O. "The Ideological Significance of the Dār al-ʿAdl in the Medieval Islamic Orient." *International Journal of Middle East Studies* 27 (1995): 3–28.

Riaz, Rafia. "The Role of State in Regulating Migration: A Study of the Arab Migration to Iraq 632–750 CE." *Journal of Islamic Studies* 51 (2012): 423–44.

Robinson, Chase F. (vol. 1), with Maribel Fierro (vol. 2), Robert W. Hefner (vol. 6), Robert Irwin (vol. 4), David O. Morgan and Anthony Reid (vol. 3), and Francis Robinson (vol. 5), ed. *The New Cambridge History of Islam*. Cambridge: Cambridge University Press, 2010.

Robinson, Chase F. *Empire and Elites After the Muslim Conquest: The Transformation of Northern Mesopotamia*. New York: Cambridge University Press, 2000.

——. "Neck-Sealing in Early Islam." *Journal of the Economic and Social History of the Orient* 48 (2005): 401–41.

Rose, Nikolas, and Peter Miller. "Political Power Beyond the State: Problematics of Government." *British Journal of Sociology* 43 (1992): 173–205.

Rosen-Ayalon, Myriam. *The Early Islamic Monuments of al-Ḥaram al-Sharīf: An Iconographic Study*. Jerusalem: Hebrew University, 1989.

Rosenthal, Erwin Isak Jakob. *Political Thought in Medieval Islam: An Introductory Outline*, Reprint. Westport, CT: Greenwood, 1985.

Rosenthal, Erwin I. J. "Islamic Political Thought: The Basic Concepts by W. Mongomery Watt." *Middle East Journal* 23 (1969): 551–52.

——. "Some Aspects of Islamic Political Thought." *Islamic Culture* 22 (1948): 1–17.

Rosenthal, Franz. *Knowledge Triumphant: The Concept of Knowledge in Medieval Islam*. Leiden: Brill, 2007.

Rubin, Zeev. "Ibn al-Muqaffaʿ and the Account of Sasanian History in the Arabic Codex Sprenger 30." *Jerusalem Studies in Arabic and Islam* 30 (2005): 52–93.

Sabra, Abdelhamid I. "The Appropriation and Subsequent Naturalization of Greek Science in Medieval Islam: A Preliminary Statement." *History of Science* 25 (1987): 223–43.

Sachedina, Abdulaziz A. *Islamic Messianism: The Idea of the Mahdī in Twelver Shīʿism*. Albany, NY: SUNY Press, 1981.

Sadan, J. "Community and Extra-Community as a Legal and Literary Problem: Strict Community Doctrines Versus Justice in Mediaeval Arabic Moral-Political Literature (Following A. K. S. Lambton's Studies on Persian Specula Regis)." *Israel Oriental Studies* 10 (1980): 102–15.

Safi, Omid. *The Politics of Knowledge in Premodern Islam: Negotiating Ideology and Religious Inquiry*. Chapel Hill, NC: University of North Carolina Press, 2006.

Ṣafwat, Aḥmad Zakī. *Jamharat Rasāʾil al-ʿArab fī al-ʿUṣūr al-ʿArabiyya al-Zāhira*. Beirut: al-Maktaba al-ʿIlmiyya, 1937.

Said, Edward W. *Culture and Imperialism*. New York: Knopf, 1994.

——. *Humanism and Democratic Criticism*. New York: Columbia University Press, 2004.

——. *Orientalism*. New York: Vintage, 2003.

Salem, Elie Adib. *Political Theory and Institutions of the Khawārij*. Baltimore, MD: Johns Hopkins University Press, 1956.

Saliba, George. *Islamic Science and the Making of the European Renaissance*. Cambridge, MA: MIT Press, 2007.

Salvatore, Armando. "Secularity Through a 'Soft Distinction' in the Islamic Ecumene? *Adab* as Counterpoint to Shariʿa." *Historical Social Research* 44 (2019): 35–51.

Saunders, John Joseph. "The Nomad as Empire Builder: A Comparison of the Arab and Mongol Conquests." *Diogenes* 52 (1965): 79–103.

Savant, Sarah Bowen. *The New Muslims of Post-Conquest Iran Tradition, Memory, and Conversion*. New York: Cambridge University Press, 2013.

Al-Sayyad, Nezar. *Cities and Caliphs: On the Genesis of Arab Muslim Urbanism*. Westport, CT: Greenwood, 1991.

Sayyid, Bobby S. *Recalling the Caliphate: Decolonisation and World Order*. London: Hurst, 2014.

Schacht, Josef. *Introduction to Islamic Law*. Oxford: Oxford University Press, 1982.

——. *The Origins of the Muhammedan Jurisprudence*. Oxford: Oxford University Press, 1950.

——. "Pre-Islamic Background and Early Development of Jurisprudence." In *The Formation of Islamic Law*, ed. Wael Hallaq, 29–57. Burlington, VT: Ashgate Variorum, 2004.

Schmitt, Carl. *Political Theology: Four Chapters on the Concept of Sovereignty*. Trans. George Schwab. Chicago: University of Chicago Press, 2005.

Sen, Sachin. "Moslem Political Thought Since 1858." *Indian Journal of Political Science* 6 (1944): 97–108.

Serjeant, R. B. "The Constitution of Medina." *Islamic Quarterly* (1964): 3–16.

Sevea, Iqbal Singh. *The Political Philosophy of Muhammad Iqbal: Islam and Nationalism in Late Colonial India*. Cambridge: Cambridge University Press, 2012.

Shaked, Shaul. "Andarz and Andarz Literature in Pre-Islamic Iran." In *Zoroastrianism: A Collection of Articles from Encyclopedia Iranica*, ed. Mahnaz Moazami, 798–810. New York: Encyclopedia Iranica Foundation, 2016.

——. "From Iran to Islam: Notes on Some Themes in Transmission, 1. 'Religion and Sovereignty are Twins' in Ibn al-Muqaffaʿ's Theory of Government. 2. The Four Sages." *Jerusalem Studies in Arabic and Islam* 4 (1984): 31–67.

——. *From Zoroastrian Iran to Islam: Studies in Religious History and Intercultural Contacts*. Farnham, Surrey: Ashgate, 2010.

Sharon, Moshe. *Black Banners from the East: The Establishment of the ʿAbbāsid State, Incubation of a Revolt*. Leiden: Brill, 1983.

Shemesh, Aharon Ben. *Taxation in Islam*, vol. III: *Abū Yūsuf's Kitāb al-Kharāj*. Trans. A. Ben Shemesh. Leiden: Brill, 1970.

Sheriff, Abdul. *Dhow Cultures of the Indian Ocean: Cosmopolitanism, Commerce and Islam*. New York: Columbia University Press, 2010.

Sherwani, Haroon Khan. *Studies in the History of Early Muslim Political Thought and Administration*. Lahore: Ashraf, 1942.

Shoufani, Elias S. *Al-Riddah and the Muslim Conquest of Arabia*. Toronto: University of Toronto Press, 1973.

Siddiqui, Sohaira Z. M. *Law and Politics Under the Abbasids: An Intellectual Portrait of al-Juwayni*. Cambridge: Cambridge University Press, 2019.

Skinner, Quentin. *Great Political Thinkers: Machiavelli*. Oxford: Oxford University Press, 1992.

——. *Visions of Politics. Volume 1 Regarding Method*. Cambridge: Cambridge University Press, 2006.

Slomkowski, Paul. *Aristotle's Topics*. Leiden: Brill, 1997.

Smith, Jonathan Z. "Religion, Religions, Religious." In *Critical Terms for Religious Studies*, ed. Mark C. Taylor, 269–84. Chicago: University of Chicago Press, 1998.

Sobieroj, Florian. "The Muʿtazila and Ṣūfism." In *Islamic Mysticism Contested: Thirteen Centuries of Controversies and Polemics*, ed. F. de Jong and Bernd Radtke, 68–92. Leiden: Brill, 1999.

Sourdel, Dominique. "La Biographie D'Ibn Al-Muqaffaʿ D'Après Les Sources Anciennes." *Arabica* 1 (1954): 307–23.

Sperl, Stefan. "Islamic Kingship and Arabic Panegyric Poetry in the Early 9th Century." *Journal of Arabic Literature* 8 (1977): 20–35.

Sprengling, M. "From Persian to Arabic." *American Journal of Semitic Languages and Literatures* 56 (1939): 175–224.

——. "From Persian to Arabic." *American Journal of Semitic Languages and Literatures* 57 (1940): 325–36.

Springborg, Patricia. *Western Republicanism and the Oriental Prince*. Cambridge: Polity, 1992.

Stewart, Devin. "Developments with Religious Sciences During the Rise and Decline of Empire." In *The Wiley Blackwell History of Islam*, ed. Armando Salvatore et al., 137–57. Hoboken, NJ: John Wiley, 2018.

Strothmann, R. *Das staatsrecht der Zaiditen*. Strassburg: Verlag von Karl J. Trübner, 1912.

Stroumsa, Guy G. *The Making of the Abrahamic Religions in Late Antiquity*. Oxford: Oxford University Press, 2017.

Suermann, Harald. *Die konstitution von medina erinnerung an ein anderes modell des zusammenlebens*. n.p.: Gorgias, 2012.

Tabatabai, Javad. "An Anomaly in the History of Persian Political Thought." In *Mirror for the Muslim Prince: Islam and the Theory of Statecraft*, ed. Mehrzad Boroujerdi, 107–21. Syracuse, NY: Syracuse University Press, 2013.

Tafazzoli, Ahmad. "Observations sur le soi-disant Mazdak-nāmag." In *Orientalia J. Duchesne-Guillemin emerito oblata. Acta Iranica. Hommages et opera minora* 9. Leiden: Brill, 1984: 507–10.

Tamari, Shemuel. *Iconotextual Studies in the Muslim Vision of Paradise*. Weisbaden: Harrasovitz, 1999.

Tannous, Jack. *Making of the Medieval Middle East: Religion, Society, and Simple Believers*. Princeton, NJ: Princeton University Press, 2018.

Taylor, Charles. *Dilemmas and Connections: Selected Essays*. Cambridge, MA: Belknap Press of Harvard University, 2014.

——. *Modern Social Imaginaries*. Durham, NC: Duke University Press, 2005.

——. *A Secular Age*. Cambridge, MA: Belknap Press of Harvard University, 2007.

——. "Secularism and Critique." *The Immanent Frame*, 2008. https://tif.ssrc.org/2008/04/24/secularism-and-critique/.

Thomas, J. Barfield. *The Nomadic Alternative*. Englewood Cliffs, NJ: Prentice Hall, 1993.

Tillier, Mathieu. "Un traité politique du IIe/VIIIe siècle L'épître de ʿUbayd Allāh b. al-Ḥasan al-ʿAnbarī au calife al-Mahdī." *Annales Islamologiques* 40 (2006): 139–70.

Tomlinson, John. *Globalization and Culture*. Chicago: University of Chicago Press, 1999.

Toorawa, Shawkat M. *Ibn Abī Ṭāhir Ṭayfūr and Arabic Writerly Culture: A Ninth Century Bookman in Baghdad*. London: Routledge, 2010.

Tor, Deborah. "Sulṭān." In *The Princeton Encyclopedia of Islamic Political Thought*, ed. Gerhard Böwering, Patricia Crone, and Mahan Mirza. Princeton, NJ: Princeton University Press, 2013.

Travis, Zadeh. *Mapping Frontiers Across Medieval Islam: Geography, Translation and the ʿAbbāsid Empire*. London: I. B. Tauris, 2011.

Trinkaus, Kathryn Maurer. "Settlement of Highlands and Lowlands in Early Islamic Damghan." *Iran* 23 (1985): 129–41.

Tucker, William F. "ʿAbdallāh b. Muʿāwiya and the Janāḥiyya: Rebels and Ideologues of the Late Umayyad Period." *Studia Islamica* 51 (1980): 39–57.

——. "Bayān b. Samʿān and the Bayāniyya: Shīʿīte Extremists of Umayyad Iraq." *Muslim World* 65 (1975): 241–53.

——. "Rebels and Gnostics: Al-Mughīra ibn Saʿīd and the Mughīriyya." *Arabica* 22 (1975): 33–47.

Turchin, Peter. "A Theory for Formation of Large Empires." *Journal of Global History* 4 (2009): 191–217.

Türkiye Diyanet Vakfi İslâm Ansiklopedisi (TDVIA). Istanbul: Türkiye Diyanet Vakfı, 2016.

Turner, Bryan S. *Marx and the End of Orientalism*. London: Allen and Unwin, 1978.

Ulrich, Brian. *Arabs in the Early Islamic Empire: Exploring Al-Azd Tribal Identity*. Edinburgh: Edinburgh University Press, 2019.

Umar, Fārūq (Omar, Farouk). *Buḥūth fī al-Tārīkh al-ʿAbbāsī*. Beirut-Baghdad: Dār al-Qalam and Maktabat al-Nahḍa, 1977.

Van Bladel, Kevin T. "The Iranian Characteristics and the Forged Greek Attributions in the Arabic Sirr al-Asrār (Secret of Secrets)." *Mélanges de l'Université Saint-Joseph* 57 (2004): 151–72.

Van Ess, Josef. "The Beginnings of Islamic Theology." In *The Cultural Context of Medieval Learning*. Boston Studies in the Philosophy of Science, vol. 26, ed. J. E. Murdoch and E. D. Sylla, 87–104. Dordrecht: Springer, 1975. https://doi.org/10.1007/978-94-010-1781-7_4.

——. "Das 'Kitāb al-Irgā' des Ḥasan b. Muḥammad b. al-Ḥanafiyya." *Arabica* 21 (1974): 20–52.

——. *Die Gedankenwelt des Ḥārit al-Muḥāsibī*. Bonn: Orientalisches Seminar der Univ. Bonn, 1961.

——. "Political Ideas in Early Islamic Religious Thought." *British Journal of Middle Eastern Studies* 28 (2001): 151–64. http://www.jstor.org/stable/826122.

——. "Some Fragments of the *Muʿaraḍat al-Qur'ān* Attributed to Ibn al-Muqaffaʿ." In *Studia Arabica et Islamica: Festschrift for Iḥsān ʿAbbās*, ed. Wadād al-Qāḍī, 151–53. Beirut: American University of Beirut, 1981.

——. *Theologie und Gesellschaft im 2. und 3. Jahrhundert Hidschra*. Berlin: De Gruyter, 1997.

——. *Theology and Society in the Second and Third Centuries of the Hijra: A History of Religious Thought in Early Islam*. Trans. Gwendolin Goldbloom. 5 vols. Leiden: Brill, 2017–2019.

Van Ess, Josef, and Hans Hinrich Biesterfeldt. *Kleine schriften*, vol. 3. Leiden: Brill, 2018.

Venturi, Franco. "Oriental Despotism." *Journal of the History of Ideas* 24 (1963): 133–42.

Viswanathan, Gauri. *Outside the Fold: Conversion, Modernity, and Belief*. Princeton, NJ: Princeton University Press, 1998.

Vries, Hent de, and Lawrence Eugene Sullivan. *Political Theologies: Public Religions in a Post-Secular World*. New York: Fordham University Press, 2009.

Walker, John. *A Catalogue of the Muhammadan Coins in the British Museum: A Catalogue of the Arab-Byzantine and Post-Reform Umaiyad Coins*, vol. 2. Oxford: British Museum, 1956.

Walzer, Richard. "Aspects of Islamic Political Thought: Al-Fārābī and Ibn Xaldūn." *Oriens* 16 (1963): 40–60.

Al-Warrāq.net. Maintained by Muḥammad Aḥmad Khalīfa al-Suwaydī. http://www.alwaraq.net/Core/index.jsp?option=1.

Wasserstrom, Steven. "The Moving Finger Writes: Mughīra b. Saʿīd's Islamic Gnosis and the Myths of Its Rejection." *History of Religions* 25 (1985–1986): 1–29.

Watson, Andrew M. *Agricultural Innovation in the Early Islamic World: The Diffusion of Crops and Farming Techniques, 700–1100*. Cambridge: Cambridge University Press, 1983.

Watt, William Montgomery. *Bell's Introduction to the Qur'an*. Edinburgh: Edinburgh University Press, 1970.

——. "God's Caliph: Qur'ānic Interpretation and Umayyad Claims." In *Iran and Islam, in Memory of the Late Vladimir Minorsky*, ed. Clifford Edmund Bosworth, 565–74. Edinburgh: Edinburgh University Press, 1971.

——. *Islamic Political Thought*. Edinburgh: Edinburgh University Press, 1998.

——. *Muhammad at Medina*. Oxford: Clarendon, 1968.

Weber, Max. *The Sociology of Religion*. Trans. Ephraim Fischoff. London: Beacon, 1963.

——. *The Vocation Lectures: "Science as a Vocation," "Politics as a Vocation."* Ed. David Owen and Tracy B. Strong. Trans. Rodney Livingstone. Indianapolis, IN: Hachette, 2004.

Weber, Max, Guenther Roth, and Claus Wittich. *Economy and Society*. Berkeley: University of California Press, 1978.

Wendell, Charles. "Baghdad: Imago Mundi and Other Foundation Lore." *International Journal of Middle East Studies* 2 (1971): 99–128.

Whitcomb, Donald. "An Umayyad Legacy for the Early Islamic City: Fusṭāṭ, and the Experience of Egypt." In *Umayyad Legacies: Medieval Memories from Syria to Spain*, ed. Antoine Borrut and Paul M. Cobb, 403–16. Leiden: Brill, 2010.

Wieseltier, Leon. "Two Concepts of Secularism." In *Isaiah Berlin: A Celebration*, ed. Isaiah Berlin, Edna Ullmann-Margalit, and Avishai Margalit, 80–99. Chicago: University of Chicago Press, 1991.

Wittfogel, Karl August. *Oriental Despotism: A Comparative Study of Total Power*. New Haven, CT: Yale University Press, 1957.

Wittgenstein, Ludwig, and G. E. M. Anscombe. *Philosophical Investigations*. Oxford: Basil Blackwell, 1972.

Wurtzel, Carl. "The Coinage of the Revolutionaries in the Late Umayyad Period." *Museum Notes (American Numismatic Society)* 23 (1978): 161–99.

Yavari, Neguin. *Advice for the Sultan: Prophetic Voices and Secular Politics in Medieval Islam*. Oxford: Oxford University Press, 2014.

——. "The Political Regard in Medieval Islamic Thought." *Historical Social Research / Historische Sozialforschung* 44 (2019): 52–73.

——. "Secularity in the Premodern Islamic World." In *Companion of the Study of Secularity*, ed. The Humanities Center for Advanced Studies (HCAS), "Multiple Secularities: Beyond the West, Beyond Modernities," 1–12. Leipzig University, 2019. https://www.multiple-secularities.de/publications/companion/secularity-in-the-premodern-islamic-world/.

Yılmaz, Hüseyin. *Caliphate Redefined: The Mystical Turn in Ottoman Political Thought*. Princeton, NJ: Princeton University Press, 2018.

——. "Containing Sultanic Authority: Constitutionalism in the Ottoman Empire Before Modernity." *Osmanlı Araştırmaları* 45 (2015): 231–64.

Yousefi, Najm al-Din. "Islam without *Fuqahā'*: Ibn al-Muqaffaʿ and His Perso-Islamic Solution to the Caliphate's Crisis of Legitimacy (70–142 AH/690–760 CE)." *Iranian Studies* (2017): 9–44.

Yücesoy, Hayrettin. "Ancient Imperial Heritage and Islamic Universal Historiography: Al-Dīnawarī's Secular Perspective." *Journal of Global History* 2 (2007): 135–55.

——. "Imamate." In *The Princeton Encyclopedia of Islamic Political Thought*, ed. Gerhard Böwering, Patricia Crone, and Mahan Mirza. Princeton, NJ: Princeton University Press, 2013.

——. "Islamic Political Theory." In *Medieval Islamic Civilization: An Encyclopedia*, ed. Yousef Meri. London: Routledge, 2006.

——. "Justification of Political Authority in Medieval Sunni Thought." In *Islam, the State, and Political Authority: Medieval Issues and Modern Concerns*, ed. Asma Afsaruddin, 9–33. New York: Palgrave Macmillan, 2011.

——. "Language of Empire: Politics of Arabic and Persian in the Abbasid World." *Publication of the Modern Language Association* 130, no. 2 (2015): 384–92.

——. *Messianic Beliefs and Imperial Politics in Medieval Islam: The ʿAbbāsid Caliphate in the Early Ninth Century*. Columbia: University of South Carolina Press, 2009.

——. "Political Anarchism, Dissent, and Marginal Groups in the Early Ninth Century: The Ṣūfīs of the Muʿtazila Revisited." In *The Lineaments of Islam: Studies in Honor of Fred McGraw Donner*, ed. Paul Cobb, 61–84. Leiden: Brill, 2012.

——. *Taṭawwur al-Fikr al-Siyāsī ʿinda Ahl al-Sunna: Fatrat al-Takwīn: min Bidāyatihi ḥatta al-Thulth al-Awwal min al-Qarn al-Rābiʿ al-Hijrī*. Amman: Dār al-Bashīr, 1993.

——. "Translation as Self-Consciousness: The Abbasid Translation Movement, Ancient Sciences, and Antediluvian Wisdom (ca. 750–850)." *Journal of World History* 20 (2009): 523–57.

Zaman, Muhammad Qasim. "The ʿAbbāsid Revolution: A Study of the Nature and Role of Religious Dynamics." *Journal of Asian History* 21 (1987): 119–49.

——. *Religion and Politics Under the Early ʿAbbasids: The Emergence of Proto-Sunni Elite*. Leiden: Brill, 1997.

Zerubavel, Eviatar. *Fine Line: Making Distinctions in Everyday Life*. Chicago: University of Chicago Press, 1993.

Index

Abbasid caliphate, 255; absolute power of, 6, 136–137; Arabian Peninsula and, 189; empire of, 261; family rule of, 34; as God's caliphs, 36; Ibn al-Muqaffaᶜ report on, 34; as imams, 36; Islam identification of, 35, 124; as messianic redeemers, 36; territorial expansion of, 42–43, 189–222, 260; Watt on breakdown of, 22; Zaman on ulema relationship with, 24

Abbasid revolt, 56, 107, 118–119, 193, 260; *The Chronicle of Zuqnin* on power struggle after, 218; for Hāshimid rule, 32–34; Ibn al-Muqaffaᶜ on, 196; Iraq-Khurasan region after, 207; Khurasani in, 191; sociopolitical change after, 232–233, 235–236; taxation after, 248–249; ulema Abbasids collaboration in, 48

Abbasids: ᶜAlids dispute with, 211–212; al-ᶜAnbarī on governing structure of, 67; Baghdad round city architectural monument, 35; empire building of, xiii, 257; Ibn Isḥāq loyalty to, 60; lay literati on sovereignty, 10; Marwān II killed by, 107, 216; on secularity in sociopolitical spaces, 11; Watt on empire under, 22

ᶜAbd al-Ḥamīd al-Kātib, 13, 82, 85, 87, 125–127; on absolute power, 136–137; Abū Hilāl on prose of, 93; beast and trainer metaphor of, 6; Ḍaḥḥāk b. Qays rebuke by, 97–98; on divine beneficence, 149; on governance, 96, 98–99; Ibn al-Muqaffaᶜ relationship with, 107, 108; letter to Hishām, 55, 92–93; "Letter to the Scribes" of, 96, 101–105, 121, 227; on military, 69, 99–100, 147, 191; on model scribe qualities, 101; political prose of, 67, 91–105, 112–113; Qadarites opposition by, 55; al-Qadi on, 95–96; on scribes in Umayyad administration, 103; on scribe vital importance, 102–103; "Testament to the Crown Prince" by, 96–100, 121, 191, 227; transitional writing of, 105

ᶜAbdallāh b. ᶜAlī, 150, 191, 216, 322n77

ᶜAbd al-Malik b. Ayyūb al-Numaryi: administrative reforms of, 189; al-Mahdī governorship appointment by, 65–66; non-Muslim taxation by, 85

Abdülhamid Ottoman sultan, Orientalists on, 16

Abrahamic monotheism, Muhammad faith of, 28

absolute power, 6; Ibn al-Muqaffaᶜ and ᶜAbd al-Ḥamīd on, 136–137

Abū Bakr (caliph), 57, 61; apostasy wars and, 29; as commander of faithful, 29; Muhammad death and, 28, 62; oath of allegiance by, 62; political authority of, 63; revisionist intervention and, 28–29; sermon on leadership of, 62; on taxation, 251

Abū Hilāl al-ᶜAskarī, 93

Abū Jaᶜfar (caliph), 211

Abū Muslim (caliph), 150, 191, 195–196, 211

Abū Yūsuf, Yaʿqūb b. Ibrāhīm, 50; on administrative matters, 78; on caliph qualities, 78–79; on good governance, 78; *ḥadīth* reliance by, 77; al-Mahdī and, 76–77; on obedience to God, 79; as al-Rashīd chief judge, 76–81
Abū Zurʿa, Damascene, 41
adab (etiquette), 126–127, 256; religious dutifulness and renunciant piety and, 8–9
Al-Adab al-Kabīr' prose, of Ibn al-Muqaffaʿ, 117–118, 121, 127, 129, 311n60, 317n35, 325n8; on authority types, 141; on elite, 227; on ruler, 325n8; on sovereignty, 139–140
Adab al-Kātib. See Etiquette for the Scribe
adab-siyasa: extrareligious discursive space creation by, 10; pragmatic secularity of, 14; regime of moral cultivation and, xiv; religion control and, 10; religion defined and political structure, 9–10; on religion role in political practice, 9; worldly ethos of, xi, 9, 124–132; sovereign cultivation by, 6; ulema practice divergence by, 10; worldliness and, 128; governance and, 255
administration: ʿAbd al-Malik reforms in, 189; Abū Yūsuf on matters of, 78; al-ʿAnbarī on justice and, 69–70; Arabic language use for caliphal, 84; caliphal practice vocabulary of early theology and, 36–37; caliph use of Arabic language in, 84; client functionaries and Umayyad caliphs, 83; effective rule from handling of, 158; of al-Manṣūr, 43; of provinces, 43; ruling proper handling of, 158; scribes and Umayyad caliph, 103; Umayyads non-Muslim and non-Arab Muslims positions in, 46
administrative efficiency: al-ʿAnbarī on, 69–70; in empire building, xiii
Agamben, Giorgio, 224, 244, 262
ahl al-ra'y (rational judgment), 178
Ahmed, Shahab, 274n56
ʿA'in-nāma. See Book of Proper Conduct
ʿAlids, 56, 60, 193, 204; Abbasids dispute with, 211–212
alms, al-ʿAnbarī on, 72–73
Althusser, Louis, 144, 154, 260
al-ʿāmma. See masses
Anas, Mālik b., 9
al-ʿAnbarī, ʿUbaydallāh b. al-Ḥasan, 3; on Abbasid governing structure, 67; on administration and justice, 69–70; on alms, 72–73; on caliphate safeguard for believers and faith, 68; on caliph authority, 73, 75; on caliph consultation with jurists, 75; caliph praise from, 68; on employment of judges, 71; on end of time, 73–74; on governance, 69; on imamate, 68–69; juristic jurisprudential writing of, 66–76; letter to caliph al-Mahdī, 50, 65–76; on al-Mahdī and Abū Yūsuf, 76–77; al-Mahdī judicial disagreements from, 66; al-Manṣūr appointment as judge of Basra, 65–66; on military, 69–70; people of trust and knowledge for caliph, 74–75; on revealed law, 75; on taxation, 67–68, 70–72, 251; on tribute revenue disbursement, 72
al-Andalus, imperial territories absence of, 190, 220–222
apostasy wars, Abū Bakr and, 29
Arabian Peninsula, Abbasid caliphate and, 189
Arabic language, xiii; caliphal administration use of, 84; empire building and, 84; Ibn al-Muqaffaʿ proficiency in, 108; learned elite prose writing in, 84–85; Persian language translation into, 85; Umayyad caliphs use of, 83
Arabic political prose, xiii; Umayyad caliphs use of, 83
Arnold, Thomas, 20; on caliphate irrational and anachronistic maintenance, 18; on Turkish National Assembly caliphate abolishment, 19
Asad, Talal, 11, 273 41
ascetics (*fiqh*), *tahdhīb* compared to, 273n37
Austin, John: Bourdieu on, xii; on language as performance, xii
authority: of imam and imamate, 1–2, 37, 39–40, 49–50, 65, 148; inheritance, 51, 52; Muhammad and, 29–30; Qur'an moral, 30; religious, 1–2, 148, 171–172, 278n98; Umayyad caliphs on theological and juridical, 41. *See also* sovereignty
authority, of caliphs: al-ʿAnbarī on, 73, 75; forms of, 36–42; pastoral authority, xiii, 257; sacred law and, 42, 165; siyasa, 141–149; sovereignty and, 42; of strength, 141; ulema contention over, 47; of whimsical temptation, 141. *See also* revealed law
Aydın, Cemil, 15
Al-Azmeh, Aziz, 23, 41

Beast and the Sovereign, The (Derrida), 6, 138
beast and trainer metaphor, of ʿAbd al-Ḥamīd, 6

Bilawhar and Yudasaf (Ibn al-Muqaffaᶜ), 117, 303n47
Biography of the Prophet (Ibn Isḥāq), 38, 49, 60
bios, Agamben on, 224, 244, 245, 261
blessing, 68, 73, 136, 246, 255, 259
Blunt, Wilfrid S., 17
body (*ṣiḥḥat al-badan/al-jasad*): collective, 49, 225; Ibn al-Muqaffaᶜ on religion and, 8, 129–130, 183; Islamist movements on formation of governing, ix
Book of Land Tax, The (*Kitāb al-Kharāj*) (Abū Yūsuf), 77–78; *ḥadīth* topics in, 79
Book of Politics, The (*Kitāb al-Siyāsa*), 296n27; Latham on, 91; ᶜA.Sālim translation of, 91
Book of Proper Conduct, The (*ᶜA'in-nāma*) (Ibn al-Muqaffaᶜ), 115–116
Book of Taxation, The (Abū Yūsuf), 50
Book of the Postponement, The (*Kitāb al-Irjā'*) (al-Ḥanafiyya), 49
Bourdieu, Pierre, xii, 121
bureaucrats: lay bureaucrat elite, 85–90; lay bureaucrat literati, 6, 10, 107–111, 258; in Umayyads, xiii
Bureau of Correspondence (*Dīwān al-Rasā'il*), documents productions by, 85

caliphal contractualism, of political authority, 37, 38; early jurists and *ḥadīth* transmitters on, 38; pre-Sunnite, 60–63
caliphal practice: Abbasids proclamation of caliphate, 33–34; administrative vocabulary of early theology, 36–37; caliphal authority forms, 36–42; foundational groups and, 31; governance ethics debate and, 31; heterogeneous polity of, 44; Hodgson on Greco-Roman and Irano-Semitic faith systems, 34–35, 294n2; intellectual capital bifurcation, 46–48; jihad military activity and, 29; al-Khaṭṭāb seniority system, 30, 286n58; military conquests of, 29; modalities of governance and, 34–36; move toward election in, 31–32; nomination-election-consent process in, 40; obedience demand, 30–31, 63, 95–96; political trajectory of new social imaginary, 28–34; provincial administrations and military expansion, 43; sociocultural differences and, 44–45; structure and meaning of, 42–46
caliphate (*khilāfa*): Abbasids proclamation of, 33–34; al-ᶜAnbarī on safeguarding for believers and faith, 68; Arnold on imperial and political potential of, 18; Arnold on irrational and anachronistic maintenance of, 18; Al-Azmeh on, 23; Blunt on England, France and Egypt claim to, 17; European scholars on Oriental despotism of, 17; Ibn al-Muqaffaᶜ on incompetence in, 233–234, 240–241; as institution, 276n79; MacDonald on English throne as holder of, 17–18; Orientalist research on, 16; as pastoral authority, xiii, 257; Qurayshite monopoly on, 61; Riḍā on establishment of, 19–20; Sunnite-juristic view of, 20; territorial consciousness and, 205–206; theory by jurists, 22; Turkish National Assembly abolishment of, 19; ulema-centric idea of, x. *See also* Abbasid caliphate
Caliphate, The (Arnold), 18
caliphs: Abū Yūsuf on qualities of, 78–79; Althusser on titles of, 144; commander of faithful military command, 36; commander of faithful readiness to listen, 314n108; discretionary sacred law code, 166; on divinely sanctioned rule, 50; election of, 40–41, 63; "Epistle on the Caliph's Privy" on, 136; Ibn al-Muqaffaᶜ on conduct of, 155; Ibn al-Muqaffaᶜ on military control by, 196–197; Ibn al-Muqaffaᶜ on titles of, 144–145; Ibn al-Muqaffaᶜ reimagination of, 134; issuance and transfer of laws, 183; jurists negotiation with, 47–48; military punitive measures of, 45; obedience of, 30–31, 63, 95–96; political, legal, and economic institutions of, 45; realm of, 149; revealed law and religious-legal structure, 172; rule after Muhammad death, 27; as ruling person, 40; sacred immutable law code of, 166; temporal or positive law code, 166; ulema interest in faith status of, 259. *See also* authority, of caliphs; Umayyad caliphs; *specific caliph*
caliphs, deconfessionalizing of, 161; rational judgment as political virtue, 154–160; siyasa caliph authority, 141–149; sovereign as beast, 134–141; sovereignty and providence dialectic, 149–154
charitable contributions, taxation and, 251
"Charter of Medina," Muhammad and, 28
chess, 10, 13, 125, 126
Chronicle of Zuqnin, The, 220; on power struggle after Abbasid revolt, 218; on Syria, 218; on taxation, 219

circle of justice, Ibn al-Muqaffaʿ and, 121–122, 305n63
civil administration, military and, 199–208
client functionaries, Umayyad caliphs administration use of, 83
codification: discretionary sacred law code, 166; imperial law theory and, 179–186; sacred immutable code, 166; temporal or positive law code, 166
co-formation of faith and empire, in self-aware political reflection, 27, 29–30
collective body. *See* community or collective body
colonial paradigm, of Islamic political thought, 14–26; Aydın on Muslim world in Afro-Eurasia, 15; Orientalists on customary knowledge practices, 15; Other essentializing in, 15; Otherness, rhetoric of, ix
colonizers, Ottoman caliphate fight against, 19
commander of faithful, 91, 201, 215, 231, 306n62, 320n25; Abū Bakr as, 29; attributes of, 36; caliph readiness to listen, 314n108; God's caliph and, 51, 52, 69; Ibn al-Muqaffaʿ on, 143–149, 155–156, 179, 181, 195, 198; military command by caliphs, 36, 96, 147, 153; obedience of, 52; privy of, 242, 328n74; taxation and, 249–250; title of, 135
common folk. *See* masses
community or collective body (*umma*): confessionalism in, 216, 219; faith, xiii, 27; Ibn al-Muqaffaʿ on, 225; ulema as guardians of, 140; ulema discourse on, 49; ulema discourse on collective body of, 49
companions (*al-ṣaḥāba*), 237; of masses, 243–244
confessionalism, x, 44–45, 250–251; in communities, 216, 219; Ibn al-Muqaffaʿ on, 224–225; in Muslim dynasties history, 16; ulema militancy and, 133
consequentialism, siyasa and, 4
constitutionalism, in Muslim state, 19
Counsel for Kings (Pseudo-Māwardī), 24–25
creation, Ibn Isḥāq *Biography of the Prophet* on, 60
Crone, Patricia, 58, 299n89, 319n8
customary knowledge practices (*ʿulūm*), 15

Dabashi, Hamid, 273n36
Ḍaḥḥāk b. Qays, ʿAbd al-Ḥamīd rebuke of, 97–98
Darling, Linda, 25
decolonial, ix, x, 1, 26
Deleuze, Gilles, 13
Derrida, Jacques, 6, 138
designation form of succession to rule, 41
dhimmī. *See* non-Muslims
dīn. *See* divine law
al-dīn. *See* revealed law
al-dīn wa al-ʿaql. *See* reason
discretionary sacred law code, of caliph, 166
discursive practices, interventions and, x, xii, 258
disenchanted politics, x, 267n2
distinctive idiom, of political rationalities, 4
divine beneficence (*niʿma*), xiv, 259; ʿAbd al-Ḥamīd on, 149; Ibn al-Muqaffaʿ on, 150, 151, 160; sovereignty as, 149–150, 255
divine law (*dīn*): as belief in and practice of laws, 7; characteristics of, 8; God teaching of, 7; in ulema discourse, 8
divine privilege, of prophets, 312n69
Dīwān al-Rasāʾil. *See* Bureau of Correspondence
Dome of the Rock in Jerusalem, 125; imamate and ulema classification and, 35; *longue-durée* Abrahamic monotheism and, 35
Dozy, Reinhart, 17
dunyawī. *See* worldliness
dynastic form, of succession to rule, 41

Egypt: Blunt on caliphate claim by, 17; Greek language use in, 83; importance of, 42–43; Mahmood on piety movement in, 2
election, of caliphs, 40–41, 63
elite (*al-khāṣṣa*), 223, 227, 229, 232, 261; functions of, 231; Ibn al-Muqaffaʿ critique on Iraq, 234; Ibn al-Muqaffaʿ on Syria, 230; Ibn al-Muqaffaʿ various description of, 228; as sovereign appropriate collaborators, 253; training of masses through, 245–246
empire: of Abbasid caliphate, 261; jurists as legal and religious establishment of, 76; ulema on sacred law of, xiv, 80–81
empire, people of, 223; elite in, 227–232; masses qualified life, 243–246; privy and challenges, 237–243; shepherd and flock, 224–227; status quo critique, 232–236; taxpaying subjects compared to nonentities, 246–253
empire building: of Abbasids, xiii, 257; administrative efficiency in, xiii; Arabic language and, 84; of Umayyads, xiii, 257
end of time, al-ʿAnbarī on, 73–74
Engels, Friedrich, 17
England: Blunt on caliphate claim by, 17; MacDonald on caliphate held by, 17–18

epistemological character, of political rationalities, 3
"Epistle" (D. Sālim), 49, 76; appeal to piety in, 58; arguments with opponents, 58; Crone and Zimmermann on, 58; on faith origin, 58; on Kharijite, Murji'ites and Fatana, 58–59; *Kitāb al-Irjā'* letter/pamphlet similarity to, 57–59
"Epistle on the Caliph's Privy" (Ibn al-Muqaffaᶜ), xiii, xiv, 5, 67, 106, 270n19, 272n27, 274n52, 307n84; on caliph, 135; on controlling legislation and law, 162; discursive practice in, 258; on elite, 227–228; on flock, 246; for Ibn al-Muqaffaᶜ personal career, 252; to al-Manṣūr, 110, 118; on masses, 244; on military, 69, 193; on order through sovereign rule, 136; on taxation, 246; themes in, 120–121
etiquette. *See* adab
Etiquette for the Scribe (*Adab al-Kātib*) (Ibn Qutayba), 132
European colonialism, Memmi on, 86
extrareligious discursive space, adab-siyasa creation of, 10

faith: Murji'ite perspective on, 57; D. Sālim "Epistle" on origin of, 58; ulema as guardians of, 140
faith community, Muhammad community rival group diversity in, 27
family form, of succession to rule, 41; of Abbasid caliphate, 34
Fanon, Frantz, 88
Fatana, D. Sālim "Epistle" on, 58–59
fiqh. *See* ascetics
flock (*raᶜiyya*), 223, 246; Ibn al-Muqaffaᶜ referral to imperial subjects as, 224–225; shepherd and, 224–227
Foucault, Michel, xii, 270n16; on common good, 5; on governance, 4, 271n20
Fowden, Garth, 35
France, Blunt on caliphate claim by, 17
free will argument, for Umayyad caliphs, 55
frontier zone, of Umayyads, 44

Gibbon, Edward, 16
global secularities, 12; early Islam and, 7–10
God: Abū Yūsuf on obedience to, 79; divine decree ruling according to law of, 51–54; qur'anic language on sovereignty of, 28; teaching of divine law, 7; von Kremer on Islam, 17
God's caliph: commander of faithful and, 51, 52, 69; Umayyad caliphs reference to, 38–39
God's caliphate: Abbasid caliphate as, 36; as political authority, 37, 38–39
good governance: of Abū Bakr, 62; Abū Yūsuf on, 78; Ibn al-Muqaffaᶜ on, 106, 118–119, 121–122, 142; siyasa on religious piety distinct from, x, 107, 259–260
governance (*tadbīr*): ᶜAbd al-Ḥamīd on, 96, 98–99; al-ᶜAnbarī on, 69; caliphil practice, 31, 34–36; Foucault on, 4, 271n20; Ibn al-Muqaffaᶜ on, 96, 98–99, 142–144; imamate on prophecy and, 255; imamate rationality of, 1–2, 106, 259; in Islamicate history, 1–7; masses elevation for social order, 245; Muhammad community rival group diversity in, 27; Muhammad message of, 280n7; Muslim intellectuals on Islamic, 20; of provinces, 44; religious authority boundaries and, 171–172; siyasa as subjects, 143; siyasa on human nature and, 255; siyasa rationality of, 2–4; sovereignty compared to, 5, 6; sultanic rulers introduction of extrareligious laws in, 14; Umayyads and debate about ethics of, 31
governmentalization: of religion after siyasa, 64–65, 77, 257; of sovereignty, 118–124, 162, 256
Grabar, Oleg, 125
grace or favor, Ibn al-Muqaffaᶜ on, 153–154
grave sinner, Umayyads as, 55; *Kitāb al-Irjā'* letter/pamphlet on, 56–57; Murji'ites position on, 56
Greco-Roman faith system, 34–35
Greek language, Syria and Egypt use of, 83
guardianship, in lay bureaucrat elite, 86–87
Guattari, Félix, 13

Habermas, Jürgen, 162–163
ḥadīth transmitter, 177–178; Abū Yūsuf reliance on, 77; *The Book of Land Tax* topics by, 79; on caliphal contractualism, 38; al-Dārimī as, 63; Ibn Isḥāq and, 60
Hallaq, Wael, 23
Ḥanafī: school of law, 76; legal methodology, 80
al-Ḥanafiyya, l-Ḥasan b. Muhammad b., 49
hard secularity, of ruler, 13–14
Hāshimid (caliph), Abbasid revolt for rule of, 32–34
Hegel, Georg W. F., 16–17
hegemonic religiosity, in history, 13

heterogeneous polity, in caliphal practice, 44
Hijaz (province), 203, 208–209
Hishām (caliph), 54; ʿAbd al-Ḥamīd letter to, 55, 92–93; ʿA. Sālim as chancellor for, 90–91
Hodgson, Marshall, 25, 26, 34–35, 294n2
al-Ḥusayn b. ʿAlī, 31

Ibn al-Muqaffaʿal-Kātib, 13, 40, 82, 85, 87, 116, 125–127, 252; on Abbasid practice, 34; ʿAbd al-Ḥamīd relationship with, 107, 108; Abū Hilāl on prose of, 93; *Al-Adab al-Kabīr*' prose of, 117–118, 121, 127, 129, 139–141, 227, 311n60, 317n35; Arabic language proficiency of, 108; on army, judiciary, revenue, taxation, 67; attempt to create politics by, 106; background of, 107–111; *Bilawhar and Yudasaf* of, 117, 303n47; on caliphate incompetence, 233–234, 240–241; on caliph conduct, 155; on caliph military control, 196–197; caliphs reimagination, 134; on caliph titles, 144–145; circle of justice and, 121–122, 305n63; on collective body, 225; on commander of faithful, 143–149, 155–156, 179, 181, 195, 198; on confessionalism, 224–225; Ḍaḥḥāk b. Qays rebuke by, 97–98; on dangerousness of masses, 244–245; death of, 109; on divine beneficence, 150, 151, 160; elite various description of, 228; on expert consultation, 229; father of, 107, 299n4; on good governance, 106, 118–119, 121–122, 142; on governance, 96, 98–99, 142–144; on grace or favor, 153–154; Ibn al-Muqaffaʿ relationship with, 107, 108; Ibn Khaldūn on, 113; imperial subjects described by, 224–225; on Iraq, 235–236; Iraq elite critique, 234; on Iraq-Khurasan region, 226, 237; Islam conversion by, 108, 110; *Kalīla and Dimna* animal fables of, 6, 113–115, 121, 132, 138, 154, 302n31; *Letter of Tansar* of, 116–117, 227, 325n1; letter to Hishām, 55, 92–93; life and political writings of, xiii, xiv, 5; on *longue-durée* imperial practices, 111, 243; on al-Manṣūr challenges, 150, 232; al-Manṣūr relationship with, 109; on merit consideration, 236; on military, 69, 99–100, 147, 192–194, 261; on model scribe qualities, 101; on Muslims, 226; on obedience, 5, 12, 56, 147–148, 159–160; political and territorial awareness of, 206–209; political prose of, 67, 91–105, 112–113; on political virtue, 157–159, 161; Qadarites opposition by, 55; al-Qadi on, 95–96; on religion and body, 8, 129–130; on religion and reason difference, 8; on revealed law, 148, 162, 167, 169, 175–176; scribe metaphor of, 137; on scribes in Umayyad administration, 103; on scribe vital importance, 102–103; on social order, 223–224, 244; on sound knowledge, 176–177; sovereign power language of, 135–136; on sovereignty, 135, 146–147, 151–152, 156; on Syria elite, 230; transitional writing of, 105; translations by, 115; ulema and writings of, xiii, 252; Umayyad caliph attacks by, 229; on vision of ideal monarchical politics, 251–252. *See also* empire, people of; "Epistle on the Caliph's Privy"; territorial consciousness
Ibn Isḥāq, 9, 38, 49, 295n15; *ḥadīth* transmitters and, 60; on Muhammad communication of God's laws, 61; Muhammad death representation by, 60, 63; on obedience, 63
Ibn Khaldūn, 22; on Ibn al-Muqaffaʿ, 113
Ibn Qutayba, 3, 132
Ibn Taymiyya, 3, 270n13
ikhtiyār (election), 37
imam (*imām*): Abbasid caliphate as, 36; imperial law and obedience to, 165, 167–173; as legitimate leader, 40; ruler of religious and secular authority, 1–2, 148; Sufis of the Muʿtazila on authority and election of, 65
imamate, 82, 268n2; al-ʿAnbarī on, 68–69; Dome of the Rock classification with, 35; on governance and prophecy, 255; governance of imam and, 1–2, 255; juristic archetype of, 65–76; language of, 49–81; legitimate authority of community by, 49–50; primary-source texts for, 2; Shiite and Kharijite positions on, 20; siyasa intertexuality in political prose with, 94–105; sovereignty of, 273n38; Strothmann on Zaydī, 21; ulema political theology of, 2; Watt on Shiite position on, 23
imamate discourse, 269n4; in caliphal world, x, 140; rationality of governance, 1–2, 106, 259; siyasa and mood and style change in, xiii; Sufis of the Muʿtazila anarchist position and, 64
imperial aristocracy, 260–261; Ibn al-Muqaffaʿ on, 253; of military, administrative elite and nobility, 223

imperial economy of military, Ibn al-Muqaffaʿ on, 200–202
imperial law theory, 162; caliph issuance and transfer of laws, 183; codification and, 179–186; jurists and, 181–183; legal disagreements in, 184–185; obedience to imam, 165, 167–173; political and legal premises, 166–167; religion and reason dialectic, 173–178; religious-legal thought critique, 163–166; theoretical and practical implications for, 186–188
imperial subjects, Ibn al-Muqaffaʿ term of flock for, 224–225
imperial universalism, Qusayr ʿAmra palace in Jordan and, 35
India, Sen on Islamic political thought in, 277n87
interpretative authority, after Muhammad death, 29–30
interventions: Abū Bakr revisionist, 28–29; analyzing statements as, xi–xii; discursive practices and, x, xii, 258
Iqbal, Muhammad: on Islamic political thought, 20; on Muslims as nation, 20–21
Irano-Semitic faith system, 34–35
Iraq: Abbasid and, 48; Ibn al-Muqaffaʿ critique of elite in, 234; Ibn al-Muqaffaʿ on, 235–236; Persian language use in, 83; Umayyads control attempts in, 32–33; Yazīd III letter to, 51, 53–54
Iraq-Khurasan region, 191, 260; after Abbasid revolt, 207; Arab population in, 204–205; as empire core, 190, 203–204; Ibn al-Muqaffaʿ on, 226, 237; military of, 189; non-Arab Muslims and non-Muslim subjects in, 226–227
Islam, 256–257; Abbasid caliphs identification with, 35, 124; Ahmed on, 275n56; global secularities and early, 7–10; Ibn al-Muqaffaʿ conversion to, 108, 110; Umayyad identification with, 35, 124; von Kremer on God, prophecy, and state in, 17; Weber on, 275n64; Yazīd III on revealed law of, 54
Islamicate history: governance in, 1–7; Hodgson on, 25, 26; soft and hard secularity in, 13–14
Islamic conservatism, 55–57
Islamic Culture (Rosenthal), 22
Islamic political thought: birth of, 20–23; as colonial paradigm, 14–26; global secularities and early Islam, x, xi, 7–10; governance in Islamicate history, 1–7; Iqbal on, 20; Kohn on, 277n89; Ottoman caliphate and Muslim state idea, 16–20; pragmatic secularity, 10–14; Sen on India, 277n87; Sherwani on, 21–22, 277n85; Strothmann on imamate and, 21
Islamic Political Thought (Watt), 22
al-Islām wa-Uṣūl al-Ḥukm (al-Rāziq), 20

al-Jāḥiẓ, 3, 130–132, 299n89
jihad, 79, 145, 193; caliphal practice and military activity of, 29
judges: Abū Yūsuf as al-Rashīd chief, 76–81; al-ʿAnbarī on employment of, 71; Umayyads and appointment of, 163
juristic archetype, of imamate, 65–76
juristic discourse, imperial turn in, 76–81
jurists: al-ʿAnbarī on caliph consultation with, 75; on caliphal contractualism, 38; caliphs negotiation with, 47–48; content of law determination by, 41–42; as empire legal and religious establishment, 76; imperial law and, 181–183; prophetic practice and, 177–178; religious-legal thought of, 164; religious scholarship monopolized by, 47–48; theory of caliphate by, 22
justice, al-ʿAnbarī on, 69–70
al-Juwaynī, 24

kalām, 2, 57, 121, 269n4
Kalīla and Dimna animal fables, of Ibn al-Muqaffaʿ, 6, 113–115, 121, 132, 302n31; on sovereignty, 138, 154
Kharijites, 31, 204; on ideal caliphate, 17; imamate position of, 20; as religiopolitical party, 17; D. Sālim "Epistle" on, 58–59
al-khāṣṣa. *See* elite
khilāfa. *See* caliphate
Khurasani: in Abbasid revolt, 191; soldiers, 193–194, 197; Umayyads control attempts in, 32–33
kingdom and kinship, 145–146; qur'anic language on, 135
kisrāwiyya, 37
Kitāb al-Irjā' letter/pamphlet: D. Sālim "Epistle" similarity to, 57–59; on Umayyads as grave sinner, 56–57
Kitāb al-Kharāj. See *Book of Land Tax, The*
Kitāb al-Siyāsa. See *Book of Politics, The*
Kitāb al-Ṭabīkh (al-Warrāq), 272n31

knowledge: qur'anic texts and legal, 164; ulema restriction attempts for, 128
Kohn, Hans, 277n89
von Kremer, Alfred, 17

language: analyzing statements as interventions, xi–xii; Austin on performance of, xii; Persian, 83, 85; qur'anic, 28, 80, 135, 164; Syria and Egypt use of Greek, 83; ulema political, xiii, 2, 255. *See also* Arabic language; imamate discourse; siyasa discourse; siyasa disruptive language; ulema discourse
language, of imamate, 49; early Islamic conservatism, 55–57; governmentalization of religion after siyasa, 64–65, 77, 257; imperial turn in juristic discourse, 76–81; juristic archetype of imamate, 65–76; pre-Sunnite caliphal contractualism, 60–63; ruling by divine decree according to God's law, 51–54; theology of resistance, 57–60; ulema-centric political theology formations, 50–51
Lapidus, Ira M., 278n98
Latham, J. D., 91, 296n29
laws: *dīn* as belief in and practice of, 7; "Epistle on the Caliph's Privy" on, 162; imperial, divine and combination bodies, 187; jurist determination of content of, 41–42; political control intersection with, xiv; sovereign as giver of, 148. *See also* imperial law theory; revealed law; sacred law
lay bureaucrat elite (*mawlā*): Fanon and, 88; guardianship in, 86–87; Memmi on, 89; shifts in, 88–89; sociocultural position of, 85–90; topics addressed by, 89–90
lay bureaucrat literati, 258; Ibn al-Muqaffaʿ background, 107–111; on monarchical politics, 6; on sovereignty, 10
leadership: imam legitimate, 40; Ottoman caliphate Muslim community spiritual, 19; sermon on Abū Bakr, 62. *See also* messianic leadership
learned elite, prose writing in Arabic language, 84–85
legal disagreements, Ibn al-Muqaffaʿ on, 184–185
legislation, 260; caliphs authority and revealed law, 165, 172; "Epistle on the Caliph's Privy" on, 162
Letter of Tansar (*Nāmah-i Tansar*) (Ibn al-Muqaffaʿ), 116–117, 227, 325n1
"Letter to the Scribes" (ʿAbd al-Ḥamīd), 96, 101–105, 121, 227
longue-durée imperial practices: Ibn al-Muqaffaʿ on, 111, 243; in Umayyads, xiii, 35, 104

MacDonald, Duncan B., 17–18
al-Mahdī (caliph), 285n57; al-ʿAnbarī judicial disagreements with, 66; al-ʿAnbarī letter to, 50, 65–66; Ibn Isḥāq and, 60; al-Numayrī governorship appointment by, 65–66
Mahmood, Saba, 2
al-Manṣūr (caliph), 211–212, 305n59; administration of, 43; al-ʿAnbarī appointment as judge of Basra, 65–66; "Epistle on the Caliph's Privy" to, 110, 119; Ibn al-Muqaffaʿ on challenges for, 150, 232; Ibn al-Muqaffaʿ relationship with, 109; Ibn Isḥāq and, 60; as messianic figure, 195; military challenges of, 191–192, 216; as second Abbasid caliph, 33–34
Marlow, Louise, 24–25
Marwān I b. al-Ḥakam (caliph), 53
Marwān II, ʿAbdallāh (caliph): Abbasids killing of, 107, 216; ʿAbd al-Ḥamīd letter to the scribes of, 96, 101–105, 121, 227; "Testament to the Crown Prince" to, 96
Marwān II b. Muhammad (caliph), 92–93
Marx, Karl, 17
Masāʾil al-Imāma (Themes of the Imamate), 3
masses (*al-ʿāmma*), 223, 261; companions of, 243–244; governance level elevation for social order, 245; life management inability of, 245; as object of politics, 246; qualified life of, 243–246; ruler use of elite for training of, 245–246
mawālī. *See* non-Arab Muslims
al-Māwardī, 2, 20, 21, 75, 129, 130, 262
mawlā. *See* lay bureaucrat elite
maʿrifat/muḥāsabat al-nafs. *See* self
Memmi, Albert, 86, 89
merit, Ibn al-Muqaffaʿ on consideration for, 236
messianic leadership: Abbasid caliphate as messianic redeemer, 36; of al-Manṣūr, 195; as political authority, 36, 39
middle-of-the-roaders, of ulema, 31, 47, 50, 61
militarization: caliphal practice and expansion of, 43; of faith community, xiii
military: ʿAbd al-Ḥamīd on, 69, 99–100, 147, 191; al-ʿAnbarī on, 69–70; civil administration and, 199–208; commander

of faithful command of, 36, 96, 147, 153; Ibn al-Muqaffaʿ critique on taxation collection by, 199–200; Ibn al-Muqaffaʿ on, 69, 99–100, 147, 192–194, 261; Ibn al-Muqaffaʿ on imperial economy of, 200–202; al-Manṣūr challenges in, 191–192, 216; religious devotion compared to soldierly virtue, 193–199
Miller, Peter, 3
mirror for princes literature, 316n23; Yavari on, 25
modernist idea, of secularism, 11
monarchical politics: Ibn al-Muqaffaʿ vision of ideal, 251–252; lay bureaucrat literati on, 6
moral authority, of Qur'an, 30
moral form, of political rationalities, 3
Muhammad (Prophet): Abrahamic monotheism faith of, 28; Abū Bakr caliph after death of, 28; caliphs rule after death of, 27; communication of God's laws, 61; Ibn Isḥāq *Biography of the Prophet* on, 60; Ibn Isḥāq on leadership of, 60; Ibn Isḥāq representation of death of, 60, 63; inheritance and succession from prophets, 51; interpretive authority birth after death of, 29–30; new social imaginary of, 28; Qur'an moral authority and memory of, 30; D. Sālim on established practice of, 59
Muhammad community, rival groups in seventh century, 27
Muir, William, 17
mulk. *See* sovereignty
al-Mulk, Niẓām, 25
multiple secularities, 12
Murji'ites: faith perspective of, 67; D. Sālim "Epistle" on, 58–59; Umayyads grave sinner position by, 56
Muslim intellectuals, 256; on Islamic governance, 20; on Muslim state political revival, 20; on Ottoman caliphate, 19
Muslims: class differential treatment of, 85–86; Ibn al-Muqaffaʿ on, 226, 253; Iqbal on nation of, 20–21. *See also* Islam
Muslim state: Arnold on caliphate imperial and political potential in, 18; constitutionalism, parliamentarism and people sovereignty in, 19; Islamic politics with modern nation-state values, 16; Muslim intellectuals on political revival of, 20; Ottoman caliphate and idea of, 16–20; Riḍā on independence of, 19–20; sacred law governance in, 16
Muʿāwiya, 31

Naṣr b. Sayyār, 86
new social imaginary, of Muhammad, 28
niʿma. *See* divine beneficence
nomination-election-consent, in caliphal practice, 40
non-Arab Muslims (*mawālī*), 294n1; Arabic language use by, 84; in Iraq-Khurasan region, 226–227; taxation obligations of, 247, 250–251; Umayyads administrative positions, 46
nonentities: taxpaying subjects compared to, 246–253; tribute revenue from, 250–251
non-Muslims (*dhimmī*): ʿAbd al-Malik taxation of, 85; Arabic language use by, 84; in Iraq-Khurasan region, 226–227; taxation obligations of, 247, 250–251; Umayyads administrative positions, 46
North Africa, imperial territories absence of, 190, 220–222

obedience: Abū Yūsuf on God, 79; of caliph, 30–31, 63, 95–96; of commander of faithful, 52; Ibn al-Muqaffaʿ on, 5, 12, 56, 147–148, 159–160; Ibn Isḥāq on, 63; to imam and imperial law, 165, 167–173; verse of, 316n7
"On Censure of the Ethics of Scribes" (al-Jāḥiẓ), 130
oppression, siyasa as opposite of, 5
Oriental despotism: European scholars on caliphate and, 17; Hegel on, 16–17; Marx and Engels on, 17
Orientialists: on Abdülhamid Ottoman sultan, 16; caliphate research by, 16
Ottoman caliphate: England Emperor of India and, 17–18; fight against colonizers and, 19; and Islamic political thought, 16–20; Muslim intellectuals on, 19; Muslim state idea and, 16–20; spiritual leadership of Muslim community by, 19

parliamentarism, in Muslim state, 19
pastoral authority, caliphate as, xiii, 257
patrimonialism, Weber on Asian political structure of, 17
PEIPT. See *Princeton Encyclopedia of Islamic Political Thought, The*

Persian humanism, Dabashi on, 273n36
Persian language: in Iraq, 83; translation into Arabic, 85
piety: movement in Egypt, 2; prudent action distinct from religious, 156–157; renunciant, 8–9; D. Sālim "Epistle" appeal to, 58; siyasa on good governance distinct from religious, x, 107, 259–260; Umayyads on Islamic, 124
Pocock, John G. A., xii
political and legal premises, for imperial law theory, 166–167
political authority: of Abū Bakr and ʿUmar, 63; of caliphal contractualism, 37–38, 60–63; God's caliphate, 37, 38–39; of messianic leadership, 36, 39; Shiite imamate, 37, 39–40
political awareness, in territorial consciousness, 189
political control: in empire building, xiii; law intersection with, xiv; of sovereignty, 6
political language, of ulema, xiii, 2, 255
political power, hegemonic religiosity and, 13
political prose: of ʿAbd al-Ḥamīd, 67, 91–105, 112–113; Arabic, xiii, 83–85; imamate and siyasa intertextuality in, 94–105; lay bureaucrat elite sociocultural position, 85–90; revolution in, 82–105; Sālim School of Siyasa, xiii, 90–94; temporal political reflection and, 83–85; Umayyad sociopolitical developments and, 85; Umayyads on sociopolitical developments in, 85
political rationalities: distinctive idiom of, 4; epistemological character of, 3; moral form of, 3
political reality, non-ulema-centric sense of, x
political subjectivity, premodern state influence on, 12
"Political Thought in Islam" (Iqbal), 20
Political thought in Medieval Islam (Rosenthal), 22
political virtue, xiv, 134, 136, 259, 260; Althusser and Skinner on, 154; Ibn al-Muqaffaʿ on, 157–159, 161; rational judgment as, 154–160
politics: Ibn al-Muqaffaʿ attempt to create, 106; masses as objects of, 246; ulema resentment of, 48, 49–50
polyphonic tenor of adab-siyasa, 14
postcolonial theories, 256
power: Abbasid caliphate absolute, 6, 136–137; hegemonic religiosity and political, 13; language of Ibn al-Muqaffaʿ, 135–136; siyasa discourse on sovereign management of, 6, 7, 154, 156, 160; sovereign actions and, 158–159, 244; sovereign disciplined, 141–142; sovereignty supreme political, 6
pragmatic secularity, 10–11; of adab-siyasa, 14; precapitalist polities and, 12; problem negotiation with practical logic, 14; religiosity and secularity relationship, 13
precapitalist polities, religiosity and secularity in, 12
premodern state, political subjectivity influenced by, 12
prepolitical, 49, 56, 60, 121
pre-Sunnite caliphal contractualism, 60–63
pre-Sunnite scholars, of ulema, 47
Princeton Encyclopedia of Islamic Political Thought, The (PEIPT), 15, 268n2
privy, 228; challenges and, 237–243; of commander of faithful, 242, 328n74
prophecy: imamate on governance and, 255; von Kremer on Islam, 17
prophetic practice (*sunna*), 180; jurists and, 177–178
prophets: divine privilege of, 312n69; sovereign compared to, 146–147. *See also* Muhammad
prose writing, 257; of learned elite in Arabic language, 84–85. *See also* political prose
providence, sovereignty dialectic and, 149–154
provinces: administration of, 43; governance of, 44; Hijaz, 203, 208–209; Yemen, 21, 203, 205, 209, 211
prudent action, religious piety distinct from, 156–157
Pseudo-Māwardī, Marlow on, 24–25
public space, 11, 126, 231, 307n86

Qadarites: ʿAbd al-Ḥamīd opposition to, 55; free will support by, 55
al-Qadi, Wadad, 95–96
qayṣariyya, 37
qiyās (legal analogy), 172, 181, 184, 185
Quarayshites, 145–146; monopoly on caliphate by, 61
Qur'an: moral authority of, 30; D. Sālim on, 59
qur'anic language: in *The Book of Land Tax*, 80; on kingdom and kingship, 135; legal knowledge and texts in, 164; organized

societies references, 28; on sovereignty of God, 28
Qusayr ᶜAmra palace in Jordan, 125; imperial universalism and, 35; siyasa and Umayyad imperial chancellery classification and, 35

al-Rashīd, Hārūn (caliph), 50; Abū Yūsuf as chief judge of, 76–81; al-Mahdī appointment of judge, 76
rational judgment, as political virtue, 154–160
ra'y. *See* sound knowledge
al-Rāziq,ᶜAlī ᶜAbd, 20
raᶜiyya. *See* flock
reason (*al-dīn wa al-ᶜaql*): Ibn al-Muqaffaᶜ on, 8, 183; religion dialectic and, 165, 173–178, 183
religion: Asad on, 11; governmentalization after siyasa, 64–65, 77, 257; Ibn al-Muqaffaᶜ on body and, 8, 129–130, 183; imamate and governmentalization of, 64–65, 77; private belief of, 10–11; reason dialectic and, 165, 173–178, 183; ulema and, 7
religiosity, 271n24; history hegemonic, 13; in precapitalist polities, 12; secularity relationship to, 13; ulema transcended, 12
religious authority: governance boundaries and, 171–172; imam as ruler with, 1–2, 148; Lapidus on, 278n98
religious devotion, soldierly virtue compared to, 193–199
religious dutifulness (*taqwā*), 8–9, 29
religious law, 162, 165, 187
religious-legal thought critique, 163, 165–166; caliph revealed law and, 172; jurists and, 164
religious ordinances, revealed law and, 172
religious piety, siyasa on good governance distinct from, x, 107, 259–260
religious politics/religious comportment, 9
religious scholarship, jurists monopolization of, 47–48
renunciant piety (*zuhd*), 8–9
republican form, of succession to rule, 41
revealed law (*al-dīn*), 54, 95–96, 141; al-ᶜAnbarī on, 75; caliph religious-legal structure and, 172; caliphs authority to legislate, 165; Ibn al-Muqaffaᶜ on, 148, 162, 167, 169, 175–176; legislation and, 165, 172; religious ordinances, 172; beyond sovereign authority, 171
revisionist intervention, Abū Bakr and, 28–29
Riḍā, Rashīd, 19–20
rival groups, plurality of faith and governance by, 27
Rose, Nikolas, 3
Rosenthal, Erwin, 22
royal authority. *See* sovereignty
ruler: *Al-Adab al-Kabīr'* prose on, 325n8; extrareligious laws in governance introduced by, 14; hard secularity form of, 13–14; imam as religious and secular authority, 1–2, 148; republican and dynastic forms of succession of, 41; response to contingency through siyasa, 4; training of masses through elite, 245–246; ulema as essential to, 47
ruling: by divine decree according to God's law, 51–54; proper handling of administration and, 158

sacred cities, of Syria, 209–210
sacred homeland, in territorial consciousness, 208–213
sacred immutable law code, of caliph, 166
sacred law (*sharīᶜa*), 7, 272n27; caliph authority and, 42, 165; characteristics of, 8; Ibn Taymiyya on governance principles according to, 3; Muslim state governance, 16; in ulema discourse, 8; ulema support for empire, xiv, 80–81
sacred roots, of Abbasids, 208–211
Safi, Omid, 274n43
al-ṣaḥāba. *See* companions
Said, Edward, 26; on self-awareness, 272n33
Sālim b. Dhakwān, 40, 49, 76; on established practice of Muhammad, 59; on Qur'an, 59; Umayyads opposition by, 59
Sālim b. ᶜAbd al-Raḥmān Abū al-ᶜAlā', 85; *The Book of Politics* translation by, 91; as chancellor for Hishām, 90–91
Sālim School of Siyasa, political prose in, xiii, 90–94
saloons, 126
Salvatore, Armando, 13
scribes: ᶜAbd al-Ḥamīd metaphor for, 137; Ibn al-Muqaffaᶜ as, 107–108; al-Jāḥiẓ on, 130–132. *See also* "Letter to the Scribes"
secular authority, imam as ruler with, 1–2, 148
secular law, 270n13
secular perpetuity, 4
secular practices, 10

secularity: adab-siyasa pragmatic, 14; Asad on, 11; concrete historical condition connection, 10; Islamic political thought and global, x, 7–10; Islamic political thought and pragmatic, 10–14; modernist idea of, 11; in precapitalist polities, 12; religiosity relationship to, 13; Salvatore and Yavari on soft and hard, 13–14; Umayyads on sociopolitical spaces in, 11; urbane conduct and, 9, 106, 107, 126, 259; worldliness and, 12, 256
Selçukid period, Yavari on, 25
Selçuks, Safi on, 274n43
Selected Narratives. See *ʿUyūn al-Akhbār*
self (*maʿrifat/muḥāsabat al-nafs*), 8; interrogation of, 272n32
self-awareness: political reflection on co-formation of faith and empire, 27, 29–30; Said on, 272n33
self-cultivation technology, siyasa functions as, 7, 259
Sen, Sachin, 277n87
sharīʿa. *See* sacred law
shepherd-flock metaphor, 223
Sherwani, Haroon Khan, 21–22, 277n85
Shiites, 31; on ideal caliphate, 17; imam, 61, 268n2; imamate as political authority, 37, 39–40; imamate position of, 20; as religiopolitical party, 17; Umayyads opposition from, 33, 204
shūra (consultation), 37, 54
Siddiqui, Sohaira, 24
ṣiḥḥat al-badan/al-jasad. *See* body
sin: ulema sociopolitical ethos of, 9; Umayyads as grave sinners, 55–57
siyasa, 268n2; ʿAbd al-Ḥamīd on, 137; ʿAbd al-Ḥamīd political prose and, 91–105; adab regime of moral cultivation, xiv; caliph authority and, 141–149; consequentialism and, 4; duties of, 2; on governance in human nature, 255; as governing subjects, 143; imamate and governmentalization of religion after, 64–65, 77, 257; imamate intertexuality in political prose with, 94–105; legal discourse of, 260; as oppression opposite, 5; Qusayr ʿAmra palace classification with, 35; Rose and Miller definition of, 3; ruler response to contingency through, 4; as temporal politics, 1, 3; self-cultivation technology function of, 7, 259; taming the sovereign role of, 6, 143–144, 259; ulema slow warm-up to term of, 3. *See also* adab-siyasa
al-siyāsa al-sharʿiyya, of Ibn Taymiyya, 270n13
siyasa discourse: in caliphal world, x; on caliphate ulema-centric idea and sovereignty, x; on empire, xiv; on good governance distinct from religious piety, x, 107, 259–260; Ibn al-Muqaffaʿ writings and, xiii; imamate mood and style change and, xiii, 82; rationality of governance, 2–4; on sovereign power management, 6, 7, 154, 156, 160
siyasa disruptive language, 106, 133; governmentalization of sovereignty, 118–124; lay bureaucrat literati Ibn al-Muqaffaʿ background, 107–111; worldly ethos of Adab-Siyasa, xi, 9, 124–132; texts as political disenchantment, 111–118
Skinner, Quentin, xii, 154
social order: Ibn al-Muqaffaʿ on, 223–224, 244; masses governance level elevation for, 245; nobility, 223, 241; sovereign and, 6, 7
sociocultural differences, caliphal practices and, 44–45
sociopolitical change, after Abbasid revolt, 232–233, 235–236
sociopolitical ideals, of ulema, 15
sociopolitical spaces, Abbasids on secularity in, 11
soft secularity, 13
soldierly virtue, religious devotion compared to, 193–199
sound knowledge (*ra'y*), Ibn al-Muqaffaʿ on, 176–177
sovereign: adab-siyasa cultivation of, 6; as beast, 134–141; disciplined power of, 141–142; elite as appropriate collaborators for, 253; Ibn al-Muqaffaʿ on order through rule of, 136, 259; as lawgiver, 148; of people in Muslim state, 19; power language of Ibn al-Muqaffaʿ, 135–136; power to act of, 158–159, 244; prophets compared to, 146–147; religious obligations observance by, 152–153; revealed law beyond authority of, 171; siyasa discourse on power management of, 6, 7, 154, 156, 160; siyasa role of taming of, 6, 143–144; social order and, 6, 7
sovereignty (*mulk*), x, 2, 273n38; ʿAbd al-Ḥamīd on, 135; *Al-Adab al-Kabīr'* on, 139–140;

Al-Azmeh on, 41; caliph authority and, 42; common good purpose of, 5, 134; as divine beneficence, 149–150, 255; evaluation of, 134; governance compared to, 5, 6; governmentalization of, 118–124, 162, 256; Ibn al-Muqaffaʿ on, 135, 146–147, 151–152, 156; *Kalīla and Dimna* on, 138, 154; providence dialectic and, 149–154; qur'anic language on God, 28; supreme political power of, 6; Umayyad and Abbasid lay literati on, 10
spiritual leadership: of Muslim community by Ottoman caliphate, 19
Das Staatsrecht der Zaiditen (Strothmann), 21
state: Safi on apparatuses of, 274n43; von Kremer on Islam, 17
strength, authority of, 141
Strothmann, Rudolf, 21
Studies in the History of Early Muslim Political Thought and Administration (Sherwani), 21–22, 277n85
subjects, taxpaying compared to nonentities, 246–253
succession to rule: designation, 41; dynastic, 51; family, 41; republican, 41
Sufis of the Muʿtazila, 62; anarchist position of, 64; on imam authority and election, 65
sunna. *See* prophetic practice
Sunnite-juristic view, of caliphate, 20
Syria, 214–215; Greek language use in, 83; Ibn al-Muqaffaʿ advice on elite in, 230; importance of, 42–43; provincialization of, 216–218; reconstitution of, 190; sacred cities of, 209–210; Umayyad and, 43, 48; as Umayyads imperial core, 190, 203, 213

tadbīr. *See* governance
taqwā. *See* religious dutifulness
taxation, 219; after Abbasid revolt, 248–249; Abū Bakr on, 251; al-ʿAnbarī on, 67, 70–72, 251; charitable contributions and, 251; commander of faithful and, 249–250; Ibn al-Muqaffaʿ critique on military collection in, 199–200; non-Arab Muslims and non-Muslims obligations for, 247, 250–251; tribute revenue compared to, 246; ulema on, 248, 250; ʿUmar II abolishment of differential, 85–86
taxpaying subjects, 224; nonentities compared to, 246–253
temporal or positive law code, of caliph, 166
temporal political morality, x, 256
temporal political practices, 3
temporal political reflection, political prose and, 83–85
temporal politics, 1; notion of, 24
temporal sociopolitical ethos, 124
temporality, 256
territorial consciousness, 42–43, 260; Abbasid dynasty and Arabian Peninsula, 189; al-Andalus absence from imperial territories, 190, 220–222; civil administration and military, 199–208; family feuds and civil wars, 211; governing of old core as imperial periphery, 213–220; Iraq-Khurasan military and, 189; North Africa absence in imperial territories, 190, 220–222; Orient of Umayyads, 190–191; political awareness in, 189; religious devotion compared to soldierly virtue, 193–199; sacred homeland in, 208–213; Syria reconstitution, 189; Western limbs of empire, 213
territorial expansion, of Abbasid caliphate, 42–43
"Testament to the Crown Prince" (ʿAbd al-Ḥamīd), 69, 99–100, 121, 191, 227; to Marwān II, 96; moral advice in, 97–98
Themes of the Imamate. *See Masā'il al-Imāma*
"Theological Sanction for the Caliphate in the Qur'an and the Traditions" (Arnold), 18
theology: caliphal practice administrative vocabulary of early, 36–37; of resistance, 57–60
"Thinking about Religion" (Asad), 273n41
tribute revenue: al-ʿAnbarī on disbursement of, 72; taxation compared to, 246
Turkish National Assembly, on caliphate abolishment, 19

ulema, 225–226; Abbasids collaboration in Abbasid revolt, 48; adab-siyasa divergence from practices of, 10; Arabic language use and, 84; on caliph faith status, 259; confessionalism and militancy of, 133; Dome of the Rock classification with, 35; empire for sacred law support by, xiv, 80–81; as essential to rulers, 47; as guardians of faith and community, 140; Ibn al-Muqaffaʿ writings and, xiii, 252; imamate

ulema (*continued*)
discourse from political language of, xiii, 2, 255; knowledge restriction attempts, 128; middle-of-the-roaders of, 31, 47, 50, 61; pre-Sunnite scholars of, 47; religion and, 7; resentment of politics by, 48, 49–50; siyasa political knowledge adoption by, 64; slow warm-up of siyasa term, 3; sociopolitical ethos of sin and, 9; sociopolitical ideals of, 15; on taxation, 248, 250; transcended religiosity of, 12; Umayyad caliphs distance from, 48; Zaman study on Abbasid caliphs relationship with, 24
ulema-centric political theology, 50–51, 261
ulema discourse: on collective body of community, 49; sacred and divine law in, 8
ʿulūm. *See* customary knowledge practices
ʿUmar I b. al-Khaṭṭāb (caliph), 57, 61, 204; caliphal practice of seniority system by, 30, 286n58; political authority of, 63
ʿUmar II b. ʿAbd al-ʿAzīz (caliph): differential tax policies abolishment, 85; reforms of, 86
Umayyad caliphs: Arabic language use by, 83; client functionaries administration use by, 83; free will argument for, 55; God's caliph reference by, 38–39; Ibn al-Muqaffaʿ attacks on, 229; loyalty and submission of subjects, 45; D. Sālim opposition to, 59; scribes in administration of, 103; ulema distance from, 48; Zurʿa on theological and juridical authority, 41
Umayyads: armed defense against, 31–32; bureaucrats in, xiii; empire building of, xiii; frontier zone of, 44; governance ethics debate and, 31; as grave sinner, 55–57; imperial chancellery and Qusayr ʿAmra palace classification, 35; Iraq and Khurasan region control attempts, 32–33; Islamic piety of, 124; Islam identification of, 35, 124; judges appointments and, 163; lay literati on sovereignty, 10; *longue-durée* imperial practices in, xiii, 35, 104; non-Muslim and non-Arab Muslims administrative positions, 46; opposition to, 31; Orient of, 190–191; political prose and sociopolitical developments of, 85; on secularity in sociopolitical spaces, 11; Shiite opposition to, 33; sovereign absolute power of, 6; Syria as imperial core of, 190, 203, 213; Syrian loyalty to, 43, 48; Watt on empire under, 22
umma. *See* community or collective body
urbane conduct, secularity and, 9, 106, 107, 126, 259
ʿUthmān (caliph), 53, 204; murder of, 57
ʿUyūn al-Akhbār (Selected Narratives) (Ibn Qutayba), 3

verse of obedience, 316n7

al-Walīd, Yazīd II b. (caliph), 49, 50; on authority inheritance, 51, 52; on caliph as deputy of God, 51; on heir appointments, 52–53; letter of, 51–53
al-Walīd, Yazīd III b. (caliph), 31, 49, 50, 92; on Islam as revealed law, 54; letter to Iraq of, 51, 53–54; al-Walīd II killed by, 54
al-Warrāq, Ibn Sayyār, 272n31
Watt, Montgomery, 22, 23
Weber, Max: on Asian political structure of patrimonialism, 17; on Islam and Muslim societies, 275n64
Weil, Gustav, 17
whimsical temptation, authority of, 141
worldliness (*dunyawī*): adab-siyasa and, 128; secularity and, 12, 256
worldly and practical character of political advice, 98
worldly and religious practices, 11
worldly attitude, 259
worldly ethos, xi, 9; of adab-siyasa, xi, 9, 124
worldly literature, 126
worldly politics/worldly comportment, 9
worldly tenor, xiii, 143
worldly ways of living, 130
Wretched of the Earth, The (Fanon), 88

Yavari, Neguin, 13–14; on mirror for princes literature, 25; on Selçukid period, 25
Yazīd II. *See* al-Walīd, Yazīd II b.
Yazīd III. *See* al-Walīd, Yazīd III b.
Yemen (province), 203, 205, 209, 211; Zaydī imamate in, 21
Yūsuf, Yaʿqūb b. Ibrāhīm Abū, 3

Zaman, Muhammad Qasim, 24
Zaydī imamate in Yemen, Strothmann on, 21
Zimmermann, Fritz, 58
zoe, Agamben on, 224, 244, 261
al-Zubayr, ʿAbdallāh b., 31
zuhd. *See* renunciant piety

GPSR Authorized Representative: Easy Access System Europe, Mustamäe tee 50, 10621 Tallinn, Estonia, gpsr.requests@easproject.com

www.ingramcontent.com/pod-product-compliance
Lightning Source LLC
Chambersburg PA
CBHW022025290426
44109CB00014B/758